THE ANNALS
OF
AMERICA

THE ANNALS OF AMERICA

Volume 17

1950 - 1960

Cold War in the Nuclear Age

William Benton, *Publisher*

ENCYCLOPÆDIA BRITANNICA, INC.

Chicago London Toronto Geneva Sydney Tokyo Manila

The editors wish to express their gratitude for permission to reprint
material from the following sources:

Kenneth Allsop for Selection 108, from *Encounter*, April 1960.

American Friends Service Committee for Selection 67, from *Speak Truth to Power: A Quaker Search for an Alternative to Violence.*

The Antioch Review and Daniel Bell for Selection 47, from *The Antioch Review*, Copyright 1953 by The Antioch Review, Incorporated, Yellow Springs, Ohio.

Ashley Famous Agency, Inc. for Selection 69, from *Holiday*, January 1955, Copyright © 1955 by The Curtis Publishing Company.

Atlantic-Little, Brown and Co. for Selection 33, from *A Creed for Free Enterprise*, by Clarence B. Randall, Copyright 1952 by Clarence B. Randall. Also for Selection 80, from *Much Ado About Me*, by Fred Allen, Copyright © 1956 by Portland Hoffa Allen (pseudonym for Mary Portland Sullivan).

The Atlantic Monthly and Marion H. Sass for Selection 74, from *The Atlantic Monthly*, November 1956, Copyright © 1956 by The Atlantic Monthly Company, Boston, Mass. The Atlantic Monthly and James H. Gray for Selection 85, from *The Atlantic Monthly*, March 1957, Copyright © 1957 by The Atlantic Monthly Company, Boston, Mass. The Atlantic Monthly and Ernest Gruening for Selection 86, from *The Atlantic Monthly*, January 1957, Copyright © 1956 by The Atlantic Monthly Company, Boston, Mass.

W. H. Auden and Encounter for Selection 70, from

The Anchor Review, Number One of a Series, 1955.

Thomas H. Benton for Selection 24, from *An Artist in America*, by Thomas H. Benton.

William Benton for Selection 26, from MS in his possession.

Columbia University Press for Selection 89, from *Negro Folk Music, U.S.A.*, ed. by Harold Courlander.

The Congressional Digest for Selection 96, from *The Congressional Digest*, Copyright 1958 by The Congressional Digest Corporation, Washington, D.C.

Polly P. Copeland for Selection 78, from *The Atlantic Monthly*, September 1956, Copyright © 1956 by The Atlantic Monthly Company, Boston, Mass.

Norman Cousins for Selection 92, from *The Saturday Review*.

Thomas Y. Crowell Company for Selection 110, from *American Poetry*, ed. by Karl Shapiro, Copyright 1960 © by Thomas Y. Crowell Company.

Agnes George de Mille and Emily Davie Kornfeld for Selection 58, from *Profile of America: An Autobiography of the U.S.A.*, ed. by Emily Davie, New York: The Viking Press, Inc., 1954.

The Devin-Adair Company for Selection 109, from *The Case for the South*, by William D. Workman, Jr., Copyright © 1960 by William D. Workman, Jr.

(continued on p. 599)

CODED SOURCES IN THIS VOLUME

Bulletin   *Department of State Bulletin.* Published weekly by the Office of Public Services, Bureau of Public Affairs. Supersedes two previous publications: *Press Releases* and *Treaty Information Bulletin.* Washington, July 1, 1939 *et seq.*

127 F. Supp. 405   *Federal Supplement.* Cases Argued and Determined in the United States District Courts and the United States Court of Claims. St. Paul, 1955. Vol. 127, pp. 405ff.

Record   *Congressional Record.* A record of the proceedings of Congress from March 3, 1873, to date, arranged by number of Congress and by session. Washington, 1874 *et seq.*

Record, App.   *Congressional Record Appendix.* A supplement to the *Congressional Record* (see above), paged separately and also arranged by Congress and session.

                  United States Reports [Supreme Court]
347 U.S. 483   Vol. 347, pp. 483ff.;
356 U.S. 44   Vol. 356, pp. 44ff.

VSD   *Vital Speeches of the Day.* Published twice a month. New York, 1934 *et seq.*

Contents

COLD WAR IN THE NUCLEAR AGE
In Pictures

Turmoil in Asia 53-66

With Europe occupied, neutralized, and, except for occasional crises
over the status of Berlin, stabilized, Cold War confrontations tended
to occur more and more in regions that had hitherto been relatively
disregarded. Asia was the main one of these; the victory of the
Chinese Communists, the war in Korea, and the continuing struggle
in Southeast Asia were the source of most of the Cold War's heat.

Cold War Crises 163-180

It was inevitable that a certain amount of jockeying for
advantage would take place between the U.S. and Russia,
particularly since the nuclear arms race was becoming
increasingly uncomfortable in a number of ways. Collision
was avoided by resort to proxy situations; the two giant
powers aligned themselves on opposite sides of smaller regional
disputes that would normally have had little to do with the
world power structure, and let others do the fighting.

A Corporate Society 269-284

The American economy moved steadily upward during the postwar
period; the gross national product rose to unheard-of levels. But
sheer productivity was by no means the whole story; new forms and
institutions were developed that profoundly affected the nation.
The corporation became a dominant institution in society,
and the lives and activities of only a very few could escape
the influence of the corporate system.

The increasingly rapid growth of urban America that marked
the postwar period was concentrated in suburban districts;
the resulting slow decay of many inner-city areas, often
including the nominally central "downtown," became one of
the critical problems of the time. The concept of urban
renewal came to the fore as the cities sought to find a means
to maintain a physical and human continuity.

There was no denying that America had achieved an economy
that was little short of miraculous. The nation had become an
island of affluence in a world whose most common feature was
poverty. Alongside and as a consequence of this wealth, however,
grew up a new complex of problems; not easily met or even
understood, they all seemed nonetheless to revolve around the
ideas of direction and purpose. It was, to some, a startling
discovery that wealth failed to bring peace and harmony.

To all the general statements about American prosperity,
abundance, and, indeed, freedom that could be made, the Negro
minority in America provided, as it always had, a painful exception.
During the 1950s, however, the cause of full equality for black
Americans, toward which only sporadic progress had been made
in the century since Emancipation, was taken up in a sustained
drive. With no distinctly marked course, with no foreseeable end,
but with a clear goal in view, the drive was destined to test severely
America's most basic assumptions and institutions.

Introduction

If one were to compare the three decades of the 1940s, the 1950s, and the 1960s, he might be forced to conclude that the 1950s — the period covered by the present volume of *Annals* — was one of relative calm and peace. Compared to the decade that preceded it, racked as it was by World War II, and the decade that followed it, with its assassination of a President, its Vietnam War, and its widespread civil disturbances, the 1950s was a time when men could breathe a little easier, and when they could hope that the promise that had been so bright at the end of World War II would at last be realized.

Perhaps it did not seem so at the time; in fact, the decade was marked by crises that aroused fear throughout the world. The first, of course, was the war in Korea. Another was the development by the Soviets, in a surprisingly short time after the American discovery, of a hydrogen bomb. A third was the Chinese Communist revolution; a fourth was the Hungarian uprising of 1956; a fifth was the Suez crisis of the same year; and a sixth was the U-2 incident of 1960. All were fraught with dangers that everyone could see, and each seemed to threaten mankind with a third, and possibly a last, world war.

But — and this is the important point — every one of these crises, terrible as they seemed at the time, was gotten through. Six times the fuse was lit; six times the bomb did not go off.

How much of the credit for this was owing to President Eisenhower and his administration probably no one can accurately say at the present time. Perhaps a century will have to pass before we know. But at the end of that century it may be possible to look back and say that whereas the Pax Romana lasted for a hundred years (it was supposed to last a thousand), the Pax Americana — a peace administered by the United States, rather than one in which it merely shared — lasted ten. If so, those ten years will have been the years covered by this volume.

The Korean War began under Truman and ended under Eisenhower. Its most dramatic event, at least from the point of view of constitutional history, occurred in the winter and spring of 1951. The first North Korean onslaught, in June 1950, had thrown the UN forces deep into South Korea; a counterattack recaptured the South and passed northward of the 38th parallel (the dividing line between North and South Korea). The UN, aware that Chinese troops and supplies were being concentrated on the North Korean-Manchurian border and fearful of bringing China into the conflict, ordered General Douglas MacArthur, the UN commander in the field, not to cross the Yalu River. MacArthur's troops nevertheless approached the river. On October 26, 1950, Chinese "volunteers" crossed into North Korea in force and stopped the UN advance; by the end of the year they had driven it south of the 38th parallel.

President Truman, taking his cue from the UN position on the matter, insisted that the war was a "police action" and that a cessation of hostilities, rather than victory, was its aim. General MacArthur sharply disagreed. Convinced that the Chinese troops on the Manchurian border must be attacked in order to control the conflict, to say nothing of winning it, MacArthur threatened China on March 25, 1951, with an air and naval bombardment unless it withdrew its "volunteers." Three weeks later Truman relieved MacArthur, replacing him with General Matthew B. Ridgway, and MacArthur returned to the United States to address a joint session of Congress on April 17. "War's very object is victory," he declared, "not prolonged indecision. In war there is no substitute for victory."

MacArthur was a popular figure. He had done valiant service in two world wars, and had been army chief of staff between them. Perhaps no American soldier in this century has had a more distinguished record. But Truman, by the Constitution, was the commander in chief. There were rumblings of discontent, and for a while some feared a revolt against the President's authority. But in the end the principle of civilian command over the military won out. (For various discussions of the early phase of the war and of the Truman-MacArthur episode, see Selections 11, 13-19, and 90.)

The Soviet ambassador to the UN proposed a Korean truce on June 23, 1951, and truce talks began on July 10. But the war was not over yet. While the delegates conferred, men on both sides continued to die. The line of battle was stabilized a few miles above the 38th parallel, and the fighting swayed back and forth in the intense cold of the winters and the heat of the summers. The main problem was the repatriation of prisoners; on October 8, 1952, the talks were called off when it seemed that they were hopelessly deadlocked over this issue. In the circumstances, Republican nominee Eisenhower's promise to go to Korea if elected had a powerful effect on the country. Ike — newspaper headline writers require a shortened form of Presidential names, and Eisenhower accepted this one — might have been elected anyway, but the prospect of having in the White House a great soldier who clearly wanted the war to come to an end ensured the defeat of his opponent, Adlai Stevenson. (For two statements by the candidates during the campaign, see Selections 40 and 41.)

For several years it had been widely anticipated that John Foster Dulles would be secretary of state if any Republican attained the presidency, and Eisenhower confirmed these expectations. Dulles had broad experience in diplomacy and was an accomplished negotiator on the international scene. Toward the Communists, however, he was intractable, a stance that subjected him to much criticism at home but also brought him the praise of many non-Communist leaders abroad. He defined diplomacy as "the ability to get to the verge [of war] without getting into the war," and declared that if "you are scared to go to the brink, you are lost." Playing brinkmanship with atomic weapons was sufficient to scare anyone, but Dulles may have been right. In any event, the bombs did not fall, and Dulles' firmness, for example in the Berlin crisis of November 1958, was respected by friend and foe alike. (For statements by Dulles, and for discussions by others of U.S. foreign policy during the decade, see Selections 4, 29-30, 42-44, 60, 67-68, 81, 85, 93, 102, and 105-106.)

On the domestic scene, the decade of the 1950s saw the end of the career of one of the most controversial figures in American history, and the beginning of one of the most significant movements. The figure, of course, was Senator Joseph R. McCarthy of Wisconsin; the movement was the so-called civil rights revolution.

McCarthy captured the headlines for the first but by no means the last time in February 1950, when, in a speech delivered in West Virginia (see Selection 5), he charged that the State Department was heavily infiltrated by Communists and Communist sympathizers. He was not on that occasion or on any others able to make his charges stick — not a single Communist was discharged from government service because of McCarthy's investigations — but he kept the country in a ferment for several years. His influence waned sharply after a series of nationally televised hearings on his charges against army officers and civilian officials in 1954, and on December 2 of that year he was condemned by the Senate, 67-22, for conduct "contrary to Senate traditions" (see Selection 61). He never again regained the great power he had had — he died in 1957 — but his spirit, as it were, marched on. McCarthyism outlived McCarthy and is with us to this day, although no longer in its most virulent form. (For discussions of these matters, see Selections 6, 12, 27, 31, 52-53, 59, 62-64, and 111.)

Earl Warren was born and educated in California, served in various municipal and state offices, and was his state's governor for three terms (1943-1953). A Republican, he was Dewey's running mate in 1948 — the only time he ever lost an election — and although he had received widespread support in California from the members of both parties, there was some dismay among liberals when he was named Chief Justice of the Supreme Court by Eisenhower in 1953.

For a while one could not be certain where Warren stood on the great issues that faced both the Court and the country in those years. Looking back on it now, there may have been, as some have suggested, a struggle for the new Chief Justice's mind between the two grand old men of the Court, Justice Hugo Black, the great liberal, and Justice Felix Frankfurter, the great conservative and advocate of strict construction. If so, Black won, a fact that was made clear by the epoch-making unanimous decision of the Court in *Brown* v. *Board of Education* in 1954 (see Selection 55) — a decision that was written by Warren himself and the unanimity of which he is said to have fought for long and hard. "In the field of public education," Warren declared, "the doctrine of 'separate but equal' has no place. Separate educational facilities are inherently unequal."

What a multitude of troubles and triumphs are represented in those two short sentences! The American Negro, who had suffered everything from humiliation to violent death — in short, every kind of injustice — for 300 years, had finally won a victory the significance of which, though everyone knew it was great, no one could fully see. Nor could anyone foresee what the refusal to heed the decision — the refusal in itself may have been predictable — would connote for the nation in the years ahead.

The Negro revolution — if that is the proper name for it — may be said, indeed, to date from that decision. Warren's words seemed to promise justice and equality in a realm in which it had always been withheld, and in which many Negro leaders saw the final satisfaction of their age-old grievances. If Negroes could attain a good education — as good a one as whites — then all the other problems, it appeared, would be solved.

But it was not to be. The task of desegregating the schools, not only in the South but also in the North, where segregation was not any the less significant for the euphemistic adjective *de facto,* proved too difficult. A few Negro students entered a few white schools in the South, and a few schools were wholly integrated in the North, but fifteen years after the decision the pattern was still largely unchanged. The situation as a whole, however, was much worse than before. The fruit had been offered and then (as it seemed to many Negroes) rudely snatched away. The crisis of the cities in the later 1960s may thus be traced — although of course there were other causes, too — to the failure to obey the law of the land as laid down in 1954. (For discussions from various points of view of Negro problems in this period, and also of education in general, see Selections 9, 33, 37, 46, 48-50, 73-74, 82, 87, 104, and 108-109. For other decisions by Chief Justice Warren, see Selections 95 and 97.)

Another theme that calls for comment here is technology, both its notable successes during the decade and its encroachment, as many observers viewed it, on social and political life. The successes were undeniable, the greatest of them being the launching, by the Soviets, of the first Sputnik on October 4, 1957, and by the Americans of Explorer I on January 31, 1958.

A race to put the first artificial satellite in orbit had been going on between the two countries for several years, and it was partly bad luck that the United States lost. But there were other factors at work, too, and the fact that the Soviet Union, which only forty years before had been one of the most backward nations in Europe, had been the first to breach the planet's atmosphere and to take a giant step toward space was a tremendous shock on this side of the Atlantic. Repercussions were felt in almost every realm of the national life, and crash programs of various kinds — in science itself, and also in education — were instituted to try to catch up. (For comments on the U.S. and Russian space programs, see Selections 88-89, 94, and 104.)

A number of different explanations were offered for the astonishing fact that the United States, supposedly the technological leader of the world, had been humiliated in this way. Our educational system was said to be defective — here was another ground on which to criticize it; we were charged with having somehow grown "soft"; and the accusation was made that some profound lack of will — both individual and national — was involved. If it was merely a question of money, that problem could obviously be solved, and immense sums were appropriated and spent in the ensuing years. But a deep and rather mysterious lack of will seemed a more difficult nut to crack, and there was much speculation at the time about ways to crack it.

Few in the 1950s were so bold as to suggest that Americans did not really want to reach the moon and to go beyond it to the planets of the solar system; even fewer took it upon themselves to say that even if we wanted to, we should not. It was not until the next decade that people began to wonder out loud whether the high cost of a space program — especially when the nation's resources were urgently needed to effect reforms at home — was justified. But there were nevertheless many who wondered whether technology in general was not receiving too high a priority in the national consciousness. Was scientific and technological progress really all that important? Was the new world we were making with our machines and our organizational skills — for the rational organization of manpower is also a branch of modern technology — as good, as desirable, as human, as the old world it was replacing?

In any event, the results of technological progress were everywhere and were changing everything. Television was just one example (see Selections 9, 45, 49, and 80), but there were many others. Perhaps the greatest worry was about the effects of automation not only on the economic position, but also on the life in general, of workers (see Selections 7 and 51). Workers had rebelled for 150 years, in all of the advanced countries of the earth, against mechanical innovations that seemed to threaten their livelihood. But the new protests seemed to be different, just as the new machines seemed to be. Old style machines had aided or replaced human muscle power. But now computers and other electronic devices seemed on the verge of replacing the human brain. Human beings had always prided themselves on the fact that they were the most intelligent beings on the earth. Would that ancient hegemony soon come to an end?

The wiser heads knew that it would not; the new machines were still built by men, and men would continue to control them in the foreseeable future. But all could not see that so clearly, and even the wisest were troubled. Change came thick and fast, and it was hard for even the best minds to keep up with it. (For discussions of these matters, from various points of view, see Selections 21, 32-35, 38-39, 44, 56-57, 63, 66, 69, 76, 78, 84-85, 98-99, and 103.)

It was therefore in an atmosphere of deep political, social, and intellectual unrest that John F. Kennedy of Massachusetts offered himself to the electorate in the fall of 1960 as somehow the representative of the new age, and as somehow able, because he was young and energetic, to deal with the vast problems that the country would have to face on many "new frontiers" in the future. He won; but his victory was one of the closest in history, and the people found it difficult to settle down to face the next decade with equanimity. How they faced it is told in the next volume.

Chronology : 1950-1960

1950

Jan. 13-Aug. 1. The Soviet Union boycotts meetings of the UN Security Council because of the latter's refusal to oust Nationalist Chinese representatives.

Jan. 31. President Truman announces U.S. program to develop a hydrogen bomb.

Feb. 7. The U.S. recognizes newly formed anti-Communist state of Vietnam, with capital at Saigon. **June 27.** President Truman announces dispatch of 35-man military mission to Vietnam to teach use of U.S. weapons. **Dec. 23.** The U.S. signs agreement with France, Vietnam, Cambodia, and Laos to provide military assistance. In the following year U.S. also agrees to provide financial assistance to Saigon government.

Feb. 11. Wisconsin Senator Joseph R. McCarthy's letter to President Truman charging that the State Department is heavily infiltrated by Communists and Communist sympathizers is made public.

May 14. Meeting of foreign ministers of U.S., Great Britain, and France, acting without the Soviet Union, announces the admission of West Germany to system of international cooperation and mutual defense.

June 25. After North Koreans invade South Korea, UN Security Council orders cease-fire in Korea and calls for UN members to supply armed forces to restore peace in the area. Resolution is not vetoed by the Soviet Union because Soviet delegate is boycotting Security Council and is not present. **June 27.** President Truman orders U.S. Air Force and Navy to Korea. **June 30.** After North Koreans have taken Seoul, capital of South Korea, President Truman authorizes the use of U.S. ground forces against the invasion in South Korea and the use of U.S. military aircraft against targets north of the 38th parallel.

July 7. U.S. government orders increased draft to supply forces for UN Korean command. **July 8.** General Douglas MacArthur is chosen head of UN forces in Korea. **July 19.** President Truman urges partial U.S. mobilization.

Aug. 1. Island of Guam in Pacific becomes an unincorporated territory of the U.S. and is granted civil rule under administration of U.S. Department of Interior. Guamanians are U.S. citizens but are not represented in Congress and do not vote in national elections.

Sept. 6. North Koreans, advancing deep into South Korea, capture P'ohangdong on east coast but are unable to drive UN forces off peninsula at Pusan beachhead. **Sept. 15.** UN counteroffensive begins when troops are landed at Inch'on on west coast; at the same time, UN forces break through surrounding lines at Pusan. **Sept. 26.** Seoul is recaptured, and Inch'on forces advance across peninsula, meeting defenders of Pusan.

Sept. 8. President Truman signs Defense Production Act, giving him extensive powers to stabilize wages and prices.

Sept. 23. Congress passes McCarran (Internal Security) Act over President Truman's veto. Act provides for stringent measures to control Communists during national emergencies and registration of Communist organizations and individuals; it also forbids entry into the U.S. of those who have belonged to totalitarian organizations. Six months later, Act is amended to allow entry of those who have been forced into these organizations when under 14 years of age.

Oct. 1. Chinese Communists declare that they cannot allow crossing of 38th parallel by UN troops. **Oct. 20.** After meeting of President Truman and General MacArthur, UN forces take P'yongyang, capital of North Korea, and head toward the Yalu River. **Nov. 26.** Chinese "volunteers" cross the Yalu in force and enter North Korea.

Nov. 1. Two Puerto Rican nationalists attempt to kill President Truman. One is shot and killed by guards; the other is wounded and later sentenced to death, but in 1952 Truman commutes sentence to life imprisonment.

Nov. 3. UN General Assembly adopts resolution asserting its power to act on "threats to peace" if UN Security Council is deadlocked or its proposed action is vetoed by any power.

Nov. 7. Fall elections show Republican gains in many states and in both House and Senate, but Democrats retain control of Congress.

Nov. 24. UN forces begin all-out offensive but are forced back by Chinese and North Korean counteroffensive. **Dec. 4-5.** UN forces, in retreat southward, abandon P'yongyang.

Nov. 29. National Council of the Churches of Christ in the United States of America is formed; organization unites 25 Protestant and 4 Eastern Orthodox groups, marking first stage of postwar movement toward Christian unity. Membership is 32 million.

Nov. 30. UN Security Council proposes resolution appealing to Chinese to withdraw from Korea and offers safeguard of Yalu River border. The Soviet Union vetoes resolution.

Dec. 6. France, which six months previously has refused to agree to rearming West Germany for service in NATO, accepts a plan for German rearmament as part of a Western Europe defense force under a supreme commander. **Dec. 18.** Foreign ministers of North Atlantic pact nations meeting in Brussels agree on plans for rearmament and defense of Western Europe, including West Germany, with U.S. participation. **Dec. 19.** General Dwight D. Eisenhower is chosen as supreme commander and in the following spring assumes command of SHAPE (Supreme Headquarters, Allied Powers in Europe), which is set up in Paris.

Dec. 24. Evacuation of about 200,000 UN troops and civilian refugees who have been pushed back by Communist counteroffensive to port of Hungnam on the east coast of North Korea is completed; it is accomplished under protection of UN aerial and naval bombardment.

1950 census shows U.S. population has increased more than 14 percent in past decade, to 150,697,000, which includes immigration of 1,035,000 since 1940. Compared with previous decade, immigration from the Americas and Asia has doubled, and that from Europe has almost doubled. People living in cities make up 64 percent of the population. Illiteracy is 3.2 percent. Since 1940 many Southern Negroes have moved northward, and many Northern cities, especially in their central areas, have doubled their Negro populations.

1950-1951

Federal Communications Commission authorizes color television broadcasting. Regular programs begin in June 1951, but limitation on manufacture because of the war and the fact that black and white sets cannot receive this type of picture force abandonment of broadcasting in October.

1950-1953

Jan. 25, 1950. As a result of second trial (the first one having ended in deadlock the previous July), Alger Hiss, former State Department official, is sentenced to five years in prison for perjury after having denied that he has engaged in espionage for the Soviet Union. **March 7.** Judith Coplon, employee of the Department of Justice, is convicted for the second time of attempted espionage for the Soviet Union. Seventeen years later she is finally freed on the ground that the Federal Bureau of Investigation (FBI) has used wiretap evidence against her. Valentin Gubitchev, her conspirator and a member of the Soviet UN staff, is also convicted at this time but agrees to return to the Soviet Union. **Dec. 9.** Harry

Gold, U.S. confederate of a British spy, is sentenced to 30 years in prison for atomic espionage. **April 5, 1951.** Ethel and Julius Rosenberg are sentenced to death for atomic espionage, and Morton Sobell, who has worked with them, to 30 years in prison. **June 19, 1953.** The Rosenbergs are executed.

1950-1954

Tranquilizer Miltown is first developed in 1950 and becomes widely used. Treatment of mental illness is advanced when, in 1952, drug reserpine is isolated from an Indian shrub and when, in 1954, tranquilizer chlorpromazine is put to use for mental disorders.

1951

Jan. 4. Huge Communist offensive forces UN troops to abandon Seoul and retreat southward.

Jan. 5-April 4. Senate holds "Great Debate" on U.S. military commitments in Europe and the relative authority of the President and Congress in fulfilling these obligations. Debate ends in triumph for collective security concept when Senate adopts substitute resolution endorsing dispatch of U.S. troops to defend Europe.

Feb. 1. The UN adopts U.S. resolution accusing Communist China of aggression in Korea.

Feb. 26. Twenty-second Amendment to the U.S. Constitution is declared ratified. Proposed in 1947, it limits the U.S. presidency to two terms; if an acting President has been in office for more than two years, the period is considered a complete first term. President Truman, however, is exempt from limitation.

March 24. General MacArthur, convinced that Chinese troops on Manchurian border must be attacked in order to win the war, threatens China with bombing and naval bombardment. April 11. President Truman relieves MacArthur of all his Far Eastern commands. MacArthur is replaced by General Matthew B. Ridgway. April 19. General MacArthur speaks at joint session of Congress, urging military action against China. May 3-June 25. Senate investigation of MacArthur's dismissal ends with adoption (June 27) by the two investigative committees of a "declaration of faith," affirming U.S. unity and warning Soviet Union of ultimate ruin if it attacks U.S.

May 18. UN General Assembly adopts resolution proposed by U.S. Congress to stop shipment of arms to Communist China and North Korea.

June 4. In decision involving 11 leaders of the U.S. Communist Party convicted in 1949 of conspiracy to overthrow the U.S. government by force, the Supreme Court upholds the Smith Act, under which they have been convicted. Dissent declares that Smith Act violates the First Amendment and that there is a difference between the teaching of Marx-Lenin principles and "conspiracy to overthrow."

June 23. Soviet UN delegate proposes Korean truce. June 29. In a broadcast to commander in chief of Communist forces in Korea, General Ridgway suggests meeting to discuss armistice. July 10. Truce talks begin in Kaesong, moving to Panmunjom in October. Sporadic battles continue during talks.

July 11. New York City's policy of allowing "released time" to children for religious study outside of schools is upheld by the New York State Court of Appeals; de-

cision is confirmed by the U.S. Supreme Court the following year.

Aug. 17. First U.S. microwave radio-relay system begins operation when call is placed and relayed 3,000 miles between New York and San Francisco by system of 107 receiving and transmitting towers built 30 miles apart. Sept. 4. The first transcontinental television broadcast by this system is President Truman's opening address at the Japanese Peace Conference in San Francisco, which is telecast over 94 stations.

Sept. 1. The U.S., Australia, and New Zealand (ANZUS Powers) sign a mutual security pact, and in the following year the first meeting of the council established by the pact is held in Honolulu to discuss defense matters of common interest.

Sept. 8. Treaty of Peace with Japan is signed in San Francisco by 48 nations but not the Soviet Union; Treaty restores Japanese sovereignty and independence, strips away all territories outside Japanese islands, and ends occupation. The U.S. is to continue occupation of the Ryukyu and Bonin islands, with the understanding that they might be placed under UN trusteeship with the U.S. as sole administrator. Separate U.S.-Japanese treaty permits the U.S. to maintain military bases in Japan.

Oct. 24. President Truman declares that the state of war with Germany is officially ended.

Dec. 21-22. At reactor testing station at Arco, Idaho, the use of atomic energy to produce electric power is demonstrated for first time.

Dec. 24. National Broadcasting Company broadcasts Gian Carlo Menotti's *Amahl and the Night Visitors,* suggested by Hieronymus Bosch's painting "Adoration of the Magi." It becomes an annual Christmas tradition and in 1953 is first commercial color telecast. Menotti's opera *The Consul,* produced in the previous year, and *The Saint of Bleecker Street,* 1954, both win Pulitzer Prizes.

Jerome David Salinger publishes his novel *Catcher in the Rye,* told in the first person by a teen-age boy in conflict with the adult world.

1951-1953

June 1951. By this month UN forces have fought back to a line a few miles north of the 38th parallel. For two years, there are no important developments in ground fighting; however, air action, with use of jet planes, is carried out between the Yalu River and the 38th parallel, and UN warships range up and down North Korean coasts bombarding installations and ports.

Investigation by House Ways and Means Subcommittee uncovers widespread corruption in the Bureau of Internal Revenue and results in hundreds of resignations and removals, including the commissioner and an assistant attorney general.

1951-1959

Lever House in New York City, completed in 1952 and designed by Skidmore, Owings & Merrill, and works of Ludwig Mies van der Rohe, especially steel and glass apartment towers in Chicago and the Seagram Building in New York City, establish functionalism coupled with refined engineering as the dominant urban architectural style. Nonconformist work of Eero Saarinen, who designs General Motors Technical Center in Warren, Michigan, and emphasis on texture in buildings by Edward Durell Stone, such as U.S. Embassy in New Delhi, India, also establish trends.

1952

Jan. 9. President Truman and British Prime Minister Winston Churchill issue communiqué reaffirming that joint bomber bases in Britain will not be used in an emergency without consent of both countries.

Jan. 12. The Soviet Union submits proposal to the UN embodying Western demand for an atomic control plan that provides for inspection on a continuing basis and for prohibition and controls to be put into operation simultaneously. West, however, is cool to the proposal because, among other things, it applies only to atomic weapons and, in addition, expresses strong opposition to international operation of atomic plants.

April 6. It is announced that U.S. is developing a hydrogen bomb. **Nov. 1.** The U.S. explodes hydrogen bomb on Eniwetok Atoll; it is the most powerful bomb yet made.

April 8. President Truman seizes steel mills to avoid strike by 600,000 steelworkers in wage-price dispute. **June 2.** The Supreme Court rules that seizure is unconstitutional in that the President has had authority of neither the Constitution nor Congress. **July 24.** Further steel strike is settled by Truman's intervention; steelworkers gain wage increase, and management gains price increase.

April 13. Federal Communications Commission ends ban on building of new television broadcasting stations and allows more than 2,000 new stations to open by allocating 70 new ultrahigh frequency (UHF) channels to augment the 12 very high frequency (VHF) channels already in existence. About 65 million persons watch the presidential nominating conventions this year.

May 27. The U.S., Britain, and five other European nations sign agreement to form European Defense Community (EDC) with joint armed forces; in August, President Truman signs protocol to North Atlantic Treaty extending its defense guarantees to include EDC; French National Assembly, however, rejects EDC.

June 27. Congress passes the Immigration and Nationality (McCarran-Walter) Act over President Truman's veto. Act removes former bans on Asiatic and Pacific immigration, retains quota principle established in 1924, stiffens law on admittance, exclusion, and deportation of aliens dangerous to national security of U.S., and gives top priority to immigrants with superior education and needed skills. Truman has called the Act inhumane and discriminatory.

July 11. Republican Convention at Chicago nominates General Dwight D. Eisenhower of Pennsylvania, who has been opposed by Senator Robert A. Taft of Ohio; Eastern internationalist Republicans, who back Eisenhower, win out over Western isolationists after dispute over credentials of Southern delegates. Senator Richard M. Nixon of California is nominated for Vice-President. **July 26.** Democrats, meeting at Chicago, nominate Governor Adlai E. Stevenson of Illinois after President Truman has announced that he will not run for a second term. (Two-term constitutional amendment does not apply to Truman, who otherwise would have been ineligible under this law.) Senator John J. Sparkman of Alabama is nominated for Vice-President. Minor party candidates are: Vincent W. Hallinan, Progressive and American Labor; Farrell Dobbs, Socialist Workers; General Douglas MacArthur, America First, Christian Nationalist, and Constitution (seven states only); Darlington Hoopes, Socialist; and Stuart Hamblen, Prohibition. Republican platform stresses government economy, criticizes Truman administration's

Asian policies, and advocates retaining the Taft-Hartley Act. Democrats advocate continuance of New Deal and Fair Deal policies, repeal of Taft-Hartley Act, and federal civil rights legislation.

July 16. President Truman signs "G.I. Bill of Rights" for Korean veterans; it provides benefits similar to those granted to World War II veterans.

Oct. 8. Korean truce talks, which are deadlocked on question of repatriation of prisoners, are recessed indefinitely by UN negotiations. Communists insist on mandatory return of North Koreans and Chinese, and the UN, believing that some have been forced into service, holds out for voluntary repatriation.

Nov. 4. General Eisenhower wins overwhelmingly in election, which gives both candidates the largest popular vote in history: Eisenhower, 33,936,000; Stevenson, 27,315,000. Electoral vote is Eisenhower, 442 (including 4 normally Democratic Southern states); Stevenson, 89. Republicans win majorities in both houses of Congress, but Senate majority is only 48 Republicans to 47 Democrats and 1 independent.

Nov. 29. In accordance with campaign promise made in October, President-elect Eisenhower leaves for Korea to inspect UN war situation. Three-day visit, in which he visits front lines, is kept secret until after he has left danger areas.

Continuing concentration of economic power is shown in report that 59 corporations, 35 of them financial rather than industrial, are in billion-dollar assets class.

By this year, various trade agreements have reduced tariffs to an average of 13 percent as opposed to the 53 percent of the early Thirties.

The *Revised Standard Version* of the Bible for Protestants is published; it has been edited by 32 scholars, who have worked since 1937, directed by Luther A. Weigle, dean emeritus of Yale Divinity School. In this same year, the Confraternity of Christian Doctrine publishes first eight books (volume 1) of the Old Testament for Roman Catholics.

1952-1953

To compete with television, Hollywood develops three-dimensional movie techniques in 1952. Natural Vision (3-D) films must be viewed through special eyeglasses and are not lastingly popular. Cinerama, made with three separate film strips and seven-channel stereophonic sound, succeeds but is prohibitively expensive. In 1953, CinemaScope, a less expensive, wide-screen system with stereophonic sound, is developed; this proves to be so successful that within a few years almost every movie theater in the U.S. has converted to Cinema-Scope projection installations.

1952-1962

Off-Broadway theater begins to grow with revival of Tennessee Williams' *Summer and Smoke*. It gains momentum, reaching its peak in 1961-1962, when there are 100 off-Broadway productions, 34 more than on Broadway.

1953

January-December. Each side in the Korean War accuses the other of atrocities. The U.S. continues to be accused of germ warfare, which it denies, appealing to the UN to investigate. UN adopts resolution accusing Communists of massacring or torturing 38,000 persons, of whom 35,000 are believed to be dead.

Feb. 2. President Eisenhower lifts U.S. fleet blockade of Chinese Nationalists on Formosa; move opens way for attacks by Nationalists on Red Chinese mainland.

March 10. Five days after death of Joseph Stalin, Senate Foreign Relations Committee shelves resolution condemning the Soviet Union for its forcible absorption of free European peoples. In January, Secretary of State John Foster Dulles has promised U.S. support to peoples behind the iron curtain. In April President Eisenhower asks that Eastern European nations be allowed their independence.

March 30. Dr. Albert Einstein announces formulas revising the unified field theory developed by him in 1945; theory aims to combine electromagnetic and gravitational equations in a single universal law. Although Einstein feels that this revision is a step forward, he is not satisfied that he has achieved his goal at the time of his death in 1955.

March 30. In a joint resolution, Congress authorizes new Cabinet-level Department of Health, Education, and Welfare, which replaces Federal Security Agency. Mrs. Oveta Culp Hobby is appointed first secretary.

April 11. UN truce team and Communists in Korea agree to exchange sick and wounded prisoners, although armistice has not yet been signed. **April 26.** Truce talks are resumed, while fighting continues. **June 8.** Agreement is reached on repatriation of prisoners of war; those who do not wish to return are to be held for up to 120 days, 90 days of which they are to be available to political persuasion. If they still refuse repatriation, they are to be freed as civilians.

April 20. U.S. government orders Communist Party to register with the Department of Justice as an organization that is controlled by the Soviet Union.

May 8. The Senate Foreign Relations Committee is told by President Eisenhower that he has granted France $60 million of aid in France's war against Vietminh (Communist) rebels in Indochina; additional financial aid to France is announced in September.

May 22. President Eisenhower signs Tidelands Oil Bill; action reverses policy of President Truman, who in January has set aside underwater oil lands as a naval petroleum reserve. Bill gives coastal states off-shore oil lands within the 3-mile limit (10½-mile limit for Texas and Florida), opening the way for immediate exploitation, and reserves to the federal government only oil lands beyond these limits (the outer Continental Shelf).

July 1. Following riots and strikes in East Germany, which are ended only by Soviet and East German military force, President Eisenhower announces that the U.S. will not intervene physically in the affairs of the iron curtain countries; he believes that people will seek their own freedom and revolt against repression. In November Secretary of State Dulles reiterates this belief, but declares that the U.S. does not morally approve of Soviet subjugation of nations.

July 27. Korean armistice is signed, and hostilities cease. Terms set up neutral zone two and a half miles wide and commissions to handle prisoners and administer the truce. The Korean War has been fought by UN forces from 16 countries, with the U.S. supplying the major number of men; in addition, medical units have been sent from 5 other countries. Communist Chinese have aided the North Koreans, and much matériel has been supplied to the North by the

Soviet Union. Casualty figures are: U.S. and other UN forces, about 39,000 killed or died while prisoners; South Korean, 70,000 military personnel killed or died, and 500,000 South Korean civilians died from disease, starvation, or as war casualties. Estimated Communist military casualties of all kinds (60 percent Chinese) are 1,600,000; in addition, about 400,000 of Communist forces have died of disease. The Korean War is the first in which helicopters have been used extensively to fly in supplies, transport the wounded, and carry troops.

Aug. 7. President Eisenhower signs Refugee Relief Act, which provides for admission to the U.S. in next three years of 214,000 victims of Communist persecution in addition to the regular quotas.

Aug. 8. Georgi Malenkov, head of Soviet government, announces that the Soviet Union has mastered production of the hydrogen bomb but declares that the Soviet Union is willing to settle all disputes by peaceful means. **Aug. 20.** The Soviet Union reveals testing of a hydrogen bomb; U.S. Atomic Energy Commission announces that the Soviet Union has conducted an atomic test on August 12 involving both fission and thermonuclear reactions.

Sept. 26. The U.S. agrees to give Spain $226 million in military and financial aid in return for the right to establish military bases in that country, although Spain does not join NATO defense organization.

September. About 90,000 Korean War prisoners have been exchanged by this month, but after talks with delegates from their home countries, many prisoners have elected to remain; these include 15,000 Chinese, almost 8,000 North Koreans, 335 South Koreans, 23 Americans, and 1 Briton. Earlier, South Korean guards on orders from President Syngman Rhee have sanctioned the escape of about 27,000 North Koreans who wish to remain in South Korea.

Oct. 20. Secretary of State Dulles confirms that the U.S. has canceled financial aid to Israel because Israel has failed to obey UN order to discontinue work on Jordan River hydroelectric project that is strongly opposed by Syria. The U.S. resumes aid after Israel agrees a week later to halt work.

Nov. 27. UN General Assembly declares Puerto Rico a self-governing political unit; although voluntarily associated with the U.S., it is no longer considered a colonial territory.

Dec. 16. It is announced that Major Charles E. Yeager has achieved air speed record of more than 1,600 miles per hour in a Bell Aircraft X-1A rocket-powered plane.

In a joint resolution, Congress proposes ending of all limitations that apply to Indian tribes of the U.S., giving individual Indians the same civil status as other citizens.

First educational television station, KUHT, operated by the University of Houston, Texas, broadcasts. Educational television, aided by public contributions and foundation grants, develops rapidly, with 52 stations by 1960.

1953-1954

June 14, 1953. At Dartmouth College commencement exercises, President Eisenhower admonishes his listeners not to join the book burners, a term applied to Republican Senator Joseph R. McCarthy, chairman of the Senate Permanent Subcommittee on Investigations, because of his campaign to remove from State Department libraries books alleged to be by Communists or their fellow travelers. **Feb. 4, 1954.** McCarthy embarks on national tour to expose "twenty years of treason" of the Democratic Party. **April 22-June 17.** Televised Army-McCarthy Senate hearings are a national sensation; McCarthy's claims of Communism in the U.S. Army, presented with clever showmanship but no substantiation, are further examples of McCarthyism, which has come to mean accusation without proof. **May 31.** Although not referring to McCarthy by name, President Eisenhower warns that thought control is endangering freedom.

Aug. 3, 1953. Congress approves Korean relief measure with appropriation of $200 million. **Jan. 26, 1954.** Senate approves U.S.-South Korea Mutual Defense Treaty; it becomes effective on November 17.

1953-1955

Dec. 8, 1953. Dr. Alton Ochsner reports that increase in lung cancer in the U.S. is caused by cigarette smoking. His findings are confirmed in the following year by the American Cancer Society. Cigarette sales decline at the time but by 1955 have begun rising again, especially sales of filter cigarettes.

1953-1957

Dec. 8, 1953. President Eisenhower makes "Atoms for Peace" proposal to the UN, urging that atomic resources and research into peaceful uses of atomic energy be turned over to an international body. **Sept. 6, 1954.** Unable to deal with the Soviet Union on "Atoms for Peace" program, President Eisenhower announces that the U.S., Great Britain, Canada, Australia, South Africa, and France are planning to form an agency to develop peaceful uses of nuclear power. **Oct. 23, 1956.** Eighty-two member states of the UN vote to establish an international agency to promote peaceful uses of atomic energy. **July 29, 1957.** International Atomic Energy Agency comes into existence officially when President Eisenhower signs ratification papers of U.S. membership.

1954

Jan. 2. Under a grant from the Rockefeller Foundation, Louisville (Kentucky) Orchestra begins series of 46 concerts featuring specially commissioned works of 19 living composers. **July 17.** Annual jazz festival is initiated at Newport, Rhode Island.

Jan. 12. Secretary of State Dulles announces shift of U.S. foreign policy from containment of the Soviet Union, as announced in the Truman Doctrine of 1947, to a plan of massive retaliation by means of its own choosing. **Jan. 21.** A reduction of military manpower and a cut of $4 billion in U.S. military budget is recommended by President Eisenhower.

Jan. 25-Feb. 18. Council of Foreign Ministers meets in Berlin, but no agreement is achieved on problem of reunification of Germany. Proposal by the Soviet Union of a security treaty covering all European nations with the U.S. and Communist China in the role of observers is turned down by the U.S., France, and Great Britain.

March 1. U.S. Atomic Energy Commission announces first of a new series of test explosions at its Pacific proving grounds in the Marshall Islands; danger of fallout is subsequently revealed. Soviet nuclear testing in the autumn also creates broad areas of fallout.

March 8. The U.S. and Japan sign mutual defense agreement guaranteeing U.S. assistance in building up Japan's defense forces.

March 16. It is reported in the French National Assembly that the U.S. has contributed more than three-fourths of France's cost of fighting Communists in Indochina. **May 7.** Although the U.S. has expected the French to win the war, Vietminh rebels take vital French fort at Dien Bien Phu during 19-nation Geneva Conference that is attempting to work out truce. **July 21.** Signing of armistice ends war of more than seven years; agreement divides Vietnam at about the 17th parallel into northern and southern parts, the north going to the Vietminh rebels and the south to the Vietnam government supported by France.

April 1. U.S. Air Force Academy is authorized. First class convenes in Denver in the following year, and the Academy moves to its permanent establishment near Colorado Springs three years later.

May 13. UN Subcommittee on Disarmament meets in London. After more than a month of discussion, the five powers are unable to agree on the banning and inspection of atomic weapons and reduction in conventional forces and armaments.

June 1. Investigating panel of U.S. Atomic Energy Commission (AEC) withdraws security clearance of J. Robert Oppenheimer, ending his work as AEC consultant, against advice of many leading scientists. Oppenheimer, who has led wartime atomic bomb effort, has been accused of being, among other things, pro-Communist; although the panel finds him loyal, it recommends that he be dismissed as lacking "enthusiasm" for the hydrogen-bomb project. In 1963 Oppenheimer receives AEC's highest honor, the Fermi Prize.

June 27. Pro-Communist regime in Guatemala is overthrown and replaced by an anti-Communist military junta. On the previous day, the U.S. and nine Latin-American nations have requested a meeting of the foreign ministers of the American states to discuss the Communist menace in Guatemala and its threat to the entire Western Hemisphere. **Sept. 1.** U.S. and Guatemala sign technical assistance agreement, which brings Point Four program in full to Guatemala.

July 22. Revised Organic Act of the Virgin Islands creates executive governorship, the governor to be appointed by U.S. President. In 1958 President Eisenhower appoints first native governor.

Aug. 2. Housing Redevelopment Act establishes policy of federal aid to urban renewal projects, with assistance in mortgage financing of new construction, rehabilitation of existing structures, and program of home building to accommodate families losing their homes as a result of slum clearance.

Aug. 5. In oil dispute between Great Britain and Iran, agreement is reached that gives right to oil production and sale to eight companies, five of which are American, with Iran to receive 50 percent of net profit.

Aug. 11. Chinese Communist leader Chou En-lai announces policy of liberation of Formosa, Nationalist Chinese island 121 miles off Chinese coast. **Aug. 17.** President Eisenhower replies that the U.S. Seventh Fleet will repel any invasion attempt. **Sept. 3-10.** Communists bombard Quemoy and Little Quemoy, Nationalist islands immediately off the Chinese coast, and Nationalists in return bombard nearby Communist island of Amoy. **Dec. 2.** Chinese Nationalists and the U.S. sign mutual defense treaty, but it does not include U.S. protection of small Nationalist islands along the Chinese coast.

Aug. 24. President Eisenhower signs Communist Control Act, which deprives in-

dividual Communists, the Communist Party, and other Communist organizations of many rights and privileges enjoyed by ordinary citizens and groups; Act also denies rights under National Labor Relations Act of 1935 to Communist-infiltrated labor unions.

Aug. 30. Atomic Energy Act allows development of peaceful atomic energy projects by private companies, which are also permitted to own nuclear materials; patents taken out must be shared for five years with other companies. Act also allows the U.S. to share information on atomic weapons and industrial uses with friendly nations. In November the U.S. and Great Britain pledge fissionable materials to international agency for research.

Sept. 1. Social Security amendments increase benefits and liberalize qualifications for receiving them, as well as adding new categories of beneficiaries, which increase rolls by 10 million people, including farm and domestic workers.

Sept. 8. South East Asia Treaty Organization (SEATO) is established by the U.S. and seven other nations, only three (Pakistan, Thailand, and the Philippines) of which are Asian; mutual security pact pledging joint military defense and promotion of political rights and economic development of area is signed. Formosa is not included in treaty.

Sept. 27. The U.S. and Canada agree to establish a line of radar stations (Distant Early Warning, or DEW, Line) across northern Canada from Greenland to Alaska. Earlier, work has been started on two other lines north of the U.S.-Canadian border — Pinetree Chain, which is already in operation, and Mid-Canada Line, which is still under construction. DEW Line begins functioning in 1957.

Oct. 27. Twenty-six comic-book publishers adopt voluntary code to eliminate from their lists obscene, vulgar, and horror comics. Protest against quality of comics is so strong that by 1955 13 states have enacted laws to control their content; although dropping from 422 to 335 titles, they still make up 35 percent of newsstand sales.

Oct. 28. Ernest Hemingway wins Nobel Prize for Literature, mainly for his latest work, *The Old Man and the Sea,* published in 1952.

Nov. 2. In close fall elections, Democrats win majority in both houses of Congress, the Senate by only one seat.

Dec. 2. Senator Joseph R. McCarthy, who has broken with Republican leaders and lost his position as head of the Senate Permanent Subcommittee on Investigations when Republicans are defeated in the fall elections, is formally condemned by a 67 to 22 Senate vote for acting contrary to Senate traditions during his investigation of Communism in government and the U.S. Army.

1954-1955

May 17, 1954. The Supreme Court, in *Brown* v. *Board of Education of Topeka,* reverses 1896 ruling allowing "separate but equal" educational facilities for Negroes. Court holds unanimously in case involving public schools that segregation is a violation of the Fourteenth Amendment, since it denies Negroes equal protection of the laws. May 31, 1955. The Supreme Court orders lower courts to use "all deliberate speed" in admitting Negro children to public schools. In some border states, compliance is almost immediate; in the deep South, decision meets with great hostility, and such groups as White Citizens' Committees are formed to fight it.

Government contract is awarded to private Dixon-Yates utility combine to build plant in West Memphis, Tennessee, to supplement electric power lost by Tennessee Valley Authority (TVA) to U.S. Atomic Energy Commission, thus enabling TVA to meet growing power needs of Memphis. Democrats accuse the Eisenhower administration of trying to dismember TVA. In the following year, Memphis announces plans to build municipal generating plant, and President Eisenhower cancels Dixon-Yates contract.

1954-1956

Feb. 23, 1954. Largest immunization test in history begins when Dr. Jonas E. Salk begins vaccinating elementary school pupils with his newly developed inactivated virus antipoliomyelitis vaccine; 2,480,000 children take part in the test. Oct. 21. Nobel Prize for Medicine and Physiology is awarded to three U.S. scientists who have discovered method of growing polio virus in quantities large enough to produce vaccine. April 12, 1955. Report on results of Salk test states that vaccine is believed to be 60 to 90 percent effective. Aug. 12. President Eisenhower signs Poliomyelitis Vaccination Assistance Act, which authorizes the U.S. Public Health Service to give $30 million to the states for purchase of poliomyelitis vaccine. By this year polio cases, which had been rising for almost a generation, have dropped sharply to about half the 1952 figure as a result of vaccination of children. In 1956 an oral (live virus) vaccine is developed; it eventually proves to be faster acting and easier to administer and is found to give protection to a community, as well as to individuals vaccinated.

Sept. 30, 1954. First atomic-powered submarine, U.S.S. *Nautilus,* is commissioned at Groton, Connecticut. In 1957, two more, the *Seawolf* and the *Skate,* are completed; the *Skate* is the first planned for assembly line production.

1954-1958

Four new man-made radioactive elements are produced: number 99, einsteinium, and number 100, fermium, in 1954; number 101, mendelevium, in 1955; and number 102, nobelium, in 1958. All are developed in the U.S. In 1955 a new atomic particle, the antiproton, is discovered, and in the following year the existence of the antineutron is confirmed; both discoveries are made at the University of California.

1954-1959

May 13, 1954. The U.S. authorizes building of the St. Lawrence Seaway in cooperation with Canada. **April 25, 1959.** The world's largest inland waterway, it opens to traffic, allowing oceangoing ships to travel 135 miles from Montreal to Lake Ontario and, through other lakes, 2,300 miles inland from the Atlantic Ocean. Related hydroelectric project has started operating in 1958.

1955

Jan. 1. The U.S., through the Foreign Operations Administration, begins giving economic assistance to Laos, Cambodia, and South Vietnam.

Jan. 28. Congress authorizes the President to use force to protect Formosa and the Pescadores from attack. **March 3.** Although Chinese Communists have been attacking smaller coastal islands, they decide risk of general war is too great when Secretary Dulles announces that U.S. protection will be extended.

Feb. 26. British physicist Cecil F. Powell estimates unofficially that by this time the U.S. has 4,000 atomic bombs stockpiled, and that the Soviet Union has 1,000, enough to kill everyone on earth several times over.

Feb. 28. Israelis and Egyptians clash on the Gaza Strip. **March 29.** The UN Security Council condemns Israel as the aggressor. **Sept. 4.** A cease-fire is worked out. **Nov. 16.** Israel asks the U.S. to sell it arms; however, no agreement is reached.

April 1. U.S. Senate ratifies treaties ending occupation of West Germany, which becomes independent, while Western occupation forces still there become security troops. One month later, West Germany formally becomes a member of NATO.

June 6. United Automobile Workers sign contract with Ford Motor Company and six days later with General Motors Corporation providing for pay during layoffs.

June 25. President Eisenhower signs peace treaty with Austria. After prolonged negotiations, treaty has been agreed to by all major powers. Pact establishes Austria's borders at 1938 pre-Hitler lines and guarantees Austria's independence.

July 21. At summit meeting of United States, Soviet Union, Great Britain, and France in Geneva, Switzerland, President Eisenhower proposes "Open Skies" policy of mutual aerial inspection by the major powers to forestall threats of war or surprise attacks. Besides disarmament, Eisenhower, British Prime Minister Anthony Eden, Soviet Premier Nikolai Bulganin, and French Premier Edgar Faure discuss unification of Germany and European security. Because of remilitarization of West Germany, the Soviet Union is opposed to its unification and rejects the West's proposals for ensuring European security, insisting instead on a European mutual defense alliance, including Germany but not the U.S. No significant agreements result.

Sept. 24. President Eisenhower suffers heart attack while in Colorado. Debate follows on how to handle possible incapacity (not death) of a President, since Eisenhower is unable to return to Washington until November.

Sept. 26. Two days after news of President Eisenhower's heart attack, stocks show sharpest drop since 1929. Dollar loss is $14 billion, greatest in U.S. history; more than 7,700,000 shares are traded in a single day.

Sept. 29. *A View from the Bridge* and *A Memory of Two Mondays,* two short plays by Pulitzer Prize playwright Arthur Miller, open in New York City; Miller's play *The Crucible,* based on the Salem witch trials and interpreted by some to refer to the McCarthy Senate hearings, has been produced the previous year.

Nov. 28-Dec. 1. White House Conference on Education recommends expanded federal aid to all levels of public education despite controversy over federal control.

Dec. 5. American Federation of Labor and Congress of Industrial Organizations merge with strong central government, equal recognition for craft and industrial unions, and an agreement to avoid competitive organizing drives. Combined AFL-CIO membership is about 16 million workers in this year.

By the end of this year, the U.S. has admitted more than 406,000 displaced persons since special admission act, passed in 1948.

By this year, electronic computers are beginning to be used widely in commerce, industry, transportation, and education.

1955-1956

Dec. 5, 1955. Negro boycott of segregated city bus lines in Montgomery, Alabama, begins. Lasting through 1956, when a Supreme Court decision forces desegregation of local transportation facilities, boycott results in loss to bus lines of much of their business. The Interstate Commerce Commission has earlier banned segregation on interstate transportation. Dr. Martin Luther King, Jr., leads movement and, with the National Association for the Advancement of Colored People (NAACP), spearheads further activity against segregation in stores, theaters, and other public places. Desegregation movement continues in spite of segregationist reprisals, such as job dismissals, mortgage foreclosures, and boycott of Negro businesses.

In these two years, private colleges, universities, and medical schools benefit from Ford Foundation education grants totaling more than $360 million; gifts are mainly for increases in faculty salaries, but more than $6 million benefits educational television.

1956

Jan. 19. Alabama Senate approves nullification of the Supreme Court decision integrating public schools. **Feb. 1.** Legislature of Virginia adopts resolution of interposition, challenging Supreme Court's outlawing of segregated public schools.

Feb. 6. Autherine Lucy, first Negro student to attempt to enter the University of Alabama, is suspended after three days of riots due to her presence. In March she is expelled because of lawsuit she has brought against the University. In this year, violence erupts in several places in the South when Negro students attempt to enroll in all-white schools and colleges.

Feb. 15. U.S. District Court in Louisiana voids all state laws that do not conform to Supreme Court's 1954 ruling on segregation.

Feb. 17. After he receives evidence of corrupt lobbying, President Eisenhower vetoes Natural Gas Bill, which provides exemption for independent producers from control by the Federal Power Commission.

March 7. The State of Virginia, which has closed its public schools after desegregation ruling of the Supreme Court, amends law to permit use of state money for private schools in attempt to defy Court's decision.

March 12. One hundred and one Southern senators and representatives publish manifesto against school integration, calling on states to disobey and resist "by all lawful means" the Supreme Court's rulings on desegregation of public schools.

March 28. Iceland demands removal of all NATO forces from the island. The U.S., unwilling to evacuate air base important to world network, is successful by November in persuading the Icelandic government to allow the U.S. to continue operating the Keflavik Air Base.

April 9. In *Slochower* v. *New York City Higher Education Board,* the Supreme Court finds that public servants may not be excluded from the protection of the Fifth Amendment of the U.S. Constitution, and that exercising the privilege against self-incrimination is not equivalent either to a confession of guilt or a conclusive presumption of perjury.

May 2. Methodist Church conference in Minneapolis demands end to racial segregation in Methodist churches.

May 28. Agricultural (Soil Bank) Act provides for paying farmers for taking cropland out of production and placing land into soil-building cover crops or trees to cut surpluses and improve land without impairing farm income.

June 29. Federal-Aid Highway Act is signed; it authorizes a 13-year program of highway construction, to be financed by various taxes on motorists. Federal funds are to cover 90 percent of the cost of a 41,000-mile interstate system and up to 50 percent of road construction within states.

July 19. After Egypt has accepted offer of financial aid for building of Aswan Dam, the U.S. retracts offer. **July 26.** Egyptian President Gamal Abd-al-Nasser announces nationalization of the Suez Canal, saying that revenue from Canal will be used to finance the Dam.

Aug. 16. At Democratic National Convention in Chicago, Adlai E. Stevenson of Illinois is nominated for President, although former President Harry S. Truman has backed Averell Harriman; the next day Senator Estes Kefauver of Tennessee is chosen for Vice-President, winning nomination over Senator John F. Kennedy of Massachusetts. **Aug. 22.** Republicans, meeting in San Francisco, renominate President Eisenhower and Vice-President Nixon. Minor party candidates are: T. Coleman Andrews, States' Rights; Enoch A. Holtwick, Prohibition; Eric Hass, Socialist Labor; and Darlington Hoopes, Socialist. Democratic and Republican platforms differ very little: both support desegregation; Democrats favor public water power, while Republicans advocate combinations of private and government organizations; both support parity payments to farmers, the Democrats fixed payments and the Republicans flexible ones.

Sept. 25. First transatlantic telephone cable begins operation; two cables, each 2,250 miles long, stretching from Newfoundland to Scotland, have three times the capacity of radio telephone circuits.

Oct. 20. Soviet Premier Bulganin's letter to President Eisenhower endorsing proposal of presidential candidate Adlai E. Stevenson that all nations stop nuclear testing is made public. Bulganin is accused by some U.S. officials of interfering in U.S. elections.

Oct. 23. Police in Budapest, Hungary, fire upon demonstrators who demand that the government form a democracy and free the country from domination by the Soviet Union. **Oct. 30.** Free elections and a policy of neutrality are promised, and Soviet troops begin leaving Budapest and apparently also Hungary. **Nov. 4.** Soviet tanks and troops sweep through Budapest, brutally crushing opposition. All resistance ends three days later. Premier Imre Nagy has appealed to the UN for help, but too late. A new Communist dictatorship is set up; about 160,000 democratic-minded students and workers flee across the borders, mostly into Austria. Two years later it is announced that Nagy and other leaders of the uprising have been executed.

Oct. 29-Nov. 1. When August international conference fails to settle Suez Canal issues, Israel, Britain, and France attack Egypt. **Nov. 6.** Pressure by the U.S. and the Soviet Union brings about cease-fire.

Nov. 6. President Eisenhower wins election by a landslide, with Stevenson taking only seven Southern states. Popular vote is Eisenhower, 35,590,000; Stevenson, 26,023,000. Electoral vote is 457 to 73 (with one Alabama elector refusing to vote for Stevenson). Election is a personal victory for Eisenhower, who runs far ahead of other Republican candidates. Congress becomes Democratic in both houses, the first time in 108 years that the party of an incoming President has not had control of at least one house of Congress.

Dec. 2. Released from prison in 1955 after serving sentence for revolutionary activities, Cuban leader Fidel Castro lands with a

small group of guerrillas in Oriente Province, determined to overthrow government of dictator Fulgencio Batista.

Dec. 6. President Eisenhower orders Defense Department to set up system of emergency air and sea transportation to bring to the U.S. 15,000 Hungarian refugees.

1956-1957

Nov. 17, 1956. The Soviet Union declares that it will accept a modified form of the "Open Skies" policy proposed by the U.S. in the previous year, but in 1957, after extended discussion between U.S. and Soviet disarmament representatives, the Soviet Union withdraws acceptance.

1956-1958

March 27, 1956. Internal Revenue officers close down Communist newspaper the *Daily Worker* for nonpayment of taxes. A week later, $4,500 partial tax payment is made, and paper resumes publication. **Jan. 13, 1958.** Because of lack of funds, it is forced to become a weekly *(The Worker)* rather than a daily.

1957

Feb. 25. On the ground that enforcement of such a law would leave nothing for adults to read except that suitable for children, the Supreme Court voids Michigan law against selling publications that might corrupt children.

March 7. Congress approves the so-called Eisenhower Doctrine, which seeks to prevent subversion or conquest of Middle Eastern countries by supplying economic and military assistance (including the use of U.S. armed forces) upon request to those countries threatened by Communist aggression. In the same year, disturbances in Jordan and Syria lead to sending of U.S. Sixth Fleet, but no intervention is necessary.

April 10. The Suez Canal reopens after UN engineering team removes sunken ships and other barriers placed in it by Egypt to render it unnavigable during the nationalization crisis.

May 2. Dave Beck, president of the Teamsters Union, is indicted for income tax evasion and 18 days later is removed from executive positions within the AFL-CIO when it is discovered that he has used union funds for his own personal gain and profit. Beck is convicted of embezzlement in December. **Dec. 6.** The AFL-CIO expels the Teamsters Union for domination by corrupt leaders, especially James Hoffa.

June 17. In *Watkins* v. *United States,* the Supreme Court voids a conviction for contempt of Congress, ruling that the freedoms of the First Amendment of the U.S. Constitution cannot be abridged in legislative inquiries and that unless a particular inquiry is justified by a specific legislative need, protected freedoms should not be jeopardized.

June 24. Three leading atomic scientists report on the possibility of producing a smaller hydrogen bomb with essentially no radioactive fallout, revealing that they have already reduced radioactive fallout from a hydrogen bomb explosion by 95 percent and that with further development the fallout will become essentially negligible.

July 1. International Geophysical Year begins; scientists of about 70 nations (including the U.S.) take part in an 18-month study of the earth, atmosphere and space, oceans and glaciers, and the sun.

July 2. To the UN Disarmament Subcommittee meeting in London, the U.S. proposes a 10-month halt in nuclear testing as a first step toward disarmament; this time could be used for setting up an inspection system. **Aug. 21.** As a concession to Soviet demands for a longer suspension, President Eisenhower announces that the U.S. has offered to suspend nuclear testing for two years on condition that the Soviet Union agree to inspection and to a halt in the production of fissionable materials for weapons purposes; the Soviet Union does not concur, and talks in London are suspended indefinitely the following month.

Aug. 29. In spite of filibuster of more than 24 hours by Senator Strom Thurmond of South Carolina, Congress passes a bill that for the first time since 1875 seeks to protect the civil rights of Negroes. Act creates a commission to investigate denial of voting rights because of race or religion and makes interference with the right to vote in national elections a federal offense. Although the number of Negroes who have registered to vote has increased, it is still much less than those eligible.

Oct. 4. Soviet scientists, investigating upper atmosphere conditions as part of International Geophysical Year program, send "Sputnik," first rocket-powered artificial earth satellite, into orbit. Second Soviet satellite, carrying a dog, is orbited on November 3. The world and the U.S., long accustomed to thinking of the U.S. as superior in all branches of advanced technology, are astonished. Critics of U.S. educational system decry lack of discipline in study of scientific fundamentals in U.S. schools, as well as failure to recruit and train bright students.

Oct. 25. Two aluminum pellets, fired into space by the U.S. Air Force, escape the earth's gravity and go into outer space.

Nov. 25. Eisenhower has a slight stroke. This illness, as well as previous heart attack and intestinal operation, causes renewed discussion of methods for dealing with incapacity of the President.

Nov. 25. In *Yates* v. *United States,* the Supreme Court holds that, under Smith Act, teaching the violent overthrow of the government in principle may not be equated with actually inciting to overthrow.

John Kerouac publishes his novel *On the Road,* a testament of the beat generation, which rejects modern society. Allen Ginsberg's book of poetry *Howl,* published in 1956, has dealt with the same theme.

1957-1958

Nov. 10, 1957. U.S. Office of Education publishes two-year survey of education in the Soviet Union, which shows that emphasis on scientific and technical education in the U.S.S.R. is far ahead of that in the U.S. **June 1958.** U.S. educators who have made a government-sponsored trip to the Soviet Union confirm these findings.

1957-1959

Sept. 24, 1957. To ensure enforcement of U.S. District Court order requiring enrollment of Negroes at the Central High School in Little Rock, Arkansas, President Eisenhower calls the Arkansas National Guard into federal service and dispatches 1,000 paratroopers to Little Rock. Nine Negro students enter guarded school on the following day. Troops remain in service until November 27. Other Southern and border states resist integration or register only token numbers of Negroes in previously all-white schools. **Sept. 1958.** The Supreme Court rejects any delay of integration in Little Rock, ruling it the duty of state and local officials to end school segregation as promptly as possible. **Aug. 12, 1959.** Following failure of a maneuver by Arkansas Governor Orval E. Faubus to segregate city

schools by changing their category to private schools, high schools in Little Rock reopen with Negro students attending under police protection.

1958

Jan. 31. In the space exploration race with the Soviet Union, the U.S. begins to close the gap by putting into orbit by a Jupiter-C rocket the artificial satellite Explorer I, weighing 31 pounds. **March 17.** The U.S. Navy launches a three-pound satellite, Vanguard I. **May 15.** The Soviet Union sends Sputnik III, a 3,000-pound capsule, into orbit. **Dec. 18.** Score, 8,800-pound Atlas missile, is orbited by the U.S. All ventures achieve firsts in space exploration: Explorer I discovers inner (Van Allen) radiation belt; Vanguard I provides first proof that the earth is (slightly) pear shaped; Sputnik III contains first space laboratory for measuring aspects of the atmosphere; and Score transmits a voice from space for the first time.

Feb. 16. In Indonesian civil war, anti-Communist rebels in Padang order American-owned oil companies to cease all shipments to Java. The U.S. adopts policy of neutrality. **Aug. 18.** After rebels are repulsed, the U.S. is reported to be shipping light military equipment to pro-Communist government.

March 6. It is revealed that President Eisenhower has rejected proposal to make the U.S. the first nation to produce planes powered by nuclear energy; he holds that such a prestige effort is wasteful of scarce materials and talent.

April 14. It is formally announced that American pianist Harvey L. ("Van") Cliburn has won the international Tchaikovsky piano competition in Moscow, playing Rachmaninoff's Third Piano Concerto;

award highlights increase in cultural exchange between the U.S. and the Soviet Union in this period.

April 16. Dr. Edward Teller says that suspension of nuclear testing may sacrifice millions of lives in case of nuclear war. **April 28.** Disagreeing with report by U.S. Atomic Energy Commission that radioactive fallout has not reached dangerous levels, Dr. Linus Pauling states that radiation from carbon 14 already released by testing will cause defects in 5 million children and millions of cancer and leukemia cases in the next 300 generations. **Aug. 10.** A UN committee reports that radiation, even in very small amounts, can cause damage to health and to the children of future generations; report states, however, that dosage varies with area, and that the situation needs further study.

April 27. Vice-President Richard M. Nixon leaves on a goodwill tour of South America. He is so hostilely received by demonstrators, especially in Venezuela and Peru, that President Eisenhower sends troops to Caribbean in case of further trouble. Nixon arrives back in U.S. on May 15.

April 29. The U.S. offers resolution to the UN Security Council that an Arctic armament inspection zone be set up, with agreements on other areas to follow. **May 2.** The proposal is vetoed by the Soviet Union.

May 3. To 11 nations conducting scientific work the U.S. proposes in the Antarctic, a treaty providing for demilitarization of the continent and international cooperation in research there. The treaty is signed in the following year by all 12 nations.

May 3. The U.S. rejects Polish proposal to denuclearize central Europe, because it could not be controlled by inspection and

would leave Western forces in Germany exposed to numerically stronger Soviet forces.

July 15. In response to an appeal by President Camille Chamoun of Lebanon, made following an uprising against his own government and the overthrow of the government of neighboring Iraq, both inspired by Arab nationalism, the U.S. sends more than 5,000 marines to restore order under the Eisenhower Doctrine. British troops enter Jordan shortly afterward when rebels threaten attack on King Hussein's government. U.S. and British troops are withdrawn in October.

July 29. National Aeronautics and Space Administration is formed to handle space research; military space investigation and activity are to be handled by the Department of Defense.

Aug. 3. U.S.S. *Nautilus*, nuclear-powered submarine, makes first submerged under-ice crossing of the North Pole on voyage from Hawaii to Iceland. **Aug. 11.** The U.S.S. *Skate* follows suit on round trip from Connecticut to North Pole. **Oct. 6.** U.S.S. *Seawolf* completes 60-day submersion.

Aug. 6. President Eisenhower signs the Defense Reorganization Act, which makes important changes in the organization of the Department of Defense, including eliminating ambiguities about command authority, centralizing research and engineering within the Department, and making each service secretary responsible to secretary of defense.

Aug. 23. Chinese Communists resume bombardment of offshore Quemoy Islands. **Sept. 3.** The U.S. fleet begins escorting supply vessels from Formosa to Quemoy, up to the three-mile territorial limit of Chinese waters. **Sept. 30.** Secretary of State Dulles suggests a cease-fire to break deadlock in negotiations with Communist China. **Oct. 6.** The Chinese Communists order the cease-fire, but on October 25 it becomes effective only on alternate days.

Aug. 25. Presidential pension law goes into effect. This is the first law ever enacted to provide an income for former U.S. Presidents.

Aug. 29. President Eisenhower signs Welfare and Pension Plans Disclosure Act, which requires reporting of management and resources of all except very small labor welfare and pension plans. Since World War II, such funds have become a major source of investment capital, but they have not been regulated to protect either the beneficiaries or the public.

Sept. 2. President Eisenhower signs National Defense Education Act which authorizes low-interest, long-term tuition loans to college and graduate students, with inducements to enter the teaching profession and special encouragements for study of mathematics, languages, and sciences. Aid to educational television is also authorized. Part of startled U.S. response to Soviet space-satellite successes, the Act is based largely on 1957 U.S. Office of Education report on education in the Soviet Union.

Sept. 22. Assistant to the President Sherman Adams resigns because of charges of improper use of official influence. During this year several cases of "conflict of interest" by corporation executives serving in federal government have been disclosed.

Oct. 4. The U.S. and Japan begin negotiations in Tokyo to revise the security treaty of 1951 in order to allow Japan greater power over its arms and military forces. U.S. occupation forces have been withdrawn from Japan in the previous year, but the Japanese (encouraged by the Soviet Union) are strongly opposed to the 1951 treaty and to occupation of former Japanese islands by the U.S.

Oct. 11. Pioneer moon rocket is launched by the U.S.; it fails to reach the moon but reaches an altitude of more than 79,000 miles, 30 times as high as any earlier man-made object.

Oct. 25. Communist China completes withdrawal of its troops from North Korea. In the following year North Korea is accused of 218 violations of the armistice by the Military Armistice Commission of the UN.

Oct. 26. Pan American World Airways begins transatlantic jet service. **Dec. 10.** Regular commercial jet flights begin within the U.S.

Nov. 4. As a result of dissatisfaction with Republican farm, labor, and foreign affairs policies, Democrats gain seats in both houses of Congress in the fall elections, acquiring 50 more seats in the House and 15 more in the Senate. Senator John F. Kennedy of Massachusetts polls the greatest plurality in the state's history.

Nov. 8. The U.S. signs agreement with the European Atomic Energy Community (Euratom) to cooperate in exchange of atomic materials and information for research.

Nov. 10. Soviet Premier Khrushchev announces that the Soviet Union is planning to turn over East Berlin to the East German government. **Nov. 21.** The U.S., alarmed at the prospect of a blockade of West Berlin by the East Germans, states that it will protect its sector of the city. **Nov. 27.** The Soviet Union proposes that West Berlin become a free, independent city and announces that it will turn over

East Berlin to East Germany by the following June.

Nov. 24. UN approves setting up a Committee on the Peaceful Uses of Outer Space in an effort to keep this field clear of political rivalries. A permanent committee is established in the following year, its members being representatives of 5 neutral, 12 Western and pro-Western, and 7 Communist nations.

Nov. 28. The U.S. fires Atlas intercontinental ballistic missile a distance of more than 6,000 miles in Atlantic Ocean testing zone.

Dec. 20. Military-civilian regime that has overthrown Venezuelan dictatorship in January alters tax laws to provide Venezuela with 60, instead of 50, percent of profits of oil companies (including U.S.).

Slowdown of business activity, with unemployment of 4,681,000, continues from last months of the previous year. Rate of national economic growth lags markedly behind growth rate of the Soviet Union.

This year, for the first time, airlines carry more transatlantic passengers than ships do.

John Kenneth Galbraith publishes *The Affluent Society,* arguing that the abundance made possible by modern technology cannot all be used up in private consumption or in investment but must be devoted to expanded public services.

The Solomon R. Guggenheim Museum, designed by Frank Lloyd Wright, is completed; it is the first and only structure of Wright's to be built in New York City. Wright dies in the following year.

U.S. churches report large increases in membership since 1950; those with greatest

percentages of gain are the Roman Catholic Church, the Southern Baptist Convention, the Churches of Christ, and the Methodists, which all together total more than 13 million new members.

1958-1959

March 31, 1958. The Soviet Union announces that it is discontinuing nuclear testing independent of Western nations but resumes testing six months later because the U.S. and Great Britain have not stopped doing so. **Oct. 31.** Representatives of the U.S., Great Britain, and the Soviet Union meet in Geneva, Switzerland, to discuss suspension of nuclear tests under international control. **Nov. 1.** UN approves U.S. resolution to suspend nuclear testing during the Geneva negotiations; the Soviet Union votes against it. **Aug. 1959.** When the U.S. announces that it is extending its nuclear test ban, Great Britain and the Soviet Union follow suit; however, everyone resumes testing two years later.

1959

Jan. 3. Alaska, with Juneau as capital, is declared the forty-ninth state of the Union. Its area is 586,400 square miles, making it the largest state, and its population is about 191,000, smallest of any state. First requested in 1916, statehood has not been approved until 1958, partly because private interests, such as canning companies, fear higher taxes and loss of federal subsidies. Addition of forty-ninth state requires change in U.S. flag, which is redesigned with a field of seven rows of seven stars each.

Jan. 19. Virginia state laws aimed at preventing school integration are ruled invalid by the Virginia Supreme Court. Two weeks later, schools in Norfolk and Arlington are desegregated with no disorders.

March 30. The Supreme Court holds that separate trials by a state and by the federal government for the same crime do not constitute double jeopardy.

April 5. The U.S. Naval Research Laboratory reports that Soviet nuclear tests made in the fall of 1958 have increased atmospheric radioactivity in the eastern U.S. by 300 percent.

April 7. Twenty-eight-year-old Negro playwright Lorraine V. Hansberry receives New York Drama Critics Circle Award for her play *A Raisin in the Sun,* the story of a Chicago Negro family struggling for a better life. Miss Hansberry dies six years later of cancer.

April 9. Seven astronauts are chosen by National Aeronautics and Space Administration to embark on a training program that will equip each of them to be ready to ride a manned space capsule in 1961.

April 15-28. Fidel Castro, head of revolutionary government in Cuba since defeat of dictator Batista, visits the U.S., where he has much support in spite of wholesale executions of Batista supporters.

May 1. Organization of American States observation group in Panama obtains surrender of small invasion force of revolutionaries, most of whom are Cuban.

May. The U.S. signs agreements with Canada, the Netherlands, Turkey, and West Germany to supply information and equipment needed to train their forces in the use of atomic weapons; agreements are the beginning of move to enable forces of these countries to take part in atomic conflicts if necessary.

July 1. It is announced that the U.S. will resume economic and technical aid to Egypt, which has joined with Syria as the United Arab Republic (U.A.R.) in the previous year. In December the U.A.R. receives from the International Bank more than $56 million for work on the Suez Canal.

July 15. Nationwide steel strike begins after two-week delay requested by President Eisenhower. **Oct. 21.** When virtually no progress is made in negotiations, U.S. District Court in Pittsburgh, at request of Eisenhower, orders 80-day injunction under the Taft-Hartley Act. **Nov. 7.** Strike ends after Supreme Court decision upholds injunction, which has been held up until now by legal argument; strike has lasted for 116 days, the longest steel strike in U.S. history. Settlement is reached the following January, the steelworkers winning major demands.

Aug. 1. Vice-President Nixon, during a visit to Moscow, tells the Soviet people over television and radio that any attempt by Premier Khrushchev to spread Communism outside the Soviet Union will result in fear and tension for them.

Aug. 21. Hawaii is proclaimed fiftieth state of the Union, after failing since 1903 to attain statehood. Population is about 656,000, half of whom live in the capital, Honolulu, on the island of Oahu. Land area is 6,424 square miles and consists of eight major islands, of which seven are inhabited, and several minor islands. Population is Japanese, Caucasian, Hawaiian, Filipino, and Chinese. Second new U.S. flag within a year is designed, with a field of five six-star rows alternating with four five-star rows, to become official on July 4, 1960.

Aug. 24. Seating of two Hawaiian senators and one representative increases number of U.S. senators to 100 and number of representatives to 437, but after the 1960 census, and becoming effective with the

1962 elections, the latter number is reduced to the 435 fixed by Congress in 1929.

Sept. 14. President Eisenhower signs Labor-Management Reporting and Disclosure Act, which seeks to control internal administration of labor unions and to protect rights of individual union members against corruption of union officials. Secondary boycott provisions of Taft-Hartley Act are also amended. Passage of the law is in part owing to disclosures before congressional committees of racketeering influences in unions.

Sept. 15-27. Soviet Premier Khrushchev visits the U.S. for informal talks with President Eisenhower and tours the U.S. After he leaves the U.S. is told that among other understandings to relieve world tension, Khrushchev has withdrawn the Soviet ultimatum on Berlin.

Dec. 30. The U.S. commissions first nuclear submarine that is able to carry and launch missiles, the *George Washington*.

During this year the U.S. and the Soviet Union continue to make advances in space exploration. Of three Soviet spacecraft, one goes into orbit around the sun, becoming the first artificial planet; one lands on the moon; and one passes around the moon, sending photographs of the hitherto unseen opposite side. Four U.S. space probes, much smaller, transmit photographs and first television pictures of the earth and information on various aspects of the atmosphere.

June 11, 1959. *Lady Chatterley's Lover* by D. H. Lawrence is banned from the U.S. mails by Postmaster General Arthur E. Summerfield as pornographic, smutty, obscene, and filthy. **March 25, 1960.** U.S. Court of Appeals rules that novel is not obscene and may be sent through the mails.

1959-1960

Nov. 30, 1959. Citizens of Panama, resentful of any equalities between Canal Zone Americans and native Panamanians, focus on question of flying Panamanian flag in the Canal Zone. Mobs attack U.S. Embassy and try unsuccessfully to invade the area. **Sept. 17, 1960.** It is announced that President Eisenhower has ordered that both flags be flown.

1960

Jan. 23. Lieutenant Don Walsh of the U.S. Navy and Jacques Piccard set new ocean diving record in the bathyscaphe *Trieste* when they descend to a depth of 35,800 feet in the Marianas Trench, near the island of Guam in the Pacific Ocean.

Feb. 2. Four Negro college students who stage sit-in to force desegregation of a lunch counter in Greensboro, North Carolina, set off series of such demonstrations throughout the South; hundreds of Negroes and whites, mostly students, take part. The following year, the first sit-in convictions to reach the Supreme Court are set aside when Court voids conviction of 16 Negroes for breach of peace; however, decision does not outlaw all restaurant segregation, nor does it cover sit-in convictions for trespassing.

April 21. Because of subterfuge practised by Southern states to keep Negroes from registering to vote, Congress passes Civil Rights Act of 1960 in spite of continuous Senate filibuster lasting more than 125 hours. Act allows federal authorities to step in when state registration practices are questionable.

May 5. Just before Paris summit meeting of President Eisenhower and Premier Khrushchev, the Soviet Union announces that a U.S. photographic reconnaissance plane (U-

2) has been shot down over Soviet territory on May 1. **May 7.** Premier Khrushchev announces that the plane's pilot, Francis Gary Powers, is alive and has confessed to having been on a spying mission. **May 9.** U.S. Secretary of State Christian Herter admits such flights have existed for several years in order to gather information to protect the West from surprise attack and asserts that flights will be continued unless the Soviet Union lessens the danger of aggression. **May 11.** Eisenhower admits that he personally has authorized the U-2 flights. **May 16.** At opening of summit conference, Eisenhower announces that U-2 flights have been suspended and are not to be resumed; Khrushchev withdraws invitation to Eisenhower to visit the Soviet Union. **May 17.** Summit conference breaks up amid charges and countercharges between East and West. **Aug. 17-19.** At trial in Moscow, Powers is found guilty of espionage for the U.S. and sentenced to 10 years' loss of liberty, 3 of which are to be spent in prison and the remainder at labor in a restricted area. The following January, Khrushchev says that he will stop making an issue out of the U-2 incident in hopes of bettering relations with Eisenhower's successor. Powers is released and flown back to the U.S. a year later in exchange for the Soviet spy Rudolf Abel.

June 16. President Eisenhower's proposed visit to Japan is canceled because of anti-U.S. riots in that country; riots are directed against new U.S.-Japanese mutual security treaty that provides for possible wartime uses of U.S. bases in Japan and equipping of Japanese forces with atomic weapons. Results of election in autumn in effect indicate approval of Japanese ratification of the treaty in June.

June 27. Disarmament conference with 10 countries represented breaks up with no agreement after long deadlock over international inspection, disarmament procedure, and Soviet demand that the U.S. withdraw from foreign military bases.

June 29. Following strong Cuban criticism of the U.S. and deterioration of relations between the two countries, during which Cuba draws closer to the Soviet Union, the U.S. protests to the Organization of American States that Cuba is causing trouble in the Caribbean. On same day, Cuba seizes U.S.-owned oil refinery. **July 6.** The U.S. cuts, and later suspends entirely, the quota of sugar sold by Cuba to the U.S. **Aug. 7.** Premier Castro announces "forcible expropriation" of all U.S.-owned companies. **Oct. 19.** U.S. blocks shipment to Cuba of all goods except medical supplies and food.

July 1. A second U.S. reconnaissance plane is shot down over Soviet territory. Two survivors are imprisoned but released in the following year.

July 13. Democratic convention at Los Angeles nominates Senator John F. Kennedy of Massachusetts on the first ballot. Senator Lyndon B. Johnson of Texas, who has rivaled Kennedy for the nomination, is chosen for Vice-President the next day. **July 27.** Republicans at Chicago nominate Vice-President Richard M. Nixon of California for President; on following day Henry Cabot Lodge of Massachusetts is chosen as his running mate. Minor party candidates are: Eric Hass, Socialist Labor; Farrell Dobbs, Socialist Workers; Rutherford L. Decker, Prohibition; and Arkansas Governor Orval Faubus, National States' Rights. Democratic platform stresses stronger civil rights legislation and federal medical care for the aged through the Social Security system, as well as denouncing the Eisenhower fiscal policy. Republicans support the Eisenhower foreign policy, a health program, increase in national defense, and a strong civil rights act.

July 20. First successful underwater launching of Polaris missiles is accomplished when they are fired from a submerged atomic submarine at targets more than 1,100 miles away.

Sept. 13. President Eisenhower signs Social Security amendments, which grant federal aid to states for medical programs for the needy aged and eventually for other needy persons; but they do not form the all-inclusive plan urged by many at this time.

Sept. 20-Dec. 21. Attended at various times by many heads of state, including Eisenhower, Khrushchev, Castro, Nasser, Macmillan, Nehru, and Tito, the opening of the fifteenth session of the UN General Assembly in New York City is probably the greatest diplomatic gathering in history. Khrushchev uses the forum to denounce Eisenhower's policies but leaves opening for a conference with a new President.

Sept. 26. In the first of four television debates Vice-President Nixon and Senator Kennedy exchange views on domestic policy. This and the subsequent debates bring contrasting personalities of the candidates before the electorate more immediately than in any previous election. To permit the debates, Congress suspends a Federal Communications Commission rule requiring that all candidates be allowed equal broadcast time.

Oct. 26. In response to Cuban government threats against U.S. military occupation of naval base at Guantánamo, Cuba (agreed to in treaty of 1903), it is announced that if necessary the U.S. will defend the base by force of arms.

Nov. 3. Dr. Willard Frank Libby of the University of California (formerly of the University of Chicago) wins Nobel Prize for Chemistry for technique of dating geological and archeological material by measuring disintegration of its radioactive carbon 14 content.

Nov. 8. Senator Kennedy wins election, in which a record number of citizens vote, taking 50.1 percent of the major party vote. Popular vote is Kennedy, 34,227,000; Nixon, 34,108,000. Electoral vote is in question for a time because of recounts demanded by some states and votes of unpledged electors from Mississippi; final electoral vote (not official until January 1961) is Kennedy, 303, with 23 states; Nixon, 219, with 26 states; and 15 electoral votes going to Senator Harry F. Byrd of Virginia. Both houses of Congress remain under Democratic control.

Nov. 8. It is announced that the U.S. will relinquish most bases in the British West Indies leased for 99 years during World War II in exchange for U.S. destroyers sent to Britain.

Nov. 14. Two elementary schools in New Orleans begin school desegregation in the Deep South amid riots and extensive absences among white children.

Nov. 16. Concerned about U.S. balance of payments deficit and drain of gold from the country, President Eisenhower orders all U.S. agencies to limit spending in foreign countries.

Nov. 17. Because of increase of tension in the Caribbean and major buildup of Cuban armed forces, it is revealed that President Eisenhower has sent U.S. naval units to the Caribbean with orders to prevent possible Cuban Communist attacks on Nicaragua and Guatemala.

Dec. 2. President Eisenhower announces appropriation of $1 million for care of those emigrating to the U.S. to escape Fidel Castro's regime in Cuba.

Dec. 15. The U.S. announces its support of rightist rebels in Laos one day before they gain control from pro-Communist coalition government. Ten days earlier, coalition government has demanded that the U.S. stop sending arms to the rebels and has agreed to a cease-fire. **Dec. 30.** New rightist government appeals to the UN, citing reported troop movements from North Vietnam. On the following day, the U.S. warns North Vietnam and Communist China to refrain from military action in Laos.

1960 census shows a U.S. population of 179,323,000 of which nearly 70 percent live in places of 2,500 or more. Immigration since the previous census has been 2,515,000. Shifts in population make it necessary to change the number of seats in the House of Representatives for 25 states; trend is mainly westward, with California gaining eight seats since 1950.

The U.S. achieves three firsts in space exploration in this year: Discoverer 13 is first capsule recovered from orbit; Discoverer 14 is first to be recovered in mid-air (at 8,500 feet); and Tiros 1 is first weather satellite, sending back to earth about 23,000 television pictures of global cloud cover. The Soviet Union succeeds in a controlled landing of animals (insects, mice, and dogs) in Sputnik 5.

The U.S. automobile industry begins shift to compact economy cars to meet falling sales and increased imports of foreign economy and sports models.

First report on a working laser is published; the laser is a nondiffusing intensified light beam that can be focused on a fine point. Its development opens new possibilities in communications, surgery, range finding, and welding.

Edmund Wilson publishes his *Apologies to the Iroquois,* which is concerned especially with injustices suffered by the people of the Iroquois Six Nations at the hands of the U.S.

America at Midcentury

The world in which the United States existed following World War II was far more complex than anything the nation's history had prepared it to cope with easily. Domestically it was a time of unprecedented prosperity, technological advancement, urbanization, business expansion, and social upheaval. Internationally, the Cold War began, interrupted frequently by small, hot wars that threatened to flare up into larger conflicts. Probably no single factor played so important a role in shaping American attitudes and policies as the threat of Communist expansion. The only balance of power seemed to be nuclear. The United States formed alliances in Europe and the Far East aimed at stemming Communist aggression, while Communist-bloc nations allied themselves in mutual defense against the "Free World."

For the first time the United States moved into the bewildering area of "limited warfare," where no conflict ever arrived at an unambiguous solution. The Korean War ended in 1953 in an uneasy stalemate. The Middle East was constantly in turmoil, with the most serious crisis of the 1950s taking place in 1956 over Egypt's seizure of the Suez Canal. The Arab-Israeli hostility in the region posed continued threats of war. In the Far East, the Geneva Conference of 1954 attempted to solve the problem of Indochina by arranging for French withdrawal and by partitioning the area. The United States committed itself to resist a Communist take-over there by either China or North Vietnam.

Within the United States increased prosperity led to greater urbanization, and to suburbanization. The phenomenon of "urban sprawl," or megalopolis, appeared on the scene as a portent of the future. Although metropolitan areas were increasing in population, most central cities were losing population to the suburbs. Thus as the social and economic problems of the cities were increasing, the more affluent and taxable citizens were no longer available to help solve them.

Maps prepared by Uni-Map Inc., Palatine, Ill.
for Encyclopaedia Britannica, Inc.

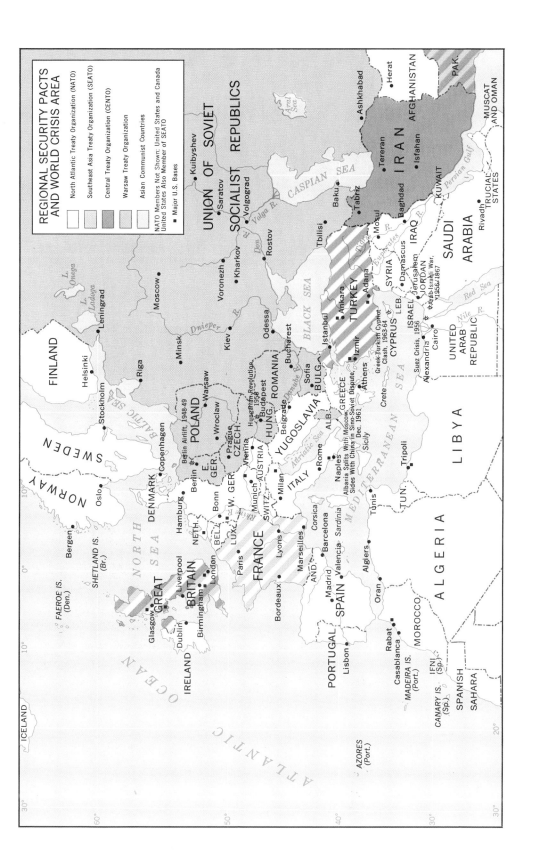

REGIONAL SECURITY PACTS
AND WORLD CRISIS AREA

North Atlantic Treaty Organization (NATO)

Southeast Asia Treaty Organization (SEATO)

Central Treaty Organization (CENTO)

Warsaw Treaty Organization

Asian Communist Countries

NATO Members Not Shown: United States and Canada
United States Also Member of SEATO

■ Major U.S. Bases

ICELAND

ATLANTIC OCEAN

FAEROE IS.
(Den.)

SHETLAND IS.
(Br.)

NORWAY

SWEDEN

FINLAND

Helsinki

Leningrad

L. Ladoga

L. Omega

Bergen

Oslo

Stockholm

BALTIC SEA

Riga

Moscow

Minsk

Voronezh

Kuibyshev

Saratov

Volgograd

Volga R.

UNION OF SOVIET

SOCIALIST REPUBLICS

Aral Sea

Ashkhabad

Herat

NORTH SEA

Bergen

IRELAND

Dublin

GREAT BRITAIN

Glasgow

Liverpool

Birmingham

London

DENMARK

Copenhagen

Hamburg

NETH.

Bonn

W. GER.

E. GER.

Berlin

Berlin Airlift, 1948-49

POLAND

Warsaw

Wroclaw

CZECH.

Prague

Minsk

Kiev

Dnieper R.

Kharkov

Kursk R.

Rostov

Don R.

Odessa

Tbilisi

Baku

CASPIAN SEA

Tabriz

Tereran

Teheran

IRAN

Isfahan

AFGHANISTAN

PAK.

Baghdad

Mosul

Euphrates R.

Tigris R.

IRAQ

KUWAIT

Persian Gulf

MUSCAT
AND OMAN

TRUCIAL
STATES

SAUDI
ARABIA

Riyadh

Paris

FRANCE

BELG.

LUX.

Bonn

Munich

SWITZ.

AUSTRIA

Vienna

Budapest

Hungarian Revolution
1956

HUNG.

ROMANIA

Bucharest

Danube R.

BULG.

Sofia

YUGOSLAVIA

Belgrade

Istanbul

BLACK SEA

Ankara

TURKEY

Adana

Izmir

Mosul

Damascus

SYRIA

Jerusalem

LEB.

ISRAEL

Arab-Israeli War,
1956-1967

JORDAN

Suez Crisis, 1956

Cairo

Alexandria

UNITED
ARAB
REPUBLIC

Nile R.

Red Sea

Bordeaux

Lyons

Marseilles

Corsica

AND.

Barcelona

Sardinia

ITALY

Milan

Rome

Naples

Sicily

Albania Splits With Moscow;
Sides With China in Sino-Soviet Dispute,
Dec. 1961

ALB.

GREECE

Athens

Crete

MEDITERRANEAN SEA

CYPRUS

Greek-Turkish Cypriot
Clash, 1963-64

Adriatic Sea

Tripoli

LIBYA

Tunis

TUN.

ALGERIA

Algiers

Oran

Valencia

Madrid

SPAIN

PORTUGAL

Lisbon

MADEIRA IS.
(Port.)

CANARY IS.
(Sp.)

IFNI
(Sp.)

MOROCCO

Rabat

Casablanca

SPANISH
SAHARA

AZORES
(Port.)

Rhine R.

30°

60°

50°

40°

30°

30°

20°

10°

0°

10°

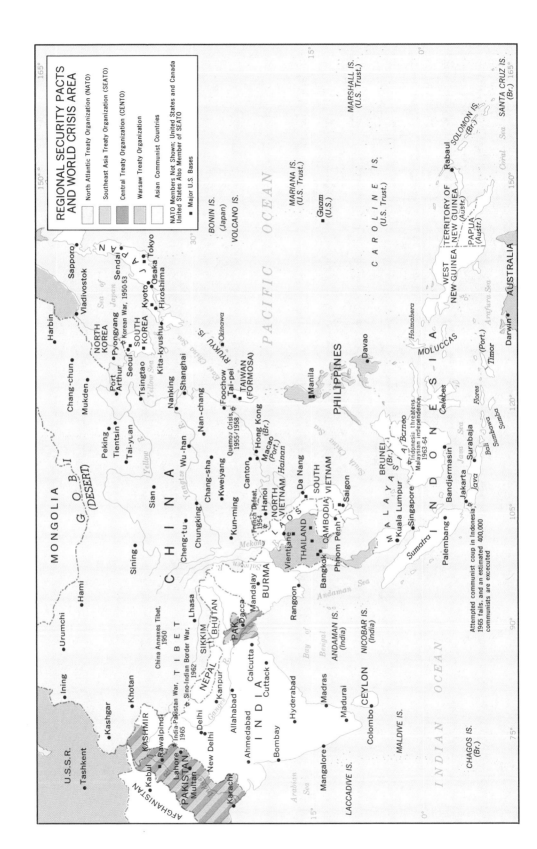

REGIONAL SECURITY PACTS AND WORLD CRISIS AREA

North Atlantic Treaty Organization (NATO)

Southeast Asia Treaty Organization (SEATO)

Central Treaty Organization (CENTO)

Warsaw Treaty Organization

Asian Communist Countries

NATO Members Not Shown; United States and Canada
United States Also Member of SEATO

■ Major U.S. Bases

U.S.S.R.

Tashkent

Ining

Urumchi

Kashgar

Khotan

MONGOLIA

G O B I
(DESERT)

Hami

Sining

Harbin

Chang-chun

Mukden

Peking

Tientsin

Tai-yu-an

Sian

C H I N A

Cheng-tu

Chungking

Sapporo

Vladivostok

Sendai

Sea of
Japan

Korean War, 1950-53

Tokyo

Osaka

Kyoto

Hiroshima

Kita-kyushu

N
A
P
A
J

Pyongyang

NORTH
KOREA

Seoul

Port
Arthur

SOUTH
KOREA

Tsingtao

Nanking

Yellow
Sea

Shanghai

Wu-han

Nan-chang

Chang-sha

Kweiyang

Yangtze R.

Foochow

Tai-pei

Quemoy Crisis,
1955/1958

RYUKYU IS.

Okinawa

East China Sea

TAIWAN
(FORMOSA)

BONIN IS.
(Japan)

VOLCANO IS.

PACIFIC OCEAN

MARIANA IS.
(U.S. Trust.)

Guam
(U.S.)

MARSHALL IS.
(U.S. Trust.)

C A R O L I N E   IS.

CAROLINE IS.
(U.S. Trust.)

Kun-ming

Canton

Hong Kong
(Br.)

Macao
(Port.)

Hainan

Da Nang

NORTH
VIETNAM

Hanoi

French Defeat,
1954

L
A
O
S

Vientiane

SOUTH
VIETNAM

Saigon

CAMBODIA

Phnom Penh

THAILAND

Bangkok

Mekong R.

Salween R.

BURMA

Mandalay

Rangoon

China Annexes Tibet,
1950

T I B E T

Lhasa

Dacca

PAK.

Sikang R.

NEPAL

SIKKIM

BHUTAN

India-Pakistan War,
1965

Sino-Indian Border War,
1962

Multan

Kabul

AFGHANISTAN

Lahore

Rawalpindi

KASHMIR

Karachi

Multan

PAKISTAN

New Delhi

Delhi

Kanpur

Allahabad

Ahmedabad

Calcutta

Cuttack

I N D I A

Ganges R.

Bombay

Hyderabad

Madras

Madurai

Mangalore

CEYLON

Colombo

MALDIVE IS.

LACCADIVE IS.

Bay of
Bengal

ANDAMAN IS.
(India)

NICOBAR IS.
(India)

Andaman
Sea

Arabian
Sea

CHAGOS IS.
(Br.)

I N D I A N   O C E A N

S. China Sea

South China Sea

MALAYA

Kuala Lumpur

Singapore

BRUNEI

Borneo

Indonesia threatens
Malaysian independence,
1963-64

PHILIPPINES

Manila

Davao

MOLUCCAS

Halmahera

Celebes

Celebes
Sea

Java Sea

Sumatra

Palembang

Bandjermasin

Jakarta

Surabaja

Bali

Flores

Java

Sumbawa

Sumba

Timor
(Port.)

Flores
Sea

I N D O N E S I A

Attempted communist coup in Indonesia
1965 fails, and an estimated 400,000
communists are executed

WEST
NEW GUINEA
(Austr.)

TERRITORY OF
NEW GUINEA
(Austr.)

PAPUA
(Austr.)

Arafura Sea

Darwin

AUSTRALIA

Coral Sea

SOLOMON IS.
(Br.)

Rabaul

SANTA CRUZ IS.
(Br.)

165°

150°

120°

105°

90°

75°

30°

15°

0°

15°

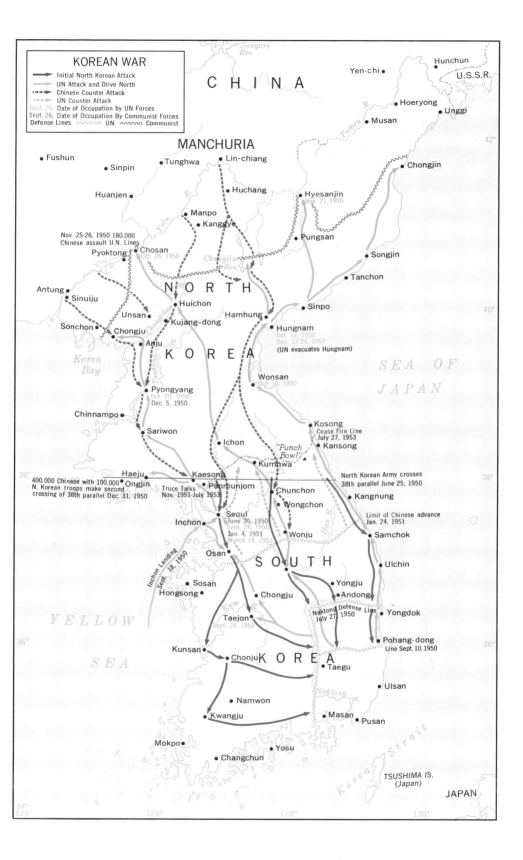

KOREAN WAR

- → Initial North Korean Attack
- → UN Attack and Drive North
- ━━▶ Chinese Counter Attack
- ┅┅▶ UN Counter Attack
- Sept. 26, Date of Occupation by UN Forces
- Sept. 26, Date of Occupation By Communist Forces
- Defense Lines ∿∿∿ UN ∿∿∿ Communist

CHINA

MANCHURIA

Hunchun
Yen-chi
U.S.S.R.
Hoeryong
Unggi
Musan
Fushun
Sinpin
Tunghwa
Lin-chiang
Chongjin
Huanjen
Huchang
Hyesanjin
Nov. 21, 1950
Manpo
Kanggye
Pungsan
Songjin
Nov. 25-26, 1950 180,000
Chinese assault U.N. Lines
Pyoktong
Chosan
Oct. 26, 1950
Chongjin
Res.
Tanchon
Antung
Sinuiju
N O R T H
Huichon
Sinpo
Unsan
Kujang-dong
Hamhung
Sonchon
Chongju
Anju
Hungnam
Oct. 17, 1950
Dec. 12-24, 1950
(UN evacuates Hungnam)
Korea
Bay
K O R E A
Pyongyang
Oct. 20, 1950
Dec. 5, 1950
Wonsan
Oct. 10, 1950
S E A   O F
J A P A N
Chinnampo
Sariwon
Kosong
Cease Fire Line
July 27, 1953
Ichon
"Punch
Bowl"
Kansong
Kumhwa
Haeju
Kaesong
North Korean Army crosses
38th parallel June 25, 1950
400,000 Chinese with 100,000
N. Korean troops make second
crossing of 38th parallel Dec. 31, 1950
Ongjin
Truce Talks
Nov. 1951-July 1953
Panmunjom
Chunchon
Kangnung
Wongchon
Seoul
June 30, 1950
Sept. 26, 1950
Jan. 4, 1951
March 14, 1951
Inchon
Wonju
Limit of Chinese advance
Jan. 24, 1951
Samchok
Osan
S O U T H
Ulchin
Sosan
Hongsong
Chongju
Yongju
Andong
Yongdok
Taejon
Sept. 28, 1950
Naktong Defense Line
July 27, 1950
Kunsan
Chonju
K O R E A
Taegu
Pohang-dong
Line Sept. 10, 1950
Y E L L O W
S E A
Namwon
Kwangju
Masan
Pusan
Ulsan
Mokpo
Yosu
Changchun
TSUSHIMA IS.
(Japan)
JAPAN

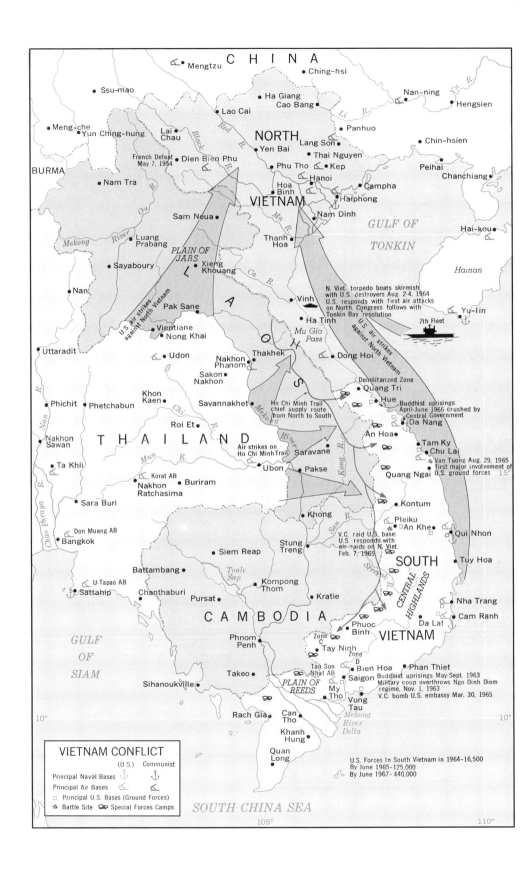

C H I N A

Mengtzu
Ssu-mao
Ching-hsi
Nan-ning
Ha Giang
Cao Bang
Hengsien
Meng-che
Yun Ching-hung
Lai Chau
Lao Cai
Panhuo
Li R.
Chin-hsien
NORTH
Lang Son
Peihai
French Defeat
May 7, 1954
Dien Bien Phu
Yen Bai
Thai Nguyen
Chanchiang
BURMA
Nam Tra
Phu Tho
Kep
Hanoi
Campha
VIETNAM
Hoa
Binh
Haiphong
Ma R.
Sam Neua
Nam Dinh
GULF OF
Luang
Prabang
Mekong River
Thanh
Hoa
TONKIN
PLAIN OF
JARS
Xieng
Khouang
Hai-kou
Sayaboury
Ca R.
Hainan
Nan
L
A
Vinh
N. Viet. torpedo boats skirmish
with U.S. destroyers Aug. 2-4, 1964
U.S. responds with first air attacks
on North. Congress follows with
Tonkin Bay resolution
Yu-lin
Pak Sane
7th Fleet
Ha Tinh
Uttaradit
O
Vientiane
Nong Khai
Mu Gia
Pass
Nakhon
Phanom
Thakhek
Dong Hoi
Udon
S
Phichit
Phetchabun
Sakon
Nakhon
Demilitarized Zone
Quang Tri
Nakhon
Sawan
Khon
Kaen
Savannakhet
Hue
Buddhist uprisings
April-June 1966 crushed by
Central Government
Ta Khli
THAILAND
Chi R.
Ho Chi Minh Trail
chief supply route
from North to South
An Hoa
Da Nang
Roi Et
Mun R.
Air strikes on
Ho Chi Minh Trail
Saravane
Tam Ky
Chu Lai
Van Tuong Aug. 29, 1965
first major involvement of
U.S. ground forces
Sara Buri
Korat AB
Nakhon
Ratchasima
Buriram
Ubon
Pakse
Quang Ngai
15°
Don Muang AB
Bangkok
Khong
Kontum
Pleiku
An Khe
Qui Nhon
V.C. raid U.S. base;
U.S. responds with
air raids on N. Viet.
Feb. 7, 1965
U-Tapao AB
Sattahip
Battambang
Chanthaburi
Pursat
Siem Reap
Stung
Treng
Kompong
Thom
Kratie
SOUTH
Tuy Hoa
CENTRAL
HIGHLANDS
Nha Trang
Cam Ranh
Tonle
Sap
CAMBODIA
Phuoc
Binh
Da Lat
GULF
OF
SIAM
Phnom
Penh
Zone C
Tay Ninh
Zone
D
VIETNAM
Takeo
Tan Son
Nhut AB
Bien Hoa
Phan Thiet
Sihanoukville
Saigon
Buddhist uprisings May-Sept. 1963
Military coup overthrows Ngo Dinh Diem
regime, Nov. 1, 1963
V.C. bomb U.S. embassy Mar. 30, 1965
PLAIN OF
REEDS
My
Tho
Vung
Tau
Rach Gia
Can
Tho
Mekong
River
Delta
10°
10°
Khanh
Hung
Quan
Long
VIETNAM CONFLICT
U.S. Forces In South Vietnam in 1964-16,500
By June 1965-125,000
By June 1967- 440,000
(U.S.)   Communist
Principal Naval Bases
Principal Air Bases
Principal U.S. Bases (Ground Forces)
Battle Site   Special Forces Camps
SOUTH CHINA SEA
105°
110°

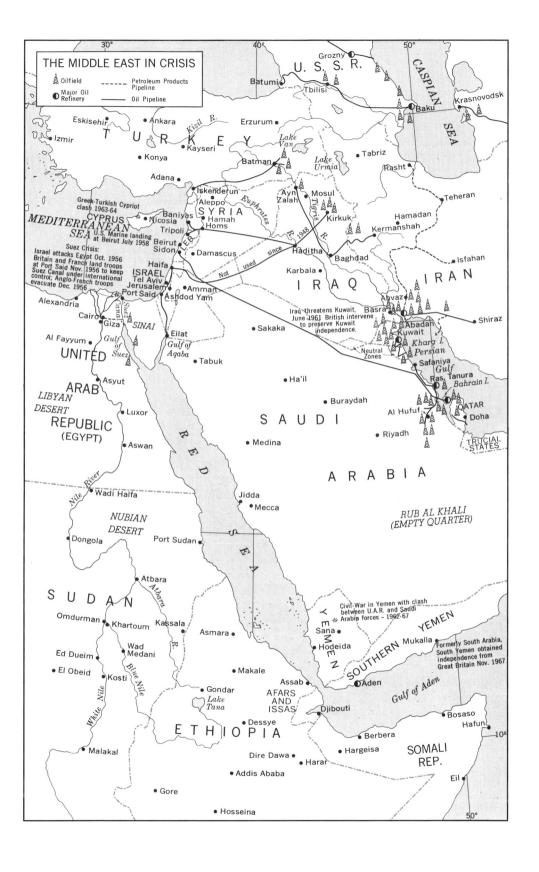

THE MIDDLE EAST IN CRISIS

Oilfield

Major Oil Refinery

Petroleum Products Pipeline

Oil Pipeline

U.S.S.R.

Grozny

Batumi

Tbilisi

CASPIAN SEA

Baku

Krasnovodsk

Eskisehir

Ankara

Kizil R.

Erzurum

T U R K E Y

Izmir

Kayseri

Lake Van

Tabriz

Rasht

Konya

Batman

Lake Urmia

Teheran

Adana

Iskenderun

Ayn Zalah

Mosul

Hamadan

Greek-Turkish Cypriot clash 1963-64

Aleppo

Euphrates

Kirkuk

Kermanshah

CYPRUS

Baniyas

SYRIA

Nicosia

Hamah

Tripoli

Homs

Tigris R. 1948

MEDITERRANEAN SEA

LEB.

Beirut

U.S. Marine landing at Beirut July 1958

Sidon

Damascus

Not used since

Haditha

Baghdad

Isfahan

Suez Crisis: Israel attacks Egypt Oct. 1956 Britain and France land troops at Port Said Nov. 1956 to keep Suez Canal under international control; Anglo-French troops evacuate Dec. 1956

Haifa

ISRAEL

Tel Aviv

Jerusalem

Karbala

I R A Q

I R A N

Ahvaz

Alexandria

Amman

Port Said

Ashdod Yam

Iraq threatens Kuwait, June 1961 British intervene to preserve Kuwait independence.

Basra

Abadan

Shiraz

Cairo

Giza

Suez Canal

SINAI

Gulf of Suez

Eilat

Gulf of Aqaba

Sakaka

Kuwait

Kharg I.

Persian

Al Fayyum

Tabuk

Ha'il

Neutral Zones

Gulf

Safaniya

Ras Tanura

Bahrain I.

UNITED

Asyut

LIBYAN DESERT

ARAB

REPUBLIC (EGYPT)

Luxor

Buraydah

Al Hufuf

QATAR

Doha

Aswan

S A U D I

Riyadh

TRUCIAL STATES

Medina

A R A B I A

RED

Wadi Halfa

Jidda

RUB AL KHALI (EMPTY QUARTER)

NUBIAN DESERT

Mecca

Dongola

Port Sudan

SEA

Atbara

Atbara

Civil War in Yemen with clash between U.A.R. and Saudi Arabia forces - 1962-67

S U D A N

Omdurman

Khartoum

Kassala

R.

YEMEN

Asmara

Sana

SOUTHERN

YEMEN

Mukalla

Ed Dueim

Wad Medani

Hodeida

Formerly South Arabia, South Yemen obtained independence from Great Britain Nov. 1967

El Obeid

Kosti

Blue Nile

Makale

Assab

AFARS AND ISSAS

Aden

Gulf of Aden

Bosaso

Hafun

Gondar

Lake Tana

Djibouti

Berbera

White Nile

Dessye

SOMALI REP.

Malakal

Dire Dawa

Hargeisa

E T H I O P I A

Harar

Gore

Addis Ababa

Eil

Hosseina

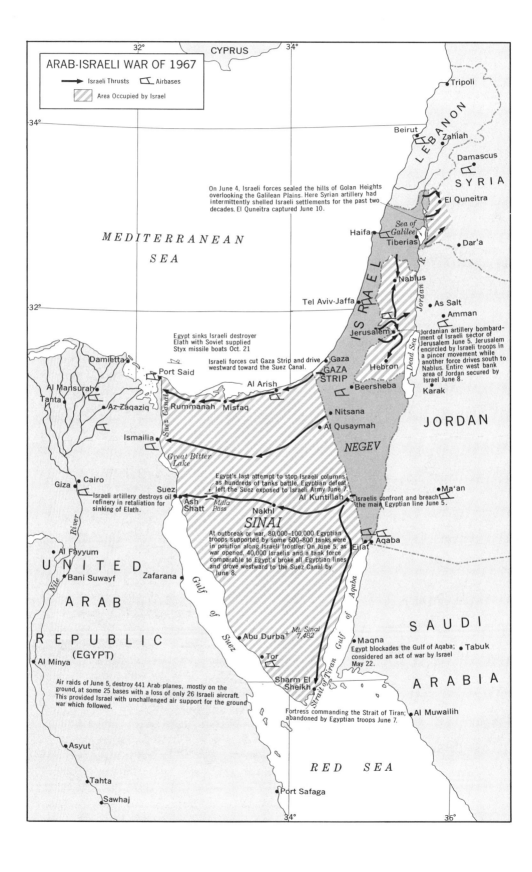

ARAB-ISRAELI WAR OF 1967

→ Israeli Thrusts ⊏ Airbases

▨ Area Occupied by Israel

CYPRUS

MEDITERRANEAN SEA

LEBANON
Tripoli
Beirut
Zahlah
Damascus
SYRIA

On June 4, Israeli forces sealed the hills of Golan Heights overlooking the Galilean Plains. Here Syrian artillery had intermittently shelled Israeli settlements for the past two decades. El Quneitra captured June 10.

El Quneitra
Haifa
Sea of Galilee
Tiberias
Dar'a

ISRAEL
Jordan R.
Nablus
Tel Aviv-Jaffa
As Salt
Amman

Egypt sinks Israeli destroyer Elath with Soviet supplied Styx missile boats Oct. 21

Jerusalem
Jordanian artillery bombardment of Israeli sector of Jerusalem June 5. Jerusalem encircled by Israeli troops in a pincer movement while another force drives south to Nablus. Entire west bank area of Jordan secured by Israel June 8.

Israeli forces cut Gaza Strip and drive westward toward the Suez Canal.

Damietta
Port Said
Al Arish
Gaza
GAZA STRIP
Hebron
Dead Sea
Karak

Al Mansurah
Tanta
Az-Zaqaziq
Rummanah
Misfaq
Beersheba
Nitsana
Al Qusaymah

JORDAN

Ismailia
Suez Canal
Great Bitter Lake

NEGEV

Egypt's last attempt to stop Israeli columns as hundreds of tanks battle. Egyptian defeat left the Suez exposed to Israeli Army June 7.

Giza
Cairo
Suez
Israeli artillery destroys oil refinery in retaliation for sinking of Elath.
Ash Shatt
Mitla Pass
Nakhl
Al Kuntillah
Israelis confront and breach the main Egyptian line June 5.

SINAI

At outbreak or war, 80,000–100,000 Egyptian troops supported by some 600-800 tanks were in position along Israeli frontier. On June 5, as war opened, 40,000 Israelis and a tank force comparable to Egypt's broke all Egyptian lines and drove westward to the Suez Canal by June 8.

Eilat
Aqaba

Al Fayyum
Zafarana
Gulf of Suez
Gulf of Aqaba

UNITED

Nile River
Bani Suwayf

ARAB

Ma'an

SAUDI

REPUBLIC
(EGYPT)

Al Minya

Abu Durba
Mt. Sinai 7,482
Tor
Maqna
Tabuk

Egypt blockades the Gulf of Aqaba; considered an act of war by Israel May 22.

ARABIA

Air raids of June 5, destroy 441 Arab planes, mostly on the ground, at some 25 bases with a loss of only 26 Israeli aircraft. This provided Israel with unchallenged air support for the ground war which followed.

Sharm El Sheikh
Strait of Tiran
Al Muwailih

Fortress commanding the Strait of Tiran, abandoned by Egyptian troops June 7.

Asyut

RED SEA

Tahta
Sawhaj
Port Safaga

1950

1.

Harry S. Truman: The Hydrogen Bomb Program

In 1945 most American military and political figures believed that the Soviet Union could not build an atomic bomb for many years. However, a number of leading scientists thought it would not take nearly so long and were not surprised when, during the summer of 1949, Russia exploded its first atomic device. By this time the United States had much more powerful atomic bombs, but the Soviet gains alarmed the public and government figures, and the argument that had been going on in the scientific community for several years was won by those who wanted America to take the next step and build not an atomic fission but a hydrogen fusion bomb. President Truman announced the decision to go ahead on a full-scale program to make such a bomb on January 31, 1950.

Source: *Bulletin*, February 13, 1950, p. 229.

It is part of my responsibility as commander in chief of the armed forces to see to it that our country is able to defend itself against any possible aggressor. Accordingly, I have directed the Atomic Energy Commission to continue its work on all forms of atomic weapons, including the so-called hydrogen or super-bomb. Like all other work in the field of atomic weapons, it is being and will be carried forward on a basis consistent with the overall objectives of our program for peace and security.

This we shall continue to do until a satisfactory plan for international control of atomic energy is achieved. We shall also continue to examine all those factors that affect our program for peace and this country's security.

2.

HENRY CABOT LODGE: For Abolishing the Electoral College

From time to time after the suffrage reforms of the 1820s, there were movements either to abolish the electoral college altogether or to alter its role in the election of U.S. Presidents. Direct reliance on the popular vote, since it reflects the will of the people more accurately than anything else can, instead of on the intervening mechanism of the electoral college has seemed more desirable to many. In 1948 Senator Henry Cabot Lodge, of Massachusetts, and Representative Ed Gossett, of Texas, introduced legislation calling for a proportional system for the election of the President and Vice-President. The following year, Lodge introduced a resolution proposing a constitutional amendment to that effect. On January 25, 1950, he spoke in defense of his proposed amendment and in opposition to an institution — the electoral college — that seems to many students of the Constitution to be an antiquated, unreliable, and potentially troublesome device. Part of the so-called Lodge Plan is reprinted here. The amendment was not passed by Congress.

Source: *Record*, 81 Cong., 2 Sess., pp. 877-881.

I DESIRE TO MAKE a presentation concerning Senate Joint Resolution 2, which proposes an amendment to the Constitution of the United States abolishing the electoral college and providing for the counting of the electoral vote for President and Vice-President in proportion to the popular vote. . . . The proposed constitutional amendment . . . does three things, principally:

First, it abolishes entirely the office of presidential elector. The electoral vote per state, which is equal to the total number of representatives and senators, is retained, but purely as an automatic counting device.

Second, it eliminates any possibility that an election may be thrown into the House of Representatives — a possibility which, as senators know, was a very real one in connection with the 1948 election.

Third, it does away with the so-called unit-rule system of counting electoral votes. Under the existing system, the candidate receiving a plurality of the popular vote in any given state is credited with all the electoral votes of that state, regardless of how infinitesimal the plurality. Under the proposed system, the electoral votes in each state are automatically divided among the candidates in direct proportion to the popular vote. . . .

Since the constitutional amendment proposed in Senate Joint Resolution 2 has as one of its objectives the correction of certain evils in our present method of electing the President, the need for reform is highlighted by a discussion of both the obvious and latent effects inherent in the electoral college-unit-rule system of choosing our President.

The indictment that can be drawn up against the present procedure is an impressive one. In general, there are three principal counts in this indictment:

First, the evils arising from the retention of the "dummy" office of presidential elector.

Second, the method of selecting a President when no candidate commands a majority of electoral votes.

Third, the defects and dangers which derive from the so-called unit-rule method of crediting all of a state's electoral votes to the plurality candidate.

An analysis of each of these three broad counts of the indictment follows:

1. *Retention of the Office of Elector.* The framers of the Constitution visioned the individual member of the electoral college as an official who would exercise independent judgment. His responsibility was a grave one and it was thought that only men of prestige and ability would be selected for that office. These characteristics no longer are associated with the office of elector. In most instances today men elected to the post of presidential elector are men whose names mean nothing whatsoever to the average voter. He is simply a strawman, or, as the phrase goes, a "man in livery," pledged in advance to vote for a certain candidate.

But it is most important to note that the individual elector is only morally bound to vote for candidates of his party for President and Vice-President. He is not legally bound. In fact, recent state and federal decisions make it very doubtful, indeed, whether a state can constitutionally impose a legal obligation on an elector to cast his vote for his party's candidate. It is possible, therefore, for individual members of the electoral college to cast their votes for whomsoever they please, utterly ignoring the mandate of the people and disregarding, if they so choose, their own pledges. Indeed, there have been several examples in the past of what I call the free-wheeling elector. In the

1948 elections a Tennessee elector, running on both the Democrat and Dixiecrat slates, cast his vote for the Dixiecrat candidate despite the fact that the state turned in a substantial plurality for the Democratic candidate. . . .

Another complication which frequently arises in connection with the individual members of the electoral college concerns the qualification of electors. The Constitution provides that members of Congress and federal officeholders are ineligible to serve as presidential electors. Surprisingly enough, it happens not infrequently . . . that ineligible electors successfully run for that office with the result that their votes for President and Vice-President, if cast, are invalid. It might well happen that these invalidated electoral votes could spell the difference between success and disaster for a presidential candidate. . . .

2. *Elections in the House of Representatives.* The second count in the indictment against the present method of electing the President concerns the constitutional provision which designates the House of Representatives as the final umpire of presidential elections in which no candidate receives a majority of the electoral votes.

A candidate, in order to win the election, must secure a majority of the whole number of electors, which at present means 266 votes. In case no person receives an electoral majority for President, the House of Representatives, voting by state units, elects the President from those receiving the three highest totals of electoral votes. A majority of the state votes — in other words, 25 — is required to settle the issue.

Each state delegation is given one vote. New York has one vote, New Jersey has one vote, Connecticut has one vote, Texas has one vote. This vote is determined by the majority of its delegation. In the event a state delegation is evenly split, the state has no vote.

I believe that at the present time the state

of New York has an odd number of representatives, but if in a redistricting there should be 48 or 46, and the election of the President were thrown into the House of Representatives, and there were 23 representatives voting for A and 23 voting for B, the entire vote of the state of New York would be excluded, and the approximately 14 million persons in New York state would be completely disfranchised.

If no candidate for Vice-President receives a majority of the electoral votes, the Senate proceeds to choose one of those who received the two highest totals of electoral votes. A majority of the senators is required to elect.

This particular aspect of our election machinery has found very few, if any, defenders. The chief criticism, of course, is the inequity that results from giving to all states, without regard to differences in population, equal power in electing the President. This procedure, it may be noted, entirely abrogates the basic principle upon which our whole approach to presidential elections is predicated, namely, that each state's relative voting power shall be measured in terms both of the state as a unit, represented by the two electoral votes for the two senators, and the state in terms of relative population, represented by the number of electoral votes for the number of representatives. This means, simply, that each state has the same number of electoral votes as it has votes in Congress. But when an election is thrown into the House of Representatives, this principle is wholly disregarded and each state stands on an equal basis with every other state.

The fundamental evil, therefore, in this system is that it furnishes no accurate or assured way of reflecting the popular will. . . .

An election procedure which is so full of dangerous uncertainties as to leave the whole result of the election unresolved, even though a plurality of the people had expressed their preference at the polls in November, is certainly one which a country founded on the principle of popular government can ill afford to condone. This danger is indeed one which needs only to be stated, not argued.

The procedure contained in the constitutional amendment proposed in Senate Joint Resolution 2 makes this danger an impossibility. The successful candidates for President and Vice-President need not obtain a majority of electoral votes; the person, to quote the language of the amendment, "having the greatest number of electoral votes for President shall be President. If two or more persons shall have an equal and the highest number of such votes," the amendment continues, "then the one for whom the greatest number of popular votes were cast shall be President." There can be no deadlocked decisions, and the universally condemned procedure of casting Congress in the role of final umpire is wholly eliminated.

3. *The Unit-Rule Method of Counting Electoral Votes.* The third count in the indictment against our existing system for electing the President deals with the unit-rule method of awarding all of a state's electoral votes to the candidate commanding even a bare plurality of the state's popular vote. This method is sometimes known as the general-ticket method of selecting electors.

It should be observed here that from the point of view of constitutional authority the states are free to adopt more equitable methods of selecting presidential electors, for Article II, Section 1 of the Constitution provides simply that each state shall appoint its electors in "such manner as the legislature thereof may direct." It is extremely unlikely, however, from a purely practical point of view, that the states could be induced severally and individually to switch from the prevailing general-ticket method. It is generally assumed, therefore, that a constitutional amendment is necessary to uproot the present system in order to establish a uniform and more accurate method of reflecting the popular will of the people.

The defects, unhealthy practices, and potential evils of the unit-rule or general-ticket procedure for counting electoral votes are many and varied. Only those of particular importance will be outlined here.

(a). The disfranchisement of voters evil. In effect, literally millions of American voters are disfranchised in every presidential election because of the unit-rule system. This contention is more than a figure of speech. It is an actuality. The 1948 elections furnish an excellent example of this point. Mr. Dewey received in the sixteen states which he carried a total of 8.6 million votes. These sixteen states gave him a total of 189 electoral votes. But in the thirty-two states which Mr. Dewey failed to carry, he had a total of 13.3 million votes. This great mass of popular votes for Mr. Dewey gave him not one single electoral vote and, therefore, counted for naught. They were of no more effect than if they had not been cast at all. . . .

(b). The "minority President" evil. The term "minority President" is frequently used with two different meanings. It may refer to a President who is elected without a majority of the popular vote, but nevertheless with more popular votes than any of his opponents. This has happened in almost half — fourteen — of the thirty-two elections for President between 1824 and 1948, inclusive. It may also refer to a President who was elected despite the fact that he had fewer popular votes than his leading opponent. This has happened three times in our history — Adams in 1824, Hayes in 1876, and Harrison in 1888. It is in this latter meaning of the term "minority President" that we discuss the phrase here.

Such a result as this is directly attributable to three characteristics of our election procedure: (1) The unit-rule method of counting electoral votes; (2) the distribution of electoral votes to states on the basis of the number of votes each state has in Congress; and (3) the fact that all save two of each state's electoral votes are awarded on the basis of population, rather than voting strength. . . .

The proponents of this constitutional amendment make no claim that it will wholly abolish the possibility of minority Presidents. But because this reform eliminates one of the three — and the principal — factors which foster such results, it is believed that possibility is greatly reduced. It can never be entirely eliminated without doing away with the two-electoral-vote bonus awarded each state regardless of population and without resorting to a direct popular election of the President, thus voiding the underlying federal principle of equality of states in the Senate which made possible the adoption of the Constitution.

In other words, so long as each state has credit for two votes, representing each senator, we are never going to get an accurate picture of the popular will. I do not claim that the proposed amendment will result in a completely accurate picture, but it will greatly improve the situation.

———————◆———————

The moral of the story of the Pilgrims is that if you work hard all your life and behave yourself every minute and take no time out for fun you will break practically even, if you can borrow enough money to pay your taxes.
WILL CUPPY, *The Decline and Fall of Practically Everybody*

3.

HENRY STEELE COMMAGER: The American Political Party

The American party system has been a subject of fascination for foreign observers since the beginning of the nineteenth century. "In America, the great moving forces are the parties," wrote James Bryce in The American Commonwealth *(1888). "The government counts for less than in Europe, the parties for more; and the fewer have become their principles and the fainter their interest in those principles, the more perfect has become their organization. The less of nature, the more of art; the less spontaneity, the more mechanism." In 1950 the distinguished American historian Henry Steele Commager wrote an essay on the institution of political parties in the United States, in the process of which he attempted to state their various functions and to identify their unique contribution to American life.*

Source: *American Scholar,* Summer 1950.

WE TEND TO TAKE our political parties for granted; when we notice them, it is to abuse or deplore them, or perhaps to apologize for them. Yet the party is our basic political institution, and perhaps our most successful one; we could get along better without the Constitution than without the party. And the party is not only a basic American institution; it is also a characteristic one. No other nation — not even Britain, Canada, or Australia — has a party system like the American.

This is not astonishing. The political party is, in a sense, an American invention; parties were unknown in eighteenth-century Europe, and British parties were what we now would call factions. The Democratic Party today is the oldest political party in the world, and the largest. Americans have had longer experience with party machinery and government than any other people; they have, inevitably, molded the party in their own image, fashioned it to their own purposes, stamped upon it their own characteristics.

It is easier to describe than to define the American political party — an observation equally appropriate to other institutions, such as democracy or constitutionalism — and it is perhaps easier to say what a party is not than to say what it is. It certainly is not Edmund Burke's "body of men united for promoting the national interest upon some particular principle upon which they are agreed"; almost the only part of that definition applicable to the American scene is the first three words — "a body of men." Indeed, insofar as a definition is possible, we can say that the party is a body of men — and women — organized to get control of the machinery of government.

This might apply, with important additions, to British and Canadian parties as well. The American party system has some singular features that do not appear in the party systems of other countries, or appear only fortuitously. First, ours is a two party system, tempered by minor parties. Second, each of the major parties is a loose federation of state and local organizations bound together chiefly by the exigencies of the presidential election system. Third, American parties are notorious for the absence of party leadership, control, agreement, and discipline, except such as are furnished by a President who is at the same time an effective party leader. Finally, the party is not only a political but a social institution, something of a fraternal organization, something of a game, something of a circus.

If we would appreciate the significance of the political party, we must look to its historical functions rather than to its forms. In the perspective of over a century and a half, those functions are clear enough; what is impressive is that they have changed so little over this period, and that they persist in the present and promise to continue into the future. Historically, the function of the political party has been to administer the government; to break down the artificial barriers of the federal system and of the separation of powers; to strengthen nationalism and ameliorate the conflicts of section, class, race, religion and interest; to advance democracy and to educate public opinion. Each of these functions requires a word of explanation.

The first job of the political party has been to run the government. The fathers of the Constitution drew up an admirable blueprint of government — and went off and left it. They made no practical provision for the day-by-day business of politics or administration. Although most of them were practical, and practising, statesmen, they apparently thought of the new government in terms of the old, and assumed that it would jog along pretty much under its own momentum. They neither anticipated nor recognized political parties; it is an interesting consideration that parties are not only unknown to the Constitution, they were unknown to law until as late as 1907. But the Constitution was neither a self-starting nor a self-operating mechanism. The first election was easy, for there could be no contest for the presidency, yet it was ominous that it was the end of April before Washington could be inaugurated, and al-

most a year later before the chief departments of the government were properly organized.

Fortunately, at a very early date, political parties came along and ran the government, and — with the assistance of a growing permanent civil service — they have been doing it ever since. They have selected men for office, conducted campaigns, managed elections, printed ballots, formulated policies and issues, taken responsibility for legislative programs — helping in the selection of cabinets and of high administrative officials, fitting together the innumerable fragments of government into an efficiently functioning machine. On the whole, they have done these things well; certainly no better system of running the business of politics and government has yet been devised.

The second of the important historical functions of the party has been that of harmonizing the federal system and the machinery of government within the various parts of that system. The Fathers of the Constitution, children of the Age of Reason, fabricated what we may call a Newtonian scheme of government, static rather than dynamic. They thought that they could create a mechanical system which, if based on sound principles of politics, could continue to operate into the indefinite future. Not only this, but since experience had taught them that all government was to be feared — that "government, like dress, is the badge of lost innocence" — they exhausted their ingenuity in devising methods of checking governmental tyranny. They manufactured to this end a complicated system of checks and balances: a federal system, the tripartite division of powers, the bicameral legislature, judicial review, frequent elections, and so forth.

Such a system, if adhered to rigorously, would result very speedily in governmental paralysis. If, for example, the members of the Electoral College really followed their own independent judgment in voting for a President — as the Framers supposed they would — the elective system would break down completely. Parties have taken charge of the whole business of electing a President — from the caucus to the convention, the campaign and the election — with the result that only three times has the election gone from the Electoral College to the House of Representatives.

Parties have made possible, too, the effective workings of a tripartite government. Theoretically, executive, legislative, and judiciary are independent and equal — so independent, indeed, that no one of them is bound to accept the interpretation of the Constitution itself by any other one or two departments. If the executive and the legislature actually insisted upon their independence, government could not function. Parties normally harmonize these two branches of the federal government. When, as occasionally happens, one party controls the executive branch and another the legislative, there is usually a deadlock. Fortunately, this happens but rarely, and when it does the good sense of American politicians finds a way out.

Equally important has been party implementation of the federal system, a system otherwise ideally designed to produce deadlock. It is the political party that harmonizes state and national interests, and integrates state and national politics. This integration has, indeed, gone too far. It is perhaps natural that presidential candidates should be taken from state governors rather than from the Senate or some other area of public life — and the majority of candidates have been governors of New York, Ohio, or Indiana in recent years — but it is scarcely natural that country, town, and village politics should operate within the framework of the national parties. That integration is, however, part of the price we pay for harmony in the federal system; it is not too high a price. The alternative is perhaps the kind of split we had in 1860 and again in 1948.

The third major function of the party has been — and still is — to strengthen nationalism and ameliorate the otherwise dangerous sectional and class divisions. It should never be forgotten that the United States is comparable to a continent rather than to the average nation, and that it contains within its spacious borders as many geographical, climatic, and economic divisions as are found in Europe or South America. We take national unity for granted, but every time we look at our map we might well say to ourselves, "There, but for the grace of God, the wisdom of the Fathers, and the work of political parties, goes South America." Normally, the sharp sectional divisions in the United States would be disintegrating, and it is relevant to recall that many of the Founding Fathers thought that a nation of continental dimensions could not possibly hold together. Fortunately, a variety of forces — historical, political, economic, social and psychological — have countered the natural particularism of the American scene. Of these forces, the most important have been the Constitution, the West, and the political party, and the party is not the least of the three.

Occasionally, to be sure, parties have come to represent purely local or sectional interests. Whenever they have done so, they have made trouble — or disappeared. The Federalists became almost wholly a sectional and class party — and went under. When in 1860 the Democratic Party split along sectional lines, and the Republican Party emerged as a strictly Northern party, the Union itself split. The re-creation of the Democratic Party as a national institution was perhaps the most effective instrument for the restoration of real union after the Civil War. Again, in the 1890s, parties were on the verge of organizing along sectional lines; fortunately, the Democratic capture of the Populist Party avoided that danger. The emergence of a purely sectional party in 1948 threatened for a time to demoralize the national political scene, throw the election into the House of Representatives, and give us a minority government; fortunately the danger was exaggerated.

But the nationalizing role of the party is not merely the negative one of overcoming sectionalism. It is positive as well. And its positive role here is closely tied to its function of selecting presidential nominees and running national campaigns. Though parties have no national bosses — Mark Hanna is the only possible exception, and Hanna could not always control his own state — they do have national leaders. It is rare that a state or local election takes precedence over a national; an astonishing number of Americans cannot name their state governor, and a substantial number do not know the name of their congressional representative. The habit of local politicians riding into Congress on the coattails of a successful presidential candidate has often been remarked, never more acidly than by Franklin Roosevelt. It has its drawbacks, to be sure, but it has its points, too. It means that for one year out of four the attention of political parties, local politicians, and the politically minded public is focused on national issues and personalities.

A parallel function of the political party has been the moderation of class antagonisms and the reconciliation of group interests. How varied those class, group, racial, and religious elements are is too familiar for rehearsal. From the beginning, one function of the party has been to serve as the great common denominator of these interests — of the whole of American society and economy. This fact is often alleged as a grave criticism of the American party — especially abroad. Parties do not, it is charged, represent real interests or groups. They do not adequately represent farmers, labor, business, the middle classes. They do not speak for the Catholics, the Protestants, the Jews; for Baptists or Methodists; for the Irish, the Germans, the Italians, the Negroes. They

even avoid issues which might give fair expression to the interests of these groups.

The charge is correct. A sound instinct has avoided the alignment of classes or racial groups into political parties. For nothing, it is clear, could be more dangerous than such an alignment, and nothing gives greater security and stability to the political system than the fact that the two dominant parties represent all classes and interests of American society and economy. Occasionally in the past a party has fallen under the control of a particular economic class or interest — the Federalists, for example, or the Democrats in the 1850s, but such yielding to particular interest groups has been fatal. Even an appearance of subservience to particular economic interests — as with the Republican Party in the 1920s — has been visited with heavy penalties.

This does not mean that a particular social or economic — or moral — interest cannot make itself felt politically. Though it is the instinct of parties to avoid issues, particular interests, if vigorous enough, can make themselves heard and felt in two ways. The first is within the major parties. Anyone familiar with the work of platform committees or of conventions, and with the compromises and concessions that go into the making of party tickets, knows that within the party conflicting interests are represented, and can, by eloquence or by political blackmail, get such attention. Nor is it impossible to persuade, or force, parties to face great issues. The major parties faced the issue of free silver in 1896, the issue of progressive reform in 1912, the issue of the social service state in 1932, the issue of intervention in 1940. The record of American parties here is not less reassuring than the record of British or French parties.

The second outlet for particular interests or groups is through the minor party — it is the fashion now to call it the splinter party.

The American party system is definitely a

two party system. There has never been a successful third party, unless the Republican Party be called that, and minor parties have rarely polled more than a very small percentage of the popular vote. Yet there have been almost innumerable minor parties — Free-Soil, Liberty, Know Nothing, Greenback, Populist, Farmer-Labor, Progressive, Socialist, Prohibitionist, Dixiecrat, and others. Sometimes — as in 1948 — these splinter parties have been merely an expression of discontent; more often — as with the antislavery or the Greenback or the Populist or the Progressive parties — they have represented genuine issues. Thus, while the function of the major parties is to be all things to all men and to avoid controversial issues, the function of the minor parties is to be something specific to a particular group of men, and to agitate controversial issues.

The business of the major parties is to capture and run the government — a task of infinite complexity, requiring compromise and concession; the business of the minor parties is to develop so great a nuisance value that one of the major parties will take over their programs or make political concessions to them. The third party is not only a useful safety valve in the American political system; it is, in a sense, the conscience of the major parties. It cannot hope to win, but it can mean defeat for a major party, and it keeps the major parties alert to protect minorities.

Finally, it may be said that the American party has been an effective instrument for democracy and for enlightenment. This is a consequence, not of any inherent quality in the party itself but rather of the dynamics of American politics. Each of the major parties has been forced to look for broad popular support, which means that parties are inevitably advocates of an extension of the suffrage. No party has ever taken the risk of openly opposing such an extension, for the consequences to it when the extension came

— as it always did — would have been disastrous. Even the appearance of hostility to democracy was disastrous to the Federalists, and the antidemocratic Dixiecrats were not able to carry a single Southern state in a fair contest. Thus, too, each of the major parties, not being committed in advance to fundamental principles, has ever been on the lookout for popular issues. Whatever issues appear to have vote-getting potentialities will inevitably be espoused by one or both major parties. Parties know, by experience, that victory goes to the party that has satisfied the most popular needs and offended the fewest groups. This does not always mean an aggressive legislative program; sometimes the public is weary of legislation and wants quiet — as in the 1920s. Sometimes it is more conscious of the burden of taxes than of the benefits of government largess. But on the whole the natural pressure of American politics is for an aggressive legislative program — witness the successful careers of Theodore Roosevelt, Woodrow Wilson, and Franklin Roosevelt.

Nor should it be overlooked in any analysis of the party system that the internal structure and organization of the party is predominantly democratic. There are exceptions here, to be sure — in the South, for example. But those who come to the fore in party politics are the willing workers, not the aristocrats or the intelligentsia. Almost every political boss has worked his way up from ward leader or county leader; the rewards do go to the workers. In this the party is much like the labor union; indeed, the analogy might profitably be carried much farther.

The two party system seems to fit the temper and character of the American people. A single party would allow no alternative to bad government and would expose government to the danger of bureaucracy, and eventually to irresponsibility. A multiparty system — requiring as it does deep convictions about principles in the body politic — would fragment the government and the nation. The two party system, working within the comfortable framework of national unity and general agreement on fundamentals, offers an amiable choice of managers and even of current policies. It is irrelevant to argue that the choice is not one of principle; it is the virtue of the American party system that it does not present the American people with the necessity of fighting about principles.

4.

Wayne L. Morse: The Need for a Bipartisan Foreign Policy

One of the benefits of America's entry into World War II was the establishment of a bipartisan foreign policy. Both Roosevelt and Truman were determined not to repeat the mistakes of the Wilson era, with its bitter partisan divisions; and the Republicans, too, under the leadership of Senator Arthur H. Vandenberg of Michigan, helped make the system a success, even during times when there were sharp differences between the parties on domestic policy. But bipartisanship in foreign policy was easier to maintain during the wartime emergency than during the Cold War, when public opinion itself became divided on such questions as Communist infiltration in government, the nuclear arms race, and aid to foreign countries. Senator Wayne L. Morse of Oregon restated the arguments for bipartisanship in foreign affairs in a speech to the American Association of School Administrators on February 26, 1950, that is reprinted here in part. Morse, then a Republican, changed his party affiliation a few years later.

Source: VSD, May 1, 1950: "The Rise or Sunset of Peace."

Shortly, in the Senate of the United States, we will be debating a proposal to appropriate funds for the extension of the Marshall Plan another year. Already the ghosts of isolationism are stalking the corridors of the national Capitol — already some senators are proposing to stop all Marshall Plan appropriations and others are proposing to cut them so drastically that the plan will break down. Statesmanship calls for finding the answer to the question, "How much money is needed to complete the job of economic rehabilitation in Europe and how much of it can America make available this next year consistent with maintaining our own economic strength here at home?"

The evidence is clear that the early suc-cess of many phases of the Marshall Plan will justify considerable reductions in previous estimates of the amount that will be needed this year. It is also clear that the Marshall Plan countries need to demonstrate a greater willingness to develop economic unity among themselves and eliminate the costly trade barriers within Europe which for so many decades have created a European pattern of economic nationalism.

The schools of America have a job of informing the public in regard to the economic problems involved in operating the Marshall Plan. Query — Will they do it? It is part of the job of winning the peace because unless the American people develop a better understanding of the direct relationship between the economic rehabilitation of Europe and the peace of the world, those of us in the Congress who are supporting the Marshall Plan will have great difficulty in preventing a scuttling of the economic phases of America's foreign policy.

That leads me to comment upon the direct relationship between the maintaining of a nonpartisan or bipartisan foreign policy and winning the peace. We shall see in our generation the sunset of peace if the American people allow themselves to become disunited over foreign policy. If partisanship replaces nonpartisanship in American foreign policy, every Communist in America and the Russian leaders in the Kremlin in Moscow will rejoice. I am satisfied that part of the infiltration tactics of the Communists is to divide us on questions of foreign policy. Here again the schools of America can function in the front lines of the fight for peace by providing the forums and spreading the truth concerning the facts of foreign affairs.

There is considerable talk these days in Washington, and elsewhere, about having the leaders of our government, and possibly of one or two other governments, make an approach to the Russian leaders for a settlement of the issue of the atomic bomb and now the hydrogen-bomb control by agreement between them. It would appear that there is some attempt to make a partisan issue of such a demand.

I seriously question the advisability of such an approach to the Russians. I regret the partisanship of the attempt to politically embarrass our President in case he does not agree to such an approach. The United States is a member of the United Nations. I believe that the best hope for peace is to be found through strengthening the United Nations, not circumventing it or weakening it. America's participation in the United Nations, in the first instance, was the direct result of a unity of action on a bipartisan basis of the leaders of the two major political parties in this country.

It is a sad fact that there have been many instances in which the spirit of bipartisanship, which characterized the great San Francisco Conference at the time the United Nations was born, has not prevailed in some other international conferences. However, mistakes in applying the principle of bipartisanship do not justify repudiating the principle. There is a growing confusion in America as to what our foreign policy is. The American people seem to be developing feelings of fear, doubt, and almost hysteria concerning our foreign policies and the trends of world affairs.

A world full of people worried by fear, nations feverish with war psychology, national economies spending more for armaments than for human welfare, time races in competitive construction of atomic and hydrogen bombs, spell war — not peace. In my judgment, the time has come for the American people, the Russian people, and the mothers and fathers everywhere on the face of this world to recognize that present world trends, unless changed, will lead to war. We will witness a sunset, not only of peace but of human happiness for generations to come, unless the leaders of our generation succeed in laying the foundation, as Senator Vandenberg has put it, of a world order based upon international justice through law.

It is my hope that you will give thoughtful consideration to the view that it is of great importance to the people of the world that the American people maintain a united front in support of a bipartisan foreign policy. That policy must seek to strengthen the forces of freedom in the world by establishing a world order capable of substituting international judicial decrees for hydrogen bombs as a means of settling international disputes.

As Nehru of India declared during his trip to this country, "There can be no doubt that a world government must come — for the only alternative is world suicide."

Yet, as we sit here tonight, we should not

ignore the fact that there are forces at work in America seeking to prejudice the thinking of our people into an acceptance of a partisan approach to foreign affairs. They are appealing to the selfish motives of those who would place immediate economic gains for themselves and the nation above the long-time security of peace. Their isolationist program is directed at the present moment of scuttling a bipartisan foreign policy. They have seized upon imperfections and mistakes in that policy as affording an opportunity to play politics with the security of our nation.

Recent statements by prominent members of the Congress, highly critical of the past, present, and supposed future policy of the United States in China and Europe, raise serious questions as to America's future course in international relations.

Is the United States on the verge of another postwar era of narrow nationalism and isolationism? Is the Republican Party about to abandon the principle of a bipartisan foreign policy which Senator Vandenberg, one of its main architects, has rightly called our best available insurance for peace?

How strong are the forces that would have America embark on an imperialistic course, characterized by dollar diplomacy and the conditioning of further Marshall Plan aid on the recipient countries adopting different policies in the conduct of their own domestic affairs?

At the Philadelphia convention in 1948, the Republican Party solidly backed the principle of bipartisanship. The platform there adopted, in anticipation of a Republican victory, pledged that the minority party would be invited to join in stopping partisan politics at the water's edge.

The Democrats likewise have repeatedly pledged a bipartisan approach to foreign-policy problems. Those who sneer at the bipartisan program need to be reminded that differences over means of implementing a united American position in international relations do not justify scuttling the principle. Rather, the shortcomings which have developed point out the need for perfecting the mechanics of cooperation.

The reasons for a bipartisan foreign policy are plain enough. Our basic objective is to achieve and maintain international peace and security in a world of free nations devoted to the protection of human rights and fundamental freedoms. To fulfill our obligations as a leader among free nations, we must have a foreign policy that is clear and consistent. Moreover, national security demands that our foreign commitments weather changes in the political direction of our government.

The necessary conditions for a workable bipartisan foreign policy are not obscure, but perhaps it may be well to restate them in view of the charge that bipartisanship means me-tooism and is no more than a Republican rubber-stamp policy.

With agreement on the desirability of a bipartisan foreign policy, its successful operation necessitates that responsible party leaders achieve an understanding of common readiness to work together, that there be full access to and sharing of information, and that there be timely consultation.

Despite the strains of three election campaigns, bipartisanship has survived. At times, its workings have been far from perfect. But now is no time to stick our heads into the sand of isolationism or refuse to put forth our best efforts toward improving the machinery of bipartisanship so that America may present a united front.

A bipartisan foreign policy carries with it the obligation upon the party in the White House, be it Democratic or Republican, to consult with the leaders of the minority party in advance of entering into international understandings which commit the United States to some definite course of action. It is a two-way street between the White House and Capitol Hill.

It is true that under our Constitution the primary responsibility for determining foreign policy rests with the President of the United States, but it is also true that whenever friction develops between the White House and the Congress over foreign policy questions, our country is greatly embarrassed. This is particularly true whenever the President makes an international commitment or agreement which later requires implementation by the Congress.

Many of the strains and stresses which American foreign policy is undergoing at the present time must be attributed to the fact that in recent years Presidents and secretaries of state have too often entered into understandings with heads of foreign governments as to which both Democratic and Republican leaders of the Congress were kept in ignorance until a misunderstanding of potentially serious proportions had developed.

It is not wise to discard entirely the use of hindsight when charting a future course of action. The shortcomings of our bipartisan foreign policy as it has developed in recent years can be seen in a much better perspective by a realistic analysis of some of the serious mistakes which have resulted from the failure of Presidents and secretaries of state to take into their confidence and to consult with congressional leaders of both parties upon whom the administration must lean, in the last analysis, for congressional support of any international commitments.

The Cairo understanding, the agreements reached at Yalta, the commitments made at Potsdam, the administration's policies in China, during and particularly since the war, are all examples of shortcomings in carrying out the basic spirit of a bipartisan foreign policy. Does anyone think for a moment that the understandings reached by the President with the representatives of foreign powers at Cairo and Yalta would have been acceptable, even at the time they were made, to the bipartisan leaders of the Senate Foreign Relations Committee?

The Cairo and Yalta commitments involved not only the prosecution of the war but the building of the peace as well. Historians will undoubtedly record that the international conferences of the Roosevelt administration involved in a very real sense an attempt to write peace treaties by the installment plan.

It is difficult to answer the charge, made in good faith by many critics of bipartisan foreign policy, that in those conferences the treaty-making clause of the Constitution was circumvented by the President of the United States. In any case, the conduct of the executive branch was not in keeping with the spirit and intent of a bipartisan foreign policy. Even the Potsdam agreement cannot escape its fair share of criticism on this score.

The administration's handling of our policy in China, particularly since the war, cannot be fitted into a traffic pattern of two-way cooperation between the White House and the Congress. For many months the State Department failed to discuss with the bipartisan leaders of the Foreign Relations Committee of the Senate its plans and policies in China, if it had any. Warning signals of dissension and criticism were raised in debate in the Senate many times during this period. On one occasion, during the Eightieth Congress, the Republican chairman of the Foreign Relations Committee — and the man who is perhaps more responsible than any other living American for a willing acceptance on the part of Republicans, and for that matter Americans generally, of the need for national unity in support of a bipartisan foreign policy — admitted under questioning on the floor of the Senate that the State Department had not consulted with the Foreign Relations Committee for many months on any phase of the China problem. He admitted in the course of that debate that the contents of the Wedemeyer Report had not been made known to the bipartisan leaders of the Foreign Relations Committee.

At that time, which was the fall of 1947, a serious crack developed in the seams of

America's bipartisan foreign policy. It should have been cemented very quickly by a mutual exchange of points of view and information between the State Department and the Senate Foreign Relations Committee. Instead, the misunderstandings and criticism in respect to American foreign policy in China became greater throughout 1947, 1948, and 1949. True, the predominant feeling in the Congress was overwhelmingly in support of any administration proposal offered in the name of a bipartisan policy. Nevertheless, those of us in the Senate who strongly supported the idea of maintaining a bipartisan foreign policy were both grieved and handicapped on many occasions over the failure of the State Department to take the bipartisan leaders of the Congress into its confidence and consultation in respect to Asia.

When the second session of the Eighty-first Congress convened on January 3, the administration faced a serious attack upon some aspects of its foreign policy, particularly those relating to China.

It is not too late to stop the trend toward partisanship in the field of American foreign policy. It is not too late to displace the distrust which some Senators have of the administration's foreign policy with a spirit of confidence and cooperation. If the administration will hasten to give not only the Congress but also the people of the United States the assurance that the leaders of both the Democratic and Republican parties in the Congress will be taken into consultation preceding formulation of policy on any major international issue by the State Department and the White House, the breach can be healed before irreparable damage is done.

That is the test of the existence of a bipartisan foreign policy. No other course of action on the part of the administration will ever satisfy those who are questioning not only the existence but the worth of a bipartisan foreign policy. No other kind of coop-

eration will give the necessary strength to the hand of the great Vandenberg by placing him in the strong position he deserves to be within the Republican Party when he is faced with laying an administration foreign policy request before the Republicans in the Senate for approval and support on a bipartisan basis.

A bipartisan foreign policy does not mean that members of the Congress should hesitate to criticize any proposed course of action contemplated by the administration in the name of a bipartisan foreign policy. Rather it is the duty of a member of the Congress to express criticisms if in his honest judgment criticisms are due. However, experience shows that mutual cooperation and mutual exchanges of points of view between the administration and the leaders of Congress in advance of international commitment usually remove any basis for fair and just criticism.

What is more, the greatest assurance the administration has of maintaining a united American people behind the foreign policy of our country is to follow a truly cooperative effort in the formulation of a bipartisan foreign policy. The American people can be counted upon to respond in united support of a foreign policy which is the result of the cooperative effort of the leaders of both the Democratic and the Republican parties. Whenever a split occurs between those leaders, then division of a serious nature is likely to develop among our people.

Rather than have the head of our government attempt to negotiate with Stalin outside the framework of the United Nations, I would prefer to have our government call for an extraordinary meeting of the General Assembly of the United Nations, to be participated in by the representatives of all nations, for the purpose of considering not only the international control of atomic and hydrogen bombs but the control of all armaments as well.

I would have both parties join forces now — this year — in a worldwide appeal through the United Nations for an end to the armament race. It seems perfectly clear to me that the position taken by the chairman of the Senate Committee on Armed Services, the distinguished senator from Maryland, Mr. Tydings, is unanswerable. He points out that unless the world agrees on some satisfactory machinery for controlling armament, the world will plunge itself into another war.

It is my opinion that the most important step the leaders of our government could take in the interests of uniting the American people in the cause of winning the peace would be to announce a coalition of Democratic and Republican leaders charged with the responsibility of developing and administering foreign policy at the State Department level. Next, it should assure the American people that it will apply a bipartisan approach to foreign policy at the congressional level by consulting and seeking advice from Democratic and Republican congressional leaders in advance of any major international negotiation. Through such a coalition of Democratic and Republican leaders working together in a spirit of patriotic, nonpartisan statesmanship, we would be able to marshal a united American people behind any program which such a coalition of leaders might present to the United Nations for the international control of atomic and hydrogen bombs and the disarming of the arsenals of the world, whose very existence are bound to be a threat to the peace. Through such coalition of Democrats and Republicans on the issue of winning the peace, I think our chances in our generation of seeing the sunrise of permanent peace would be greatly improved.

5.

JOSEPH R. MCCARTHY: Communists in the State Department

The beginning of the meteoric career of Joseph R. McCarthy, the senator from Wisconsin who gave his name to an era of American history, may be traced to an address he delivered on the night of February 9, 1950, at Wheeling, West Virginia. McCarthy later inserted in the Congressional Record *a text of the speech — probably modified — which is reprinted here. McCarthy asserted at that time that American reversals in the postwar period, especially the fall of China to Communism, were the result of Communist infiltration into the highest levels of the American government, particularly the State Department. The source of the figures cited by McCarthy in the speech was never identified, and in fact no Communists were actually ever discovered as a direct result of his charges, but he nevertheless succeeded in keeping both the government and the country in a turmoil for several years.*

Source: *Record*, 81 Cong., 2 Sess., pp. 1952-1957.

Ladies and gentlemen:

Tonight as we celebrate the one hundred and forty-first birthday of one of the greatest men in American history, I would like to be able to talk about what a glorious day today is in the history of the world. As we celebrate the birth of this man, who with his whole heart and soul hated war, I would like to be able to speak of peace in our time, of war being outlawed, and of worldwide disarmament. These would be truly appropriate things to be able to mention as we celebrate the birthday of Abraham Lincoln.

Five years after a world war has been won, men's hearts should anticipate a long peace, and men's minds should be free from the heavy weight that comes with war. But this is not such a period — for this is not a period of peace. This is a time of the "cold war." This is a time when all the world is split into two vast, increasingly hostile armed camps — a time of a great armaments race. Today we can almost physically hear the mutterings and rumblings of an invigorated god of war. You can see it, feel it, and hear it all the way from the hills of Indochina, from the shores of Formosa, right over into the very heart of Europe itself.

The one encouraging thing is that the "mad moment" has not yet arrived for the firing of the gun or the exploding of the bomb which will set civilization about the final task of destroying itself. There is still a hope for peace if we finally decide that no longer can we safely blind our eyes and close our ears to those facts which are shaping up more and more clearly. And that is that we are now engaged in a showdown fight — not the usual war between nations for land areas or other material gains but a war between two diametrically opposed ideologies.

The great difference between our Western Christian world and the atheistic Communist world is not political, ladies and gentlemen, it is moral. There are other differences, of course, but those could be reconciled. For instance, the Marxian idea of confiscating the land and factories and running the entire economy as a single enterprise is momentous. Likewise, Lenin's invention of the one-party police state as a way to make Marx's idea work is hardly less momentous. Stalin's resolute putting across of these two ideas, of course, did much to divide the world. With only those differences, however, the East and the West could most certainly still live in peace.

The real, basic difference, however, lies in the religion of immoralism — invented by Marx, preached feverishly by Lenin, and carried to unimaginable extremes by Stalin. This religion of immoralism, if the Red half of the world wins — and well it may — this religion of immoralism will more deeply wound and damage mankind than any conceivable economic or political system.

Karl Marx dismissed God as a hoax, and Lenin and Stalin have added in clear-cut, unmistakable language their resolve that no nation, no people who believe in a God can exist side by side with their communistic state.

Karl Marx, for example, expelled people from his Communist Party for mentioning such things as justice, humanity, or morality. He called this soulful ravings and sloppy sentimentality.

While Lincoln was a relatively young man in his late thirties, Karl Marx boasted that the Communist specter was haunting Europe. Since that time, hundreds of millions of people and vast areas of the world have fallen under Communist domination. Today, less than 100 years after Lincoln's death, Stalin brags that this Communist specter is not only haunting the world but is about to completely subjugate it.

Today we are engaged in a final, all-out battle between communistic atheism and Christianity. The modern champions of communism have selected this as the time. And, ladies and gentlemen, the chips are down — they are truly down.

Lest there be any doubt that the time has been chosen, let us go directly to the leader of communism today — Joseph Stalin. Here is what he said — not back in 1928, not before the war, not during the war — but two years after the last war was ended: "To think that the Communist revolution can be carried out peacefully, within the framework of a Christian democracy means one has either gone out of one's mind and lost all normal understanding, or has grossly and openly repudiated the Communist revolution."

And this is what was said by Lenin in 1919, which was also quoted with approval by Stalin in 1947: "We are living," said Lenin, "not merely in a state but in a system of states, and the existence of the Soviet Republic side by side with Christian states for a long time is unthinkable. One or the other must triumph in the end. And before that end supervenes, a series of frightful collisions between the Soviet Republic and the bourgeois states will be inevitable."

Ladies and gentlemen, can there be anyone here tonight who is so blind as to say that the war is not on? Can there be anyone who fails to realize that the Communist world has said, "The time is now" — that this is the time for the show-down between the democratic Christian world and the Communist atheistic world? Unless we face this fact, we shall pay the price that must be paid by those who wait too long.

Six years ago, at the time of the first conference to map out the peace — Dumbarton Oaks — there was within the Soviet orbit 180 million people. Lined up on the antitotalitarian side there were in the world at that time roughly 1,625,000,000 people. Today, only six years later, there are 800 million people under the absolute domination of Soviet Russia — an increase of over 400 percent. On our side, the figure has shrunk to around 500 million. In other words, in less than six years the odds have changed from 9 to 1 in our favor to 8 to 5 against us. This indicates the swiftness of the tempo of Communist victories and American defeats in the cold war. As one of our outstanding historical figures once said, "When a great democracy is destroyed, it will not be because of enemies from without but rather because of enemies from within." The truth of this statement is becoming terrifyingly clear as we see this country each day losing on every front.

At war's end we were physically the strongest nation on earth and, at least potentially, the most powerful intellectually and morally. Ours could have been the honor of being a beacon in the desert of destruction, a shining, living proof that civilization was not yet ready to destroy itself. Unfortunately, we have failed miserably and tragically to arise to the opportunity.

The reason why we find ourselves in a position of impotency is not because our only powerful, potential enemy has sent men to invade our shores, but rather because of the traitorous actions of those who have been treated so well by this nation. It has not been the less fortunate or members of minority groups who have been selling this nation out, but rather those who have had all the benefits that the wealthiest nation on earth has had to offer — the finest homes, the finest college education, and the finest jobs in government we can give.

This is glaringly true in the State Department. There the bright young men who are born with silver spoons in their mouths are the ones who have been worst.

Now I know it is very easy for anyone to condemn a particular bureau or department in general terms. Therefore, I would like to cite one rather unusual case — the case of a man who has done much to shape our foreign policy.

When Chiang Kai-shek was fighting our war, the State Department had in China a young man named John S. Service. His task, obviously, was not to work for the communization of China. Strangely, however, he sent official reports back to the State Department urging that we torpedo our ally Chiang Kai-shek and stating, in effect, that communism was the best hope of China.

Later, this man — John Service — was picked up by the Federal Bureau of Investigation for turning over to the Communists secret State Department information. Strangely, however, he was never prosecuted. However, Joseph Grew, the undersecretary of state, who insisted on his prosecution, was forced to resign. Two days after Grew's successor, Dean Acheson, took over as undersecretary of state, this man — John Service — who had been picked up by the FBI and who had previously urged that communism was the best hope of China, was not only reinstated in the State Department but promoted; and, finally, under Acheson, placed in charge of all placements and promotions. Today, ladies and gentlemen, this man Service is on his way to represent the State Department and Acheson in Calcutta — by far and away the most important listening post in the Far East.

Now, let's see what happens when individuals with Communist connections are forced out of the State Department. Gustave Duran, who was labeled as (I quote) "a notorious international Communist," was made assistant to the assistant secretary of state in charge of Latin-American affairs. He was taken into the State Department from his job as a lieutenant colonel in the Communist International Brigade. Finally, after intense congressional pressure and criticism, he resigned in 1946 from the State Department — and, ladies and gentlemen, where do you think he is now? He took over a high-salaried job as chief of Cultural Activities Section in the office of the assistant secretary-general of the United Nations.

Then there was a Mrs. Mary Jane Kenny, from the Board of Economic Warfare in the State Department, who was named in an FBI report and in a House committee report as a courier for the Communist Party while working for the government. And where do you think Mrs. Kenny is — she is now an editor in the United Nations Document Bureau.

Another interesting case was that of Julian H. Wadleigh, economist in the Trade Agreements Section of the State Department for eleven years and was sent to Turkey and Italy and other countries as United States representative. After the statute of limitations had run so he could not be prosecuted for treason, he openly and brazenly not only admitted but proclaimed that he had been a member of the Communist Party . . . that while working for the State Department he stole a vast number of secret documents . . . and furnished these documents to the Russian spy ring of which he was a part.

You will recall last spring there was held in New York what was known as the World Peace Conference — a conference which was labeled by the State Department and Mr. Truman as the sounding board for Communist propaganda and a front for Russia. Dr. Harlow Shapley was the chairman of that conference. Interestingly enough, according to the new release put out by the Department in July, the secretary of state appointed Shapley on a commission which acts as liaison between UNESCO and the State Department.

This, ladies and gentlemen, gives you somewhat of a picture of the type of individuals who have been helping to shape our foreign policy. In my opinion the State Department, which is one of the most important government departments, is thoroughly infested with Communists.

I have in my hand fifty-seven cases of individuals who would appear to be either card-carrying members or certainly loyal to the Communist Party, but who nevertheless are still helping to shape our foreign policy.

One thing to remember in discussing the Communists in our government is that we are not dealing with spies who get thirty pieces of silver to steal the blueprints of a new weapon. We are dealing with a far more sinister type of activity because it permits the enemy to guide and shape our policy. . . .

This brings us down to the case of one Alger Hiss, who is important not as an individual anymore but rather because he is so representative of a group in the State Department. It is unnecessary to go over the sordid events showing how he sold out the nation which had given him so much. Those are rather fresh in all of our minds. However, it should be remembered that the facts in regard to his connection with this international Communist spy ring were made known to the then Undersecretary of State Berle three days after Hitler and Stalin signed the Russo-German Alliance Pact. At that time one Whittaker Chambers — who was also part of the spy ring — apparently decided that with Russia on Hitler's side, he could no longer betray our nation to Russia. He gave Undersecretary of State Berle — and this is all a matter of record — practically all, if not more, of the facts upon which Hiss's conviction was based.

Undersecretary Berle promptly contacted Dean Acheson and received word in return that Acheson (and I quote) "could vouch for Hiss absolutely" — at which time the matter was dropped. And this, you understand, was at a time when Russia was an ally of Germany. This condition existed while Russia and Germany were invading and dismembering Poland, and while the Communist groups here were screaming "warmonger" at the United States for their support of the allied nations.

Again in 1943, the FBI had occasion to investigate the facts surrounding Hiss's contacts with the Russian spy ring. But even after that FBI report was submitted, nothing was done.

Then, late in 1948 — on August 5 — when the Un-American Activities Committee called Alger Hiss to give an accounting, President Truman at once issued a presidential directive ordering all government agencies to refuse to turn over any information whatsoever in regard to the Communist activities of any government employee to a congressional committee.

Incidentally, even after Hiss was convicted, it is interesting to note that the President still labeled the exposé of Hiss as a "red herring."

If time permitted, it might be well to go into detail about the fact that Hiss was Roosevelt's chief adviser at Yalta when Roosevelt was admittedly in ill health and tired physically and mentally . . . and when, according to the secretary of state, Hiss and Gromyko drafted the report on the conference.

According to the then Secretary of State Stettinius, here are some of the things that Hiss helped to decide at Yalta: (1) the establishment of a European High Commission; (2) the treatment of Germany — this you will recall was the conference at which it was decided that we would occupy Berlin with Russia occupying an area completely circling the city, which, as you know, resulted in the Berlin airlift which cost thirty-one American lives; (3) the Polish question; (4) the relationship between UNRRA and the Soviet; (5) the rights of Americans on control commissions of Rumania, Bulgaria, and Hungary; (6) Iran; (7) China — here's where we gave away Manchuria; (8) Turkish Straits question; (9) international trusteeships; (10) Korea.

Of the results of this conference, Arthur Bliss Lane of the State Department had this to say: "As I glanced over the document, I could not believe my eyes. To me, almost every line spoke of a surrender to Stalin."

As you hear this story of high treason, I know that you are saying to yourself, "Well, why doesn't the Congress do something about it?" Actually, ladies and gentlemen, one of the important reasons for the graft, the corruption, the dishonesty, the disloyalty, the treason in high government positions — one of the most important reasons why this continues — is a lack of moral uprising on the part of the 140 million American people. In the light of history, however, this is not hard to explain.

It is the result of an emotional hangover and a temporary moral lapse which follows every war. It is the apathy to evil which people who have been subjected to the tremendous evils of war feel. As the people of the world see mass murder, the destruction of defenseless and innocent people, and all of the crime and lack of morals which go with war, they become numb and apathetic. It has always been thus after war. However, the morals of our people have not been destroyed. They still exist. This cloak of numbness and apathy has only needed a spark to rekindle them. Happily, this spark has finally been supplied.

As you know, very recently the secretary of state proclaimed his loyalty to a man guilty of what has always been considered as the most abominable of all crimes — of being a traitor to the people who gave him a position of great trust. The secretary of state, in attempting to justify his continued devotion to the man who sold out the Christian world to the atheistic world, referred to Christ's Sermon on the Mount as a justification and reason therefor, and the reaction of the American people to this would have made the heart of Abraham Lincoln happy. When this pompous diplomat in striped pants, with a phony British accent, proclaimed to the American people that Christ on the Mount endorsed communism, high treason, and betrayal of a sacred trust, the blasphemy was so great that it awakened the dormant indignation of the American people.

He has lighted the spark which is resulting in a moral uprising and will end only when the whole sorry mess of twisted, warped thinkers are swept from the national scene so that we may have a new birth of national honesty and decency in government.

6.

HERBERT H. LEHMAN: Freedom and Individual Security

The national agitation over Communist activity both at home and abroad during the late 1940s and early 1950s opened the way for renewed attacks on the New Deal and its descendant, the Fair Deal. Critics of "welfare state" legislation denounced it as Communistic or at least socialistic, decried the alleged encroachment of the federal government on the ordinary life of citizens, and asserted that "big government" was inimical to the true welfare of the people as it would eventually deprive them of their freedom. Liberal statesmen did not agree. Senator Herbert H. Lehman of New York voiced the opposition to such criticisms in a symposium on "Freedom and the Welfare State" in New York City in April 1950. His speech, originally titled "Freedom and the General Welfare," is reprinted here.

Source: *Freedom and the Welfare State,* A Symposium . . . on the Occasion of the 45th Anniversary of the League for Industrial Democracy, New York, n.d.

IT HAS BECOME FASHIONABLE in circles of political reaction to attack the concept of the welfare state as being prejudicial to individual liberty and freedom. These reactionaries view with fright and alarm the current and proposed activities of government in the fields of housing, health, and social security.

"These are steps on the road to Communism," the alarmists cry. But these same men uttered the same cries in the same tones of fear and outrage when President Roosevelt proposed the Securities and Exchange Act, the Fair Labor Standards Act, the Holding Company Act, the Federal Deposit Insurance Act, and many other pieces of legislation which even reactionaries would not dare to attack today. The same cries were raised when Woodrow Wilson proposed the Federal Trade Commission Act in 1913 and when the Railway Labor Act was first placed on the statute books in 1926. I could cite laws and programs by the score enacted over the violent opposition of the reactionaries — laws and programs which were assailed as communistic at the time — but which are now accepted even in the most conservative circles.

This cry of state tyranny has been raised during the last half century whenever the community has attempted to interfere with the right of a few to destroy forests, exploit little children, operate unsanitary and unsafe shops, indulge in racial or religious discrimination, and pursue other policies endangering the health, safety, and welfare of the community. These few have completely ignored the fact that, when their license to exploit the community was restricted, the freedom of the many from ignorance, insecurity, and want — the freedom of the many to live the good life — was measurably enhanced.

I do not believe that our federal government should seek to assume functions which properly belong to the individual or to the family, to the local community, or to free organizations of individuals. But I do believe that our federal government should and must perform those functions which, in this complex and interdependent society, the individual, the family, or the community cannot practicably perform for themselves.

Today we in America and in the entire freedom-loving world are confronted with a worldwide threat to that principle which we hold most dear, the principle of individual dignity and of individual freedom. For the preservation of that principle we are willing to dedicate our lives, if it should prove necessary. But while this is a threat which we face on the world front, we face another danger here at home. That is the threat to our freedom from those within our own country who would identify individual freedom with special privilege. Any move to diminish privilege, to stamp out discrimination, and to bring security to our citizens is branded by these people as un-American.

Not so long ago an American political leader said that "the governments of the past could fairly be characterized as devices for maintaining in perpetuity the place and position of certain privileged classes. The government of the United States, on the other hand, is a device for maintaining in perpetuity the rights of the people, with the ultimate extinction of all privileged classes." Was it some Communist, some irresponsible radical or reformer, who made that statement? No, it was not. It was the late President Calvin Coolidge in a speech at Philadelphia in 1924.

It is my firm belief that the extinction of special privilege is an essential and basic program of the welfare state. Today the forces of special privilege provide the chief opposition and raise the wildest cries of alarm against economic security for all.

In addition to the forces of special privilege who are opposed, on principle, to all social legislation, there are some who, while paying lip service to liberalism, claim to be troubled by the expanding scope of government in its direct concern with the welfare of the individual citizen. These people, while conceding merit to the specific programs of the welfare state, and while approving the welfare state programs of the past, join with the forces of privilege in contending that if the government provides any further services, it is moving in the direction of totalitarianism.

In my opinion these men of little vision have lost sight of the most important — and to me the most obvious — truth of our times — that a government which has secured the greatest degree of welfare for its people is the government which stands most firmly against totalitarianism. The critics of the welfare state do not understand this simple fact. They spend their time looking for Communists in and out of government and at the same time attack those measures which would deprive Communists and would-be Communists of their ammunition — and of their audience. The measures which would provide for the welfare of the people are the surest weapons against totalitarianism.

The Communist International, its leaders, and their philosophy have been responsible for many designs which we in the democratic world consider the quintessence of evil. Certainly the suppression of basic rights — the police state and the slave labor camp — constitutes the most repulsive and obnoxious way of life we can imagine.

But, as a liberal, I have a *special* resentment against the Communists. I feel that one of their greatest disservices to the cause of human progress has been their identification of economic security with the suppression of freedom. It is their claim that in order to achieve the solution of the economic needs of the many, it is necessary to curb the freedoms of all. They say, in effect, that you cannot have a full stomach and a free mind at the same time.

I reject this concept! I reject it as being the ultimate in reaction. This is but another demonstration of the basic affinity between Communists and reactionaries in their thinking about man and his problems. *Both* groups believe that a nation of freemen cannot possibly conquer the scourges of hunger, disease, lack of shelter, intolerance, and ignorance. And they *both* have much to gain if they convince enough people that freedom and security are incompatible.

It is a strange paradox that the same conservatives and reactionaries who pose as champions of national security express the greatest antagonism toward individual security. Most of us readily acknowledge that the nations of the world cannot be free if

they are not secure. It seems equally logical to me that *individuals* cannot be free if they are beset by fear and insecurity. To my mind the welfare state is simply a state in which people are free to develop their individual capacities, to receive just awards for their talents and to engage in the pursuit of happiness, unburdened by fear of actual hunger, actual homelessness or oppression by reason of race, creed or color.

The fear of old age, the fear of sickness, the fear of unemployment, and the fear of homelessness are not — as some would have us believe — essential drives in a productive society. These fears are not necessary to make free competitive enterprise work. The fear of insecurity is rather a cancer upon free competitive enterprise. It is the greatest threat which confronts our economic system. I hasten to add that I believe in free competitive enterprise. I believe it is the best system yet devised by man. But it is not a goal in itself. It must always serve the public interest.

We have had twenty years of the New Deal and the Fair Deal. Who would say that the American worker, the American farmer, and the ordinary American businessman is less free than he was twenty years ago? Actually, freedom in the true sense flourishes more generally and more widely today than ever before in our history. The worker, the farmer, and the businessman have vastly more freedom than they ever had before. They are freer to enjoy the fruits and benefits of a productive economy and a full life. But they are not yet free enough.

We are still far from the goal we seek. Insecurity still haunts millions. Inadequate housing poisons the wells of family life in vast numbers of cases. Inadequate schooling handicaps a great segment of our people. And the fear of sickness and old age still clutches at the hearts of many if not most of our fellow citizens. Until we solve all these problems and quiet all these fears, our people will not be truly free.

24

Joe Glazer: "Too Old To Work"

In the late 1940s the big American industrial unions began a campaign for company-paid pensions for workers to supplement what seemed to be inadequate government social security payments. The unions' slogan was "Too Old to Work, Too Young to Die," which gave Joe Glazer the refrain for this song, written in 1950. Glazer was inspired, he said, by hearing Walter Reuther "ripping into the automobile employers" in a speech. Glazer remembered Reuther telling a story of the mine mules that pulled the coal cars in West Virginia. During slack times the mules were well cared for — "but did they put the coal miner out to pasture? Did they feed him and keep him healthy? They did not. And you know why? Because it cost fifty bucks to get another mule, but they could always get another coal miner for nothing."

Source: *Songs of Work and Freedom,* Edith Fowke and Joe Glazer, eds., New York, 1960.

TOO OLD TO WORK

You work in the factory all of your life,
Try to provide for your kids and your wife.
When you get too old to produce any more,
They hand you your hat and they show you the door.

Chorus:
Too old to work, too old to work,
When you're too old to work and you're too young to die,
Who will take care of you, how'll you get by,
When you're too old to work and you're too young to die?

You don't ask for favors when your life is through;
You've got a right to what's coming to you.
Your boss gets a pension when he is too old;
You helped him retire — you're out in the cold.

They put horses to pasture, they feed them on hay;
Even machines get retired some day.
The bosses get pensions when their days are through;
Fat pensions for them, brother; nothing for you.

There's no easy answer, there's no easy cure;
Dreaming won't change it, that's one thing for sure;
But fighting together we'll get there some day,
And when we have won we will no longer say.

8.

MARTHA WOLFENSTEIN AND NATHAN LEITES:
American Film Plots

*As late as 1950 most Americans were still attending the movies once or twice a week.
A number of observers and social critics tried to evaluate this extraordinary fidelity
to an entertainment medium on the assumption that a habit so deeply ingrained
in an entire people must imply something about American cultural values. It was not
easy, however, to determine just what those values were. Martha Wolfenstein and
Nathan Leites published a work in 1950 in which they tried to pinpoint the elements in
Hollywood's productions that seemed most pervasive and most "American." Part of
the book's concluding chapter, on American film plots, is reprinted here.*

Source: *Movies: A Psychological Study*, Glencoe, Ill., 1950, pp. 293-301.

DRAMATIC PRODUCTIONS may show human fate in various ways. The story may be of love and we may see the happy lovers joined as in a dream while seeming obstacles melt away before them. Or love may contend with other powerful motives in the lover, or be opposed by strong antagonists. Love may overstep the bounds of licit choice. Lovers who defy the law to come together may be overwhelmed by punishers who overtake them or by their own conscience. Or conscience may run on ahead of longing, chastening their wishes and sending them apart without their ever having been together. Rivals in love may be brought into deadly conflict, or to renunciation. The lover may find he is not loved in return; his love may change to rage or self-destruction, or he may find someone else. And so again confusion may be sorted out and each one find a partner.

Thus wishes working their way through various hazards may win happy fulfillment, may be denied, or may by being fulfilled bring down hard penalties. The plot may be of violence, and we may see the hero carrying out acts we wish but dread to do. He commits the dreamed-of crime but also bears its awful recompense. Or injury may justify his deeds, or call for deeds he cannot bring himself to do. Battles may be won or lost; victory may be dimmed by regrets for the loser, or gladdened by assurance of a righteous cause. Justice may be done or may miscarry. We may feel both triumph and pain as we see the hero undergo inevitable punishment for his rash deeds. Or we may see the fallibility of human justice as misplaced penalties fall on the innocent.

The world may appear in various aspects, as beautiful or dangerous or sordid, ruled over by benign or punitive gods or none at all. The main point of the drama may be not to exhibit conflicts between protagonists who may win or lose but to show the opposition of human wishes to the nature of life itself. The contest becomes one in which we all lose in the end, and the aim of the drama may be to reconcile us to this eventuality.

The dramatic productions of a particular culture at a particular time, or even over a considerable period, tend to exhibit a distinctive plot configuration. This configuration gives the various individual dramas the distinctive atmosphere which we can recognize as pervading them all. Obviously a group of plots or even a single plot is exceedingly complex. Nevertheless a certain basic plan may be discerned; we can see that one pattern from among the range of dramatic alternatives has been chosen for major emphasis. . . .

The major plot configuration in American films contrasts with both the British and the French. Winning is terrifically important and always possible though it may be a tough fight. The conflict is not an internal one; it is not our own impulses which endanger us nor our own scruples that stand in our way. The hazards are all external, but they are not rooted in the nature of life itself. They are the hazards of a particular situation with which we find ourselves confronted. The hero is typically in a strange town where there are apt to be dangerous men and women of ambiguous character and where the forces of law and order are not to be relied on. If he sizes up the situation correctly, if he does not go off halfcocked but is still able to beat the other fellow to the punch once he is sure who the enemy is, if he relies on no one but himself, if he demands sufficient evidence of virtue from the girl, he will emerge triumphant. He will defeat the dangerous men, get the right girl, and show the authorities what's what.

When he is a child, he is the comic hero, showing off, blundering, cocky, scared, called on to perform beyond his capacities, and pulling through by surprising spurts of activity and with the help of favorable circumstances. He is completely harmless, free from sexual or aggressive impulses, and the world around him reflects his own innocuous character. Its threats are playful and its reproaches ridiculous. When he is a man he is the melodrama hero and the world changes to reflect his changed potentialities; it becomes dangerous and seriously accusing, and launches him on his fighting career.

The majority of the melodramas show him coming through successfully. A minority reveal various perils which lie off the main track; they are cautionary tales. The hero may succumb to his attacker; this is his bad dream. The men around him may be less dangerous than he suspects. Under the delusion that he attacks in self-defense, he may initiate hostilities; then he will lose. In this case he is crazy. Without being deluded to this extent, out of greed and overconfidence, he may try to get away with murder; he commits the crime of which he is usually only suspected and he has to pay for it. The girl may turn out to be worse than he believed. He will have to go off without her; then he is lonely. He may not be able to produce anyone on whom to pin the blame for the crimes of which he is falsely accused; then he is a victim of circumstances. If circumstances fail to collaborate with his need to blame someone else, he may even end by blaming himself. These are the various hazards which the usual melodrama hero safely passes on the way.

The fantasy which provides for defeating dangerous men, winning the right girl, and coming out in the clear is produced under the auspices of two major mechanisms: projection and denial. Self-accusations are embodied in the blundering police and destructive impulses in the unprovoked attacker. The beloved woman seems to be involved with another man but investigation ends in the gratifying demonstration that she never loved anyone but the hero. The love disappointment to which the French movie hero is repeatedly exposed is here denied.

The external world may be dangerous but manageable, or, at other times, uncontrollable but gratifying. Where things seem to get out of control the results turn out to be wish-fulfilling. The overturning automobile throws the girl into the hero's arms, the rocking boat tosses the heroine's rival into the waves. The world that is uncontrollable but gratifying expresses an omnipotence fantasy while at the same time eliminating guilt. As soon as an internal problem is replaced by an external one, we can see the promise of success. The hero suffering from kleptomania becomes involved in investigating the activities of a gang of thieves; the amnesiac hero pursues his memories only long enough to unearth clues of someone else's crime before he rises impatiently from the psychiatrist's couch to embark on a successful detective job.

The world, which is not effectively policed, does not need to be policed at all. The hero, the self-appointed investigator and agent of justice, is able to set things right independently. The world thus appears as a kind of workable anarchic arrangement where, although hostilities are far from eliminated, life need not be nasty, brutish, and short, at any rate not for anyone we care about. The unofficial supervisors of private morals, the comic onlookers, are just as superfluous as the police. No one has any intention of doing anything naughty; only the mistakenly suspicious onlooker fails to recognize the natural goodness of the clean-cut young people.

American film plots are pervaded by false appearances. In this shadowy but temporarily vivid guise, the content of what is projected and denied tends to reappear. It is in false appearances that the forbidden wishes are realized which the hero and heroine so rarely carry into action. In a false appearance the heroine is promiscuous, the hero is a murderer, the young couple carry on an illicit affair, two men friends share the fa-

vors of a woman. This device makes it possible for us to eat our cake and have it, since we can enjoy the suggested wish-fulfillments without emphatic guilt; we know that the characters with whom we identify have not done anything. The contention of American films is that we should not feel guilty for mere wishes. The hero and heroine are threatened with penalties for the incriminating appearance but in the end are absolved. The misguided police or the foolish onlooker in comedies convey a self-accusation from which the hero and heroine struggle to dissociate themselves, a vestige of archaic conscience which is to be dispensed with.

What the plot unfolds is a process of proof. Something is undone rather than done: the false appearance is negated. The hero and heroine do not become committed to any irretrievable act whose consequences they must bear. Nor do they usually undergo any character transformation, ennoblement or degradation, gain or loss of hope, acceptance of a new role or the diminution and regrets of age. They succeed in proving what they were all along. They emerge from the shadow of the false appearance. What has changed is other people's impressions of them. In so far as the hero and heroine may be unsure of who or what they are except as they see themselves mirrored in the eyes of others, they have succeeded in establishing for themselves a desirable identity. In so far as they struggle against a projected archaic conscience that persecutes the wish as if it were the act, they win a victory for a more tolerant and discriminating morality.

———————◆———————

Hollywood is a place where the people from Iowa mistake each other for stars.
                                                    FRED ALLEN

9.

GILBERT SELDES: Pandora's Box — Television

Television began to take over from the movies and radio as the most popular form of entertainment in America around 1950. The new medium did not have to suffer some of the growing pains of the old: programming and advertising practices were adopted from radio, and the basic uses of the TV camera were imitated from the movies. Moreover, the national networks already existed, and the Federal Communications Commission had gained experience since its establishment in 1934 in controlling network policy and determining licensing requirements. But there were nevertheless a number of knowledgeable Americans who had serious doubts about the role — obviously immense — that television was destined to play in American life. One of these was Gilbert Seldes, who had been director of TV programming for CBS during the war, when a limited schedule of broadcasts was maintained by the network. A chapter from Seldes' book, The Great Audience, *is reprinted here in part.*

Source: *The Great Audience,* New York, 1950, pp. 160-173.

WITHOUT A MOMENT'S HESITATION, the American people have given over control of television to the networks, the stations, and the sponsors who have established the standards of radio broadcasting. It is a remarkable vote of confidence, and the masters of this new instrument have every right to be proud. Nothing the intellectuals, the bureaucrats, or the anti-capitalists have said against radio has had the slightest effect; television has a free hand.

If television were developing as the movies did half a century ago, spottily, without a sense of direction, pushed now one way, now another, by a hundred separate exploiters, all criticism of its present state and all guesses about the future would be premature. It is, on the contrary, being directed chiefly by the big broadcasters, who have analyzed their past experience and know precisely what they want; they are building television from a blueprint, eliminating the structural weaknesses of early radio; they are working from a master plan, the grand outlines of which are already visible.

The economics of television, as the chronological child-and-destroyer of radio, are paradoxical, but one thing is certain: in the early days of movies and of radio a program style could be tried and thrown away without much loss; in television the cost of any operation is so great that from the start broadcasters have a vested interest to protect. The chances for experiment are slimmer; whatever succeeds now will set the standards for the next ten years. If the direction now taken is in any way unsatisfactory, the moment to call a halt, to reconsider, and to change cannot be postponed.

That television would be used substantially for the same purposes as AM broadcasting became inevitable years ago, perhaps as far back as 1929, when Vladimir Zworykin went to work for the Radio Corporation of America, developed the iconoscope in their research laboratories, and automatically delivered modern television into the broadcasters' hands. If he had been working for any part of the movie industry, the control of television might have been rooted in

Hollywood; if he had been a researcher for the Navy, the course of television again would have been altered. Considering the enormous RCA investment in radio, as manufacturer of equipment and the parent company of two radio networks, its enterprise in pushing television is extraordinary. Some competition, especially in Great Britain, has existed, but RCA was for a long time in a position to slow up the growth of television, and did not do so. By using NBC as an experimental station, it has forced CBS and eventually all other broadcasters to take the first steps, and so set in motion the forces which are making television a part of the radio industry, leaving the movies far behind.

Given that situation, and the capacity of television to act as a universal transmitter of virtually all forms of communication and entertainment, the development now taking definite shape is this:

Television will be used as the primary force in the creation of a unified entertainment industry which will include sports, the theater and the movies, newsreels, radio, night clubs, vaudeville, as well as any minor activities, and will profoundly affect newspapers, magazines, books, the fine arts, and ultimately education. Coexisting within this pyramid of entertainment there will be a highly unified communications industry affecting political life.

Under our present laws we are not likely to get a single monolithic entertainment industry; but each network will be, in effect, a vertical trust, creating or subsidizing its own sports events, its own movies, investing in plays; and all the TV broadcasters together will profoundly influence the outlying independents in many fields, just as the movies now influence the production of plays and books and, to an extent, the writing of short stories.

It was commonly said, when television was beginning, that the great problem was not the size of the screen or the cost of the production or the reluctance of sponsors;

the essential thing was to get into Madison Square Garden; without access to the great fights and other events held there, a broadcaster would not be able to compete for an audience. The Garden is not now the exclusive property of a single broadcaster; but each one can make exclusive contracts with the management of individual events.

Before television could demonstrate that it did, or did not, hurt attendance, several new ways of handling sports were worked out. To compete with the NBC monopoly on the fights arranged by the Twentieth Century Club, CBS invested in the Tournament of Champions, becoming in effect a sports promoter. Even more illuminating was the progress of the Roller Derby. The spectacle of young women with long and powerful legs, skating around an arena, jockeying for position, and eventually mauling and tearing at one another, had attracted moderate attention in its native habitat; transferred to television it became a sensation. The ABC network put the Roller Derby under a five-year contract, and the owner could count on such a large income from sponsorship that his primary economic interest veered to television; the techniques of the sport were adapted at least as much to the requirements of the cameras as to those of the arena audience.

The major baseball clubs have not yet been affected, but they are receiving substantial sums for telecasts of their games, and one predictable result is that there will be more night games, which come over brilliantly on the TV screen, because the available audience is greater, and this will in turn affect movies, theaters, and restaurants, especially if baseball as a spectator sport is carefully promoted for women, following the precedent set by the cigarette industry. To a degree, the pattern set by baseball will apply to other sports; after two years of television the Garden was asking, according to the *New York Times*, sixty thousand dollars for a series of professional basketball or hockey, and as much as a hundred and fifty thousand for a somewhat longer series of college basketball games. (As neither networks nor colleges seem to have a strong historical sense, it may be worth noting that in 1930 the president of NBC said, "We have refused to permit on our system the sponsoring of football games by commercial institutions. . . . With all these youngsters . . . I just did not quite like to see the Yale-Harvard game announced 'through the courtesy of so-and-so.'" Most colleges and most so-and-sos have not been permanently barred by the scruples of Merlin Aylseworth.)

The telecasting of sports was a turning point in the first phase of TV history. It shocked the idealists who saw a great instrument of imagination and social significance turned to the mean estate of reporting not only a World's Series, but phony wrestling matches and third-rate prizefights as well; and it shook the practical men, because for a moment it seemed that television was moving from the atmosphere of the home (an ideal place for selling clothes, soap, cars, and the other commodities supporting radio) to the saloon, where, according to persistent rumor, it didn't even increase the sale of beer, the spectators being so attentive to the sport that they forgot to order.

A few commodities are naturals for sports broadcasts, whether they are received at home or in public places: cigarettes, beer, razor blades, and so on. But these events present their own special difficulties: they cannot be reduced to the specific durations of other programs scheduled for the same time each week; and most of them are long enough to become automatically the feature of an entire evening, so that the rest of the schedule has to be built around them. They are nevertheless ideal material for television, fulfilling some of its essential requirements, giving it a chance to do what no other medium can do; in sports, television transmits instantaneously and completely an actual event the outcome of which cannot be fore-

told. The condensed movie version of a prizefight, cutting out the dull moments, splicing in slow motion for the knockout, pausing to call attention in advance to the unexpected blow or the disputed foul, is in every way a superior document; but no one (except perhaps Fred Allen's Titus Moody) ever bet on a newsreel prizefight.

The intellectual dislike for spectator sports will make no headway against the combination of their inherent attraction and the still miraculous opportunity of seeing them happen, the moment they happen, fifty or a thousand or eventually three thousand miles away. When the coaxial cable and relay systems extend to all parts of the country, citizens in the eastern time zone will be able to watch sports from the first game of a doubleheader at one o'clock in the afternoon to the last round of a prizefight at Gilmore Field in Los Angeles at one the next morning, by his own watch. The God-favored Californian will be able to start watching sports as early as eleven A.M. When network television is complete, the added interest may lead to an extension of the Major Leagues to the Coast; the jump from St. Louis to Los Angeles by plane will take no longer than did the trip from New York to Chicago in the days when the Leagues were founded. The obstacle at present is that, except for World's Series games, transmission is local, not national.

If the sports promoters prove uncooperative, the path of the broadcasters has already been mapped by CBS and ABC: they can create their own events, and the engines of publicity at their disposal will go into high gear to make the sports created by broadcasters more popular than those withheld from transmission. They will not need to create rivals to the National and American Leagues, the chances being that baseball will be happy to increase its paying audience by telecasting the games; but the TV broadcasters will always have it in their power to undermine any uncooperative sport by filling the air with other entertainments calculated to keep the customers looking at the screen instead of going to the field or the arena.

The interaction of sports and television is significant. In the past twenty years Americans have enormously increased their outlay as spectators; professional baseball quadrupled its take in that period; pro football went up a thousand percent; hockey and college football did not rise so far, but their increase was two to four times as great as the rise in movie receipts; and the relative newcomer, dog racing, went up nearly two thousand percent, and did as well as the old established horse racing. (The figures were given by Charles Sawyer, Secretary of Commerce, in an address to the Theatre Owners of America, whom he tried to console for their humiliating increase of a mere hundred percent in the same years by reflecting that their take was still three times as great as the combined receipts of all other spectator amusements.) There has also been an increase in active sports, and bowling and basketball are among the leading diversions of the entire country. A medium which can deliver an event as completely as television does is bound to exploit all its capacities to the full, and while fights and wrestling may go down for a while, the only possible effect on sports as a whole must be to multiply its attractions.

They are magnetic enough as it is. In one of its more abstract and lofty essays, the magazine *Life* analyzed the American pursuit of happiness; as a prelude to the discussion, *Life* went through its files and published twenty-five separate pictures showing how we use our inalienable right. The pictures ranged from religious dedication to beauty contests; one-fifth were specifically connected with sport; three-fifths were preadult, and only four of the twenty-five were pictures of mature men and women. The number of columns of text devoted to sport in such a sober journal as the *New York Times* is often greater than that assigned to

all the arts and sciences, education, the special interests of women, editorials, and human-interest stories put together; in Boston, morning papers make mid-season baseball the lead story on the front page although the actual results of games have been known for twelve hours, and West Coast papers often do the same for stories about the Major League baseball teams which their readers have never seen.

The irritated intellectual knows that all this sitting around and watching other people hit or kick or throw a ball isn't "good"; he knows that professional sport is dubiously linked with large-scale gambling, with corruption and crime; he feels something artificial in the passion of the Dodger fan and suspects that shrewd promotion lies behind it. From critics in the Soviet Union he hears that the build-up of spectator sports is only another device to keep the American people in a state of perpetual adolescence, and he may recall the remark of Thorstein Veblen that, unlike the proletariat of ancient Rome, who got in free, the Americans have to pay for their circuses. All this may be true; but in relation to mass entertainment the critic has standing only in one limited way. If television is not only to satisfy, but actively to exploit and exaggerate, the appetite for looking at sports, the general level of its entertainment will not rise in any marked degree above the sports-lovers' limitations. There will be exceptions; but a mass medium creates its audience by its average.

It was great fun to read that the saloon audience shouted "turn on the fights" when the first grand opera was transmitted from the Metropolitan; but one who likes grand opera even less than second-rate fights may wonder whether television intends to build up a mass-minority audience at the sports level, satisfying only one ruling passion, and leaving untouched all the other interests and curiosities and appetites that human beings, including sports-lovers, enjoy. The ready-made (and in part radio-made) audience, eager for baseball and prizefights in television, is not a moronic fringe of the population; if it shows symptoms of delayed maturity when it throws bottles at an umpire, it may be retreating into adolescence for a holiday; and the same people that sit in the grandstands and bleachers are responsible craftsmen and husbands and citizens at other times. But the audience that television will create if it excites and feeds only one group of appetites will be lower in the scale of human values simply because so many natural human wants will go unsatisfied and so many capacities will atrophy from disuse.

For if the television audience is conceived and created in the image of the robot man, all the other entertainments absorbed into television will be squeezed into the same zone of interest. The process by which the movies reduce Dumas to farce or Flaubert to melodrama, and radio reduces relativity to a series of puns, will continue; the reluctance of producers to stage a play that has no chance in Hollywood will find a parallel wherever the "television angle" will be the decisive factor. (A woman with a pleasing voice was supplanted on the TV version of a radio program by a singer not nearly so good; the radio singer was fat, the other slender.) The area of effect will depend on what is popular at any moment. Night clubs and resurgent vaudeville will come under the influence of television at once, since they depend on personalities, on flash popularity, which television can build; from there the effects will radiate to musical shows. If television goes in for a series of short dramatizations, the writers of short stories will be touched; if methods are found to visualize fantasy, Superman and Batman and the rest will be written with television in mind. . . .

The relation between television and the movies may work out in several different ways. The essential factor is that until now the audience for television is substantially the same as the movie audience. Nothing in the quality of the product stands in the way of a merger of interests; and if no agreement is reached, each will be the mortal enemy of the other.

In Hollywood are huge studios, magnificent equipment, trained technicians, and the most popular of all entertainers; also a backlog of several thousand feature films. Owned by Hollywood, and not necessarily on the credit side at this moment, are theater buildings all over the country. The studios can use what they have to make pictures for the theaters; or they can, after some revolutionary adjustments, make pictures for the television industry and bring into the theaters both their own pictures and certain types of TV studio programs.

Or they can compromise. They can act as a manufacturing unit for television, preparing pictures to the specifications of broadcasting, and at the same time reach out for the audience neither Hollywood nor television attracts. This would follow the pattern set by the theater after the movies came to Broadway; the melodrama of the 1890s disappeared, and the parlor comedy followed when the movies offered their own version; some plays were put on in the hope of sale to the movies, but for a generation the theater survived by attracting a non-movie-going audience. It was not done without bankruptcies and heartbreak; but the theater survived long enough for new talent to come into it. Whether the movies with their enormous overhead can afford anything like this purging experience is doubtful; but if they get a substantial income out of the pictures made for television, they may have time to reorient themselves.

The movies may, however, take their bearings and go off into a wilderness of Westerns and musical extravaganzas. In these departments television cannot compete. Networks and sponsors may commission short films or cheaply made longer ones; if they cannot get them from the major studios, they will find independents to make them, or they will go into the business themselves. But the spectacular film, well made, in color (which will not be generally available to television for several years) is too costly. It may be a risky thing, but if Hollywood chooses to fight television, competing for the same audience, these noisy and infantile productions are available; and local theaters may make a deal with independent television stations to pipe in sporting events and quizzes so they will have some form of television to offer. The audiences attracted by this combination of the least significant elements in the two media would not tolerate the best of Hollywood's current product, and the net result would be a further lowering of movie standards.

10.

WILLIAM FAULKNER: Nobel Prize Acceptance Speech

William Faulkner, the author of half a dozen of the most admired, but also the most difficult, American novels of the twentieth century, was awarded the Nobel Prize for Literature for 1949. His acceptance speech, delivered in Stockholm on December 10, 1950, and reprinted here, was a surprise to some of his critics and even to some of his devotees. Faulkner had been better known for complexity than for simplicity of language, and for delvings into the evils of human nature than for affirmations of man's "highest" qualities. But the speech was marked by a striking plainness and forthrightness, and its message was one of exalted hope rather than despair. All in all, it is a singularly eloquent statement of the writer's creed.

I FEEL THAT THIS AWARD was not made to me as a man, but to my work — a life's work in the agony and sweat of the human spirit, not for glory and least of all for profit, but to create out of the materials of the human spirit something which did not exist before. So this award is only mine in trust. It will not be difficult to find a dedication for the money part of it commensurate with the purpose and significance of its origin. But I would like to do the same with the acclaim too, by using this moment as a pinnacle from which I might be listened to by the young men and women already dedicated to the same anguish and travail, among whom is already that one who will someday stand where I am standing.

Our tragedy today is a general and universal physical fear so long sustained by now that we can even bear it. There are no longer problems of the spirit. There is only the question: When will I be blown up? Because of this, the young man or woman writing today has forgotten the problems of the human heart in conflict with itself which alone can make good writing because only that is worth writing about, worth the agony and the sweat.

He must learn them again. He must teach himself that the basest of all things is to be afraid; and, teaching himself that, forget it forever, leaving no room in his workshop for anything but the old verities and truths of the heart, the old universal truths lacking which any story is ephemeral and doomed — love and honor and pity and pride and compassion and sacrifice. Until he does so, he labors under a curse. He writes not of love but of lust, of defeats in which nobody loses anything of value, of victories without hope and, worst of all, without pity or compassion. His griefs grieve on no universal bones, leaving no scars. He writes not of the heart but of the glands.

Until he relearns these things, he will write as though he stood among and watched the end of man. I decline to accept the end of man. It is easy enough to say that man is immortal simply because he will endure; that when the last ding-dong of doom has clanged and faded from the last worthless rock hanging tideless in the last red and dying evening, that even then there will still be one more sound: that of his puny, inexhaustible voice, still talking.

I refuse to accept this. I believe that man will not merely endure: he will prevail. He is immortal, not because he alone among creatures has an inexhaustible voice, but because he has a soul, a spirit capable of compassion and sacrifice and endurance. The poet's, the writer's duty is to write about these things. It is his privilege to help man endure by lifting his heart, by reminding him of the courage and honor and hope and pride and compassion and pity and sacrifice which have been the glory of his past. The poet's voice need not merely be the record of man; it can be one of the props, the pillars to help him endure and prevail.

11.

Harry S. Truman: United Nations Police Action in Korea

The failure of the United States and the Soviet Union to create a unified Korea after World War II left that country divided into two hostile parts by an arbitrary line drawn east and west at the 38th parallel of latitude. The southern half of the country became the Republic of Korea in 1948, following UN-sponsored elections. The Democratic People's Republic of Korea was established in the northern part, largely as a result of Russian urgings; it claimed jurisdiction over the whole country. Relations between the two halves of Korea became more and more strained as the Cold War intensified in other parts of the world. American occupation troops were withdrawn from South Korea in 1949, leaving the area almost completely unprotected. On June 25, 1950, civil war broke out when North Korean troops invaded the south. Two days later President Truman released the following statement of the American government's attitude toward the Korean crisis.

Source: *Bulletin,* July 3, 1950, p. 5.

In Korea, the government forces, which were armed to prevent border raids and to preserve internal security, were attacked by invading forces from North Korea. The Security Council of the United Nations called upon the invading troops to cease hostilities and to withdraw to the 38th parallel. This they have not done, but, on the contrary, have pressed the attack. The Security Coun-

cil called upon all members of the United Nations to render every assistance to the United Nations in the execution of this resolution. In these circumstances, I have ordered United States air and sea forces to give the Korean government troops cover and support.

The attack upon Korea makes it plain beyond all doubt that Communism has passed beyond the use of subversion to conquer independent nations and will now use armed invasion and war. It has defied the orders of the Security Council of the United Nations issued to preserve international peace and security. In these circumstances, the occupation of Formosa by Communist forces would be a direct threat to the security of the Pacific area and to United States forces performing their lawful and necessary functions in that area.

Accordingly, I have ordered the Seventh Fleet to prevent any attack on Formosa. As a corollary of this action, I am calling upon the Chinese government on Formosa to cease all air and sea operations against the mainland. The Seventh Fleet will see that this is done. The determination of the future status of Formosa must await the restoration of security in the Pacific, a peace settlement with Japan, or consideration by the United Nations.

I have also directed that United States forces in the Philippines be strengthened and that military assistance to the Philippine government be accelerated.

I have similarly directed acceleration in the furnishing of military assistance to the forces of France and the Associated States in Indochina and the dispatch of a military mission to provide close working relations with those forces.

I know that all members of the United Nations will consider carefully the consequences of this latest aggression in Korea in defiance of the Charter of the United Nations. A return to the rule of force in international affairs would have far-reaching effects. The United States will continue to uphold the rule of law.

12.

HARRY S. TRUMAN: Veto of the Internal Security Act

A number of federal laws prohibiting or limiting Communist activities had been passed by the beginning of 1950, but the onset of the Korean War heightened public feeling against Communism and led to demands for even more stringent legislation. Congress responded to these pressures by passing the McCarran Internal Security Act on September 20, 1950. The Act required the registration of organizations listed by the attorney general as either Fascist or Communist, prohibited the employment of Communists and certain Communist sympathizers in national defense work, and denied Communists the right to enter the country. President Truman, feeling that the new law went too far, vetoed it on September 22. The McCarran Act was repassed over his veto the following day. A portion of his veto message is reprinted here.

Source: 81 Congress, 2 Session, House Document No. 708.

I RETURN HEREWITH, without my approval, H. R. 9490, the proposed Internal Security Act of 1950.

I am taking this action only after the most serious study and reflection and after consultation with the security and intelligence agencies of the government. The Department of Justice, the Department of Defense, the Central Intelligence Agency, and the Department of State have all advised me that the bill would seriously damage the security and the intelligence operations for which they are responsible. They have strongly expressed the hope that the bill would not become law.

This is an omnibus bill containing many different legislative proposals with only one thing in common — they are all represented to be "anti-Communist." But when the many complicated pieces of the bill are analyzed in detail, a startling result appears.

H. R. 9490 would not hurt the Communists. Instead, it would help them.

It has been claimed over and over again that this is an "anti-Communist" bill — a "Communist control" bill. But in actual operation the bill would have results exactly the opposite of those intended. . . .

Specifically, some of the principal objections to the bill are as follows:

1. It would aid potential enemies by requiring the publication of a complete list of vital defense plants, laboratories, and other installations.

2. It would require the Department of Justice and its Federal Bureau of Investigation to waste immense amounts of time and energy attempting to carry out its unworkable registration provisions.

3. It would deprive us of the great assistance of many aliens in intelligence matters.

4. It would antagonize friendly governments.

5. It would put the government of the United States in the thought-control business.

6. It would make it easier for subversive aliens to become naturalized as United States citizens.

7. It would give government officials vast powers to harass all of our citizens in the exercise of their right of free speech.

Legislation with these consequences is not necessary to meet the real dangers which Communism presents to our free society. Those dangers are serious, and must be met. But this bill would hinder us, not help us, in meeting them. Fortunately, we already have on the books strong laws which give us most of the protection we need from the real dangers of treason, espionage, sabotage, and actions looking to the overthrow of our government by force and violence. Most of the provisions of this bill have no relation to these real dangers. . . .

I therefore most earnestly request the Congress to reconsider its action. I am confident that on more careful analysis most members of Congress will recognize that this bill is contrary to the best interests of our country at this critical time. . . .

Sections 22 and 25 of this bill would make sweeping changes in our laws governing the admission of aliens to the United States and their naturalization as citizens. The ostensible purpose of these provisions is to prevent persons who would be dangerous to our national security from entering the country or becoming citizens. In fact, present law already achieves that objective.

What these provisions would actually do is to prevent us from admitting to our country, or to citizenship, many people who could make real contributions to our national strength. The bill would deprive our government and our intelligence agencies of the valuable services of aliens in security operations. It would require us to exclude and to deport the citizens of some friendly non-Communist countries. Furthermore, it would actually make it easier for subversive aliens to become United States citizens. Only the Communist movement would gain from such actions.

Section 24 and Sections 26 through 30 of this bill make a number of minor changes in the naturalization laws. None of them is of great significance — nor are they particularly relevant to the problem of internal security. These provisions, for the most part, have received little or no attention in the legislative process. I believe that several of them would not be approved by the Congress if they were considered on their merits, rather than as parts of an omnibus bill.

Section 31 of this bill makes it a crime to attempt to influence a judge or jury by public demonstration, such as picketing. While the courts already have considerable power to punish such actions under existing law, I have no objection to this section.

Sections 100 through 117 of this bill (Title II) are intended to give the government power, in the event of invasion, war, or insurrection in the United States in aid of a foreign enemy, to seize and hold persons who could be expected to attempt acts of espionage or sabotage, even though they had as yet committed no crime. It may be that legislation of this type should be on the statute books. But the provisions in H. R. 9490 would very probably prove ineffective to achieve the objective sought, since they would not suspend the writ of habeas corpus, and under our legal system to detain a man not charged with a crime would raise serious constitutional questions unless the writ of habeas corpus were suspended. Furthermore, it may well be that other persons than those covered by these provisions would be more important to detain in the event of emergency. This whole problem, therefore, should clearly be studied more thoroughly before further legislative action along these lines is considered.

In brief, when all the provisions of H. R. 9490 are considered together, it is evident that the great bulk of them are not directed toward the real and present dangers that exist from Communism. Instead of striking blows at Communism, they would strike blows at our own liberties and at our position in the forefront of those working for freedom in the world. At a time when our young men are fighting for freedom in Korea, it would be tragic to advance the objectives of Communism in this country, as this bill would do.

Because I feel so strongly that this legislation would be a terrible mistake, I want to discuss more fully its worst features — Sections 1 through 17 and Sections 22 and 25.

Most of the first seventeen sections of H. R. 9490 are concerned with requiring registration and annual reports, by what the bill calls "Communist-action organizations" and "Communist-front organizations," of names of officers, sources and uses of funds, and, in the case of "Communist-action organizations," names of members. The idea of requiring Communist organizations to divulge information about themselves is a simple and attractive one. But it is about as practical as requiring thieves to register with the sheriff. Obviously, no such organization as the Communist Party is likely to register voluntarily.

Under the provisions of the bill, if an organization which the attorney general believes should register does not do so, he must request a five-man "Subversive Activities Control Board" to order the organization to register. The attorney general would have to produce proof that the organization in question was in fact a "Communist-action" or a "Communist-front organization." To do this he would have to offer evidence relating to every aspect of the organization's activities. The organization could present opposing evidence. Prolonged hearings would be required to allow both sides to present proof and to cross-examine opposing witnesses.

To estimate the duration of such a proceeding involving the Communist Party, we need only recall that on much narrower issues the trial of the eleven Communist leaders under the Smith Act consumed nine months. In a hearing under this bill, the difficulties of proof would be much greater and would take a much longer time.

The bill lists a number of criteria for the Board to consider in deciding whether or not an organization is a "Communist-action" or "Communist-front" organization. Many of these deal with the attitudes or states of mind of the organization's leaders. It is frequently difficult in legal proceedings to establish whether or not a man has committed an overt act, such as theft or perjury. But under this bill the attorney general would have to attempt the immensely more difficult task of producing concrete legal evidence that men have particular ideas or opinions. This would inevitably require the disclosure of many of the FBI's confidential sources of information and thus would damage our national security. . . .

Thus the net result of the registration provisions of this bill would probably be an endless chasing of one organization after another, with the Communists always able to frustrate the law-enforcement agencies and prevent any final result from being achieved. It could only result in wasting the energies of the Department of Justice and in destroying the sources of information of its FBI. To impose these fruitless burdens upon the FBI would divert it from its vital security duties and thus give aid and comfort to the very Communists whom the bill is supposed to control.

Unfortunately, these provisions are not merely ineffective and unworkable. They represent a clear and present danger to our institutions.

Insofar as the bill would require registration by the Communist Party itself, it does not endanger our traditional liberties. However, the application of the registration requirements to so-called Communist-front organizations can be the greatest danger to freedom of speech, press, and assembly since the Alien and Sedition Laws of 1798. This danger arises out of the criteria or standards to be applied in determining whether an organization is a Communist-front organization.

There would be no serious problem if the bill required proof that an organization was controlled and financed by the Communist Party before it could be classified as a Communist-front organization. However, recognizing the difficulty of proving those matters, the bill would permit such a determination to be based solely upon "the extent to which the positions taken or advanced by it from time to time on matters of policy do not deviate from those" of the Communist movement.

This provision could easily be used to classify as a Communist-front organization any organization which is advocating a single policy or objective which is also being urged by the Communist Party or by a Communist foreign government. In fact, this may be the intended result, since the bill defines "organization" to include "a group of persons . . . permanently or temporarily associated together for joint action on any subject or subjects." Thus, an organization which advocates low-cost housing for sincere humanitarian reasons might be classified as a Communist-front organization because the Communists regularly exploit slum conditions as one of their fifth-column techniques.

It is not enough to say that this probably would not be done. The mere fact that it could be done shows clearly how the bill would open a Pandora's box of opportunities for official condemnation of organizations and individuals for perfectly honest opinions which happen to be stated also by Communists.

The basic error of these sections is that they move in the direction of suppressing opinion and belief. This would be a very dangerous course to take, not because we have any sympathy for Communist opinions but because any governmental stifling of the free expression of opinion is a long step toward totalitarianism.

There is no more fundamental axiom of American freedom than the familiar statement: In a free country we punish men for the crimes they commit but never for the opinions they have. And the reason this is so fundamental to freedom is not, as many suppose, that it protects the few unorthodox from suppression by the majority. To permit freedom of expression is primarily for the benefit of the majority, because it protects criticism, and criticism leads to progress.

We can and we will prevent espionage, sabotage, or other actions endangering our national security. But we would betray our finest traditions if we attempted, as this bill would attempt, to curb the simple expression of opinion. This we should never do, no matter how distasteful the opinion may be to the vast majority of our people. The course proposed by this bill would delight the Communists, for it would make a mockery of the Bill of Rights and of our claims to stand for freedom in the world.

And what kind of effect would these provisions have on the normal expression of political views? Obviously, if this law were on the statute books, the part of prudence would be to avoid saying anything that might be construed by someone as not deviating sufficiently from the current Communist-propaganda line. And since no one could be sure in advance what views were safe to express, the inevitable tendency would be to express no views on controversial subjects. The result could only be to reduce the vigor and strength of our political life — an outcome that the Communists would happily welcome, but that freemen should abhor.

We need not fear the expression of ideas — we do need to fear their suppression.

Our position in the vanguard of freedom rests largely on our demonstration that the free expression of opinion, coupled with government by popular consent, leads to national strength and human advancement. Let us not, in cowering and foolish fear, throw away the ideals which are the fundamental basis of our free society.

Not only are the registration provisions of this bill unworkable and dangerous, they are also grossly misleading in that all but one of the objectives which are claimed for them are already being accomplished by other and superior methods — and the one objective which is not now being accomplished would not in fact be accomplished under this bill either.

It is claimed that the bill would provide information about the Communist Party and its members. The fact is, the FBI already possesses very complete sources of information concerning the Communist movement in this country. If the FBI must disclose its sources of information in public hearings to require registration under this bill, its present sources of information and its ability to acquire new information will be largely destroyed.

It is claimed that this bill would deny income-tax exemptions to Communist organizations. The fact is that the Bureau of Internal Revenue already denies income-tax exemptions to such organizations.

It is claimed that this bill would deny passports to Communists. The fact is that the government can and does deny passports to Communists under existing law.

It is claimed that this bill would prohibit the employment of Communists by the federal government. The fact is that the employment of Communists by the federal government is already prohibited and, at least in the executive branch, there is an effective program to see that they are not employed.

It is claimed that this bill would prohibit the employment of Communists in defense plants. The fact is that it would be years before this bill would have any effect of this nature — if it ever would. Fortunately, this objective is already being substantially achieved under the present procedures of the Department of Defense, and if the Congress would enact one of the provisions I have recommended — which it did not include in this bill — the situation would be entirely taken care of, promptly and effectively. . . .

Section 4(a) of the bill, like its registration provisions, would be ineffective, would be subject to dangerous abuse, and would seek to accomplish an objective which is already better accomplished under existing law. This provision would make unlawful any agreement "to perform any act which would substantially contribute to the establishment within the United States" of a foreign-controlled dictatorship. Of course, this provision would be unconstitutional if it infringed upon the fundamental right of the American people to establish for themselves by constitutional methods any form of government they choose. To avoid this, it is provided that this section "shall not apply to the proposal of a constitutional amendment." If this language limits the prohibition of the section to the use of unlawful methods, then it adds nothing to the Smith Act, under which eleven Communist leaders have been convicted, and would be more difficult to enforce. Thus, it would accomplish nothing. Moreover, the bill does not even purport to define the phrase, unique in a criminal statute, "substantially contribute." A phrase so vague raises a serious constitutional question.

Sections 22 and 25 of this bill are directed toward the specific questions of who should be admitted to our country and who should be permitted to become a United States citizen. I believe there is general agreement that the answers to those questions should be: We should admit to our country, within the available quotas, anyone with a legitimate purpose who would not endanger our security, and we should admit to citizenship any immigrant who will be a loyal and constructive member of the community. Those are essentially the standards set by existing law. Under present law we do not admit to our country known Communists because we believe they work to overthrow our government, and we do not admit Communists to citizenship because we believe they are not loyal to the United States.

The changes which would be made in the present law by Sections 22 and 25 would not reinforce those sensible standards. Instead, they would add a number of new standards, which, for no good and sufficient reason, would interfere with our relations with other countries and seriously damage our national security.

Section 22 would, for example, exclude from our country anyone who advocates any form of totalitarian or one-party government. We, of course, believe in the democratic system of competing political parties, offering a choice of candidates and policies. But a number of countries with which we maintain friendly relations have a different form of government.

Until now no one has suggested that we should abandon cultural and commercial relations with a country merely because it has a form of government different from ours. Yet Section 22 would require that. As one instance, it is clear that under the definitions of the bill, the present government of Spain, among others, would be classified as "totalitarian." As a result, the attorney general would be required to exclude from the United States all Spanish businessmen, students, and other nonofficial travelers who support the present government of their country. I cannot understand how the sponsors of this bill can think that such an action would contribute to our national security.

Moreover, the provisions of Section 22 of this bill would strike a serious blow to our national security by taking away from the government the power to grant asylum in this country to foreign diplomats who repudiate Communist imperialism and wish to escape its reprisals. It must be obvious to anyone that it is in our national interest to persuade people to renounce Communism and to encourage their defection from Communist forces. Many of these people are extremely valuable to our intelligence operations. Yet under this bill the government would lose the limited authority it now has to offer asylum in our country as the great incentive for such defection.

In addition, the provisions of Section 22 would sharply limit the authority of the government to admit foreign diplomatic representatives and their families on official business. Under existing law we already have the authority to send out of the country any person who abuses diplomatic privileges by working against the interests of the United States. But under this bill a whole series of unnecessary restrictions would be placed on the admission of diplomatic personnel. This is not only ungenerous for a country which eagerly sought and proudly holds the honor of being the seat of the United Nations; it is also very unwise because it makes our country appear to be fearful of "foreigners," when in fact we are working as hard as we know how to build mutual confidence and friendly relations among the nations of the world.

Section 22 is so contrary to our national interests that it would actually put the government into the business of thought control by requiring the deportation of any alien who distributes or publishes, or who is affiliated with an organization which distributes or publishes, any written or printed matter advocating (or merely expressing belief in) the economic and governmental doctrines of any form of totalitarianism. This provision does not require an evil intent or purpose on the part of the alien, as does a similar provision in the Smith Act. Thus, the attorney general would be required to deport any alien operating or connected with a well-stocked bookshop containing books on economics or politics written by supporters of the present governments of Spain, of Yugoslavia, or any one of a number of other countries. Section 25 would make the same aliens ineligible for citizenship. There should be no room in our laws for such hysterical provisions. The next logical step would be to "burn the books."

This illustrates the fundamental error of these immigration and naturalization provisions. It is easy to see that they are hasty and ill-considered. But far more significant — and far more dangerous — is their apparent underlying purpose. Instead of trying to encourage the free movement of people, subject only to the real requirements of national security, these provisions attempt to bar movement to anyone who is, or once

was, associated with ideas we dislike and, in the process, they would succeed in barring many people whom it would be to our advantage to admit.

Such an action would be a serious blow to our work for world peace. We uphold — or have upheld till now, at any rate — the concept of freedom on an international scale. That is the root concept of our efforts to bring unity among the free nations and peace in the world.

The Communists, on the other hand, attempt to break down in every possible way the free interchange of persons and ideas. It will be to their advantage, and not ours, if we establish for ourselves an "iron curtain" against those who can help us in the fight for freedom.

Another provision of the bill which would greatly weaken our national security is Section 25, which would make subversive aliens eligible for naturalization as soon as they withdraw from organizations required to register under this bill, whereas under existing law they must wait for a period of ten years after such withdrawal before becoming eligible for citizenship. This proposal is clearly contrary to the national interest and clearly gives to the Communists an advantage they do not have under existing law.

I have discussed the provisions of this bill at some length in order to explain why I am convinced that it would be harmful to our security and damaging to the individual rights of our people if it were enacted.

Earlier this month, we launched a great crusade for freedom, designed, in the words of General Eisenhower, to fight the big lie with the big truth. I can think of no better way to make a mockery of that crusade and of the deep American belief in human freedom and dignity which underlie it than to put the provisions of H. R. 9490 on our statute books.

I do not undertake lightly the responsibility of differing with the majority in both houses of Congress who have voted for this bill. We are all Americans; we all wish to safeguard and preserve our constitutional liberties against internal and external enemies. But I cannot approve this legislation, which instead of accomplishing its avowed purpose would actually interfere with our liberties and help the Communists against whom the bill was aimed.

This is a time when we must marshal all our resources and all the moral strength of our free system in self-defense against the threat of Communist aggression. We will fail in this and we will destroy all that we seek to preserve if we sacrifice the liberties of our citizens in a misguided attempt to achieve national security.

There is no reason why we should fail. Our country has been through dangerous times before without losing our liberties to external attack or internal hysteria. Each of us, in government and out, has a share in guarding our liberties. Each of us must search his own conscience to find whether he is doing all that can be done to preserve and strengthen them.

No considerations of expediency can justify the enactment of such a bill as this, a bill which would so greatly weaken our liberties and give aid and comfort to those who would destroy us. I have, therefore, no alternative but to return this bill without my approval, and I earnestly request the Congress to reconsider its action.

13.

DEAN ACHESON: The Strategy of Freedom

During the first summer of the Korean War, a large number of Americans were confused and dismayed by America's seemingly paradoxical involvement in a conflict thousands of miles from home. Especially confusing was the question of the government's aims. Did President Truman and his military chiefs want to win the war? And if they did, were they going about it in anything like the right way? If they did not want to win, then why not? And in that case, what did they want? A number of administration spokesmen, as well as the President himself, tried at various times to explain this first in a series of "limited" engagements that would occupy most of the attention of the country for the next decade and a half. One of these spokesmen was Secretary of State Dean Acheson, whose address of November 29, 1950, three days after Chinese Communist troops had swept across the border into Korea and attacked the UN forces at the Yalu River, is reprinted here in part.

Source: *Bulletin,* December 18, 1950.

WHAT COURSE OF ACTION will enable us to maintain our freedom and bring about a peaceful resolution of this world crisis; or, if despite our best efforts aggression does take place, will provide a basis for defeating it? . . .

The main elements of the strategy by which we are seeking to carry out this course of action — the Strategy of Freedom — are now well established as national policy. They have emerged as practical responses to the problems we have encountered, and they have found general support in the nation. I want to try to bring these elements together and develop their interrelationships because it is essential that the whole pattern and single purpose of our actions be clear to us.

There are six main elements in the Strategy of Freedom.

First is the development of an international order for the preservation of peace and freedom under the United Nations. The Charter of the United Nations expresses the universal aspirations of mankind, and the organization itself is a symbol of these aspirations. But the United Nations is also more than a symbol. It is a means through which we can take practical, day-by-day steps toward the building of a stable international community. As an organization in which most nations participate, the United Nations can also help to bring about the accommodations of interest and the adjustments of differences which are essential to peace in a world of change.

Our action in Korea . . . is intended to support the authority of the United Nations against aggression. In the current session of the General Assembly, we have initiated a number of measures designed to increase the effectiveness of the United Nations action against aggression. We intend to do our full part in helping the United Nations to grow in strength.

The second element in the Strategy of Freedom is the development of regional groupings, within the framework of the United Nations. To insure their collective security, free nations are engaged in cooperative defense measures, not possible on a universal basis at the present time. The keystone of the defense system of the free world is being built in the North Atlantic community, and among the states of the Western Hemisphere.

A whole network of cooperative institutions has been developing among the free nations of the North Atlantic and Western European area, each a practical response to a felt need. The problems they face are extremely complex, but progress has been made toward overcoming ancient national hostilities and in developing a common will and a sense of confidence in the potentialities of the North Atlantic community, working together as a community.

In this hemisphere, the accomplishments of the Organization of American States in promoting unity of action have been remarkable. Support of this organization is fundamental to our policy.

The essential ingredient in these regional developments has been a sense of community interest among neighbor nations. The development of further regional organizations depends in the first instance upon the existence of this community sense among the people of other areas.

The third element in our Strategy of Freedom is the *rapid* building up of military strength at home and among our allies. I stress the word "rapid" because the period of greatest danger is directly before us. Our defense must not only be strong enough, it must come soon enough.

There is only one test of whether our defense preparations are adequate: That is to measure them against a sober calculation of the danger which faces us. So measured, the defense efforts of the United States and other free nations are inadequate. A greatly increased scale and tempo of effort is required on the part of all free nations to enable them to overcome this inadequacy at the earliest possible moment.

The fourth element is economic cooperation. This has a dual character. It contributes powerfully to the building of our defenses against external attack. It also is an instrument for helping to build healthy societies in which the vitality and the promise of freedom find practical expression — in comparison with which the decadence and despair of Communist tyranny is starkly exposed.

Although the amount of resources available for economic assistance is limited by the defense requirements imposed upon us by Soviet action, even under the burden of rearmament, free societies can more effectively provide for human well-being and advancement than tyrannical regimes. The productive power of freemen, who are aware of the dangers that face them and who are determined to meet the challenge to their freedom, cannot be matched by authoritarian societies.

With our technical assistance, the resolve of the free peoples of Latin America, Asia, Africa, and the Middle East to better the conditions of their lives can become a powerful drive against the age-old banes of poverty and disease and the political instability which often accompanies them. Men everywhere have awakened to the opportunities for progress which modern science and technology have opened. We can help them to help themselves, and it is in our interest to do so.

Our technical assistance is not philanthropy, for here our principles and our self-interest coincide. As the people of underdeveloped areas rise from poverty, not only will our own economy benefit, but also and even more important the real promise of freedom will expose the false promises of Bolshevik imperialism, and the peoples of these countries will grow in their recognition of the common interest and purpose of the free nations.

So far as possible, economic cooperation, like defense cooperation and collective security programs, is being carried on through the United Nations and regional organizations in order to strengthen international institutions devoted to peace and security.

The fifth element in the Strategy of Freedom is a readiness at all times to negotiate just settlements of international disputes and to find just accommodations of conflicting interests. Our experience has demonstrated that the Soviet rulers cannot be expected to accept fair and equal negotiation so long as they feel capable of imposing their own terms or exacting their own price. Their concept of negotiation is that it should record the facts of power rather than the requirements of justice. We shall not seek to use our power in this way, but as the free world develops strength, the Soviet rulers may find it advantageous to adjust differences equitably rather than to seek to impose their demands. The free nations must always be prepared to enter into genuine negotiations, and even to take the initiative in efforts to bring about honest negotiation.

If the issues are clear, free men will not be prey to unrealistic expectations, nor to propaganda abuse of the negotiating process. It is in the long perspective that results may be expected, not in the fits and starts of shifting tactics.

Because our earnest desire is peace, we shall remain constantly receptive to genuine negotiation. With the confidence that comes of strength and the humility that comes from our devotion to Christian principles, we shall be endlessly patient in working for peace. And we shall at the same time be endlessly alert to defend the bases of our national life.

The sixth element in the Strategy of Freedom is a firm adherence in all our actions, at home and abroad, to the moral values which give meaning to our lives.

We are a young country, an enthusiastic people, and despite our great interest in material progress, we are an idealistic nation. The principles to which our common life is dedicated are powerful forces for good in the world. The affirmative values of our society have been deeply inspiring to those who have seen and felt their great creative force. We do not always present our best side to the world. In our enthusiasm and drive we often do not take care to make ourselves understood, and expect others to recognize us for what we are. We have launched a greatly expanded information program to bring knowledge of ourselves to other peoples, a program which the President has called "The Campaign of Truth."

It is our purpose to carry to all parts of

the world the facts about what is happening in America and in the world, because it is a fundamental part of our democratic faith that people, if informed of the truth, will make sound judgments. What is even more important than what we say to the world is how we conduct ourselves at home and abroad. The force of example and action is the factor which finally determines what our influence is to be.

If we are to be worthy of the leadership that derives from our power, we must be sure that we are true to the values and principles upon which our society is founded. It is the example of democracy at work, vigorous, healthy, respectful of its first principles, growing in freedom and justice and opportunity, that can inspire ourselves and others to meet the tasks ahead with hope and confidence.

Without this, which depends on every one of us, on the everyday conduct of each citizen, the Strategy of Freedom would "become as sounding brass or a tinkling cymbal."

These are the elements of our national foreign policy of the Strategy of Freedom. This is the course by which we seek to avoid war and to secure peace. No one can guarantee that war will not come. The present crisis is extremely serious. Whether reason will prevail is only partly for us to decide. We must hope and strive for the best while we prepare for the worst.

This is a responsibility, not just of a few public officials, not just of the Congress, but of the whole American people. The qualities we must demonstrate — steadiness, moderation, restraint, constancy of purpose, and flexibility in action, imagination, wisdom, maturity — these qualities are possible for us as a nation only if the American people participate as individuals in striving to make our society worthy of the hopes that free men everywhere have placed in it.

A deep understanding of the forces we are dealing with, and the role we must play, must be acquired by each of us. Every single individual has a share of this responsibility.

The six elements of the Strategy of Freedom — support of the United Nations, development of regional organizations, the rapid building up of our strength in partnership with our allies, economic cooperation, readiness to negotiate, and a firm adherence to the fundamental purposes and principles of our society — constitute a national policy, not a party policy. They have emerged from a long process of discussion and consideration as the practical requirements of a policy adequate to the problems which confront us. They are rooted in our traditions. They find general support in both parties.

It is right and proper that there should be differences of opinion among us about the execution of this policy, and about questions of emphasis, priorities, application and administration. No one has a monopoly of wisdom and the vigor and vitality of a democratic society derive from free discussion and debate and the consent which flows from understanding. However vigorous our debates may be, it should be made clear to all that our country is united in its determination to hew to the Strategy of Freedom which is our national policy.

The nation's peril is our challenge. The united will of the people must be our answer.

So we won't have to fight in Wichita.

> CAPTAIN JAMES JABARA, of Wichita, when asked why we were fighting in Korea; quoted by Adlai Stevenson in a speech

14.

HERBERT HOOVER: Military Policy for the Cold War

The common prewar posture of outright and uncompromising isolationism was almost wholly abandoned during World War II, and after the war this attitude toward the world and America's relation to it did not revive as it had in the 1920s. The reason was simple enough: most citizens believed that the country had the responsibility, whether it was a pleasant one or not, of protecting other, weaker nations against Communist aggression, either real or threatened. Nevertheless, a type of isolationism did make its appearance in the strife-torn years of the Cold War. Called the "fortress America" program, it was advocated by, among others, former President Herbert Hoover, who explained the position in a radio broadcast on December 20, 1950. December was probably the darkest month of the Korean War, for the entry of China into the conflict at the end of November had thrown the UN troops, mainly Americans, out of North Korea and south of the 38th parallel.

Source: *Addresses Upon the American Road, 1950-1955*, Stanford, Calif., 1955, pp. 3-10.

I HAVE RECEIVED hundreds of requests that I appraise the present situation and give my conclusions as to our national policies.

I speak with a deep sense of responsibility. And I speak tonight under the anxieties of every American for the nation's sons who are fighting and dying on a mission of peace and the honor of our country.

No appraisal of the world situation can be final in an unstable world. However, to find our national path we must constantly reexamine where we have arrived and at times revise our direction. I do not propose to traverse the disastrous road by which we reached this point.

We may first survey the global military situation. There is today only one center of aggression on the earth. That is the Communist-controlled Asian-European land mass of 800 million people. They have probably over 300 trained and equipped combat divisions with over 30,000 tanks, 10,000 tactical planes, and further large reserves they can put in action in ninety days. But they are not a great sea power. Their long-range air power is limited. This congeries of over thirty different races will some day go to pieces. But in the meantime they furnish unlimited cannon fodder.

Facing this menace on the Eastern front there are about 100 million non-Communist island people in Japan, Formosa, the Philippines, and Korea. Aside from Korea . . . they have probably only twelve effective combat divisions with practically no tanks, air, or navy.

Facing this land mass on the south are the Indies and the Middle East of about 600 million non-Communist people. There are about 150 million further non-Communist people in North Africa and Latin America. Except Turkey and Formosa, these 850 million non-Communist people have little military force which they would or could spare. But they could contribute vital economic and moral strength.

Facing this menace on the Continental European front there are about 160 million further non-Communist people who, excluding Spain, have less than twenty combat divisions now available, few tanks, and little air or naval force. And their will to defend themselves is feeble and their disunities are manifest.

Of importance in military weight at this moment there is the British Commonwealth of 150 million people, with probably thirty combat divisions under arms, a superior Navy, considerable Air Force, and a few tanks.

And there are 150 million people in the United States preparing 3.5 million men into a gigantic Air Force and Navy, with about thirty equipped combat divisions.

Thus there are 1,310,000,000 non-Communist people in the world, of whom today only about 320 million have any military potency.

If we weigh these military forces as they stand today, we must arrive at certain basic conclusions:

1. We must face the fact that to commit the sparse ground forces of the non-Communist nations into a land war against this Communist land mass would be a war without victory, a war without a successful political terminal. The Germans failed with a magnificent army of 240 combat divisions and with powerful air and tank forces. That compares with only 60 divisions proposed today for the North Atlantic Pact nations. Even were Western Europe armed far beyond any contemplated program, we could never reach Moscow. Therefore, any attempt to make war on the Communist mass by land invasion, through the quicksands of China, India, or Western Europe, is sheer folly. That would be the graveyard of millions of American boys and would end in the exhaustion of this Gibraltar of Western civilization.

2. Equally, we Americans alone, with sea and air power, can so control the Atlantic and Pacific Oceans that there can be no possible invasion of the Western Hemisphere by Communist armies. They can no more reach Washington in force than we can reach Moscow.

3. In this military connection we must realize the fact that the atomic bomb is a far less dominant weapon than it was once thought to be.

4. It is obvious that the United Nations have been defeated in Korea by the aggression of Communist China. There are no available forces in the world to repel them. Even if we sacrifice more American boys to hold a bridgehead, we know we shall not succeed at the present time in the mission given to us by the fifty members of the United Nations.

We may explore our American situation still further. The 150 million American people are already economically strained by government expenditures. It must not be forgotten that we are carrying huge burdens from previous wars, including obligations to veterans and $260 billion of bond and currency issues from those wars. In the fiscal year 1952, federal and local expenditures are likely to exceed $90 billion. That is more than our total savings. We must finance huge deficits by further government issues. Inflation is already moving. The dollar has in six months fallen 15 or 20 percent in purchasing power. But we might with stern measures avoid the economic disintegration of such a load for a very few years. If we continued long on this road, the one center of resistance in the world will collapse in economic disaster.

We may also appraise the diplomatic front. Our great hope was in the United Nations. We have witnessed the sabotage of its primary purpose of preserving peace. It has been, down to last week, a forum for continuous smear on our honor, our ideals, and our purposes. It did stiffen up against raw aggression last July in Korea. But in its call for that military action, America had to furnish over 90 percent of the foreign forces and suffer over 90 percent of their dead and injured. That effort now comes at least to a measurable military defeat by the aggression of Communist hordes.

Whether or not the United Nations is to

Wide World

Herbert Hoover, 76-year-old former President, addressing the nation on the dangers of becoming involved in a war with the Soviet Union, 1951

have a moral defeat and suffer the collapse of its whole moral stature now depends on whether it has the courage to:

1. Declare Communist China an aggressor.

2. Refuse admission of this aggressor to its membership.

3. Demand that each member of the United Nations cease to furnish or transport supplies of any kind to Communist China that can aid in their military operations. Such a course honestly carried out by the non-Communist nations is not economic sanctions nor does it require military actions. But it would constitute a great pressure for rectitude.

4. For once, pass a resolution condemning the infamous lies about the United States.

Any course short of such action is appeasement.

And now I come to where we should go from here. . . .

First, the foundation of our national policies must be to preserve for the world this Western Hemisphere Gibraltar of Western civilization.

Second, we can, without any measure of doubt, with our own air and naval forces, hold the Atlantic and Pacific Oceans with one frontier on Britain (if she wishes to cooperate); the other, on Japan, Formosa, and the Philippines. We can hold open the sea lanes for our supplies. And I devoutly hope that a maximum of cooperation can be established between the British Commonwealth and ourselves.

Third, to do this we should arm our air and naval forces to the teeth. We have little need for large armies unless we are going to Europe or China. We should give Japan her independence and aid her in arms to defend herself. We should stiffen the defenses of our Pacific frontier in Formosa and the Philippines. We can protect this island chain by our sea and air power.

Fourth, we could, after initial outlays for more air and navy equipment, greatly reduce our expenditures, balance our budget, and free ourselves from the dangers of inflation and economic degeneration.

Fifth, if we toil and sacrifice as the President has so well asked, we can continue aid to the hungry of the world. Out of our productivity, we can give aid to other nations when they have already displayed spirit and strength in defense against Communism. We have the stern duty to work and sacrifice to do it.

Sixth, we should have none of appeasement. Morally there is no appeasement of Communism. Appeasement contains more dangers than Dunkirks. We want no more Teherans and no more Yaltas. We can retrieve a battle but we cannot retrieve an appeasement. We are grateful that President Truman has denounced such a course.

Seventh, we are not blind to the need to preserve Western civilization on the continent of Europe or to our cultural and religious ties to it. But the prime obligation of defense of Western Continental Europe rests upon the nations of Europe. The test is whether they have the spiritual force, the will, and acceptance of unity among them by their own volition. America cannot create their spiritual forces; we cannot buy them with money.

You can search all the history of mankind and there is no parallel to the effort and sacrifice we have made to elevate their spirit and to achieve their unity. To this date it has failed. Their minds are confused with fears and disunities. They exclude Spain, although she has the will and means to fight. They higgle with Germany, although she is their frontier. They vacillate in the belief that they are in little danger and they hope to avoid again being a theater of war. And Karl Marx has added to their confusions. They still suffer from battle shock. Their highly organized Communist parties are a menace that we must not ignore.

In both World War I and World War II (including West Germany) those nations placed more than 250 trained and equipped combat divisions in the field within sixty days, with strong air and naval forces. They have more manpower and more productive capacity today than in either one of those wars. To warrant our further aid they should show they have spiritual strength and unity to avail themselves of their own resources. But it must be far more than pacts, conferences, paper promises, and declarations. Today it must express itself in organized and equipped combat divisions of such huge numbers as would erect a sure dam against the red flood. And that before we land another man or another dollar on their shores. Otherwise we shall be inviting another Korea. That would be a calamity to Europe as well as to us. Our policy in this quarter of the world should be confined to a period of watchful waiting before we take on any commitments.

There is a proper urge in all Americans for unity in troubled times. But unless unity is based on right principles and right action it is a vain and dangerous thing. Honest difference of views and honest debate are not disunity. They are the vital process of policymaking among free men.

A right, a specific, an open foreign policy must be formulated which gives confidence in our own security before we can get behind it.

American eyes should now be opened to these hordes in Asia.

These policies I have suggested would be no isolationism. Indeed, they are the opposite. They would avoid rash involvement of our military forces in hopeless campaigns. They do not relieve us of working to our utmost. They would preserve a stronghold of Christian civilization in the world against any peradventure.

With the policies I have outlined, even without Europe, Americans have no reason for hysteria or loss of confidence in our security or our future. And in American security rests the future security of all mankind.

It would be an uneasy peace, but we could carry it on with these policies indefinitely even if the Communists should attack our lines on the seas.

We can hope that in time the more than a billion of other non-Communist peoples of the world will rise to their dangers. We can hope that sometime the evils of Communism and the crumbling of their racial controls will bring their own disintegration. It is a remote consolation, but twice before in world history Asiatic hordes have swept over a large part of the world and their racial dissensions dissolved their empires.

Our people have braved difficult and distressing situations in these three centuries we have been on this continent. We have faced our troubles without fear and we have not failed. We shall not fail in this, even if we have to stand alone. But we need to realize the whole truth and gird ourselves for troubled times. The truth is ugly. We face it with prayer and courage. The Almighty is on our side.

15.

The Issue of Limited War in Korea

Red China's entry into the Korean War in November 1950 made of the conflict, in General MacArthur's words, "an entirely new war." It seemed for a time that World War III had broken out, and a violent debate ensued over America's whole foreign policy. Stated simply, the issue was this: Should the United States undertake the responsibility of defending against Communist aggression anywhere in the world, or should it distinguish between areas deemed essential to American security and those that could be left to fend for themselves? Neo-isolationists proposed the "fortress America" program, the essence of which was defense of the Western Hemisphere. The following exchange of communications in December 1950 between General MacArthur, commanding in Korea, and the Joint Chiefs of Staff illustrates a few of the problems posed by the Chinese intervention.

Source: *Military Situation in the Far East, Hearings Before the Committee on Armed Services and the Committee on Foreign Relations, U.S. Senate,* 82 Congress, 1 Session, Washington, 1951, Pt. 3, pp. 2179-2180.
Courtney Whitney, *MacArthur: His Rendezvous With History,* New York, 1956, pp. 432-434.

I.

The Joint Chiefs of Staff to General MacArthur

CHINESE COMMUNISTS now appear, from estimates available, capable of forcing evacuation by forces of UN. By committing substantial United States forces which would place other commitments, including safety of Japan, in serious jeopardy, or by inflicting serious losses on him, enemy might be forced to abandon exercise of his capability. If, with present UN strength, successful resistance at some position in Korea without our incurring serious losses could be accomplished and apparent military and political prestige of Chinese Communists could be deflated, it would be of great importance to our national interests. In the face of increased threat of general war, JCS believe commitment of additional United States ground forces in Korea should not be made, since our view is that major war should not be fought in Korea.

Not considered practicable to obtain at this time significant additional forces from other United Nations. Therefore, in light of present situation, your basic directive, of furnish to ROK assistance as necessary to repel armed attack and restore to the area security and peace, is modified. Your directive now is to defend in successive positions, subject to safety of your troops as your primary consideration, inflicting as much damage to hostile forces in Korea as is possible.

In view of continued threat to safety of Japan and possibility of forced withdrawal from Korea, it is important to make advance determination of last reasonable opportunity for orderly evacuation. It appears here that if Chinese Communists retain force capability of forcing evacuation after having driven UN forces to rear, it would be necessary to direct commencement of your withdrawal. Request your views on these conditions which should determine evacuation. You should consider your mission of defending Japan and limitation on troops available to you. Definite directive on conditions for initiation of evacuation will be provided when your views are received.

For the present this message which has been handled with ultimate security should be known only to your chief of staff and to Ridgway and his chief of staff.

II.

General MacArthur to the Joint Chiefs of Staff

Courtesy, Lewis, "Milwaukee Journal"

"Keep to the Right"; cartoon by Lewis in the "Milwaukee Journal," 1951

ANY ESTIMATE of relative capabilities in the Korean campaign appears to be dependent upon political-military policies yet to be formulated vis-à-vis Chinese military operations being conducted against our forces. It is quite clear now that the entire military resource of the Chinese nation, with logistic support from the Soviet, is committed to a maximum effort against the United Nations command. In implementation of this commitment a major concentration of Chinese force in the Korean-Manchurian area will increasingly leave China vulnerable in areas whence troops to support Korean operations have been drawn. Meanwhile, under existing restrictions, our naval and air potential are being only partially utilized and the great potential of Chinese Nationalist force on Formosa and guerrilla action on the mainland are being ignored. Indeed, as to the former, we are preventing its employment against the common enemy by our own naval force.

Should a policy determination be reached by our government or through it by the United Nations to recognize the state of war which has been forced upon us by the Chinese authorities and to take retaliatory measures within our capabilities, we could: (1) blockade the coast of China; (2) destroy through naval gunfire and air bombardment China's industrial capacity to wage war; (3) secure reinforcements from the Nationalist garrison in Formosa to strengthen our position in Korea if we decided to continue the fight for that peninsula; and (4) release existing restrictions upon the Formosan garrison for diversionary action (possibly leading to counterinvasion) against vulnerable areas of the Chinese mainland.

I believe that by the foregoing measures we could severely cripple and largely neutralize China's capability to wage aggressive war and thus save Asia from the engulfment otherwise facing it. I believe furthermore that we could do so with but a small part of our overall military potential committed to the purpose. There is no slightest doubt but that this action would at once release the pressure upon our forces in Korea, whereupon determination could be reached as to whether to maintain the fight in that area or to affect a strategic displacement of our forces with the view to strengthening our defense of the littoral island chain while continuing our naval and air pressure upon China's military potential. I am fully conscious of the fact that this course of action has been rejected in the past for fear of provoking China into a major war effort, but we must now realistically recognize that China's commitment thereto has already been fully and unequivocably made and that nothing we can do would further aggravate the situation as far as China is concerned.

Whether defending ourselves by way of military retaliation would bring in Soviet military intervention or not is a matter of speculation. I have always felt that a Soviet decision to precipitate a general war would depend solely upon the Soviet's own estimate of relative strengths and capabilities with little regard to other factors. . . . If we are forced to evacuate Korea without taking military measures against China proper as suggested in your message, it would have the most adverse affect upon the people of Asia, not excepting the Japanese, *and a material reinforcement of the forces now in this theater would be mandatory if we are to hold the littoral defense chain against determined assault.*

Moreover, it must be borne in mind that evacuation of our forces from Korea under any circumstances would at once release the bulk of the Chinese forces now absorbed by that campaign for action elsewhere — quite probably in areas of far greater importance than Korea itself. . . .

I understand thoroughly the demand for European security and fully concur in doing everything possible in that sector, but not to the point of accepting defeat anywhere else — an acceptance which I am sure could not fail to insure later defeat in Europe itself. The preparations for the defense of Europe, however, by the most optimistic estimate are aimed at a condition of readiness two years hence. The use of forces in the present emergency in the Far East could not in any way prejudice this basic concept. To the contrary, it would ensure thoroughly seasoned forces for later commitment in Europe synchronously with Europe's own development of military resources. . . .

So far as your tactical estimate of the situation in Korea is concerned, under the conditions presently implied, viz.: no reinforcements, continued restrictions upon Chinese Nationalist action, no military measures against China's continental military potential, and the concentration of Chinese military force solely upon the Korean sector, would seem to be sound. The tactical plan of a successively contracting defense line south to the Pusan beachhead is believed the only possible way which the evacuation could be accomplished. In the execution of this plan it would not be necessary for you to make an anticipatory decision for evacuation until such time as we may be forced to that beachhead line.

───────◆───────

That's the way the ball bounces.
                                        Army saying, Korean War

Brian Blake from Rapho Guillumette
Red Chinese youth on parade

TURMOIL IN ASIA

In the aftermath of World War II, and especially during the 1950s, Asia became more and more an area of concern for the United States. The major event was the victory of the Chinese Communists in the mainland and the consequent exile of the Nationalist regime to the island of Formosa. American aid during and after the war had attempted in vain to bolster the corrupt and inefficient government of Chiang Kai-shek; aid was continued after his defeat in 1949, and Formosa became an armed camp under essentially a military dictatorship. Chiang maintained the illusion of representing all of China; the U.S. supported this position for, while the Communist nations and many NATO allies recognized the Communist government of China, the U.S. consistently refused to do so and opposed its admission to the UN. Support for Chiang became a partisan issue at home; with the American tradition of yellow-perilism never

far from the surface, the more extremely anti-Communist elements pushed the unrealistic policy of "unleashing Chiang" to attack the mainland and quite probably precipitate a major war. The Korean War, stemming from the partition and double-occupation scheme also applied to Germany, was fought to a standstill; the major test of Truman's containment policy, it too was the subject of partisan debate, though there was little difference between Truman's and Eisenhower's policies. With the Korean armistice, attention shifted to Southeast Asia where communism was involved in the anti-colonial struggles of several small nations. The Cold War rhetoric, the domestic Red Scare, and the growing trend of neutralism among emerging Asian and African nations made the development of a consistent and realistic policy difficult. The reliance on military solutions was, however, becoming clearly less rewarding.

OPPOSITE PAGE: (Top) Laborers at the Ming Tombs Dam near Peking, China, where much of the construction was done without the aid of machinery; (bottom left) Chinese youths at an anti-U.S. demonstration; (bottom right) Chinese elementary school

(Right) Herblock cartoon from 1950 criticizing aid to Chiang's government; (center) French soldiers fighting in Vietnam; (bottom) French and Vietnamese officials at the ceremony establishing Bao Dai's government, 1948

"You Can Still Catch The Boat If You Hurry!"

Courtesy, Herblock, "The Washington Post"

Library of Congress

Library of Congress

Security Council in session in November 1950 at the time that Chinese Communists entered the war

The reunification of Korea, divided by Soviet and American occupation along the 38th parallel, was delayed by both internal dissension and Soviet recalcitrance. A UN mission sent in 1948 to supervise all-Korean elections was denied admission to the North; consequently a UN-recognized government was established in the South, while the North became a pro-Soviet People's Republic. In June 1950 the North launched an all-out attack on the Southern Republic.

(Left) Woman nurses her injured husband amid ruins of Seoul; (below) Marines on the road near Wonsan, North Korea, December 1950

Bert Handy — Pix from Publix

(Above) Marines begin the invasion of Inch'on, September 1950, one of the major offensives of the Korean War; (below) United Nations forces move in on the Communists to recapture Seoul, capital city of South Korea, September 1950

U.S. Army Photo

UPI — Compix

(Left) U.S. Air Force planes drop napalm bombs on a Communist supply center in North Korea; (above) bodies of Communist soldiers killed by napalm; (below) ground fighting against Chinese

European Picture Service
UPI — Compix

"We've Been Using More Of A Roundish One"

Courtesy, Herblock, "The Washington Post"

Modern General?

Courtesy, Edward Kuekes, "Cleveland Plain Dealer"

Two cartoonists' views of MacArthur's position as leader of the United Nations forces in Korea

When North Korea ignored a UN resolution demanding a withdrawal of forces behind the 38th parallel, a UN peace force was created largely of U.S. troops under the command of Gen. MacArthur. South Korean defenses crumbled and by the time the UN force was mobilized at an effective strength, nearly all of South Korea was in Northern hands.

(Right) MacArthur confers with President Truman on Wake Island, October 1950; (below) parade honors MacArthur after he returned to the United States in early 1951

UPI — Compix

Bob Gelberg — Pix from Publix

(Above) Members of a U.S. Cavalry Division move up under fire from the Chinese Communists in an attack near Chipyang; (below) infantrymen atop "Old Baldy" sniping at the enemy

The UN counteroffensive rapidly gained momentum and by October the 38th parallel was regained. Discounting threats of Chinese intervention, MacArthur moved quickly into North Korea. Worthless intelligence estimates of the Chinese military and political position led to a smashing defeat when China poured in 300,000 men in November 1950. The UN forces retired to the 38th parallel around which the war revolved until the armistice in July 1953. Ordered to obtain prior clearance from Washington for policy statements, MacArthur was relieved by Truman in April 1951 after the general continued to criticize Truman's reluctance to risk war with China or Russia in order to reunite Korea.

(Top) R.O.K. soldier patroling the streets of Inch'on; (center) United Nations representatives arrive at Kaesong during truce talks with the Communists, 1951; (bottom) armistice commission in session in 1953

(Above) **Farmer plowing along a roadside as French soldiers move to front line, 1954; (below) French and Vietnamese soldiers pass a child killed during the conflict with the Communists**

The U.S. had opposed the French reentry into Indochina after World War II; it recognized the French-sponsored Bao Dai government of 1948, however, and under the pressure of the Korean War began supplying aid to French troops in their battle against the northern Viet Minh regime. The Korean armistice released Chinese support to the Viet Minh, and the French were finally defeated in 1954. A Geneva conference agreed on a cease-fire, temporary partition of Vietnam, and reunifying elections to be held by 1956. The U.S. did not sign the accords.

French Army Photo

Battle of Dien Bien Phu: (Top) American plane brings supplies to the French; (center left) wounded soldier carried away from front lines; (right) reinforcements parachute into the besieged French outpost; (bottom left) French soldiers in the trenches during a break in fighting

Keystone Press

Keystone Press

Francois Sully from Black Star

European Picture Service

French Army Photo

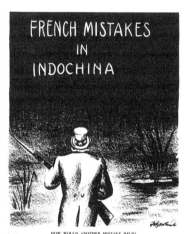

FRENCH MISTAKES
IN
INDOCHINA

HOW WOULD ANOTHER MISTAKE HELP?

Courtesy, Daniel Fitzpatrick, "St. Louis Post-Dispatch"

(Top) U.S. supplies land at Haiphong to aid France's campaign in Indochina; (center left) American general visits the French at Dien Bien Phu; (center right) cartoonist's view of U.S. aid to the French; (bottom) Mendes-France and Chou En-lai at Geneva

Keystone Press

(Top) Delegates plan the Southeast Asia Treaty Organization, 1954; **(bottom left)** Dulles visits in Vietnam, 1955; **(bottom right)** John Foster Dulles, secretary of state for Eisenhower

After 1954 the U.S. supplied military and economic aid directly to South Vietnam. In 1955 a rigged referendum vote gave Ngo Dinh Diem control and he quickly assumed dictatorial power. Though U.S. aid was ostensibly aimed at creating a viable, democratic, and anti-Communist regime able to compete with, and eventually replace, the Communist government in the North, under Diem reform was nullified, local political structures were destroyed, and repression grew steadily. The all-Vietnam elections called for at Geneva were not allowed to take place. In 1960 Communist and non-Communist opposition to Diem coalesced in the National Liberation Front whose armed branch, the Viet Cong, began guerrilla operations.

(Above) Anti-American poster displayed in New Delhi, India; (bottom left) Jawaharlal Nehru, prime minister of India; (bottom right) Chinese Premier Chou En-lai at Bandung Conference

Following its independence, India became a major influence in Asian affairs, pursuing an independent and, in Cold War terms, anomalous course. While grappling with the difficulties of establishing a socialistic state in an unindustrial nation, India developed, more than any other country, the neutralist position. Despite border disputes and occasional clashes, India strongly advocated UN membership for Communist China; it accepted economic aid from the U.S. and Russia but refused to enter military alliances.

16.

William R. Tansill: Civil Supremacy Over the Military

Throughout its history the United States has never ceased to maintain the view that civil authority — in the person of the President, constitutionally the commander in chief — should reign supreme over the military. From time to time, however, and never more vigorously than during the period following World War II, this traditional policy has been questioned. Once it was said that war was too important to be left to the generals; it began to be said that peace was too important to be left to the civilians. The National Security Act of 1947, as amended in 1949, established the Department of Defense and integrated all of the armed forces into one branch of government. The consequent increase in efficiency of administration, along with the fact that military men stationed in far-flung places were often as aware of developments in their areas as members of the diplomatic corps, strengthened the arguments of those who felt that the traditional policy should be abandoned, at least in part. In a paper prepared for the Library of Congress Legislative Reference Service in 1950, William R. Tansill examined these and allied questions. A portion of the pamphlet appears here.

Source: *The Concept of Civil Supremacy Over the Military in the United States*, Public Affairs Bulletin No. 94, February 1951, Washington.

A. Discussion of the Military in Its New Role

THE PROMINENCE IN WORLD AFFAIRS — political as well as military — attained by America's top military figures since the advent of World War II and the high incidence of succession by our generals and admirals to major civil responsibility have constituted one of the most important public developments of the postwar period. It would appear to Arthur Krock, well-known editorial writer of the *New York Times,* that "If the world remains an armed camp possibly aspirants to public life should investigate the curricula of [America's] service academies."

There is no doubt that the second global war, which enlisted the active services of more Americans than ever before,

has left the American people with a greater disposition than at any previous time to trust professional military opinion and to employ the military method in foreign policy. It is clear that if armies increase in size and if military experience extends to a larger and larger proportion of the population, the military mind is more likely to become characteristic of the national mind.

If this is an accurate description of the present situation, conditions are far different from those obtaining before the turn of the century, when Lord Bryce first analyzed the American scene. The renowned British observer was cheered by the inconspicuous role played by the military in our way of life. He happily pointed out that

> freedom of the country from militarism of spirit and policy . . . conduced not only to the slightness of a branch of expenditure which European states find almost insupportable, but also to the exemption of this republic from a source of danger which other republics have found so serious — the ambition of unsuccessful generals, and the interference of the army in political strifes. Strong and deep-rooted as are the constitutional traditions of the United States there have been moments, even in her history, when the existence of a great standing army might have menaced or led to civil war. Patriotism has not suffered, as Europeans sometimes fancy it must suffer, by long-continued peace. . . .
>
> In no country can a military despotism, such as that which has twice prevailed in France and once in England, be deemed less likely to arise [than in the United States]. . . .
>
> Caesarism is the last danger likely to menace America. In no nation is civil order more stable. None is more averse to the military spirit. No political system would offer a greater resistance to an attempt to create a standing army or centralize the administration.

President Franklin D. Roosevelt placed several career military men (e.g., Admiral Leahy, who served as ambassador to Vichy France and as personal chief of staff to both Roosevelt and Truman) in diplomatic and administrative positions. President Truman has followed that lead to an extent which gives alarm to many observers.

Several reasons explain in part President Truman's apparent predilection for appointing military personnel to civilian posts. First, our career generals and admirals are always available for any assignment, military or civil. On the other hand, the relatively low salaries in government service, coupled with the public abuse to which officials are often subject, have discouraged

many top-flight civilians in business and industry from entering public life. In the second place, many military men have had considerable administrative experience. Third, they are used to serving the public rather than a special interest. The fourth, and perhaps the most important, motive is that these men, having participated in a war of global dimensions, are necessarily acquainted with world affairs.

Objections to the use of the military in civil positions are also impressive. The career soldier may be dictatorial and uncompromising — a natural result of lifelong discipline. He tends to ignore public opinion and, sometimes, even to slight civilian rights, and military methods of organization have been known to make for inefficiency when applied to civilian projects.

An important check on military pretensions in foreign policy has been the civilian leadership of the Department of State, War, and Navy. Foreign affairs, at least in the initiation of contacts, have always been exclusively within the province of the President and his State Department, while tradition has decreed, generally speaking, that the War and Navy secretaries be civilians. It has been only in times of peace, however, that the President has been able to rely primarily and almost exclusively on the civilian Department of State for advice on foreign policy and on the civilian chiefs of the defense departments for guidance relative to military matters. In wartime the limitations to military influence on the President are stretched drastically. In war, military operations necessarily are connected with foreign policy; and the President, as commander in chief, is constrained to keep unbroken and active his contact with leaders of the armed forces.

General Bradley, present chairman of the Joint Chiefs of Staff, calls for a union of soldier and civilian in working out our world interests and responsibilities:

The conduct of foreign affairs is a civilian responsibility. Military policy in our democratic America must always remain the servant of national arms. But today, amid new global dangers, neither the diplomat nor the soldier alone can lead the American people to wise international action. Both voices must be heard if the course pursued is to be realistic and effective.

The soldier can see strategic perils that the civilian might readily overlook. The soldier must not direct the civilian policy, but the civilian must never overcommit the soldier. We must never have a foreign policy that sends our armed forces to world tasks beyond their capabilities.

It has been urged in some quarters that soldiers be barred from doubling as diplomats, if only because the use of the military in key civil posts, especially in the foreign service, has led friendly observers abroad to wonder whether the United States has become imperialist-minded.

It has appeared to some analysts of the military scene that the influence of the soldier on both foreign and national policy in late years has been disproportionately large. These critics point especially to four major developments as military-inspired. First, the United States, it is claimed, practically annexed Japan's Pacific mandates. This action reduced the effectiveness of our protests against Russian expansion in Eastern Europe. Second, the administration of Japan under General MacArthur has been virtually "unilateral." In the third place, official Washington's attitude toward the Peron government in Argentina had softened markedly by 1947; the change has been attributed to a desire, allegedly abetted by the military, to establish a sphere of influence in South America as a counterweight to Russian dominance in Europe. Fourth, considerable agitation for the adoption of universal military training arose in the immediate postwar period, inspired in no small mea-

sure by veterans' groups and the professional military.

The Presidential Advisory Commission on Universal Military Training, composed of civilians and headed by Dr. Karl T. Compton, supported such training. The group even suggested that those who participated in the program receive no compensation. Hanson Baldwin was shocked by such an attitude. To Mr. Baldwin, involuntary military service without pay was alarmingly akin to the forced service in Russian labor camps. Americans in general, nevertheless, registered little protest over the Commission's suggestion.

In matters of military policy, civilian insight the world over has sometimes been more acute than that displayed by soldiers. "Lloyd George in England and Rathenau in Germany seemed to have appreciated better than the military men the character of World War I as a production enterprise and the importance of bringing the national economy into full utilization for war purposes." On the other hand, the military mind has often been the repository of invaluable advice and experience; all too frequently has this resource been ignored or discredited.

B. The Issue of Atomic
Energy Control

By early 1946, when legislation according varying degrees of authority to the military in a proposed Atomic Energy Commission was pending before Congress, the controversy over the control of atomic energy had become a subject of wide and heated discussion in both official and private forums. It was often mistakenly assumed by elements of the public that the issue was merely civilian versus military control. In reality the conflict of ideas was not so confined in scope; the basic issue was the extent of the military's participation in the atomic energy program under civilian leadership. All parties directly concerned in the controversy asserted that *fundamentally* they supported the principle of civilian control.

Secretary of War Robert P. Patterson declared before the House Committee on Military Affairs in October 1945 that the War Department was no longer interested in retaining its wartime control of atomic energy, as it "recognized that the problems we now face go far beyond the purely military sphere." The secretary amended his position somewhat at a press conference called in March of the following year, when he stated, according to the *New York Times,* that his department "approved civilian control of atomic energy development, but wanted military 'participation' in developments for military uses, and also in decisions involving security." He added that the War Department "*in general,* would leave authority with [a civilian] commission to adopt security regulations."

Major General Leslie R. Groves, wartime chief of atomic energy projects, affirmed before a Senate committee in February 1946 that he "believed that the Commission should be primarily civilian . . . [but that] the Army and Navy would have to be represented." He proposed that the membership of the Commission include from two to four military men, on either active or retired status, who would, however, serve as individuals and not as representatives of the War and Navy Departments.

Secretary of the Navy James V. Forrestal, in testifying before the same committee a month earlier, protested that it was "illogical" to accord the Commission "no specific responsibility for the national defense, while at the same time [that body] was charged with the development of atomic weapons. . . ." Forrestal felt that "responsibility and the authority for development must go together"; consequently, that the Commission should include as members the secretaries of war and of the Navy.

Dr. Harrison Davies, of the Federation of Atomic Scientists, informed this Senate committee that his group wished

> to go on record most strongly as favoring complete exclusion of the military from any policy-making functions on the Commission, [although] by this [they did] not mean to exclude efficient liaison between the Commission and the armed forces. . . . A subject fraught with such tremendous significance to our foreign policy as the development of atomic energy in this country must certainly be freed from every vestige of military control.

Hanson W. Baldwin advocated compromise:

> Today [1946] atomic energy is military power and nothing more, and to bar the military from representation on a policy-making control commission, as the scientists would do, is to set up virtually an entirely new department of war, separate from, and outside of, the War and Navy Departments. It makes no sense. As long as atomic energy is to be used for military purposes in the world, our military must have a hand in it or our own national defense will be hopelessly crippled. Of course, in any atomic energy control legislation that is passed the principle of civilian preeminence and civilian control over the military — fundamental to our type of government — must be upheld, and secrecy restrictions must be liberalized as much as possible. Otherwise we shall defeat our own purposes — the preservation of democracy and the fostering of scientific research.

In a joint letter to Senator Brien McMahon in March 1946, seventeen widely different organizations, including the National League of Women Voters, the Southern Conference on Human Welfare, and the National Lawyers Guild, listed six major reasons for the entrusting of atomic energy to civilian control. Civilian supremacy

> is the cornerstone of our form of government. It is part of the great tradition of the United States of America. . . .

[It] is essential for national defense. . . .

[It] is essential to scientific progress. . . .

[It] is essential for the protection of free enterprise. . . .

[It] is essential for education. . . .

[It] is essential to the development of any adequate program of world control [of atomic energy].

President Truman personally preferred a commission "composed exclusively of civilians," although "former military personnel" should not be disqualified from membership. As approved by the President, on Aug. 1, 1946, the Atomic Energy Act of 1946 provided for an Atomic Energy Commission "composed of five members." It was stipulated that no member "shall engage in any other business, vocation, or employment than that of serving as a member of the Commission." The military was to serve the Commission in an advisory capacity, through a Military Liaison Committee.

C. The Debate on National Security and Unification of the Military

THROUGHOUT THE DEBATES on the promotion of defense and the unification of the armed services, it was assumed virtually by everyone that defense policies were to be under the guidance exclusively of civilians, chief among whom was to be the secretary of defense. Some representative views were as follows:

Senator McClellan. Is there anything in the bill which would prevent a high-ranking officer from resigning his commission in order to accept one of these appointments as secretary [of defense, or of the Army, Navy, or Air Force]?

Senator Thomas. There is nothing in the bill [S. 2044, of the 79th Congress]. I doubt very much whether that would ever follow under our scheme.

Senator Hill. The language in the bill concerning these secretaries reads . . .

"who shall be appointed from civilian life by the President. . . ." Of course, if a man resigned I take it that he would go back to civilian life, but it would be a clear violation of what would seem to me to be the spirit of this act.

Senator Magnuson. You don't think the Senate would confirm him, do you?

Senator Hill. I don't think it would, and I don't think the President . . . would appoint him in the first instance. So far as I am concerned I wouldn't object to an amendment saying that no man who has held a commission in the Army or Navy would be eligible, but there you would run into the difficulty of where you might have a man who had served for a short period during the wartime.

Senator Gerry. Well, you might want some man who was in the Army or the Navy. I don't see any objection to it.

Senator McClellan. I am not raising any objection. I merely state that as I understand the spirit of this bill it is to try to keep it in civilian hands.

Senator Brooks. There are three outstanding examples in taking General Bradley to run the Veterans' Bureau, General Marshall to be special representative to China, and General Smith as ambassador to Russia. We are certainly on a trend of pulling them out of military service and putting them where we want to, so if you want to keep it separate you had better write such a provision in, because your precedents are all against you.

Senator Magnuson. My idea was to discourage the trend of military men taking those jobs.

Senator Baldwin. Many times, when the subject of reorganization of our armed forces has come before the Congress, it has been opposed by some on the basis that it would pave the way to military control of our government, and to its ultimate overthrow, and military dictatorship. It is very well that Americans should be fearful of that possibility. . . . [But under this bill,]

Of course, the secretary of national security will be a civilian. . . . [The] bill in no way lessens . . . civilian control. In fact, if anything, [it] increases that control by one echelon; that is by the addition of a secretary of national security.

Senator Morse. Even with the elimination of the single military chief of staff, there have been voiced objections that the proposed single secretary of national security, albeit a civilian, would have too much power to be safe, would abrogate the powers of the President, and would become a czar-like authority unto himself — a dire menace to our form of government. It has been further contended that to put any man short of the President, whether he be civilian or military, over the armed forces would cause our security establishment to become unbalanced because the top man might neglect one of the forces through favoritism toward another one. This fear of even civilian control of the armed forces has been perhaps unreasonable since, after all, what kind of control do we want if not civilian? . . . The traditional civilian control of our armed forces is guaranteed. The civilian secretary of national security is superior to the three military commanders — Army, Navy, and Air Force. There is no single military chief of staff. The top secretary views the overall problem of national security impartially and on a broad basis, and is a principal assistant to the President and adviser to the Congress on the general subject.

Representative Wadsworth. . . . The secretary of defense must be a civilian.

Representative Martin of Iowa. Mr. Chairman, several of the opponents . . . have alleged that this pending unification bill will permit military domination of the United States. To me such a fear is pure rubbish. I have never been able to understand just how this domination by the military is supposed to come about. This bill provides for an increase in civilian control of the military rather than the diminution thereof.

Representative Brown of Ohio. In my mind the people are afraid of just one thing in connection with this bill . . . and that is they are afraid of a military government, some sort of a super-dictatorship which might arise in this country. . . . I will agree . . . that it is entirely possible that you might have a military officer who would like to do that; but I know one thing, that if you require a civilian to be the head of this agency then you will not have any danger within the agency of military influence or military dictatorship.

The National Security Act of 1947, approved by the President on July 26, 1947, provided that

> There shall be a secretary of defense, who shall be appointed from civilian life by the President, by and with the advice and consent of the Senate: *Provided,* that a person who has within ten years been on active duty as a commissioned officer in a regular component of the armed services shall not be eligible for appointment as secretary of defense. The secretary of defense shall be the principal assistant to the President in all matters relating to the national security.

———◆———

[War] is like an aging actress: more and more dangerous, and less and less photogenic.

Robert Capa

1951

17.

Harry S. Truman: Message to Douglas MacArthur

Communist China's entry into the Korean War made for feelings of uncertainty regarding what was now to be done in the Far East. Some proposed pulling out of Korea altogether and making Japan the focal point of defense, while others urged that American troops, reinforced as strongly as need be, remain in Korea in the hope of regaining the lost territory south of the 38th parallel and perhaps even of taking all of Korea up to the Chinese border. Sharp differences of opinion existed between General MacArthur, commanding in the field, and President Truman and members of his National Security Council, who were concerned about overall problems of defense, not only in Asia but also in Europe. In an attempt to clear up what was becoming an increasingly muddled situation, the President sent the following cable to MacArthur on January 13, 1951, spelling out the government's position regarding the war in the Far East.

I WANT YOU TO KNOW that the situation in Korea is receiving the utmost attention here and that our efforts are concentrated upon finding the right decisions on this matter of the gravest importance to the future of America and to the survival of free peoples everywhere.

I wish in this telegram to let you have my views as to our basic national and international purposes in continuing the resistance to aggression in Korea. We need your judgment as to the maximum effort which could reasonably be expected from the United Nations forces under your command to support the resistance to aggression which we are trying rapidly to organize on a worldwide basis. This present telegram is not to be taken in any sense as a directive. Its purpose is to give you something of what is in our minds regarding the political factors.

1. A successful resistance in Korea would serve the following important purposes:

a. To demonstrate that aggression will not be accepted by us or by the United Nations and to provide a rallying point around which the spirits and energies of the free world can be mobilized to meet the worldwide threat which the Soviet Union now poses.

b. To deflate the dangerously exaggerated political and military prestige of Communist China which now threatens to undermine the resistance of non-Communist Asia and to consolidate the hold of Communism on China itself.

c. To afford more time for and to give direct assistance to the organization of non-Communist resistance in Asia, both outside and inside China.

d. To carry out our commitments of honor to the South Koreans and to demonstrate to the world that the friendship of the United States is of inestimable value in time of adversity.

e. To make possible a far more satisfactory peace settlement for Japan and to contribute greatly to the post-treaty security position of Japan in relation to the continent.

f. To lend resolution to many countries not only in Asia but also in Europe and the Middle East who are now living within the shadow of Communist power and to let them know that they need not now rush to come to terms with Communism on whatever terms they can get, meaning complete submission.

g. To inspire those who may be called upon to fight against great odds if subjected to a sudden onslaught by the Soviet Union or by Communist China.

h. To lend point and urgency to the rapid build-up of the defenses of the Western world.

i. To bring the United Nations through its first great effort on collective security and to produce a free-world coalition of incalculable value to the national security interests of the United States.

j. To alert the peoples behind the Iron Curtain that their masters are bent upon wars of aggression and that this crime will be resisted by the free world.

2. Our course of action at this time should be such as to consolidate the great majority of the United Nations. This majority is not merely part of the organization but is also the nations whom we would desperately need to count on as allies in the event the Soviet Union moves against us. Further, pending the buildup of our national strength, we must act with great prudence insofar as extending the area of hostilities is concerned. Steps which might in themselves be fully justified and which might lend some assistance to the campaign in Korea would not be beneficial if they thereby involved Japan or Western Europe in large-scale hostilities.

3. We recognize, of course, that continued resistance might not be militarily possible with the limited forces with which you are being called upon to meet large Chinese armies. Further, in the present world situation, your forces must be preserved as an effective instrument for the defense of Japan and elsewhere. However, some of the important purposes mentioned above might be supported, if you should think it practicable and advisable, by continued resistance from offshore islands of Korea, particularly from Cheju-do, if it becomes impracticable to hold an important portion of Korea itself. In the worst case, it would be important that, if we must withdraw from Korea, it be clear to the world that that course is forced upon us by military necessity and that we shall not accept the result politically or militarily until the aggression has been rectified.

4. In reaching a final decision about Korea, I shall have to give constant thought to the main threat from the Soviet Union and to the need for a rapid expansion of our armed forces to meet this great danger.

5. I am encouraged to believe that the free world is getting a much clearer and re-

alistic picture of the dangers before us and that the necessary courage and energy will be forthcoming. Recent proceedings in the United Nations have disclosed a certain amount of confusion and wishful thinking, but I believe that most members have been actuated by a desire to be absolutely sure that all possible avenues to peaceful settlement have been fully explored. I believe that the great majority is now rapidly consolidating and that the result will be an encouraging and formidable combination in defense of freedom.

6. The entire nation is grateful for your splendid leadership in the difficult struggle in Korea and for the superb performance of your forces under the most difficult circumstances.

18.

Harry S. Truman: Korea and the Policy of Containment

The differences between General MacArthur and the Truman administration over Korean War policy intensified during the spring of 1951, when the UN troops, made up mostly of Americans, faced upwards of 400,000 Red Chinese "volunteers" in addition to the well-trained and Soviet-equipped divisions of North Korea. The issue was simple enough: MacArthur wanted an all-out war, including permission to bomb bases in China itself, in order to assure not only victory in Korea itself but also an end to the uneasy stalemate in the Far East as a whole. The administration, on the contrary, with its eye on Russia in Europe as well as Asia, was determined to confine the war to Korea and to end it if possible with a negotiated settlement. MacArthur was under orders from his commander in chief not to make any public policy statements, but on April 5 Congressman Joseph Martin of Massachusetts made public a letter he had received from MacArthur that expressed the general's disapproval of the administration's limited goals in no uncertain terms. At this juncture Truman removed MacArthur from his command. The President broadcast the following message to the nation on April 11, defining the government's aims in Korea and explaining MacArthur's recall.

Source: *Bulletin*, April 16, 1951, pp. 603-605.

I WANT TO TALK PLAINLY to you tonight about what we are doing in Korea and about our policy in the Far East. In the simplest terms, what we are doing in Korea is this: We are trying to prevent a third world war.

I think most people in this country recognized that fact last June. And they warmly supported the decision of the government to help the Republic of Korea against the Communist agressors. Now, many persons, even some who applauded our decision to defend Korea, have forgotten the basic reason for our action.

It is right for us to be in Korea. It was right last June. It is right today. I want to remind you why this is true.

The Communists in the Kremlin are engaged in a monstrous conspiracy to stamp out freedom all over the world. If they were to succeed, the United States would be numbered among their principal victims. It must be clear to everyone that the United States cannot — and will not — sit idly by and await foreign conquest. The only question is: When is the best time to meet the threat and how?

The best time to meet the threat is in the beginning. It is easier to put out a fire in the beginning when it is small than after it has become a roaring blaze. And the best way to meet the threat of aggression is for the peace-loving nations to act together. If they don't act together, they are likely to be picked off, one by one.

If they had followed the right policies in the 1930s — if the free countries had acted together to crush the aggression of the dictators, and if they had acted in the beginning, when the aggression was small, there probably would have been no World War II.

If history has taught us anything, it is that aggression anywhere in the world is a threat to peace everywhere in the world. When that aggression is supported by the cruel and selfish rulers of a powerful nation who are bent on conquest, it becomes a clear and present danger to the security and independence of every free nation. This is a lesson that most people in this country have learned thoroughly. This is the basic reason why we joined in creating the United Nations. And since the end of World War II we have been putting that lesson into practice — we have been working with other free nations to check the aggressive designs of the Soviet Union before they can result in a third world war.

That is what we did in Greece when that nation was threatened by the aggression of international communism. The attack against Greece could have led to general war. But this country came to the aid of Greece. The United Nations supported Greek resistance. With our help, the deter-

mination and efforts of the Greek people defeated the attack on the spot.

Another big Communist threat to peace was the Berlin blockade. That too could have led to war. But again it was settled because freemen would not back down in an emergency.

The aggression against Korea is the boldest and most dangerous move the Communists have yet made. The attack on Korea was part of a greater plan for conquering all of Asia.

I would like to read to you from a secret intelligence report which came to us after the attack. It is a report of a speech a Communist army officer in North Korea gave to a group of spies and saboteurs last May, one month before South Korea was invaded. The report shows in great detail how this invasion was part of a carefully prepared plot. Here is part of what the Communist officer, who had been trained in Moscow, told his men: "Our forces," he said, "are scheduled to attack South Korean forces about the middle of June. . . . The coming attack on South Korea marks the first step toward the liberation of Asia."

Notice that he used the word "liberation." That is Communist double-talk meaning "conquest."

I have another secret intelligence report here. This one tells what another Communist officer in the Far East told his men several months before the invasion of Korea. Here is what he said: "In order to successfully undertake the long-awaited world revolution, we must first unify Asia. . . . Java, Indochina, Malaya, India, Tibet, Thailand, Philippines, and Japan are our ultimate targets. . . . The United States is the only obstacle on our road for the liberation of all countries in southeast Asia. In other words, we must unify the people of Asia and crush the United States."

That is what the Communist leaders are telling their people, and that is what they have been trying to do. They want to control all Asia from the Kremlin.

This plan of conquest is in flat contradiction to what we believe. We believe that Korea belongs to the Koreans, that India belongs to the Indians — that all the nations of Asia should be free to work out their affairs in their own way. This is the basis of peace in the Far East and everywhere else.

The whole Communist imperialism is back of the attack on peace in the Far East. It was the Soviet Union that trained and equipped the North Koreans for aggression. The Chinese Communists massed forty-four well-trained and well-equipped divisions on the Korean frontier. These were the troops they threw into battle when the North Korean Communists were beaten.

The question we have had to face is whether the Communist plan of conquest can be stopped without general war. Our government and other countries associated with us in the United Nations believe that the best chance of stopping it without general war is to meet the attack in Korea and defeat it there.

That is what we have been doing. It is a difficult and bitter task. But so far it has been successful. So far, we have prevented World War III. So far, by fighting a limited war in Korea, we have prevented aggression from succeeding and bringing on a general war. And the ability of the whole free world to resist Communist aggression has been greatly improved.

We have taught the enemy a lesson. He has found out that aggression is not cheap or easy. Moreover, men all over the world who want to remain free have been given new courage and new hope. They know now that the champions of freedom can stand up and fight and that they will stand up and fight. Our resolute stand in Korea is helping the forces of freedom now fighting in Indochina and other countries in that part of the world. It has already slowed down the timetable of conquest.

In Korea itself, there are signs that the enemy is building up his ground forces for a new mass offensive. We also know that there have been large increases in the enemy's available air forces. If a new attack comes, I feel confident it will be turned back. The United Nations fighting forces are tough and able and well-equipped. They are fighting for a just cause. They are proving to all the world that the principle of collective security will work. We are proud of all these forces for the magnificent job they have done against heavy odds. We pray that their efforts may succeed, for upon their success may hinge the peace of the world.

The Communist side must now choose its course of action. The Communist rulers may press the attack against us. They may take further action which will spread the conflict. They have that choice, and with it the awful responsibility for what may follow. The Communists also have the choice of a peaceful settlement which could lead to a general relaxation of tensions in the Far East. The decision is theirs, because the forces of the United Nations will strive to limit the conflict if possible.

We do not want to see the conflict in Korea extended. We are trying to prevent a world war — not to start one. The best way to do that is to make it plain that we and the other free countries will continue to resist the attack.

But you may ask: Why can't we take other steps to punish the aggressor? Why don't we bomb Manchuria and China itself? Why don't we assist Chinese Nationalist troops to land on the mainland of China?

If we were to do these things we would be running a very grave risk of starting a general war. If that were to happen, we would have brought about the exact situation we are trying to prevent. If we were to do these things, we would become entangled in a vast conflict on the continent of Asia and our task would become immeasurably more difficult all over the world.

What would suit the ambitions of the

Kremlin better than for our military forces to be committed to a full-scale war with Red China?

It may well be that, in spite of our best efforts, the Communists may spread the war. But it would be wrong — tragically wrong — for us to take the initiative in extending the war.

The dangers are great. Make no mistake about it. Behind the North Koreans and Chinese Communists in the front lines stand additional millions of Chinese soldiers. And behind the Chinese stand the tanks, the planes, the submarines, the soldiers, and the scheming rulers of the Soviet Union.

Our aim is to avoid the spread of the conflict. The course we have been following is the one best calculated to avoid an all-out war. It is the course consistent with our obligation to do all we can to maintain international peace and security. Our experience in Greece and Berlin shows that it is the most effective course of action we can follow.

First of all, it is clear that our efforts in Korea can blunt the will of the Chinese Communists to continue the struggle. The United Nations forces have put up a tremendous fight in Korea and have inflicted very heavy casualties on the enemy. Our forces are stronger now than they have been before. These are plain facts which may discourage the Chinese Communists from continuing their attack.

Second, the free world as a whole is growing in military strength every day. In the United States, in Western Europe, and throughout the world, freemen are alert to the Soviet threat and are building their defenses. This may discourage the Communist rulers from continuing the war in Korea — and from undertaking new acts of aggression elsewhere.

If the Communist authorities realize that they cannot defeat us in Korea, if they realize it would be foolhardy to widen the hostilities beyond Korea, then they may recognize the folly of continuing their aggression. A peaceful settlement may then be possible. The door is always open.

Then we may achieve a settlement in Korea which will not compromise the principles and purposes of the United Nations.

I have thought long and hard about this question of extending the war in Asia. I have discussed it many times with the ablest military advisers in the country. I believe with all my heart that the course we are following is the best course. I believe that we must try to limit the war to Korea for these vital reasons: to make sure that the precious lives of our fighting men are not wasted; to see that the security of our country and the free world is not needlessly jeopardized; and to prevent a third world war.

A number of events have made it evident that General MacArthur did not agree with that policy. I have therefore considered it essential to relieve General MacArthur so that there would be no doubt or confusion as to the real purpose and aim of our policy. It was with the deepest personal regret that I found myself compelled to take this action. General MacArthur is one of our greatest military commanders. But the cause of world peace is more important than any individual.

The change in commands in the Far East means no change whatever in the policy of the United States. We will carry on the fight in Korea with vigor and determination in an effort to bring the war to a speedy and successful conclusion. The new commander, Lt. Gen. Matthew Ridgway, has already demonstrated that he has the great qualities of military leadership needed for this task.

We are ready, at any time, to negotiate for a restoration of peace in the area. But we will not engage in appeasement. We are only interested in real peace. Real peace can be achieved through a settlement based on the following factors:

1. The fighting must stop.

2. Concrete steps must be taken to insure that the fighting will not break out again.

3. There must be an end to the aggression.

A settlement founded upon these elements would open the way for the unification of Korea and the withdrawal of all foreign forces.

In the meantime, I want to be clear about our military objective. We are fighting to resist an outrageous aggression in Korea. We are trying to keep the Korean conflict from spreading to other areas. But at the same time we must conduct our military activities so as to insure the security of our forces. This is essential if they are to continue the fight until the enemy abandons its ruthless attempt to destroy the Republic of Korea. That is our military objective — to repel attack and to restore peace.

In the hard fighting in Korea, we are proving that collective action among nations is not only a high principle but a workable means of resisting aggression. Defeat of aggression in Korea may be the turning point in the world's search for a practical way of achieving peace and security.

The struggle of the United Nations in Korea is a struggle for peace. The free nations have united their strength in an effort to prevent a third world war. That war can come if the Communist rulers want it to come. But this nation and its allies will not be responsible for its coming.

We do not want to widen the conflict. We will use every effort to prevent that disaster. And in so doing we know that we are following the great principles of peace, freedom, and justice.

19.

Douglas MacArthur: Farewell Address to Congress

President Truman's removal of General MacArthur from the Korean command produced an emotional and political crisis in the United States, for the general had wide popular support and sympathy. He was met by cheering crowds on his return and was honored by the traditional ticker-tape parade down Broadway. On April 19, 1951, MacArthur appeared before a special session of Congress and delivered a valedictory address at the close of a distinguished career. The address is reprinted here. In fact, the country weathered the storm more easily than some observers feared, partly because MacArthur himself maintained throughout those hectic days an attitude of complete respect for the President and his decision.

Source: *Record*, 82 Cong., 1 Sess., pp. 4123-4125.

Mr. President, Mr. Speaker, and distinguished members of the Congress:

I stand on this rostrum with a sense of deep humility and great pride — humility in the wake of those great American architects of our history who have stood here before me, pride in the reflection that this forum of legislative debate represents human liberty in the purest form yet devised. Here are centered the hopes, and aspirations, and faith of the entire human race.

I do not stand here as advocate for any partisan cause, for the issues are fundamental and reach quite beyond the realm of partisan consideration. They must be resolved on the highest plane of national interest if our course is to prove sound and our future protected. I trust, therefore, that you will do me the justice of receiving that which I have to say as solely expressing the considered viewpoint of a fellow American. I address you with neither rancor nor bitterness in the fading twilight of life with but one purpose in mind — to serve my country.

The issues are global and so interlocked that to consider the problems of one sector, oblivious to those of another, is but to court disaster for the whole.

While Asia is commonly referred to as the gateway to Europe, it is no less true that Europe is the gateway to Asia, and the broad influence of the one cannot fail to have its impact upon the other.

There are those who claim our strength is inadequate to protect on both fronts — that we cannot divide our effort. I can think of no greater expression of defeatism. If a potential enemy can divide his strength on two fronts, it is for us to counter his effort.

The Communist threat is a global one. Its successful advance in one sector threatens the destruction of every other sector. You cannot appease or otherwise surrender to communism in Asia without simultaneously undermining our efforts to halt its advance in Europe.

Beyond pointing out these general truisms, I shall confine my discussion to the general areas of Asia. Before one may objectively assess the situation now existing there, he must comprehend something of Asia's past and the revolutionary changes which have marked her course up to the present. Long exploited by the so-called colonial powers, with little opportunity to achieve any degree of social justice, individual dignity, or a higher standard of life such as guided our own noble administration of the Philippines, the peoples of Asia found their opportunity in the war just past to throw off the shackles of colonialism, and now see the dawn of new opportunity, a heretofore unfelt dignity and the self-respect of political freedom.

Mustering half of the earth's population and 60 percent of its natural resources, these peoples are rapidly consolidating a new force, both moral and material, with which to raise the living standard and erect adaptations of the design of modern progress to their own distinct cultural environments. Whether one adheres to the concept of colonization or not, this is the direction of Asian progress and it may not be stopped. It is a corollary to the shift of the world economic frontiers, as the whole epicenter of world affairs rotates back toward the area whence it started. In this situation it becomes vital that our own country orient its policies in consonance with this basic evolutionary condition rather than pursue a course blind to the reality that the colonial era is now past and the Asian peoples covet the right to shape their own free destiny.

What they seek now is friendly guidance, understanding, and support, not imperious direction; the dignity of equality, not the shame of subjugation. Their prewar standards of life, pitifully low, are infinitely lower now in the devastation left in war's wake. World ideologies play little part in Asian thinking and are little understood. What the people strive for is the opportunity for a little more food in their stomachs, a little better clothing on their backs, a little firmer roof over their heads, and the realization of the normal nationalist urge for political freedom. These political-social conditions have but an indirect bearing upon our own national security, but do form a backdrop to contemporary planning which must be thoughtfully considered if we are to avoid the pitfalls of unrealism.

Of more direct and immediate bearing upon our national security are the changes wrought in the strategic potential of the Pacific Ocean in the course of the past war.

Prior thereto, the western strategic frontier of the United States lay on the littoral line of the Americas with an exposed island salient extending out through Hawaii, Midway, and Guam to the Philippines. That salient proved not an outpost of strength but an avenue of weakness along which the enemy could and did attack. The Pacific was a potential area of advance for any predatory force intent upon striking at the bordering land areas.

All this was changed by our Pacific victory. Our strategic frontier then shifted to embrace the entire Pacific Ocean, which became a vast moat to protect us as long as we hold it. Indeed, it acts as a protective shield for all of the Americas and all free lands of the Pacific Ocean area. We control it to the shores of Asia by a chain of islands extending in an arc from the Aleutians to the Marianas held by us and our free allies.

From this island chain we can dominate with sea and air power every Asiatic port from Vladivostok to Singapore and prevent any hostile movement into the Pacific. Any predatory attack from Asia must be an amphibious effort. No amphibious force can be successful without control of the sea lanes and the air over those lanes in its avenue of advance. With naval and air supremacy and modest ground elements to defend bases, any major attack from continental Asia toward us or our friends of the Pacific would be doomed to failure. Under such conditions the Pacific no longer represents menacing avenues of approach for a prospective invader — it assumes instead the friendly aspect of a peaceful lake. Our line of defense is a natural one and can be maintained with a minimum of military effort and expense. It envisions no attack against anyone nor does it provide the bastions essential for offensive operations, but properly maintained would be an invincible defense against aggression.

The holding of this littoral defense line in the western Pacific is entirely dependent upon holding all segments thereof, for any major breach of that line by an unfriendly power would render vulnerable to determined attack every other major segment. This is a military estimate as to which I have yet to find a military leader who will take exception. For that reason I have strongly recommended in the past as a matter of military urgency that under no circumstances must Formosa fall under Communist control. Such an eventuality would at once threaten the freedom of the Philippines and the loss of Japan, and might well force our western frontier back to the coasts of California, Oregon, and Washington.

To understand the changes which now appear upon the Chinese mainland, one must understand the changes in Chinese character and culture over the past fifty years. China up to fifty years ago was completely nonhomogeneous, being compartmented into groups divided against each other. The warmaking tendency was almost nonexistent, as they still followed the tenets of the Confucian ideal of pacifist culture. At the turn of the century, under the regime of Chan So Lin, efforts toward greater homogeneity produced the start of a nationalist urge. This was further and more successfully developed under the leadership of Chiang Kai-shek, but has been brought to its greatest fruition under the present regime, to the point that it has now taken on the character of a united nationalism of increasingly dominant aggressive tendencies.

Through these past fifty years, the Chinese people have thus become militarized in their concepts and in their ideals. They now constitute excellent soldiers, with competent staffs and commanders. This has produced a new and dominant power in Asia which for its own purposes is allied with Soviet Russia, but which in its own concepts and methods has become aggressively imperialistic with a lust for expansion and increased power normal to this type of imperialism. There is little of the ideological concept either one way or another in the Chinese makeup. The standard of living is so low and the capital accumulation has been so thoroughly dissipated by war that the masses are desperate and avid to follow any leadership which seems to promise the alleviation of local stringencies.

I have from the beginning believed that the Chinese Communists' support of the North Koreans was the dominant one. Their interests are at present parallel to those of the Soviet, but I believe that the aggressiveness recently displayed not only in Korea but also in Indochina and Tibet, and pointing potentially toward the south, reflects predominantly the same lust for the expansion of power which has animated every would-be conqueror since the beginning of time.

The Japanese people since the war have undergone the greatest reformation recorded in modern history. With a commendable will, eagerness to learn, and marked capacity to understand, they have, from the ashes left in war's wake, erected in Japan an edifice dedicated to the primacy of individual liberty and personal dignity, and in the ensuing process there has been created a truly representative government committed to the advance of political morality, freedom of economic enterprise, and social justice. Politically, economically, and socially, Japan is now abreast of many free nations of the earth and will not again fail the universal trust. That it may be counted upon to wield a profoundly beneficial influence over the course of events in Asia is attested by the magnificent manner in which the Japanese people have met the recent challenge of war, unrest, and confusion surrounding them from the outside, and checked communism within their own frontiers without the slightest slackening in their forward progress.

I sent all four of our occupation divisions to the Korean battlefront without the slightest qualms as to the effect of the resulting power vacuum upon Japan. The re-

sults fully justified my faith. I know of no nation more serene, orderly, and industrious — nor in which higher hopes can be entertained for future constructive service in the advance of the human race.

Of our former wards, the Philippines, we can look forward in confidence that the existing unrest will be corrected and a strong and healthy nation will grow in the longer aftermath of war's terrible destructiveness. We must be patient and understanding and never fail them, as in our hour of need they did not fail us. A Christian nation, the Philippines stand as a mighty bulwark of Christianity in the Far East, and its capacity for high moral leadership in Asia is unlimited.

On Formosa, the government of the Republic of China has had the opportunity to refute by action much of the malicious gossip which so undermined the strength of its leadership on the Chinese mainland. The Formosan people are receiving a just and enlightened administration with majority representation on the organs of government; and politically, economically, and socially they appear to be advancing along sound and constructive lines.

With this brief insight into the surrounding areas I now turn to the Korean conflict. While I was not consulted prior to the President's decision to intervene in support of the Republic of Korea, that decision, from a military standpoint, proved a sound one as we hurled back the invaders and decimated his forces. Our victory was complete and our objectives within reach when Red China intervened with numerically superior ground forces. This created a new war and an entirely new situation — a situation not contemplated when our forces were committed against the North Korean invaders — a situation which called for new decisions in the diplomatic sphere to permit the realistic adjustment of military strategy. Such decisions have not been forthcoming.

While no man in his right mind would advocate sending our ground forces into continental China, and such was never given a thought, the new situation did urgently demand a drastic revision of strategic planning if our political aim was to defeat this new enemy as we had defeated the old.

Apart from the military need as I saw it to neutralize the sanctuary protection given the enemy north of the Yalu, I felt that military necessity in the conduct of the war made mandatory:

1. The intensification of our economic blockade against China.

2. The imposition of a naval blockade against the China coast.

3. Removal of restrictions on air reconnaissance of China's coast areas and of Manchuria.

4. Removal of restrictions on the forces of the Republic of China on Formosa with logistical support to contribute to their effective operations against the common enemy.

For entertaining these views, all professionally designed to support our forces committed to Korea and bring hostilities to an end with the least possible delay and at a saving of countless American and Allied lives, I have been severely criticized in lay circles, principally abroad, despite my understanding that from a military standpoint the above views have been fully shared in the past by practically every military leader concerned with the Korean campaign, including our own Joint Chiefs of Staff.

I called for reinforcements, but was informed that reinforcements were not available. I made clear that if not permitted to destroy the buildup bases north of the Yalu; if not permitted to utilize the friendly Chinese force of some 600,000 men on Formosa; if not permitted to blockade the China coast to prevent the Chinese Reds from getting succor from without; and if there were to be no hope of major reinforcements, the position of the command from the military standpoint forbade victory. We could hold in Korea by constant maneuver and at an approximate area where our supply line advantages were in balance with the supply line disadvantages of the enemy, but we could hope at best for only an indecisive campaign, with its terrible and constant attrition upon our forces if the enemy utilized his full military potential.

I have constantly called for the new political decisions essential to a solution. Efforts have been made to distort my position. It has been said, in effect, that I am a warmonger. Nothing could be further from the truth. I know war as few other men now living know it, and nothing to me is more revolting. I have long advocated its complete abolition as its very destructiveness on both friend and foe has rendered it useless as a means of settling international disputes. Indeed, on the 2nd of September, 1945, just following the surrender of the Japanese nation on the battleship *Missouri,* I formally cautioned as follows:

Men since the beginning of time have sought peace. Various methods through the ages have been attempted to devise an international process to prevent or settle disputes between nations. From the very start, workable methods were found insofar as individual citizens were concerned, but the mechanics of an instrumentality of larger international scope have never been successful. Military alliances, balances of power, leagues of nations, all in turn failed, leaving the only path to be by way of the crucible of war. The utter destructiveness of war now blots out this alternative. We have had our last chance. If we will not devise some greater and more equitable system, Armageddon will be at our door. The problem basically is theological and involves a spiritual recrudescence and improvement of human character that will synchronize with our almost matchless advances in science, art, literature, and all material and cultural developments of the past 2,000 years. It must be of the spirit if we are to save the flesh.

But once war is forced upon us, there is no other alternative than to apply every available means to bring it to a swift end. War's very object is victory — not prolonged indecision. In war, indeed, there can be no substitute for victory.

There are some who for varying reasons would appease Red China. They are blind to history's clear lesson; for history teaches with unmistakable emphasis that appeasement but begets new and bloodier war. It points to no single instance where the end has justified that means — where appeasement has led to more than a sham peace. Like blackmail, it lays the basis for new and successively greater demands, until, as in blackmail, violence becomes the only other alternative.

Why, my soldiers asked of me, surrender military advantages to an enemy in the field? I could not answer. Some may say to avoid spread of the conflict into an all-out war with China; others, to avoid Soviet intervention. Neither explanation seems valid. For China is already engaging with the maximum power it can commit and the Soviet will not necessarily mesh its actions with our moves. Like a cobra, any new enemy will more likely strike whenever it feels that the relativity in military or other potential is in its favor on a worldwide basis.

The tragedy of Korea is further heightened by the fact that as military action is confined to its territorial limits, it condemns that nation, which it is our purpose to save, to suffer the devastating impact of full naval and air bombardment, while the enemy's sanctuaries are fully protected from such attack and devastation. Of the nations of the world, Korea alone, up to now, is the sole one which has risked its all against communism. The magnificence of the courage and fortitude of the Korean people defies description. They have chosen to risk death rather than slavery. Their last words to me were "Don't scuttle the Pacific."

I have just left your fighting sons in Korea. They have met all tests there and I can report to you without reservation they are splendid in every way. It was my constant effort to preserve them and end this savage conflict honorably and with the least loss of time and a minimum sacrifice of life. Its growing bloodshed has caused me the deepest anguish and anxiety. Those gallant men will remain often in my thoughts and in my prayers always.

I am closing my fifty-two years of military service. When I joined the Army, even before the turn of the century, it was the fulfillment of all my boyish hopes and dreams. The world has turned over many times since I took the oath on the plain at West Point, and the hopes and dreams have long since vanished. But I still remember the refrain of one of the most popular barrack ballads of that day which proclaimed most proudly that —

> Old soldiers never die;
> they just fade away.

And like the old soldier of that ballad, I now close my military career and just fade away — an old soldier who tried to do his duty as God gave him the light to see that duty.

Good-by.

I hate war as only a soldier who has lived it can, only as one who has seen its brutality, its futility, its stupidity.

DWIGHT D. EISENHOWER

20.

Senate Report on Organized Crime

That a highly complex and efficient criminal organization existed in the United States had been acknowledged as early as 1915, when a crime commission asserted as much in Chicago. But many people still refused to believe it until 1950, when the Senate Crime Investigating Committee, under the leadership of Estes Kefauver of Tennessee (later to be Adlai Stevenson's running mate in 1956), conducted a series of hearings into the activities of crime syndicates in interstate commerce. The televised hearings surprised and shocked many Americans; especially memorable were the hands of one New York racketeer who had agreed to testify only on condition that his face would not be shown. "A nationwide crime syndicate does exist in the United States of America," Kefauver declared, "despite the protestations of a strangely assorted company of criminals, self-serving politicians, plain blind fools, and others who may be honestly misguided." The committee published a Third Interim Report on May 1, 1951, a part of which appears here.

Source: 82 Congress, 1 Session, Senate Report No. 307, pp. 1-5.

1. Organized criminal gangs operating in interstate commerce are firmly entrenched in our large cities in the operation of many different gambling enterprises, such as bookmaking, policy, slot machines, as well as in other rackets, such as the sale and distribution of narcotics and commercialized prostitution. They are the survivors of the murderous underworld wars of the Prohibition era. After the repeal of the Prohibition laws, these groups and syndicates shifted their major criminal activities to gambling. However, many of the crime syndicates continued to take an interest in other rackets such as narcotics, prostitution, labor and business racketeering, black marketing, etc.

2. Criminal syndicates in this country make tremendous profits and are due primarily to the ability of such gangs and syndicates to secure monopolies in the illegal operations in which they are engaged. These monopolies are secured by persuasion, intimidation, violence, and murder.

The committee found in some cities that law-enforcement officials aided and protected gangsters and racketeers to maintain their monopolistic position in particular rackets. Mobsters who attempted to compete with these entrenched criminal groups found that they and their followers were being subjected to arrest and prosecution while protected gang operations were left untouched.

3. Crime is on a syndicated basis to a substantial extent in many cities. The two major crime syndicates in this country are the Accardo-Guzik-Fischetti syndicate, whose headquarters are Chicago; and the Costello-Adonis-Lansky syndicate based on New York. Evidence of the operations of the Accardo-Guzik-Fischetti syndicate was found by the committee in such places as Chicago, Kansas City, Dallas, Miami, Las Vegas, Nev., and the West Coast. Evidence of the Costello-Adonis-Lansky operations was found in New York City, Saratoga,

Bergen County, N.J., New Orleans, Miami, Las Vegas, the West Coast, and Havana, Cuba. These syndicates, as well as other criminal gangs throughout the country, enter profitable relationships with each other. There is also a close personal, financial, and social relationship between top-level mobsters in different areas of the country.

4. There is a sinister criminal organization known as the Mafia operating throughout the country with ties in other nations, in the opinion of the committee. The Mafia is the direct descendant of a criminal organization of the same name originating in the island of Sicily. In this country, the Mafia has also been known as the Black Hand and the Unione Siciliano. The membership of the Mafia today is not confined to persons of Sicilian origin. The Mafia is a loose-knit organization specializing in the sale and distribution of narcotics, the conduct of various gambling enterprises, prostitution, and other rackets based on extortion and violence. The Mafia is the binder which ties together the two major criminal syndicates as well as numerous other criminal groups throughout the country. The power of the Mafia is based on a ruthless enforcement of its edicts and its own law of vengeance, to which have been creditably attributed literally hundreds of murders throughout the country.

5. Despite known arrest records and well-documented criminal reputations, the leading hoodlums in the country remain, for the most part, immune from prosecution and punishment, although underlings of their gangs may, on occasion, be prosecuted and punished. This quasi-immunity of top-level mobsters can be ascribed to what is popularly known as the "fix." The fix is not always the direct payment of money to law-enforcement officials, although the committee has run across considerable evidence of such bribery. The fix may also come about through the acquisition of political power by contributions to political organizations or otherwise, by creating economic ties with apparently respectable and reputable businessmen and lawyers, and by buying public goodwill through charitable contributions and press relations.

6. Gambling profits are the principal support of big-time racketeering and gangsterism. These profits provide the financial resources whereby ordinary criminals are converted into big-time racketeers, political bosses, pseudo-businessmen, and alleged philanthropists. Thus, the $2 horse bettor and the 5-cent numbers player are not only suckers because they are gambling against hopeless odds, but they also provide the moneys which enable underworld characters to undermine our institutions.

The legalization of gambling would not terminate the widespread predatory activities of criminal gangs and syndicates. The history of legalized gambling in Nevada and in other parts of the country gives no assurance that mobsters and racketeers can be converted into responsible businessmen through the simple process of obtaining state and local licenses for their gambling enterprises. Gambling, moreover, historically has been associated with cheating and corruption.

The committee has not seen any workable proposal for controlled gambling which would eliminate the gangsters or the corruption.

7. Rapid transmission of racing information and gambling information about other sporting events is indispensable to big-time bookmaking operations. This information is presently being provided by a monopoly operated by the Continental Press Service. The Continental Press Service, at critical times and in crucial places where monopoly of bookmaking is at stake, yields to the domination and control of the Accardo-Guzik-Fischetti crime syndicate, to which it is beholden for its own monopoly in the wire-service field. The wire service is so vital to large bookmakers that they are compelled to pay what the traffic will bear to the Continental Press Service. This makes it

possible for the Accardo-Guzik-Fischetti crime syndicate to participate in the profits of bookmaking operations throughout the country.

8. The backbone of the wire service which provides gambling information to bookmakers is the leased wires of the Western Union Telegraph Co. This company, in many parts of the country, has not been fully cooperative with law-enforcement officials who have been trying to suppress organized criminal rackets which make use of telegraph facilities. By permitting its facilities to be used by bookmakers, Western Union has given aid and comfort to those engaged in violation of gambling laws. In some cases, Western Union officials and employees actually participated in book-making conspiracies by accepting bets and transmitting them to bookmakers. It should be noted that during the latter months of the committee's investigation, Western Union has taken steps to prevent this practice and has been more cooperative with the committee.

In many areas, of which New York is a notable example, the telephone companies have cooperated fully with law-enforcement officials. However, in still other areas, telephone companies have been much less cooperative. Local legislation is apparently necessary in many states to require telephone company officials to refuse facilities and remove existing facilities of suspected bookmakers and to call to the attention of local law-enforcement officials the use of telephone facilities by bookmakers.

9. Crime is largely a local problem. It must be attacked primarily at the local level, with supplementary aid, where appropriate, from state and federal authorities. The conduct of various forms of gambling enterprises, houses of prostitution, the distribution of narcotics, the use of intimidation, violence, and murder to achieve gang objectives are all violations of state laws. The public must insist upon local and state law-enforcement agencies meeting this challenge, and must not be deceived by the aura of romanticism and respectability deliberately cultivated by the communities' top mobsters.

10. The federal government has the basic responsibility of helping the states and local governments in eliminating the interstate activities and interstate aspects of organized crime, and in facilitating exchange of information with appropriate safeguards between the federal government and local and state law-enforcement agencies, as well as between law-enforcement agencies in the various states.

The task of dealing with organized crime is so great that the public must insist upon the fullest measure of cooperation between law-enforcement agencies at all levels of government without buck-passing. The committee feels that it has fully demonstrated the need for such cooperation. The time for action has arrived.

11. Wide-open gambling operations and racketeering conditions are supported by out-and-out corruption in many places. The wide-open conditions which were found in these localities can easily be cleaned up by vigorous law enforcement. This has been demonstrated in the past in many different communities and has received added demonstration during the life of our committee. The outstanding example is Saratoga, N.Y., which ran wide-open through the racing season of 1949 but was closed down tight in 1950.

12. Venal public officials have had the effrontery to testify before the committee that they were elected on "liberal" platforms calling for wide-open towns. The committee believes that these officials were put in office by gamblers and with gamblers' money, and that 'in the few cases where the public was convinced that gambling is good for business, this myth was deliberately propagated by the paid publicists of the gambling interests. In many wide-open communities, so-called political leaders and law-enforcement officials have sabotaged ef-

forts of civic-minded citizens to combat such wide-open conditions and the crime and corruption that they entailed.

13. The Treasury of the United States has been defrauded of huge sums of money in tax revenues by racketeers and gangsters engaged in organized criminal activities. Huge sums in cash handled by racketeers and gangsters are not reflected in their income tax returns. Income tax returns filed with the federal government have been inadequate since, as a rule, they contained no listing of the sources of income nor any itemization of the expenses. Gangsters and racketeers, moreover, do not keep books and records from which it might be possible to check tax returns.

14. Mobsters and racketeers have been assisted by some tax accountants and tax lawyers in defrauding the government. These accountants and lawyers have prepared and defended income tax returns which they knew to be inadequate. At the very least, those who are guilty of such practices could be convicted of a misdemeanor and sent to jail for a year for every year in which they have failed to comply with the law.

The Bureau of Internal Revenue states that it has, to the best of its ability, considering its limited manpower, been investigating these returns. It states further that when it pursues the case of one of these individuals, it prefers to set up against him a case of criminal tax evasion, which is a felony, rather than the lesser offense of failing to keep proper books and records, which is a misdemeanor.

Despite this, the committee believes that the Bureau of Internal Revenue could, and should, make more frequent use of the sanctions provided for failure to keep proper books and records than it has heretofore. In any event, the Bureau of Internal Revenue should insist on adequate returns and proper books.

While the great majority of agents of the Bureau of Internal Revenue are honest and efficient, there have been relatively few instances in different parts of the country of lack of vigorous and effective action to collect income taxes from gangsters and racketeers.

15. A major question of legal ethics has arisen in that there are a number of lawyers in different parts of the country whose relations to organized criminal gangs and individual mobsters pass the line of reasonable representation. Such lawyers become true "mouthpieces" for the mob. In individual cases, they have become integral parts of the criminal conspiracy of their clients.

16. Evidence of the infiltration by organized criminals into legitimate business has been found, particularly in connection with the sale and distribution of liquor, real-estate operations, night clubs, hotels, automobile agencies, restaurants, taverns, cigarette-vending companies, juke-box concerns, laundries, the manufacture of clothing, and the transmission of racing and sport news. In some areas of legitimate activity, the committee has found evidence of the use by gangsters of the same methods of intimidation and violence as are used to secure monopolies in criminal enterprise. Gangster infiltration into business also aggravates the possibility of black markets during a period of national emergency such as we are now experiencing. Racketeers also have used labor unions as fronts to enable them to exploit legitimate businessmen.

17. In some instances legitimate businessmen have aided the interests of the underworld by awarding lucrative contracts to gangsters and mobsters in return for help in handling employees, defeating attempts at organization, and in breaking strikes. And the committee has had testimony showing that unions are used in the aid of racketeers and gangsters, particularly on the New York waterfront.

21.

Russell W. Davenport *et al.:* The Transformation of American Capitalism

U.S.A. The Permanent Revolution *appeared first as a series of articles in* Fortune *magazine and was then published in book form. The work, written by the editors of* Fortune *under the direction of Russell W. Davenport, was a serious and widely admired attempt to sum up the historical development of American capitalism and to show how it had been transformed in recent years into an institution "that neither Karl Marx nor Adam Smith ever dreamed of." The book argued that business, particularly Big Business, had accepted a new social responsibility, and asserted that "in all the world there [was] no more hopeful economic phenomenon" than this new attitude on the part of American industrialists. Portions of the fourth chapter are reprinted here.*

Source: *U.S.A. The Permanent Revolution*, New York, 1951, pp. 65-88.

FIFTY YEARS AGO American capitalism seemed to be what Marx predicted it would be and what all the muckrakers said it was — the inhuman offspring of greed and irresponsibility, committed by its master, Wall Street, to a long life of monopoly. It seemed to provide overwhelming proof of the theory that private ownership could honor no obligation except the obligation to pile up profits. It was, indeed, close to the capitalism that Andrei Vishinsky today keeps on denouncing so laboriously and humorlessly. And it was the capitalism that millions of people abroad and many even at home, to the immense aid and comfort of the Communists, still think American capitalism is.

But American capitalism today is actually nothing of the kind. There has occurred a great transformation, of which the world as a whole is as yet unaware, the speed of which has outstripped the perception of the historians, the commentators, the writers of business books — even many businessmen themselves. No important progress whatever can be made in the understanding of America unless the nature of this transformation is grasped and the obsolete intellectual stereotypes discarded.

Many evidences of the transformation are at hand, though they have never yet been drawn together into what is very urgently needed — a restatement of capitalistic theory in modern American terms. Take, for example, the all-pervasive character of American capitalism, as stressed in "The American Way of Life." There has been a vast dispersion of ownership and initiative, so that the capitalist system has become intimately bound in with the political system and takes nourishment from its democratic roots. What might be called the influence of Main Street has become vastly more important than the control of Wall Street. U.S.

capitalism is *popular* capitalism, not only in the sense that it has popular support, but in the deeper sense that the people as a whole participate in it and use it.

But perhaps the transformation can best be understood by looking at what has happened to "Big Business," which once was supposed to have controlled the economy from its headquarters in Wall Street. The fact is that Wall Street no longer wields much power over Big Business, which in turn is far from being the most powerful sector of the economy. For economic power boils down to the ability to decide who makes what and who gets what and in what proportions, and business alone no longer decides this. "The class struggle in America," writes Professor Clair Wilcox in the *Harvard Business Review*, "is not a struggle between the proletariat and the bourgeoisie. It is a struggle between functional groups possessing concentrated power — a struggle to control the products of industry." These groups, as Professor Wilcox describes them, are Big Labor, Big Agriculture, Big Little Business, and Big Business. Of them all, Big Business, if only because it is subject to the most pressure, exercises its power with a strong and growing sense of responsibility. It has led the way to the formation of a kind of capitalism that neither Karl Marx nor Adam Smith ever dreamed of. . . .

THE CATACLYSM OF THE DEPRESSION, which forever broke apart the old business universe, also heaved up the bright new stars of the unions and the farmers. With between 14 and 16 million members in labor unions, labor leaders now enjoy tremendous industrial power. This power is exercised through the familiar method of tying up an entire industry in order to win certain gains for the workers, whether these gains be "economic" or not. In the face of such power, industry is impotent; and since the national welfare is often enough at stake,

the White House itself becomes directly involved. The danger of such power is obvious, and was recently accented by John L. Lewis, who put his miners on a three-day week, not merely to enforce a wage demand, but to keep the price of coal up by creating a scarcity. Here, indeed, is a problem that the permanent revolution has not yet solved, although certain solutions are beginning to emerge. . . . The point to note here is that the power of Wall Street, which has declined in any case, has been met, and sometimes overmatched, by the power of modern labor; a development that has played an enormous role in the transformation of American capitalism.

The power of the farmer, if less direct than that of labor, is likewise formidable. Represented in Congress out of proportion to his numbers, the farmer has been championed by legislators and bureaucrats who have effectively insulated him from the law of supply and demand. By restricting output, fixing prices, and storing up surpluses at government expense, they have done for agriculture what a watertight cartel would do for a group of manufacturers of widely varying efficiency. They have not only saddled the public with high prices, they have . . . tended to prevent American farming from becoming as efficient as it ought to be and can be. For they have spread a price umbrella over the farmers that has enabled the worst of them to do all right and the best of them to make fantastic and undeserved profits without necessarily encouraging any of them to become more efficient. The $23-billion farm industry, furthermore, is hardly comparable to any one industry; it is more comparable to all industry — to all industry cartelized, subsidized, and rigidified. In terms of deciding who makes what and who gets what, it is one of the most powerful blocs in American history.

AND WHERE, IN THIS REGROUPING of U.S. economic power, do we find the sense of responsibility that ought to go with the power if the nation is to increase its productivity? Labor, with a few exceptions, does not yet show much of it, and agriculture shows even less. The only place it can be found in any force is in the individual business enterprise, which now has the initiative that might have remained in Wall Street had not the transformation taken place.

One of the two chief characteristics of big modern enterprise is that it is run by hired management. As Berle and Means put it, the power inherent in the control of the "active property" — the plant, organization, and goodwill — has superseded the power inherent in "passive property" — the stocks and bonds. Even companies whose owners are managers may be described as management-run. The Ford Company, for example behaves not as an organization solely dedicated to earning the maximum number of dollars for the Ford family, but as an organization dedicated first of all to its own perpetuation and growth.

The other chief characteristic of the big modern enterprise is that management is becoming a profession. This means, to begin with, that a professional manager holds his job primarily because he is good at it. Often he has begun at the bottom and worked his way up by sheer merit. Or more often he has been carefully and even scientifically chosen from a number of bright and appropriately educated young men, put through an executive-training course, and gradually insinuated into the activities for which he shows the most talent. Since even at the top he generally functions as a member of a committee rather than as a final authority, his talents are so well balanced that none of them protrude excessively. He lives on what he makes, and even when he is well paid he doesn't have much left after taxes. Generally he is gregarious, and usually he is not a colossal "personality." But if he is not a General MacArthur,

neither is he a Mr. Milquetoast. And if he is expected not to give arbitrary orders, he is also expected not to take them. In most well-run big enterprises, an executive is by definition a man who would object officially to a policy decision he disapproved.

More important, the manager is becoming a professional in the sense that like all professional men he has a responsibility to society as a whole. This is not to say that he no longer needs good, old-fashioned business sense. He does, and more than ever. The manager is responsible primarily to his company as a profit-earning mechanism, and current talk about the corporation as a nonprofit institution is more than a little naive. Any self-respecting businessman would rightly suspect a colleague who allowed he was in business not to make money. The modern enterpriser *should* be in business to make money. His ability to make money is the prime measure of his company's efficiency. If it cannot prosper in the service it supplies to society, or if it cannot persuade society to pay it enough to prosper, it does not deserve to stay in business. Moreover, the good, efficient manager *likes* to make money, and it is mainly because he likes to make money that he does a first-rate job. As the Russians have discovered, when the profit motive does not exist it has to be invented.

But the great happy paradox of the profit motive in the American system is that management, precisely because it is in business to make money years on end, cannot concentrate exclusively on making money here and now. To keep on making money years on end, it must, in the words of Frank Abrams, Chairman of the Standard Oil Co. of New Jersey, "conduct the affairs of the enterprise in such a way as to maintain an *equitable and working balance* among the claims of the various directly interested groups — stockholders, employees, customers, and the public at large." Not all pundits have understood this vital point. In his romantic *Managerial Revolution*, for example, James Burnham described the trend accurately enough but conveyed the idea that somehow the corporate manager is destined to become the Western equivalent of a King Farouk or perhaps an unusually favored commissar. The corporate manager neither is nor is becoming, anything of the kind. He is part of a group that enjoys power only so long as it does not abuse it — in other words, precisely so long as it does not exercise power the way men and groups of men used to before the capitalistic transformation.

THUS IT IS NOT TOO DIFFICULT to define management's responsibility to the stockholder. Management is no longer occupied exclusively with the interests of the stockholder, who often has become a kind of contingent bondholder rather than a part owner, and who rarely exerts any direct influence on the affairs of the company. But management cannot flagrantly disregard stockholders' interests, at least not for long. As the management of Bethlehem and U.S. Steel know well, stockholders can be a considerable nuisance. Even when widely dispersed, they can be induced to take a point of view by proxy. And on the whole, management is treating the stockholders well — despite "abuses" like the habit of holding annual meetings in some out-of-the-way railway station or in Wilmington, Delaware. Almost any good manager can honestly argue that the growing importance of the hired management and its policy of self-capitalization have been to the benefit of the stockholder. Above all, he can argue that the stockholder's long-term interests lie in letting competent, responsible management build up the company and deal justly with employees, customers, and the public.

But modern management exhibits also a sense of responsibility toward its employees, not only to prevent or anticipate the demands of labor unions (though this motive has often been strong) but for the simple, obvious, and honest reason that a satisfied, loyal group of employees is at least as much of an asset as a modern plant or a vital piece of machinery. The trend toward more enlightened employment policies has been growing for years, and while there is still a great distance to go, an old-style capitalist would be appalled by the wide variety of benefits that modern corporations offer those who work for them.

There is a growing tendency on the part of blue-chip management to regard a job in the company as a kind of employment package, complete with pensions, savings plan, and numerous "fringe" benefits such as severance pay, maternity leave, hospitalization and medical insurance. Other managements specialize in certain types of benefits. Some, for instance, go in for stabilization of employment. ATF, Inc., as an example, which recently bought into the furniture business, has succeeded in almost eliminating the highly seasonal character of that work. Some companies (Procter & Gamble, Nunn-Bush, Hormel) carry employment stabilization to the point of guaranteeing an annual wage. Others have developed forecasting techniques to anticipate trends and to stabilize employment by leveling out production. Almost every important company now has a pension plan or is in the process of getting one. Many, like Sears, Roebuck, combine pensions with savings plans, so that when an employee retires he takes with him a sizeable capital sum. Others, backed by the Council of Profit-Sharing Industries (276 members), give the workers a cut of profits, with annual bonuses running up to 100 percent of base wages.

But material benefits, as Elton Mayo and others have demonstrated, are often not as important as job satisfaction — the feeling of having done a good job, and of having it recognized by people who know what a good job is. Related and equally important is the question of real participation in the

"Another in a Year of Record Breaking Figures"; cartoon by Lewis in the "Milwaukee Journal," 1955

company's affairs. The problem involved here is tremendous, and it cannot be solved merely by the resolution to do something about it. In one of the Standard Oil affiliates, for example, management was stumped by a case of group dissatisfaction until the president of the company began to talk to the men informally about some of the problems that were plaguing him and his board. "The men showed an immediate and extraordinary interest, and that gradually revealed the source of their dissatisfaction," recalls Frank Abrams. "They had been 'left out of things.'" The point to be noted here is that not every president could have done that. This president obviously had the "something" it takes to put a man across with his employees. And the gradual cultivation of that something is one of the unfinished tasks ahead of management.

This fundamental point is met, and is combined with material incentives, by the "participation" school, which is growing, and whose most promising development is that fostered by Joseph Scanlon of M.I.T. The Scanlon approach actually brings the worker into the enterprise system by giving him a share in productivity decisions and a cut in productivity profits. Since January 1950, at least a dozen firms, including Stromberg-Carlson of Rochester, New York, have adopted the Scanlon system, and many more are preparing for it. This approach can hardly fail to revolutionize American industrial relations and thus carry further the great transformation in which American capitalism is engaged.

How well American management has actually done by its employees is a question that leads to inevitable debate. The fact is incontestable, however, that it has done better than management anywhere else — and, for that matter, better than management ever dreamed it could, under the old form of capitalism. The problem, indeed, may be to prevent management from becoming overgenerous. For when a company distributes employee benefits that are not compensated by rising productivity, it must in the long run pass the cost increase on to the consumer. Obviously a company *can* be tempted to win employee cooperation easily; a few producers and a single union can combine to gang up on the public.

Thus far, however, it is the modern manager's sense of responsibility to his customer and the general public that gives him his best claim to being progressive. More goods at lower cost (and prices) is the basic principle of American industry, and even companies regarded as anything but socially minded have built themselves upon it. Many a chemical, for example, has been sold at a progressively lower price without the spur of competition, simply to encourage the market. And most modern managers do worry a good deal about the related subjects of prices, monopoly, and competition. Competition has come a long way since the time of Lord Dewar, who cracked that "competition is the life of trade, and competition is the death of profits." The alternatives today are not monopoly or all-out competition. The Darwinian concept of all-out competition has given way to the concept of a pragmatic or "workable" competition, which, far from being the death of profits, provides, as smart companies know, the soundest way to ensure their survival.

Aside from its value as a foil to antitrust, which can be exaggerated, healthy, workable competition provides a good check on how a company is doing. Take du Pont, which, though almost unique, may well set a precedent. Pursued by the hounds of antitrust (unjustly, it maintains), du Pont spent more than a year looking for a competitor willing to put $20 million into a cellophane plant. Having found one in Olin Industries, it is building the plant for Olin and supplying the necessary technical assistance. And that is not all. Because du Pont was the only market source for sodium metal, it induced National Distillers to make the stuff. And recently it turned over its nylon patents to the Chemstrand Co.

Other companies have learned that a similar self-discipline is the best price policy in the long run. The recent furor about rolling back the prices of automobiles obscures the fact that the automobile companies had conducted themselves with a notable respect for public opinion. Had they let the law of supply and demand take its course in the sellers' market of the past four or five years, they could have priced their cars much higher. Their dealers, it is true, sometimes did extract a premium from eager buyers. But it was the manufacturers' list prices that in the main determine the price level, and the auto makers' refusal to charge what the traffic would bear must be reckoned as an extraordinary example of the transformation of the capitalistic mind.

ONE OF THE MOST PRESSING concerns of almost every large company today is what people are going to think about it. Board meetings often turn into self-examination sessions, with managers defending or explaining their actions as if before accusing judges. At a recent board meeting of a large consumer-goods company, the president rose up and remarked that the foremen had in effect built up a block between management and labor, and that management was mostly at fault. Fully two hours were devoted to soul-searching and discussion. There was also the matter of closing an old mill in a small town. Not only was the specific situation explored thoroughly, but the history of other similar cases was brought up. This problem was solved, after a full hour's discussion, by the decision to move a storage plant into the town and thus absorb nearly all the displaced employees. As one executive remarked, "At least half our time is taken up with discussing the repercussions of what we propose to do. And this is what the boys who write the books call the managerial revolution."

What may set a new high in business' concern with fundamental values and questions is a current project of Corning Glass Works, which is celebrating its centennial in 1951. On the premise that "As long as there are men making and operating machines, there will be a humanistic problem as well as a scientific and technological problem in an industrial society." Corning has joined the American Council of Learned Societies in sponsoring a conference on "Living in Industrial Civilization." The conference was held in May 1951, at the Corning Glass Center, and attended by academicians and men of affairs from all over the world. They discussed such topics as Work and Human Values; Leisure and Human Values; the Individual's Sense of Community; Confidence in Life.

NOTHING PERHAPS IS MORE INDICATIVE of the corporation's awareness of its responsibilities than the growth of public-relations activities. Upwards of 4,000 companies now go in for public-relations "programs." Although many of them are hardly more than publicity campaigns, more and more managers understand tolerably well that good business public relations is good performance publicly appreciated, because adequately communicated. Now the mere comprehension of a moral axiom, as all parents know, does not guarantee its observance. But its constant iteration does make the subject more and more acutely aware of its importance, and thus eventually influences his behavior. As Paul Garrett of G.M. has been saying for years, "Our program is finding out what people like, doing more of it; finding out what people don't like, doing less of it."

All of which should not be interpreted to mean that business is already rolling us down the six-lane, highspeed highway to economic paradise. We have concerned ourselves here with the pace-setters of American management, and do not presume to imply that all managers and all other companies are doing as well. Many still give precedence to the big, quick profit. Many incline to regard the stockholder mainly as a convenient personification of the profit goal, labor as a lamentably sensitive kind of commodity, and the customer as the man who gets rolled. Like many a labor and agricultural leader, these businessmen try to increase their share of the national product regardless of their contribution to that product. What Professor Wilcox calls Big (or organized) Little Business, for example, is responsible for or protected by most of the fair-trade laws, licensing systems, local bidding laws, and other legal devices that maintain prices independently of the market.

Big Business, too, has something to answer for. Just how much power it has, for example, to fix prices, and to what extent it uses or abuses that power are right now the subjects of much expert contention. Some economists maintain that "Oligopoly is by all evidence the ruling market form in the modern economy" — *i.e.*, since the nation's corporate assets are concentrated in a relatively few companies, the market is made up of a few sellers, who can administer prices. Other economists, attacking the statistics on which such conclusions are based, maintain that only 20 percent of the national income is provided by unregulated oligopoly, and that an analysis of competition in terms of market realities, which nobody has yet completed, will show that the American economy is becoming more, not less, competitive. It is to be hoped that such an important analysis will be undertaken soon. But whatever its results, it is not likely to reveal that business, socially speaking, has yet attained perfection.

What counts, however, is that certain business leaders *are* setting the pace, and *are* being followed. What counts is that the old concept that the owner has a right to use his property just the way he pleases has evolved into the belief that ownership carries social obligations, and that a manager is a trustee not only for the owner but for society as a whole. Such is the Transformation of American Capitalism. In all the world there is no more hopeful economic phenomenon.

22.

John Courtney Murray: The State-Church and Democratic Society

The Catholic Church's teachings on relations between church and state came in for sharp criticism during the 1950s, the best-known attack being launched by Paul Blanshard in his American Freedom and Catholic Power *(1949). Partly to meet these criticisms, and partly to alter what he himself considered to be antiquated church views, John Courtney Murray, distinguished theologian and Jesuit priest, sought in a series of essays and books to find a way of bringing Catholic principles and American democratic ideas into a compatible union. In the essay, originally titled "The Problem of State Religion," and reprinted here in part, Murray asserted that the American conception of the freedom of religious worship was both more reasonable and more Christian than the traditional Catholic theory of a state-church. Murray, who died in 1967, was an important influence on Vatican II, which adopted the view shared by Murray and others on this matter.*

Source: *Theological Studies,* June 1951.

THE PRINCIPLES OF THE CHURCH in the matter of her relation to the state do not change; but the reality to which she must relate herself is a variable, not only in its institutional forms and processes but also in the idea that men make of it. There are indeed absolute principles of politics, universal in their application; but their application is relative to complex historical factors, and even the theoretical statement of them is subject to revision in the light of enlarged political experience. For instance, the idea of the political relationship ("governors-governed") is permanently valid as an idea, a necessity of nature and reason. But its institutionalization, and the concept held of it, shows enormous variations, as realized in the ancient patrimonial or patriarchal state, in a feudal regime, in the city-state of the late Middle Ages, in the classical French monarchy, in a modern dictatorship, in a republic on the Revolutionary model, in a democracy in the Anglo-Saxon tradition.

What therefore the Church must seek, and has sought, in every age is such a vital application of her principles, such an institutional embodiment of them, as will make them operative in particular temporal contexts towards the permanent ends, human and supernatural, which she has always in view. The history of Church-State relations is the history of this manner of adaptive application. It records many compromises, but no ideal realizations.

The legal institution known as the state-church, and the later embodiment in the written constitutional law of territorial states of the concept of Catholicism as "the religion of the state," represent an application of Catholic principles (and of the medieval tradition, itself an adaptation) to the complex political, social, religious, and cultural conditions prevailing in the modern state, as it appeared on the dissolution of medieval Christendom, took form in the era of political absolutism, flourished in the era of "confessional absolutism" (to use Eder's phrase) under the royal governments in the "Catholic nations" of post-Reformation Europe, and sought reinstatement in the monarchic restorations of the nineteenth century.

As a necessary adaptation of principle this legal institution was at first tolerated by the Church; later, in the circumstances of fixed religious divisions, it became the object of more positive acquiescence; still later, in the circumstances created by the French Revolution, it was defended against the laicizing monism of Continental Liberalism, which destroyed the institution of the state-church in consequence of its denial of the Catholic thesis of juridical and social dualism under the primacy of the spiritual, of which the institution was, however defectively, an expression. In the course of this defense the application of the thesis was identified with the thesis itself — an identification that was never canonized by the Church.

Since the institution of the state-church was an adaptation to a particular historical context, it does not represent a permanent and unalterable exigence of Catholic principles, to be realized in any and all historical situations in which there is verified the general hypothesis of a "Catholic population." This legal institution need not be defended by Catholics as a sort of transtemporal "ideal," the single and only institutionalized form of Catholic-State relationships which can claim the support of principles, the unique "thesis" beside which all other solutions to the Church-State problem must be regarded as "hypothesis," provisional concessions to *force majeure*.

Where the conditions of its origin still more or less prevail, the institution of the state-church is still the object of defense. But the long history of the Church's adaptation of her permanent principles to perpetually changing political realities has not come to a climax and an end with this institution, in such wise that the only valid present effort must be in the direction of a restoration of what existed in a particular epoch of the past — the national state-church by law established, with legal disabilities for dissenters.

On the contrary, the Church can, if she will (and if Catholic thinkers clarify the way for her), consent to other institutionalizations of Church-State relationships and regard them as *aequo iure* valid, vital, and necessary adaptations of principle to legitimate political and social developments.

Such a development is presented by the democratic state. The term does not designate the special type of state which issued from French Revolutionary ideology and Continental Liberalism, which was merely another form of the absolutist state. The term refers to the political idea of the state derived from "the liberal tradition" of the West, which has been best preserved, though not guarded in its purity, in the Anglo-Saxon democratic tradition. Continental Liberalism was a deformation of the liberal tradition; it was in effect simply another form of absolutist state-monism, to which the liberal tradition stands in opposition.

Democracy today presents itself with all the force of an idea whose time has come. And there are two reasons why the present task of Catholics is to work toward the purification of the liberal tradition (which is their own real tradition) and of the democratic form of state in which it finds expression, by restoring both the idea and the institutions of democracy to their proper Christian foundations. First, this form of state is presently man's best, and possibly last, hope of human freedom. Secondly, this form of state presently offers to the Church as a spiritual power as good a hope of freedom as she has ever had; it offers to the Church as the Christian people a means, through its free political institutions, of achieving harmony between law and social organization and the demands of their Christian conscience; finally, by reason of its aspirations towards an order of personal and associational freedom, political equality, civic friendship, social justice, and cultural advancement, it offers to the Church the kind of cooperation which she presently needs, and it merits in turn her cooperation in the realization of its own aspirations.

Consequently, the theological task of the moment is not simply to carry on the polemic against Continental Liberalism. It is also to explore, under the guidance of the Church, the possibilities of a vital adaptation of Church-State doctrine to the constitutional structure, the political institutions, and the ethos of freedom characteristic of the democratic state. To this task the theologian is urged by Pius XII's affirmation of the validity of the democratic development and the new concept of "the people" that it has brought into being. The concept of "the people" is the crucial one in this present day, as it was in the past age that saw the birth of the institution of the state-church, which was itself based on a particular concept of "the people."

The political teaching of Pius XII (and of Pius XI) represents considerable progress over the political teaching of Leo XIII, and this progress invites to a commensurate development of the theory of Church-State relations. In order that this development may be organic in the Catholic sense, a work of discernment has to be done on tradition — the rational political tradition of the West, the Church's theological tradition, and her tradition of practical conduct in the face of the changing realities of the political order.

It is not a matter of debating the "thesis" versus the "hypothesis"; these categories are related to a particular and predominantly polemic state of the question. The doctrinal problem is to discern in their purity the principles that are at the heart of tradition. The categories of discussion are "principle" and "application of principle," or (what comes to the same) "ideas" and "institutions."

Certainly in the conditions of the twentieth century, when a new revolutionary movement has violently altered the nineteenth-century state of the question, it would be an abdication of the theological task, if the theologian were to remain simply the literal exegete of Leo XIII, as if somehow the total doctrine and practice of Church-State relations had reached their definitive and ultimate stage of development in the Leonine *corpus*. Such an abrupt closure of development would be altogether untraditional. It would be to repeat the mistake of the fourteenth- and fifteenth-century canonists who supposed that with the "traditional" theory of society expressed in the Bull *Unam Sanctam* and with the "traditional" canonical doctrine of the direct power Catholic tradition had received in every respect its permanent and unalterable statement. Leo XIII did not fall into this mistake; if he had, *Immortale Dei* would never have been written.

Concretely, the present problem concerns the provision guaranteeing "the free exercise of religion" that has become characteristic of the democratic state constitution. At least, this is usually conceived to be the major aspect of the problem. In fuller form the problem may be stated as follows: can the Church accept, as a valid adaptation of principle to the legitimate idea of democratic government and to the historically developed idea of "the people" (to which democratic government appeals for its legitimacy), a constitutional system of Church-State relations with these three characteristics: (1) the freedom of the Church is guaranteed in a guarantee to the people of the free exercise of religion; (2) the harmony of law and social institutions with the demands of the Christian conscience is to be effected by the people themselves through the medium of free political institutions and freedom of association; (3) the cooperation between Church and state takes these three forms: (*a*) constitutional protection of the freedom of the Church and all her institutional activities; (*b*) the effort of the state to perform its own function of justice, social welfare, and the favoring within society of those conditions of order and freedom necessary for human development; (*c*) the effort of the Church, through the action of a laity conscious of its Christian and civic responsibilities, to effect that christianization of society in all its dimensions which will enable and oblige the state, as the instrument of society, to function in a Christian sense.

This lengthy question is not to be transformed into a brief tendentious one: Can the Church at last come to terms with Continental Liberalism? The answer to that nineteenth-century question is still the nineteenth-century answer: No. But when the nineteenth-century question has been given its nineteenth-century answer, the twentieth-century question still remains unanswered. To it, as put, I am inclined to answer in the affirmative. The Church can, if she wishes, permit her principles of freedom, harmony, and cooperation thus to be applied to the political reality of the democratic state. The application of each of the three principles (freedom, harmony, cooperation) can be justified in terms of traditional Catholic thought, political and theological.

The resulting system would not indeed be some "ideal" realization of Church-State relations, some sort of "new thesis." The point is that no "ideal" realizations are possible in history; no application of principle can claim to be a "thesis." For instance, in the series of Concordats beginning with the Council of Constance (1418) and ending with the Concordat with Francis I (1516) the Church first undertook to assume an historical attitude to the emerging modern state; in these Concordats were likewise laid the juridical foundations for the institution of the state-church in the *ancien régime*. Yet no one would say that the system of Church-State relationships set forth in these Concordats, and the institutions through which the system operated, represented some "ideal" realization of principle —

least of all an ideal realization of the principle of the freedom of the Church. In every respect principle was adapted to political reality — to a political reality, it should be added, that was much less justifiably rational, because absolutist, than is the contemporary democracy of the liberal tradition. One should therefore expect the Church's attitude toward democracy to be only what her attitude toward absolute monarchy was — a valid and vital, because purposeful, application of principle. Not an "ideal," not a "thesis."

With regard to the special problem of religious freedom one remark may be made. There would seem to be a valid analogy between the constitutional provision for religious freedom in the democratic state and the legal institution of the state-church in the post-Reformation monarchic states, in the sense that both represent an analogical adaptation to analogous situations. The latter institution was an adaptation to two facts: (1) the emergence of the modern state as a "person," as autonomous, with an autonomy that extended to state determination of the religion of the people; with this fact is allied the concept of "the people" as purely passive in the face of government, whose purposes are determined apart from consultation of the people; (2) the religious division of universal Christian society into separate and autonomous Catholic and Protestant nations and states.

The former institution is an adaptation to two analogous facts: (1) the emergence of "the people" into active self-consciousness, into a spiritual autonomy that extends to a rejection of governmental determination or even tutelage of their religion; with this fact is allied the concept of "the state" as the instrument of the people for limited purposes sanctioned by the people; (2) the religious divisions within territorial states between persons of different religions. When they are viewed in this historical perspective, it is difficult to see why one institution is any less, or more, an adaptation of principle than the other, why one should be considered more valid and vital than the other, why one has a greater right to claim the support of principle than the other.

Actually, from the standpoint of principle the crucial point is not the fact of religious unity or disunity, with the former basing a "thesis" and the latter an "hypothesis"; for both situations are predicated on a disruption of Catholic unity in the proper sense. The crucial question is whether the concept of the state and the concept of the people that undergirds the legal institution of the state-church is any more rational than the concept of the state and the concept of the people that undergirds the legal institution of religious freedom. The answer would seem to be that the latter concepts are certainly more rational and better founded in Christian thought.

The foregoing propositions set forth, simply in outline, the major points of a theory of Church-State relationships which may, I think, be considered tenable in the light of the full Catholic tradition of thought and practice in the matter.

23.

Paul Campbell (The Weavers): "Kisses Sweeter Than Wine"

A revolution occurred in American popular music in the 1950s, when folk songs were "discovered" by the public at large. Up to that time the enthusiasm almost exclusively of a small coterie of collectors, folk-song records became big sellers and appeared on juke boxes around the country in the company of rock and roll and "country and western" songs. One of the first great folk-song successes — it was actually not a folk song, since it was written by Paul Campbell of the Weavers in conjunction with Huddie Ledbetter, better known as "Leadbelly" — was "Kisses Sweeter Than Wine," which sold more than a million records in the Weavers' version. In its refusal to emphasize romantic love to the exclusion of everything else, the song was typical of the genre, which can tell stories, incorporate social and political criticism, and express feelings shared by both young and old.

Source: *The Weavers' Song Book*, New York, 1960. Copyright 1951 Folkways Music Publishers, Inc., New York, N.Y.

KISSES SWEETER THAN WINE

When I was a young man and never been kissed
I got to thinking it over what I had missed.
I got me a girl, I kissed her and then,
Oh Lord, I kissed her again.

Chorus:
Oh, kisses sweeter than wine,
Oh, kisses sweeter than wine.

He asked me to marry and be his sweet wife,
And we would be so happy all of our life.
He begged and he pleaded like a natural man, and then,
Oh Lord, I gave him my hand.

I worked mighty hard and so did my wife,
Workin' hand in hand to make a good life.
Corn in the field and wheat in the bins, I was,
Oh Lord, the father of twins.

Our children numbered just about four,
And they all had sweethearts knockin' at the door.
They all got married and didn't hesitate; I was,
Oh Lord, the grandmother of eight.

Now we are old, and ready to go,
We get to thinkin' what happened a long time ago.
Had a lot of kids, trouble and pain, but,
Oh Lord, we'd do it again.

24.

THOMAS HART BENTON: Regionalism

Throughout his long and distinguished career, Thomas Hart Benton continued, in common with a group of his fellow artists called Regionalists, to paint scenes of daily life that, in their fidelity to "reality," were meaningful to average citizens. Regionalism connotes a turning away from the dominant abstract and nonobjective styles of the century and an avoidance of the obscure. In the following extract from the revised version of his autobiography, which was published in 1951, Benton describes his own career as a Regionalist.

Source: *An Artist in America*, Revised edition, New York, 1951, pp. 314-321.

JOHN STEUART CURRY and Grant Wood rose along with me to public attention in the '30s. They were very much a part of what I stood for and made it possible for me in my lectures and interviews to promote the idea that an indigenous art with its own aesthetics was a growing reality in America. Without them, I would have had only personal grounds to stand on for my pronouncements.

We were, the three of us, pretty well along before we ever became acquainted or were linked under the now famous name of Regionalism. We were different in our temperaments and many of our ideas, but we were alike in that we were all in revolt against the unhappy effects which the Armory show of 1913 had had on American painting. We objected to the new Parisian aesthetics which was more and more turning art away from the living world of active men and women into an academic world of empty pattern. We wanted an American art which was not empty, and we believed that only by turning the formative processes of art back again to meaningful subject matter, in our cases specifically American subject matter, could we expect to get one. . . .

The term [Regionalism] was, so to speak, wished upon us. Borrowed from a group of Southern writers who were interested in their regional cultures, it was applied to us somewhat loosely, but with a fair degree of appropriateness. However, our interests were wider than the term suggests. They had their roots in that general and country-wide revival of Americanism which followed the defeat of Woodrow Wilson's universal idealism at the end of World War I and which developed through the subsequent periods of boom and depression, until the new internationalisms of the Second World War pushed it aside. This Americanist period had many facets, some dark, repressive, and suggestive of an ugly neo-Fascism, but on the whole it was a time of general improvement in democratic idealism.

After the break of 1929, a new and effective liberalism grew over the country and the battles between that liberalism and the entrenched moneyed groups, which had inherited our post-Civil War sociology and were in defense of it, brought out a new and vigorous discussion of the intended nature of our society. This discussion and the political battles over its findings, plus a new flood of historical writing concentrated the '30s on our American image. It was this country-wide concentration more probably than any of our artistic efforts which raised Wood, Curry, and me to prominence in the national scene. We symbolized aesthetically what the majority of Americans had in mind — America itself.

Our success was a popular success. Even where some American citizens did not agree with the nature of our images, instanced in the objections to my state-sponsored murals in Indiana and Missouri, they understood them. What ideological battles we had were in American terms and were generally comprehensible to Americans as a whole. This was exactly what we wanted. The fact that our art was arguable in the language of the street, whether or not it was liked, was proof to us that we had succeeded in separating it from the hothouse atmosphere of an imported and, for our country, functionless aesthetics. With that proof we felt that we were on the way to releasing American art from its subservience to borrowed forms. In the heyday of our success, we really believed we had at last succeeded in making a dent in American aesthetic colonialism.

However, as later occurrences have shown, we were well off the beam on that score. As soon as the Second World War began, substituting in the public mind a world concern for the specifically American concerns which had prevailed during our rise, Wood, Curry, and I found the bottom knocked out from under us. In a day when the problems of America were mainly exterior, our interior images lost public significance. Losing that, they lost the only thing which could sustain them because the critical world of art had, by and large, as little use for our group front as it had for me as an individual. The coteries of highbrows, of critics, college art professors, and museum boys, the tastes of which had been thoroughly conditioned by the new aesthetics of 20th-century Paris, had sustained themselves in various subsidized ivory towers and kept their grip on the journals of aesthetic opinion all during the Americanist period. These coteries, highly verbal but not always notably intelligent or able to see through momentarily fashionable thought patterns, could never accommodate our populist leanings. They had, as a matter of fact, a vested interest in aesthetic obscurity, in highfalutin' symbolisms and devious and indistinct meanings.

The entertainment of these obscurities, giving an appearance of superior discernment and extraordinary understanding, enabled them to milk the wealthy ladies who went in for art and the college and museum trustees of the country for the means of support. Immediately after it was recognized that Wood, Curry, and I were bringing American art out into a field where its meanings had to be socially intelligible to justify themselves and where aesthetic accomplishment would depend on an effective representation of cultural ideas, which were themselves generally comprehensible, the ivory tower boys and girls saw the danger to their presumptions and their protected positions. They rose with their supporting groups of artists and highbrowish disciples to destroy our menace. . . .

I profited greatly by their fulminations and so, for a while, did Wood and Curry. However, in the end, they succeeded in destroying our Regionalism and returning American art to that desired position of obscurity and popular incomprehensibility which enabled them to remain its chief prophets. The Museum of Modern Art, the Rockefeller-supported institution in New York, and other similar culturally rootless artistic centers, run often by the most neurotic of people, came rapidly, as we moved through the war years, to positions of predominant influence over the artistic life of our country. As the attitudes of these cultist groups were grounded on aesthetic events which had occurred or were occurring in cultures overseas, their ultimate effect was to return American art to the imitative status from which Wood, Curry, and I had tried to extricate it.

The younger artists of America were left, in this situation, only with an extenuating function. The sense of this humiliating state of affairs led many of them, and notably some of the most talented of my old stu-

dents, to a denial of all formal values and they began pouring paint out of cans and buckets just to see what would happen, or tying pieces of wire to sticks and smacking them around in the air in the name of a new mobility. This American contribution to "modern" aesthetics, though it suggests the butler trying to outdo his master's manners, received wide applause in our cultist circles, and it went out from there to the young ladies' colleges and to the small-town art schools and into the minds of all those thousands of amateurs over the land who took themselves to be artists. These latter saw immediately the wonderful opportunities for their own ego advancement which this "free expression" afforded and embraced it enthusiastically.

Now, all this anarchic idiocy of the current American art scene cannot be blamed solely on the importation of foreign ideas about art or on the existence in our midst of institutions which represent them. It is rather that our artists have not known how to deal with these. In other fields than art, foreign ideas have many times vastly benefited our culture. In fact, few American ideas are wholly indigenous, nor in fact are those of any other country, certainly not in our modern world. But most of the imported ideas which have proved of use to us were able to become so by intellectual assimilation. They were thoughts which could be thought of.

The difficulty in the case of aesthetic ideas is that intellectual assimilation is not enough — for effective production. Effective aesthetic production depends on something beyond thought. The intellectual aspects of art are not art nor does a comprehension of them enable art to be made. It is in fact the over-intellectualization of modern art and its separation from ordinary life intuitions which have permitted it, in this day of almost wholly collective action, to remain psychologically tied to the "public be damned" individualism of the last century and, thus, in spite of its novelties, to represent a cultural lag.

Art has been treated by most American practitioners as if it were a form of science where like processes give like results all over the world. By learning to carry on the processes by which imported goods were made, the American artist assumed that he would be able to end with their expressive values. This is not perhaps wholly his fault because a large proportion of the contemporary imports he studied were themselves laboratory products, studio experiments in process, with pseudo-scientific motivations which suggested that art was, like science, primarily a process evolution. This put inventive method rather than a search for the human meaning of one's life at the center of artistic endeavor and made it appear that aesthetic creation was a matter for intellectual rather than intuitive insight. Actually, this was only illusory, and art's modern flight from representation to technical invention has only left it empty and stranded in the backwaters of life. Without those old cultural ties which used to make the art of each country so expressive of national and regional character, it has lost not only its social purpose but its very techniques for expression.

It was against the general cultural inconsequence of modern art and the attempt to create by intellectual assimilation that Wood, Curry, and I revolted in the early twenties and turned ourselves to a reconsideration of artistic aims. We did not do this by agreement. We came to our conclusions separately but we ended with similar convictions that we must find our aesthetic values, not in thinking but in penetrating to the meaning and forms of life as lived. For us this meant, as I have indicated, American life and American life as known and felt by ordinary Americans. We believed that only by our own participation in the reality of American life, and that very definitely included the folk patterns which sparked it

and largely directed its assumptions, could we come to forms in which Americans would find an opportunity for genuine spectator participation. This latter, which we were, by the example of history, led to believe was a corollary, and in fact, a proof of real artistic vitality in a civilization, gave us that public-minded orientation which so offended those who lived above and believed that art should live above "vulgar" contacts. The philosophy of our popularism was rarely considered by our critics. It was much easier, especially after international problems took popular press support away from us, to dub us conventional chauvinists, Fascists, isolationists, or just ignorant provincials, and dismiss us.

When we were left to the mercies of the art journals, the professors, and the museum boys, we began immediately to lose influence among the newly budding artists and the young students. The band-wagon practitioners, and most artists are unhappily such, left our regionalist banner like rats from a sinking ship and allied themselves with the now dominant internationalisms of the highbrow aesthetes. The fact that these internationalisms were for the most part emanations from cultural events occurring in the Bohemias of Paris, and thus as local as the forms they deserted, never once occurred to any of our band-wagon fugitives.

Having long been separated from my teaching contacts, I did not immediately notice the change of student attitude which went with our loss of public attention. But Wood and Curry, still maintaining their university positions, were much affected, and in the course of time, under the new indifference, and sometimes actual scorn, of the young, began feeling as if their days were over.

It was one of the saddest experiences of my life to watch these two men, so well known and, when compared with most artists, enormously successful, finish their lives in ill health and occasional moods of deep despondency. After the time we came to be publicly associated in the early thirties, we had for all our differences developed a close personal friendship and this loss of self-confidence by my friends was disturbing to me. It was, as a matter of fact, sort of catching and I had more than a few low moments of my own.

Wood and Curry, and particularly Curry, were oversensitive to criticism. They lacked that certain core of inner hardness, so necessary to any kind of public adventure, which throws off the opinions of others when these set up conflicts within the personality. Thus to the profound self-doubts, which all artists of stature experience, was added in these two an unhappy oversusceptibility to the doubts of others. Such a susceptibility in times of despondency or depression is likely to be disastrous. It was most emphatically so for Wood and Curry.

Small men catch the weaknesses of their famous brothers very quickly, and in the universities where Wood and Curry taught, there were plenty of these to add their tormenting stings to the mounting uncertainties of my two companions. Oddly enough . . . our friendly encouragements never seemed to equal the discouragements which Wood's and Curry's campus brothers worked up to annoy them. Wood was pestered almost from the beginning of his university career by departmental highbrows who could never understand why an Iowa small-towner received world attention while they, with all their obviously superior endowments, received none at all.

By the time we moved over into the '40s, both Wood and Curry were in a pretty bad way physically and even psychologi-cally. They had their good moments but these seemed to be rare and short-lived. In the end, what with worry over his weighty debts and his artistic self-doubts, Wood came to the curious idea of changing his identity. Wood was a man of many curious and illusory fancies, and, when I went to see him in 1942 as he lay dying of a liver cancer in an Iowa hospital, he told me that when he got well he was going to change his name, go where nobody knew him, and start all over again with a new style of painting. This was very uncanny because I'm sure he knew quite well he would never come out of that hospital alive. It was as if he wanted to destroy what was in him and become an empty soul before he went out into the emptiness of death. So far as I know, Grant had no God to whom he could offer a soul with memories.

John Curry died slowly in 1946 after operations for high blood pressure and a general physical failure had taken his big body to pieces little by little. He made a visit to Martha's Vineyard the autumn before he died. Sitting before the fire on a cold, gray day when a nor'easter was building up seas outside, I tried to bolster his failing spirits.

"John," I ventured, "you must feel pretty good now, after all your struggles, to know that you have come to a permanent place in American art. It's a long way from a Kansas farm to fame like yours."

"I don't know about that," he replied, "maybe I'd have done better to stay on the farm. No one seems interested in my pictures. Nobody thinks I can paint. If I *am* any good, I lived at the wrong time."

This is the way my two famous associates came to their end.

25.

Mark Van Doren: "No Word, No Wind"

*Many American poets have tried to express the spirit of places and regions in the
United States — so much so, indeed, that this may almost be said to be an American
genre. An example of this kind of poetry is Mark Van Doren's "No Word, No Wind,"
which attempts to sum up the author's feelings about the Middle West, the region
where he was born but which he left for New York and New England around 1920.
Van Doren's belief — if belief it actually is — that Middle Westerners are "so far,
not a thoughtful people," and that they have as yet no "articulate Deity," is shared
by many Americans — who love the Middle West nonetheless for its other virtues,
some of which are also described in the poem.*

Source: *In That Far Land*, Iowa City, 1951.

NO WORD, NO WIND

I

What god was there
When the slow buggy, appearing and disappearing,
Slipped in and out of moon and maple shadow, down
Those least of earth's depressions, up those low,
Those prairie rises? Eighteen miles
From town to sleepy town, and not a lamp
In any passing window — oh, so slowly
Passing, as the mare's feet
Shuffled, and the delicate wheels
Answered, invisible in windless
Dust. No weather then,
No breath of any god, no loud intelligence
Looking. Nothing blown out of the north,
No word.
What understanding, nevertheless, what hidden listener
Brooded? For the whole of that great place
Consented — I remember it —
Consented, and we nodded in the narrow
Seat, and safely crawled up hills
That were no hills, down grades that were but folded
Ground, with gentle pockets of cool air
Where the night sighed, considering itself.
No rain, no sun, no sting of snow,
No sound of rivers, sluggish, far away among their sycamores

In bottom land, forgotten.
And no wind.
What god, if nothing breathed? I might go back there,
Maybe, and find out. But that same night
Is not there now;
Never again, I think, will such a stillness
Be, and not be spoken to.
No word, no wind — I swear it,
Not one sign
That the world knew we went that way at all.

II

Whereas in whirling March — oh, I remember —
Or the dog days,
Or knee deep in the Christmas drifts
That crusted later — all white ice
Both ways a thousand miles to where the mountains were,
And are, that leave that valley to itself,
Lonesome, and vast, and unreportable —
Or mournfully, in fall,
When the pale corn, suffering the southwest
Trade winds, rustled by night, by day, as if a dead sea
Whispered, pitying the labor
Of its own waves, interminable, intentless —
Then what mind presided? Father
Or mother of all those men,
Those midland children, what lost mind
Like theirs looked down and listened,
Sharing it with them, that great place
To which they both consented? Someone did,
And does. Or are they several, enormous, many
Minded, with no single
Voice that yet can sing, that yet can say,
As some day it may do, what meaning lies
In the long vacancy between those silent mountains?
So far, not a thoughtful
People; so far, not an articulate
Deity, unless that world of weather
Itself is god, is goddess, trying
Their patience whom alternately it blasts
And lulls to slumber
On hot nights
When grain but not idea grows. I might go back there,
Maybe, and look sharp; and shall,
Some day, and listen. There is no other
Sky that I would rather, after these distant
Years, see face to face.

26.

WILLIAM BENTON: For the Expulsion of Senator McCarthy

Many citizens both in and out of government felt that Wisconsin Senator Joseph R. McCarthy's tactics were irresponsible and that his charges were unfounded, and when no Communists were actually turned up as a result of his efforts some members of Congress became concerned lest his actions injure the reputation of the Senate. An investigating committee under Senator Millard Tydings of Maryland concluded in 1950 that McCarthy's own highly publicized investigations were "a fraud and a hoax perpetrated on the Senate of the United States and on the American people." Tydings was defeated in the fall of 1950 after a campaign in which McCarthy was later shown to have played a questionable part; and the campaign itself was the subject of an investigation in 1951 by the Senate Subcommittee on Privileges and Elections. On September 28, 1951, Senator William Benton of Connecticut appeared before this subcommittee and, after reviewing McCarthy's actions during the campaign and at other times, urged that the Senate expel or at least censure him. By this courageous action Benton became one of the first to confront the McCarthy challenge, which was not only to the Senate but also to traditional American institutions and practices. A portion of Benton's testimony is reprinted here.

Source: Manuscript in the possession of William Benton.

MR. CHAIRMAN, I KNOW that all of us this morning are conscious of the many implications of our meeting here and of the gravity of this morning's hearings.

Today I shall lay before your committee pertinent facts and information which bear on the right and fitness of a member of the United States Senate to retain his seat. This question of fitness is a perennial question, and an unresolved one. I believe I can quickly show that it has never been more important than now.

The framers of the Constitution foresaw just the contingency which this committee is facing today. They provided that the United States Senate should be the judge of the qualifications of its own members. They further provided a procedure for the expul-sion of a member of the Senate. This right to expel has been construed broadly. Chief Justice Story, in his treatise on the Constitution, had this to say: "That the right to expel extends to all cases where the offense is such as in the judgment of the Senate is inconsistent with the trust and duty of a member."

The first instance of an expulsion from the Senate was that involving Senator William Blount of Tennessee, who was expelled in 1797. The Select Committee which considered the case found as follows:

When they (the Committee) consider his (Blount's) attempts to seduce Carey from his duty as a faithful interpreter, and to employ him as an engine to alienate the affections and confidence of the

Indians from the public officers of the United States residing among them, the measures he has proposed to excite a temper which must produce the recall or expulsion of our superintendent from the Creek Nation, his insidious advice tending to the advancement of his own popularity and consequence, at the expense and hazard of the good opinion which the Indians entertain of the government, and of the treaties subsisting between us and them, your committee have no doubt that Mr. Blount's conduct has been inconsistent with his public duty, renders him unworthy of a further continuance of his public trust in this body, and amounts to a high misdemeanor.

Mr. Chairman, the fact that the Senate has in a number of cases denied seats to senators-elect before the oath could be administered is better known than the fact that in eighteen cases sitting senators have been formally expelled. Further, three sitting senators have resigned when it has seemed apparent to them that a Senate expulsion vote would go against them. Thus there is ample precedent for the action proposed by this resolution upon which you are holding hearings today.

However, Mr. Chairman and members of the Committee, I want to make it clear that I believe that action on the resolution you are considering today is urgent and indeed imperative even were there no precedents for it. I am therefore here to urge upon you a favorable report on this resolution. For the reasons I shall present today, I deem such action essential to the well-being and security of the American people.

The prestige of the United States in today's world depends not only on our military power and our economic strength but also on our national achievement of a reputation for integrity and character. Without such a reputation, how can we hope to win and retain loyal allies? Without it, how can we hope permanently to undermine the strength and the faith of potential foes?

Mr. Chairman, the United States Senate is often acclaimed as the most important legislative body in the world. In foreign eyes, the character of the Senate is a measure of the objectives and the quality of the people of the United States and of their government and their foreign policy. The measure of the Senate is its membership. Standing at all times in the blinding light of world attention, a United States senator carries the heavy burden of his country's prestige and honor.

This is far more important today than ever before. This is one of the many consequences of our world power which we, in the Senate, must now face up to in our own thinking about ourselves as senators. I submit that the United States Senate is not yet as alert as it must become to these grave consequences, applied to our own actions as senators and the impact of our actions upon the national security. This new urgency for a high sense of responsibility on the part of each and every senator is one reason why, in line with my own experience in the field of foreign policy, I have felt that it was my duty as a senator to demand the expulsion of Senator McCarthy from the Senate. As I shall show today, he himself has created for himself, not only a record of irresponsibility but one of lack of integrity and of character.

Is it not a part of our duty as senators to encourage within and for the Senate the standards of morality and justice which we wish proudly to proclaim to the world as representative of the best qualities of our country? I submit that the failure of any senator to set a high standard of morality is not the failure of a man alone. In the eyes of the world, it is the failure of a nation. Thus the question of standards of character for a senator cannot be deemed a matter of merely local concern for a single state, or merely a matter of personal concern for the senator or his family. The question we are to discuss today is not only a matter of national but of world concern.

The issue here this morning is thus not merely the issue of the moral conduct of a single senator. It is the mighty symbolism of the Senate itself. If your committee, with its high responsibilities, tolerates corruptibility and mendacity in a United States senator, shame is brought to a whole people. Such toleration undermines on a world scale the capacity for leadership of that people in a world desperately requiring their leadership.

Senate Resolution 187, which you are considering this morning, and which I submitted on August 6, quotes certain paragraphs dealing with Senator McCarthy's actions during the 1950 senatorial election in Maryland, as reported to the Senate by your committee. Your report shows that Senator McCarthy was deeply involved in actions described as a "despicable backstreet campaign." These were actions which your committee "vigorously denounced" and which led your committee to call for legislation which would make "acts of defamation, slander, and libel sufficient grounds for presentment to the Senate for the purpose of declaring a Senate seat vacant."

Senate Resolution 187 asks that the Rules Committee

> make such further investigation with respect to the participation of Senator Joseph R. McCarthy in the 1950 senatorial campaign of Senator John Marshall Butler and *such investigation with respect to his other acts since his election to the Senate* as may be appropriate to enable such committee to determine whether or not it should initiate action with a view toward the expulsion from the United States Senate of the said Senator McCarthy.

My presentation today will prove to you, I hope, that you should at once launch the further investigation called for by this resolution. If I give you only one case story today which indicates the need for a more extended investigation, I submit to the com-

mittee that I shall have proved my point. I of course am persuaded that my own testimony of this morning will develop for you ample evidence to show that Senator McCarthy should be expelled, but at minimum I hope your committee will agree that further investigation is not only warranted but imperative.

Perhaps it may prove helpful to this committee if I now make clear what I shall *not* attempt to do at this hearing today.

I shall raise no question about the issue of congressional immunity or about present efforts to put curbs upon it or to develop methods for the protection of those who suffer from the reckless and irresponsible assaults upon their reputations which congressional immunity makes possible. In support of congressional immunity the Constitution provides that senators and representatives "shall not be questioned *in any other place*" for what they say. The clear intent of the Constitution is that senators should be accountable *to the Senate*. That is what I propose today — to call Senator McCarthy to account before his fellow senators.

Next, I shall not this morning — nor would I at any time — question the absolute freedom of any senator to report to the Senate any facts he believes to be true, to express any opinion he elects to hold; or to advance any interpretation of fact or opinion he chooses to make. I state this categorically and at once to make clear that today we are not discussing any issue involving freedom of speech or debate for senators or for anyone else.

Next, I shall not today attempt to appraise the total record and background of Senator McCarthy, even though a review of his actions before he became a senator would prove most germane, in my opinion, to the deliberations of your committee. You may decide to extend your inquiry into the record of Joseph R. McCarthy in the years prior to his entrance into the U.S. Senate. This record of the earlier roots of the pattern of conduct I shall outline this morning can help illumine and explain his actions as a United States senator. As the members of the committee must know, many unusual claims and charges have been published which support the thesis that Senator McCarthy's is a pattern of conduct sustained over a period of many years, and repeated again and again, rather than merely a series of events between '47 to '51.

Finally, I shall not try to cover the many events, during Senator McCarthy's four and a half years in the Senate, which have been brought to my attention and which would, it seems to me, further prove the case I shall develop this morning. I shall seek only to advance enough examples of Senator McCarthy's conduct so that the pattern is crystal clear, for all to see. . . .

Freedom to lie is not a freedom which membership in the U.S. Senate confers upon any man; nor does membership confer the freedom to commit unethical acts of any kind.

My evidence today will, I hope, help your committee find the answers to pertinent questions as to whether Senator McCarthy has borne false witness and as to whether he has deliberately and repeatedly corrupted and subverted facts. It will help you determine whether he has committed perjury and whether he has practised calculated deceit and falsehood on both the U.S. Senate and the American people. Finally, it will help you decide whether it is incumbent upon you to make a further investigation as to whether his conduct as a United States senator has been in such gross violation of senatorial ethics — both the express and implied obligations of office for a senator — and whether also his conduct has so gravely reflected on the integrity of the Senate itself that he should now and forthwith be called to account.

Mr. Chairman, I shall submit a group of case studies, ten in all, to help illustrate the general charges I have just made. All my

Senator William Benton, of Connecticut

case studies are of the same general pattern. . . .

Mr. Chairman, I am nearing the end of my presentation. It has been such a lengthy one that I feel it wise briefly to summarize the ten case stories previously cited as supporting evidence for my general charges against Senator McCarthy of perjury and deception of the Senate, and, through his role as a senator, deception of the American people:

Case No. 1 establishes that Senator McCarthy apparently lied under oath to a Senate Foreign Relations subcommittee last year by denying he had said in a speech at Wheeling, W.Va., that "I have here in my hand a list of 205 names that were made known to the secretary of state as being members of the Communist Party." This case further indicates deliberate deception of the Senate by Senator McCarthy in altering the text of that sensational speech when he read it into the *Congressional Record*.

Case No. 2 illuminates the lack of character, ethical standards, and integrity of Senator McCarthy by detailing his acceptance of $10,000 from the Lustron Corp., a corporation which had had a vital interest in the outcome of the deliberations of a Senate housing committee presided over by Senator McCarthy as acting chairman and vice-chairman, and a corporation dependent on the RFC, which in turn is the concern of the Banking and Currency Committee, of which Senator McCarthy was a member.

Case No. 3 highlights Senator McCarthy's efforts to hoax the Senate with the incredible charge that Gen. George Catlett Marshall has been part of a "conspiracy so immense and an infamy so black as to dwarf any previous such venture in the history of man."

Case No. 4 establishes that Senator McCarthy practised calculated deceit on the United States Senate and the people of the country by falsely stating on the Senate floor that Senator Tydings had forced him to make public the names of government officials against whom his unsubstantiated charges of communism were directed.

Case No. 5 reviews the fraud and deceit practised by Senator McCarthy on the Senate, on the people of the United States, and on the people of Maryland through taking major responsibility for what this subcommittee, in its investigation of the Maryland elections, already has branded as "a despicable, back-street campaign," and in particular through responsibility for the lies in its campaign tabloid *From the Record.*

Case No. 6 examines an instance of deliberate deception of the Senate by Senator McCarthy in offering to repeat off the floor, away from the umbrella of senatorial immunity, libelous statements which he later refused to repeat off the floor.

Case No. 7 shows Senator McCarthy pressing on the Senate a claim to possess a so-called FBI chart consisting of photostats listing Communists in the State Department, when, in fact, on the word of J. Edgar Hoover, the FBI "did not send any such chart to the State Department and, of course, made no evaluation of information as was indicated. . . ."

Case No. 8 illustrates conscious and deliberate deception of the Senate in Senator McCarthy's promise to list the names of 81 Communists for any Senate committee — a promise on which he was forced to renege — after implying they were the fruit of his own investigations — because in fact his cases obviously came from a three-year-old list of unnamed cases previously compiled by a House committee.

Case No. 9 raises the question whether Senator McCarthy falsely accused Americans and excused convicted Germans involved in the infamous Malmedy massacre, possibly on the say-so of a member of the German underground, and whether Senator McCarthy deliberately lied about the Malmedy affair on the floor of the Senate.

Case No. 10 adds to the evidence that Senator McCarthy himself committed perjury the further evidence that he continues to employ a man described by a Senate committee as his administrative assistant who, while in his employ, is charged with committing perjury, as well as with other serious misdeeds.

Mr. Chairman, the preparation of this testimony has been a long and arduous task — one that I have not relished. I am sure that listening to it has not been pleasant for your distinguished colleagues. I felt a compunctive duty to undertake this self-imposed job to document the pattern of conduct of Senator McCarthy which has cast such grave reflections on the integrity of the United States Senate that I feel it can no longer be tolerated by us as senators.

I do not suggest that these ten case stories which I have submitted to you by any means exhaust the flood of material that has poured in upon me and my office staff. Quite the contrary. These could be multiplied to an extent I've had no time to determine.

I shall not attempt to tell the members of this committee how to assess the ten individual stories I have submitted as evidence, or what to do about them. I put my faith, Mr. Chairman, in the wisdom and the judicial integrity of the members of your most eminent group.

I have regarded it as my principal duty here only to present some pertinent facts in an effort to help this committee determine whether the record now requires a further investigation as to Senator McCarthy's fitness to sit in the United States Senate. It is you who must determine the degree of his guilt and, if he is guilty, the most suitable form of punishment.

There have been three cases in modern times, I am told, where a vote of censure has been deemed more suitable than outright expulsion. This possibility has been mentioned to me informally by several senators. While my own personal conviction, as expressed in my resolution, looks to expulsion as the appropriate action, I have learned that many senators seem so gun-shy of the injunction in the Constitution that the Senate is responsible for the qualifications of its members that I fear some might even prefer to let a state send a proved scoundrel to the Senate to any attempt at his expulsion. I concede further that there is appeal in the argument often advanced to me that it won't be long before the voters of Wisconsin will have their chance to expel Senator McCarthy.

If it is the judgment of this committee that a resolution of censure is at this time more suitable and more practical, I shall with confidence look to Wisconsin, awakened to the problem by such a resolution of censure, to see to it that my conviction is acted upon and that Senator McCarthy is expelled at the polls.

Mr. Chairman, I cannot conclude my testimony without expressing my great pride in the United States Senate of which I have the honor to be a member. In my twenty months service in it, as well as through my close work with many senators and Senate committees in my three previous assignments in Washington, I have found that almost all U.S. senators are deeply conscious of their great responsibilities. I have found that membership in the Senate in itself evokes in men a capacity to rise above themselves, to rise to the highest and noblest call of their country's need and its highest aspirations. I wish and hope this might be true of every single senator. Human nature being what it is, it is amazing the extent to which it is true.

Mr. Chairman, among the high aspirations of our country is the ideal of fair play. Fair play — this is what we try to inculcate into our children. That is what we try to measure up to in our own eyes.

In conclusion, I submit that there is one act of hypocrisy which most offends the deepest convictions of the Christian conscience and also the American spirit of justice and fair play. That act is to put the brand of guilt on an innocent man. I submit that there is no one who has erred more recklessly and maliciously in this respect than Senator Joseph McCarthy. Let us now remember the words of Isaiah: "Woe unto them that call evil good and good evil."

———◆———

The Democratic label is now the property of men and women who have been unwilling to recognize evil or who bent to whispered pleas from the lips of traitors . . . men and women who wear the political label stitched with the idiocy of a Truman, rotted by the deceit of an Acheson, corrupted by the Red slime of a White.

JOSEPH R. MCCARTHY, speech, Madison, 1954

1952

27.

WILLIAM O. DOUGLAS: The Black Silence of Fear

McCarthyism — as the political and social turmoil stirred up by Senator McCarthy of Wisconsin had come to be called by 1952 — was a source of distress to many Americans, who opposed it more because of its unpleasant side effects than because McCarthy had failed to discover any actual Communists in the U.S. government. In the opinion of numerous observers, a pernicious political orthodoxy was being imposed on the country, one result of which was that all differences of opinion, dissent, and original thought had become suspect. Despite the widespread opposition, however, not much was said in public — which was one point made by Supreme Court Justice William O. Douglas in an article published in January 1952.

Source: *New York Times Magazine*, January 13, 1952.

THERE IS AN OMINOUS TREND in this nation. We are developing tolerance only for the orthodox point of view on world affairs, intolerance for new or different approaches. Orthodoxy normally has stood in the path of change. Orthodoxy was always the stronghold of the status quo, the enemy of new ideas — at least new ideas that were disturbing. He who was wedded to the orthodox view was isolated from the challenge of new facts.

The democratic way of life rejects standardized thought. It rejects orthodoxy. It wants the fullest and freest discussion, within peaceful limits, of all public issues. It encourages constant search for truth at the periphery of knowledge.

We as a people have probably never lived up to that standard in any of our communities. But it has been an ideal toward which most of our communities have strived. We have over the years swung from tolerance to intolerance and back again. There have been eras of intolerance when the views of minorities have been suppressed. But there probably has not been a period of greater intolerance than we witness today.

To understand this, I think one has to leave the country, go into the back regions of the world, lose himself there, and become absorbed in the problems of the peoples of different civilizations. When he returns to America after a few months he probably will be shocked. He will be shocked, not at the intentions or purposes or ideals of the American people. He will be shocked at the arrogance and intolerance of great segments of the American press, at the arrogance and intolerance of many leaders in public office, at the arrogance and intolerance reflected in many of our attitudes toward Asia. He will find that thought is being standardized, that the permissible area for calm discussion is being narrowed, that the range of ideas is being limited, that many minds are closed to the receipt of any ideas from Asia.

This is alarming to one who loves his country. It means that the philosophy of strength through free speech is being forsaken for the philosophy of fear through repression.

That choice in Russia is conscious. Under Lenin the ministers and officials were encouraged to debate, to advance new ideas and criticisms. Once the debate was over, however, no dissension or disagreement was permitted. But even that small degree of tolerance for free discussion that Lenin permitted disappeared under Stalin. Stalin maintains a tight system of control, permitting no free speech, no real clash in ideas, even in the inner circle. We are, of course, not emulating either Lenin or Stalin. But we are drifting in the direction of repression, drifting dangerously fast.

What is the cause of this drift? What are the forces behind it? It is only a drift, for certainly everything in our tradition would make the great majority of us reject that course as a conscious choice. The drift goes back, I think, to the fact that we carried over to days of peace the military approach to world affairs. Diplomacy, certainly in our relations with Asia, took a back seat. The military approach conditioned our thinking and our planning. The military, in fact, determined our approach to the Asians and their problems. That has been a great tragedy in Asia. And the tragedy to us at home has been about as great.

Military thinking continued to play a dominant role in our domestic affairs. The conspiratorial role of Soviet communism in the world scene was apparent to all who could read. This conspiratorial role of Soviet communism was, of course, backed by Russia's military strength. We, therefore, had to be strong in a military sense to hold off Russia. But we soon accepted the military role as the dominant one. We thought of Asia in terms of military bases, not in terms of peoples and their aspirations. We wanted the starving people of Asia to choose sides, to make up their minds whether they were for us or against us, to cast their lot with us and against Russia.

We did not realize that to millions of these people the difference between Soviet dictatorship and the dictatorship under which they presently live is not very great. We did not realize that in some regions of Asia it is the Communist Party that has identified itself with the so-called reform program, the other parties being mere instruments for keeping a ruling class in power. We did not realize that the choice between democracy and communism is not, in the eyes of millions of illiterates, the critical choice it is for us.

We forgot that democracy in many lands is an empty word; that the appeal is hollow when made to illiterate people living at the subsistence level. We asked them to furnish staging grounds for a military operation whose outcome, in their eyes, had no perceptible relation to their own welfare. Those who rejected our overtures must be Communists, we said. Those who did not fall in with our military plans must be secretly aligning with Russia, we thought. This was the result of our military thinking, of our absorption in military affairs. In Asia it has brought us the lowest prestige in our existence.

The military effort has been involving more and more of our sons, more and more of our budget, more and more of our thinking. The military policy has so completely absorbed our thoughts that we have mostly forgotten that our greatest strength, our enduring power is not in guns but in ideas. Today in Asia we are identified not with ideas of freedom, but with guns. Today at home we are thinking less and less in terms of defeating communism with ideas, more and more in terms of defeating communism with military might.

The concentration on military means has helped to breed fear. It has bred fear and insecurity partly because of the horror of atomic war. But the real reason strikes deeper. In spite of our enormous expenditures, we see that Soviet imperialism continues to expand and that the expansion proceeds without the Soviets firing a shot. The free world continues to contract without a battle for its survival having been fought. It becomes apparent, as country after country falls to Soviet imperialistic ambitions, that military policy alone is a weak one; that military policy alone will end in political bankruptcy and futility. Thus fear mounts.

Fear has many manifestations. The Communist threat inside the country has been magnified and exalted far beyond its realities. Irresponsible talk by irresponsible people has fanned the flames of fear. Accusations have been loosely made. Character assassinations have become common. Suspicion has taken the place of goodwill. Once we could debate with impunity along a wide range of inquiry. Once we could safely explore to the edges of a problem, challenge orthodoxy without qualms, and run the gamut of ideas in search of solutions to perplexing problems. Once we had confidence in each other. Now there is suspicion. Innocent acts become telltale marks of disloyalty. The coincidence that an idea parallels Soviet Russia's policy for a moment of time settles an aura of suspicion around a person. Suspicion grows until only the orthodox idea is the safe one. Suspicion grows until only the person who loudly proclaims that orthodox view, or who, once having been a Communist, has been converted, is trustworthy. Competition for embracing the new orthodoxy increases. Those who are unorthodox are suspect. Everyone who does not follow the military policymakers is suspect. Everyone who voices opposition to the trend away from diplomacy and away from political tactics takes a chance. Some who are opposed are indeed "subversive." Therefore, the thundering edict commands that all who are opposed are "subversive." Fear is fanned to a fury. Good and honest men are pilloried. Character is assassinated. Fear runs rampant.

Fear even strikes at lawyers and the bar. Those accused of illegal Communist activity — all presumed innocent, of course, until found guilty — have difficulty getting reputable lawyers to defend them. Lawyers have talked with me about it. Many are worried. Some could not volunteer their services, for if they did they would lose clients and their firms would suffer. Others could not volunteer because if they did they would be dubbed "subversive" by their community and put in the same category as those they would defend. This is a dark tragedy. Fear has driven more and more men and women in all walks of life either to silence or to the folds of the orthodox. Fear has mounted — fear of losing one's job, fear of being investigated, fear of being pilloried. This fear has stereotyped our thinking, narrowed the range of free public discussion, and driven many thoughtful people to despair. This fear has even entered universities, great citadels of our spiritual strength, and corrupted them. We have the spectacle of university officials leading themselves to one of the worst witch hunts we have seen since early days.

This fear has affected the youngsters. Youth has played a very important role in our national affairs. It has usually been the oncoming generation — full of enthusiasm, full of idealism, full of energy — that has challenged its elders and the status quo. It is from this young group that the country has received much of its moral power. They have always been prone to question the stewardship of their fathers, to doubt the wisdom of traditional practices, to explode clichés, to quarrel with the management of public affairs. Youth — like the opposition party in a parliamentary system — has served a powerful role. It has cast doubts on our policies, challenged our inarticulate major premises, put the light on our prejudices, and exposed our inconsistencies. Youth has made each generation indulge in self-examination.

But a great change has taken place. Youth is still rebellious; but it is largely holding its tongue. There is the fear of being labeled a "subversive" if one departs from the orthodox party line. That charge — if leveled against a young man or young woman — may have profound effects. It may ruin a youngster's business or professional career. No one wants a Communist in his organization nor anyone who is suspect. And so the lips of the younger generation have become more and more sealed. Repression of ideas has taken the place of debate. There may not be a swelling crowd of converts to the orthodox, military view. But the voice of the opposition is more and more stilled; and youth, the mainstay in early days of the revolt against orthodoxy, is largely immobilized.

This pattern of orthodoxy that is shaping our thinking has dangerous implications. No one man, no one group can have the answer to the many perplexing problems that today confront the management of world affairs. The scene is a troubled and complicated one. The problems require the pooling of many ideas, the exposure of different points of view, the hammering out in public

discussions of the pros and cons of this policy or of that.

There are few who know first hand the conditions in the villages of Asia, the South Pacific, South America, and Africa. There are few who really know the powerful forces operating from the grass roots in those areas — forces that are reflected in the attitudes of the men who head up the governments in those countries. But unless we know those attitudes, we cannot manage intelligently. Unless we know, we will waste our energies and our resources. Unless we know, we are not in position to win even political alliances of an enduring nature. Unless we are eager to know, unless we invite a flood of information on these problems, unless we encourage every avenue of approach to them, we will live and act in ignorance.

There are those who think that our present policy toward Asia will lead to disaster — for us. There are those who believe that in Asia we are fast becoming the symbol of what the people of Asia fear and hate. There are those who believe that the most effective bases we can get in Asia are bases in the hearts of Asia's millions, not bases on their lands. There are those who believe that we must substitute a political for a military strategy in Asia; that when there is a cease-fire in Korea, we must make a political settlement with Red China; that if we apply to China the attitude we are now brilliantly exploiting in Yugoslavia, we can manage to make Soviet imperialism crumble. There are those who are deeply opposed, many of whom put that issue beyond the pale of discussion. There are even some who make the crucial test of one's loyalty or sanity his acceptance or rejection of our present policy toward Asia.

The question of our Asian policy illustrates the need for a wide range of free public discussion. Asia poses probably the most critical issues of the day. Certain it is that if Asia, like China, is swept into the political orbit of Soviet Russia, the Soviets will then command or be able to immobilize

—— *the bulk of the people of the world*
—— *the bulk of the wealth of the world.*

If that happens, it is doubtful if we, with all our atomic bombs, could even win a war.

The great danger of this period is not inflation, nor the national debt, nor atomic warfare. The great, the critical danger is that we will so limit or narrow the range of permissible discussion and permissible thought that we will become victims of the orthodox school. If we do, we will lose flexibility. We will lose the capacity for expert management. We will then become wedded to a few techniques, to a few devices. They will define our policy and at the same time limit our ability to alter or modify it. Once we narrow the range of thought and discussion, we will surrender a great deal of our power. We will become like the man on the toboggan who can ride it but who can neither steer it nor stop it.

The mind of man must always be free. The strong society is one that sanctions and encourages freedom of thought and expression. When there is that freedom, a nation has resiliency and adaptability. When freedom of expression is supreme, a nation will keep its balance and stability. Our real power is our spiritual strength, and that spiritual strength stems from our civil liberties. If we are true to our traditions, if we are tolerant of a whole market place of ideas, we will always be strong. Our weakness grows when we become intolerant of opposing ideas, depart from our standards of civil liberties, and borrow the policeman's philosophy from the enemy we detest.

That has been the direction of our drift. . . . The demands of orthodoxy already have begun to sap our strength — and to deprive us of power. One sees it from far-off Asia. From Asia one sees an America that is losing its humanity, its idealism, and its Christian character. From Asia one sees an America that is strong and rich and powerful, and yet crippled and ineffective because of its limited vision.

When we view this problem full face, we are following the American tradition. The times demand a renaissance in freedom of thought and freedom of expression, a renaissance that will end the orthodoxy that threatens to devitalize us.

———————◆———————

It is often easier to fight for principles than to live up to them.
ADLAI STEVENSON, speech to American Legion, New York, August 1952

28.

Charles B. Marshall: The Limits of Power Politics

One of the perennial problems in American foreign policy has been the role of principles — mainly moral ones — in the making of decisions in this area. The issue may be stated thus: Should foreign policy be based on concrete political realities, or should it be guided by normative considerations, i.e., considerations of what ought to be rather than what is? The question became especially important during the Cold War period, when America's overseas commitments were worldwide and foreign problems became more intricate and sensitive than ever before. There was much public discussion of the matter in the early 1950s, and Charles Marshall of the State Department's Policy Planning staff addressed himself to it in an article published in March 1952, part of which is reprinted here. The article was originally titled "The Nature of Foreign Policy."

Source: *Bulletin,* March 17, 1952.

THE WORLD SITUATION concerning us in the recent past and the present has been characterized by five main elements.

The first is the result of complex historic changes, notably two world wars. A falling away in power among several nations once of primary greatness has occurred. This leaves two states of first magnitude, each with a great geographic span and great resources of power. One of these is our country.

The second relates to the situation of the other main element in this bipolar world of power, the Soviet Union. . . .

As the third element, I cite the climate of intimidation and fear in much of the world resulting from the circumstance that the Soviet Union has great military forces, either under direct control or amenable to its purposes, and that these forces are deployed along a huge span bearing on northern and central Europe, the Mediterranean area, the Middle East, Southeast Asia, and Japan.

Fourth, the dislocation of economic patterns and the exhaustion and demoralization of peoples in consequence of invasion, occupation, and oppression in World War II have created situations affording special opportunities for Soviet communism working within other countries as a conspiratorial force in the service of the Soviet rulers.

Fifth, the weakening of old restraints in Africa, the Middle East, and East Asia, and the impulse to wayward use of freedom among peoples unaccustomed to the usages of responsibility and preoccupied with redressing old grievances, real or fancied, have created opportunities for the Soviet Union, alert as it is to the quest of advantage in the troubles of others.

In these circumstances our endeavor has been along four general lines.

First, we have sought to develop stronger situations in the areas where the choices made by the peoples and governments in the great confrontation coincide with ours.

We have done this so as to relieve the sense of anxiety — and with it the intimidatory power of the Kremlin — among the nations disposed to go along with us. In this category I put our alliances, military and economic assistance to our allies, and our efforts to return our former enemies to full relationships with other nations.

Second, we have sought to insure that the areas where the crisis of politics is sharpest — the areas of contest, such as Southeast Asia, the Middle East, and the Arab areas — shall not be lost.

Third, we have sought to exercise leadership in working toward the ideas of responsibility and peaceful adjustment in contradistinction to the Soviet pattern of turmoil and conflict. This aim enlightens our attitude of trying to combine responsibility with new-found freedom among the Middle Eastern and the Southeast Asian countries. It reflects itself in our support of the United Nations pattern, in our confrontation of aggression in Korea, and in our attempts to bring about a system of arms limitation that will not reward faithless performance.

Fourth, we have sought to steer away from the tragedy of another world war.

I am referring here, not to objectives divided into neat categories distinct from each other but to concurrent phases of a process. That sounds very bureaucratic, but I do not know how better to convey the idea that in reality these things do not have such nice separateness as they seem to have when one talks or writes about them. These interrelated aims tend in part to support each other, and in part they also tend to contradict each other.

For example, at a certain point the pace of generating military strength may run counter to the requirements for a sound economic basis among our allies. In another instance, the effort at countering aggression might be carried to lengths that bear against the aim to avoid a general war. In still another, the impulse to deal sympathetically

with the aspirations of a people new to freedom and not adjusted to its obligations may run counter to the economic necessities of another country which is allied with us or to the strategic necessities of our allies and ourselves. Again, trying to help with the military needs of one area may require the diversion of arms and supplies from others who also need them.

Such are the dilemmas that arise when our power is not sufficient for doing all the things we want to do. . . .

As an accountable government, our government must stay within the limits permitted by public opinion. To the degree that unrealistic notions about what is feasible are factors in public opinion, unnecessary limits are imposed on the scope of action in foreign affairs, and rigidities harmful to our true interests result. This is borne constantly upon the mind of anyone having responsibilities in the making of foreign policy.

Several things occur to me as sources of the expectation of complete efficacy.

One of them is the consciousness of an extraordinarily successful past. The diplomatic course in the evolution from a colonial beachhead to a power of highest magnitude was one of matchless performance. Just as a man may lose his perspectives in calling up his departed youth, it is all too easy for us to lose a sense of proportion about our national problems by harking back to what we did when horizons were open and distance and the balance of power afforded us a shield.

Another influence I might call faith in engineering. That stems from our natural pride in the physical development of our country. Popular tradition treasures the idea that in the realm of creation all things are possible to those who will them. The margins available to us have made this almost true so far as the development of our own country is concerned.

Some of the popular ideas derived from science reflect this same material optimism.

I think these are due not so much to the leaders of science themselves as to the popular interpreters of scientific achievement. From them we get the notion that cumulative knowledge can solve anything and that every problem is by definition solvable. Whatever may be the validity of this notion in the material relations which are the field of science, an error comes in trying to apply it as a universal.

Another contributing circumstance is that so much of foreign policy now stems from legislation. Legislation is law, law is to be obeyed, and an objective expressed in law is bound to be achieved. So goes the notion. This idea bears particularly on congressional expectations in relation to foreign aid. The Congress has written into foreign aid legislation as conditions upon recipients many purposes whose consummation is devoutly to be wished. Some of these are such that they could be realized only in considerable spans of time and under government with great margins of political power derived from energized and purposeful public support. The lack of such conditions in Europe is the heart of the difficulty. I find incredible the idea that phrases enacted by one country's legislature can *ipso facto* solve problems, the solution of which requires redressing the factors of political power in another country.

This topic came up the other day in a conversation with a friend of mine who serves very ably in the House of Representatives. He was perturbed at the lag among European nations in realizing some of the domestic and international reforms prescribed by the Congress in the foreign aid legislation. I commented along the same line as I have spoken here. He agreed with me. Then he added that the Congress would have to write the conditions tighter next time. Thus runs the endless faith in the compulsiveness of law.

Besides faith in making laws, let me mention faith in advertising. Where a perfume

is marketed, not only for its odor but also as a guarantee of domestic bliss; where automobiles are sold as means to capture the esteem of neighbors as well as means of transport; and where life insurance is offered, not only as protection but also as a help for insomnia, it is natural to demand of foreign policy not only that it should handle the problems at hand but also that it should lead to a transfiguration of history.

This idea and all its implications are fit to be spurned. I shudder whenever I hear anyone refer to "selling" our foreign policy. Let me say for my Planning Staff colleagues and for myself that we regard foreign policy not as a commodity but as a responsibility, the American public not as our customers but as our masters, and ourselves not as salesmen but as stewards.

I spoke along these lines recently to a very able group of businessmen visiting the State Department, Sloan Foundation Fellows from the Massachusetts Institute of Technology. One of them commented that by disclosing its foreign policy too much in terms of moral purposes rather than in terms of actual problems to be handled within practical limits of capability, the government itself encouraged the tendency that I was decrying.

That was a good point. I was reminded of the story that at the Battle of New Orleans, General Jackson, seeing that the targets were being missed, ordered his artillerymen to elevate the guns a little lower. That counsel applies here.

As one other influence, a very important one, giving rise to the expectation of perfect performance, I shall cite the confusion of force and power.

By force I mean, first, the capacity to transmit energy and so to expend it as to do vital harm to a foe; and second, the deterrent, compulsive effect exerted by the existence of this capacity. The capacity for force is only one of many elements in a nation's power reservoir. The others pertain to its economic strength, the internal integrity of its political position, the degree of confidence and goodwill which it commands abroad, and many other factors.

A nation's intentions and its power interact on each other. What we seek is in part determined by what we can do. What we can do is determined in part by what we are after. Furthermore, our own aims and power acting as functions of each other are in an interactive relation with adversary intentions and capabilities, which also relate to each other as interdependent variables.

Foreign affairs are a complex business. Gross errors result in the attempt to treat them on the basis of the misleading notion that all the problems of power can be reduced to the nice simplicity of calculations of force. Wars occur when nations seek to impose their wills by effecting drastic changes in the ratios of power through radical action in the factors of force. The force factors are susceptible of precision in military planning. The elements are concrete. The speeds of ships, their capabilities for carrying men and cargo, the distances, the fuel requirements of planes and tanks, and the fire power of divisions, and so on are known factors.

The military planning process, insofar as it relates to the ponderables of real or hypothetical campaigns, turns out tidy and complete results. I do not mean that battles and campaigns are fought according to preconceived schedules. I mean only that insofar as advance planning is employed in the military field, the quotients are precise, the columns are even, and the conclusions concrete. Furthermore, within the time and space limits of a campaign, the problem of force can be brought to an absolute solution. It really is possible to achieve the surrender of all of an enemy's forces or to eliminate armed resistance in a particular place for a particular time.

I speak here in no sense of professional disdain for military methods. I have served more of my life as a staff officer in the Army than in the line of foreign policy. I recognize the utility and necessity of military methods of thinking for military purposes. I am aware also of their limitations for other purposes.

It is easy for the unwary to jump to a fallacious conclusion that if all human affairs were laid out with the precision of military plans, then all problems could be brought to as complete solution as can the problem of force in the conduct of a victorious military campaign. This is the sort of thing one gets to when one tries to find the solution of all of the nation's problems in the world, instead of taking the historically realistic view that the job is one of managing the problems, not of getting rid of them.

It is only a few steps from the notion of solution to the notion of employing force as a solvent. This is an easy fallacy for those souls anxious for history to be tidy and all conclusions certain. The exercise of force, however, is only an incident. The problems of power are endless. Wars only occur. Politics endures.

Some of my colleagues who bore with me as I tried out these comments thought I discounted too heavily the qualitative importance of objectives in foreign policy and reflected too somber an outlook. Let me make the proportions clear.

I do not disparage the importance of objectives. Only in the light of ultimate purposes can one know how to proceed problem by problem in this field. Moreover, I do not believe that good is forever beyond reach, but I am sure that the way to it is difficult and long.

The young Gladstone was advised by his mentor that politics was an unsatisfactory business and that he would have to learn to accept imperfect results. That advice has wisdom for the conduct of a foreign policy.

The never-ending dilemmas inherent in measuring what we would like to do against what we can do impose great moral burdens. These are beyond the capacity of some individuals to bear. Sometimes they become intolerable for whole societies. The rebellion against that burden sometimes takes the form of an abdication of will, and relief is sought in a passive fatalism about the problems of national existence. Again the rebellion may take the form of resorting to the counsel of violence as the solvent for the difficulties and restraints which life imposes. In either form, the rejection is a rejection of life itself, for life imposes on nations, as on men, the obligation to strive without despair even though the way may be long and the burdens heavy.

29.

John Foster Dulles: A Policy of Instant Retaliation

Most of the policies (and also the slogans) associated with John Foster Dulles' tenure of office as secretary of state — he served under Eisenhower from 1953 until shortly before his death in 1959 — were adumbrated in statements and articles by him in the year before he entered the Cabinet. "Brinkmanship," "instant and massive retaliation," and "liberation of captive peoples" were all phrases that Dulles had used to try to express his conception of a more effective foreign policy than had obtained (he believed) under President Truman. The basis of Dulles' policy was unyielding opposition to the Soviet system, which, he felt, implied not only containing Russian power but also "rolling it back." In "A Policy of Boldness," reprinted here in part, Dulles indicated the general approach he would take to foreign affairs.

Source: *Life*, May 19, 1952.

Soviet Communism confronts our nation with its gravest peril. To meet its long-term strategy of encirclement and strangulation, we have adopted a series of emergency measures which are fantastically costly not only in money but in their warping of our American way of life.

No one would begrudge the cost of what we are doing if, in fact, it was adequate and was ending the peril, and if there was no better way. Actually, our policies are *inadequate* in scope. They are *not* ending the peril. There *is* a better way.

The costs of our present policies are perilously high in money, in freedom, and in friendships.

The Administration's "security policies" would this year cost us, in money, about 60 billion, of which about 99 percent goes for military purposes and for equipment (which will quickly become obsolete and demand replacement indefinitely). Such gigantic expenditures unbalance our budget and require taxes so heavy that they discourage incentive. They so cheapen the dollar that savings, pensions, and Social Security reserves have already lost much of their value.

What is worse, this concentration on military matters is — to use George Washington's words — "inauspicious to liberty." It leads to encroachments on civil rights and transfers from the civilian to the military decisions which profoundly affect our domestic life and our foreign relations.

We are also rapidly expending our friendships and prestige in the world. Increasing numbers turn away from our policies as too militaristic, too costly, too erratic and too inconclusive for them to follow. Our far-flung, extravagant, and surreptitious military projects are frightening many who feel that we are conducting a private feud with Russia, which may endanger them, rather than performing a public service for peace.

All these are, indeed, perilously high costs.

There are times when nations have to pay such costs to win a victory and end a peril. We know that from the last two World Wars. But today our policies are not designed to win a victory conclusively.

If you will think back over the past six years, you will see that our policies have largely involved emergency action to try to "contain" Soviet Communism by checking it here or blocking it there. We are not working, sacrificing, and spending in order to be able to live *without* this peril — but to be able to live *with* it, presumably forever. . . .

A nation with our resourcefulness should be able to devise better policies. But we cannot take it for granted that better policies will automatically result from a change of Administration. Conceivably policies could be worse rather than better.

In Korea, for all our failure to deter attack, we did respond nobly when the attack came. President Truman's decision that the United States should go to the defense of the Korean Republic was courageous, righteous, and in the national interest.

In Europe, thanks in great part to the commanding presence of General Eisenhower, we are promoting a defense community with political and military unity.

In Japan, General MacArthur's loftily conceived occupation policies provided the foundation for a good peace, and we added sound security arrangements with Japan, Australia, New Zealand, and the Philippines.

There are a few Republicans — and some Democrats — who would turn their backs on all the world's problems and wrap the United States in some magically "impregnable" isolation.

Such policies would really give 100 percent cooperation to the Soviet Communist effort to encircle and isolate us, as a preliminary to a final assault. Once Asia, Europe, Africa, and probably South America were consolidated against us, our plight would be desperate.

The mere fact that such a retreat is seriously discussed shows that the frustration of past hopes is inducing a somewhat morbid state of mind which minimizes our assets pathetically and exaggerates those of Soviet Communism ludicrously. It assumes we are *lacking* strength rather than that we are *misusing* it.

Looked at in any impartial way, we are the world's greatest and strongest power. The only commodity in which we seem deficient is faith. In all material things we have a productivity far exceeding that of Russia: our steel production is about three and one half times that of the Soviet Union, and in aluminum, petroleum, and electric power our superiority is even greater. Our people have a standard of education, an inventive talent, and a technical skill unmatched by any of the peoples under Soviet rule.

On the Soviet side a dozen people in the Kremlin are attempting to rule 800 million human beings — while trying to conquer more. All except a privileged few work under conditions which sternly deny them the "pursuit of happiness." Within Russia itself the discontent can be judged by the 15 million prisoners in forced labor camps — more than twice the membership of the Soviet Communist Party. Even the leaders are suspicious of each other as each wonders whether the other plots his purge.

In satellite countries, such as Poland and Czechoslovakia, the situation is worse, because there it is aggravated by the repression of patriotism. Leaders in the Czech Communist Party have been liquidated one after another. In China the party tries to frighten the people into subjection by staging wholesale public executions.

All of this reflects not strength but weakness. The "dictatorship of the proletariat" is like other tyrannies that went before. They may present a formidable exterior, but they are "like unto whited sepulchers, which indeed appear beautiful outward, but are within full of dead men's bones and of all uncleanness."

The free should not be numbed by the sight of this vast graveyard of human liberties. It is the despots who should feel haunted. They, not we, should fear the future.

As we stop fretting and start thinking, the first problem to tackle is the strictly military one. It comes in the form of a paradox: for we must seek a military formula more effective than any devised to date — that we may no longer be so overridingly preoccupied with purely military necessity.

The dimensions of the problem are plain: at least 3 million Soviet soldiers regularly under arms, another 3 million to 4 million in the Chinese Red armies. These forces, poised in a central area could strike with massive power east, south or west at any one of more than 20 nations along the 20,000-mile boundary which runs from near Alaska down by Japan, through East Asia and South Asia, along the Middle and Near East to Europe and up through Central Europe to the North Cape. By the very existence of this dangerous menace, free governments are intimidated; creative effort is paralyzed, and local Communist parties can exploit mass fear of the Red armies' advance. Thus do these armies serve as a savagely effective political weapon.

Our military program, vast as it is, falls far short of meeting this threat. . . . *There*

is one solution and only one: that is for the free world to develop the will and organize the means to retaliate instantly against open aggression by Red armies, so that, if it occurred anywhere, we could and would strike back where it hurts, by means of our choosing.

The principle involved is as simple as that of our municipal police forces. We do not station armed guards at every house to stop aggressors — that would be economic suicide — but we deter potential aggressors by making it probable that if they aggress, they will lose in punishment more than they can gain by aggression. . . .

Today atomic energy, coupled with strategic air and sea power, provides the community of free nations with vast new possibilities of organizing a community power to stop open aggression before it starts and reduce, to the vanishing point, the risk of general war. So far these weapons are merely part of national arsenals for use in fighting general war when it has come. If that catastrophe occurs, it will be because we have allowed these new and awesome forces to become the ordinary killing tools of the soldier when, in the hands of the statesmen, they could serve as effective political weapons in defense of the peace.

This does not mean that old ways of defending the peace should be abandoned where they can still be efficacious. The United States should maintain a strong military force of a kind befitting our responsibilities. Western Europe, which has historically demonstrated great military power, should promptly redevelop that potential, if only to restore its own self-confidence and sense of self-respect. Everywhere free nations should have ability to resist attack from within so that they will dare to put up sturdy resistance to Communist inroads.

But these old methods are quite inadequate to match the 20,000-mile scope of the present military peril; and if we strain to make them adequate, we shall succumb to the twin evils of militarism and bankruptcy. New methods of defense are needed to save the free nations from the dilemma, which present policies impose, of choosing between murder from without or suicide from within.

That is the enlightened and effective way to proceed. It is a way that we can afford to live with, and until there is effective international disarmament, it is the way we cannot afford to live without.

Once the free world has established a military defense, it can undertake what has been too long delayed — a political offense.

It is ironic and wrong that we who believe in the boundless power of human freedom should so long have accepted a static political role. It is also ironic and wrong that we who so proudly profess regard for the spiritual should rely so utterly on material defenses while the avowed materialists have been waging a winning war with social ideas, stirring humanity everywhere.

There are three truths which we need to recall in these times:

1. The dynamic prevails over the static; the active over the passive. We were from the beginning a vigorous, confident people, born with a sense of destiny and of mission. That is why we have grown from a small and feeble nation to our present stature in the world.

2. Nonmaterial forces are more powerful than those that are merely material. Our dynamism has always been moral and intellectual rather than military or material. During most of our national life we had only a small military establishment and during the last century we had to borrow money abroad to develop our expanding economy. But we always generated political, social and industrial ideas and projected them abroad where they were more explosive than dynamite.

3. There is a moral or natural law not made by man which determines right and wrong and in the long run only those who conform to that law will escape disaster.

This law has been trampled by the Soviet rulers, and for that violation they can and should be made to pay. This will happen when we ourselves keep faith with that law in our practical decisions of policy.

We should let these truths work in and through us. We should be *dynamic,* we should use *ideas* as weapons; and these ideas should conform to *moral* principles. That we do this is right, for it is the inevitable expression of a faith — and I am confident that we still do have a faith. But it is also expedient in defending ourselves against an aggressive, imperialistic despotism. For even the present lines will not hold unless our purpose goes beyond confining Soviet Communism within its present orbit.

Consider the situation of the 20-odd non-Western nations which are next door to the Soviet world. These exposed nations feel that they have been put in the "expendable" class, condemned in perpetuity to be the ramparts against which the angry waves of Soviet Communism will constantly hurl themselves. They are expected to live precariously, permanently barred from areas with which they normally should have trade, commerce, and cultural relations. They cannot be enthusiastic about policies which would merely perpetuate so hazardous and uncomfortable a position. Today they live close to despair because the United States, the historic leader of the forces of freedom, seems dedicated to the negative policy of "containment" and "stalemate."

As a matter of fact, some highly competent work is being done, at one place or another, to promote liberation. Obviously such activities do not lend themselves to public exposition. But liberation from the yoke of Moscow will not occur for a very long time, and courage in neighboring lands will not be sustained, *unless the United States makes it publicly known that it wants and expects liberation to occur.* The mere statement of that wish and expectation would change, in an electrifying way, the mood of the captive peoples. It would put heavy new burdens on the jailers and create new opportunities for liberation.

Here are some specific acts which we could take:

1. We could make it clear, on the highest authority of the President and the Congress, that U.S. policy seeks as one of its peaceful goals the eventual restoration of genuine independence in the nations of Europe and Asia now dominated by Moscow, and that we will not be a party to any "deal" confirming the rule of Soviet despotism over the alien peoples which it now dominates.

2. We could welcome the creation in the free world of political "task forces" to develop a freedom program for each of the captive nations. Each group would be made up of those who are proved patriots, who have practical resourcefulness, and who command confidence and respect at home and abroad.

3. We could stimulate the escape from behind the Iron Curtain of those who can help to develop these programs.

4. The activities of the Voice of America and such private committees as those for Free Europe and Free Asia could be coordinated with these freedom programs. The agencies would be far more effective if given concrete jobs to do.

5. We could coordinate our economic, commercial, and cultural relations with the freedom programs, cutting off or licensing intercourse as seemed most effective from time to time.

6. We could end diplomatic relations with present governments which are in fact only puppets of Moscow, if and when that would promote the freedom programs.

7. We could seek to bring other free nations to unite with us in proclaiming, in a great new Declaration of Independence, our policies toward the captive nations.

We do not want a series of bloody uprisings and reprisals. There can be peaceful separation from Moscow, as Tito showed, and enslavement can be made so unprofitable that the master will let go his grip. Such results will not come to pass overnight. But we can know, for history proves, that the spirit of patriotism burns unquenched in Poles, Czechs, Hungarians, Rumanians, Bulgarians, Chinese, and others, and we can be confident that within two, five, or ten years substantial parts of the present captive world can peacefully regain national independence. That will mark the beginning of the end of Soviet despotism's attempt at world conquest.

The positive policies we have outlined would create new and refreshing conditions of opportunity. Political aggression can then be ended. The local Communist parties would lose much of their vigor and belligerence as the Soviet Communist Party became ever more preoccupied with its own "home work" of coping with the growing restiveness of the captive peoples. The free governments, no longer intimidated by the Red armies and heartened by their own growing military power, would have the self-confidence and the capacity to deal ruggedly with threats to domestic tranquillity. The free nations could then move ahead to creative accomplishments that would restore the waning prestige of freedom. . . .

Only a united America can unify the free world.

We cannot provide effective leadership if we ourselves are so divided that the President cannot get his treaties ratified, or if he cannot get the money to implement his foreign policies, or if foreign governments know that the President's policies may be reversed by the next congressional or presidential election.

I can testify, from personal knowledge, that the President and the Secretary of

State really want bi-partisanship and congressional cooperation in foreign policy. I know also that leading Republicans and Democrats in and out of Congress accept the need of working together in these dangerous times.

Cooperation, however, requires enough foresight and initiative on the part of the Executive so that his representatives can sit down and talk out *in advance* with congressional leaders of both parties what the United States should do. We had that in relation to the Japanese Peace Treaty and the Pacific Security Treaties. We could have it in relation to the kind of policies which are proposed here, because then the initiative would be ours. But we cannot have an honest meeting of Executive-congressional and Democratic-Republican minds so long as the Administration accepts a purely defensive role in its foreign policy. Such a role means that we are constantly surprised and kept off balance — and enormously preoccupied — by a series of cleverly timed and varied Soviet offensives spotted neatly around the globe. These have condemned us to improvised reactions, which at times have been magnificent, as in the case of the Berlin air lift and some aspects of Korea. But our policy makers have not found policies which would put us in command of the situation. Under these conditions domestic cooperation can only be of the "shotgun" variety. That is not good enough to stand the strains and stresses of these dangerous days.

30.

Eleanor Roosevelt: Defense of American Territorial Policies

The battle lines of the Cold War were drawn up not only in Korea, where the war entered its third year in the summer of 1952, but also in the world's underdeveloped and emerging nations, where the conflict was more ideological than military. Both of the Cold War opponents — the United States and the Soviet Union — offered aid and assistance to the new countries, and they also traded charges about the other's offers. The American position was that Russian help was intended to subvert the new countries and to bring them into the Communist sphere, while the Russians claimed that American aid was an aspect of a new kind of imperialism and colonialism. The Russian charges were answered by Mrs. Eleanor Roosevelt in the following remarks to a committee of the United Nations on November 24, 1952. The President's widow was serving at the time as U.S. representative to the General Assembly.

Source: *Bulletin*, December 29, 1952, pp. 1032-1033.

I should like to express the appreciation of my delegation for the serious and responsible way in which most of the members of this committee have conducted this debate on the self-determination of peoples — a matter on which practically all of us have very strong feelings. We are also appreciative of the interest and understanding which our amendments to resolution A have so generally received.

Unfortunately, during the course of this debate, an effort has been made by certain delegations to distort and discredit, not only our motives in this debate but also U.S. policies, particularly with regard to the territories under our administration. So familiar and so stereotyped have such attacks become that we who have heard them over and over again are inclined to react to them much as we do to a bit of disagreeable weather. However, so that the principal misstatements may not remain unchallenged in the records, and so that those who are not familiar with these misstatements may not be misled, I should like to introduce a few facts to set the record straight.

The distinguished representative of the Belorussian Soviet Socialist Republic at our meeting of November 13 spoke at some length on what he called the "deplorable conditions" in Puerto Rico. Among other things, he alleged that the national culture had been annihilated. This is indeed a strange charge when one considers that after fifty-four years of U.S. administration, less than 25 percent of the people know English well. While English is taught in the schools, Spanish is the predominant language. The preamble to the 1952 constitution of the Commonwealth of Puerto Rico, written by the Puerto Rican people and ratified by them in a popular referendum, "recognizes as one of the determining factors in their life the coexistence in Puerto Rico of the two great cultures of the American hemisphere." This duality of culture, with full freedom of choice, is expressly recognized in Puerto Rican political life. For example, there is a qualification that a member of the legislative assembly must be able to read and write either the Spanish or the English language.

The distinguished representative of Belorussia alleged that the economy of Puerto Rico was adapted solely to the needs of the United States. It is hard to reconcile such a statement with the fact that the Puerto Ricans have freely chosen to retain the same tariff and trade protections as enjoyed by states of the United States and that under their own economic development program they have experienced over the past ten years a notable expansion of local industry and enterprise. He charged that large numbers of Puerto Ricans had been deprived of their lands. Not only is this a gross distortion of the facts but he said nothing of the agrarian reform introduced in 1941. This was undertaken through the establishment of the Land Authority to enforce the law prohibiting corporate ownership of over 500 acres of land and to aid *agregados,* or landless peasants, to acquire land on which to build homes.

He referred to certain statistics on the extent of unemployment. Unemployment in Puerto Rico is admittedly a serious problem, but he failed to point out that it is, in fact, a result of improved conditions and consequent population growth and that the Puerto Ricans are, with our help, overcoming the problem. This is illustrated by the fact that the number of persons employed in 1951 increased by 20,000 over the previous year.

The representative of Belorussia also made some charges concerning the average annual wage in Puerto Rico. If he had based himself on the official information supplied to the United Nations by my government instead of on a magazine article, he would have given quite a different impression. For example, on page 45 of our latest report on Puerto Rico it is stated that the average wage rate in all industries in Puerto Rico in 1950 (the most recent year for which statistics have been supplied) was 44 cents an hour. While this is not a high rate when compared with wages in the United States, it is much higher than the figure quoted by the representative of Belorussia, and it compares favorably with wage rates in the region. Furthermore, as the report also shows, wage rates in Puerto Rico have in almost all cases been steadily rising from year to year, while between 1948 and 1950 the consumer's price index rose only about 1 percent, a situation which many of us might envy.

Similarly, in the fields of health and education, where the Puerto Rican and U.S. governments made no effort to hide the difficult problems that exist, the representative of Belorussia, by ignoring the substantial progress made in overcoming these problems, left no doubt that the purpose of his comments was to mislead and confuse.

As for his reference to the new Puerto Rican constitution, it may be that his failure to understand the free democratic processes by which it was drawn up by elected representatives of the Puerto Rican people and ratified in a popular referendum by an overwhelming majority is due to a lack of personal familiarity with such democratic processes.

With regard to the Trust Territory of the Pacific Islands administered by the United States under a trusteeship agreement with the United Nations, it is scarcely necessary to deal here with the wholesale charges made by the distinguished representatives of Belorussia and the Ukraine. These charges have been made before by Soviet representatives in the Trusteeship Council and have been answered fully and frankly by U.S. representatives. It is perhaps sufficient to point out that after examining the most recent report on the Pacific Islands, the Trusteeship Council, with the sole exception of the Soviet representative, "noted with approval the progress made in the political,

economic, social, and educational fields during the period under review."

In closing, I cannot help commenting on the bitter irony in hearing certain representatives among us support the self-determination of peoples, when we are convinced that the system they represent is devoted to the systematic denial of that principle. One of the ideas expressed by Secretary Acheson in his opening statement to this Assembly is highly pertinent to this aspect of our present discussion. I refer to that passage in which he said:

The unfortunate fact is that we cannot approach this problem, or indeed any other problem before this Assembly, without being mindful of the events that are taking place in another part of the world. There, whole nations have been swallowed up and submerged by a new colonialism. Others have been reduced to a state of servile dependence. The tragic events behind this dark boundary not only are in stark contrast with the evolutionary process toward self-government [in non-self-governing territories] . . . but they are so fraught with danger to all of us that we can never afford to forget them.

Thus, in our present discussion of the self-determination of peoples, we must not forget the vast populations who have been deprived of their self-determination. I am sure none of us will be deceived for a moment by the pretended support of this principle by the representatives of a movement which purges all those who seek any form of self-determination which differs from that dictated by their leaders.

There are only two kinds of wars — Indian wars and coalition wars. All wars of the future are coalition wars and we have to learn how to fight them.
ALFRED GRUENTHER

31.

Harry S. Truman: Veto of the McCarran-Walter Immigration Act

The McCarran-Walter Immigration Act of 1952 was essentially a restatement of the immigrant quota system set up by the Johnson-Reed Act of 1924. But the new act also made provision for keeping suspected subversives out of the country and for deporting "dangerous" aliens and even some naturalized citizens. President Truman disapproved of the bill for the reasons stated in his veto message of June 25, 1952, part of which is reprinted here. The veto was overridden on June 26 by the House and on June 27 by the Senate.

Source: 82 Congress, 2 Session, House Document No. 520.

I RETURN HEREWITH, without my approval, H. R. 5678, the proposed Immigration and Nationality Act.

In outlining my objections to this bill, I want to make it clear that it contains certain provisions that meet with my approval. This is a long and complex piece of legislation. It has 164 separate sections, some with more than 40 subdivisions. It presents a difficult problem of weighing the good against the bad and arriving at a judgment on the whole.

H. R. 5678 is an omnibus bill which would revise and codify all of our laws relating to immigration, naturalization, and nationality. A general revision and modernization of these laws unquestionably is needed and long overdue, particularly with respect to immigration. But this bill would not provide us with an immigration policy adequate for the present world situation. Indeed, the bill, taking all its provisions together, would be a step backward and not a step forward. In view of the crying need for reform in the field of immigration, I deeply regret that I am unable to approve H. R. 5678.

In recent years our immigration policy has become a matter of major national concern. Long dormant questions about the effect of our immigration laws now assume first-rate importance. What we do in the field of immigration and naturalization is vital to the continued growth and internal development of the United States — to the economic and social strength of our country — which is the core of the defense of the free world. Our immigration policy is equally, if not more, important to the conduct of our foreign relations and to our responsibilities of moral leadership in the struggle for world peace.

In one respect, this bill recognizes the great international significance of our immigration and naturalization policy, and takes a step to improve existing laws. All racial bars to naturalization would be removed, and at least some minimum immigration quota would be afforded to each of the free nations of Asia.

I have long urged that racial or national barriers to naturalization be abolished. This was one of the recommendations in my civil rights message to the Congress on Feb. 2,

1948. On Feb. 19, 1951, the House of Representatives unanimously passed a bill to carry it out.

But now this most desirable provision comes before me embedded in a mass of legislation which would perpetuate injustices of long standing against many other nations of the world, hamper the efforts we are making to rally the men of the East and West alike to the cause of freedom, and intensify the repressive and inhumane aspects of our immigration procedures. The price is too high and, in good conscience, I cannot agree to pay it.

I want all our residents of Japanese ancestry, and all our friends throughout the Far East, to understand this point clearly. I cannot take the step I would like to take and strike down the bars that prejudice has erected against them without, at the same time, establishing new discriminations against the peoples of Asia and approving harsh and repressive measures directed at all who seek a new life within our boundaries. I am sure that with a little more time and a little more discussion in this country the public conscience and the good sense of the American people will assert themselves, and we shall be in a position to enact an immigration and naturalization policy that will be fair to all.

In addition to removing racial bars to naturalization, the bill would permit American women citizens to bring their alien husbands to this country as nonquota immigrants, and enable alien husbands of resident women aliens to come in under the quota in a preferred status. These provisions would be a step toward preserving the integrity of the family under our immigration laws and are clearly desirable. . . .

But these few improvements are heavily outweighed by other provisions of the bill which retain existing defects in our laws and add many undesirable new features.

The bill would continue, practically without change, the national origins quota system, which was enacted into law in 1924

and put into effect in 1929. This quota system — always based upon assumptions at variance with our American ideals — is long since out of date and more than ever unrealistic in the face of present world conditions.

This system hinders us in dealing with current immigration problems, and is a constant handicap in the conduct of our foreign relations. As I stated in my message to Congress on March 24, 1952, on the need for an emergency program of immigration from Europe:

> Our present quota system is not only inadequate to meet present emergency needs, it is also an obstacle to the development of an enlightened and satisfactory immigration policy for the long-run future.

The inadequacy of the present quota system has been demonstrated since the end of the war, when we were compelled to resort to emergency legislation to admit displaced persons. If the quota system remains unchanged, we shall be compelled to resort to similar emergency legislation again in order to admit any substantial portion of the refugees from communism or the victims of overcrowding in Europe.

With the idea of quotas in general there is no quarrel. Some numerical limitation must be set so that immigration will be within our capacity to absorb. But the overall limitation of numbers imposed by the national origins quota system is too small for our needs today, and the country-by-country limitations create a pattern that is insulting to large numbers of our finest citizens, irritating to our allies abroad, and foreign to our purposes and ideals.

The overall quota limitation, under the law of 1924, restricted annual immigration to approximately 150,000. This was about one-seventh of 1 percent of our total population in 1920. Taking into account the growth in population since 1920, the law now allows us but one-tenth of 1 percent of our total population. And since the largest national quotas are only partly used, the number actually coming in has been in the neighborhood of one-fifteenth of 1 percent. This is far less than we must have in the years ahead to keep up with the growing needs of our nation for manpower to maintain the strength and vigor of our economy.

The greatest vice of the present quota system, however, is that it discriminates, deliberately and intentionally, against many of the peoples of the world. The purpose behind it was to cut down and virtually eliminate immigration to this country from southern and eastern Europe. A theory was invented to rationalize this objective. The theory was that in order to be readily assimilable, European immigrants should be admitted in proportion to the numbers of persons of their respective national stocks already here as shown by the census of 1920. Since Americans of English, Irish, and German descent were most numerous, immigrants of those three nationalities got the lion's share — more than two-thirds — of the total quota. The remaining third was divided up among all the other nations given quotas.

The desired effect was obtained. Immigration from the newer sources of southern and eastern Europe was reduced to a trickle. The quotas allotted to England and Ireland remained largely unused, as was intended. Total quota immigration fell to a half or a third — and sometimes even less — of the annual limit of 154,000. People from such countries as Greece or Spain or Latvia were virtually deprived of any opportunity to come here at all simply because Greeks or Spaniards or Latvians had not come here before 1920 in any substantial numbers.

The idea behind this discriminatory policy was, to put it baldly, that Americans with English or Irish names were better people and better citizens than Americans with Italian or Greek or Polish names. It was thought that people of West European origin made better citizens than Rumanians or Yugoslavs or Ukrainians or Hungarians or Balts or Austrians. Such a concept is utterly unworthy of our traditions and our ideals. It violates the great political doctrine of the Declaration of Independence that "all men are created equal." It denies the humanitarian creed inscribed beneath the Statue of Liberty proclaiming to all nations, "Give me your tired, your poor, your huddled masses yearning to breathe free." It repudiates our basic religious concepts, our belief in the brotherhood of man, and in the words of St. Paul that "there is neither Jew nor Greek, there is neither bond nor free . . . for ye are all one in Christ Jesus."

The basis of this quota system was false and unworthy in 1924. It is even worse now. At the present time this quota system keeps out the very people we want to bring in. It is incredible to me that, in this year of 1952, we should again be enacting into law such a slur on the patriotism, the capacity, and the decency of a large part of our citizenry.

Today, we have entered into an alliance, the North Atlantic Treaty, with Italy, Greece, and Turkey against one of the most terrible threats mankind has ever faced. We are asking them to join with us in protecting the peace of the world. We are helping them to build their defenses, and train their men, in the common cause. But, through this bill we say to their people: You are less worthy to come to this country than Englishmen or Irishmen; you Italians, who need to find homes abroad in the hundreds of thousands — you shall have a quota of 5,645; you Greeks, struggling to assist the helpless victims of a Communist civil war — you shall have a quota of 308; and you Turks, you are brave defenders of the Eastern flank, but you shall have a quota of only 225.

Today, we are "protecting" ourselves, as we were in 1924, against being flooded by immigrants from Eastern Europe. This is fantastic. The countries of Eastern Europe have fallen under the Communist yoke — they are silenced, fenced off by barbed wire and minefields — no one passes their borders but at the risk of his life. We do not need to be protected against immigrants from these countries — on the contrary we want to stretch out a helping hand, to save those who are brave enough to escape from barbarism, to welcome and restore them against the day when their countries will, as we hope, be free again. But this we cannot do, as we would like to do, because the quota for Poland is only 6,500, as against the 138,000 exiled Poles, all over Europe, who are asking to come to these shores; because the quota for the now subjugated Baltic countries is little more than 700 — against the 23,000 Baltic refugees imploring us to admit them to a new life here; because the quota for Rumania is only 289, and some 30,000 Rumanians, who have managed to escape the labor camps and the mass deportations of their Soviet masters, have asked our help. These are only a few examples of the absurdity, the cruelty of carrying over into this year of 1952 the isolationist limitations of our 1924 law. . . .

The time to shake off this dead weight of past mistakes is now. The time to develop a decent policy of immigration — a fitting instrument for our foreign policy and a true reflection of the ideals we stand for, at home and abroad — is now. In my earlier message on immigration, I tried to explain to the Congress that the situation we face in immigration is an emergency — that it must be met promptly. I have pointed out that in the last few years we have blazed a new trail in immigration through our displaced persons program. Through the combined efforts of the government and private agencies, working together not to keep people out but to bring qualified people in, we summoned our resources of goodwill and human feeling to meet the task. In this program we have found better techniques

to meet the immigration problems of the 1950s.

None of this fruitful experience of the last three years is reflected in this bill before me. None of the crying human needs of this time of trouble is recognized in this bill. But it is not too late. The Congress can remedy these defects, and it can adopt legislation to meet the most critical problems before adjournment.

The only consequential change in the 1924 quota system which the bill would make is to extend a small quota to each of the countries of Asia. But most of the beneficial effects of this gesture are offset by other provisions of the bill. The countries of Asia are told in one breath that they shall have quotas for their nationals and, in the next, that the nationals of the other countries, if their ancestry is as much as 50 percent Asian, shall be charged to these quotas.

It is only with respect to persons of Oriental ancestry that this invidious discrimination applies. All other persons are charged to the country of their birth. But persons with Asian ancestry are charged to the countries of Asia, wherever they may have been born or however long their ancestors have made their homes outside the land of their origin. These provisions are without justification.

I now wish to turn to the other provisions of the bill, those dealing with the qualifications of aliens and immigrants for admission, with the administration of the laws, and with problems of naturalization and nationality. In these provisions, too, I find objections that preclude my signing this bill.

The bill would make it even more difficult to enter our country. Our resident aliens would be more easily separated from homes and families under grounds of deportation, both new and old, which would specifically be made retroactive. Admission to our citizenship would be made more diffi-

YOUR NATIONALITY QUOTA IS FILLED, YOU CAN'T SPEAK ENGLISH, YOU DON'T HAVE A MARITIME UNION CARD, SO YOU CAN'T LAND HERE TO DISCOVER AMERICA

Courtesy, Lewis, "Milwaukee Journal"

Cartoon by Lewis in the "Milwaukee Journal," 1953

cult; expulsion from our citizenship would be made easier. Certain rights of native-born, first-generation Americans would be limited. All our citizens returning from abroad would be subjected to serious risk of unreasonable invasions of privacy. Seldom has a bill exhibited the distrust evidenced here for citizens and aliens alike — at a time when we need unity at home and the confidence of our friends abroad.

We have adequate and fair provisions in our present law to protect us against the entry of criminals. The changes made by the bill in those provisions would result in empowering minor immigration and consular officials to act as prosecutor, judge, and jury in determining whether acts constituting a crime have been committed. Worse, we would be compelled to exclude certain people because they have been convicted by "courts" in Communist countries that know no justice. Under this provision, no matter how construed, it would not be possible for us to admit many of the men and women who have stood up against totalitarian repression and have been punished for doing so. I do not approve of substituting

totalitarian vengeance for democratic justice. I will not extend full faith and credit to the judgments of the Communist secret police. . . .

I am asked to approve the reenactment of highly objectionable provisions now contained in the Internal Security Act of 1950 — a measure passed over my veto shortly after the invasion of South Korea. Some of these provisions would empower the attorney general to deport any alien who has engaged or has had a purpose to engage in activities "prejudicial to the public interest" or "subversive to the national security." No standards or definitions are provided to guide discretion in the exercise of powers so sweeping. To punish undefined "activities" departs from traditional American insistence on established standards of guilt. To punish an undefined "purpose" is thought control.

These provisions are worse than the infamous Alien Act of 1798, passed in a time of national fear and distrust of foreigners, which gave the President power to deport any alien deemed "dangerous to the peace and safety of the United States." Alien residents were thoroughly frightened and citizens much disturbed by that threat to liberty.

Such powers are inconsistent with our democratic ideals. Conferring powers like that upon the attorney general is unfair to him as well as to our alien residents. Once fully informed of such vast discretionary powers vested in the attorney general, Americans now would and should be just as alarmed as Americans were in 1798 over less drastic powers vested in the President.

Heretofore, for the most part, deportation and exclusion have rested upon findings of fact made upon evidence. Under this bill, they would rest in many instances upon the "opinion" or "satisfaction" of immigration or consular employees. The change from objective findings to subjective feelings is not compatible with our system of justice. The result would be to restrict or eliminate judicial review of unlawful administrative action.

The bill would sharply restrict the present opportunity of citizens and alien residents to save family members from deportation. Under the procedures of present law, the attorney general can exercise his discretion to suspend deportation in meritorious cases. In each such case, at the present time, the exercise of administrative discretion is subject to the scrutiny and approval of the Congress. Nevertheless, the bill would prevent this discretion from being used in many cases where it is now available, and would narrow the circle of those who can obtain relief from the letter of the law. This is most unfortunate, because the bill, in its other provisions, would impose harsher restrictions and greatly increase the number of cases deserving equitable relief.

Native-born American citizens who are dual nationals would be subjected to loss of citizenship on grounds not applicable to other native-born American citizens. This distinction is a slap at millions of Americans whose fathers were of alien birth.

Children would be subjected to additional risk of loss of citizenship. Naturalized citizens would be subjected to the risk of denaturalization by any procedure that can be found to be permitted under any state law or practice pertaining to minor civil-law suits. Judicial review of administrative denials of citizenship would be severely limited and impeded in many cases, and completely eliminated in others. I believe these provisions raise serious constitutional questions. Constitutionality aside, I see no justification in national policy for their adoption. . . .

Many of the aspects of the bill which have been most widely criticized in the public debate are reaffirmations or elaborations of existing statutes or administrative procedures. Time and again, examination discloses that the revisions of existing law that would be made by the bill are intended to solidify some restrictive practice of our immigration authorities, or to overrule or modify some ameliorative decision of the Supreme Court or other federal courts. By and large, the changes that would be made by the bill do not depart from the basically restrictive spirit of our existing laws — but intensify and reinforce it.

These conclusions point to an underlying condition which deserves the most careful study. Should we not undertake a reassessment of our immigration policies and practices in the light of the conditions that face us in the second half of the twentieth century? The great popular interest which this bill has created, and the criticism which it has stirred up, demand an affirmative answer. I hope the Congress will agree to a careful reexamination of this entire matter.

To assist in this complex task, I suggest the creation of a representative commission of outstanding Americans to examine the basic assumptions of our immigration policy, the quota system and all that goes with it, the effect of our present immigration and nationality laws, their administration, and the ways in which they can be brought into line with our national ideals and our foreign policy.

32.

Peter F. Drucker: Productivity Is an Attitude

*During the Second World War, and largely because of it, the U.S. economy developed
from one of scarcity to one of abundance. The enormous growth of the industrial
system, the vast increase in the gross national product, and the general spread of
affluence made America the wealthiest and most powerful nation on earth in a few
short years. One result was that for the first time European businessmen began to
look with more than passing interest on the achievements of American capitalism.
Peter Drucker described this growing interest in an article first published in
April 1952 and reprinted here.*

Source: *Nation's Business*, April 1952.

DURING THE PAST few years the American business system has been examined, probed, and dissected as no other economic system has ever been looked over.

Several thousand hand-picked experts — businessmen, technicians, educators, workers, and union officials, coming from every country of Western Europe and from almost every industry — have been touring the U.S. since 1949 to find out for themselves what causes American productivity. Organized in some 200 "productivity teams" under the Marshall Plan — and financed mostly by the funds the European governments themselves provide as their share — they have looked at foundries, textile mills, business schools, breweries, printing companies, and labor unions. And most of them have stayed long enough — some as long as nine months — to get more than a tourist's view.

Officially the program goes by the name of "Technical Assistance"; and the purpose is to find American techniques for European use. The bias toward techniques is further emphasized by the selection of the teams who normally come either from one industry, locomotive building for instance, or from one technical specialty, such as cost accounting or industrial engineering. No wonder then, that the teams arrive here expecting to find the cause of American productivity in techniques and processes, if not in gadgets. Yet, I know of no team that did not speedily discover for itself that techniques are not the really important thing and are certainly not the real cause of our productivity.

"Productivity is an attitude of mind," the report of the team from the British letterpress printing industry summed it up; and in one way or another every team has said the same. Attitude, social organization, and moral value, those, the experts from the other side report, underlie and explain America's industrial achievement.

Even in such a seemingly "technical" area as the use of machinery, the visitors see the main cause for America's lead in attitudes rather than in the abundance of capital, the lack of wartime destruction, etc. A British team investigating the making of brushes, for instance, remarks that machinery, including automatic, is being used successfully in the United States "in operations normally regarded in British practice as unsuitable for mechanization."

This difference in attitude the team credits with the major share of the enormous difference in productivity: there are only one-third more production workers in the American brush industry than there are in the British — 15,500 against 12,000 men — yet the American industry turns out almost four times as many brushes. And the American brush industry is not one of those mass-production industries organized in giant plants, which to most Europeans stand for "American productivity," but a small industry composed of small units producing a tremendous variety of products — in brief, exactly the type of industry in which most Europeans (and many Americans) are wont to attribute superiority to Europe.

Five things, in particular, impress our visitors as being fundamental and at the same time as presenting the greatest contrast to Europe:

1. *The discovery of management.* "The United States has made a major discovery — that it is management that makes the wheels go round," a successful French manufacturer summed up to me the main impressions of his team. "We are still largely organized on the belief that all a business needs is a supply of capital, after which it will run itself. In your country the basic decisions are made by men who know the business from the ground up, who consider it their main interest in life, and who got their job because of their competence. With us it is still largely the absentee-owner — a family group or a banker — who really decides; the people who run the business are rarely much more than technicians or badly paid chief clerks. As a result, business attracts the best minds in your country, and that, more than anything else, explains how you got where you are today."

Every report stresses this central importance of a management, responsible for the success of the business, familiar with it and chosen for competence. But the most glowing tribute to management and to its importance came from a group of British labor leaders: "We are convinced that it is efficient management who set the pace of productivity in American industry. . . . American trades union officials can rely on management to be sufficiently progressive." Every trade unionist on the teams comments with awe on the confidence in management's competence, fairness, and integrity that he finds among American workers and trade union leaders — a comment that strikes many American management men of my acquaintance as amusing were it not for the lurid light it casts on labor's attitude on the other side.

2. *Productivity as a social principle.* Every team believes that its own country must raise productivity to survive. Yet most of the visitors, whether labor or management men, still tend to look upon increased productivity as primarily a way to increase individual business profits. But our visitors find that we look upon profits not as the rationale of increased productivity but as the reward for the social benefits it brings with it — higher wages, cheaper prices, and more goods for the consumer. They report that managements, and successful managements, of profitable companies hardly mention "profits" when they discuss productivity but stress the duty of business to increase productivity even if no immediate increase in profits results.

The visitors also find — to their amazement — that American industry does not only talk this way but acts it too. They find it taken for granted in labor negotiations that an increase in productivity justifies a corresponding increase in wages. They find in companies, large and small, that management salaries and bonuses take into account performance, efficiency, and productivity rather than profit figures alone. They find elaborate attempts, such as the suggestion system they mention over and over again, to reward individual workers for contributions to productive efficiency.

It is to this concept of productivity that our visitors attribute the basic American attitude toward technological progress. Precisely because in this country increased productivity is a social if not a moral responsibility, American industry and American labor — so our visitors report — believe in, and accept, technological change rather than resist it.

3. *The attitude toward the market.* Our visitors cannot be blamed for believing when they arrive here what we ourselves have been telling them: that the major factor in our distributive system is the continental span of our market. But few productivity teams have departed, as far as I know, without having learned better.

Of course, the United States is a market larger both in territory and in numbers than any country of Western Europe. But it is not the width of the market that constitutes the real difference; after all, France, Italy, Germany, and England each offers a larger market than that actually covered by the majority of American businesses with their concentration on one region or area. It is in depth that the American market differs basically from European concepts and business practice — a qualitative rather than a quantitative difference.

One example — and it is given again and again by visitors — is the structure of the American automobile market in which last year's car will compete directly with a new model. Another one equally apparent to them is the television market. But what struck one team the most was a comparison between the Sears Roebuck catalog and that of an expensive Fifth Avenue sporting goods store, a store definitely in the luxury class. They found that practically every kind of merchandise offered by the Fifth Avenue store also was to be found in the Sears catalog. "That the American is rich beyond our wildest dreams, we know in Europe," they said; "but that 'wealth' here is not just an economic term but a social one, that it means that there are the same things for the rich and for the poor, this none of us understood — and it is much more important."

Closely connected with the concept of the mass market is our attitude toward the capacity of the market. "We put our stress on the actually existing market which we tend to take for granted. You look for the potential market," is one way some of the teams put it: Or: "We consider it our job to fill existing demands; you in the United States go out to create demands."

Basically the European businessman's concept is that of a given, static market. Hence a new product is seen as cutting into the markets of all the existing products; competition as taking away sales. Our concept — or so our visitors report — is that the market is indefinitely expandable. New products create their own, new demand; competition broadens the market for all.

It is to this that our visitors attribute, for instance, our emphasis on research — technical, market, product, the pricing policy of our progressive companies who often price a new product according to its expected eventual market rather than according to present cost or immediate sales, or the willingness to develop a new product first and to worry about its market later. All of these our visitors consider significant factors in America's high level of productivity.

4. *Productivity based on diversity and experimentation.* Practically every team starts its tour by asking: "What is the standard American cost-accounting system?" "Does the typical labor contract give the union a voice in the setting of production standards?" "What is the typical American pricing policy?" "What is the foreman training program?" etc. When told that there is no

such thing as "the American policy," they are incredulous.

It is not only that they are steeped in the prevailing European myth of American uniformity. In their own country or their own industry such things are usually uniform, set by government, by an industry-wide labor contract, a nationwide labor law, compulsory nationwide arbitration, or by trade association or cartel. In fact, most of the teams cannot, at first, imagine that important practices and policies could be anything but uniform. But most of the teams eventually come to the conclusion that our diversity is a major cause of our productivity. It means constant experimentation with new methods, ideas, and approaches. "Almost every company we have seen," wrote a Scandinavian team, "was working on something new, something it was experimenting with, in foundry techniques or in personnel methods, in accounting or in merchandise. No two companies were alike. As a result, the entire industry is forever questioning its methods, working on improvements, trying to find a better way."

A group of European trade union leaders stressed in their talk to me the value of diversity and experimentation in American labor relations, even though it runs counter to European trade-union tradition. "As long as you can maintain the union local and the individual management as the centers of labor relations," they said, "you will not only be safe from Communism; you will be able to make labor relations productive socially and economically. Bad labor relations can be made on an industry-wide or nationwide basis. Sound labor relations — that you have taught us here — require vigorous and imaginative unionism at the bottom as well as at the top. They require a national union policy, but also constant experimentation, constant adaptation in the actual plant."

Even less expected and more baffling is the prevailing cooperation and the free interchange of ideas and experiences that our visitors find. They know when they arrive that American business is highly competitive; and they find even more competition than they usually expected — too much for most tastes. But intensive competition, they believe, must mean secretiveness. It must mean refusal to disclose anything that might help the competitor — if it does not mean absence of any contact with the outside world. This explains why a group of European automobile men considered its visit to the annual meeting of the Society of Automotive Engineers its most interesting experience. "There were men from all the companies reading papers and telling everybody what they were doing, how it worked out, what difficulties they were running into, and what future plans they had. Everybody answered the most searching questions frankly, and each finished the discussion of his paper by inviting the men in the meeting to write to him or to call on him should they have any further question. And everyone sounded as if he really meant it."

5. *The importance of the human being.* Industrial training, management development programs, the opportunity for workers to rise to the top are important factors in America's productive capacity. Such factors as the informality in plants and offices, the attention paid to making work easy for the worker, the skill of the foreman in leading his people are only a few of the things every visiting team noticed and remarked on. Even our labor relations seem to them to be based on deep respect for human beings.

The "close cooperation" between stewards and management is remarked upon again and again; and several teams have underlined the "friendly and relaxed" atmosphere of our labor negotiations. That they are sincere in these compliments is shown by the fact that we are always being asked to include a labor relations expert in the American management teams that go to Europe.

What it all adds up to in the minds of our foreign visitors is that this country avails itself of a much larger percentage of its human resources than their own. We have not, of course, done a perfect job, perhaps not even a good job — as witness the need in almost all our major companies for elaborate programs to find, train, and develop potential management men. But we have at least not thrown away altogether all major human resources in industry.

Just how much of these American attitudes have the productivity teams taken home with them? Techniques, processes, gadgets Europe has adopted wholesale — and with good success in many cases. The productivity teams would be the first to stress, however, that techniques and processes without the underlying attitudes won't do much good. Yet precisely because it is attitudes that are important, success has been slow. For attitudes do not transplant fast or well. An added difficulty is that the top men in European companies can rarely spare six months — or even three — for a trip to the U.S.; hence teams have been largely composed of middle-management people who, when they get home, have a difficult time "selling the big boss."

The greatest obstacle, however, has been that the American beliefs and principles require something of which Europe has an incredible shortage: management. (In fact, it becomes quite obvious in talking to European teams that the major reason for the stranglehold of the cartel system on the Eu-ropean economy is not protectionism but simply the absence of management; the cartel largely eliminates the need for management by eliminating problems of pricing, merchandising, competition, labor relations, or technical efficiency, and gets rid of whatever remains by unloading it on the cartel secretary.) For this reason the emphasis on the training and development of management on all levels that has recently emerged in the Marshall Plan countries represents a major victory; but it also means that progress will be slow.

Yet there have been spectacular "conversions" — with equally spectacular results in practically every country of Western Europe. And because the important things are attitudes, principles, and policies rather than techniques, machines, and processes, the one convert filled with evangelical fervor may well have the greatest impact.

After all, though we today take for granted the basic attitudes to which Europe credits our productivity, every one of them was, thirty or forty years ago, nothing but the pet obsession of a few "visionary crackpots"; the concept of management, of productivity, of the mass market, the idea that human resources are the basic resource, etc. Certainly, the productivity teams supply something to Europe neither American dollars nor arms can supply: a constructive program, a goal and a vision. And when you talk to Europeans about the program, you come to feel that it is also the most effective "Voice of America" reaching Europe today.

———◆———

Private property began the instant somebody had a mind of his own.

E. E. CUMMINGS

33.

Clarence B. Randall: American Industry and Executive Recruitment

The new technology that was one of the most notable results of World War II brought with it changes in the managerial structure of many corporations. The success or failure of a firm depended on its ability to hire and hold executives and technicians in whose hands the task of decision making and planning would be placed. Big companies went directly to the colleges to recruit new employees, and competition among companies for new talent became intense. Clarence B. Randall of Inland Steel Company discussed the criteria for selection of college men for business in a book published in 1952.

Source: *A Creed for Free Enterprise,* Boston, 1952, pp. 121-137.

How to pick the right group of college seniors for seeding into a company, and what to do with them after they are selected, are fascinating and altogether baffling problems, about which there are as many different viewpoints as there are individual executives who are concerned. I happen to hold strong opinions, but they are strictly personal, and some of my closest friends think I am wrong in many particulars. This variety of approach, however, as among companies even in the same industry is wholesome, and is once more typical of the strength of free enterprise.

To begin with, I am not too happy with the intense zeal of some of the college placement officers who are apt to fall into the habit of mind of scoring their own performance and that of their institution on the basis of the number of seniors whom they place with the so-called good companies. Like the justice of the peace who performs hasty marriages, they sometimes start a train of circumstances that brings unhappiness later. One of their sins, in my opinion,

for example, is the coaching they give the boy on the day before he is interviewed by the company representative. Like a horse being groomed for the show ring they want him to appear well for their own sakes or that of the college. So they tell the senior to be crisp and decisive in his answers, and to give the appearance of knowing his own mind.

But how can a boy be wisely crisp and decisive when he is torn by inner doubts and fears? How can a youngster who has never tried to sell anything know that he wants to enter a sales department? Or can he be sure that just because he had a good mark in physics he will do well in production? For myself, I am always wary of the senior who knows his own mind, since I am quite sure that indecision and uncertainty are normal at that time in one's life. The recruiters whom I have trained, therefore, never ask the senior what it is he wants to do, but devote themselves to trying to discover what sort of boy it is they are talking to. And the decisions as to where those selected are to be placed in the company are postponed as long as possible in the training period, to permit the boy to learn all he can about what actually goes on in the company, and the staff to learn all they can about the boy. Complete mutual understanding is a better basis for the future than snap judgment on both sides in March of senior year.

Another fundamental in my creed is that we never select a man for what he knows. It is his capacity to learn that excites me, and particularly his capacity to learn that which he knows nothing about. If he is to be a leader he will spend most of his mature life doing things for which he is not specially trained, and to be effective he must have the intellectual courage and facility to have a go at any problem, no matter how strange. A metallurgist who is afraid of a balance sheet because he had no accounting in college will never rise above the level of technician. Proven competence in some field, plus intense intellectual curiosity and audacity are the essential qualities, it seems to me. The trick is how to detect them in a twenty-minute interview.

Scholastic marks are important. It is of course true that many a man with poor grades comes to great success in later life, usually because his maturing process was slow, but as a matter of cold calculation there will be fewer such among the C's than among the B's, and fewer there than among the A's. Once the intellectual capacity is established, the interviewer can turn to the other desired qualities, but to choose a dull mind because the boy is pleasant is not being fair to the future.

The list of the other qualities must start with character. There is no substitute for character — the awareness of moral problems, and the courage to do the right thing under all conditions of life. The brilliant but dishonest mind and heart may bring disaster to the company in later years, and no young man is worthy who lacks rugged integrity.

Then comes an instinct for human relations. Here is where the intellectual must be watched carefully, for if he is too intent on the processes of the mind to be aware of what people think of him, he will not understand team play in industry.

And then comes the capacity for self-expression. Many a brilliant mind has burned itself out in industry because the man could not communicate to those of lesser intellectual power the advanced ideas which he had conceived. Writing and speaking English clearly and concisely are indispensable as working tools in modern business.

This is not intended as a complete list of qualities that may attract an interviewer, but rather to point up the opinion that I hold that there is no single scholastic discipline or training that is the best preparation for the steel industry, or any other business. Such qualities are to be found among the seniors of every school, and among students of science or students of the liberal arts. It is the qualities that we seek, and not specific knowledge acquired by the student in a particular field of concentration. And if we base our decisions on the qualities, wherever they may be found, we will surely at the same time give our companies a wide variety of educational backgrounds.

Personally, I like a full year of company training for the seeded player before he is assigned to a job, a sort of postgraduate course in the particular affairs of the one institution. This should be as broad as possible, for once he is in a groove it will be many years before the young man can look around again. That year is his own golden opportunity to equip himself with a breadth of background which may thereafter lie fallow until he approaches middle age. He should see not only things but people, and all of the key officials should study him as he studies them. If possible, he should work with his hands and not be merely an observer, but that is very hard to accomplish as he moves from department to department, since he cannot remain long enough to receive the necessary training. At any rate, he should live in the plant community, and be urged to seek every opportunity of forming friendships with employee families. If the trainees form a group, they should be encouraged to take their meals together in order that the bull session may be continuous. The cross-currents of comment that flow back and forth between the technically trained and those from the liberal arts are very humbling and very salutary on both sides, and as mutual respect develops comradeships are formed that mean a great deal in future years.

Actual placement at the end of the training year is seldom difficult. The first to be weeded out are those occasional ones who find neither the industry nor the company to their liking, and much later heartache will be avoided if such are encouraged to leave without the slightest feeling of moral obligation for the year of training. Those who remain are the keen ones who sense that this is precisely the company they want to work for, and who now are so well informed about the whole organization that they want to try out for a particular job. The indecision of senior year has given way to confidence born of knowledge and experience.

Occasionally, there is the black sheep who casts discredit on his generation and breeds cynicism in the heart of his boss — the boy who signs on with his tongue in his cheek, never intending to stay permanently, but planning deliberately to steal two or three more years of training and then sell his services in the market of those employers who are too lazy to provide training. The dishonesty lies in the fact that he permits himself to be overpaid during the early years, and leaves before he has pulled his weight.

Once the boy is placed the real battle begins, and it is one that tries the soul of the most understanding executive. Seeded players are temperamental, whether on the tennis courts or in industry, and to bring the unusual young man safely through the restiveness of his first five years is a ticklish task in human engineering. To begin with, his immediate superior will probably not be helpful. If he is not a college man himself, he may resent college men. If he happens to have one of the slower minds, he resents the facile speech and mental quickness of the boy who led his class. Having come up the hard way himself, he withholds information and assigns the newcomer repetitive tasks that fill him with dismal boredom. And the understanding boss must bite his fingernails through all this, for if he so much as inquires about the youngster he gives the kiss of death to his advancement on merit. It must always be clear that the boy is not teacher's pet, and he must have no promotion that has not been won in competition with all comers, or where his ability has not been fully recognized by all concerned. Only the boy himself can lick the problem, and he does it by infinite patience, an honest smile, and faith in his own future.

About a third of them can't take it, however, and jump during the first five years. They become morbidly convinced that they have been forgotten, that they are getting nowhere, and that the road ahead is too long for them to endure. In college they found fresh intellectual challenge as they began each new course, and to perform the same task each day for even six months in industry establishes a boredom in their lives which soon exhausts their scant supply of patience. So they walk out, and the man who came up the hard way smiles knowingly at the worthlessness of the youngsters of today.

Almost invariably they jump to small companies, proud of the fifty-dollar-a-month increase which the new employer is glad to give them because it has saved him the trouble of recruiting, and buoyed up with hope that soon they will have genuine responsibility. And usually that happens. It is ordinarily true that in the early years young men advance more rapidly both in compensation and in authority in small companies than in so-called big business. Larger organizations with well-developed personnel programs protect themselves in depth with talent so far as possible, and not only have substitutes in the line of succession but substitutes for the substitutes. The ultimate target is the thing, however, and that is something which is very difficult to explain to a young man about to be married to whom an immediate pay increase is the most important thing in life.

Vaguely he thinks that at forty he will be eagerly sought after and that he will then go back to a fine job in a large institution, but it seldom works out that way. Large companies go outside for talent only as a last resort and because someone failed in their personnel planning, for they must reward those who didn't jump. And nothing makes an older man more heartsick than to watch through the years the career of a boy who jumped, and find him eventually stymied in a job too small for him, just because economic circumstances doomed his company to stagnation. And to talk to him before he leaves about the greater security to be found in a large organization is wasted effort that he sits through with reluctance, for what is to happen to him at sixty-five has less gravitational pull with him than the moon has on a millpond.

But over the years — and this process in one form or another has been going on for a long time — these jumpers, the seeded players who leave the large companies to sign on with the small, have had a marked influence on our economy. No one who has sat as I have on boards of business and civic organizations made up of men drawn from every section of the country and all industries can have failed to observe with some chagrin that the brilliant creative minds and the courageous natural leaders seem to be found more often in the smaller companies than in the large. I am afraid that this is a process of natural selection. Too many men who dare, jump, and eventually a man who didn't have the courage to leave becomes president of the large institution by seniority, simply because he was there. So the problem of the large companies is to find a way to bring the seeded players, the would-be jumpers, the men of spark and audacity through the restive period into the tranquillity of recognized opportunity.

This requires subtlety and an ever-watchful eye on the part of the top management. One useful technique is what I like to call horizontal promotion, by which the promising man, whether a seeded player or one who came up the hard way, is not kept too long on one job or in one sequence. He will do much to train himself for future responsibility if given the chance, but unusual ability, like a fine machine, must be tuned up by use. The larger the company the greater degree of specialization, and if that process is not resisted it will give the company of the future a magnificent group of technicians with no one qualified to direct them. The breadth of judgment required of a seasoned executive at middle life is a function of experience, but the man of promise can acquire that experience only if his boss consciously makes it possible.

Similarly the experience in civic responsibility which these future leaders must have if the free enterprise system is to be perpetuated can be made possible only by conscious stimulation and intelligent recognition on the part of the senior executives. No longer may they gibe at the patriotic youngster who wants to serve in the National Guard: "What's the matter, haven't you got enough to do around here?" On the contrary, they must suggest the names of likely juniors to civic organizations who are recruiting workers, and go out of their way to compliment those who volunteer for such assignments. Likewise they must watch for signs of the articulate quality, and encourage the youngsters to try their wings at speaking about their own fields of interest to church groups, luncheon clubs, etc. Above all, they themselves must set a worthy example in all these things.

There is one habit which we older men have in dealing with employment which I deplore, but I must confess that in holding my opinions I find myself in a most exclusive minority. Actually, the attitude of which I complain is a piece of unreasoned folklore that is commonly accepted and practised because, in my view, it is not thought through. These are the usual circumstances. In even those companies that for years have been outstanding in their personnel planning and administration there come emergencies. Perhaps the number two in a sequence resigns, and the senior suffers a coronary, all in the same month, leaving a key spot without coverage, and creating a situation so desperate that the management has no alternative but to go outside for a replacement. There isn't time to bring in a junior by lateral transfer and give him the necessary training, for immediate experience is demanded at a mature level. Invariably under those conditions the management casts covetous eyes on the number two in the same sequence in the organization of a strong competitor, and the question arises of whether the consent of that company should be secured before the man is approached. The accepted code is that such consent must always be obtained, and that the matter should be dropped if the other company demurs.

Personally I do not consider myself bound by that code, nor do I ask others to respect it in dealing with me, for it seems to me that the practice plainly violates the freedom of individual action which we are seeking so earnestly to preserve. Who am I to decide for one of my subordinates a matter which vitally touches his whole life? He is entitled to make his own decisions as to whether the opportunity offered by the other company is greater than that of his present prospect, and it is not in keeping with our concept of the worth of the individual in a democracy to bargain about him like a piece of merchandise without his knowledge. If he leaves our company, and I am unhappy, it would indicate that we have underpaid him, or withheld from him an insight into the future to which he was entitled. So I hire the competitor's man if I want to, and make no preliminary telephone call.

And there is then one final phobia that I have about young men in which again I am sadly in the minority, though again I like to think that the conventional attitude receives wide acceptance because the individual executives do not pause to think it through. It has to do with industrial deferment from military service. Beginning in my war back in 1917, and coming strongly into favor in the last war, as well as in the successive crises since 1945, has been the concept that the chemist, the metallurgist, the engineer, and the other technically trained students must not bear arms. They constitute a special reserve of brains which the nation must not jeopardize. They are to stay in the factories and devise new weapons while the liberal arts boys do the dying. Yet from among those same impractical students of the humanities and the social sciences might come the future Churchills, the men of ideals and character, who would hold aloft the torch of leadership in their country for either war or peace. So I cannot think it is just to have a planned economy in death. The grim burden should be shared by all alike.

But I must close . . . as I began . . . by paying my respect once more to the youth in American industry today, and expressing my warm affection for them. They are magnificent, and the question is not whether they will fail us, but rather whether we will fail them.

34.

John Kenneth Galbraith: Countervailing Power

John Kenneth Galbraith is probably the most influential and widely read economist of the mid-twentieth century in America. As an adviser to President Kennedy and as ambassador to India during the Kennedy administration, Galbraith gained a distinguished reputation as a public figure; but it is his economic works, starting with American Capitalism *(1952) and continuing with* The Affluent Society *(1958) and* The New Industrial State *(1967), that will probably give him his most enduring fame. The selection below is taken from the first of these books, in which Galbraith developed his theory of what he called countervailing power. According to this theory, other centers of power besides the giant corporations are bound to rise in a free enterprise system, partly as inevitable economic responses to concentrated control, and partly because the people desire them.*

Source: *American Capitalism: The Concept of Countervailing Power*, Boston, 1952, Ch. 9.

As WITH SOCIAL EFFICIENCY, and its neglect of technical dynamics, the paradox of the unexercised power of the large corporation begins with an important oversight in the underlying economic theory. In the competitive model — the economy of many sellers each with a small share of the total market — the restraint on the private exercise of economic power was provided by other firms on the same side of the market. It was the eagerness of competitors to sell, not the complaints of buyers, that saved the latter from spoliation. It was assumed, no doubt accurately, that the nineteenth-century textile manufacturer who overcharged for his product would promptly lose his market to another manufacturer who did not. If all manufacturers found themselves in a position where they could exploit a strong demand, and mark up their prices accordingly, there would soon be an inflow of new competitors. The resulting increase in supply would bring prices and profits back to normal.

As with the seller who was tempted to use his economic power against the customer, so with the buyer who was tempted to use it against his labor or suppliers. The man who paid less than prevailing wage would lose his labor force to those who paid the worker his full (marginal) contribution to earnings. In all cases the incentive to socially desirable behavior was provided by the competitor. It was to the same side of the market and thus to competition that economists came to look for the self-regulatory mechanism of the economy.

They also came to look to competition exclusively and in formal theory still do. The notion that there might be another regulatory mechanism in the economy has been almost completely excluded from economic thought. Thus, with the widespread disappearance of competition in its classical form and its replacement by the small group of firms if not in overt, at least in conventional or tacit collusion, it was easy to suppose that since competition had dis-

John Kenneth Galbraith

appeared, all effective restraint on private power had disappeared. Indeed this conclusion was all but inevitable if no search was made for other restraints and so complete was the preoccupation with competition that none was made.

In fact, new restraints on private power did appear, to replace competition. They were nurtured by the same process of concentration which impaired or destroyed competition. But they appeared not on the same side of the market but on the opposite side, not with competitors but with customers or suppliers. It will be convenient to have a name for this counterpart of competition and I shall call it *countervailing power.*

To begin with a broad and somewhat too dogmatically stated proposition, private economic power is held in check by the countervailing power of those who are subject to it. The first begets the second. The long trend toward concentration of industrial enterprise in the hands of a relatively few firms has brought into existence not only strong sellers, as economists have supposed, but also strong buyers as they have failed to

see. The two develop together, not in precise step but in such manner that there can be no doubt that the one is in response to the other.

The fact that a seller enjoys a measure of monopoly power, and is reaping a measure of monopoly return as a result, means that there is an inducement to those firms from whom he buys or those to whom he sells to develop the power with which they can defend themselves against exploitation. It means also that there is a reward to them, in the form of a share of the gains of their opponents' market power, if they are able to do so. In this way the existence of market power creates an incentive to the organization of another position of power that neutralizes it.

The contention I am here making is a formidable one. It comes to this: Competition which, at least since the time of Adam Smith, has been viewed as the autonomous regulator of economic activity and as the only available regulatory mechanism apart from the state, has, in fact, been superseded. Not entirely, to be sure. There are still important markets where the power of the firm as (say) a seller is checked or circumscribed by those who provide a similar or a substitute product or service. This, in the broadest sense that can be meaningful, is the meaning of competition. The role of the buyer on the other side of such markets is essentially a passive one. It consists in looking for, perhaps asking for, and responding to the best bargain. The active restraint is provided by the competitor who offers, or threatens to offer, a better bargain. By contrast, in the typical modern market of few sellers, the active restraint is provided not by competitors but from the other side of the market by strong buyers. Given the convention against price competition, it is the role of the competitor that becomes passive.

It was always one of the basic presuppositions of competition that market power exercised in its absence would invite the competitors who would eliminate such exercise of power. In other words competition was regarded as a *self-generating* regulatory force. The doubt whether this was in fact so after a market had been preempted by a few large sellers, after entry of new firms had become difficult and after existing firms had accepted a convention against price competition, was what destroyed the faith in competition as a regulatory mechanism. Countervailing power is also a self-generating force and this is a matter of great importance. Something, although not very much, could be claimed for the regulatory role of the strong buyer in relation to the market power of sellers, did it happen that, as an accident of economic development, such strong buyers were frequently juxtaposed to strong sellers. However it is far more important that, as with the ancient presupposition concerning competition, the regulatory role of the strong buyer, in relation to the market power of the strong seller, is also self-generating. As noted, power on one side of a market creates both the need for, and the prospect of reward to, the exercise of countervailing power from the other side. In the market of small numbers, the self-generating power of competition is a chimera. That of countervailing power, by contrast, is readily assimilated to the common sense of the situation and its existence, once we have learned to look for it, is readily subject to empirical verification.

Market power can be exercised by strong buyers against weak sellers as well as by strong sellers against weak buyers. In the competitive model, competition acted as a restraint on both kinds of exercise of power. This is also the case with countervailing power. In turning to its practical manifestations, it will be convenient, in fact, to begin with a case where it is exercised by weak sellers against strong buyers.

THE OPERATION of countervailing power is to be seen with the greatest clarity in the labor market where it is also most fully developed. Because of his comparative immobility, the worker has long been highly vulnerable to private economic power. The customer of any particular steel mill, at the turn of the century, could always take himself elsewhere if he felt he was being overcharged. Or he could exercise his sovereign privilege of not buying steel at all. The worker had no comparable freedom if he felt he was being underpaid. Normally he could not move and he had to have work. Not often has the power of one man over another been used more callously than in the American labor market after the rise of the large corporation. As late as the early twenties, the steel industry worked a twelve-hour day and seventy-two-hour week with an incredible twenty-four-hour stint every fortnight when the shift changed.

No such power is exercised today and for the reason that its earlier exercise stimulated the counteraction that brought it to an end. In the ultimate sense it was the power of the steel industry, not the organizing abilities of John L. Lewis and Philip Murray, that brought the United Steel Workers into being. The economic power that the worker faced in the sale of his labor — the competition of many sellers dealing with few buyers — made it necessary that he organize for his own protection. There were rewards to the power of the steel companies in which, when he had successfully developed countervailing power, he could share.

As a general though not invariable rule there are strong unions in the United States only where markets are served by strong corporations. And it is not an accident that the large automobile, steel, electrical, rubber, farm-machinery and non-ferrous metal-mining and smelting companies all bargain with powerful CIO unions. Not only has the strength of the corporations in these industries made it necessary for workers to develop the protection of countervailing power, it has provided unions with the opportunity for getting something more as well. If successful they could share in the fruits of the corporation's market power. By contrast there is not a single union of any consequence in American agriculture, the country's closest approach to the competitive model. The reason lies not in the difficulties in organization; these are considerable, but greater difficulties in organization have been overcome. The reason is that the farmer has not possessed any power over his labor force, and at least until recent times has not had any rewards from market power, which it was worth the while of a union to seek. As an interesting verification of the point, in the Great Valley of California, the large farmers of that area have had considerable power vis-à-vis their labor force. Almost uniquely in the United States, that region has been marked by persistent attempts at organization by farm workers.

The other industries which are not marked by any high degree of concentration, and accordingly are not especially powerful in their labor market, do not normally have strong unions. The textile industry, boot and shoe manufacture, lumbering and other forest industries in most parts of the country, and smaller wholesale and retail enterprises, are all cases in point. I do not advance the theory of countervailing power as a monolithic explanation of trade-union organization; in the case of bituminous-coal mining and the clothing industry, for example, the unions have emerged as a supplement to the weak market position of the operators and manufacturers. They have assumed price- and market-regulating functions that are the normal functions of management. Nevertheless, as an explanation of the incidence of trade-union strength in the American economy, the theory of countervailing power clearly fits the broad contours of experience.

THE LABOR MARKET SERVES admirably to illustrate the incentives to the development of countervailing power and it is of great importance in this market. However, its de-velopment, in response to positions of market power, is pervasive in the economy. As a regulatory device one of its most important manifestations is in the relation of the large retailer to the firms from which it buys. The way in which countervailing power operates in these markets is worth examining in some detail.

One of the seemingly harmless simplifications of formal economic theory has been the assumption that producers of consumers' goods sell their products directly to consumers. All business units are held, for this reason, to have broadly parallel interests. Each buys labor and materials, combines them and passes them along to the public at prices that, in some sense, maximize returns. Were this in fact the case, the lot of the consumer would be an unhappy one.

In practice, goods pass to retailers whose interests, normally, are at sharp variance with those of their suppliers. The typical retailer is deeply concerned with his volume of sales. This is uniquely important for minimizing inventory risk, it is a prime factor in the prestige of the concern, and, of course, it is one of the dimensions of profit. The convention that excludes cutthroat price competition — in the case of retailers the cutting of gross margins — is observed by retailers as by other firms. Nonetheless, lower prices — a low level in general as well as low prices in relation to those of other firms — are regarded by one whole class of retailers as the major device for obtaining and maintaining volume. It is in their interest accordingly to resist any exercise of market power by their suppliers that results in higher prices. More important, any power retailers can exercise to reduce their supplier's prices will redound to their benefit. It will enable them to use price as an inducement without breaking the convention against destructive cutting of their own margins.

Such an opportunity exists only when

their suppliers are enjoying something that can be taken away, *i.e.*, when they are enjoying the fruits of market power from which they can be separated. Thus, in precise parallel with the labor market, we find the retailer with both a protective and profit incentive to develop countervailing power whenever his supplier is in possession of market power. The practical manifestation of this, over the last half-century, has been the spectacular rise of the food chains, the variety chains, the mail-order houses (now graduated into chain stores), the department-store chains, and the cooperative buying organizations of the surviving independent department and food stores.

This development has been the countervailing response to previously established positions of power. The gains from invading these positions have been considerable. The rubber tire industry is a fairly commonplace example of oligopoly. Four large firms are dominant in the market. In the thirties, Sears, Roebuck & Co. was able, by exploiting its role as a large and indispensable customer, to procure tires from Goodyear Tire & Rubber Company at a price from twenty-nine to forty percent lower than the going market. These it resold to thrifty motorists for from a fifth to a quarter less than the same tires carrying the regular Goodyear brand.

One consequence of the failure of the government to recognize the role of countervailing power is that many hundreds of pages of court records have detailed the exercise of this power by the Great Atlantic & Pacific Tea Company. There is little doubt that this firm has used the countervailing power it has developed with considerable artistry. In 1937, a survey by the company indicated that, for an investment of $175,000, it could supply itself with corn flakes. Assuming that it charged itself the price it then was paying to one of the three companies manufacturing this delicacy, it could earn a modest sixty-eight percent on the outlay. Armed with this information, and the threat to go into the business which its power could readily make effective, it had no difficulty in bringing down the price by approximately ten percent. Such gains from the exercise of countervailing power, it will be clear, could only occur where there is an exercise of original market power with which to contend. The A & P could have reaped no comparable gains in buying staple products from the farmer. Committed as he is to the competition of the competitive model, the farmer has no gains to surrender. Provided, as he is, with the opportunity of selling all he produces at the impersonally determined market price, he has nôt the slightest incentive to make a special price to A & P beyond that which might be associated with the simple economies of bulk sale.

The examples of the exercise of countervailing power by Sears, Roebuck and A & P just cited show how this power is deployed in its most dramatic form. The day-to-day exercise of the buyer's power is a good deal less spectacular but also a good deal more significant. At the end of virtually every channel by which consumers' goods reach the public there is, in practice, a layer of powerful buyers. In the food market there are the great food chains; in clothing there are the department stores, the chain department stores and the department store buying organizations; in appliances there are Sears, Roebuck and Montgomery Ward and the department stores; these latter firms are also important outlets for furniture and other house furnishings; the drug and cosmetic manufacturer has to seek part of his market through the large drug chains and the department stores; a vast miscellany of consumers' goods pass to the public through Woolworth's, Kresge's and the other variety chains.

In all of these cases buyers deal directly with the manufacturer and there are few of the latter who, in setting prices, do not have to reckon with the attitude and reaction of their powerful customers. The retail buyers have a variety of weapons at their disposal to use against the market power of their suppliers. Their ultimate sanction is to develop their own source of supply as the food chains, Sears, Roebuck and Montgomery Ward have extensively done. They can also concentrate their entire patronage on a single supplier and, in return for a lower price, give him security in his volume and relieve him of selling and advertising costs.

The more commonplace but more important exercise of countervailing power consists, merely, in keeping the seller in a state of uncertainty as to the intentions of a buyer who is indispensable to him. The larger of the retail buying organizations place orders around which the production schedules and occasionally the investment of even the largest manufacturers become organized. A shift in this custom imposes prompt and heavy loss. The threat or even the fear of this sanction is enough to cause the supplier to surrender some or all of the rewards of his market power. He must, frequently, make a more conditional surrender to less potent buyers if he is not to be more than ever in the power of his large customers. It will be clear that in this operation there are rare opportunities for playing one supplier off against another.

A measure of the importance which large retailing organizations attach to the deployment of their countervailing power is the prestige they accord to their buyers. These men (and women) are the key employees of the modern large retail organization; they are highly paid and they are among the most intelligent and resourceful people to be found anywhere in business. In the everyday course of business, they are considerably better known, both for their capacities and their power, than the salesmen from whom they buy.

There are producers of consumers' goods who have secured themselves from exercise of countervailing power. Some, like the automobile and the oil industry, have done so either by integrating their distribution through to the consumer or because they have an organization of small and dependent and therefore fairly powerless dealers. It seems probable that in a few industries, tobacco manufacture for example, the members are strong enough and have sufficient solidarity to withstand any pressure applied to them even by the most powerful buyer. However, even the tobacco manufacturers, under conditions that were especially favorable to the exercise of countervailing power in the thirties, were forced to make liberal price concessions, in the form of advertising allowances, to the A & P and possibly also to other large consumers. When the comprehensive representation of large retailers in the various fields of consumers' goods distribution is considered, it is reasonable to conclude — the reader is warned that this is an important generalization — that most positions of market power in the production of consumers' goods are covered by positions of countervailing power.

Countervailing power also manifests itself, although less visibly, in producers' goods markets. For many years the power of the automobile companies, as purchasers of steel, has sharply curbed the power of the steel mills as sellers. Detroit is the only city where the recently outlawed basing-point system was not used to price steel. Under the basing-point system, all producers regardless of location quoted the same price at any particular point of delivery. This minimized the opportunity of a strong buyer to play one seller off against the other. The large firms in the automobile industry had developed the countervailing power which enabled them to do precisely this. They were not disposed to tolerate any limitations on their exercise of such power. In explaining the quotation of "arbitrary prices" on Detroit steel, a leading student of the basing-point system has recently recognized, implicitly, the role of countervailing power by observing that "it is difficult to apply high cartel prices to particularly large and strong customers such as the automobile manufacturers in Detroit."

The more normal operation of countervailing power in producers' goods markets turns on the relatively small number of customers which firms in these industries typically have. Where the cigarette or soap manufacturer numbers his retail outlets by the hundreds of thousands and his final consumers by the millions, the machinery or equipment manufacturer counts his customers by the hundreds or thousands and, very often, his important ones by the dozen. The latter are important to the seller as individuals and are able to collect the rewards of that importance. As elsewhere, the market pays a premium to those who develop power as buyers that is equivalent to the market power of those from whom they buy. The reverse is true where weak sellers do business with strong buyers.

THERE IS AN OLD SAYING, or should be, that it is a wise economist who recognizes the scope of his own generalizations. While countervailing power is of decisive importance in regulating the exercise of private economic power, it is not universally effective. Some industries, because they are integrated through to the consumer or because their product passes through a dependent dealer organization, have not been faced with countervailing power. As noted, there are a few cases where a very strong market position has proved impregnable even against the attacks of strong buyers. And there are cases where the dangers from countervailing power have, apparently, been recognized and where it has been successfully resisted.

An example of successful resistance to countervailing power is the residential-building industry. No segment of American capitalism evokes less pride. Yet anyone approaching the industry with the preconceptions of competition in mind is unlikely to see, very accurately, the reasons for its shortcomings. There are many thousands of individual firms in the business of building houses. Nearly all are small — the capital of the typical housebuilder runs from a few hundred to a few thousand dollars. The members of the industry oppose little market power to the would-be house owner. Except in times of extremely high building activity there is aggressive competition for business.

The industry does show many detailed manifestations of guild restraint. Builders are frequently in alliance with each other, the unions, and local politicians to protect prices, wages and to maintain established building techniques. These derelictions have been seized upon avidly by the critics of the industry. Since they represent its major departure from the competitive model, they have been assumed to be the cause of the poor performance of the housing industry.

Unhappily, were the restraints on contract prices, materials, and techniques in the industry swept away, it seems improbable that the prices of new houses would be much changed and the satisfaction of customers with what they get for what they pay much enhanced. The reason is that the typical builder would still be a small and powerless figure contending with unions that are far stronger than he and buying his building materials in small quantities at high cost from suppliers with effective market power. It is these factors which, very largely, determine the cost of the house.

The builder is kept without power. With few exceptions, the manufacturers of building supplies decline to sell direct to the builder. This prevents any one of the latter from bringing pressure to bear on his source of supply; at the same time it helps keep all builders relatively small and powerless by uniformly denying them the economies of direct purchase. All must pay jobbers' and retailers' margins. A few builders — a spectacular case is Levitt & Sons of Long Island — have managed to circumvent this ban. As the result of more effective buying, a much stronger position in dealing with labor, and the savings from large-scale production of houses, they have notably increased the satisfaction of customers with what they receive for their money. Few can doubt that the future of the industry, if its future is to improve on its past, lies with such firms.

Thus it is the notion of countervailing power, not of competition, which points the way to progress in the housing industry. What is needed is fewer firms of far greater scale with resulting capacity to bring power to bear upon unions and suppliers. It is the absence of such firms, and of the resulting economies, which helps explain why one sector of this industry — low-cost housing where cost is especially important in relation to ability-to-pay — has passed under government management. In the absence of an effective regulating mechanism within the industry in the form of countervailing power, private entrepreneurship has been superseded.

35.

William J. Grede: America, A Frontier

In the four decades between World War I and the first Eisenhower administration the National Association of Manufacturers reflected the social and economic attitudes of the great majority of American businessmen. After World War II, however, with the rise of the giant or "mature" corporation (as economist J. K. Galbraith has called it), there arose a split in the ranks of business, with the result that there grew up a divergence of opinion between the giant corporations, on the one hand, and the majority of members of the NAM, on the other. The attitudes of small businessmen toward the federal government, welfare legislation, taxation, and economic control are reflected in the following address by William J. Grede, president of the NAM, delivered before a meeting of the American Association of Blood Banks in Milwaukee on October 10, 1952. Portions of the address are reprinted here.

Source: VSD, November 15, 1952.

As the 1952 president of the National Association of Manufacturers, which seems to be my principal job this year . . . I do feel compelled to give you a little NAM commercial. This is the National Association of Manufacturers that you have heard so frequently described as the powerful force of big business, and here they come to this little burg of Milwaukee and select a foundryman as its president.

The National Association of Manufacturers has in its membership about 18,500 industrial concerns and you will be interested to know that nearly 85 percent of them employ less than 500 people. Now, I use the figure 500 because the Bureau of Labor Statistics says that anybody who employs less than 500 is small business, and anybody who employs more than 500 is big business, so under that definition, the NAM is the biggest small business organization in the world — nearly half of our members employ less than 100 employees.

That does not mean we do not have some of the large corporations in our membership — we do. We wish we had more, not only for their support and advice and counsel but our dues are based on net worth, and that is very helpful to the budget.

I find, however, as I travel about the country, meeting with our members and talking with American audiences, that Americans do not divide as sharply as the Bureau of Labor Statistics would divide us. I find that big business and little business all have identical problems, and when I face an audience in the community in which I am not particularly well acquainted, I cannot pick out the presidents of the big corporations and the presidents of the small corporations.

The NAM, like your association, is people, and, of course, to most businessmen, anybody whose business is bigger than yours is big business and it is the same way with nearly every other division that the enemies of freedom in America would like to make of Americans — they divide us into the have and have-nots, and employer and employee, and big and small, producers and consumers, rich and poor. Anybody that has more money than you have is rich — that is about as sharp a definition as you can make. . . .

No, this freedom business, you know, is on both sides of the street. Freedom is related to people and there is no middle road of freedom — if we are going to have freedom, it must be on both sides of the street.

Socialism sort of creeps up on us and many times organizations like yours, nonprofit and human welfare organizations, forget that progress grows out of competition, for many of us, even the well and able-bodied, have feared the rigors of competition, this process so often described as the selfish ambition for gain.

Let us look at the American free, private, competitive enterprise system, this system under which men struggle to reduce costs and make better products at lower prices so that they can sell more products and make more money. It is that selfishness, if that is what you call it, which has produced in America the highest standard of living and the greatest social, medical, and educational development in the history of the world.

Some day I am going to write a book on the virtue of selfishness! Just ponder the by-products of our American competitive selfishness — everyone is better off. But do not confuse selfishness with covetousness. By our selfish competition, we are constantly increasing the size of the pie, which means opportunity, so our piece will grow, but so does everyone else's.

The covetousness of pressure groups and government planners is to take for themselves what others have. They describe it as a struggle between the have's and have-nots, and they want to make their piece of pie bigger by taking some of yours. That is not selfish nor in their own self-interest — that is covetousness and will eventually destroy the whole pie, because it will destroy incentive and opportunity.

We must all do our part to keep America free and keep big government and big pressure groups out of our economics and out of our charity. No government can provide opportunity or security; the best they can provide is alms.

Sometimes we get impatient with our progress and are inclined to ask government for help. We somehow get the idea that federal money is free money, and so, gradually, powerful central government and socialism develops. . . . If the American people had ever been given an outright, clear-cut opportunity to decide on the question of socialism, they would have unhesitatingly and overwhelmingly voted "no," but, unfortunately, the issue has never been presented to the people in any such honest and manly fashion. Instead, the federal government has artfully been feeding the nation with dose after dose of socialism, sugarcoating each dose with such terms as democracy, liberalism, progressive, and the abundant life. It began with small doses and steadily increased as our tolerance increased and our resistance weakened.

These amazingly diverse and cleverly disguised series of government measures add up to an alarmingly deep penetration by government of our traditional rights of freedom. The most obvious indication of this infiltration and sabotage of our free American system is found in the rapidity and degree to which our central government has increased in size. In 1928, the executive branch of the federal government had less than 450 component parts; today it has some 1,800 bureaus and agencies.

In 1928, the federal government was spending less than $4 billion annually; today our government is spending at the rate of $79 billion — and don't be fooled by the spenders' smoke-screen arguments that there are certain elements fixed in the budget that they cannot reduce. Even if you take only the 15 percent that some folks say is the only part that you can investigate, that is $12 billion and there is ample opportunity for savings; but the NAM and others have each year analyzed the federal budget and they have pointed out to the Congress substantial savings that could be made and in which departments specifically it could be made. In this year's $84-billion budget, the NAM study indicates that without impairing any of our civilian services or our defense effort, $14 billion could be saved.

As a taxpayer, I am vitally interested both in how much and how the federal government spends the revenue it collects and borrows, but as a freedom-loving American, I am even more concerned about the fact that to an increasing degree we are being compelled ourselves to pay out of our own substance for the violation of our own rights and freedom. We are forced to surrender to government a percent of our incomes, and then a part of the income surrendered is used by the government to regulate, control, and interfere with the way we live and work and earn our income.

The more obvious form of government control and interference consists in regulating the prices at which we buy and sell and the rates we pay and profits we may retain and the rate at which we may depreciate our plant for tax purposes, the unions we must recognize and the rates of interest we must pay, welfare funds, pension funds, crops we sow and reap and either destroy or sell to the government.

These are serious invasions of freedom. However, it would be fatal if at this point we halted our inquiry with the deceptive reflection that our problem consists chiefly in dealing with the overgrown, spendthrift, meddlesome government. We must rather recognize that we are confronted and threatened by central government which steadily increases its power and uses that power to hobble and undermine the free market that is the heart of our system of capitalism — in brief, a government that is either blundering or stumbling into socialism or one that is plotting and maneuvering us into a Socialist state.

Consider a few examples of how this federal government has been invading major elements of our economy. In 1939 the federal government taxes siphoned off slightly more than 6 percent of the national income; for the year ended last June 30, federal taxes took 22 percent of our national income and state and local taxes another 10 percent or 12 percent — one-third of our national income for taxes.

Now, consider some of the ways in which this federal money is used to make people, communities, and states political wards of a super-state being built with our money. Seventeen and a half million individual Americans receive regular monthly checks from the federal government, and this does not include checks to veterans for vocational rehabilitation or readjustment payment, nor does it include the federal government unemployment checks nor checks to the part-time government AAA workers, or the almost 3 million farmers who receive government checks under the Agriculture Conservation Program.

Twenty-five percent of the nation's total land area is now owned by the federal government and supervised by some sixty federal agencies. Wholly owned government enterprises have a total lending authority of about $66 billion as of last June 30. This is $10 billion more than the total outstanding loans of all commercial banks.

Government-sponsored life insurance approximates $325 billion, as contrasted with $300 billion of life insurance issued by private firms. And consider, too, what the government is endeavoring to accomplish in the field you know best — the field of health and medical care. Recently a series of hearings were held by the President's Commission on Health Needs. In spite of the fact that there is no health emergency at this time, and that our health standards have never been higher, nevertheless these hearings were held for the expressed purpose of exploring the whole vast field of national health needs. However, the meetings themselves have led many people to wonder if there has not been undue influence on the part of several who are open proponents of compulsory health programs.

Naturally, sympathetic planners and controllers and other elements quickly availed themselves of this sounding-board to plug for a broad national health program. The friends of socialized medicine were given every opportunity to speak their standard patter. And, strangely enough, the managers of this federal medicine show somehow "overlooked" making provisions for representatives of management to be heard at the meetings.

There is here certainly no quarrel with the worthy objective of high standards of medical care. But one has reason to look with apprehension upon devices and schemes that propagandize aspects of socialism disguised as welfare. Everyone desires improving medical care but there is no indication that government could ever do the job as well as private individuals and institutions are doing it now.

Incidentally, I might mention that the National Association of Manufacturers has been active in encouraging and assisting private industry to achieve better in-plant health and safety and generally to accept its responsibility for the protection of the health and safety of employees from on-the-job as well as off-the-job causes.

Moreover, American industry increasingly recognizes the desirability of improving general standards of health and medical care through group health and accident plans and through the support of voluntary prepaid hospital and medical plans on a contributory basis. Specifically, the NAM has called upon employers to exercise initiative and leadership in improving health protection through voluntary participation at the local level.

Although we have examined some of the specifically socialistic activities of the federal government, nevertheless it is even more important to recognize the overall and certainly more fundamental consequences flowing from a central government suffering delusions of its own grandeur and omnipotence.

For example, big government rejects and endeavors to stamp out the rich and constructive diversity of American life that functions in the community, state, and region by federal standardization. Now, certainly, we do not oppose some standardization, but as I explained to you earlier, America is people and you cannot standardize people.

Big government attempts to impose a rigidly uniform pattern of economic, social, political, and cultural principles and practices and destroys free enterprise and incentive and opportunity: Even in charitable activities, a necessary part of the American system, big government aims to replace God-given freedom with a dictatorial conformity, imposing blind discipline. Therefore, every extra dollar of revenue and every service and function that local and state governments surrender to the federal octopus enlarge the size and increase the strength of the kind of government that could utterly destroy the principles, traditions, and practices that have made us a spiritually vigorous and materially strong people.

It is right and necessary that we should fight for economy in government and fight against government squandering itself into socialism. But it is equally required of us that we find a complete and lasting alternative to the big, centralized government that is severing the American people from the roots that have given them their strength and freedom.

There is no choice but to return to the states and localities all the services and responsibilities that fall logically and naturally within their governmental provinces and which they have traditionally initiated, controlled, and administered, unaided by the federal government, and return to the people their normal responsibilities in the free economy.

Service responsibilities should be performed by the smallest unit of government able to perform them well and efficiently. Then they will be done more competently and economically. The dangerous people in the community are not always the Communists; so many times we have folks who think that a badge of liberalism is to sort of say and feel that they are just a little socialistic themselves. I say to you that they are the dangerous people, who are Socialists and do not know it, and who, when their own community seems to need some help, rush to the federal government for so-called free money to proceed with their responsibilities instead of taking them themselves.

Your worthy organizations are working at preserving this American principle of community-self-reliance and self-responsibility. Each of your organizations is an admirable example of what people — individual, private people — can and should do in their communities. It is an admirable example of exactly what I have been talking about. You are proving both the desirability and the feasibility of keeping government at home.

If we do not get government back home, we shall be in progressively greater danger of the federal government dominating our lives, destroying our freedom, and killing the way of life we have cherished here in America. . . .

I think we should understand that what we call freedom is related to people; it is not freedom for this or freedom from that; it is not freedom of the press or of religion; it is freedom, and there is no middle road of freedom. Freedom is related to people. Freedom in America, as we understand it in America, is not an economic nor a political discovery.

In the last analysis, people are important in our scheme of things, and freedom is a religious discovery; the religions of the ages have struggled to relate the individual person to his Deity. The Judeo-Christian philosophy of our Bible in the Old and the New Testaments was replete with the philosophy of individualism; the sanctity of persons and their individual relationship with God are all-important; and our forefathers in 1776, when they set up this nation, for the first time in the history of the world wove that religious conviction into the political fabric of government. Our Declaration of Independence and our Constitution do not use the word "democracy," but they do refer to the Creator.

So frequently America is referred to as the last bulwark of democracy. It is not a democracy in the true meaning of the word, and it is not a last bulwark. America is a frontier, it is a spiritual frontier of freedom; and as we face our responsibilities today in America and around the world, let us have the faith and the courage of our forefathers and sound in America a new call for freedom!

36.

FLORENCE R. KLUCKHOHN: American Women and American Values

As with all other aspects of American society, the Second World War worked a decisive change in the status of women. The most obvious change was the great increase in the number of women employed outside the home. The war opened up many new avenues of employment, especially in industry, that had hitherto been largely reserved for men. With the position of wage earner came new responsibilities as well as a new freedom. Shortly after the war sociologists, psychologists, economists, and others began to examine the new roles played by women in American society. In the following selection, Florence Kluckhohn assesses the new position of women in America.

Source: *Facing the Future's Risks*, Lyman Bryson, ed., New York, 1952, pp. 193-198.

THE VICIOUS ALTERNATIVE of extreme feminism, marriage *or* career, has been changed by modern women to marriage *and* career, or at least marriage and the job. The switch of conjunctions is a meaningful one, and the issue as now phrased will undoubtedly be recorded in future history of the feminine role as the major one of the mid-twentieth century. This prediction is, however, general and does not state which of several possible phrasings will finally be given to the issue. Certainly, to some extent, both the final phrasing and the effects it may have for family life and the whole society will depend upon what thoughtful men and women think and do in the near future. A trend once started may be difficult to stay, but few Americans submit to the view that human beings can have no say in the direction trends will take.

Being myself a majority American, I would like, in conclusion, first to summarize briefly the three factors which I believe to be the main reasons for the formulation of this current issue and then offer three suggestions for ways in which that issue may be altered to the advantage of everyone.

The three main factors in the order of their importance are: the changes which have come in the wife-mother role; woman's growing dissatisfaction with typically feminine activities outside the home; the character of woman's education.

There is little reason to doubt that for a vast majority of American women the wife-mother role is still the dominant component in the total role. Although there are women who refuse to become wives and mothers because they believe the marital state hampering to self-expression, they are few. Most of America's single women are not single by choice. They either failed to find and attract a man who also attracted, or they gave him up for reasons of pride or duty to others.

The idealization of the American woman is primarily an idealization of her motherhood. As one writer has caustically remarked, American men more often seek mothers in their marriages than wives. It is also as mothers that women are most often self-consciously critical of themselves. And of all family relational bonds, the mother-child relationship has the greatest emotional strength and depth. Although it was real insight which led an English anthropologist to label Mother's Day an American rite of atonement, we all know that there is a profound attitude of devotion underlying the commercialized sentimentality about mothers which fills American magazines in the month of May.

No, there certainly is not much danger that women either are developing or will develop completely negative attitudes toward their wife-mother role. I see no substantial evidence for the argument that women, in their desire to seek self-fulfillment outside family life, are the main cause of increases in delinquency and divorce rates and the mounting list of neurotic symptoms discovered in both children and adults. All these various symptoms are related and to some extent have a common origin, but rather than say simply that the cause is woman's wish for self-expression, it would seem more logical and accurate to place this wish, too, on the list of symptoms. But even though I cannot agree with those who blame women so much, I concur in the opinion that a majority of women now find, and will continue to find it difficult to be both adequate wives and mothers and also successful competitors in the occupations. Why, then, if it is so difficult, are so many women already attempting to do both, others expressing the wish that they could, and still others showing signs of frustrations because they do not or cannot?

The changes in the wife-mother role itself

provide part of the answer to the question. However important the role may still be, it has lost both meaning and scope in recent years. Meaning is undeniably lost when the role is separated in the minds of men and women alike from its inevitable counterpart, the housewife role, and the tasks of that counterpart greatly demeaned in value. Work which is done because one has to do it, and which does not have a value worthy of an adequate training for it, is not apt to be rewarding. Moreover, the negative attitudes can so easily lead to the expression, either consciously formulated or unconsciously made known in behavior, of a belief that mother deserves much because she has given up so much and done so many things she did not really enjoy.

The scope of the role has been narrowed because modern families are both small in size and share so many of their functions with a host of other organizations. Not only is the mother of today freed from many of the worrisome problems that colonial women always faced, she is also all too soon out of a mother's job. As Dr. Margaret Mead has said:

> Every social pressure to which she is subjected tells her that she should not spoil her children's lives, that she should let them lead their own lives, that she should make them independent and self-sufficient. Yet the more faithfully she obeys these injunctions, the more she is working herself out of a job. Some day, while she is still a young woman . . . she will be alone, quite alone, in a home of her own.

In an action-oriented, future time-minded society, having no job to do engenders a feeling of uselessness which in turn creates emotional disturbance. Most of us have witnessed the disoriented behavior and emotional stress of women whose children have grown up and gone. Some respond by clinging to children, others try desperately to fit into jobs with the outmoded skills they learned and used years ago; others become unnecessarily fussy housewives; some are merely restless.

There would be many fewer occurrences of any of these responses if the evaluation of women's activities outside the home was sufficiently high to provide the needed feelings of usefulness and accomplishment. But such is not the case; hence we have the second of the reasons why more and more women are trying to combine marriage with a career.

In whatever part of the history of woman's role we look, we note that being a status symbol, a glamour girl, especially an *old* glamour girl, or even a culture bearer, does not bring many badges of merit in our kind of society. Not even in community work are there many satisfactions left for women today. Here again men have damaged the value of the work by often adopting an attitude that it, too, is secondary to business and safely left in the hands of women until conditions become really bad or the issues extreme. Then, of course, they plan to step in and put things on a businesslike basis.

But more than the attitudes of men, it has been the professionalization of community activities which has deflated women's interest in them. It is the way of Americans to organize and professionalize everything which becomes important. Welfare work, many community services, and even recreational programs in cities of any size are now large scale and important. The formulation of their policies and their administration are, therefore, matters which require professional competence. What is left to the well-intentioned but untrained woman who must work part-time and as a volunteer is neither much nor very important. Sometimes volunteer services are not accepted at all. More than a few of my former students report a refusal of their services in any capacity. They are told, kindly enough, to go back to school, obtain the necessary degree, and then apply for a paid position.

This situation is enough to discourage women in their efforts to play their variant role. It is worsened, however, by the kind of education these women have had, a training which I have elsewhere labeled a *contingency education.* Educational opportunities are no longer refused women, although in some colleges there are still some professors who let it be known that they consider a higher education for women both a nuisance and a waste of time. Nor is the education girls receive different from that given to boys. Throughout childhood and youth the girl child goes to school with boys and is trained in accord with masculine patterns. From babyhood on, she learns the ways of being independent and autonomous. Even though little sister still finds a doll in a carriage under the Christmas tree while brother has a train for his or father's amusement, she is expected to learn to look after herself all through adolescence and beyond, even forever if need be. The hope is expressed that she will not have to remain independent and therefore need not use much of what she has learned. Instead, and this is the great problem, she is expected, upon her marriage or certainly after children are born, to give her attention to other things for which she has not been well trained.

These are the powerful factors which are making women look to the occupations for the means of becoming dominant Americans. I find it difficult to criticize any woman for what she either does or does not do as long as she is left so much in doubt as to what is expected of her.

Are there ways of eliminating confusion and cutting away contradictions? I have said that I would suggest three. The first I mentioned long ago: we should change our attitudes toward domestic tasks and accord them a worth which will challenge women to truly creative accomplishments. Cooking, planned marketing, home management, flower arrangement, and interior decoration are no less worthy of thoughtful attention and long hours of concentration than what goes on in offices. They just seem so because that is what we are taught to believe. As for the more humdrum tasks, it is doubtful that washing the same dish ten times is intrinsically a more boring chore than filing the same folder ten times in the same office cabinet.

A change in attitudes will, of course, necessitate some alteration in the present methods of educating women — and men too. This could well begin at home, where so often domestically indifferent mothers pass on their prejudices to daughters without even knowing it. It was only a few years ago that one woman remarked to me, "I understand you think women should give more attention to houses and domestic things than they do. I agree with you and am worried about my daughter. I try so hard to get her into the kitchen, but she resists. I tell her that, Heaven knows, I hate it, but we do have to eat and it is easier to learn now than later."

Some change of program in schools and colleges may also be required, and this will not be easy. But neither is it impossible, for no proposal is being made that women should be segregated from men and taught only feminine tasks and interests. Should anyone have this fear, the next proposal will quickly dispel it.

Women should also be trained for and allowed to have their regular place in the occupations, but preferably it should be the kind of job, or career, which is limited in time and scope. I avoid the term "part-time jobs" so commonly used because it has come to mean a fill-in job with few responsibilities or incentives. Some women, whether from necessity or from choice, will want a full-time job, and it is their right as Americans to have it without discrimination. However, for most women, and especially during the years of motherhood, the limited job seems much the better solution.

Whether these solutions are liked or not, whether or not they are better than other possible ones, it is a fact that as long as America retains its particular values (individualism, a future-time orientation, a belief in mastering nature, the conception of human nature as evil but perfectible, and a high evaluation of men of action) women will go on striving for the right to participate fully in the spheres of activity which best express them.

But need Americans cling so tenaciously to these particular values which virtually force us to judge the worth of a person by what he is doing or may accomplish in the job world rather than by what kind of person he is or may become? My third suggestion, which goes far beyond women and their role in American life, is that some of the other interests and goals which human beings always have within them as potentials be raised to a value status that is at least the equal of that accorded to economic affairs. American men are not by nature more anti-intellectual than other men and are not more aesthetically gauche. They undoubtedly have surprising gifts of both kinds which they would enjoy expressing. Women, too, have more capacities than those of mere appreciation. But of greater importance than the gains to men as men or to women as women would be the widened area of common interests for men and women, for husbands and wives.

Indeed, each of the suggestions offered really has this as its fundamental aim because, contrary to what some persons seem to believe, it is the husband-wife relationship in the American family, and not the mother-child one, which is in greatest need of the thoughtful attention of all of us. And the most strategic point for a first focusing of that attention is the feminine role itself. Once this role is defined to the better satisfaction of women, once the husband-wife relationship is strengthened and given new and richer meaning, the many problems which psychologists and others are finding in parent-child relations will be easily solved. Most of them may just disappear.

U.S. soldier on guard duty at a missile base in a West German forest, 1958

COLD WAR CRISES

The Cold War concept, springing from the U.S.-Russian antagonism of the immediate postwar years and the alignment of power blocs around divided Europe, came to full fruition during the Eisenhower years. Under the leadership of John Foster Dulles, American foreign policy developed an essentially simplistic view of the world as divided between Communism and the Free World; this view grew into a creed, and anomalies such as Tito's Yugoslavia, Latin-American dictatorships, or African imperial colonies, were tortured to fit or ignored.

Though Eisenhower and Dulles had repudiated as ineffective the containment policy of Truman and promised a more active anti-Communist program, the general stance of foreign policy remained static while the rhetoric escalated. As Russia entered a period of post-Stalinist "peaceful coexistence," the thaw seemed to expose American policy as operating on two independent levels, that of Eisenhower's personal diplomacy, and that of the hard-line State Department; many saw a similar schism in the Soviet Union.

Truman had proven an effective postwar president. The Marshall Plan, NATO, loyalty oaths and investigations for federal employees, and the National Security Act of 1947, establishing among others the Central Intelligence Agency, were all parts of his administration. There was no real hope for a Democratic victory in 1952, however; the custom of postwar Republicanism and the vast popularity of Eisenhower combined to defeat Adlai Stevenson in 1952 and again in 1956. The keynote of Eisenhower's years was moderate conservatism, a late version of normalcy; except in foreign policy, the administration was calm and undemanding.

Joe Covello from Black Star

UPI — Compix

(Left) Heavy machinery being manufactured for distribution through the Marshall Plan, 1951; (below) members of the Congress look on as President Truman signs the NATO alliance pact, 1949

(Above) Adlai Stevenson (second left), Democratic presidential candidate, 1952 and 1956, with other party leaders; (below) Eisenhower campaigning for the presidency in 1952

Elliott Erwitt from Magnum

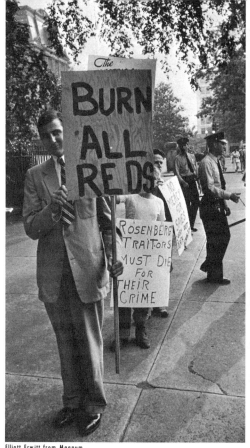

Elliott Erwitt from Magnum

"It's Okay—We're Hunting Communists"

(Above left) Protesters picket White House in an attempt to stay the execution of the Rosenbergs as Communist spies; (above right) pickets in support of the Rosenberg conviction; (right) Herblock cartoon drawn during the House Un-American Activities Committee's investigations of 1947

Eve Arnold from Magnum

Courtesy, Daniel Fitzpatrick, "St. Louis Post-Dispatch"

(Above) Roy Cohn and Joseph McCarthy during an investigation into Communist infiltration of the government; (right) cartoonist views McCarthy's tactics

The new Red Scare posed serious threats to civil liberties during the 1950s and once again demonstrated the possibility of demagoguery in a democracy. The rabid anti-communism that was Cold War dogma was bolstered by the Hiss case and the trial of the Rosenbergs as atomic spies. Taking the cue, Sen. Joseph McCarthy began a campaign to seek out "Communist" infiltrators in government. Wild claims, unsubstantiated charges, and complete disregard for either standards of justice or the liberty of individuals were the method; the victims were chosen practically at random. The climax of the McCarthy campaign was the televised Army hearings in 1954; the viciousness and slander of the "investigation" proved too much even for an acquiescent Congress. McCarthy was condemned by the Senate in December 1954.

THE SUPREME COURT OF SOMETHING OR OTHER

Party leaders at the funeral of Soviet dictator Josef Stalin, March 1953

The reunification of Germany remained an insoluble dilemma. Russia, with vulnerable borders in the west, was wary of a rearmed, sovereign Germany; the U.S. and its Allies refused to consider a Communist or neutral Germany. Conferences in 1954 and 1955 failed to solve the problem as no genuine compromise plan was offered by either side. The rearmament of West Germany, long opposed by France, became a priority aim; in May 1955 West Germany was granted full sovereignty and membership in NATO with an obligation to set up armed forces within the NATO system.

Berlin uprising in June 1953: (Left) Two demonstrators hurl stones at Soviet tanks; (below) East Berliners view fires of protest

European Picture Service

Keystone Press

Wide World

(Top) American Army assists in training the new German forces; (center) Dulles greets Soviet leaders Bulganin and Khrushchev and Germany's Adenauer; (below) Geneva Conference of 1955

Comet Photo from Black Star

(Above) Hungarian freedom fighter in Budapest; (left) Premier Imre Nagy, who failed to win free government for Hungary

A relaxation of Russia's rigid control of Hungary followed Stalin's death in 1953, but was reversed in 1955. Opposition to the government mounted and in October 1956 a student demonstration demanding an end to Soviet domination and the return of democracy sparked a revolution. Premier Nagy announced Hungary's withdrawal from the Warsaw Pact and appealed in vain for UN aid and recognition. And despite Dulles' earlier dedication of U.S. foreign policy to the "liberation of captive peoples," America failed to take any action during the crisis. On November 4 Soviet troops entered Budapest and crushed the revolt.

Europress — Pix from Publix

(Above) Soviet tanks moving into Hungary to put down the revolt; (below) Hungarian patriots burn Soviet books and propaganda in the protest against Communist rule

Erich Lessing from Magnum

The end of the revolt: (Above) Hungarian refugees slip across the border into Austria; (below) dead Soviet soldier in the ruins of Budapest after the Soviet suppression of the uprising

Keystone Press

Social and economic reform had been relatively successful in Egypt under the nationalist — and anti-Communist — leadership of Gamal Abd-al-Nasser, who had become increasingly prominent among both Arab and neutralist leaders. An attack by Israel on frontier positions in February 1955 led Nasser to appeal for Western arms; he was refused and, while the U.S. and Britain moved to weaken Egypt's cotton trade, was forced to seek aid from Communist Czechoslovakia. The U.S. then reneged on its promised assistance in the construction of the Aswan Dam.

(Top) Sunken ships block entrance to the Suez Canal at Port Said; (bottom) British soldiers fighting in the town of Ismailia, following Egyptian seizure of the Suez Canal

European Picture Service

(Above) United Nations Security Council meeting to hear Anglo-French complaint against Egypt; (below) Londoners protest against their country's actions in the Middle East, 1956

(Above) Dulles at ceremonies for the founding of SEATO; (right) American seaman participates in U.S. maneuvers in Lebanon; (below) American soldiers patrol streets of a Lebanese village

Nasser nationalized the Suez Canal in July 1956 and announced that tolls would be used to finance the Aswan Dam. Israel attacked again in October. Britain and France issued a cease-fire ultimatum and, when Egypt rejected it, began joint bombardment of Egypt. The U.S., aware beforehand of Anglo-French intentions, sponsored a UN cease-fire resolution; Anglo-French troops were defiantly landed on November 5. A UN-supervised cease-fire and withdrawal was finally arranged. To stem doubts of its support of European allies, the U.S. sent its own troops to Lebanon in July 1958 to halt a pro-Nasser revolt.

SAC
COMMUNICATIONS
CENTER
EYES AND EARS OF THE
STRATEGIC AIR COMMAND
NERVE CENTER OF THE
FREE WORLD

DUTY OFFICER
LT. RADLEIN   LT. LYNCH
DUTY NCO
S/SGT SNIPES

PLEASE DISPLAY BADGE

U.S. Air Force Photo

U.S. Air Force Photo

Eisenhower and Dulles repudiated the Truman containment theory of quick but localized reaction to Communist pressure anywhere along the front and instituted instead the rhetoric of deterrence and massive retaliation. In the new terms, while conventional armed forces were to be maintained — on a reduced scale — to deal with "brush-fire" wars, America's main reliance was to be placed on a large atomic force capable of striking back instantly at the Soviet homeland. Essential to this theory was the credibility factor, the requirement that potential enemies fully believe America's ability and determination to wreak utter destruction. Maintaining this credibility required the further willingness to advance to "the brink of war" in any crisis to discourage foolish aggressors.

(Left) Airman on duty to check identification at the Communications Center of the Strategic Air Command; (below) B-52 stratofortress during an operational readiness inspection

(Above) Jets at the American air base Wheelus, near Tripoli in North Africa; (below) radar equipment at the Wheelus base

(Above) Barbed wire surrounding an American missile base in West Germany; (left) Air Force launches a Minuteman intercontinental ballistic missile from Cape Kennedy in 1963

The new military requirements for increasingly efficient — and costly — atomic delivery systems and defensive detection networks were quickly fulfilled; the nation's defense expenditures rose sharply and whole new industries were born of the rapidly advancing technology of war. In 1955 the first atomic-powered submarine was launched and was followed in a few years by a submarine capable of firing several missiles equipped with atomic warheads. The giant and constantly patrolling bombers of the Strategic Air Command were gradually superseded by permanent emplacements of intercontinental ballistic missiles across the country. Behind the fanfare announcing the perfection of a radar detection system that would give a full 15 minutes warning of a Soviet attack, a civil defense program emphasizing both private and mass fallout shelters was largely ignored by the public.

(Above) Looking down onto a combat-ready Titan II missile at McConnell Air Force Base in Kansas;
(below) atomic-powered submarine "Nautilus" returns from first sea trials, 1955

President Eisenhower welcomes Nikita Khrushchev to United States in 1959

As the vastly expensive arms race began, some critics raised the possibility that the stockpiling of bombs and missiles might actually increase the chances of war; it was certain that all-out war would see inconceivable destruction. At the same time, however, the Khrushchev "thaw" and Eisenhower's personal diplomacy eased somewhat the tensions at the top. A cordial summit meeting in 1955, the Russians' suspension of atomic testing in 1958, and Khrushchev's visit to the U.S. in 1959 seemed encouraging signs that a head-on confrontation could be avoided.

Khrushchev tours an American farm with Secretary of Agriculture Ezra Taft Benson

37.

John Dewey: On Progressive Education

Few men have influenced American education in the twentieth century so deeply as John Dewey, who for more than fifty years was education's most severe critic as well as its most imaginative innovator. The program known as "progressive education" is probably his best-known achievement, but his ideas resulted in many other changes and improvements as well. Dewey was asked in 1952 to write an introduction for a volume titled The Use of Resources in Education, *and he took the opportunity afforded by the request to survey the educational scene as he had known it throughout his long career. Part of his Introduction to the work is reprinted here.*

Source: Elsie R. Clapp, *The Use of Resources in Education*, New York, 1952.

IN THE COURSE OF MORE than half a century of participation in the theory and practice of education, I have witnessed many successes and many failures in what is most popularly known as "progressive education," but is also known as "the new education," "modern education," and so on. These designations are singular but they cover a plurality of different movements which have in common the general objective of improving the educational system but which differ from one another in many specific respects — ideas, principles, policies, and programs. The confusion in public discussion of educational problems does not arise from using the term "progressive education" instead of "new education" or vice versa. It arises from using these designations as if they were proper names, denoting a singular entity. This is hardly the place to enter into terminological problems; however, it is in place to point out that I shall use the designations "progressive education" and "the progressive education movement" as common names, that is, as convenient linguistic means of referring to the whole complex of diversified movements and efforts to improve the practice and theory of education.

During the past few years, organized attacks on the achievements of progressive education have become more extensive and virulent than ever before. The current effort to turn the clock back in education is a real cause for alarm but not for surprise. The educational system is part of the common life and cannot escape suffering the consequences that flow from the conditions prevailing outside the school building. When repressive and reactionary forces are increasing in strength in all our other institutions — economic, social, and political — it would be folly to expect the school to get off free.

For the same reason, it is folly to think that the progressive education movement was something thought up and put over by the teachers all by themselves. On the intellectual side, it was part of the wider movement of thought, the inquiries into the nature and problems of growth which constitute the great contribution of the second half of the 19th century to the advancement of human knowledge in the biological, psychological, and sociological sciences. On the social side, it was part of the widespread effort to liberate individuals and institutions from bondage to repressive modes of life.

Without the support of the progressive and enlightening forces in the community, intellectual and social, the teachers of new vision would have been at best like Arnold's Shelley, ineffectual angels, born out of their time, and all their best plans and ideas would have had little or no effect on the educational system.

The most widespread and marked success of the progressive education movement has been in bringing about a significant change in the life-conditions in the classroom. There is a greater awareness of the needs of the growing human being, and the personal relations between teachers and students have been to a noticeable extent humanized and democratized. But the success in these respects is as yet limited; it is largely atmospheric; it hasn't yet really penetrated and permeated the foundations of the educational institution. The older gross manifestations of the method of education by fear and repression — physical, social, and intellectual — which was the established norm for the educational system before the progressive education movement began have, generally speaking, been eliminated. But the basic attitudes underlying the gross manifestations have in many areas still to be rooted out. The fundamental authoritarianism of the old education persists in various modified forms. There is a great deal of talk about education being a cooperative enterprise in which teachers and students participate democratically, but there is far more talk about it than the doing of it. To be sure, many teachers, particularly in the kindergarten and elementary schools, take the children into sharing with them to an extent impossible and inconceivable under the old system whose supreme achievement of educational wisdom is enshrined in its maxim: spare the rod and spoil the child.

In the secondary schools and colleges, however, there isn't much sharing on the part of teachers in the needs and concerns of those whom they teach. Of course, the conditions still too largely prevailing in the school — the size of the classes, the load of work, and so on — make it difficult to carry on the educative process in any genuinely cooperative, democratic way. These conditions, however, are not the sole causes for the failures in educational democracy, as is evident from the fact that in "progressive" schools where these deplorable conditions do not exist education as thoroughgoing sharing is often rather more a theme of discourse in various courses in the curriculum than a practice observable in the conduct of the school. . . .

It should be a commonplace, but unfortunately it is not, that no education — or anything else for that matter — is progressive unless it is making progress. Nothing is more reactionary in its consequences than the effort to live according to the ideas, principles, customs, habits, or institutions which at some time in the past represented a change for the better but which in the present constitute factors in the problems confronting us. The fact that a given change was made in order to realize a desirable end in view signifies that the life-conditions before and after are different. In the process of attaining that good, a new situation was created. A new complex of life-conditions was brought into existence presenting its own distinctive characteristics and problems. Blind attachment to what was good for a state of affairs that no longer exists prevents recognition of the needs of the present and blots out of view the desirable ends that those needs should generate. As Emerson puts it, the attained good tends to become the enemy of the better.

New problems cannot be met intelligently by routine application of ideas and principles which were developed in solving different problems. New problems demand for their intelligent solution the projection of new purposes, new ends in view; and new ends necessitate the development of new means and methods. Of course, the "new" is, in all cases, relatively, not absolutely, new. Even though something absolutely new may be desirable, and some may delude themselves into thinking they have something absolutely new, the continuities in culture and experience exclude the possibility of anything having in fact this absolute character. The danger of cutting through all relations and connections inherited from the past is purely chimerical. The real danger is in perpetuating the past under forms that claim to be new but are only disguises of the old.

What has just been said is illustrated in the history of the progressive education movement — as in every other area of human effort and advance. It accounts for the failure in the movement which can no more be attributed to the teachers alone than can its successes. To change long-established habits in the individual is a slow, difficult, and complicated process. To change long-established institutions — which are social habits organized in the structure of the common life — is a much slower, more difficult, and far more complicated process. The drive of established institutions is to assimilate and distort the new into conformity with themselves. This drive or tendency in the educational institution is perhaps most glaringly evident in the way the ideas and principles of the educational philosophy I have had a share in developing are still for the most part taught, more than half a century after they began to find their way in various parts of the school. In teachers colleges and elsewhere the ideas and principles have been converted into a fixed subject matter of ready-made rules, to be taught and memorized according to certain standardized procedures and, when occasion arises, to be applied to educational problems externally, the way mustard plasters, for example, are applied.

In other words, habits of "learning" institutionalized and perpetuated for centuries

seek to transform into their own image ideas and principles which explicitly emphasize that learning is a method of growth and that the educative process does not consist in acquiring a kit of tools but is a process of learning means and methods of human growth which can never be fixed but must be constantly developed for the intelligent solution of new problems or more adequate solution of old problems partially solved. Considered from the most general philosophical point of view, this conversion — or perversion — of means and methods into a fixed, self-sufficient subject matter is due to the persistence and power of the traditional notion that the qualities of ideas are inherent, eternal, and immutable essences. On this theory, the principles of progressive education (of whatever sort they may be) are "inherently progressive" and anyone who can recite them is *ipso facto* a "progressive" teacher.

It may perhaps be said that to train teachers in the right principles the wrong way is an improvement over teacher training that is wrong in both respects. But it is not much of an improvement. For the *method* of training — inside or outside the school — forms character. The *method* of teacher training in teachers colleges is not of course the sole determinant of the characters of the future teachers; but insofar as the method of training is successful it forms their character *as teachers,* and hence is a significant determinant of their moral development. Training in the right principles the wrong way means in effect to create a split between the moral and intellectual training of teachers. The principles they learn to recite acquire the function of a verbal veneer. To the extent that their training is effective and until it is modified (for better or worse) by post-training experiences, they will teach as they were taught in fact, not as they were taught *about* teaching as a subject of educational theory.

Speaking again from the most general

philosophical standpoint, this authoritarian principle in education and the consequences that flow from it in the conduct of the school will never be effectively eradicated as long as the traditional notion prevails that the qualities of ideas are inherent essences. For it follows from this notion or doctrine that the education of teachers consists in transmitting to them certain collections of fixed, immutable subject matter which they in turn are to transmit to the students under them. The educational regimen thus consists of authorities at the upper end handing down to the receivers at the lower end what they must accept. This is not education but indoctrination, propaganda. It is a type of "education" fit for the foundations of a totalitarian society and, for the same reason, fit to subvert, pervert, and destroy the foundations of a democratic society.

For the creation of a democratic society we need an educational system where the process of moral-intellectual development is in practice as well as in theory a cooperative transaction of inquiry engaged in by free, independent human beings who treat ideas and the heritage of the past as means and methods for the further enrichment of life, quantitatively and qualitatively, who use the good attained for the discovery and establishment of something better.

38.

Aaron Copland: The Composer in Industrial America

Serious music in America has been called the orphan of the arts. American literature is known and admired both at home and abroad, and American painting and sculpture have recently, at least, attained the reputation of being among the best being produced in the world at the present time. But American music, apart from popular songs and jazz, is not accorded much respect even by Americans themselves. This fact, together with the reasons for it, was discussed by composer Aaron Copland in a book, Music and Imagination, *published in 1952. Copland's thesis was not only that Americans should know their own music better, but also that American composers should try harder to produce music appropriate to the new industrial culture of the country.*

Source: *Music and Imagination*, Cambridge, 1952, Ch. 6.

My years in Europe from the age of twenty to twenty-three made me acutely conscious of the origins of the music I loved. Most of the time I spent in France, where the characteristics of French culture are evident at every turn. The relation of French music to the life around me became increasingly manifest. Gradually, the idea that my personal expression in music ought somehow to be related to my own back-home environment took hold of me. The conviction grew inside me that the two things that seemed always to have been so separate in America — music and the life about me — must be made to touch. This desire to make the music I wanted to write come out of the life I had lived in America became a preoccupation of mine in the '20s. It was not so very different from the experience of other young American artists, in other fields, who had gone abroad to study in that period; in greater or lesser degree, all of us discovered America in Europe.

In music our problem was a special one: it really began when we started to search for what Van Wyck Brooks calls a usable past. In those days the example of our American elders in music was not readily at hand. Their music was not often played except perhaps locally. Their scores were seldom published and, even when published, were expensive and not easily available to the inquiring student. We knew, of course, that they too had been to Europe as students, absorbing musical culture, principally in Teutonic centers of learning. Like us, they came home full of admiration for the treasures of European musical art, with the self-appointed mission of expounding these glories to their countrymen.

But when I think of these older men, and especially of the most important among them — John Knowles Paine, George Chadwick, Arthur Foote, Horatio Parker — who made up the Boston school of composers at the turn of the century, I am aware of a fundamental difference between their attitude and our own. Their attitude was founded upon an admiration for the European art work and an identification with it that made the seeking out of any other art formula a kind of sacrilege. The challenge of the continental art work was not: can we do better or can we also do something truly our own, but merely, can we do as well. But of course one never does "as well." Meeting Brahms or Wagner on his own terms one is certain to come off second best. They loved the masterworks of Europe's mature culture not like creative personalities but like the schoolmasters that many of them became. They accepted an artistic authority that came from abroad, and seemed intent on conforming to that authority.

I do not mean to underestimate what they accomplished for the beginnings of serious American musical composition. Quite

the contrary. Within the framework of the German musical tradition in which most of them had been trained, they composed industriously, they set up professional standards of workmanship, and encouraged a seriousness of purpose in their students that long outlasted their own activities. But judged purely on their merits as composers, estimable though their symphonies and operas and chamber works are, they were essentially practitioners in the conventional idiom of their own day, and therefore had little to offer us of a younger generation. No doubt it is trite to say so, but it is nonetheless true, I think, that a genteel aura hangs about them. There were no Dostoyevskys, no Rimbauds among them; no one expired in the gutter like Edgar Allan Poe. It may not be gracious to say so, but I fear that the New England group of composers of that time were in all their instincts overgentlemanly, too well-mannered, and their culture reflected a certain museumlike propriety and bourgeois solidity.

In some strange way Edward MacDowell, a contemporary of theirs, managed to escape some of the pitfalls of the New Englanders. Perhaps the fact that he had been trained from an early age in the shadow of the Conservatoire at Paris and had spent many subsequent years abroad gave him a familiarity in the presence of Europe's great works that the others never acquired. This is pure surmise on my part; but it is fairly obvious that, speaking generally, his music shows more independence of spirit, and certainly more personality than was true of his colleagues around 1900. It was the music of MacDowell, among Americans, that we knew best, even in 1925. I cannot honestly say that we dealt kindly with his work at that period; his central position as "foremost composer of his generation" made him especially apt as a target for our impatience with the weaknesses and orthodoxies of an older generation. Nowadays, although his music is played less often than it once was, one can appreciate more justly what

MacDowell had: a sensitive and individual poetic gift, and a special turn of harmony of his own. He is most successful when he is least pretentious. It seems likely that for a long time MacDowell's name will be secure in the annals of American music, even though his direct influence as a composer can hardly be found in present-day American music.

The search for a usable past, for musical ancestors, led us to examine most closely, as was natural, the music of the men who immediately preceded our own time — the generation that was active after the death of MacDowell in 1908. It was not until about that period that some of our composers were able to shake off the all-pervasive German influence in American music. With Debussy and Ravel, France had reappeared as a world figure on the international musical scene, and French impressionism became the new influence. Composers like Charles Martin Loeffler and Charles T. Griffes were the radicals of their day. But we see now that if the earlier Boston composers were prone to take refuge in the sure values of the academic world, these newer men were in danger of escaping to a kind of artistic ivory tower. As composers, they seemed quite content to avoid contact with the world they lived in. Unlike the poetry of Sandburg or the novels of Dreiser or Frank Norris, so conscious of the crude realities of industrial America, you will find no picture of the times in the music of Loeffler or Griffes. The danger was that their music would become a mere adjunct to the grim realities of everyday life, a mere exercise in the poetic, the exotic-medievalism, Hinduisms, Gregorian chants, *chinoiseries*. Even their early critics stressed the "decadent" note in their music.

Despite this *fin-de-siècle* tendency, Charles Griffes is a name that deserves to be remembered. He represents a new type of composer as contrasted with the men of Boston. Griffes was just an ordinary small-town boy from Elmira, New York. He never knew the important musical people of his time and he never managed to get a better job than that of music teacher in a private school for boys, outside Tarrytown, New York. And yet there are pages in his music where we recognize the presence of the truly inspired moment. His was the work of a sentient human being, forward-looking, for its period, with a definite relationship to the impressionists and to Scriabin. No one can say how far Griffes might have developed if his career had not been cut short by death in his thirty-sixth year in 1920. What he gave those of us who came after him was a sense of the adventurous in composition, of being thoroughly alive to the newest trends in world music and to the stimulus that might be derived from such contact.

Looking backward for first signs of the native composer with an interest in the American scene one comes upon the sympathetic figure of Henry F. Gilbert. His special concern was the use of Negro material as a basis for serious composition. This idea had been given great impetus by the arrival in America in 1892 of the Bohemian composer, Anton Dvořák. His writing of the New World Symphony *in* the new world, using melodic material strongly suggestive of Negro spirituals, awakened a desire on the part of several of the younger Americans of that era to write music of local color, characteristic of one part, at least, of the American scene. Henry Gilbert was a Boston musician, but he had little in common with his fellow New Englanders, for it was his firm conviction that it was better to write a music in one's own way, no matter how modest and restricted its style might be, than to compose large works after a foreign model. Gilbert thought he had solved the problem of an indigenous expression by quoting Negro or Creole themes in his overtures and ballets. What he did was suggestive on a primitive and pioneering level, but the fact is that he lacked the technique and musicianship for expressing his ideals in a significant way. . . .

Through a curious quirk of musical history the man who was writing such a music — a music that came close to approximating our needs — was entirely unknown to us. I sometimes wonder whether the story of American music might have been different if Charles Ives and his work had been played at the time he was composing most of it — roughly the twenty years from 1900 to 1920. Perhaps not; perhaps he was too far in advance of his own generation. As it turned out, it was not until the '30s that he was discovered by the younger composers. As time goes on, Ives takes on a more and more legendary character, for his career as composer is surely unique not only in America but in musical history anywhere. . . .

Ives had an abiding interest in the American scene as lived in the region with which he was familiar. He grew up in Danbury, Connecticut, but completed his schooling at Yale University, where he graduated in 1898. Later he moved on to New York, where he spent many years as a successful man of business. Throughout his life one gets the impression that he was deeply immersed in his American roots. He was fascinated by typical features of New England small-town life: the village church choir, the Fourth of July celebration, the firemen's band, a barn dance, a village election, George Washington's birthday. References to all these things and many similar ones can be found in his sonatas and symphonies. Ives treated this subject matter imaginatively rather than literally. Don't think for an instant that he was a mere provincial with a happy knack for incorporating indigenous material into his many scores. No, Ives was an intellectual, and what is most impressive is not his evocation of a local landscape but the overall range and comprehensiveness of his musical mind.

Nevertheless Ives had a major problem in attempting to achieve formal coherence in the midst of so varied a musical material. He did not by any means entirely succeed in this difficult assignment. At its worst his music is amorphous, disheveled, haphazard — like the music of a man who is incapable of organizing his many different thoughts. Simultaneity of impression was an idea that intrigued Ives all his life. As a boy he never got over the excitement of hearing three village bands play on different street corners at the same time. Ives tried a part solution for reproducing this simultaneity of effect which was subsequently dubbed "musical perspective" by one music critic.

He composed a work which is a good example of this device. It is called "Central Park in the Dark," dates from 1907, and, like many of Ives's work, is based on a poetic transcription of a realistic scene. The composer thought up a simple but ingenious method for picturing this scene, thereby enhancing what was in reality a purely musical intention. Behind a velvet curtain he placed a muted string orchestra to represent the sounds of the night, and before the curtain he placed a woodwind ensemble which made city noises. Together they evoke Central Park in the dark. The effect is almost that of musical cubism, since the music seems to exist independently on different planes. This so-called musical perspective makes use of music realism in order to create an impressionistic effect.

The full stature of Ives as composer will not be known until we have an opportunity to judge his output as a whole. Up to now, only a part of his work has been deciphered and published. But whatever the total impression may turn out to be, his example in the Twenties helped us not at all, for our knowledge of his work was sketchy — so little of it had been played. . . .

[This] desire of mine to find a musical vernacular, which, as language, would cause no difficulties to my listeners, was perhaps nothing more than a recrudescence of my old interest in making a connection between music and the life about me. Our serious composers have not been signally successful at making that kind of connection. Oblivious to their surroundings, they live in constant communion with great works, which in turn seems to make it *de rigueur* for them to attempt to emulate the great works by writing one of their own on an equivalent plane. Do not misunderstand me. I entirely approve of the big gesture for those who can carry it off. What seems to me a waste of time is the self-deceiving "major" effort on the part of many composers who might better serve the community by the writing of a good piece for high school band. Young composers are especially prone to overreaching themselves — to making the grand gesture by the writing of ambitious works, often in a crabbed style, that have no future whatever. It is unrealistic and a useless aping, generally of foreign models.

I have no illusion, of course, that this good advice will be heeded by anyone. But I like to think that in my own work I have, by example, encouraged the notion that a composer writes for different purposes and from different viewpoints. It is a satisfaction to know that in the composing of a ballet like *Billy the Kid* or in a film score like *Our Town,* and perhaps in the *Lincoln Portrait,* I have touched off for myself and others a kind of musical naturalness that we have badly needed along with "great" works.

An honest appraisal of the position of the American composer in our society today would find much to be proud of, and also much to complain about. The worst feature of the composer's life is the fact that he does not feel himself an integral part of the musical community. There is no deep need for his activities as composer, no passionate concern in each separate work as it is written. (I speak now not of my own personal experience but of my observation of the general scene.) When a composer is played, he is usually surrounded by an air of mild approval; when he is not played, no one demands to hear him. Performances in any case are rare events, with the result that

very few composers can hope to earn a livelihood from the music they write. The music-teaching profession has therefore been their principal resource, and the composing of music an activity reserved for their spare time. These are familiar complaints, I know, perhaps immemorial ones; but they show little sign of abatement, and in the aggregate they make composers as a group an unhappy lot, with the outward signs of unhappiness ranging from open resentment to inner frustration.

On the brighter side of the ledger there is the cheering fact that numerically there are many more active composers than there once were. There is private encouragement on the part of certain foundations and individuals, and prizes and commissions are much more frequently given. An occasional radio station or recording company will indicate a spurt of interest. The publishers have shown signs of gratifying awakening, by a willingness to invest in the future of unknowns. The music critics are, generally speaking, more open-minded in their attitude, more ready to applaud than they were a quarter of a century ago. And best of all there appears to be a continual welling up of new talents from all parts of America that augurs well for our composing future.

In the final analysis the composer must look for keenest satisfaction in the work that he does — in the creative art itself. In many important respects creation in an industrial community is little different from what it has always been in any community. What, after all, do I put down when I put down notes? I put down a reflection of emotional states: feelings, perceptions, imaginings, intuitions. An emotional state, as I use the term, is compounded of everything we are: our background, our environment, our convictions. Art particularizes and makes actual these fluent emotional states. Because it particularizes and because it makes actual, it gives meaning to *la condition humaine.* If it gives meaning it necessarily has purpose. I would even add that it has moral purpose.

One of the primary problems for the composer in an industrial society like that of America is to achieve integration, to find justification for the life of art in the life about him. I must believe in the ultimate good of the world and of life as I live it in order to create a work of art. Negative emotions cannot produce art; positive emotions bespeak an emotion about something. I cannot imagine an artwork without implied convictions; and that is true also for music, the most abstract of the arts.

It is this need for a positive philosophy which is a little frightening in the world as we know it. You cannot make art out of fear and suspicion; you can make it only out of affirmative beliefs. This sense of affirmation can be had only in part from one's inner being; for the rest it must be continually reactivated by a creative and yea-saying atmosphere in the life about one. The artist should feel himself affirmed and buoyed up by his community. In other words, art and the life of art must mean something, in the deepest sense, to the everyday citizen. When that happens, America will have achieved a maturity to which every sincere artist will have contributed.

39.

Harold Rosenberg: Action Painting

The style of painting known as Abstract Expressionism came to the fore in the years after World War II. Americans were its leading practitioners, and it was the first American school of art to influence European painters rather than the other way around. Art critic Harold Rosenberg discussed the new style, which he dubbed "action painting," in an article published in 1952 and reprinted here. He emphasized its significance, not only as a largely American contribution to the Western world's art, but also as reflecting radical changes — here, in the "painting-viewer relationship" — that have tended to mark all of the arts in the postwar period.

Source: *Art News*, December 1952: "The American Action Painters."

WHAT MAKES ANY DEFINITION of a movement in art dubious is that it never fits the deepest artists in the movement — certainly not as well as, if successful, it does the others. Yet without the definition something essential in those best is bound to be missed. The attempt to define is like a game in which you cannot possibly reach the goal from the starting point but can only close in on it by picking up each time from where the last play landed.

MODERN ART? OR AN ART OF THE MODERN?

SINCE THE WAR every twentieth-century style in painting is being brought to profusion in the United States: thousands of "abstract" painters — crowded teaching courses in Modern Art — a scattering of new heroes — ambitions stimulated by new galleries, mass exhibitions, reproductions in popular magazines, festivals, appropriations.

Is this the usual catching up of America with European art forms? Or is something new being created? . . . For the question of novelty, a definition would seem indispensable.

Some people deny that there is anything original in the recent American painting. Whatever is being done here now, they claim, was done thirty years ago in Paris. You can trace this painter's boxes of symbols to Kandinsky, that one's moony shapes to Miró or even back to Cézanne.

Quantitatively, it is true that most of the symphonies in blue and red rectangles, the wandering pelvises and birdbills, the line constructions and plane suspensions, the virginal dissections of flat areas that crowd the art shows are accretions to the "School of Paris" brought into being by the fact that the mode of production of modern masterpieces has now been all too clearly rationalized. There are styles in the present displays which the painter could have acquired by putting a square inch of a Soutine or a Bonnard under a microscope. . . . All this is training based on a new conception of what art is, rather than original work demonstrating what art is about to become.

At the center of this wide practising of the immediate past, however, the work of some painters has separated itself from the rest by a consciousness of a function for painting different from that of the earlier "abstractionists," both the Europeans themselves and the Americans who joined them in the years of the Great Vanguard.

This new painting does not constitute a School. To form a School in modern times not only is a new painting consciousness needed but a consciousness of that consciousness — and even an insistence on certain formulas. A School is the result of the linkage of practice with terminology — different paintings are affected by the same words. In the American vanguard the words, as we shall see, belong not to the art

but to the individual artists. What they think in common is represented only by what they do separately.

GETTING INSIDE THE CANVAS

AT A CERTAIN MOMENT the canvas began to appear to one American painter after another as an arena in which to act — rather than as a space in which to reproduce, redesign, analyze or "express" an object, actual or imagined. What was to go on the canvas was not a picture but an event.

The painter no longer approached his easel with an image in his mind; he went up to it with material in his hand to do something to that other piece of material in front of him. The image would be the result of this encounter.

It is pointless to argue that Rembrandt or Michelangelo worked in the same way. You don't get Lucrece with a dagger out of staining a piece of cloth or spontaneously putting forms into motion upon it. She had to exist some place else before she got on the canvas, and the paint was Rembrandt's means for bringing her here. Now, everything must have been in the tubes, in the painter's muscles and in the cream-colored sea into which he dives. If Lucrece should come out she will be among us for the first time — a surprise. To the painter, she *must* be a surprise. In this mood there is no point in an act if you already know what it contains.

"B. is not modern," one of the leaders of this mode said to me the other day. "He works from sketches. That makes him Renaissance."

Here the principle, and the difference from the old painting, is made into a formula. A sketch is the preliminary form of an image the *mind* is trying to grasp. To work from sketches arouses the suspicion that the artist still regards the canvas as a place where the mind records its contents

— rather than itself the "mind" through which the painter thinks by changing a surface with paint.

If a painting is an action, the sketch is one action, the painting that follows it another. The second cannot be "better" or more complete than the first. There is just as much significance in their difference as in their similarity.

Of course, the painter who spoke had no right to assume that the other had the old mental conception of a sketch. There is no reason why an act cannot be prolonged from a piece of paper to a canvas. Or repeated on another scale and with more control. A sketch can have the function of a skirmish.

Call this painting "abstract" or "Expressionist" or "Abstract-Expressionist," what counts is its special motive for extinguishing the object, which is not the same as in other abstract or Expressionist phases of modern art.

The new American painting is not "pure art," since the extrusion of the object was not for the sake of the aesthetic. The apples weren't brushed off the table in order to make room for perfect relations of space and color. They had to go so that nothing would get in the way of the act of painting. In this gesturing with materials the aesthetic, too, has been subordinated. Form, color, composition, drawing, are auxiliaries, any one of which — or practically all, as has been attempted, logically, with unpainted canvases — can be dispensed with. What matters always is the revelation contained in the act. It is to be taken for granted that in the final effect, the image, whatever be or be not in it, will be a *tension*.

DRAMAS OF AS IF

A PAINTING THAT IS AN ACT is inseparable from the biography of the artist. The painting itself is a "moment" in the adulterated mixture of his life — whether "moment" means, in one case, the actual minutes taken up with spotting the canvas or, in another, the entire duration of a lucid drama conducted in sign language. The act-painting is of the same metaphysical substance as the artist's existence. The new painting has broken down every distinction between art and life.

It follows that anything is relevant to it. Anything that has to do with action — psychology, philosophy, history, mythology, hero worship. Anything but art criticism. The painter gets away from Art through his act of painting; the critic can't get away from it. The critic who goes on judging in terms of schools, styles, form, as if the painter were still concerned with producing a certain kind of object (the work of art), instead of living on the canvas, is bound to seem a stranger.

Some painters take advantage of this stranger. Having insisted that their painting is an act, they then claim admiration for the act as art. This turns the act back toward the aesthetic in a petty circle. If the picture is an act, it cannot be justified *as an act of genius* in a field whose whole measuring apparatus has been sent to the devil. Its value must be found apart from art. Otherwise the "act" gets to be "making a painting" at sufficient speed to meet an exhibition date.

Art — relation of the painting to the works of the past, rightness of color, texture, balance, etc. — comes back into painting, by way of psychology. As Stevens says of poetry, "it is a process of the personality of the poet." But the psychology is the psychology of creation. Not that of the so-called psychological criticism that wants to "read" a painting for clues to the artist's sexual preferences or debilities. The work, the act, translates the psychologically given into the intentional, into a "world" — and thus transcends it.

With traditional aesthetic references discarded as irrelevant, what gives the canvas its meaning is not psychological data but *role,* the way the artist organizes his emotional and intellectual energy as if he were in a living situation. The interest lies in the kind of act taking place in the four-sided arena, a dramatic interest.

Criticism must begin by recognizing in the painting the assumptions inherent in its mode of creation. Since the painter has become an actor, the spectator has to think in a vocabulary of action: its inception, duration, direction — psychic state, concentration, and relaxation of the will, passivity, alert waiting. He must become a connoisseur of the gradations between the automatic, the spontaneous, the evoked.

"IT'S NOT THAT, IT'S NOT THAT, IT'S NOT THAT"

WITH A FEW IMPORTANT EXCEPTIONS, most of the artists of this vanguard found their way to their present work by being cut in two. Their type is not a young painter but a reborn one. The man may be over forty, the painter around seven. The diagonal of a grand crisis separates him from his personal and artistic past.

Many of the painters were "Marxists" (WPA unions, artists' congresses) — they had been trying to paint Society. Others had been trying to paint Art (Cubism, Post-Impressionism) — it amounts to the same thing.

The big moment came when it was decided to paint. . . . Just TO PAINT. The gesture on the canvas was a gesture of liberation, from Value — political, aesthetic, moral.

If the war and the decline of radicalism in America had anything to do with this sudden impatience, there is no evidence of it. About the effects of large issues upon their emotions, Americans tend to be either reticent or unconscious. The French artist thinks of himself as a battleground of history; here one hears only of private Dark Nights. Yet it is strange how many segregated individuals came to a dead stop within the past ten years and abandoned, even physically destroyed, the work they had been doing. A far-off watcher, unable to realize that these events were taking place in silence, might have assumed they were being directed by a single voice.

At its center the movement was away from rather than towards. The Great Works of the Past and the Good Life of the Future became equally nil.

The refusal of Value did not take the form of condemnation or defiance of society, as it did after World War I. It was diffident. The lone artist did not want the world to be different, he wanted his canvas to be a world. Liberation from the "nature," society and art already there. It was a movement to leave behind the self that wished to choose his future and to nullify its promissory notes to the past.

With the American, heir of the pioneer and the immigrant, the foundering of Art and Society was not experienced as a loss. On the contrary, the end of Art marked the beginning of an optimism regarding himself as an artist. The American vanguard painter took to the white expanse of the canvas as Melville's Ishmael took to the sea.

On the one hand, a desperate recognition of moral and intellectual exhaustion; on the other, the exhilaration of an adventure over depths in which he might find reflected the true image of his identity. Painting could now be reduced to that equipment which the artist needed for an activity that would be an alternative to both utility and idleness. Guided by visual and somatic memories of paintings he had seen or made — memories which he did his best to keep from intruding into his consciousness — he gesticulated upon the canvas and watched for what each novelty would declare him and his art to be.

Based on the phenomenon of conversion the new movement is, with the majority of the painters, essentially a religious movement. In every case, however, the conversion has been experienced in secular terms. The result has been the creation of private myths. The tension of the private myth is the content of every painting of this vanguard. The act on the canvas springs from an attempt to resurrect the saving moment in his "story" when the painter first felt himself released from Value — myth of past self-recognition. Or it attempts to initiate a new moment in which the painter will realize his total personality — myth of future self-recognition. Some formulate their myth verbally and connect individual works with its episodes. With others, usually deeper, the painting itself is the exclusive formulation, it is a Sign.

The revolution against the given, in the self and in the world, which since Hegel has provided European vanguard art with theories of a New Reality, has re-entered America in the form of personal revolts. Art as action rests on the enormous assumption that the artist accepts as real only that which he is in the process of creating. "Except the soul has divested itself of the love of created things . . ." The artist works in a condition of open possibility, risking, to follow Kierkegaard, the anguish of the aesthetic, which accompanies possibility lacking in reality. To maintain the force to refrain from settling anything, he must exercise in himself a constant No.

APOCALYPSE AND WALLPAPER

THE MOST COMFORTABLE INTERCOURSE with the void is mysticism, especially a mysticism that avoids ritualizing itself. Philosophy is not popular among American painters. For most, thinking consists of the various arguments that TO PAINT is something different from, say, to write or to criticize: a mystique of the particular activity. Lacking ver-

bal flexibility, the painters speak of what they are doing in a jargon still involved in the metaphysics of *things:* "My painting is not Art; it's an Is." "It's not a picture of a thing; it's the thing itself." "It doesn't reproduce Nature; it is Nature." "The painter doesn't think; he knows." Etc. etc. "Art is not, not not not not . . ." As against this, a few reply, art today is the same as it always has been.

Language has not accustomed itself to a situation in which the act itself is the "object." Along with the philosophy of TO PAINT appear bits of Vedanta and popular pantheism.

In terms of American tradition, the new painters stand somewhere between Christian Science and Whitman's "gangs of cosmos." That is, between a discipline of vagueness by which one protects oneself from disturbance while keeping one's eyes open for benefits; and the discipline of the Open Road of risk that leads to the farther side of the object and the outer spaces of the consciousness.

What made Whitman's mysticism serious was that he directed his "cosmic 'I'" towards a Pike's-Peak-or-Bust of morality and politics. He wanted the ineffable in *all* behavior — he wanted it *to win the streets.*

The test of any of the new paintings is its seriousness — and the test of its seriousness is the degree to which the act on the canvas is an extension of the artist's total effort to make over his experience. A good painting in this mode leaves no doubt concerning its reality as an action and its relation to a transforming process in the artist. The canvas has "talked back" to the artist not to quiet him with Sibylline murmurs or to stun him with Dionysian outcries but to provoke him into a dramatic dialogue. Each stroke had to be a decision and was answered by a new question. By its very nature, action painting is painting in the medium of difficulties.

Weak mysticism, the "Christian Science" side of the new movement, tends in the opposite direction, toward *easy* painting — never so many unearned masterpieces! Works of this sort lack the dialectical tension of a genuine act, associated with risk and will. When a tube of paint is squeezed by the Absolute, the result can only be a Success. The painter need keep himself on hand solely to collect the benefits of an endless series of strokes of luck. His gesture completes itself without arousing either an opposing movement within itself nor his own desire to make the act more fully his own. Satisfied with wonders that remain safely inside the canvas, the artist accepts the permanence of the commonplace and decorates it with his own daily annihilation. The result is an apocalyptic wallpaper.

The cosmic "I" that turns up to paint pictures but shudders and departs the moment there is a knock on the studio door brings to the artist a megalomania which is the opposite of revolutionary. The tremors produced by a few expanses of tone or by the juxtaposition of colors and shapes purposely brought to the verge of bad taste in the manner of Park Avenue shop windows are sufficient cataclysms in many of these happy overthrows of Art. The mystical dissociation of painting as an ineffable event has made it common to mistake for an act the mere sensation of having acted — or of having been acted upon. Since there is nothing to be "communicated," a unique signature comes to seem the equivalent of a new plastic language. In a single stroke the painter exists as a Somebody — at least on a wall. That this Somebody is not he seems beside the point.

Once the difficulties that belong to a real act have been evaded by mysticism, the artist's experience of transformation is at an end. In that case what is left? Or to put it differently: What is a painting that is not an object nor the representation of an object nor the analysis or impression of it nor whatever else a painting has ever been —

and which has also ceased to be the emblem of a personal struggle? It is the painter himself changed into a ghost inhabiting The Art World. Here the common phrase, "I have bought an O." (rather than a painting by O.) becomes literally true. The man who started to remake himself has made himself into a commodity with a trademark.

MILIEU: THE BUSY NO-AUDIENCE

WE SAID THAT THE NEW PAINTING calls for a new kind of criticism, one that would distinguish the specific qualities of each artist's act.

Unhappily for an art whose value depends on the authenticity of its mysteries, the new movement appeared at the same moment that Modern Art *en masse* "arrived" in America: Modern architecture, not only for sophisticated homes, but for corporations, municipalities, synagogues; Modern furniture and crockery in mail-order catalogues; Modern vacuum cleaners, can openers; beer-ad "mobiles" — along with reproductions and articles on advanced painting in big-circulation magazines. *Enigmas for everybody.* Art in America today is not only nouveau, it's news.

This new painting came into being fastened to Modern Art and without intellectual allies — in literature everything had found its niche. From this isolated liaison it has derived certain superstitions comparable to those of a wife with a famous husband. Superiorities, supremacies even, are taken for granted. It is boasted that modern painting in America is not only original but an "advance" in world art (at the same time that one says "to hell with world art").

Everyone knows that the label Modern Art no longer has any relation to the words that compose it. To be Modern Art a work need not be either modern nor art; it need not even be a work. A three thousand-year-old mask from the South Pacific qualifies as

Modern and a piece of wood found on a beach becomes Art. When they find this out, some people grow extremely enthusiastic, even, oddly enough, proud of themselves; others become infuriated.

These reactions suggest what Modern Art actually is. It is not a certain kind of art object. It is not even a Style. It has nothing to do either with the period when a thing was made nor with the intention of the maker. It is something that someone has had the power to designate as psychologically, aesthetically or ideologically relevant to our epoch. The question of the driftwood is: *Who* found it?

Modern Art in America represents a revolution of taste — and serves to identify power of the caste conducting that revolution. Responses to Modern Art are primarily responses to claims to social leadership. For this reason Modern Art is periodically attacked as snobbish, Red, immoral, etc., by established interests in Society, politics, the church. Comedy of a revolution that restricts itself to weapons of taste — and which at the same time addresses itself to the masses: Modern-design fabrics in bargain basements, Modern interiors for office girls living alone, Modern milk bottles.

Modern art is educational, not with regard to art but with regard to life. You cannot explain Mondrian's painting to people who don't know anything about Vermeer, but you can easily explain the social importance of admiring Mondrian and forgetting about Vermeer.

Through Modern Art the expanding caste of professional enlighteners of the masses — designers, architects, decorators, fashion people, exhibition directors — informs the populace that a supreme Value has emerged in our time, the Value of the NEW, and that there are persons and things that embody that Value. This Value is a completely fluid one. As we have seen, Modern Art does not have to be actually new; it only has to be new to *somebody* — to the last lady who

found out about the driftwood — and to win neophytes is the chief interest of the caste.

Since the only thing that counts for Modern Art is that a work shall be NEW, and since the question of its newness is determined not by analysis but by social power and pedagogy, the vanguard painter functions in a milieu utterly indifferent to the content of his work.

Unlike the art of nineteenth-century America, advanced paintings today are not bought by the middle class. Nor are they by the populace. Considering the degree to which it is publicized and feted, vanguard painting is hardly bought at all. It is *used* in its totality as material for educational and profit-making enterprises: color reproductions, design adaptations, human-interest stories. Despite the fact that more people see and hear about works of art than ever before, the vanguard artist has an audience of nobody. An interested individual here and there, but no audience. He creates in an environment not of people but of functions. His paintings are employed not wanted. The public for whose edification he is periodically trotted out accepts the choices made for it as phenomena of The Age of Queer Things.

AN ACTION is not a matter of taste.

You don't let taste decide the firing of a pistol or the building of a maze.

As the Marquis de Sade understood, even experiments in sensation, if deliberately repeated, presuppose a morality.

To see in the explosion of shrapnel over No Man's Land only the opening of a flower of flame, Marinetti had to erase the moral premises of the act of destruction — as Molotov did explicitly when he said that Fascism is a matter of taste. Both M's were, of course, speaking the driftwood language of the Modern Art International.

Limited to the aesthetics, the taste bureaucracies of Modern Art cannot grasp the human experience involved in the new action paintings. One work is equivalent to another on the basis of resemblances of surface, and the movement as a whole a modish addition to twentieth-century picture making. Examples in every style are packed side by side in annuals and in the heads of newspaper reviewers like canned meats in a chain store — all standard brands.

To counteract the obtuseness, venality, and aimlessness of the Art World, American vanguard art needs a genuine audience — not just a market. It needs understanding — not just publicity.

In our form of society, audience and understanding for advanced painting have been produced, both here and abroad, first of all by the tiny circle of poets, musicians, theoreticians, men of letters, who have sensed in their own work the presence of the new creative principle.

So far, the silence of American literature on the new painting all but amounts to a scandal.

40.

Adlai E. Stevenson: Acceptance Speech

Adlai Stevenson won the governorship of Illinois by an unprecedented plurality of over half a million votes in 1948, and during the next four years his name began to be mentioned as a possible Democratic candidate for the presidency in 1952. However, he did not seek the nomination, even after President Truman announced on March 29, 1952, that he would not be a candidate for reelection; thus when Stevenson was named on the third ballot at Chicago after trailing Estes Kefauver of Tennessee on the first two, he became the first presidential nominee to be drafted since Garfield in 1880. Stevenson's acceptance speech, delivered to the Democratic Convention on July 26, electrified the country — or at least the Democrats in the country — by its eloquence and wit. Political oratory of this high quality, it was widely asserted, had not been heard for years. The speech is reprinted here.

Source: *Major Campaign Speeches of Adlai E. Stevenson, 1952,* New York, 1953, pp. 7-10.

I accept your nomination — and your program.

I should have preferred to hear those words uttered by a stronger, a wiser, a better man than myself. But, after listening to the President's speech, I feel better about myself!

None of you, my friends, can wholly appreciate what is in my heart. I can only hope that you may understand my words. They will be few.

I have not sought the honor you have done me. I *could* not seek it because I aspired to another office, which was the full measure of my ambition. One does not treat the highest office within the gift of the people of Illinois as an alternative or as a consolation prize. I *would* not seek your nomination for the presidency because the burdens of that office stagger the imagination. Its potential for good or evil now and in the years of our lives smothers exultation and converts vanity to prayer.

I have asked the merciful Father — the

Father of us all — to let this cup pass from me. But from such dread responsibility one does not shrink in fear, in self-interest, or in false humility. So, "If this cup may not pass from me, except I drink it, Thy will be done."

That my heart has been troubled, that I have not sought this nomination, that I could not seek it in good conscience, that I would not seek it in honest self-appraisal, is not to say that I value it the less. Rather it is that I revere the office of the presidency of the United States.

And now, my friends, that you have made your decision, I will fight to win that office with all my heart and soul. And, with your help, I have no doubt that we will win.

You have summoned me to the highest mission within the gift of any people. I could not be more proud. Better men than I were at hand for this mighty task, and I owe to you and to them every resource of mind and of strength that I possess to make your deed today a good one for our country and for our party. I am confident, too, that your selection of a candidate for vice-president will strengthen me and our party immeasurably in the hard, the implacable work that lies ahead for all of us.

I know you join me in gratitude and respect for the great Democrats and the leaders of our generation whose names you have considered here in this convention, whose vigor, whose character, whose devotion to the republic we love so well have won the respect of countless Americans and have enriched our party. I shall need them, we shall need them, because I have not changed in any respect since yesterday. Your nomination, awesome as I find it, has not enlarged my capacities. So I am profoundly grateful and emboldened by their comradeship and their fealty, and I have been deeply moved by their expressions of goodwill and support.

And I cannot, my friends, resist the urge

to take the one opportunity that has been afforded me to pay my humble respects to a very great and good American, whom I am proud to call my kinsman, Alben Barkley of Kentucky.

Let me say, too, that I have been heartened by the conduct of this convention. You have argued and disagreed, because as Democrats you care and you care deeply. But you have disagreed and argued without calling each other liars and thieves, without despoiling our best traditions in any naked struggles for power. And you have written a platform that neither equivocates, contradicts, nor evades. You have restated our party's record, its principles and its purposes, in language that none can mistake, and with a firm confidence in justice, freedom, and peace on earth that will raise the hearts and the hopes of mankind for that distant day when no one rattles a saber and no one drags a chain.

For all these things I am grateful to you. But I feel no exultation, no sense of triumph. Our troubles are all ahead of us. Some will call us appeasers; others will say we are the war party. Some will say we are reactionary. Others will say that we stand for socialism. There will be the inevitable cries of "Throw the rascals out"; "It's time for a change"; and so on and so on.

We'll hear all those things and many more besides. But we will hear nothing that we have not heard before. I am not too much concerned with partisan denunciation, with epithets and abuse, because the workingman, the farmer, the thoughtful businessmen all know that they are better off than ever before and they all know that the greatest danger to free enterprise in this country died with the Great Depression under the hammer blows of the Democratic Party.

Nor am I afraid that the precious two-party system is in danger. Certainly the Republican Party looked brutally alive a couple of weeks ago, and I mean both Republican parties! Nor am I afraid that the Democratic Party is old and fat and indolent. After 150 years it has been old for a long time; and it will never be indolent as long as it looks forward and not back, as long as it commands the allegiance of the young and the hopeful who dream the dreams and see the visions of a better America and a better world.

You will hear many sincere and thoughtful people express concern about the continuation of one party in power for twenty years. I don't belittle this attitude. But change for the sake of change has no absolute merit in itself. If our greatest hazard is preservation of the values of Western civilization, in our self-interest alone, if you please, is it the part of wisdom to change for the sake of change to a party with a split personality; to a leader whom we all respect but who has been called upon to minister to a hopeless case of political schizophrenia?

If the fear is corruption in official position, do you believe with Charles Evans Hughes that guilt is personal and knows no party? Do you doubt the power of any political leader, if he has the will to do so, to set his own house in order without his neighbors having to burn it down?

What does concern me, in common with thinking partisans of both parties, is not just winning the election but how it is won, how well we can take advantage of this great quadrennial opportunity to debate issues sensibly and soberly. I hope and pray that we Democrats, win or lose, can campaign not as a crusade to exterminate the opposing party, as our opponents seem to prefer, but as a great opportunity to educate and elevate a people whose destiny is leadership, not alone of a rich and prosperous, contented country as in the past but of a world in ferment.

And, my friends, more important than winning the election is governing the nation. That is the test of a political party —

the acid, final test. When the tumult and the shouting die, when the bands are gone and the lights are dimmed, there is the stark reality of responsibility in an hour of history haunted with those gaunt, grim specters of strife, dissension, and materialism at home, and ruthless, inscrutable, and hostile power abroad.

The ordeal of the 20th century — the bloodiest, most turbulent era of the Christian age — is far from over. Sacrifice, patience, understanding, and implacable purpose may be our lot for years to come. Let's face it. Let's talk sense to the American people. Let's tell them the truth, that there are no gains without pains, that we are now on the eve of great decisions, not easy decisions, like resistance when you're attacked, but a long, patient, costly struggle which alone can assure triumph over the great enemies of man — war, poverty, and tyranny — and the assaults upon human dignity which are the most grievous consequences of each.

Let's tell them that the victory to be won in the 20th century, this portal to the Golden Age, mocks the pretensions of individual acumen and ingenuity. For it is a citadel guarded by thick walls of ignorance and of mistrust which do not fall before the trumpets' blast or the politicians' imprecations or even a general's baton. They are, my friends, walls that must be directly stormed by the hosts of courage, of morality and of vision, standing shoulder to shoulder, unafraid of ugly truth, contemptuous of lies, half truths, circuses, and demagoguery.

The people are wise — wiser than the Republicans think. And the Democratic Party is the people's party, not the labor party, not the farmers' party, not the employers' party — it is the party of no one because it is the party of everyone. That I think, is our ancient mission. Where we have deserted it, we have failed. With your help there will be no desertion now. Better we lose the election than mislead the people; and better we lose than misgovern the people.

Help me to do the job in this autumn of conflict and of campaign; help me to do the job in these years of darkness, doubt, and of crisis which stretch beyond the horizon of tonight's happy vision, and we will justify our glorious past and the loyalty of silent millions who look to us for compassion, for understanding, and for honest purpose. Thus we will serve our great tradition greatly.

I ask of you all you have; I will give to you all I have, even as he who came here tonight and honored me, as he has honored you — the Democratic Party — by a lifetime of service and bravery that will find him an imperishable page in the history of the republic and of the Democratic Party — President Harry S. Truman.

And, finally, my friends, in the staggering task you have assigned me, I shall always try "to do justly and to love mercy and to walk humbly with my God."

41.

Dwight D. Eisenhower: I Shall Go to Korea

It was inevitable that the Korean War should become an issue in the 1952 campaign, particularly since the Republican candidate was the renowned American general who had led the Allies to victory in Europe less than a decade before. Eisenhower did not claim to have any magical solutions for the conflict, but his reputation for solid military competence combined with prudence in emergencies gave him a great advantage over Stevenson, who had had comparatively little war experience. Eisenhower would probably have won in any event, but his election was assured when, in a campaign speech at Detroit on October 24, 1952, he pledged to go to Korea immediately after election day if he were chosen. He did win, and he did go to Korea, on December 2. The Detroit speech is reprinted here.

Source: *New York Times*, October 25, 1952.

IN THIS ANXIOUS AUTUMN for America, one fact looms above all others in our people's mind. One tragedy challenges all men dedicated to the work of peace. One word shouts denial to those who foolishly pretend that ours is not a nation at war.

This fact, this tragedy, this word is: Korea.

A small country, Korea has been, for more than two years, the battleground for the costliest foreign war our nation has fought, excepting the two world wars. It has been the burial ground for 20,000 American dead. It has been another historic field of honor for the valor and skill and tenacity of American soldiers.

All these things it has been — and yet one thing more. It has been a symbol — a telling symbol — of the foreign policy of our nation. It has been a sign — a warning sign — of the way the administration has conducted our world affairs. It has been a measure — a damning measure — of the quality of leadership we have been given.

Tonight I am going to talk about our foreign policy and of its supreme symbol —

the Korean War. I am not going to give you elaborate generalizations but hard, tough facts. I am going to state the unvarnished truth.

What, then, are the plain facts?

The biggest fact about the Korean War is this: It was never inevitable; it was never inescapable; no fantastic fiat of history decreed that little South Korea — in the summer of 1950 — would fatally tempt Communist aggressors as their easiest victim. No demonic destiny decreed that America had to be bled this way in order to keep South Korea free and to keep freedom itself self-respecting.

We are not mute prisoners of history. That is a doctrine for totalitarians; it is no creed for freemen.

There is a Korean War — and we are fighting it — for the simplest of reasons: Because free leadership failed to check and to turn back Communist ambition before it savagely attacked us. The Korean War — more perhaps than any other war in history — simply and swiftly followed the collapse of our political defenses. There is no other reason than this: We failed to read and to outwit the totalitarian mind.

I know something of this totalitarian mind. Through the years of World War II, I carried a heavy burden of decision in the free world's crusade against the tyranny then threatening us all. Month after month, year after year, I had to search out and to weigh the strengths and weaknesses of an enemy driven by the lust to rule the great globe itself.

World War II should have taught us all one lesson. The lesson is this: To vacillate, to hesitate — to appease even by merely betraying unsteady purpose — is to feed a dictator's appetite for conquest and to invite war itself. That lesson — which should have firmly guided every great decision of our leadership through these later years — was ignored in the development of the administration's policies for Asia since the end

of World War II. Because it was ignored, the record of these policies is a record of appalling failure.

The record of failure dates back — with red-letter folly — at least to September of 1947. It was then that Gen. Albert Wedemeyer — returned from a presidential mission to the Far East — submitted to the President this warning: "The withdrawal of American military forces from Korea would result in the occupation of South Korea by either Soviet troops or, as seems more likely, by the Korean military units trained under Soviet auspices in North Korea." That warning and his entire report were disregarded and suppressed by the administration.

The terrible record of these years reaches its dramatic climax in a series of unforgettable scenes on Capitol Hill in June of 1949. By then the decision to complete withdrawal of American forces from Korea — despite menacing signs from the North — had been drawn up by the Department of State. The decision included the intention to ask Congress for aid to Korea to compensate for the withdrawal of American forces.

This brought questions from Congress. The administration parade of civilian and military witnesses before the House Foreign Affairs Committee was headed by the secretary of state. He and his aides faced a group of Republican congressmen, both skeptical and fearful. What followed was historic and decisive. I beg you to listen carefully to the words that followed, for they shaped this nation's course from that date to this. Listen, then.

First: Republican Congressman John Lodge of Connecticut asked, "[Do] you feel that the Korean government is able to fill the vacuum caused by the withdrawal of the occupation forces?"

The administration answered: "Definitely."

Second: A very different estimate of the risk involved came from Republican Congressman Walter Judd of Minnesota. He warned: "I think the thing necessary to give security to Korea at this stage of the game is the presence of a small American force and the knowledge (on the Soviet side) that attack upon it would bring trouble with us." "I am convinced," Representative Judd continued, "that if we keep even a battalion there, they are not going to move. And if the battalion is not there" — listen now to his warning — "the chances are they will move within a year."

What a tragedy that the administration shrugged off that so-accurate warning!

Third: The secretary of state was asked if he agreed that the South Koreans alone — and I quote — "will be able to defend themselves against any attack from the northern half of the country." To this the secretary answered briskly: "We share the same view. Yes, sir."

Rarely in congressional testimony has so much misinformation been compressed so efficiently into so few words.

Fourth: Republican Congressman Lodge had an incisive comment on all this. "That," he said, "is wishful thinking. . . . I am afraid it confesses a kind of fundamental isolationism that exists in certain branches of the government, which I think is a very dangerous pattern. I think the presence of our troops there is a tremendous deterrent to the Russians."

Finally: This remarkable scene of the summer of 1949 ends with a memorable document. The minority report of five Republican members of the House Foreign Affairs Committee on July 26, 1949, submitted this solemn warning. Listen to it:

It is reliably reported that Soviet troops, attached to the North Korean puppet armies, are in position of command as well as acting as advisers. . . . This development may well presage the launching of a full-scale military drive across the 38th Parallel.
Our forces . . . have been withdrawn from South Korea at the very instant when logic and common sense both demanded no retreat from the realities of the situation.

The report continues:

Already along the 38th Parallel aggression is speaking with the too-familiar voices of howitzers and cannons. Our position is untenable and indefensible. The House should be aware of these facts.

These words of eloquent, reasoned warning were spoken eleven months before the Korean War broke.

Behind these words was a fervent, desperate appeal. That appeal was addressed to the administration. It begged at least some firm statement of American intention that might deter the foreseen attack.

What was the administration answer to that appeal?

The first answer was silence — stubborn, sullen silence, for six months. Then, suddenly, came speech — a high government official at long last speaking out on Asia. It was now January of 1950. What did he say? He said, "The United States government will not provide military aid or advice to Chinese forces on Formosa." Then, one week later, the secretary of state announced his famous "defense perimeter" — publicly advising our enemies that so far as nations outside this perimeter were concerned "no person can guarantee these areas against military attack." Under these circumstances, it was cold comfort to the nations outside this perimeter to be reminded that they could appeal to the United Nations.

These nations, of course, included Korea. The armies of communism, thus informed, began their big build-up. Six months later they were ready to strike across the 38th Parallel. They struck on June 25, 1950. On that day, the record of political and diplomatic failure of this administration was completed and sealed.

The responsibility for this record cannot be dodged or evaded. Even if not a single

Republican leader had warned so clearly against the coming disaster, the responsibility for the fateful political decisions would still rest wholly with the men charged with making those decisions — in the Department of State and in the White House. They cannot escape that responsibility now or ever.

When the enemy struck on that June day of 1950, what did America do? It did what it always has done in all its times of peril — it appealed to the heroism of its youth. This appeal was utterly right and utterly inescapable. It was inescapable not only because this was the only way to defend the idea of collective freedom against savage aggression. That appeal was inescapable because there was now in the plight into which we had stumbled no other way to save honor and self-respect.

The answer to that appeal has been what any American knew it would be. It has been sheer valor — valor on all the Korean mountainsides that each day bear fresh scars of new graves.

Now — in this anxious autumn — from these heroic men there comes back an answering appeal. It is no whine, no whimpering plea. It is a question that addresses itself to simple reason. It asks: Where do we go from here? When comes the end? Is there an end?

These questions touch all of us. They demand truthful answers. Neither glib promises nor glib excuses will serve. They would be no better than the glib prophecies that brought us to this pass.

To these questions there are two false answers — both equally false. The first would be any answer that dishonestly pledged an end to war in Korea by any imminent, exact date. Such a pledge would brand its speaker as a deceiver. The second and equally false answer declares that nothing can be done to speed a secure peace. It dares to tell us that we, the strongest nation in the history of freedom, can only wait — and wait — and wait. Such a statement brands its speaker as a defeatist.

My answer — candid and complete — is this: The first task of a new administration will be to review and reexamine every course of action open to us with one goal in view — to bring the Korean War to an early and honorable end. That is my pledge to the American people.

For this task a wholly new administration is necessary. The reason for this is simple. The old administration cannot be expected to repair what it failed to prevent.

Where will a new administration begin? It will begin with its President taking a simple, firm resolution. That resolution will be: To forgo the diversions of politics and to concentrate on the job of ending the Korean War — until that job is honorably done.

That job requires a personal trip to Korea. I shall make that trip. Only in that way could I learn how best to serve the American people in the cause of peace.

I shall go to Korea.

That is my second pledge to the American people.

Carefully, then, this new administration, unfettered by past decisions and inherited mistakes, can review every factor — military, political, and psychological — to be mobilized in speeding a just peace.

Progress along at least two lines can instantly begin. We can, first, step up the program of training and arming the South Korean forces. Manifestly, under the circumstances of today, United Nations forces cannot abandon that unhappy land. But just as troops of the Republic of Korea covet and deserve the honor of defending their frontiers, so should we give them maximum assistance to insure their ability to do so. Then, United Nations forces in reserve positions and supporting roles would be assurance that disaster would not again strike.

We can, secondly, shape our psychological warfare program into a weapon capable of cracking the Communist front.

Beyond all this we must carefully weigh all interrelated courses of action. We will, of course, constantly confer with associated free nations of Asia and with the cooperating members of the United Nations. Thus we could bring into being a practical plan for world peace.

That is my third pledge to you.

As the next administration goes to work for peace, we must be guided at every instant by that lesson I spoke of earlier. The vital lesson is this: To vacillate, to appease, to placate is only to invite war — vaster war, bloodier war. In the words of the late Senator Vandenberg, appeasement is not the road to peace; it is only surrender on the installment plan.

I will always reject appeasement.

And that is my fourth pledge to you.

A nation's foreign policy is a much graver matter than rustling papers and bustling conferences. It is much more than diplomatic decisions and trade treaties and military arrangements. A foreign policy is the face and voice of a whole people. It is all that the world sees and hears and understands about a single nation. It expresses the character and the faith and the will of that nation. In this, a nation is like any individual of our personal acquaintance; the simplest gesture can betray hesitation or weakness, the merest inflection of voice can reveal doubt or fear. It is in this deep sense that our foreign policy has faltered and failed.

For a democracy, a great election, such as this, signifies a most solemn trial. It is the time when — to the bewilderment of all tyrants — the people sit in judgment upon the leaders. It is the time when these leaders are summoned before the bar of public decision. There they must give evidence both to justify their actions and explain their intentions.

In the great trial of this election, the judges — the people — must not be deceived into believing that the choice is between isolationism and internationalism. That is a debate of the dead past. The vast majority of Americans of both parties know that to keep their own nation free they bear a majestic responsibility for freedom through all the world. As practical people, Americans also know the critical necessity of unimpaired access to raw materials on other continents for our own economic and military strength.

Today, the choice — the real choice — lies between policies that assume that responsibility awkwardly and fearfully, and policies that accept that responsibility with sure purpose and firm will. The choice is between foresight and blindness, between doing and apologizing, between planning and improvising.

In rendering their verdict, the people must judge with courage and with wisdom. For, at this date, any faltering in America's leadership is a capital offense against freedom.

In this trial, my testimony, of a personal kind, is quite simple. A soldier all my life, I have enlisted in the greatest cause of my life — the cause of peace. I do not believe it a presumption for me to call the effort of all who have enlisted with me a crusade. I use that word only to signify two facts. First, we are united and devoted to a just cause of the purest meaning to all humankind. Second, we know that — for all the might of our effort — victory can come only with the gift of God's help.

In this spirit — humble servants of a proud ideal — we do soberly say: This is a crusade.

1953

42.

JOHN FOSTER DULLES: Containment or Liberation?

It was no secret that Eisenhower would name John Foster Dulles as his secretary of state, and the new President wasted no time in confirming everyone's expectations. Dulles was asked to testify on the policies that he would follow, and concerning which he had given many hints in the past year, to the Senate Committee on Foreign Relations on January 15, 1953, five days before the new administration took office. The main subject of the questioning was Dulles' policy of "liberation," which the Republicans throughout the campaign had opposed to the Democrats' policy of "containment," calling the latter "negative, futile, and immoral." Portions of Dulles' testimony are reprinted here.

Source: *Nomination of John Foster Dulles, Secretary of State-Designate, Hearing Before the Committee on Foreign Relations, U.S. Senate,* 83 Congress, 1 Session, Washington, 1953.

THERE ARE A NUMBER of policy matters which I would prefer to discuss with the committee in executive session, but I have no objection to saying in open session what I have said before: namely, that we shall never have a secure peace or a happy world so long as Soviet Communism dominates one-third of all of the peoples that there are, and is in the process of trying at least to extend its rule to many others.

These people who are enslaved are people who deserve to be free, and who, from our own selfish standpoint, ought to be free; because if they are the servile instruments of aggressive despotism, they will eventually be welded into a force which will be highly dangerous to ourselves and to all of the free world. Therefore, we must always have in mind the liberation of these captive peoples.

Now, liberation does not mean a war of liberation. Liberation can be accomplished by processes short of war. We have, as one example — not an ideal example, but it illustrates my point — the defection of Yugoslavia under Tito from the domination of Soviet Communism. Well, that rule of Tito is not one which we admire, and it has many aspects of despotism itself; but at least it illustrates that it is possible to disintegrate this present monolithic structure which, as I say, represents approximately one-third of all the people that there are in the world.

The present tie between China and Moscow is an unholy arrangement, which is contrary to the traditions, the hopes, the aspirations of the Chinese people. Certainly we cannot tolerate a continuance of that, or a welding of the 450 million people of China into the servile instruments of Soviet aggression.

Therefore, a policy which only aims at containing Russia where it now is, is, in itself, an unsound policy; but it is a policy which is bound to fail because a purely defensive policy never wins against an aggressive policy. If our only policy is to stay where we are, we will be driven back. It is only by keeping alive the hope of liberation, by taking advantage of that wherever opportunity arises, that we will end this terrible peril which dominates the world, which imposes upon us such terrible sacrifices and so-great fears for the future. But all of this can be done and must be done in ways which will not provoke a general war, or in ways which will not provoke an insurrection which would be crushed with bloody violence, such as was the case, for example, when the Russians instigated the Polish revolt, under General Bor, and merely sat by and watched them when the Germans exterminated those who were revolting.

It must be and can be a peaceful process, but those who do not believe that results can be accomplished by moral pressures, by the weight of propaganda, just do not know what they are talking about.

I ask you to recall the fact that Soviet Communism, itself, has spread from controlling 200 million people some seven years ago to controlling 800 million people today, and it has done that by methods of political warfare, psychological warfare and propaganda, and it has not actually used the Red Army as an open aggressive force in accomplishing that.

Surely what they can accomplish, we can accomplish. Surely if they can use moral and psychological force, we can use it; and to take a negative defeatist attitude is not an approach which is conducive to our own welfare or in conformity with our own historical ideas. . . .

The threat of Soviet Communism, in my opinion, is not only the gravest threat that ever faced the United States but the gravest threat that has ever faced what we call Western civilization, or, indeed, any civilization which was dominated by a spiritual faith.

Soviet Communism is atheistic in its philosophy and materialistic. It believes that human beings are nothing more than somewhat superior animals, that they have no soul, no spirit, no right to personal dignity, and that the best kind of a world is that world which is organized as a well-managed farm is organized, where certain animals are taken out to pasture, and they are fed and brought back and milked, and they are given a barn as shelter over their heads, and that is a form of society which is most conducive to the material welfare of mankind — that is their opinion. That can be made into a persuasive doctrine if one does not believe in the spiritual nature of man.

If you do believe in the spiritual nature of man, it is a doctrine which is utterly unacceptable and wholly irreconcilable.

I do not see how, as long as Soviet Communism holds those views, and holds also the belief that its destiny is to spread those views throughout the world, and to organize the whole world on that basis, there can be any permanent reconciliation.

That does not exclude the possibility of coming to working agreements of a limited character; but basically, between the doctrine of Soviet Communism and the doctrine of a Christian or Jewish or, indeed, any religion, this is an irreconcilable conflict.

43.

J. Robert Oppenheimer: Atomic Weapons and American Policy

It was the scientists who had produced it, rather than the statesmen and the military men who, in many cases, did not fully understand it, who were most vocal during the postwar period in calling for international control of atomic energy. At first it was hoped that the United Nations might be turned into a workable world government, which would solve the problem by making control of the awesome new power in effect a domestic matter, but as this grew obviously less and less feasible owing to the continued strife between America and the Soviet Union, the scientists began to cast about for alternatives. Some of these were explored in an article published in July 1953 by J. Robert Oppenheimer, wartime head of the Los Alamos laboratory that had made the first atomic bomb and, from 1947 to 1966, director of the Institute for Advanced Study at Princeton, New Jersey. The article is reprinted here in part.

Source: Reprinted by special permission from *Foreign Affairs,* July 1953.

It is possible that in the large light of history, if indeed there is to be history, the atomic bomb will appear not very different than in the bright light of the first atomic explosion. Partly because of the mood of the time, partly because of a very clear prevision of what the technical developments would be, we had the impression that this might mark, not merely the end of a great and terrible war but the end of such wars for mankind.

Two years later Colonel Stimson was to write in *Foreign Affairs,* "The riven atom, uncontrolled, can be only a growing menace to us all. . . ." In the same paragraph he wrote, "Lasting peace and freedom cannot be achieved until the world finds a way toward the necessary government of the whole." Earlier, shortly after the war's end, the government of the United States had put forward some modest suggestions, responsive to these views, for dealing with the atom in a friendly, open, cooperative way. We need not argue as to whether these proposals were stillborn. They have been very dead a long, long time, to the surprise of only a few. Openness, friendliness, and cooperation did not seem to be what the Soviet government most prized on this earth.

It should not be beyond human ingenuity for us to devise less friendly proposals. We need not here detail the many reasons why they have not been put forward, why it has appeared irrelevant and grotesque to do so. These reasons range from the special difficulties of all negotiation with the Soviet Union, through the peculiar obstacles presented by the programmatic hostility and the institutionalized secretiveness of Communist countries, to what may be regarded as the more normal and familiar difficulties of devising instruments for the regulation of armaments in a world without prospect of political settlement.

Instead we came to grips, or began to come to grips, with the massive evidences of Soviet hostility and the growing evidences of Soviet power, and with the many almost inevitable, yet often tragic, elements of weakness, disharmony, and disunity in what we have learned to call the Free World. In these preoccupations — one wholly negative and one largely positive, though very difficult — the atom, too, was given a simple role, and the policy followed was a fairly simple one. The role was to be one ingredient of a shield: a shield composed also in part of the great industrial power of America, and in part of the military and, even more, the political weaknesses of the Soviet Union. The rule for the atom was: "Let us keep ahead. Let us be sure that we are ahead of the enemy."

Today it would seem that, however necessary these considerations and these policies may be, they are no longer nearly sufficient. The reason for that one can see when one looks at the character of the arms race. The reason for that one can see when one compares the time-scale of atomic developments here and abroad with the probable time-scale of deep political changes in the world.

It is easy to say "let us look at the arms race." I must tell about it without communicating anything. I must reveal its nature without revealing anything; and this I propose to do.

There are three countries embarked on this race — the United Kingdom — and of that we need to note only that it is unfortunate that so talented and hard-pressed a country, so close to us in history and tradition, should be doing all this separately from us — ourselves, and the U.S.S.R.

As for the U.S.S.R., it has recently been said officially, and thus may be repeated with official sanction, that it has produced three atomic explosions and is producing fissionable material in substantial quantities. I should like to present the evidence for this; I cannot. We do need one word of warning: This is evidence which could well be evidence of what the government of the U.S.S.R. wants us to think rather than evidence of what is true. I may, however, record my own casual, perhaps too rough, guess as to how the U.S.S.R. stands in relation to us in the field of atomic munitions. This does not refer at all to other elements of armament. I think that the U.S.S.R. is about four years behind us. And I think that the scale of its operations is not as big as ours was four years ago. It may be something like half as big as ours then was. This is consistent with the facts known to us. It has not been proven by them, by any means.

This sounds comfortably reassuring. It sounds as though the job of keeping ahead were being satisfactorily accomplished. But in order to assay what it means, we have to know something of what it is that they are four years behind, how fast the situation is likely to change, and what it means to be half as big as we are.

When Hiroshima was bombed, there was a single plane. There was no air opposition. We flew straight in at medium height, at rather low speed, over the city of Hiroshima; we dropped one bomb with an energy release the equivalent of about fifteen thousand tons of TNT. It killed more than seventy thousand people and produced a comparable number of casualties; it largely destroyed a medium-sized city. That we had in mind. But we also had in mind, and we said, that it was not a question of one bomb. It would become a question of ten, and then one hundred, and then a thousand, and then ten thousand, and then maybe one hundred thousand. We knew — or, rather, we did not know, but we had very good reason to think — that it was not a question of ten thousand tons but of one hundred thousand, and then a million tons, and then ten million tons, and then maybe one hundred million tons.

We knew that these munitions could be adapted, not merely to a slow medium bomber operating where we had almost complete air supremacy but to methods of delivery more modern, more flexible, harder to intercept, and more suitable for combat as it might be encountered today.

Today all of this is in train. It is my opinion that we should all know — not precisely but quantitatively and, above all, authoritatively — where we stand in these matters; that we should all have a good idea of how rapidly the situation has changed and of where we may stand, let us say, three, four, or five years ahead, which is about as far as one can see. I shall revert to the reasons why I think it important that we all know of these matters. I cannot write of them.

What I can say is this: I have never discussed these prospects candidly with any responsible group, whether scientists or statesmen, whether citizens or officers of the government, with any group that could steadily look at the facts, that did not come away with a great sense of anxiety and somberness at what they saw. The very least we can say is that, looking ten years ahead, it is likely to be small comfort that the Soviet Union is four years behind us, and small comfort that they are only about half as big as we are. The very least we can conclude is that our twenty-thousandth bomb, useful as it may be in filling the vast munitions pipelines of a great war, will not in any deep strategic sense offset their two-thousandth. The very least we can say is that, as Mr. Gordon Dean has emphasized, there will come a time when, even from the narrowest technical point of view, the art of delivery and the art of defense will have a much higher military relevance than supremacy in the atomic munitions field itself.

There are other aspects of the arms race; though they may be well known, they are worth mentioning. We developed the atomic bomb under the stimulus of the fear that the Germans might be at it. We deliberated at length on the use of the bomb against Japan; indeed, it was Colonel Stimson who initiated and presided over these thorough deliberations. We decided that it should be used. We have greatly developed and greatly increased our atomic activities. This growth, though natural technically, is not inevitable. If the Congress had appropriated no money, it would not have occurred. We have made our decision to push our stockpiles and the power of our weapons. We have from the first maintained that we should be free to use these weapons; and it is generally known we plan to use them. It is also generally known that one ingredient of this plan is a rather rigid commitment to their use in a very massive, initial, unremitting strategic assault on the enemy.

This arms race has other characteristics. There has been relatively little done to secure our defense against the atom; and in the far more tragic and difficult problem of defending our allies in Europe still less has been done. This does not promise to be an easy problem.

Atomic weapons are not just one element of an arsenal that we hope may deter the Soviet government, or just one of the means we think of for putting an end to a war, once started. It is, perhaps, almost the only military measure that anyone has in mind to prevent, let us say, a great battle in Europe from being a continuing, agonizing, large-scale Korea. It is the only military instrument which brings the Soviet Union and the United States into contact — a most uncomfortable and dangerous contact — with one another.

Atomic weapons, as everyone knows,

have been incorporated in the plans for the defense of Europe. They have been developed for many tactical military uses, as in the anti-submarine campaign, the air campaign, and the ground campaign in the European theater; and these potential applications continue to ramify and multiply. Yet the Europeans are rather in ignorance what these weapons are, how many there may be, how they will be used, and what they will do. It thus needs to be remarked, as we shall need to remark again, that for Europe the atomic weapon is both a much needed hope of effective defense and a terrible immediate peril, greater even than for this country.

These are some of the peculiarities of this arms race, marked for us by a very great rigidity of policy and a terrifyingly rapid accumulation, probably on both sides, of a deadly munition. When we think of the terms in which we in this country tend to talk of the future, the somberness with which thoughtful men leave a discussion of the subject is not wholly ununderstandable. There are two things that everyone would like to see happen; but few people, if any, confidently believe that they will happen soon. One is a prompt, a happily prompt, reform or collapse of the enemy. One is a regulation of armaments as part of a general political settlement — an acceptable, hopeful, honorable, and humane settlement to which we could be a party.

There is nothing repugnant in these prospects; but they may not appear to be very likely in the near future. Most of us, and almost all Europeans, appear to regard the outbreak of war in this near future as a disaster. Thus the prevailing view is that we are probably faced with a long period of cold war in which conflict, tension, and armaments are to be with us. The trouble then is just this — during this period the atomic clock ticks faster and faster. We may anticipate a state of affairs in which two

J. Robert Oppenheimer

Great Powers will each be in a position to put an end to the civilization and life of the other, though not without risking its own. We may be likened to two scorpions in a bottle, each capable of killing the other, but only at the risk of his own life.

This prospect does not tend to make for serenity; and the basic fact that needs to be communicated is that the time in which this will happen is short, compared to the time in which reasonable men may have some confidence in a reasonable amelioration or even alteration of the great political troubles of our time.

In this prospect, surely, we shall need all the help and wisdom and resourcefulness we can muster. This, in all probability, is a very tough fix. There are three things we need to remember, three things that are very sharp. It is perilous to forget any one of them. One is the hostility and the power of the Soviet. Another is the touch of weakness — the need for unity, the need for some stability, the need for armed strength on the part of our friends in the Free World. And the third is the increasing peril of the atom. The problem is straightforward, if not easy, if we forget the last. It is easy if we forget the first. It is hard if we remember all three. But they are all there.

We need the greatest attainable freedom of action. We need strength to be able to ask whether our plans for the use of the atom are, all things considered, right or wrong. We need the freedom of action necessary — and we do not have it today — to be able to negotiate should an opportunity for that at some future time appear. . . .

The political vitality of our country largely derives from two sources. One is the interplay, the conflict of opinion and debate, in many diverse and complex agencies, legislative and executive, which contribute to the making of policy. The other is a public opinion which is based on confidence that it knows the truth.

Today public opinion cannot exist in this field. No responsible person will hazard an opinion in a field where he believes that there is somebody else who knows the truth and where he believes that he does not know it. It is true that there are and always will be, as long as we live in danger of war, secrets that it is important to keep secret, at least for an appropriate period, if not for all time; some of these, and important ones, are in the field of atomic energy. But knowledge of the characteristics and probable effects of our atomic weapons, of — in rough terms — the numbers available, and of the changes that are likely to occur within the next years, this is not among the things to be kept secret. Nor is our general estimate of where the enemy stands.

Many arguments have been advanced against making public this basic information. Some of these arguments had merit in times past. One is that we might be giving vital information to the enemy. My own view is that the enemy has this information. It is available to anyone who will trouble to make an intelligence analysis of what has been published. Private citizens do not do this; but we must expect that the enemy does. It is largely available by other means as well. It is also my view that it is good for the peace of the world if the enemy knows these basic facts — very good indeed, and very dangerous if he does not.

There is another source of worry — that public knowledge of the situation might induce in this country a mood of despair, or a too-ready acceptance of what is lightheartedly called preventive war. I believe that until we have looked this tiger in the eye, we shall be in the worst of all possible dangers, which is that we may back into him. More generally, I do not think a country like ours can in any real sense survive if we are afraid of our people.

As a first step, but a great one, we need the courage and the wisdom to make public at least what, in all reason, the enemy must now know: to describe in rough but authoritative and quantitative terms what the atomic armaments race is. It is not enough to say, as our government so often has, that we have made "substantial progress." When the American people are responsibly informed, we may not have solved, but we shall have a new freedom to face, some of the tough problems that are before us.

44.

Dwight D. Eisenhower: Atoms for Peace

President Truman declared that the United States would undertake the development of a hydrogen bomb on January 31, 1950. On April 6, 1952, it was announced that the U.S. was already manufacturing such a bomb; on November 1 of the same year the first bomb containing hydrogen ingredients was exploded at Eniwetok Island in the South Pacific. The new weapon made the old atomic bomb that had destroyed Hiroshima and Nagasaki seem like a child's toy. Tests of various hydrogen devices continued throughout 1953, and there was widespread fear that fallout from these experiments would contaminate the atmosphere even if the explosions themselves did not start a "chain reaction" that would destroy the entire earth. In this climate of mounting terror President Eisenhower appeared before the United Nations on December 8, 1953, and delivered the speech reprinted here in part, which spelled out the alternatives facing the peoples of the world in the face of the awesome new power.

Source: *United Nations: Official Records of the General Assembly, Eighth Session, Plenary Meetings,* September 15-December 9, 1953, pp. 450-452.

I FEEL IMPELLED TO SPEAK today in a language that in a sense is new, one which I, who have spent so much of my life in the military profession, would have preferred never to use. That new language is the language of atomic warfare.

The Atomic Age has moved forward at such a pace that every citizen of the world should have some comprehension, at least in comparative terms, of the extent of this development, of the utmost significance to every one of us. Clearly, if the peoples of the world are to conduct an intelligent search for peace, they must be armed with the significant facts of today's existence.

My recital of atomic danger and power is necessarily stated in United States terms, for these are the only incontrovertible facts that I know. I need hardly point out to this Assembly, however, that this subject is global, not merely national in character.

On July 16, 1945, the United States set off the world's biggest atomic explosion. Since that date in 1945, the United States of America has conducted forty-two test explosions. Atomic bombs are more than twenty-five times as powerful as the weapons with which the atomic age dawned, while hydrogen weapons are in the ranges of millions of tons of TNT equivalent.

Today, the United States stockpile of atomic weapons, which, of course, increases daily, exceeds by many times the total equivalent of the total of all bombs and all shells that came from every plane and every gun in every theater of war in all the years of World War II. A single air group, whether afloat or land based, can now deliver to any reachable target a destructive cargo exceeding in power all the bombs that fell on Britain in all World War II.

In size and variety, the development of atomic weapons has been no less remarkable. The development has been such that atomic weapons have virtually achieved conventional status within our armed services. In the United States, the Army, the Navy, the Air Force, and the Marine Corps are all capable of putting this weapon to military use.

But the dread secret and the fearful engines of atomic might are not ours alone. In the first place, the secret is possessed by our friends and allies, the United Kingdom and Canada, whose scientific genius made a tremendous contribution to our original discoveries and the designs of atomic bombs. The secret is also known by the Soviet Union. The Soviet Union has informed us that, over recent years, it has devoted extensive resources to atomic weapons. During this period the Soviet Union has exploded a series of atomic devices, including at least one involving thermonuclear reactions.

If at one time the United States possessed what might have been called a monopoly of atomic power, that monopoly ceased to exist several years ago. Therefore, although our earlier start has permitted us to accumulate what is today a great quantitative advantage, the atomic realities of today comprehend two facts of even greater significance. First, the knowledge now possessed by several nations will eventually be shared by others, possibly all others. Second, even a vast superiority in numbers of weapons, and a consequent capability of devastating retaliation, is no preventive, of itself, against the fearful material damage and toll of human lives that would be inflicted by surprise aggression.

The free world, at least dimly aware of these facts, has naturally embarked on a large program of warning and defense systems. That program will be accelerated and extended. But let no one think that the expenditure of vast sums for weapons and systems of defense can guarantee absolute safety for the cities and citizens of any nation. The awful arithmetic of the atomic bomb does not permit of any such easy solution. Even against the most powerful defense, an aggressor in possession of the effective minimum number of atomic bombs for a surprise attack could probably place a sufficient number of his bombs on the chosen targets to cause hideous damage.

Should such an atomic attack be launched against the United States, our reactions would be swift and resolute. But for me to say that the defense capabilities of the United States are such that they could inflict terrible losses upon an aggressor, for me to say that the retaliation capabilities of the United States are so great that such an aggressor's land would be laid waste, all this, while fact, is not the true expression of the purpose and the hopes of the United States.

To pause there would be to confirm the hopeless finality of a belief that two atomic colossi are doomed malevolently to eye each other indefinitely across a trembling world. To stop there would be to accept helplessly the probability of civilization destroyed, the annihilation of the irreplaceable heritage of mankind handed down to us from generation to generation, and the condemnation of mankind to begin all over again the age-old struggle upward from savagery toward decency and right and justice. . . .

Most recently we have received from the Soviet Union what is in effect an expression of willingness to hold a four-power meeting. Along with our allies, the United Kingdom and France, we were pleased to see that this note did not contain the unacceptable preconditions previously put forward. . . . The United States, the United Kingdom, and France have agreed promptly to meet with the Soviet Union.

The government of the United States approaches this conference with hopeful sincerity. We will bend every effort of our minds to the single purpose of emerging from that conference with tangible results towards peace, the only true way of lessening international tension.

We never have, and never will, propose

or suggest that the Soviet Union surrender what rightfully belongs to it. We will never say that the peoples of the U.S.S.R. are an enemy with whom we have no desire ever to deal or mingle in friendly and fruitful relationship. On the contrary, we hope that this coming conference may initiate a relationship with the Soviet Union which will eventually bring about a freer mingling of the peoples of the East and of the West — the one sure, human way of developing the understanding required for confident and peaceful relations.

Instead of the discontent which is now settling upon Eastern Germany, occupied Austria, and the countries of Eastern Europe, we seek a harmonious family of free European nations, with none a threat to the other, and least of all a threat to the peoples of the U.S.S.R. Beyond the turmoil and strife and misery of Asia, we seek peaceful opportunity for these peoples to develop their natural resources and to elevate their lot.

These are not idle words or shallow visions. Behind them lies a story of nations lately come to independence, not as a result of war but through free grant or peaceful negotiation. There is a record already written of assistance gladly given by nations of the West to needy peoples and to those suffering the temporary effects of famine, drought, and natural disaster. These are deeds of peace. They speak more loudly than promises or protestations of peaceful intent.

But I do not wish to rest either upon the reiteration of past proposals or the restatement of past deeds. The gravity of the time is such that every new avenue of peace, no matter how dimly discernible, should be explored.

There is at least one new avenue of peace which has not been well explored — an avenue now laid out by the General Assembly of the United Nations. In its resolution of Nov. 28, 1953 this General Assembly suggested

that the Disarmament Commission study the desirability of establishing a subcommittee consisting of representatives of the powers principally involved, which should seek in private an acceptable solution and report . . . on such a solution to the General Assembly and to the Security Council not later than Sept. 1, 1954.

The United States, heeding the suggestion of the General Assembly of the United Nations, is instantly prepared to meet privately with such other countries as may be "principally involved," to seek "an acceptable solution" to the atomic armaments race which overshadows not only the peace but the very life of the world.

We shall carry into these private or diplomatic talks a new conception. The United States would seek more than the mere reduction or elimination of atomic materials for military purposes. It is not enough to take this weapon out of the hands of the soldiers. It must be put into the hands of those who will know how to strip its military casing and adapt it to the arts of peace.

The United States knows that if the fearful trend of atomic military build-up can be reversed, this greatest of destructive forces can be developed into a great boon for the benefit of all mankind. The United States knows that peaceful power from atomic energy is no dream of the future. That capability, already proved, is here today. Who can doubt that, if the entire body of the world's scientists and engineers had adequate amounts of fissionable material with which to test and develop their ideas, this capability would rapidly be transformed into universal, efficient, and economic usage?

To hasten the day when fear of the atom will begin to disappear from the minds of the people and the governments of the East and West, there are certain steps that can be taken now. I therefore make the following proposals:

The governments principally involved, to

the extent permitted by elementary prudence, should begin now and continue to make joint contributions from their stockpiles of normal uranium and fissionable materials to an international atomic energy agency. We would expect that such an agency would be set up under the aegis of the United Nations. The ratios of contributions, the procedures and other details would properly be within the scope of the "private conversations" I referred to earlier.

The United States is prepared to undertake these explorations in good faith. Any partner of the United States acting in the same good faith will find the United States a not unreasonable or ungenerous associate.

Undoubtedly, initial and early contributions to this plan would be small in quantity. However, the proposal has the great virtue that it can be undertaken without the irritations and mutual suspicions incident to any attempt to set up a completely acceptable system of worldwide inspection and control.

The atomic energy agency could be made responsible for the impounding, storage, and protection of the contributed fissionable and other materials. The ingenuity of our scientists will provide special safe conditions under which such a bank of fissionable material can be made essentially immune to surprise seizure.

The more important responsibility of this atomic energy agency would be to devise methods whereby this fissionable material would be allocated to serve the peaceful pursuits of mankind. Experts would be mobilized to apply atomic energy to the needs of agriculture, medicine, and other peaceful activities. A special purpose would be to provide abundant electrical energy in the power-starved areas of the world.

Thus the contributing powers would be dedicating some of their strength to serve the needs rather than the fears of mankind.

The United States would be more than willing — it would be proud — to take up with others "principally involved" the development of plans whereby such peaceful use of atomic energy would be expedited. Of those "principally involved" the Soviet Union must, of course, be one.

I would be prepared to submit to the Congress of the United States, and with every expectation of approval, any such plan that would, first, encourage worldwide investigation into the most effective peacetime uses of fissionable material, and with the certainty that the investigators had all the material needed for the conducting of all experiments that were appropriate; second, begin to diminish the potential destructive power of the world's atomic stockpiles; third, allow all peoples of all nations to see that, in this enlightened age, the great powers of the earth, both of the East and of the West, are interested in human aspirations first rather than in building up the armaments of war; fourth, open up a new channel for peaceful discussion and initiative, at least, a new approach to the many difficult problems that must be solved in both private and public conversations if the world is to shake off the inertia imposed by fear and is to make positive progress towards peace.

Against the dark background of the atomic bomb, the United States does not wish merely to present strength but also the desire and the hope for peace.

The coming months will be fraught with fateful decisions. In this Assembly, in the capitals and military headquarters of the world, in the hearts of men everywhere, be they governed or governors, may they be the decisions which will lead this world out of fear and into peace.

To the making of these fateful decisions, the United States pledges before you, and therefore before the world, its determination to help solve the fearful atomic dilemma — to devote its entire heart and mind to finding the way by which the miraculous inventiveness of man shall not be dedicated to his death, but consecrated to his life.

45.

George Gallup: Mass Information or Mass Entertainment

The quality of both the information and the entertainment supplied to their vast audience by the mass media has been a subject of discussion in America for more than a generation. From one point of view, the Americans are the best informed people on earth, for literacy is almost universal and there is a television set in almost every home. From another point of view, however, Americans are ill informed because of the low level of what they see on television, hear on radio, and read in popular magazines. The question was discussed by George Gallup, director of the American Institute of Public Opinion, and one of the country's pioneer pollsters, in a speech at the University of Iowa (formerly State University of Iowa) on April 14, 1953. The address is reprinted here.

Source: VSD, May 15, 1953.

ONE OF THE REAL THREATS to America's future place in the world is a citizenry which daily elects to be entertained and not informed. From the time the typical citizen arises and looks at his morning newspaper until he turns off his radio or television set before going to bed, he has unwittingly cast his vote a hundred times for entertainment or for education. Without his knowing it, he has helped to determine the very character of our three most important media of communication — the press, radio, and television.

The sad and irrefutable fact is that the choice of the American public is going so heavily in favor of entertainment that we may, as the saying goes, eventually "kill ourselves laughing."

What is the evidence? Let's look first at television. To appreciate the extent to which entertainment has taken over this medium, one should glance over the newspaper listing of the programs for just one week. Or, better still, study the popularity ratings of all shows on TV. The variety shows, mysteries, comedies, Westerns completely dominate the lists. You'll find only a handful of shows which I would describe as truly informational.

The fault can't be attributed to the medium nor to the advertisers who make the final decision as to which shows they will sponsor. The fault is almost entirely with the television viewers. I have known many a valiant attempt on the part of advertisers to put information shows on the air, only to be compelled by good business practice to withdraw them after it was clearly demonstrated that the public was not interested in this type of serious fare. Those who own and control the networks and independent stations of the country would prefer a better balance, if the public could somehow be induced to give relatively more time to information and less to entertainment.

The present lack of interest in the informative type of television show is shocking. The total number of hours devoted by the American public to just *two* shows, "I Love Lucy" and the "Show of Shows," is greater than the total number of hours spent on all information or educational shows put together.

And perhaps here I need to make myself clear on one point. I am not in any sense opposed to entertainment shows. The American public cannot be criticized for its love of entertainment. That is one of our more attractive qualities as a people. I do wish to argue strenuously, however, that there should be a better balance between entertainment and education.

The situation in respect to radio programs is essentially the same as in the case of television. In the entire history of this medium not one serious, educational show has ever reached top rating. And most programs of this type have such small audiences that they are kept on the air solely for prestige purposes, that is to say, to prove to legislators and critics that it is possible to find a few educational shows among the hundreds of entertainment shows offered weekly by this medium.

There has been a rash of quiz shows on radio and, to a lesser extent, on television. But I have never found much justification for listing these as educational. It seems to me that it makes little difference whether the people of this country know how long a fly can stand on the ceiling or whether Martha Washington has an upper plate. Without the lavish prizes that are handed out to almost anyone who can remember his own name, these shows would all have died a-borning.

The newspaper itself has had to make great concessions to this ever growing demand on the part of the public to be entertained. Within the last two decades the number of comic strips printed daily and Sunday has increased by many times. And don't for one minute assume that only children read them. Actually, more adults read the most popular comic strip on a typical day than read the most important news story on the front page.

During the last war one of the saddest sights to me was to see grown men, most of them with high school or college training, poring over comic books in railroad and bus stations and apparently wholly unconcerned with the happenings in the world which would almost certainly affect their destiny.

In a recent study of metropolitan newspapers, it was found that the average amount of time which a reader spends daily on the important news of his country and of the world is less than four minutes. He spends ten times as much time on sports, local gossip, and the service and entertainment features.

For many years I have been interested in the problems of the motion-picture industry, the chief of which is, of course, the problem of making pictures which net a profit. In estimating picture "grosses," we discovered that one question is absolutely essential on the questionnaires given to moviegoers. He is asked to tell whether, on the basis of the title and a synopsis of the story, he believes the picture to be "educational." If the answer is "yes," it is safe to predict almost certain failure for the picture at the box office.

From the field of book reading comes further evidence of our lack of intellectual interests. For many years I have had the opportunity to probe into the book-reading habits of the American people. Despite the fact that we have the highest level of formal education in the world, fewer people buy and read books in this nation than in any other modern democracy. The typical Englishman, with far less formal education, reads nearly three times as many books as our typical citizen. In fact, an Englishman who leaves school at the age of fourteen reads about as many books as our college graduate.

This lack of interest in books is reflected

by the number of bookstores in the United States. In this country, about 1,450 stores sell a fairly complete line of books. In Denmark, a nation whose population is just about half that of New York City, there are some 650 full-fledged bookstores. If we had the same proportion in this country as Denmark, we would have not 1,450 bookstores — but 23,000!

But some will say that whereas we have few bookstores we have a great many free libraries. We do, but certainly not to the extent of the Scandinavian countries. In the United States there are about 7,500 free public libraries. In Sweden, a nation only one twenty-fifth the size of the United States in population, there are 6,500 free public libraries. Or, to put this comparison in another way, the United States would have to have not 7,500 libraries but 150,000 to equal Sweden!

Recent reports from Moscow tell of the great interest in books in that city. Frank Rounds, Jr., in the *United States News,* describes the numerous bookstores in Moscow and the large number of persons who read serious books on the subways. The libraries of Moscow open at 9 A.M. and close at 11:30 P.M., and all day long people queue up to get into them.

Have you seen any queues in front of our libraries lately?

It is understandable perhaps why citizens in the United States who have had little or no schooling would not be interested in books. The discouraging fact is that our high school and college trained citizens read so few books of a serious nature.

In a recent survey of college graduates which I undertook, it was discovered that five out of every six had not done any reading of a serious nature in the few months just prior to the interview — that is, reading which was not immediately connected with their business or occupation. Of the entire group, only a little more than half — 55 percent — could name any recently published book which they would like to read.

The ignorance of these college graduates about the classics was overwhelming. Only one in ten could name the author of *Tom Jones;* three out of four could not name the author of *Wealth of Nations;* six in ten could not name the author of *Vanity Fair.* One college graduate interviewed frankly admitted that he had not read a book since he left college ten years ago. He knew nothing about any of the current best sellers. In answer to some questions which attempted to probe into his knowledge of authors, he "guessed that" Shakespeare wrote *Canterbury Tales,* and that an author he identified as "longsworth" wrote *Tom Jones.* And yet this man is a Bachelor of Arts.

I have heard it said that pocket-size books, which sell at every newsstand and drugstore, now meet America's requirement for books and that the sensational growth in sales of these inexpensive, paperbound books really explains why book sales are low and why libraries are so empty. Actually, more than 200 million pocketbooks will be sold this year. This could give us a lot of comfort were it not for two important statistics. The first is that three-fourths of all pocketbooks are bought by approximately 10 percent of the population — 72 million persons have never bought a single copy in their lives. The second statistic is that it is not the books of cultural value which account for the bulk of the 200 million sales, but the Westerns, mysteries, and raw sex stories.

Another answer sometimes offered to explain why Americans read so few books is that we are a magazine-reading nation. It is true that we buy millions and millions of copies of magazines, just as we buy some 54 million copies of newspapers daily. The strange fact is that, despite this great circulation of newspapers and magazines, we manage to remain rather poorly informed on many of the vital issues of the day.

You may recall the attention accorded the two political conventions last summer by newspapers and magazines. During the two conventions, American newspapers gave over most of their front pages and inside pages to reports on convention happenings. The news magazines, likewise, went all-out to provide complete coverage of these events. Moreover, you could hear or see little else on radio and television. Even so, only one adult in every four throughout the country could name the two men selected as vice-presidential candidates.

It is the daily experience of polltakers to discover how little high school and college graduates as a group know about tariffs, about the progress of the North Atlantic Treaty Organization, our Point Four Program, the struggle in Asia, and similar issues which affect not only their pocketbooks but their very lives.

Even simple matters of geography which should have been learned in grade school remain a mystery — such things, for example, as the location of Formosa, Manchuria, Yugoslavia; or the population of China, Canada, France. In fact, a good many college students and former students cannot take an outline map of the United States and put their finger on the state of Illinois.

I trust that I am not one who places too much emphasis upon "book learning." In the course of polling the American public over a period of nearly two decades, I have found that our people are wonderfully endowed with what is best described as "horse sense." The collective judgment of the people, up to this point in history, has been extraordinarily sound. There is a mountain of evidence to prove that the public is generally right in its opinions and usually far ahead of its representatives in government.

If I could be sure that the problems of the world would become less complex, if I thought that all nations might lapse into that blissful state of "innocuous desuetude"

once described by one of our Presidents, then I would feel far less concerned.

What can we do to help restore a proper balance in this country between entertainment and education? Ultimately, the responsibility must rest on each individual. The media of communication can do many things to make information more palatable to their readers or listeners. Some interesting work is now being undertaken by a number of newspapers, and particularly by the International Press Institute headed by Lester Markel of the *New York Times.* The Ford Foundation is attempting to develop educational programs for television which will attract large audiences, and our leading magazines are constantly trying to get more persons to read the serious material which they publish, in contrast to the fiction and service material.

Without doubt the outstanding success of the 20th century in making worthwhile information interesting to the great mass of readers is *The Reader's Digest,* whose success has extended throughout the world. If any persons in the communications world today deserve to be called geniuses, De Witt and Lila Wallace are those persons.

While I believe that every individual owes it to himself and to his country to be reasonably well informed, and while it is true that the various media of communication are daily working on the problem of getting more readers and listeners to attend to the important rather than to the entertaining, I believe that the great hope of the future must lie in our educational system.

I am thoroughly convinced that we must change our whole basic philosophy of education. We must begin to recognize that the years *after* graduation from grade school, high school, or college are the really important years, and not the years spent in school. We must realize that self-education is all-important and that formal education received in the schools is good only to the extent that it aids and abets self-education.

Too many students today hold the belief that when they are "through" school, that is to say, when they have been graduated, they "have had it." And too many of our teachers, oddly enough, never attempted in any way to disabuse them of this belief. We must begin to understand that the process of learning is a process which must continue throughout life. As Sir Richard Livingstone has said, "Who can suppose that spiritual and intellectual growth ceases and knowledge and wisdom are finally achieved when a university degree is taken, or that the need of knowledge does not grow more urgent with the passing of the years?"

The importance of the years after school can be arrived at through simple arithmetic. The typical high school student is graduated at age seventeen or eighteen; the typical college student, at age twenty-two. If we consider the normal life span, the college graduate spends fifty years after leaving college; the high school graduate, fifty-four.

The opportunity to learn and to increase one's mental stature is thus far greater in the nonschool years than in school years, even though only part of the time of an adult can be devoted to study. Experience in life adds meaning to learning and gives it direction. So, in a real sense, the education of every person should begin and not end with graduation.

If we are ever to make this transition, if we are ever to place full emphasis on self-education, we must start at the college level, as they do in the universities of Europe. I have always resisted the idea, widely held in this country, that college students are too immature to be left to make any but the most simple type of decisions for themselves. And I have always resisted the idea that college students must be shepherded about as if they were still adolescent.

Students enrolled in European universities are more carefully selected than ours. Yet I cannot help believing that if we transferred most of the responsibility, not only for learning but for conduct, to the students themselves, our students would mature much faster.

After studying the operation of European universities and in the light of my own experience in teaching college courses here, I have come reluctantly but inevitably to the conclusion that the enemies of learning at the university level are the textbook, the classroom lecture, and our course system. At Oxford, for example, the student is left pretty much on his own. He reports at weekly or biweekly intervals to his professor or don, who offers his guidance and criticism. But there are no lectures which he *must* attend. His reading covers a broad field, and to a great extent the books which he consults in the course of preparing papers are books of his own selection.

In this country, we lean heavily on textbooks which consist for the most part of bits and pieces of knowledge cannibalized from other textbooks. Too often the teacher, in his classroom lecture, merely repeats the material covered by the textbooks. And the student, once he has memorized and then regurgitated the textbook material in a true-false quiz, can forget the whole business.

The heavy emphasis which we place upon memorizing facts in contrast to learning how to use facts was pointed out by a British student now taking graduate work in Princeton; in an article written for the *Daily Telegraph* of London he wrote:

> The student in the United States must have a thousand streamlined facts at his fingertips, and be able to retell everything in answer to a question, like a tic-tac man giving the latest odds on the next horse race. He must scan the scurrying fashions in ideas as Paris dressmakers watch London.

Obviously the whole school system, from the grades up to college, must be revised if we are to turn out a more mature product. And it occurs to me that the way to do this is rather simple. The first step is to agree on the goals of education. And the second is to test our graduates to see how successfully they attain these goals.

In conversations with college professors throughout the country, I have found rather general agreement on these goals. Most educators will agree that our universities should train students (1) to think independently; (2) to write reasonably well; (3) to know something about the world of today and the world of yesterday; and (4) to want to enlarge their intellectual horizons.

I am confident that if we were to study our graduates who have been out of college for one, ten, or twenty years, we would be appalled at how far short of these goals most of them fall. And I am equally confident that our whole basic philosophy of education would change as a result of this knowledge. If an intellectual renaissance is to get under way in this country, the natural place for it to be born is in our universities.

If our teachers and our schools lead the way, we will have less reason to worry about an uninformed citizenry. And our media of communication can devote an increasing amount of time and space to enlightening a receptive public.

46.

MIKE MANSFIELD: Tidelands Oil for Education

On January 16, 1953, President Truman, shortly before leaving office and hoping perhaps to resolve a long disputed problem, issued an executive order "setting aside the submerged lands of the Continental Shelf as a naval petroleum reserve." This policy was reversed by the incoming Republican administration, which introduced a bill, giving the states title to submerged lands, that was passed by the House on April 1, 1953, and by the Senate on May 5. Senate passage was achieved after a vigorous debate that was marked by a 22-hour, 26-minute filibuster by Senator Wayne Morse of Oregon, an opponent of the bill. Senator Mansfield of Montana, another Democratic opponent, inserted the following statement summing up his views in the Congressional Record *for May 4. The law as passed affirmed U.S. title to the resources of the outer Continental Shelf, a region from which, at the time, oil could not be economically raised.*

Source: *Record,* 83 Cong., 1 Sess., pp. 4362-4363.

ON THE BASIS OF DECISIONS already made by the Supreme Court, I believe that title in the submerged lands has been vested in the United States and, unless legislation such as the Holland Bill is enacted, will remain so.

The Supreme Court of the United States on June 23, 1947, rendered an opinion in the case of United States against California and on June 5, 1950, rendered opinion in the cases of United States against Texas, holding that the United States has paramount rights in, and full dominion and power over, the submerged lands of the Continental Shelf adjacent to the shores of California, Louisiana, and Texas, and stated that the respective states do not own the submerged lands of the Continental Shelf within their boundaries.

At the present time the American system of primary, secondary, and higher education faces a financial crisis of severe magnitude because of the unusually large growth in the school-age population, because of the inadequate supply of teachers, and because of the deteriorating and infirm physical plant of the American educational system. In my opinion the children of the United States — not oil — are this nation's most precious natural resource and their education has from the beginnings of this republic been traditionally held most dear by all Americans.

It is not my purpose to join in the complicated and technical controversy revolving around the ownership of these offshore lands. The Supreme Court of the United States has twice determined the question in unmistakable language. The high court has ruled that this oil, which the Geological Survey has estimated to be worth at least $40 billion — others up to $300 billion at present prices — belongs to all the people of all the states. In my view the issue of ownership has been settled.

It is, however, my desire to emphasize once more to the members of the Senate the crucial financial crisis which our American educational system faces. I know that it is not precisely a secret to any of my colleagues. I do, however, believe the actual bare figures will bring a new sense of shock to them as they did to me despite our mutual awareness of the crisis.

Our children, yours and mine, and those of our constituents, are the most precious asset this nation has. They are America's greatest single natural resource. Their independence of mind, their individuality, their ability to think for themselves and to speak and act for themselves are what we hold most dear. It is their heritage as it was ours. As often as we are confronted with today's specter of Communist totalitarianism just as

often do we take comfort in the ability of our young Americans to take care of themselves. They have always had this ability in the past. It is in the American tradition. But they have had it mainly because of our great system of education, a system which today is deteriorating and is in serious danger of breaking down.

We have been blessed in times of international danger with the engineers, the chemists, the inventors, the technicians, the mechanics, the scientists, the military leaders who have always been imaginative and ingenious enough to protect our people. Are we today so sure that this supply of American talent will always be available to us in the future? Ten years, twenty years from now, what kind of education can our children thank us for? Let us take a look at the record.

In 1947 the elementary-school enrollment in public and private schools was 20.3 million children. By 1957 it is estimated that this enrollment will be 29.5 million. In this ten-year period our school-age children will have increased 50 percent.

Although there has been considerable school construction in the years since the war, the school buildings going up are merely replacing obsolete and unsafe school plants. They do not even begin to touch the problem created by the increased enrollments. It has been authoritatively estimated that it would cost around $11 billion over the next ten years to construct the classrooms to meet the needs of our growing school population. This neglect now puts us in a serious dilemma. First the Depression and then World War II brought school construction to a standstill. At the same time, building costs have doubled over the past twenty-five years. The longer we have waited the more we must pay.

Also, just as more and more of our children reach school age, so are more and more of our teachers leaving the schools. This is just as true today as it was during

World War II. The labor supply is tightening and the teachers are leaving their low-paid jobs to go into defense work. During World War II, 350,000 teachers left the profession. Most of them did not return. Why? The answer was given in one paragraph from the lead editorial in *Collier's* for July 28, 1951.

> The average pay for elementary teachers during the past school year was less than $40 a week in ten states, according to NEA figures. Twenty-one states paid less than $50 a week, and thirty-seven states, less than $60 a week.

There are not enough replacements coming up. The 1951 National Teachers Supply and Demand Study reveals that this year only 32,000 qualified elementary-school teachers will graduate. That is the national supply. What is the demand? In 1953, this year, we will need 60,000 teachers merely to replace those who retire; we will need 10,000 teachers to meet the demands of increased enrollments; we will need another 10,000 teachers merely to relieve overcrowding; and we need thousands more to replace unqualified temporary teachers.

In the postwar years, very little, not much, has been done to raise teachers' salaries. But the few raises have long ago been wiped out by our spiraling inflation. Teachers' pay has not kept pace with our people's pay. In 1949 they earned 99 percent more than in 1940, yet the average employed person earned 120 percent more.

School financing is a serious local problem. As the federal government takes more in taxes for purposes of defense, there is less for our local tax systems, which have in the past taken care of our school problems, and that is one great additional virtue of the oil-for-education amendment. It puts no additional burden whatsoever on the back of the taxpayer, since, whatever grants-in-aid are made to the forty-eight states will not come out of his pocket but out of oil royalties.

I have summarized as briefly as I can the financial crisis in the education of America's children. We must supplement the funds for education or in a few short years our own children will be inadequately educated. Our illiteracy rates will start rising again.

In 1949 we spent approximately $5 billion for the cost of public schools, private schools, parochial schools, colleges, and universities. In that same year we spent more than $7 billion for foreign aid and $12 billion for defense. In my opinion, the dollars for foreign aid and national defense were money wisely spent. But we did not spend enough to educate our children at home. This amendment is a method for increasing our educational facilities without spending more tax money.

Tidelands oil has been a controversial issue for the past twelve years. It has been fought out on the political platforms, in the courts, and in the Congress. I suggest to all of you that here in this oil-for-education amendment you will find a reasonable — in fact, an idealistic — compromise for both sides. In accepting this compromise we will be contributing in the most direct way possible to the future of America.

Amendments have been offered to allocate royalties from submerged lands to reduce expenditures and curtail taxation. Unfortunately, these amendments, like the oil-for-education amendment, have been defeated.

The danger, once this bill passes and becomes law, lies in the possibility that, in addition to this giveaway, there will be additional takeaways. Bills have already been introduced in both houses to take away from the federal government the mineral rights it possesses in the states and also to reduce the grazing authority of the United States government on the public domain in the West. These are only indications of what may happen and I sincerely hope that what I anticipate may not come to pass.

47.

Daniel Bell: Crime, Ethnic Groups, and Urban Politics

The investigations into organized crime in America that were conducted by a Senate committee under Estes Kefauver of Tennessee in 1950-1951 were a revelation to many Americans. The televised hearings shocked a large proportion of viewers and led to a demand that something be done. The more knowing, however, were not surprised by Kefauver's findings and tended to be skeptical about most of the plans for action against crime that were suggested. Sociologist Daniel Bell, for instance, saw the hearings as but one more in a long series of oversimplified explanations of a complex social phenomenon. Bell analyzed the committee's findings in an article published in June 1953. Originally titled "Crime as an American Way of Life," the article is reprinted here in part.

Source: *Antioch Review*, June 1953.

Americans have had an extraordinary talent for compromise in politics and extremism in morality. The most shameless political deals (and "steals") have been rationalized as expedient and realistically necessary. Yet in no other country have there been such spectacular attempts to curb human appetites and brand them as illicit, and nowhere else such glaring failures.

From the start America was at one and the same time a frontier community where "everything goes," and the fair country of the Blue Laws. At the turn of the century the cleavage developed between the Big City and the small-town conscience. Crime as a growing business was fed by the revenues from prostitution, liquor, and gambling that a wide-open urban society encouraged and which a middle-class Protestant ethos tried to suppress with a ferocity unmatched in any other civilized country. Catholic cultures rarely have imposed such restrictions, and have rarely suffered such excesses. Even in prim and proper Anglican England, prostitution is a commonplace of Piccadilly night life, and gambling one of the largest and most popular industries. In America the enforcement of public morals has been a continuing feature of our history.

Some truth may lie in Svend Ranulf's generalization that moral indignation is a peculiar fact of middle-class psychology and represents a disguised form of repressed envy. The larger truth lies perhaps in the brawling nature of American development and the social character of crime. Crime, in many ways, is a Coney Island mirror, caricaturing the morals and manners of a society. The jungle quality of the American business community, particularly at the turn of the century, was reflected in the mode of "business" practised by the coarse gangster elements, most of them from new immigrant families, who were "getting ahead," just as Horatio Alger had urged. In the older, Protestant tradition the intense acquisitiveness, such as that of Daniel Drew, was rationalized by a compulsive moral fervor.

But the formal obeisance of the ruthless businessman in the workaday world to the church-going pieties of the Sabbath was one that the gangster could not make. Moreover, for the young criminal, hunting in the asphalt jungle of the crowded city, it was not the businessman with his wily manipulation of numbers but the "man with the gun" who was the American hero. "No amount of commercial prosperity," once wrote Teddy Roosevelt, "can supply the lack of the heroic virtues." The American was "the hunter, cowboy, frontiersman, the soldier, the naval hero." And in the crowded slums, the gangster. He was a man with a gun, acquiring by personal merit what was denied to him by complex orderings of a stratified society. And the duel with the law was the morality play *par excellence*: the gangster, with whom rides our own illicit desires, and the prosecutor, representing final judgment and the force of the law.

Yet all this was acted out in a wider context. The desires satisfied in extralegal fashion were more than a hunger for the "forbidden fruits" of conventional morality. They also involved, in the complex and ever shifting structure of group, class, and ethnic stratification, which is the warp and woof of America's "open" society, such "normal" goals as independence through a business of one's own, and such "moral" aspirations as the desire for social advancement and social prestige. For crime, in the language of the sociologists, has a "functional" role in the society, and the urban rackets — the illicit activity organized for continuing profit rather than individual illegal acts — is one of the queer ladders of social mobility in American life. Indeed, it is not too much to say that the whole question of organized crime in America cannot be understood unless one appreciates (1) the distinctive role of organized gambling as a function of a mass-consumption economy; (2) the specific role of various immigrant groups as they one after another became involved in marginal business and crime; and (3) the relation of crime to the changing character of the urban political machines.

As a society changes, so does, in lagging fashion, its type of crime. As American society became more "organized," as the American businessman became more "civilized" and less "buccaneering," so did the American racketeer. And just as there were important changes in the structure of business enterprise, so the "institutionalized" criminal enterprise was transformed too.

In the America of the last fifty years the main drift of society has been toward the rationalization of industry, the domestication of the crude self-made captain of industry into the respectable man of manners, and the emergence of a mass-consumption economy. The most significant transformation in the field of "institutionalized" crime was the increasing relative importance of gambling as against other kinds of illegal activity. And, as a multi-billion-dollar business, gambling underwent a transition parallel to the changes in American enterprise as a whole.

This parallel was exemplified in many ways: in gambling's industrial organization (*e.g.*, the growth of a complex technology such as the national racing wire service and the minimization of risks by such techniques as lay-off betting); in its respectability, as was evidenced in the opening of smart and popular gambling casinos in resort towns and in "satellite" adjuncts to metropolitan areas; in its functional role in a mass-consumption economy (for sheer volume of money changing hands, nothing has ever surpassed this feverish activity of fifty million American adults); in the social acceptance of the gamblers in the important status world of sport and entertainment, *i.e.*, "café society." . . .

ALTHOUGH IT NEVER SHOWED UP in the gross national product, gambling in the last decade was one of the largest industries in the United States. The Kefauver Committee estimated it as a twenty-billion-dollar business. This figure has been picked up and widely quoted, but in truth no one knows what the gambling "turnover" and "take" actually is, nor how much is bet legally (pari-mutuel, etc.) and how much illegally. In fact, the figure cited by the committee was arbitrary and arrived at quite sloppily. As one staff member said: "We had no real idea of the money spent. . . . The California crime commission said twelve billion. Virgil Peterson of Chicago estimated thirty billion. We picked twenty billion as a balance between the two."

If comprehensive data are not available, we do know, from specific instances, the magnitude of many of the operations. Some indications can be seen from these items culled at random:

— James Carroll and the M & G syndicate did a 20-million-dollar annual business in St. Louis. This was one of the two large books in the city.

— The S & G syndicate in Miami did a 26-million-dollar volume yearly; the total for all books in the Florida resort reached 40 millions.

— Slot machines were present in 69,786 establishments in 1951 (each paid $100 for a license to the Bureau of Internal Revenue); the usual average is three machines to a license, which would add up to 210,000 slot machines in operation in the United States. In legalized areas, where the betting is higher and more regular, the average gross "take" per machine is $50 a week.

— The largest policy wheel (i.e., "numbers") in Chicago's "Black Belt" reported taxable net profits for the four-year period from 1946 through 1949, after sizable deductions for "overhead," of $3,656,968. One of the large "white" wheels reported in 1947 a gross income of $2,317,000 and a net profit of $205,000. One CIO official estimated that perhaps 15 percent of his union's lower echelon officials are involved in the numbers racket (a steward, free to roam a plant, is in a perfect situation for organizing bets).

If one considers the amount of betting on sports alone — an estimated six billion on baseball, a billion on football pools, another billion on basketball, six billion on horse

racing — then Elmo Roper's judgment that "only the food, steel, auto, chemical, and machine-tool industries have a greater volume of business" does not seem too far-fetched.

While gambling has long flourished in the United States, the influx of the big mobsters into the industry — and its expansion — started in the '30s when repeal of Prohibition forced them to look about for new avenues of enterprise. Gambling, which had begun to flower under the nourishment of rising incomes, was the most lucrative field in sight. To a large extent the shift from bootlegging to gambling was a mere transfer of business operations. In the East, Frank Costello went into slot machines and the operation of a number of ritzy gambling casinos. He also became the "banker" for the Erickson "book," which "laid-off" bets for other bookies. Joe Adonis, similarly, opened up a number of casinos, principally in New Jersey. Across the country, many other mobsters went into bookmaking. As other rackets diminished, and gambling, particularly horse-race betting, flourished in the '40s, a struggle erupted over the control of racing information. . . .

The mobsters were able, where they wished, to "muscle in" on the gambling business because the established gamblers were wholly vulnerable, not being able to call on the law for protection. The senators, however, refusing to make any distinction between a gambler and a gangster, found it convenient to talk loosely of a nationwide conspiracy of "illegal" elements. Senator Kefauver asserted that a "nationwide crime syndicate does exist in the United States, despite the protestations of a strangely assorted company of criminals, self-serving politicians, plain blind fools, and others who may be honestly misguided, that there is no such combine."

The Senate Committee report states the matter more dogmatically:

There is a nationwide crime syndicate known as the Mafia. . . . Its leaders are

Courtesy, F. O. Alexander, "The Bulletin"

"City Birds of Prey"; cartoon by Alexander in "The Bulletin," Philadelphia, 1956

usually found in control of the most lucrative rackets in their cities. There are indications of a centralized direction and control of these rackets. . . . The Mafia is the cement that helps to bind the Costello-Adonis-Lansky syndicate of New York and the Accardo-Guzik-Fischetti syndicate of Chicago. . . . These groups have kept in touch with Luciano since his deportation from the country.

Unfortunately for a good story — and the existence of the Mafia would be a whale of a story — neither the Senate Crime Committee in its testimony, nor Kefauver in his book, presented any real evidence that the Mafia exists as a functioning organization. One finds police officials asserting before the Kefauver Committee their *belief* in the Mafia; the Narcotics Bureau *thinks* that a worldwide dope ring allegedly run by Luciano is part of the Mafia; but the only other "evidence" presented — aside from the incredulous responses both of Senator Kefauver and Rudolph Halley when nearly all the Italian gangsters asserted that they didn't know about the Mafia — is that certain crimes bear "the earmarks of the Mafia."

The legend of the Mafia has been fostered in recent years largely by the peephole writing team of Jack Lait and Lee Mortimer. In their *Chicago Confidential,* they rattled off a series of names and titles that made the organization sound like a rival to an Amos and Andy Kingfish society. Few serious reporters, however, give it much credence. Burton Turkus, the Brooklyn prosecutor who broke up the "Murder, Inc." ring, denies the existence of the Mafia. Nor could Senator Kefauver even make out much of a case for his picture of a national crime syndicate. He is forced to admit that "as it exists today [it] is an elusive and furtive but nonetheless tangible thing," and that "its organization and machinations are not always easy to pinpoint." His "evidence" that many gangsters congregate at certain times of the year in such places as Hot Springs, Arkansas, in itself does not prove much; people "in the trade" usually do, and as the loquacious late Willie Moretti of New Jersey said, in explaining how he had met the late Al Capone at a racetrack, "Listen, well-charactered people you don't need introductions to; you just meet automatically."

Why did the Senate Crime Committee plump so hard for its theory of the Mafia and a national crime syndicate? In part, they may have been misled by their own hearsay. The Senate Committee was not in the position to do original research, and its staff, both legal and investigative, was incredibly small. Senator Kefauver had begun the investigation with the attitude that with so much smoke there must be a raging fire. But smoke can also mean a smoke screen. Mob activities is a field in which busy gossip and exaggeration flourish even more readily than in a radical political sect.

There is, as well, in the American temper, a feeling that "somewhere," "somebody" is pulling all the complicated strings to which this jumbled world dances. In politics the labor image is "Wall Street," or "Big Business"; while the business stereotype was the

"New Dealers." In the field of crime, the side-of-the-mouth low-down was "Costello."

The salient reason, perhaps, why the Kefauver Committee was taken in by its own myth of an omnipotent Mafia and a despotic Costello was its failure to assimilate and understand three of the more relevant sociological facts about institutionalized crime in its relation to the political life of large urban communities in America, namely: (1) the rise of the American-Italian community, as part of the inevitable process of ethnic succession, to positions of importance in politics, a process that has been occurring independently but almost simultaneously in most cities with large Italian constituencies — New York, Chicago, Kansas City, Los Angeles; (2) the fact that there are individual Italians who play prominent, often leading roles today in gambling and in the mobs; and (3) the fact that Italian gamblers and mobsters often possessed "status" within the Italian community itself and a "pull" in city politics. These three items are indeed related — but not so as to form a "plot." . . .

IRONICALLY, THE SOCIAL DEVELOPMENT which made possible the rise to political influence sounds, too, the knell of the Italian gangster. For it is the growing number of Italians with professional training and legitimate business success that both prompts and permits the Italian group to wield increasing political influence; and increasingly it is the professionals and businessmen who provide models for Italian youth today, models that hardly existed twenty years ago. Ironically, the headlines and exposés of "crime" of the Italian "gangsters" came years after the fact. Many of the top "crime" figures long ago had forsworn violence, and even their income, in large part, was derived from legitimate investments (real estate in the case of Costello, motor haulage and auto dealer franchises in the case of Adonis), or from such quasi-legitimate but socially respectable sources, as gambling casinos. Hence society's "retribution" in the jail sentences for Costello and Adonis was little more than a trumped-up morality that disguised a social hypocrisy.

Apart from these considerations, what of the larger context of crime and the American way of life? The passing of the Fair Deal signalizes, oddly, the passing of an older pattern of illicit activities. The gambling fever of the past decade and a half was part of the flush and exuberance of rising incomes, and was characteristic largely of new upper-middle-class rich having a first fling at conspicuous consumption. This upper-middle-class rich, a significant new stratum in American life (not rich in the nineteenth century sense of enormous wealth, but largely middle-sized businessmen and entrepreneurs of the service and luxury trades — the "tertiary economy" in Colin Clark's phrase — who by the tax laws have achieved sizable incomes often much higher than the managers of the super-giant corporations) were the chief patrons of the munificent gambling casinos.

During the war decade when travel was difficult, gambling and the lush resorts provided important outlets for this social class. Now they are settling down, learning about Europe and culture. The petty gambling, the betting and bingo which relieve the tedium of small-town life, or the expectation among the urban slum dwellers of winning a sizable sum by a "lucky number" or a "lucky horse" goes on. To quote Bernard Baruch: "You can't stop people from gambling on horses. And why should you prohibit a man from backing his own judgment? It's another form of personal initiative." But the lush profits are passing from gambling, as the costs of coordination rise. And in the future it is likely that gambling, like prostitution, winning tacit acceptance as a necessary fact, will continue on a decentralized, small-entrepreneur basis.

But passing, too, is a political pattern, the

system of political "bosses" which in its reciprocal relation provided "protection" for and was fed revenue from crime. The collapse of the "boss" system was a product of the Roosevelt era. Twenty years ago Jim Farley's task was simple; he had to work only on some key state bosses. Now there is no longer such an animal. New Jersey Democracy was once ruled by Frank Hague; now there are five or six men each top dog, for the moment, in his part of the state or faction of the party. Within the urban centers, the old Irish-dominated political machines in New York, Boston, Newark, and Chicago have fallen apart. The decentralization of the metropolitan centers, the growth of suburbs and satellite towns, the break-up of the old ecological patterns of slum and transient belts, the rise of functional groups, the increasing middle-class

character of American life, all contribute to this decline.

With the rationalization and absorption of some illicit activities into the structure of the economy, the passing of an older generation that had established a hegemony over crime, the general rise of minority groups to social position, and the break-up of the urban boss system, the pattern of crime we have discussed is passing as well. Crime, of course, remains as long as passion and the desire for gain remain. But big, organized city crime, as we have known it for the past seventy-five years, was based on more than these universal motives. It was based on certain characteristics of the American economy, American ethnic groups, and American politics. The changes in all these areas means that it too, in the form we have known it, is at an end.

48.

Langston Hughes: Bop

Langston Hughes was the author of half a dozen books of poems, a novel, a collection of short stories, one or two plays, and an autobiography, but it is likely that his most enduring creation was Simple, the Negro protagonist of several books in which Hughes expressed his deep understanding of his race and of its relation to, and role in, the white man's world. In the vignettes that make up the Simple books, Hughes commented, in a humorous style that was only occasionally sardonic, on the paradoxes of the Negro's life in the land of the free. An example of Simple at his best is the short disquisition reprinted here, which first appeared in Simple Takes a Wife *(1953).*

Source: *The Best of Simple,* New York, 1961.

SOMEBODY UPSTAIRS in Simple's house had the combination turned up loud with an old Dizzy Gillespie record spinning like mad filling the Sabbath with Bop as I passed.

"Set down here on the stoop with me and listen to the music," said Simple.

"I've heard your landlady doesn't like tenants sitting on her stoop," I said.

"Pay it no mind," said Simple. "Ool-ya-koo," he sang. "Hey Ba-Ba-Re-Bop! Be-Bop! Mop!"

"All that nonsense singing reminds me of

Cab Calloway back in the old *scat* days," I said, "around 1930 when he was chanting, 'Hi-de-*hie*-de-ho! Hee-de-*hee*-de-hee!'"

"Not at all," said Simple, "absolutely not at all."

"Re-Bop certainly sounds like scat to me," I insisted.

"No," said Simple, "Daddy-o, you are wrong. Besides, it was not *Re*-Bop. It is *Be*-Bop."

"What's the difference," I asked, "between *Re* and *Be?*"

"A lot," said Simple. "Re-Bop was an imitation like most of the white boys play. Be-Bop is the real thing like the colored boys play."

"You bring race into everything," I said, "even music."

"It is in everything," said Simple.

"Anyway, Be-Bop is passé, gone, finished."

"It may be gone, but its riffs remain behind," said Simple. "Be-Bop music was certainly colored folks' music — which is why white folks found it so hard to imitate. But there are some few white boys that latched onto it right well. And no wonder, because they sat and listened to Dizzy, Thelonius, Tad Dameron, Charlie Parker, also Mary Lou, all night long every time they got a chance, and bought their records by the dozens to copy their riffs. The ones that sing tried to make up new Be-Bop words, but them white folks don't know what they are singing about, even yet."

"It all sounds like pure nonsense syllables to me."

"Nonsense, nothing!" cried Simple. "Bop makes plenty of sense."

"What kind of sense?"

"You must not know where Bop comes from," said Simple, astonished at my ignorance.

"I do not know," I said. "Where?"

"From the police," said Simple.

"What do you mean, from the police?"

"From the police beating Negroes' heads," said Simple. "Every time a cop hits a Negro with his billy club, that old club says, 'BOP! BOP! . . . BE-BOP! . . . MOP! . . . BOP!'

"That Negro hollers, 'Ooool-ya-koo! Ou-o-o!'

"Old Cop just keeps on, 'MOP! MOP! . . . BE-BOP! . . . MOP!' That's where Be-Bop came from, beaten right out of some Negro's head into them horns and saxophones and piano keys that plays it. Do you call that nonsense?"

"If it's true, I do not," I said.

"That's why so many white folks don't dig Bop," said Simple. "White folks do not get their heads beat *just for being white.* But me — a cop is liable to grab me almost any time and beat my head — *just* for being colored.

"In some parts of this American country as soon as the polices see me, they say, 'Boy, what are you doing in this neighborhood?'

"I say, 'Coming from work, sir.'

"They say, 'Where do you work?'

"Then I have to go into my whole pedigree because I am a black man in a white neighborhood. And if my answers do not satisfy them, BOP! MOP! . . . BE-BOP! . . . MOP! If they do not hit me, they have already hurt my soul. *A dark man shall see dark days.* Bop comes out of them dark days. That's why real Bop is mad, wild, frantic, crazy — and not to be dug unless you've seen dark days, too. Folks who ain't suffered much cannot play Bop, neither appreciate it. They think Bop is nonsense — like you. They think it's just *crazy* crazy. They do not know Bop is also MAD crazy, SAD crazy, FRANTIC WILD CRAZY — beat out of somebody's head! That's what Bop is. Them young colored kids who started it, they know what Bop is."

"Your explanation depresses me," I said.

"Your nonsense depresses me," said Simple.

49.

Dwight Macdonald: Mass Culture

*America has been a world leader in the creation of a so-called mass culture — one
that is enjoyed by the millions but that they have little or no part in creating. The
question of whether such a culture can produce good or "high" art has engaged the
attention of critics both in America and in Europe at least since the 1920s when the
terms "highbrow" and "lowbrow" were popular. Dwight Macdonald, one of the
more vocal critics of mass culture, examined this and allied matters in an article
published in 1953. In the piece, which is reprinted here in part, Macdonald
emphasized the important role of eccentric or avant-garde groups as an antidote
to the articulators of mass culture, despite the evidence that even these groups
were fighting a losing battle.*

Source: *Diogenes,* Summer 1953: "A Theory of Mass Culture."

For about a century, Western culture has really been two cultures: the traditional kind — let us call it "High Culture" — that is chronicled in the textbooks, and a "Mass Culture" manufactured wholesale for the market. In the old art forms, the artisans of Mass Culture have long been at work: in the novel, the line stretches from Eugène Süe to Lloyd C. Douglas; in music, from Offenbach to Tin-Pan Alley; in art, from the chromo to Maxfield Parrish and Norman Rockwell; in architecture, from Victorian Gothic to suburban Tudor. Mass Culture has also developed new media of its own, into which the serious artist rarely ventures: radio, the movies, comic books, detective stories, science-fiction, television.

It is sometimes called "Popular Culture," but I think "Mass Culture" a more accurate term, since its distinctive mark is that it is solely and directly an article for mass consumption, like chewing gum. A work of High Culture is occasionally popular, after all, though this is increasingly rare. Thus Dickens was even more popular than his contemporary G. A. Henty, the difference being that he was an artist, communicating his individual vision to other individuals, while Henty was an impersonal manufacturer of an impersonal commodity for the masses.

THE NATURE OF MASS CULTURE

The historical reasons for the growth of Mass Culture since the early 1800s are well known. Political democracy and popular education broke down the old upper-class monopoly of culture. Business enterprise found a profitable market in the cultural demands of the newly awakened masses, and the advance of technology made possible the cheap production of books, periodicals, pictures, music, and furniture, in sufficient quantities to satisfy this market. Modern technology also created new media like the movies and television which are specially well adapted to mass manufacture and distribution.

The phenomenon is thus peculiar to modern times and differs radically from what was hitherto known as art or culture. It is true that Mass Culture began as, and to some extent still is, a parasitic, a cancerous growth on High Culture. As Clement Greenberg pointed out in "Avant-Garde and Kitsch" (*Partisan Review*, Fall, 1939): "The precondition of *kitsch* [a German term for "Mass Culture"] is the availability close at hand of a fully matured cultural tradition, whose discoveries, acquisitions, and perfected self-consciousness *kitsch* can take advantage of for its own ends." The connection, however, is not that of the leaf and the branch but rather that of the caterpillar and the leaf. *Kitsch* "mines" High Culture the way improvident frontiersmen mine the soil, extracting its riches and putting nothing back. Also, as *kitsch* develops, it begins to draw on its own past, and some of it evolves so far away from High Culture as to appear quite disconnected from it.

It is also true that Mass Culture is to some extent a continuation of the old Folk Art which until the Industrial Revolution was the culture of the common people, but here, too, the differences are more striking than the similarities. Folk Art grew from below. It was a spontaneous, autochthonous expression of the people, shaped by themselves, pretty much without the benefit of High Culture, to suit their own needs. Mass Culture is imposed from above. It is fabricated by technicians hired by businessmen; its audiences are passive consumers, their participation limited to the choice between buying and not buying. The Lords of *kitsch*, in short, exploit the cultural needs of the masses in order to make a profit and/or to maintain their class rule — in Communist countries, only the second purpose obtains. (It is very different to *satisfy* popular tastes, as Robert Burns's poetry did, and to *exploit* them, as Hollywood does.)

Folk Art was the people's own institution, their private little kitchen-garden walled off from the great formal park of their masters' High Culture. But Mass Culture breaks down the wall, integrating the masses into a debased form of High Culture and thus becoming an instrument of political domination. If one had no other data to go on, the nature of Mass Culture would reveal capitalism to be an exploitative class society and not the harmonious commonwealth it is sometimes alleged to be. . . .

GRESHAM'S LAW IN CULTURE

THE SEPARATION OF FOLK ART and High Culture in fairly watertight compartments corresponded to the sharp line once drawn between the common people and the aristocracy. The irruption of the masses onto the political stage has broken down this compartmentation, with disastrous cultural results. Whereas Folk Art had its own special quality, Mass Culture is at best a vulgarized reflection of High Culture. And whereas High Culture could formerly ignore the mob and seek to please only the *cognoscenti*, it must now compete with Mass Culture or be merged into it.

The problem is acute in the United States and not just because a prolific Mass Culture exists here. If there were a clearly defined cultural *élite*, then the masses could have their *kitsch* and the *élite* could have its High Culture, with everybody happy. But the boundary is blurred. A statistically significant part of the population, I venture to guess, is chronically confronted with a choice between going to the movies or to a concert, between reading Tolstoy or a detective story, between looking at old masters or at a TV show; *i.e.*, the pattern of their cultural lives is "open" to the point of being porous. Good art competes with *kitsch*, serious ideas compete with commercialized formulae — and the advantage lies all on one side.

There seems to be a Gresham's Law in cultural as well as monetary circulation: bad stuff drives out the good, since it is more easily understood and enjoyed. It is this facility of access which at once sells *kitsch* on a wide market and also prevents it from achieving quality. Clement Greenberg writes that the special aesthetic quality of *kitsch* is that it "predigests art for the spectator and spares him effort, provides him with a shortcut to the pleasures of art that detours what is necessarily difficult in genuine art" because it includes the spectator's reactions in the work of art itself instead of forcing him to make his own responses. Thus "Eddie Guest and the Indian Love Lyrics are more 'poetic' than T. S. Eliot and Shakespeare." And so, too, our "collegiate Gothic" like the Harkness Quadrangle at Yale is more picturesquely Gothic than Chartres, and a pin-up girl smoothly airbrushed by Petty is more sexy than a real naked woman.

When to this ease of consumption is added *kitsch*'s ease of production because of its standardized nature, its prolific growth is easy to understand. It threatens High Culture by its sheer pervasiveness, its brutal, overwhelming *quantity*. The upper classes, who begin by using it to make money from the crude tastes of the masses and to dominate them politically, end by finding their own culture attacked and even threatened with destruction by the instrument they have thoughtlessly employed. (The same irony may be observed in modern politics, where most swords seem to have two edges; thus Nazism began as a tool of the big bourgeoisie and the army *Junkers* but ended by using *them* as *its* tools.) . . .

ACADEMICISM AND AVANT-GARDISM

UNTIL ABOUT 1930, HIGH CULTURE tried to defend itself against the encroachments of Mass Culture in two opposite ways: Academicism, or an attempt to compete by imitation; and Avant-gardism, or a withdrawal from competition.

Academicism is *kitsch* for the *élite:* spurious High Culture that is outwardly the real thing but actually as much a manufactured article as the cheaper cultural goods produced for the masses. It is recognized at the time for what it is only by the Avant-gardists. A generation or two later, its real nature is understood by everyone and it quietly drops into the same oblivion as its franker sister-under-the-skin. Examples are painters like Bougereau and Rosa Bonheur, critics like Edmund Clarence Stedman and Edmund Gosse, the Beaux Arts school of architecture, composers like the late Sir Edward Elgar, poets like Stephen Phillips, and novelists like Alphonse Daudet, Arnold Bennett, James Branch Cabell, and Somerset Maugham.

The significance of the Avant-garde movement (by which I mean poets like Rimbaud, novelists like Joyce, composers like Stravinsky, and painters like Picasso) is that it simply refused to compete. Rejecting Academicism — and thus, at a second remove, also Mass Culture — it made a desperate attempt to fence off some area where the serious artist could still function. It created a new compartmentation of culture, on the basis of an intellectual rather than a social *élite*. The attempt was remarkably successful: to it we owe almost everything that is living in the art of the last fifty or so years. In fact, the High Culture of our times is pretty much identical with Avant-gardism.

The movement came at a time (1890-1930) when bourgeois values were being challenged both culturally and politically. (In this country, the cultural challenge did not come until World War I, so that our Avant-garde flourished only in the '20s.) In the '30s the two streams mingled briefly, after each had spent its real force, under the aegis of the Communists, only to sink together at the end of the decade into the sands of the wasteland we still live in. The rise of Nazism and the revelation in the Moscow Trials of the real nature of the new society in Russia inaugurated the present period, when men cling to the evils they know rather than risk possibly greater ones by pressing forward. Nor has the chronic state of war, hot or cold, the world has been in since 1939 encouraged rebellion or experiment in either art or politics.

A MERGER HAS BEEN ARRANGED

IN THIS NEW PERIOD, THE COMPETITORS, as often happens in the business world, are merging. Mass Culture takes on the color of both varieties of the old High Culture, Academic, and Avant-garde, while these latter are increasingly watered down with Mass elements. There is slowly emerging a tepid, flaccid Middlebrow Culture that threatens to engulf everything in its spreading ooze. *Bauhaus* modernism has at last trickled down, in a debased form of course, into our furniture, cafeterias, movie theaters, electric toasters, office buildings, drugstores, and railroad trains. Psychoanalysis is expounded sympathetically and superficially in popular magazines, and the psychoanalyst replaces the eccentric millionaire as the *deus ex machina* in many a movie. T. S. Eliot writes *The Cocktail Party* and it becomes a Broadway hit. (Though in some ways excellent, it is surely inferior to his *Murder in the Cathedral*, which in the unmerged '30s had to depend on WPA to get produced at all.) The type creator of *kitsch* today, at least

in the old media, is an indeterminate specimen. There are no widely influential critics so completely terrible as, say, the late William Lyon Phelps was. Instead we have such gray creatures as Clifton Fadiman and Henry Seidel Canby. The artless numbers of an Eddie Guest are drowned out by the more sophisticated though equally commonplace strains of Benet's *John Brown's Body*. Maxfield Parrish yields to Rockwell Kent, Arthur Brisbane to Walter Lippmann, Theda Bara to Ingrid Bergman. We even have what might be called *l'avant-garde pompier* (or, in American, "phoney Avant-gardism"), as in the buildings of Raymond Hood and the later poetry of Archibald MacLeish, as there is also an academic Avant-gardism in *belles lettres* so that now the "little" as well as the big magazines have their hack writers.

All this is not a raising of the level of Mass Culture, as might appear at first, but rather a corruption of High Culture. There is nothing more vulgar than sophisticated *kitsch*. Compare Conan Doyle's workmanlike and unpretentious Sherlock Holmes stories with the bogus "intellectuality" of Dorothy M. Sayers, who, like many contemporary detective-story writers, is a novelist *manquée* who ruins her stuff with literary attitudinizing. Or consider the relationship of Hollywood and Broadway.

In the '20s, the two were sharply differentiated, movies being produced for the masses of the hinterland, theater for an upper-class New York audience. The theater was High Culture, mostly of the Academic variety (Theatre Guild) but with some spark of Avant-garde fire (the "little" or "experimental" theater movement). The movies were definitely Mass Culture, mostly very bad but with some leaven of Avant-gardism (Griffiths, Stroheim) and Folk Art (Chaplin and other comedians). With the sound film, Broadway and Hollywood drew closer together. Plays are now produced mainly to sell the movie rights, with many being directly financed by the film companies. The merger has standardized the theater to such an extent that even the early Theatre Guild seems vital in retrospect, while hardly a trace of the "experimental" theater is left.

And what have the movies gained? They are more sophisticated, the acting is subtler, the sets in better taste. But they too have become standardized: they are never as awful as they often were in the old days, but they are never as good either. They are better entertainment and worse art. The cinema of the '20s occasionally gave us the fresh charm of Folk Art or the imaginative intensity of Avant-gardism. The coming of sound, and with it Broadway, degraded the camera to a recording instrument for an alien art form, the spoken play. The silent film had at least the *theoretical possibility,* even within the limits of Mass Culture, of being artistically significant. The sound film, within those limits, does not. . . .

SHERLOCK HOLMES TO MIKE HAMMER

THE ROLE OF SCIENCE IN MASS CULTURE has similarly changed from the rational and the purposive to the passive, accidental, even the catastrophic. Consider the evolution of the detective story, a genre which can be traced back to the memoirs of Vidocq, the master-detective of the Napoleonic era. Poe, who was peculiarly fascinated by scientific method, wrote the first and still the best detective stories: *The Purloined Letter, The Gold Bug, The Mystery of Marie Roget, The Murders in the Rue Morgue.* Conan Doyle created the great folk hero Sherlock Holmes, like Poe's Dupin a mage whose wizard's wand was scientific deduction (Poe's "ratiocination"). Such stories could only appeal to — in fact, only be *comprehensible* to — an audience accustomed to

think in scientific terms: to survey the data, set up a hypothesis, test it by seeing whether it caught the murderer. The very idea of an art genre cast in the form of a problem to be solved by purely intellectual means could only have arisen in a scientific age.

This kind of detective fiction, which might be called the "classic" style, is still widely practised (well by Agatha Christie and John Dickson Carr, badly by the more popular Erle Stanley Gardiner), but of late it has been overshadowed by the rank, noxious growth of works in the "sensational" style. This was inaugurated by Dashiel Hammett (whom André Gide was foolish enough to admire) and has recently been enormously stepped up in voltage by Mickey Spillane, whose six books to date have sold 13 million copies. The sensationalists use what for the classicists was the point — the uncovering of the criminal — as a mere excuse for the minute description of scenes of bloodshed, brutality, lust, and alcoholism. The cool, astute, subtle Dupin-Holmes is replaced by the crude man-of-action whose prowess is measured, not by intellectual mastery but by his capacity for liquor, women, and mayhem (he can "take it" as well as "dish it out" — Hammett's *The Glass Key* is largely a chronicle of the epic beatings absorbed by the hero before he finally staggers to the solution).

Mike Hammer, Spillane's aptly named hero, is such a monumental blunderer that even Dr. Watson would have seen through him. According to Richard W. Johnston (*Life,* June 23, 1952), "Mike has one bizarre and memorable characteristic that sets him apart from all other fictional detectives: sheer incompetence. In the five Hammer cases, forty-eight people have been killed, and there is reason to believe that if Mike had kept out of the way, thirty-four of them — all innocent of the original crime — would have survived." A decade ago, the late George Orwell, apropos a "sensationalist" detective story of the time, *No*

Orchids for Miss Blandish, showed how the brutalization of this genre mirrors the general degeneration in ethics from 19th-century standards. What he would have written had Mickey Spillane's works been then in existence I find it hard to imagine.

FRANKENSTEIN TO HIROSHIMA

THE REAL HEIRS OF THE "CLASSIC" detective story today, so far as the exploitation of science is concerned, are the writers of science fiction, a genre begun by Jules Verne and H. G. Wells that has of late become very popular. Or at least of the more sophisticated kinds of science fiction, where the marvels and horrors of the future must always be "scientifically possible" — just as Sherlock Holmes drew on no supernatural powers. This is the approach of the bourgeoisie, who think of science as their familiar instrument. The masses are less confident, more awed in their approach to science, and there are vast lower strata of science fiction where the marvelous is untrammeled by the limits of knowledge.

To the masses, science is the modern *arcanum arcanorum,* at once the supreme mystery and the philosopher's stone that explains the mystery. The latter concept appears in comic strips like "Superman" and in the charlatan-science exploited by "health fakers" and "nature fakers." Taken this way, science gives man mastery over his environment and is beneficent. But science itself is not understood, therefore not mastered, therefore terrifying because of its very power. Taken *this* way, as the supreme mystery, science becomes the stock-in-trade of the "horror" pulp magazines and comics and movies. It has got to the point, indeed, that if one sees a laboratory in a movie, one shudders, and the white coat of the scientist is as blood-chilling a sight as Count Dracula's black cloak. These "horror" films have apparently an indestructible popularity:

"Frankenstein" is still shown, after twenty-one years, and the current revival of "King Kong" is expected to gross over $2 million.

If the scientist's laboratory has acquired in Mass Culture a ghastly atmosphere, is this perhaps not one of those deep popular intuitions? From Frankenstein's laboratory to Maidenek and Hiroshima is not a long journey. Was there a popular suspicion, perhaps only half-conscious, that the 19th-century trust in science, like the 19th-century trust in popular education, was mistaken, that science can as easily be used for anti-human as for pro-human ends, perhaps even more easily? For Mrs. Shelley's Frankenstein, the experimenter who brought disaster by pushing his science too far, is a scientific folk-hero older than and still as famous as Mr. Doyle's successful and beneficent Sherlock Holmes.

THE PROBLEM OF THE MASSES

CONSERVATIVES LIKE ORTEGA Y GASSET and T. S. Eliot argue that since "the revolt of the masses" has led to the horrors of totalitarianism (and of California roadside architecture), the only hope is to rebuild the old class walls and bring the masses once more under aristocratic control. They think of the popular as synonymous with the cheap and vulgar. Marxian radicals and liberals, on the other hand, see the masses as intrinsically healthy but as the dupes and victims of cultural exploitation by the Lords of *kitsch* — in the style of Rousseau's "noble savage" idea. If only the masses were offered good stuff instead of *kitsch,* how they would eat it up! How the level of Mass Culture would rise! Both these diagnoses seem to me fallacious: they assume that Mass Culture is (in the conservative view) or could be (in the liberal view) an expression of *people,* like Folk Art, whereas actually it is an expression of *masses,* a very different thing.

There are theoretical reasons why Mass

Culture is not and can never be any good. I take it as axiomatic that culture can only be produced by and for human beings. But insofar as people are organized (more strictly, disorganized) as masses, they lose their human identity and quality. For the masses are in historical time what a crowd is in space: a large quantity of people unable to express themselves as human beings because they are related to one another neither as individuals nor as members of communities — indeed they are not related *to each other* at all but only to something distant, abstract, nonhuman: a football game or bargain sale in the case of a crowd, a system of industrial production, a party or a State, in the case of the masses.

The Mass man is a solitary atom, uniform with and undifferentiated from thousands and millions of other atoms who go to make up "the lonely crowd," as David Riesman well calls American society. A folk or a people, however, is a community, *i.e.,* a group of individuals linked to each other by common interests, work, traditions, values, and sentiments; something like a family, each of whose members has a special place and function as an individual while at the same time sharing the group's interests (family budget), sentiments (family quarrels), and culture (family jokes). The scale is small enough so that it "makes a difference" what the individual does, a first condition for human — as against mass — existence. He is at once more important as an individual than in mass society and at the same time more closely integrated into the community, his creativity nourished by a rich combination of individualism and communalism. (The great culture-bearing *élites* of the past have been communities of this kind.)

In contrast, a mass society, like a crowd, is so undifferentiated and loosely structured that its atoms, insofar as human values go, tend to cohere only along the line of the least common denominator; its morality

sinks to that of its most brutal and primitive members, its taste to that of the least sensitive and most ignorant. And in addition to everything else, the scale is simply too big, there are just *too many people.*

Yet this collective monstrosity, "the masses," "the public," is taken as a human norm by the scientific and artistic technicians of our Mass Culture. They at once degrade the public by treating it as an object, to be handled with the lack of ceremony and the objectivity of medical students dissecting a corpse, and at the same time flatter it, pander to its level of taste and ideas by taking these as the criterion of reality (in the case of questionnaire-sociologists and other "social scientists") or of art (in the case of the Lords of *kitsch*). When one hears a questionnaire-sociologist talk about how he will "set up" an investigation, one feels he regards people as a herd of dumb animals, as mere congeries of conditioned reflexes, his calculation being which reflex will be stimulated by which question. At the same time, of necessity, he sees the statistical majority as the great Reality, the secret of life he is trying to find out; like the *kitsch* Lords, he is wholly without values, willing to accept any idiocy if it is held by many people.

The aristocrat and the democrat both criticize and argue with popular taste, the one with hostility, the other in friendship, for both attitudes proceed from a set of values. This is less degrading to the masses than the "objective" approach of Hollywood and the questionnaire-sociologists, just as it is less degrading to a man to be shouted at in anger than to be quietly assumed to be part of a machine. But the *plebs* have their dialectical revenge: complete indifference to their human *quality* means complete prostration before their statistical *quantity,* so that a movie magnate who cynically "gives the public what it wants" — *i.e.,* assumes it wants trash — sweats with terror if box-office returns drop 10 percent.

THE FUTURE OF HIGH CULTURE: DARK

THE CONSERVATIVE PROPOSAL TO SAVE culture by restoring the old class lines has a more solid historical base than the Marxian hope for a new democratic, classless culture, for, with the possible (and important) exception of Periclean Athens, all the great cultures of the past were *élite* cultures. Politically, however, it is without meaning in a world dominated by the two great mass nations, U.S.A. and U.S.S.R., and becoming more industrialized, more mass-ified all the time. The only practical thing along those lines would be to revive the *cultural élite* which the Avant-garde created. As I have already noted, the Avant-garde is now dying, partly from internal causes, partly suffocated by the competing Mass Culture, where it is not being absorbed into it. Of course this process has not reached 100 percent, and doubtless never will unless the country goes either Fascist or Communist. There are still islands above the flood for those determined enough to reach them, and to stay on them: as Faulkner has shown, a writer can even use Hollywood instead of being used by it, if his purpose is firm enough.

But the homogenization of High and Mass Culture has gone far and is going farther all the time, and there seems little reason to expect a revival of Avant-gardism, that is, of a successful countermovement to Mass Culture. Particularly, not in this country, where the blurring of class lines, the absence of a stable cultural tradition, and the greater facilities for manufacturing and marketing *kitsch* all work in the other direction. The result is that our intelligentsia is remarkably small, weak, and disintegrated. One of the odd things about the American cultural scene is how many brain-workers there are and how few intellectuals, defining the former as specialists whose thinking is pretty much confined to their limited "fields" and the latter as persons who take all culture for their province. Not only are there few intellectuals, but they don't hang together, they have very little *esprit de corps,* very little sense of belonging to a community; they are so isolated from each other they don't even bother to quarrel — there hasn't been a really good fight among them since the Moscow Trials.

THE FUTURE OF MASS CULTURE: DARKER

IF THE CONSERVATIVE PROPOSAL TO SAVE our culture via the aristocratic Avant-garde seems historically unlikely, what of the democratic-liberal proposal? Is there a reasonable prospect of raising the level of Mass Culture? In his recent book, *The Great Audience*, Gilbert Seldes argues there is. He blames the present sad state of our Mass Culture on the stupidity of the Lords of *kitsch*, who underestimate the mental age of the public; the arrogance of the intellectuals, who make the same mistake and so snobbishly refuse to work for mass media like radio, TV, and movies; and the passivity of the public itself, which doesn't insist on better Mass Cultural products. This diagnosis seems to me superficial in that it blames everything on subjective, moral factors: stupidity, perversity, failure of will. My own feeling is that, as in the case of the alleged responsibility of the German (or Russian) people for the horrors of Nazism (or Soviet Communism), it is unjust to blame social groups for this result.

Human beings have been caught up in the inexorable workings of a mechanism that forces them, with a pressure only heroes can resist (and one cannot *demand* that anybody be a hero, though one can *hope* for it), into its own pattern. I see Mass Culture as a reciprocating engine, and who is to say, once it has been set in motion, whether the stroke or the counterstroke is "responsible" for its continued action?

The Lords of *kitsch* sell culture to the masses. It is a debased, trivial culture that voids both the deep realities (sex, death, failure, tragedy) and also the simple, spontaneous pleasures, since the realities would be too real and the pleasures too *lively* to induce what Mr. Seldes calls "the mood of consent": *i.e.,* a narcotized acceptance of Mass Culture and of the commodities it sells as a substitute for the unsettling and unpredictable (hence unsalable) joy, tragedy, wit, change, originality, and beauty of real life. The masses, debauched by several generations of this sort of thing, in turn come to demand trivial and comfortable cultural products. Which came first, the chicken or the egg, the mass demand or its satisfaction (and further stimulation) is a question as academic as it is unanswerable. The engine is reciprocating and shows no signs of running down.

Indeed, far from Mass Culture getting better, we will be lucky if it doesn't get worse. When shall we see another popular humorist like Sholem Aleichem, whose books are still being translated from the Yiddish and for whose funeral in 1916, 100,000 inhabitants of the Bronx turned out? Or Finley Peter Dunne, whose Mr. Dooley commented on the American scene with such wit that Henry Adams was a faithful reader and Henry James, on his famous return to his native land, wanted to meet only one American author, Dunne?

Since Mass Culture is not an art form but a manufactured commodity, it tends always downward, toward cheapness — and so standardization — of production. Thus, T. W. Adorno has noted, in his brilliant essay "On Popular Music" (*Studies in Philosophy and Social Science,* New York, No. 1,

1941) that the chorus of every popular song *without exception* has the same number of bars; while Mr. Seldes remarks that Hollywood movies are cut in a uniformly rapid tempo, a shot rarely being held more than forty-five seconds, which gives them a standardized effect in contrast to the varied tempo of European film cutting. This sort of standardization means that what may have begun as something fresh and original is repeated until it becomes a nerveless routine, *vide* what happened to Fred Allen as a radio comedian.

The only time Mass Culture is good is at the very beginning, before the "formula" has hardened, before the money-boys and efficiency experts and audience-reaction analysts have moved in. Then for a while it may have the quality of real Folk Art. But the Folk artist today lacks the cultural roots and the intellectual toughness (both of which the Avant-garde artist has relatively more of) to resist for long the pressures of Mass Culture. His taste can easily be corrupted, his sense of his own special talent and limitations obscured, as in what happened to Disney between the gay, inventive early Mickey Mouse and "Silly Symphony" cartoons and the vulgar pretentiousness of "Fantasia" and heavy-handed sentimentality of "Snow White," or to Westbrook Pegler who has regressed from an excellent sports writer, with a sure sense of form and a mastery of colloquial satire, into the rambling, coarse-grained, garrulous political pundit of today.

Whatever virtues the Folk artist has, and they are many, staying power is not one of them. And staying power is the essential virtue of one who would hold his own against the spreading ooze of Mass Culture.

50.

DYLAN THOMAS: Life Among the Culture Vultures

*Dylan Thomas was one (but not the last) of a long, long line of foreign (mainly but not exclusively English and European) poets, novelists, painters, sculptors, musicians, journalists, philosophers, scientists, politicians, and every other kind of intellectual and pseudo-intellectual who have, over the last century and a half or so, come to the United States on a "lecture tour," the point of which, for them, was profit, and for the audiences, culture. Thomas was also not alone in bemoaning his fate —
Charles Dickens, Matthew Arnold, George Bernard Shaw, and a host of others before him had also written scathingly of the difficulties and dangers of such endeavors. The selection reprinted here in part was a speech recorded by Thomas in 1953 for delivery over the BBC, and later revised by him for publication. The recorded speech was broadcast on March 30, 1954, five months after his untimely death in New York City.*

Source: *Quite Early One Morning,* New York, 1954: "A Visit to America."

ACROSS THE UNITED STATES of America, from New York to California and back, glazed, again, for many months of the year, there streams and sings for its heady supper a dazed and prejudiced procession of European lecturers, scholars, sociologists, economists, writers, authorities on this and that and even, in theory, on the United States of America. And, breathlessly, between addresses and receptions, in planes and trains and boiling hotel bedroom ovens, many of these attempt to keep journals and diaries.

At first, confused and shocked by shameless profusion and almost shamed by generosity, unaccustomed to such importance as they are assumed, by their hosts, to possess, and up against the barrier of a common language, they write in their notebooks like demons, generalizing away, on character and culture and the American political scene. But, towards the middle of their middle-aged whisk through Middle-Western clubs and universities, the fury of the writing flags; their spirits are lowered by the spirit with which they are everywhere strongly greeted and which, in ever increasing doses, they themselves lower; and they begin to mistrust themselves, and their reputations — for they have found, too often, that an audience will receive a lantern-lecture on, say, Ceramics, with the same uninhibited enthusiasm that it accorded the very week before to a paper on the Modern Turkish Novel. And, in their diaries, more and more do such entries appear as, "No way of escape!" or "Buffalo!" or "I am beaten," until at last they cannot write a word. And, twittering all over, old before their time, with eyes like rissoles in the sand, they are helped up the gangway of the home-bound liner by kind bosom friends (of all kinds and bosoms) who boister them on the back, pick them up again, thrust bottles, sonnets, cigars, addresses, into their pockets, have a farewell party in their cabin, pick them up again, and, snickering and yelping, are gone: to wait at the dockside for another boat from Europe and another batch of fresh, green lecturers.

There they go, every spring, from New

York to Los Angeles: exhibitionists, polemicists, histrionic publicists, theological rhetoricians, historical hoddy-doddies, balletomanes, ulterior decorators, windbags and bigwigs and humbugs, men in love with stamps, men in love with steaks, men after millionaires' widows, men with elephantiasis of the reputation (huge trunks and teeny minds), authorities on gas, bishops, best sellers, editors looking for writers, writers looking for publishers, publishers looking for dollars, existentialists, serious physicists with nuclear missions, men from the B.B.C. who speak as though they had the Elgin marbles in their mouths, potboiling philosophers, professional Irishmen (very lepricorny), and, I am afraid, fat poets with slim volumes.

And see, too, in that linguacious stream, the tall monocled men, smelling of saddle soap and club armchairs, their breath a nice blending of whisky and fox's blood, with big protruding upper-class tusks and county mustaches, presumably invented in England and sent abroad to advertise *Punch,* who lecture to women's clubs on such unlikely subjects as "The History of Etching in the Shetland Islands"; and the brassy-bossy men-women, with corrugated-iron perms, and hippo hides, who come, self-announced, as "ordinary British housewives," to talk to rich minked chunks of American matronhood about the iniquity of the Health Services, the criminal sloth of the miners, the *visible* tail and horns of Mr. Aneurin Bevan, and the fear of everyone in England to go out alone at night because of the organized legions of coshboys against whom the police are powerless owing to the refusal of those in power to equip them with revolvers and to flog to ribbons every adolescent offender on any charge at all.

And there shiver and teeter also, meek and driven, those British authors unfortunate enough to have written, after years of unadventurous forgotten work, one bad novel which became enormously popular on both sides of the Atlantic. At home, when success first hit them, they were mildly delighted; a couple of literary luncheons went sugar-tipsy to their heads, like the washing sherry served before those luncheons; and perhaps, as the lovely money rolled lushly in, they began to dream, in their moony writers' way, of being able to retire to the country, keep wasps (or was it bees?) and never write another lousy word. But in come the literary agent's triggermen and the publisher's armed narks: "You must go to the States and make a Personal Appearance. Your novel is *killing* them over there, and we're not surprised either. You must go round the States lecturing to women." And the inoffensive writers, who have never dared lecture anyone, let alone women — they are frightened of women, they do not understand them women, they write about women as creatures that never existed, and the women lap it up — these sensitive plants cry out, "But what shall we lecture about?"

"The English Novel."

"I don't read novels."

"Great Women in Fiction."

"I don't like fiction *or* women."

But off they are wafted, first class, in the plush bowels of the *Queen Victoria,* with a list of engagements long as a New York menu or a half-hour with a book by Charles Morgan, and soon they are losing their little cold-as-goldfish paw in the great general glutinous handshake of a clutch of enveloping hostesses. . . .

See the garrulous others, also, gabbing and garlanded from one nest of culture-vultures to another: people selling the English way of life and condemning the American way as they swig and guzzle through it; people resurrecting the theories of surrealism for the benefit of remote parochial female audiences who did not know it was dead, not having ever known it had been alive; people talking about Etruscan pots and pans to a bunch of dead pans and wealthy pots in Boston. And there, too, in the sticky thick of lecturers moving across the continent black with clubs, go the foreign poets, catarrhal troubadours, lyrical one-night-standers, dollar-mad nightingales, remittance-bards from at home, myself among them booming with the worst.

Did we pass one another, en route, all unknowing, I wonder; one of us spry-eyed, with clean, white lectures and a soul he could call his own, going buoyantly west to his remunerative doom in the great state university factories; another returning dog-eared as his clutch of poems and his carefully typed impromptu asides? I ache for us both. There one goes, unsullied as yet, in his Pullman pride, toying — oh boy! — with a blunderbuss bourbon, being smoked by a large cigar, riding out to the wide-open spaces of the faces of his waiting audience. He carries, besides his literary baggage, a new, dynamic razor, just on the market, bought in New York, which operates at the flick of a thumb, but cuts the thumb to the bone; a tin of new shaving-lather which is worked with the other, un-bleeding, thumb, and covers not only the face but the whole bathroom and, instantly freezing, makes an arctic, icicled cave from which it takes two sneering bellboys to extract him; and, of course, a nylon shirt. This, he dearly believes, from the advertisements, he can himself wash in his hotel, hang to dry overnight, and put on, without ironing, in the morning. (In my case, no ironing was needed, for, as someone cruelly pointed out in print, I looked, anyway, like an unmade bed.)

He is vigorously welcomed at the station by an earnest crew-cut platoon of giant collegiates, all chasing the butterfly culture with net, notebook, poison bottle, pin and label, each with at least thirty-six terribly white teeth, and nursed away, as heavily gently as though he were an imbecile rich aunt with a short prospect of life, into a motorcar in which, for a mere fifty miles or

so traveled at poet-breaking speed, he assures them of the correctness of their assumption that he is half-witted by stammering inconsequential answers in an over-British accent to their genial questions about what international conference Stephen Spender might be attending at the moment, or the reactions of British poets to the work of a famous American whose name he did not know or catch. He is then taken to a small party of only a few hundred people all of whom hold the belief that what a visiting lecturer needs before he trips on to the platform is just enough martinis so that he can trip off the platform as well. And, clutching his explosive glass, he is soon contemptuously dismissing, in a flush of ignorance and fluency, the poetry of those androgynous literary ladies with three names who produce a kind of verbal ectoplasm to order as a waiter dishes up spaghetti — only to find that the fiercest of these, a wealthy huntress of small, seedy lions (such as himself), who stalks the middle-western bush with ears and rifle cocked, is his hostess for the evening. Of the lecture, he remembers little but the applause and maybe two questions: "Is it true that the young English intellectuals are *really* psychological?" or, "I always carry Kierkegaard in my pocket. What do you carry?"

Late at night, in his room, he fills a page of his journal with a confused, but scathing, account of his first engagement; summarizes American advanced education in a paragraph that will be meaningless tomorrow; and falls to sleep where he is immediately chased through long, dark thickets by a Mrs. Mabel Frankincense Mehaffey, with a tray of martinis and lyrics.

And there goes the other happy poet bedraggledly back to New York which struck him all of a sheepish never-sleeping heap at first, but which seems to him now, after the ulcerous rigors of a lecturer's spring, a haven cozy as toast, cool as an icebox, and safe as skyscrapers.

51.

Joe Glazer: "Automation"

The development of automation since 1900, and especially since World War II, has been called the Second Industrial Revolution. The machine became a new kind of employee, performing many of the operations that hitherto were accomplished by man — and doing them in much less time with much more precision and accuracy. "Labor welcomes these technological changes," George Meany, later president of the AFL-CIO, once said. "The new techniques offer promise of higher living standards for all, greater leisure, and more pleasant working conditions." But many workers feared this new technological revolution — they were afraid of losing their jobs to a machine. Joe Glazer's song, "Automation," reflects their concern.

Source: *Songs of Work and Freedom*, Edith Fowke and Joe Glazer, eds., New York, 1960.

AUTOMATION

I went down, down, down to the factory
Early on a Monday morn.
When I got down to the factory
It was lonely, it was forlorn.
I couldn't find Joe, Jack, John, or Jim;
Nobody could I see:
Nothing but buttons and bells and lights
All over the factory.

I walked, walked, walked into the foreman's office
To find out what was what.
I looked him in the eye and I said, "What goes?"
And this is the answer I got:
His eyes turned red, then green, then blue
And it suddenly dawned on me —
There was a robot sitting in the seat
Where the foreman used to be.

I walked all around, all around, up and down
And across that factory.
I watched all the buttons and the bells and the lights —
It was a mystery to me.
I hollered "Frank, Hank, Ike, Mike, Roy, Ray, Don, Dan,
Bill, Phil, Ed, Fred, Pete!"
And a great big mechanical voice boomed out:
"All your buddies are obsolete."

I was scared, scared, scared, I was worried, I was sick
As I left that factory.
I decided that I had to see the president
Of the whole darn company.
When I got up to his office he was rushing out the door
With a scowl upon his face,
'Cause there was a great big mechanical executive
Sitting in the president's place.

I went home, home, home to my ever-loving wife
And told her 'bout the factory.
She hugged me and she kissed me and she cried a little bit
As she sat on my knee.
I don't understand all the buttons and the lights
But one thing I will say —
I thank the Lord that love's still made
In the good old-fashioned way.

52.

A Letter to Presbyterians

During the early 1950s the unceasing search for Communist influence carried out by the Senate Permanent Subcommittee on Investigations under the leadership of Senator Joseph R. McCarthy of Wisconsin reached into almost every area of American life. In 1953 one of McCarthy's aides published an article in a national magazine asserting that the Protestant clergy numbered in its ranks "the largest single group supporting the Communist apparatus in the United States today." The severity of this and of similar charges by the McCarthy committee led to widespread protest. An example was the letter reprinted here, which was drafted by John A. Mackay of Princeton Theological Seminary and published by the General Council of the Presbyterian Church in the United States on October 21, 1953.

Source: *A Letter to Presbyterians Concerning the Present Situation in Our Country and in the World,* October 21, 1953, issued through the Office of the General Assembly, Philadelphia.

THE GENERAL COUNCIL of the Presbyterian Church in the United States of America is instructed under the constitution of the Church, "to cultivate and promote the spiritual welfare of the whole church," and "to correspond with and advise the General Councils of Presbyteries. . . ."

Profoundly concerned about the present situation in our country and the world, the Council addresses itself to fellow-Presbyterians through the Presbyteries and the ministers and officers of the congregations. In doing so it is guided by the historic witness of our Church and the deliverances of successive General Assemblies. The Council hopes that the following statement may help to clarify certain important problems and at the same time initiate a process of thought by which our Church can contribute toward their solution.

The 165th General Assembly made the following pronouncement for the guidance of Presbyterians:

> All human life should be lived in accordance with the principles established by God for the life of men and of nations. This is a tenet of Biblical religion. It is also a basic emphasis in our Presbyterian heritage of faith.
>
> As individuals and as a group, Christians are responsible for adjusting their thought and behavior to those everlasting principles of righteousness which God has revealed in Holy Scripture. It is no less their responsibility, as citizens of their nation, to seek as far as their influence may extend, to bring national life and all the institutions of society into conformity with the moral government of God, and into harmony with the spirit of Jesus Christ.

In full accordance with this deliverance, the General Council would share with our Church constituency the following thoughts:

Things are happening in our national life and in the international sphere which should give us deep concern. Serious thought needs to be given to the menace of Communism in the world of today and to the undoubted aim on the part of its leaders to subvert the thought and life of the United States. Everlasting vigilance is also needed, and appropriate precautions should be constantly taken to forestall the insidious intervention of a foreign power in the internal affairs of our country. In this connection Congressional committees, which are an important expression of democracy in action, have rendered some valuable services to the nation.

At the same time the citizens of this country, and those in particular who are Protestant Christians, have reason to take a grave view of the situation which is being created by the almost exclusive concentration of the American mind upon the problem of the threat of Communism.

Under the plea that the structure of American society is in imminent peril of being shattered by a satanic conspiracy, dangerous developments are taking place in our national life. Favored by an atmosphere of intense disquiet and suspicion, a subtle but potent assault upon basic human rights is now in progress. Some Congressional inquiries have revealed a distinct tendency to become inquisitions. These inquisitions, which find their historic pattern in medieval Spain and in the tribunals of modern totalitarian states, begin to constitute a threat to freedom of thought in this country. Treason and dissent are being confused. The shrine of conscience and private judgment, which God alone has a right to enter, is being invaded. Un-American attitudes toward ideas and books are becoming current. Attacks are being made upon citizens of integrity and social passion which are utterly alien to our democratic tradition. They are particularly alien to the Protestant religious tradition which has been a main source of the freedoms which the people of the United States enjoy.

There is something still more serious. A great many people, within and without our government, approach the problem of Communism in a purely negative way. Communism, which is at bottom a secular religious faith of great vitality, is thus being dealt with as an exclusively police problem. As a result of this there is growing up over against Communism a fanatical negativism. Totally devoid of a constructive program of action, this negativism is in danger of leading the American mind into a spiritual vacuum. Our national house, cleansed of one demon, would invite by its very emptiness the entrance of seven others. In the case of a national crisis this emptiness could, in the high-sounding name of security, be occupied with ease by a Fascist tyranny.

We suggest, therefore, that all Presbyterians give earnest consideration to the following three basic principles and their implications for our thought and life.

I. The Christian Church has a prophetic function to fulfill in every society and in every age

WHATEVER CONCERNS MAN and his welfare is a concern of the Church and its ministers. Religion has to do with life in its wholeness. While being patriotically loyal to the country within whose bounds it lives and works, the Church does not derive its authority from the nation but from Jesus Christ. Its supreme and ultimate allegiance is to Christ, its sole Head, and to His Kingdom, and not to any nation or race, to any class or culture. It is, therefore, under obligation to consider the life of man in the light of God's purpose in Christ for the world. While it is not the role of the Christian Church to present blueprints for the organization of society and the conduct of government, the Church owes it to its own members and to men in general to draw attention to violations of those spiritual bases of human relationship which have been established by God. It has the obligation also to proclaim those principles, and to instill that spirit, which are essential for social health, and which form the indispensable foundation of sound and stable policies in the affairs of state.

II. The majesty of truth must be preserved at all times and at all costs

LOYALTY TO TRUTH is the common basis of true religion and true culture. Despite the lofty idealism of many of our national leaders, truth is being subtly and silently dethroned by prominent public figures from the position it has occupied hitherto in our American tradition. The state of strife known as "cold war," in which our own and other nations, as well as groups within nations, are now engaged, is producing startling phenomena and sinister personalities. In this form of warfare, falsehood is frequently preferred to fact if it can be shown to have greater propaganda value. In the interests of propaganda, truth is deliberately distorted or remains unspoken. The demagogue, who lives by propaganda, is coming into his own on a national scale. According to the new philosophy, if what is true "gives aid and comfort" to our enemies, it must be suppressed. Truth is thus a captive in the land of the free. At the same time, and for the same reason, great words like "love," "peace," "justice," and "mercy," and the ideas which underlie them, are becoming suspect.

Communism, as we know to our sorrow, is committed on principle to a philosophy of lying; democracy, in fighting Communism, is in danger of succumbing, through fear and in the name of expediency, to the self-same philosophy. It is being assumed, in effect, that, in view of the magnitude of the issues at stake, the end justifies the means. Whatever the outcome of such a war, the moral consequences will be terrifying. People will become accustomed to going through life with no regard for rules or sanctities.

A painful illustration of this development is that men and women should be publicly condemned upon the uncorroborated word of former Communists. Many of these witnesses have done no more, as we know, than transfer their allegiance from one authoritarian system to another. Nothing is easier for people, as contemporary history has shown, than to make the transition from one totalitarianism to another, carrying their basic attitudes along with them. As a matter of fact, the lands that have suffered most from Communism, or that are most menaced by it today, Russia and Italy, for example, are lands which have been traditionally authoritarian in their political or their religious life. And yet the ex-Communists to whose word Congressional committees apparently give unqualified credence are in very many instances people whose basic philosophy authorizes them now, as in the past, to believe that a lie in a good cause is thoroughly justified.

III. God's sovereign rule is the controlling factor in history

WE SPEAK of "This nation under God." Nothing is more needed today than to explore afresh and to apply to all the problems of thought and life in our generation what it means to take God seriously in national life. There is an order of God. Even in these days of flux and nihilism, of relativism and expediency, God reigns. The American-born poet T. S. Eliot has written these prophetic words:

Those who put their faith in worldly
    order
Not controlled by the order of God,
In confident ignorance, but arrest
    disorder,
Make it fast, breed fatal disease,
Degrade what they exalt.

Any attempt to impose upon society, or the course of history, a purely man-made order, however lofty the aims, can have no more than temporary success. Social disorder and false political philosophies cannot be adequately met by police measures, but only by a sincere attempt to organize society in accordance with the everlasting principles of God's moral government of the world. It is, therefore, of paramount importance that individuals, groups, and nations should adjust themselves to the order of God. God's character and God's way with man provide the pattern for man's way with his fellowman.

That we have the obligation to make our nation as secure as possible, no one can dispute. But there is no absolute security in human affairs, nor is security the ultimate human obligation. A still greater obligation, as well as a more strategic procedure, is to make sure that what we mean by security, and the methods we employ to achieve it, are in accordance with the will of God. Otherwise, any human attempt to establish a form of world order which does no more than exalt the interest of a class, a culture, a race, or a nation, above God and the interests of the whole human family, is foredoomed to disaster. Ideas are on the march, forces are abroad whose time has come. They cannot be repressed and they will bring unjust orders to an end. In the world of today all forms of feudalism, for example, are foredoomed. So too are all types of imperialism. The real question is how to solve the problems presented by these two forms of outmoded society in such a way that the transition to a better order will be gradual and constructive.

Let us frankly recognize that many of the revolutionary forces of our time are in great part the judgment of God upon human selfishness and complacency, and upon man's forgetfulness of man. That does not make these forces right; it does, however, compel us to consider how their driving power can be channeled into forms of creative thought and work. History, moreover, makes it abundantly clear that wherever a religion, a political system, or a social order does not interest itself in the common people, violent revolt eventually takes place.

On the other hand, just because God rules in the affairs of men, Communism as a solution of the human problem is foredoomed to failure. No political order can prevail which deliberately leaves God out of account. Despite its pretention to be striving after "liberation," Communism enslaves in the name of freedom. It does not know that evil cannot be eradicated from human life by simply changing a social structure. Man, moreover, has deep spiritual longings which Communism cannot satisfy. The Communistic order will eventually be shattered upon the bedrock of human nature, that is, upon the basic sins, and the abysmal needs, of man and society. For that reason Communism has an approaching rendezvous with God and the moral order.

Nevertheless, Communists, Communist nations, and Communist-ruled peoples should be our concern. In hating a system let us not allow ourselves to hate individuals or whole nations. History and experience teach us that persons and peoples do change. Let us ever be on the lookout for the evidence of change in the Communist world, for the effects of disillusionment, and for the presence of a God-implanted hunger. Such disillusionment and hunger can be met only by a sympathetic approach and a disposition to listen and confer.

There is clear evidence that a post-Communist mood is actually being created in many parts of Europe and Asia. Let us seek to deepen that mood. Let us explore afresh the meaning of mercy and forgiveness and recognize that both can have social and political significance when they are sincerely and opportunely applied.

Let us always be ready to meet around a conference table with the rulers of Communist countries. There should be, therefore, no reluctance to employ the conference method to the full in the settling of disputes with our country's enemies. Let us beware of the cynical attitude which prevails in certain official' circles to regard as a forlorn hope any negotiated solution of the major issues which divide mankind.

In human conflicts there can be no substitute for negotiation. Direct personal conference has been God's way with man from the beginning. "Come, now, and let us reason together," was the word of God to Israel through the Prophet Isaiah. We must take the risk, and even the initiative, of seeking face-to-face encounter with our enemies. We should meet them officially, whatever their ignominious record, and regardless of the suffering they may have caused us. We too have reasons for penitence and stand in need of forgiveness. In any case, talk, unhurried talk, talk which does not rule out in advance the possibility of success, talk which takes place in private, and not before reporters or microphones or television, is the only kind of approach which can lead to sanity and fruitful understanding. Let the process of conference be private, but let its conclusions, its complete conclusions, be made public.

In this connection such an organization as the United Nations is in harmony with the principles of God's moral government. American Presbyterians should remember with pride that it is the successor of a former organization which was the creation of a great American who was also a great Presbyterian. While the United Nations organization is very far from perfection and it functions today under great handicaps, it is yet the natural and best available agent for international cooperation and the settlement of disputes among nations. It is imperative, therefore, that it be given the utmost support. It stands between us and war.

While we take all wise precautions for defense, both within and outside our borders, the present situation demands spiritual calm, historical perspective, religious faith, and an adventurous spirit. Loyalty to great principles of truth and justice has made our nation great; such loyalty alone can keep it great and ensure its destiny.

May God give us the wisdom and courage to think and act in accordance with His Will.

53.

Harry S. Truman: Reply to a Congressional Subpoena

The issue of Communists in government was an important one in the 1952 presidential campaign, even though the Republican candidate, Eisenhower, did not associate himself with the charge of the more extreme elements in his party that the Roosevelt and Truman administrations had added up to "twenty years of treason." After Eisenhower was elected, the extremists in the party continued the attack, calling in question the loyalty of former President Truman as well as many of his aides and appointees. On November 6, 1953, Attorney General Herbert Brownell, Jr., charged that Truman had knowingly appointed a Soviet spy, Harry Dexter White, to a government position. The House Un-American Activities Committee thereupon subpoenaed Truman to appear before it and explain the reasons for the appointment. Adhering to a tradition more than a century old, Truman declined to appear. His reply to the committee is reprinted here.

I HAVE YOUR SUBPOENA dated Nov. 9, 1953, directing my appearance before your committee on Friday, November 13, in Washington. The subpoena does not state the matters upon which you seek my testimony, but I assume from the press stories that you seek to examine me with respect to matters which occurred during my tenure of the presidency of the United States.

In spite of my personal willingness to cooperate with your committee, I feel constrained by my duty to the people of the United States to decline to comply with the subpoena. In doing so, I am carrying out the provisions of the Constitution of the United States, and am following a long line of precedents, commencing with George Washington himself in 1796. Since his day, Presidents Jefferson, Monroe, Jackson, Tyler, Polk, Fillmore, Buchanan, Lincoln, Grant, Hayes, Cleveland, Theodore Roosevelt, Coolidge, Hoover, and Franklin D. Roosevelt have declined to respond to sub-poenas or demands for information of various kinds by Congress.

The underlying reason for this clearly established and universally recognized constitutional doctrine has been succinctly set forth by Charles Warren, one of our leading constitutional authorities, as follows:

> In this long series of contests by the Executive to maintain his constitutional integrity, one sees a legitimate conclusion from our theory of government. . . . Under our Constitution, each branch of the government is designed to be a coordinate representative of the will of the people. . . . Defense by the Executive of his constitutional powers becomes in very truth, therefore, defense of popular rights — defense of power which the people granted to him.

It was in that sense that President Cleveland spoke of his duty to the people not to relinquish any of the powers of his great office. It was in that sense that President Buchanan stated the people have rights and prerogatives in the execution of his office by the President which every President is under a duty to see "shall never be violated in his person" but "passed to his successors unimpaired by the adoption of a dangerous precedent." In maintaining his rights against a trespassing Congress, the President defends not himself but popular government; he represents not himself but the people.

President Jackson repelled an attempt by the Congress to break down the separation of powers in these words: "For myself I shall repel all such attempts as an invasion of the principles of justice as well as of the Constitution, and I shall esteem it my sacred duty to the people of the United States to resist them as I would the establishment of a Spanish Inquisition."

I might commend to your reading the opinion of one of the committees of the House of Representatives in 1879, House Report 141, March 3, 1879, 45th Congress, Third Session, in which the House Judiciary Committee said the following: "The Executive is as independent of either house of Congress as either house of Congress is independent of him, and they cannot call for the records of his actions, or the action of his officers against his consent, any more than he can call for any of the journals or records of the House or Senate."

It must be obvious to you that if the doctrine of separation of powers and the independence of the presidency is to have any validity at all, it must be equally applicable to a President after his term of office has expired when he is sought to be examined with respect to any acts occurring while he is President.

The doctrine would be shattered, and the President, contrary to our fundamental theory of constitutional government, would become a mere arm of the legislative branch of the government if he would feel during his term of office that his every act might be subject to official inquiry and possible distortion for political purposes.

If your intention, however, is to inquire into any acts as a private individual either before or after my presidency and unrelated to any acts as President, I shall be happy to appear.

———◆———

In my experience all very successful commanders are prima donnas, and must be so treated.

GEORGE S. PATTON, JR.

1954

54.

JOHN FOSTER DULLES: The Strategy of Massive Retaliation

John Foster Dulles' foreign policy, particularly with regard to America's Cold War foe, the Soviet Union, was based on two main principles: "liberation of captive peoples" rather than "containment" of Communism, and "massive retaliation" against Communist aggression rather than "limited" military response confined to the area of the attack. One result of the second point was Dulles' emphasis on nuclear weapons rather than conventional forces, and another was the periodic crises, or "brinks," that the U.S. and the U.S.S.R. approached from time to time during the 1950s. Dulles explained his policy of overwhelming deterrent force in a speech to the Council on Foreign Relations in New York City on January 12, 1954. Part of the speech is reprinted here.

Source: *Bulletin*, January 25, 1954, pp. 107-110.

WE LIVE IN A WORLD where emergencies are always possible, and our survival may depend upon our capacity to meet emergencies. Let us pray that we shall always have that capacity. But, having said that, it is necessary also to say that emergency measures — however good for the emergency — do not necessarily make good permanent policies. Emergency measures are costly; they are superficial; and they imply that the enemy has the initiative. They cannot be depended on to serve our long-time interests. This "long-time" factor is of critical importance.

The Soviet Communists are planning for what they call "an entire historical era," and we should do the same. They seek, through many types of maneuvers, gradually to divide and weaken the free nations by overextending them in efforts which, as Lenin put it, are "beyond their strength, so that they come to practical bankruptcy." Then, said Lenin, "our victory is assured." Then, said Stalin, will be "the moment for the decisive blow."

In the face of this strategy, measures cannot be judged adequate merely because they ward off an immediate danger. It is essential to do this, but it is also essential to do so without exhausting ourselves.

When the Eisenhower administration applied this test, we felt that some transformations were needed.

It is not sound military strategy permanently to commit U.S. land forces to Asia to a degree that leaves us no strategic reserves. It is not sound economics or good foreign policy to support permanently other countries; for, in the long run, that creates as much ill will as goodwill. Also, it is not sound to become permanently committed to military expenditures so vast that they lead to "practical bankruptcy."

Change was imperative to assure the stamina needed for permanent security. But it was equally imperative that change should be accompanied by understanding of our true purposes. Sudden and spectacular change had to be avoided. Otherwise, there might have been a panic among our friends and miscalculated aggression by our enemies. We can, I believe, make a good report in these respects.

We need allies and collective security. Our purpose is to make these relations more effective, less costly. This can be done by placing more reliance on deterrent power and less dependence on local defensive power. This is accepted practice so far as local communities are concerned. We keep locks on our doors, but we do not have an armed guard in every home. We rely principally on a community security system so well equipped to punish any who break in and steal that, in fact, would-be aggressors are generally deterred. That is the modern way of getting maximum protection at a bearable cost.

What the Eisenhower administration seeks is a similar international security system. We want, for ourselves and the other free nations, a maximum deterrent at a bearable cost.

Local defense will always be important. But there is no local defense which alone will contain the mighty landpower of the Communist world. Local defenses must be reinforced by the further deterrent of massive retaliatory power. A potential aggressor must know that he cannot always prescribe battle conditions that suit him. Otherwise, for example, a potential aggressor, who is glutted with manpower, might be tempted to attack in confidence that resistance would be confined to manpower. He might be tempted to attack in places where his superiority was decisive.

The way to deter aggression is for the free community to be willing and able to respond vigorously at places and with means of its own choosing.

So long as our basic policy concepts were unclear, our military leaders could not be selective in building our military power. If an enemy could pick his time and place and method of warfare — and if our policy was to remain the traditional one of meeting aggression by direct and local opposition — then we needed to be ready to fight in the Arctic and in the Tropics; in Asia, the Near East, and in Europe; by sea, by land, and by air; with old weapons and with new weapons.

The total cost of our security efforts, at home and abroad, was over $50 billion per annum, and involved, for 1953, a projected budgetary deficit of $9 billion; and $11 billion for 1954. This was on top of taxes comparable to wartime taxes; and the dollar was depreciating in effective value. Our allies were similarly weighed down. This could not be continued for long without grave budgetary, economic, and social consequences.

But before military planning could be changed, the President and his advisers, as represented by the National Security Council, had to take some basic policy decisions. This has been done. The basic decision was to depend primarily upon a great capacity to retaliate, instantly, by means and at places of our choosing. Now the Department of Defense and the Joint Chiefs of Staff can shape our military establishment to fit what is *our* policy instead of having to try to be ready to meet the enemy's many choices. That permits of a selection of military means instead of a multiplication of means. As a result, it is now possible to get and share more basic security at less cost. . . .

We do not, of course, claim to have found some magic formula that insures against all forms of Communist successes. It is normal that at some times and at some places there may be setbacks to the cause of freedom. What we do expect to insure is that any setbacks will have only temporary and local significance, because they will leave unimpaired those free-world assets which in the long run will prevail.

If we can deter such aggression as would mean general war, and that is our confident resolve, then we can let time and fundamentals work for us. We do not need self-imposed policies which sap our strength.

The fundamental, on our side, is the richness — spiritual, intellectual, and material — that freedom can produce and the irresistible attraction it then sets up. That is why we do not plan ourselves to shackle freedom to preserve freedom. We intend that our conduct and example shall continue, as in the past, to show all men how good can be the fruits of freedom.

If we rely on freedom, then it follows that we must abstain from diplomatic moves which would seem to endorse captivity. That would, in effect, be a conspiracy against freedom. I can assure you that we shall never seek illusory security for ourselves by such a "deal." We do negotiate about specific matters but only to advance the cause of human welfare.

President Eisenhower electrified the world with his proposal to lift a great weight of fear by turning atomic energy from a means of death into a source of life. Yesterday, I started procedural talks with the Soviet government on that topic.

We have persisted, with our allies, in seeking the unification of Germany and the liberation of Austria. Now the Soviet rulers have agreed to discuss these questions. We expect to meet them soon in Berlin. I hope they will come with a sincerity which will equal our own.

We have sought a conference to unify Korea and relieve it of foreign troops. So far, our persistence is unrewarded; but we have not given up.

These efforts at negotiation are normal initiatives that breathe the spirit of freedom. They involve no plan for a partnership division of world power with those who suppress freedom.

If we persist in the courses I outline, we shall confront dictatorship with a task that is, in the long run, beyond its strength. For unless it changes, it must suppress the human desires that freedom satisfies — as we shall be demonstrating. If the dictators persist in their present course, then it is they who will be limited to superficial successes while their foundation crumbles under the tread of their iron boots.

The power of positive brinking.
ADLAI STEVENSON, of the Eisenhower-Dulles foreign policy

55.

EARL WARREN: *Brown et al.* v. *Board of Education of Topeka et al.*

The outset of the Negro or civil rights movement of the 1950s and 1960s may be said to have occurred on May 17, 1954, when the Supreme Court handed down its decision in Brown v. Board of Education of Topeka. *The decision, written by Chief Justice Warren for a unanimous Court, directly reversed the famous ruling in* Plessy v. Ferguson *(1896). In the earlier case the Court had upheld a Louisiana law requiring separate railroad facilities, on the grounds that if equality of accommodations existed Negroes had no recourse under the equal protection of the laws clause of the Fourteenth Amendment. The 1954 ruling held, on the contrary, that even if educational opportunities for Negroes were equal to those for whites, Negroes were nevertheless deprived under the same clause of the same amendment.*

Source: 347 U.S. 483.

THESE CASES COME TO US from the states of Kansas, South Carolina, Virginia, and Delaware. They are premised on different facts and different local conditions, but a common legal question justifies their consideration together in this consolidated opinion.[1]

In each of the cases, minors of the Negro race, through their legal representatives, seek the aid of the courts in obtaining admission to the public schools of their community on a nonsegregated basis. In each instance, they had been denied admission to

1. In the Kansas case, *Brown* v. *Board of Education,* the plaintiffs are Negro children of elementary-school age residing in Topeka. They brought this action in the United States District Court for the District of Kansas to enjoin enforcement of a Kansas statute which permits, but does not require, cities of more than 15,000 population to maintain separate school facilities for Negro and white students. Kan. Gen. Stat. Sec. 72-1724 (1949). Pursuant to that authority, the Topeka Board of Education elected to establish segregated elementary schools. Other public schools in the community, however, are operated on a nonsegregated basis. The three-judge District Court, convened under 28 U.S.C. Sec. 2281 and 2284, found that segregation in public education has a detrimental effect upon Negro children, but denied relief on the ground that the Negro and white schools were substantially equal with respect to buildings, transportation, curricula, and educational qualifications of teachers. 98 F. Supp. 797. The case is here on direct appeal under 28 U.S.C. Sec. 1253.

In the South Carolina case, *Briggs* v. *Elliott,* the plaintiffs are Negro children of both elementary and high-school age residing in Clarendon County. They brought this action in the United States District Court for the Eastern District of South Carolina to enjoin enforcement of provisions in the state constitution and statutory code which require the segregation of Negroes and whites in public schools. S.C. Const., Art. XI, Sec. 7; S.C. Code Sec. 5377 (1942). The three-judge District Court, convened under 28 U.S.C. Sec. 2281 and 2284, denied the requested relief. The court found that the Negro schools were inferior to the white schools and ordered the defendants to begin immediately to equalize the facilities. But the court sustained the validity of the contested provisions and denied the plaintiffs admission to the white schools during the equalization program. 98 F. Supp. 529. This Court vacated the District Court's judgment and remanded the case for the purpose of obtaining the court's views on a report filed by the defendants concerning the progress made in the equalization program.

schools attended by white children under laws requiring or permitting segregation according to race. This segregation was alleged to deprive the plaintiffs of the equal protection of the laws under the Fourteenth Amendment. In each of the cases other than

342 U.S. 350. On remand, the District Court found that substantial equality had been achieved except for buildings and that the defendants were proceeding to rectify this inequality as well. 103 F. Supp. 920. The case is again here on direct appeal under 28 U.S.C. Sec. 1253.

In the Virginia case, *Davis* v. *County School Board*, the plaintiffs are Negro children of high-school age residing in Prince Edward County. They brought this action in the United States District Court for the Eastern District of Virginia to enjoin enforcement of provisions in the state constitution and statutory code which require the segregation of Negroes and whites in public schools. Va. Const., Sec. 140; Va. Code Sec. 22-221 (1950). The three-judge District Court, convened under 28 U.S.C. Sec. 2281 and 2284, denied the requested relief. The court found the Negro school inferior in physical plant, curricula, and transportation, and ordered the defendants forthwith to provide substantially equal curricula and transportation and to "proceed with all reasonable diligence and dispatch to remove" the inequality in physical plant. But, as in the South Carolina case, the court sustained the validity of the contested provisions and denied the plaintiffs admission to the white schools during the equalization program. 103 F. Supp. 337. The case is here on direct appeal under 28 U.S.C. Sec. 1253.

In the Delaware case, *Gebhart* v. *Belton*, the plaintiffs are Negro children of both elementary and high-school age residing in New Castle County. They brought this action in the Delaware Court of Chancery to enjoin enforcement of provisions in the state constitution and statutory code which require the segregation of Negroes and whites in public schools. Del. Const., Art. X, Sec. 2; Del. Rev. Code Sec. 2631 (1935). The chancellor gave judgment for the plaintiffs and ordered their immediate admission to schools previously attended only by white children on the ground that the Negro schools were inferior with respect to teacher training, pupil-teacher ratio, extracurricular activities, physical plant, and time and distance involved in travel. 87 A. 2d 862. The chancellor also found that segregation itself results in an inferior education for Negro children (see note 10, *infra*), but did not rest his decision on that ground. *Id.*, at 865. The chancellor's decree was affirmed by the Supreme Court of Delaware, which intimated, however, that the defendants might be able to obtain a modification of the decree after equalization of the Negro and white schools had been accomplished. 91 A. 2nd 137, 152. The defendants, contending only that the Delaware courts had erred in ordering the immediate admission of the Negro plaintiffs to the white schools, applied to this Court for certiorari. The writ was granted, 344 U.S. 891. The plaintiffs, who were successful below, did not submit a cross-petition.

the Delaware case, a three-judge federal District Court denied relief to the plaintiffs on the so-called "separate but equal" doctrine announced by this Court in *Plessy* v. *Ferguson*, 163 U.S. 537. Under that doctrine, equality of treatment is accorded when the races are provided substantially equal facilities, even though these facilities be separate. In the Delaware case, the Supreme Court of Delaware adhered to that doctrine, but ordered that the plaintiffs be admitted to the white schools because of their superiority to the Negro schools.

The plaintiffs contend that segregated public schools are not "equal" and cannot be made "equal," and that hence they are deprived of the equal protection of the laws. Because of the obvious importance of the question presented, the Court took jurisdiction.[2] Argument was heard in the 1952 Term, and reargument was heard this Term on certain questions propounded by the Court.[3]

Reargument was largely devoted to the circumstances surrounding the adoption of the Fourteenth Amendment in 1868. It covered exhaustively consideration of the amendment in Congress, ratification by the states, then-existing practices in racial segregation, and the views of proponents and opponents of the amendment. This discussion and our own investigation convince us that, although these sources cast some light, it is not enough to resolve the problem with which we are faced. At best, they are inconclusive. The most avid proponents of the postwar amendments undoubtedly intended them to remove all legal distinctions among "all persons born or naturalized in the United States." Their opponents, just as certainly, were antagonistic to both the letter and the spirit of the amendments and

2. 344 U.S. 1, 141, 891.
3. 345 U.S. 972. The attorney general of the United States participated both Terms as *amicus curiae*.

wished them to have the most limited effect. What others in Congress and the state legislatures had in mind cannot be determined with any degree of certainty.

An additional reason for the inconclusive nature of the amendment's history, with respect to segregated schools, is the status of public education at that time.[4] In the South, the movement toward free common schools, supported by general taxation, had not yet taken hold. Education of white children was largely in the hands of private groups. Education of Negroes was almost nonexistent, and practically all of the race were illiterate. In fact, any education of Negroes was forbidden by law in some states. Today, in contrast, many Negroes have achieved outstanding success in the arts and sciences as well as in the business and professional world. It is true that public-school education at the time of the amendment had advanced further in the North, but the effect of the amendment on Northern states was generally ignored in the congressional debates.

4. For a general study of the development of public education prior to the amendment, see Butts and Cremin, *A History of Education in American Culture* (1953), Pts. I, II; Cubberley, *Public Education in the United States* (1934 ed.), cc. II-XII. School practices current at the time of the adoption of the Fourteenth Amendment are described in Butts and Cremin, *supra*, at 269-275; Cubberley, *supra*, at 288-339, 408-431; Knight, *Public Education in the South* (1922), cc. VIII, IX. See also H. Ex. Doc. No. 315, 41st Cong., 2nd Sess. (1871). Although the demand for free public schools followed substantially the same pattern in both the North and the South, the development in the South did not begin to gain momentum until about 1850, some twenty years after that in the North. The reasons for the somewhat slower development in the South (*e.g.*, the rural character of the South and the different regional attitudes toward state assistance) are well explained in Cubberley, *supra*, at 408-423. In the country as a whole, but particularly in the South, the war virtually stopped all progress in public education. *Id.*, at 427-428. The low status of Negro education in all sections of the country, both before and immediately after the war, is described in Beale, *A History of Freedom of Teaching in American Schools* (1941), 112-132, 175-195. Compulsory school-attendance laws were not generally adopted until after the ratification of the Fourteenth Amendment, and it was not until 1918 that such laws were in force in all the states. Cubberley, *supra*, at 563-565.

Even in the North, the conditions of public education did not approximate those existing today. The curriculum was usually rudimentary; ungraded schools were common in rural areas; the school term was but three months a year in many states; and compulsory school attendance was virtually unknown. As a consequence, it is not surprising that there should be so little in the history of the Fourteenth Amendment relating to its intended effect on public education.

In the first cases in this Court construing the Fourteenth Amendment, decided shortly after its adoption, the Court interpreted it as proscribing all state-imposed discriminations against the Negro race.[5] The doctrine of "separate but equal" did not make its appearance in this Court until 1896 in the case of *Plessy* v. *Ferguson, supra,* involving not education but transportation.[6] American

5. *Slaughter-House Cases,* 16 Wall. 36, 67-72 (1873); *Strauder* v. *West Virginia,* 100 U. S. 303, 307-308 (1880): "It ordains that no state shall deprive any person of life, liberty, or property, without due process of law, or deny to any person within its jurisdiction the equal protection of the laws. What is this but declaring that the law in the states shall be the same for the black as for the white; that all persons, whether colored or white, shall stand equal before the laws of the states, and, in regard to the colored race, for whose protection the amendment was primarily designed, that no discrimination shall be made against them by law because of their color? The words of the amendment, it is true, are prohibitory, but they contain a necessary implication of a positive immunity, or right, most valuable to the colored race — the right to exemption from unfriendly legislation against them distinctively as colored — exemption from legal discriminations, implying inferiority in civil society, lessening the security of their enjoyment of the rights which others enjoy, and discriminations which are steps toward reducing them to the condition of a subject race." See also *Virginia* v. *Rives,* 100 U.S. 313, 318 (1880); *Ex parte Virginia,* 100 U.S. 339, 344-345 (1880).

6. The doctrine apparently originated in *Roberts* v. *City of Boston,* 59 Mass. 198, 206 (1850), upholding school segregation against attack as being violative of a state constitutional guarantee of equality. Segregation in Boston public schools was eliminated in 1855. Mass. Acts 1855, c. 256. But elsewhere in the North, segregation in public education has persisted in some communities until recent years. It is apparent that such segregation has long been a nationwide problem, not merely one of sectional concern.

courts have since labored with the doctrine for over half a century.

In this Court there have been six cases involving the "separate but equal" doctrine in the field of public education.[7] In *Cumming* v. *County Board of Education,* 175 U. S. 528, and *Gong Lum* v. *Rice,* 275 U. S. 78, the validity of the doctrine itself was not challenged.[8] In more recent cases, all on the graduate-school level, inequality was found in that specific benefits enjoyed by white students were denied to Negro students of the same educational qualifications. *Missouri ex rel. Gaines* v. *Canada,* 305 U. S. 337; *Sipuel* v. *Oklahoma,* 332 U. S. 631; *Sweatt* v. *Painter,* 339 U. S. 629; *McLaurin* v. *Oklahoma State Regents,* 339 U. S. 637. In none of these cases was it necessary to reexamine the doctrine to grant relief to the Negro plaintiff. And in *Sweatt* v. *Painter, supra,* the Court expressly reserved decision on the question whether *Plessy* v. *Ferguson* should be held inapplicable to public education.

In the instant cases, that question is directly presented. Here, unlike *Sweatt* v. *Painter,* there are findings below that the Negro and white schools involved have been equalized, or are being equalized, with respect to buildings, curricula, qualifications and salaries of teachers, and other "tangible" factors.[9] Our decision, therefore,

7. See also *Berea College* v. *Kentucky,* 211 U.S. 45 (1908).
8. In the *Cumming* case, Negro taxpayers sought an injunction requiring the defendant school board to discontinue the operation of a high school for white children until the board resumed operation of a high school for Negro children. Similarly, in the *Gong Lum* case, the plaintiff, a child of Chinese descent, contended only that state authorities had misapplied the doctrine by classifying him with Negro children and requiring him to attend a Negro school.
9. In the Kansas case, the court below found substantial equality as to all such factors. 98 F. Supp. 797, 798. In the South Carolina case, the court below found that the defendants were proceeding "promptly and in good faith to comply with the court's decree." 103 F. Supp. 920, 921. In the Virginia case, the court below noted that the equalization program was already "afoot and progressing" (103 F. Supp. 337, 341); since then, we have

cannot turn on merely a comparison of these tangible factors in the Negro and white schools involved in each of the cases. We must look instead to the effect of segregation itself on public education.

In approaching this problem, we cannot turn the clock back to 1868 when the amendment was adopted, or even to 1896 when *Plessy* v. *Ferguson* was written. We must consider public education in the light of its full development and its present place in American life throughout the nation. Only in this way can it be determined if segregation in public schools deprives these plaintiffs of the equal protection of the laws.

Today, education is perhaps the most important function of state and local governments. Compulsory school-attendance laws and the great expenditures for education both demonstrate our recognition of the importance of education to our democratic society. It is required in the performance of our most basic public responsibilities, even service in the armed forces. It is the very foundation of good citizenship. Today it is a principal instrument in awakening the child to cultural values, in preparing him for later professional training, and in helping him to adjust normally to his environment. In these days, it is doubtful that any child may reasonably be expected to succeed in life if he is denied the opportunity of an education. Such an opportunity, where the state has undertaken to provide it, is a right which must be made available to all on equal terms.

We come then to the question presented: Does segregation of children in public schools solely on the basis of race, even though the physical facilities and other "tangible" factors may be equal, deprive the children of the minority group of equal ed-

been advised, in the Virginia attorney general's brief on reargument, that the program has now been completed. In the Delaware case, the court below similarly noted that the state's equalization program was well under way. 91 A. 2d 137, 149.

ucational opportunities? We believe that it does.

In *Sweatt* v. *Painter, supra,* in finding that a segregated law school for Negroes could not provide them equal educational opportunities, this Court relied in large part on "those qualities which are incapable of objective measurement but which make for greatness in a law school." In *McLaurin* v. *Oklahoma State Regents, supra,* the Court, in requiring that a Negro admitted to a white graduate school be treated like all other students, again resorted to intangible considerations: ". . . his ability to study, to engage in discussions and exchange views with other students, and, in general, to learn his profession." Such considerations apply with added force to children in grade and high schools. To separate them from others of similar age and qualifications solely because of their race generates a feeling of inferiority as to their status in the community that may affect their hearts and minds in a way unlikely ever to be undone. The effect of this separation on their educational opportunities was well stated by a finding in the Kansas case by a court which nevertheless felt compelled to rule against the Negro plaintiffs:

> Segregation of white and colored children in public schools has a detrimental effect upon the colored children. The impact is greater when it has the sanction of the law; for the policy of separating the races is usually interpreted as denoting the inferiority of the Negro group. A sense of inferiority affects the motivation of a child to learn. Segregation with the sanction of law, therefore, has a tendency to [retard] the educational and mental development of Negro children and to deprive them of some of the benefits they would receive in a racial[ly] integrated school system.[10]

Whatever may have been the extent of psychological knowledge at the time of *Plessy*

v. *Ferguson,* this finding is amply supported by modern authority.[11] Any language in *Plessy* v. *Ferguson* contrary to this finding is rejected.

We conclude that in the field of public education the doctrine of "separate but equal" has no place. Separate educational facilities are inherently unequal. Therefore, we hold that the plaintiffs and others similarly situated for whom the actions have been brought are, by reason of the segregation complained of, deprived of the equal protection of the laws guaranteed by the Fourteenth Amendment. This disposition makes unnecessary any discussion whether such segregation also violates the due process clause of the Fourteenth Amendment.[12]

Because these are class actions, because of the wide applicability of this decision, and because of the great variety of local conditions, the formulation of decrees in these cases presents problems of considerable complexity. On reargument, the consideration of appropriate relief was necessarily subordinated to the primary question — the constitutionality of segregation in public education. We have now announced that such segregation is a denial of the equal protection of the laws. In order that we may have the full assistance of the parties in formulating decrees, the cases will be restored to the docket, and the parties are requested to

---

10. A similar finding was made in the Delaware case: "I conclude from the testimony that, in our Delaware society, state-imposed segregation in education itself results in the Negro children, as a class, receiving educational opportunities which are substantially inferior to those available to white children otherwise similarly situated." 87 A. 2d 862, 865.

11. K. B. Clark, *Effect of Prejudice and Discrimination on Personality Development* (Midcentury White House Conference on Children and Youth, 1950); Witmer and Kotinsky, *Personality in the Making* (1952), c. VI; Deutscher and Chein, "The Psychological Effects of Enforced Segregation: A Survey of Social Science Opinion," *26 J. Psychol.* 259 (1948); Chein, "What are the Psychological Effects of Segregation Under Conditions of Equal Facilities?" *3 Int. J. Opinion and Attitude Res.* 229 (1949); Brameld, *Educational Costs, in Discrimination and National Welfare* (MacIver, ed., 1949), 44-48; Frazier, *The Negro in the United States* (1949), 674-681. And see generally Myrdal, *An American Dilemma* (1944).

12. See *Bolling* v. *Sharpe, post,* p. 497, concerning the due process clause of the Fifth Amendment.

present further argument on Questions 4 and 5 previously propounded by the Court for the reargument this Term.[13] The attorney general of the United States is again invited to participate. The attorneys general

of the states requiring or permitting segregation in public education will also be permitted to appear as *amici curiae* upon request to do so by Sept. 15, 1954, and submission of briefs by Oct. 1, 1954.[14]

---

13. "4. Assuming it is decided that segregation in public schools violates the Fourteenth Amendment
"(a) would a decree necessarily follow providing that, within the limits set by normal geographic school districting, Negro children should forthwith be admitted to schools of their choice, or
"(b) may this Court, in the exercise of its equity powers, permit an effective gradual adjustment to be brought about from existing segregated systems to a system not based on color distinctions?
"5. On the assumption on which questions 4 (a) and (b) are based, and assuming further that this Court will exercise its equity powers to the end described in question 4 (b),
"(a) should this Court formulate detailed decrees

in these cases;
"(b) if so, what specific issues should the decrees reach;
"(c) should this Court appoint a special master to hear evidence with a view to recommending specific terms for such decrees;
"(d) should this Court remand to the courts of first instance with directions to frame decrees in these cases, and if so what general directions should the decrees of this Court include and what procedures should the courts of first instance follow in arriving at the specific terms of more detailed decrees?"
14. See Rule 42, Revised Rules of this Court (effective July 1, 1954).

56.

David M. Potter: Democracy and Abundance

World War II brought with it for the United States intensive technological development, vastly increased industrial growth, and reduced unemployment. One result was a redistribution of wealth that meant affluence for a greater proportion of the population than had ever enjoyed it before. But America's prosperity was not shared by most of the people of Asia, Africa, and South America, who found themselves hampered not only by a tradition of poverty but also by a rising birthrate that more than overcame any economic advances. To these people, many of them citizens of struggling new nations, the abundant wealth of America stood out in stark contrast. In his book People of Plenty, *published in 1954, historian David M. Potter examined the history of American abundance and discussed the mission of America* vis-à-vis *the poor and undeveloped nations of the earth. A portion of Chapter Six is reprinted here.*

Source: *People of Plenty*, Chicago, 1954: "Abundance and the Mission of America."

TODAY, WHEN THE FOUR FREEDOMS seem as much an illusion as the Big Four who were jointly to underwrite them, the frustration of the belief in an American mission is too poignant to admit of dispassionate comment. Consistently, throughout our history, we have assumed that we had a message for

the world, a democratic message, and, some would say, a message of redemption. Consistently we have scanned the horizon, looking for signs that the message was being received. Hopefully we have attempted to convince ourselves that other movements were intrinsically at one with our own, despite local differences of complexion: that French Jacobinism was American democracy reacting against a greater accumulation of grievances and acts of oppression than America had known; that Latin-American *caudillos* were merely American political bosses strutting in gaudy uniforms; that the Soviets of 1919 and 1920 were merely extending American political democracy into the economic orbit and were carrying on from where we had stopped; that the Chinese Communists were, at bottom, Jeffersonian Democrats who mouthed the phrases of Marx but thought the thoughts of the independent agrarian man.

Ironically, those who have embraced the principles of democracy — those who have adopted the system that we desired to spread — have been indebted to us only in a minor sense for their ideas. Britain enacted her Reform Bill of 1832 at a time when America was regarded with widespread contempt by the British; Canada received her dominion status upon the recommendation of a British peer and without any instigation by the United States; Australia and New Zealand worked out their democratic regimes almost as if the United States were on another planet; and the republics of Western Europe owe their self-government very much more to European socialist thought than to American democratic thought.

Although democracy in American style never seemed to gain ascendancy in other parts of the globe, there was a long interval, extending over most of the nineteenth century, during which American ideals seemed a beacon light to poor and humble folk all over the world. Millions of these poor came to America because it was a refuge for the oppressed, and millions of others who remained at home were inspired by the American dream. The moral authority of our ideals of equality, of freedom, and of opportunity was immense, and we were entitled to believe that for every aristocrat who disparaged us or condescended to us

there were scores of plain men and women who shared in and were heartened by our aspirations for human welfare. The rapidity and eagerness with which our immigrants embraced Americanism gave tangible proof of this response, and thus our people, who have always been solicitous for the approval of others, could find comfort in the assurance that the heart of humanity responded to the creed of our democracy. This assurance went far to mitigate our disappointment at the failure of American democracy to take root overseas.

But today this consolation has utterly vanished, and we now harbor few illusions as to the affection which we can command from the mass of humanity. Ever since the days of Calvin Coolidge, when Uncle Sam first heard himself being called "Uncle Shylock," we have grown increasingly used to finding American motives misrepresented and American ideals greeted with skepticism and indifference. In the last decade many Americans have come sadly to believe that the only influence which we can command is of that precarious kind which is bought and paid for, not once but repeatedly. Insofar as we do find friends, they are less among the oppressed than among the propertied and conservative classes.

In these circumstances one is almost constrained to wonder whether, in reality, we have had a message for the world at all. If we did, why this series of frustrations in delivering it? Why have we, who applauded at the birth of so many revolutions, so consistently found those revolutions defeating the very ends which we hoped they would promote? Why has our country, which championed the cause of ordinary humanity, received its most vicious attacks from the spokesmen of the proletariat?

In some respects this is the question behind all the questions which confront America today, and, as such, it has an overwhelming importance which should discourage a casual approach. The immense difficulty of the problem automatically discredits all simple solutions, and it is challenge enough even to define the problem. It is, therefore, with some hesitation that I point out one possible aspect in which the factor of American abundance bears upon this problem and thus may be of some use in defining it, even though it could hardly be of any direct use in dealing with it.

The thought is not original with me, but what I would suggest is this: that we have been historically correct in supposing that we had a revolutionary message to offer but we have been mistaken in our concept of what that message was. We supposed that our revelation was "democracy revolutionizing the world," but in reality it was "abundance revolutionizing the world" — a message which we did not preach and scarcely understood ourselves, but one which was peculiarly able to preach its own gospel without words.

It is perhaps significant that it took a European to perceive the true impact which the United States had upon the rest of the world. As early as 1932, André Siegfried, in an address to a group of French Protestant businessmen, made these very pregnant observations: "The West," he said, "has thought for a long time, not without a certain naïveté, that it represented spirituality in the world. But is spirituality really the message we have taken along with us everywhere? What has been borrowed from us, as I have so often observed, is our mechanisms. Today, in the most remote, most ancient villages, one finds the automobile, the cinema, the radio, the telephone, the phonograph, not to mention the airplane, and it is not the white men, nor the most civilized, who display the greatest enthusiasm for them."

This comment applies to the influence of Western civilization as a whole, but, with specific reference to America, Siegfried said, "The United States is presiding at a general reorganization of the ways of living throughout the entire world."

As to what we have imparted, "the one really new gospel we have introduced is the revelation, after centuries of passively endured privations, that a man may at last free himself of poverty, and, most fantastic innovation of all, that he may actually enjoy his existence. . . . And so, without our wishing it, or even knowing it, we appear as the terrible instigators of social change and revolution." . . .

For a country destined, as ours has been, to play such a role it was a tragic fallacy that we conceived of democracy as an absolute value, largely ideological in content and equally valid in any environment, instead of recognizing that our own democratic system is one of the major by-products of our abundance, workable primarily because of the measure of our abundance. . . .

On the domestic scene, the fallacy was more or less academic in its consequences, which is perhaps why we have been slow to perceive it. The only adverse result was to bring us to the right operative conclusions for the wrong reasons.

But on the international front this fallacy has had most far-reaching results, in that it has consistently impelled us to proselyte for converts to the democratic faith in places where the economic prerequisites for democracy have not been established. This, I believe, has a great deal to do with the widespread impression in the world that the Americans are, somehow, hypocrites. In our own country the promise of equality meant the right to advance, without discrimination, to easily attainable ends. Hence the principle of equality could be upheld with genuine sincerity. Freedom meant the removal of barriers to advancement from one position to another, more advantageous one. But in countries where even decency, much less comfort, lay beyond the point of attainability for most people — where the number of advantageous positions was negligible — it seemed a kind of deception to offer the individual as good a chance as anyone to compete for nonexistent prizes or to assure him of his freedom to go where he wished, when there was, in fact, nowhere to go.

This anomalous relationship between the permissive and the protective aspects of freedom has always required adjustment, both at the domestic and at the international level. Thus Franklin Roosevelt, who, on the domestic front, shifted the emphasis from freedom as immunity to control, to freedom as immunity to social privation, also recognized the need for giving new connotations to the term "freedom" on the international scene. Hence his four freedoms — freedom of speech, freedom of religion, freedom from want, and freedom from fear — were two parts freedom in the classic liberal sense and two parts security under the label of "freedom."

If Roosevelt had been able to fulfill his formula, the whole nature of this problem would be different; but he was not, and we revert to the fact that American liberals throughout our history have misunderstood the nature of our own economic revolution and have also misunderstood what the revolutionists of other countries wanted. Jefferson and his landowning, independent, backwoods farmers, who had conducted a political revolution against Britain without social upheaval, were not prepared for the convulsions that an oppressed class of serfs and a Paris mob would regard as a necessary part of any reform that was worth making in France. Henry Clay and the expansive westerners did not appreciate that in Latin America, behind the few idealists who believed in liberty, there was a local ruling class which saw no reason why absentees in Europe should continue to share in the exploitation of the Indians and who proposed to monopolize this exploitation for themselves. The idealists who felt it a national obligation to liberate Cuba in 1898 did not appreciate that the Cubans were revolting against economic conditions which resulted

even more from the McKinley Tariff than from the iniquities of Bourbon misrule. American liberals in 1919 and 1920 failed to grasp the fact that Russian revolutionaries were overthrowing the ruthless regime of the tsars not because they wanted to substitute a more humanitarian regime in its place but because they wanted to substitute a more efficient ruthlessness, and one which would be operated by a different class.

The most effective means by which we could have promoted humanitarian and democratic principles abroad was not by applauding revolutions conducted in the name of such principles but by imparting to other parts of the world the means that we have developed for raising the standard of living. . . .

But no less important than the original, easily accessible wealth was the fact that this wealth stimulated our technology and our entire productive system in such a way that we developed an unparalleled aptitude for converting many previously inconvertible materials and sources of power into forms that also constituted wealth. If we were unique in the original heritage, we are not at all unique in the possession of potential assets whose value may be realized by the application of technological skill. Thus we are in position to affirm to the world that, although we are in many respects set apart by our natural plenty, in many other respects we are qualified to show other countries the path that may lead them to a plenty like our own. But we have thrown away this opportunity by failing to display the processes which others might emulate and by showing, instead, the end-product — our standard of living — which they can only envy. Then we have deepened the alienation by blaming other peoples for failing to embrace the political ideals which our standard of living supports.

In spite of the early export of such American technological devices as the McCormick reaper and in spite of attempts, through the Point Four program, to stimulate production in undeveloped countries, it remains painfully true that we have urged other nations to adopt our democracy as their own, while encouraging them to draw upon our abundance in such a way (by the importation of consumer goods) that it remains distinctively our own. Democracy has been held up as a matter of political morality, involving privileges of citizenship which mean little to people below a certain economic level, and it has not been presented as a highly flexible social system conducive to the economic energy and growth which provide abundance. Abundance has been presented as an entirely separate feature of American life and has been manifested to the world primarily in the form of consumer goods which excite the international envy of those whose needs they satisfy, without in any way removing either the sources of envy or the sources of need. Consequently, America's abundance has probably done more to cut us off from actual moral leadership than it has done to enhance such leadership. And certainly it has placed American generosity — much of which is both genuine and unselfish — under the curse of chronic envy.

As a result, our message to the world has become involved in a dilemma: to other peoples, our democracy has seemed attainable but not especially desirable; our abundance has seemed infinitely desirable but quite unattainable. But, if the realities of the relationship between democracy and abundance had been understood by people of other countries or, what is more to the point, by those Americans who were seeking to impart our message, our democracy would have seemed more desirable, and our abundance would have seemed more attainable. Both these changes would have had

the effect of strengthening the moral influence of the United States.

In this brief consideration of a tremendously complex subject which has challenged all the skill of large staffs of trained workers in our government, there is no intention to imply that a simple and easy solution for international difficulties lies ready at hand. Nor would I suggest that these workers have universally lacked insight into the relationship between democracy and abundance. But, insofar as they may have possessed such insight, certainly they must have been hindered by the general lack of understanding of this matter both at home and abroad. We have talked so much about "free enterprise" as if we just meant laissez-faire economics (which all too often is what we did mean) and so much about "democracy" as if we meant some vague, yearning fraternalism (which, again, is too often what we did mean) that we have failed to make the point that democracy paced the growth of our abundance and abundance broadened the base of our democracy.

Thus our whole conception of our mission in the world was distorted by our failure to understand what the world regarded as most significant in our development and what the essential conditions of democratic life in the American sense really are. The factor of abundance, which we first discovered as an environmental condition and which we then converted by technological change into a cultural as well as a physical force, has not only influenced all the aspects of American life in a fundamental way but has also impinged upon our relations with the peoples of the world, and our failure to realize the nature of the relationship between this abundance and our democracy has played a critical part in frustrating our attempts to fulfill the mission of America.

The typewriter was the American woman's frontier.
DAVID M. POTTER

57.

Adolf A. Berle: The Capitalist Revolution and "The City of God"

In no epoch of American history has the country's basic economic structure remained static, and the period since World War I has been marked by particularly notable changes. Wealth remained concentrated, but its control changed hands and the power of the capitalist sharply diminished. The capitalists and bankers gave way first to the corporation managers, and latterly the managers themselves have given up some of their control to technicians and experts. These changes and others in the American corporate structure were examined by Adolf A. Berle in a book published in 1954. The following selection is taken from the chapter titled "Corporate Capitalism and 'The City of God.'"

Source: *The 20th Century Capitalist Revolution*, New York, 1954, pp. 164-188.

IN THE LONG VIEW OF HISTORY, it is quite probable that the capitalist revolution will be found to be one branch, and not the least significant, of the revolution which the twentieth century has wrought around the world. In many countries of the old world, its instrument was one or another form of socialist organization. In the United States, the chief instrument has proved to be the modern giant corporation.

Only at the middle point of the century has corporate capitalism begun to be aware of this aspect of its function. In process, the real significance was difficult to apprehend. In retrospect, the currents pushing corporate capitalism into the realm of political organization are reasonably clear. Concentration of economic power occurred, driven by the deepest force of the time. Demand for a high standard of living required mass production and mass distribution. Technological advance made this production possible in many of the goods and services considered most essential to the life of a modern population. But, in the quantity and at the prices desired, it had to be accomplished by mass organization. Factually that organization was achieved by great corporate units.

The resulting phenomenon of production in large units in turn set up a grouping within many industries. These groups, although (or perhaps because) they disposed of great powers in their own organizations, in time were oftener than not compelled to attempt or join in planning operations, often embodied in statutory schemes of regulation or legalized stabilization, in lower or higher order of development. In greater or less degree, the practice of national industrial planning is now familiar throughout great areas of the twentieth-century corporate capitalist system. Participation in it is frequently a function, and in any case an occupational hazard, of the managements of large corporations.

Now planning all or any fragment of an economy has enormous implications. This is why any "planned economy" has been feared in America; why economy planned by the state has usually been bitterly fought; why emergence of planning power immediately raises doubts and wonders in the minds of the constituency affected. Naturally; any plan (if it is not a naked power-grab) must be a plan for something, and affects or limits people. Planning, however limited in scope, means planning for some kind of a community, or at least some aspect of a community, deemed by some group to be desirable. Capacity to plan, united with power to give effect to the plan, is perhaps the highest trust granted to statesmen. Its devolution has forced into the hands of many businessmen a complex of problems far beyond their chosen fields, problems overpassing those of producing oil or electrical supplies, of manufacturing steel or motor cars, as the case may be. It may have been naïve public relations for an officer of General Motors, proposed for confirmation as Secretary of Defense in the Cabinet of the United States, to say that what was good for General Motors was good for the country, and what was good for the country was good for General Motors; but he could have adduced an impressive array of statistical fact to back up his statement.

For the fact seems to be that the really great corporation managements have reached a position for the first time in their history in which they must consciously take account of philosophical considerations. They must consider the kind of a community in which they have faith, and which they will serve, and which they intend to help to construct and maintain. In a word, they must consider at least in its more elementary phases the ancient problem of the "good life," and how their operations in the community can be adapted to affording or fostering it. They may endeavor to give their views exact statement, or they may merely proceed on undisclosed premises; but, explicitly or implicitly, the premises are there.

Businessmen charged with commercial enterprise are not accustomed to this sort of thinking. As a rule, they reject the idea that this is part of their function. Most corporation executives are acutely aware of the fact that foresight is extremely difficult. Many believe quite frankly, and not without justification, that community welfare is as likely to be developed soundly by hazard as by plan.

The greatest leaders in the corporate field take a contrary view. They forcefully argue that corporations are always citizens of the community in which they operate, while large ones necessarily play a mighty part in the life of their time. It is not possible for them, these men state, to carry on great corporate businesses apart from the main context of American life. If private business and businessmen do not assume community responsibilities, government must step in and American life will become increasingly statist. In consequence, they have urged that corporations must share the burdens of supporting the non-governmental philanthropic and educational institutions which have played so stately a role in the development of twentieth-century America.

Mr. Irving Olds, at the time Chairman of the Board of Directors of U.S. Steel Company, made a brilliant and moving address at Yale University, insisting that corporations must contribute to the general educational facilities of the country, such as universities and graduate schools, and that the duties of big business overpass their traditional power to make gifts to those minor or local charities incident to plant and sales operations. He was forcefully supported by Mr. Frank Abrams, Chairman of the Board of Standard Oil Company of New Jersey. Both corporations gave emphatic proof of assent by voting substantial gifts to liberal arts colleges.

Twenty-nine states have already passed statutes authorizing corporations, both presently existing and subsequently organized, to make contributions to philanthropy and education. Constitutional validity of one of these statutes — that of New Jersey — was the subject of a recent test case (*A. P. Smith Manufacturing Company* v. *Ruth Barlow et al.*) and was forthrightly upheld by the New Jersey Supreme Court. The Supreme Court of the United States dismissed appeal, holding that no Federal question was involved. For practical purposes, the state has authorized corporations to withhold from their shareholders a portion of their profits, channeling it to schools, colleges, hospitals, research, and other good causes.

Twenty years ago, the writer had a controversy with the late Professor E. Merrick Dodd, of Harvard Law School, the writer holding that corporate powers were powers in trust for shareholders while Professor Dodd argued that these powers were held in trust for the entire community. The argument has been settled (at least for the time being) squarely in favor of Professor Dodd's contention.

All this certainly underlines the central philosophical problem. If corporations are to make industrial plans, what are the criteria of these plans? If they are to make gifts to support philanthropy, what kind of philanthropy shall they support? If they are trustees for the community, what kind of community interests do they forward? In narrower range, they are explicitly expected to discharge a more or less specialized function by running their businesses and providing a given set of goods and services for the community and in doing so must provide employment for a great number of people. The goods and services they provide, their manner of marketing, the employment conditions they create, the plants they build, all exert powerful influence on the framework of community life. Corporations must also, one supposes, do something for their stockholders as indeed they do, and usually well, even though stockholders do not hold the center of the corporate stage just now. Provision must also be made, it seems, for continued advance in the art and technique of their chosen field or fields.

In larger aspect, the great corporations frequently join, by their own desire or under community pressure, in constructing, setting up, and operating countrywide and national plans tending to assure the continued stability, health, and serviceability of their industries. These are of many kinds, and the means of achieving them have been diverse; but, in the aggregate, plans of some kind cover the more essential parts of the economic machinery of America.

Large corporations, lying outside the range of any nationwide industry planning as some do, nevertheless within their own operating sphere, appreciably affect community development. They have power to apportion their capital expenditures, on which often depends continued growth in one or another section of the country. Limitations likewise show signs of appearing: there is increasing sentiment, not yet crystallized in law, that they may not withdraw from a community, leaving it a ghost town because business factors offer greater profit-making opportunities somewhere else.

In the widest of all scenes — the great stage of world politics and world developments — American corporations have begun to appear as active and significant elements. . . .

Growing consciousness of the power thus achieved and its implications has excited a very considerable discussion in the corporate world. Directors, especially those of the largest and most responsible companies, are acutely aware of the problems thus raised. A division of opinion is reported in these circles. One group believes it necessary to pick up the load and tackle the immense responsibilities foreshadowed as did Mr. Olds and Mr. Abrams. Another group take the view that this is not their affair, that they are not equipped to meet it, and that they should find ways of avoiding so great a burden. After all, a board of directors is chosen primarily for its ability in running a particular business. It cannot properly or effectively enter into a whole series of extraneous problems extending all the way from methods of administering individual justice to community development, community organization and community values. This school of thought believes that teachers, scholars, philosophers, and possibly politicians and governments, have to wrestle with these questions: boards of directors cannot. Both views are expressed with honesty and great sincerity.

Corporations still have, perhaps, some range of choice: they can either take an extended view of their responsibility, or a limited one. Yet the choice is probably less free than would appear. Power has laws of its own. One of them is that when one group having power declines or abdicates it, some other directing group immediately picks it up; and this appears constant throughout history. The choice of corporate managements is not whether so great a power shall cease to exist; they can merely determine whether they will serve as the nuclei of its organization or pass it over to someone else, probably the modern state. The present current of thinking and insistence that private rather than governmental decisions are soundest for the community are clearly forcing the largest corporations toward a greater rather than a lesser acceptance of the responsibility that goes with power.

Men squarely facing this problem, in small or in large application, now find themselves, with some surprise, in the realm of philosophy. They have not, it is true, been assigned the job of sketching an Utopia; they only have to take — indeed, can only take — one step at a time. But they can hardly avoid determining the direction of the steps, and the aggregate of their steps in the second half of the twentieth century must necessarily go far toward determining

the framework of the American community of the twenty-first. Some sort of hypothesis, however hazy, as to what that community should be, should do, and should look like, seems implicit in this situation.

Some corporations, knowing this, have sought outside advice — General Motors, for example, retained Mr. Peter Drucker for this purpose and his book, *The Concept of the Corporation*, is one of the fruits of it. Others seek guidance from different sources: a famous New York bank has a section which handles corporate foundations set up to discharge their charitable organizations, while the National Industrial Conference Board, an organization of large corporations, works up studies in business policy which it circulates effectively in the corporate field. Still others rely on contacts of their directors with great figures — university presidents, leaders of thought, and eleemosynary foundations, and are guided by them. Occasionally suggestions are made that corporations interested in discharging their novel obligations ought to have a joint working committee, a sort of expanded Community Chest organization, which could make recommendations — and this would have the effect of concentrating still further the mass impact of these great organizations on the future. At least two great business schools — Harvard and Columbia — have offered programs of background information and thinking in the larger ranges of social organization to selected business executives.

All this is matrix work, tending toward a body of sophisticated thinking whose aim, properly analyzed, is a conception of a community making for the good life. It seems that, in diverse ways, we are nibbling at the edges of a vast, dangerous, and fascinating piece of thinking. Despite the absence of clear mandate, in broadest outline we are plotting the course by which the twentieth century in America is expected to produce an evolving economic Utopia, and, apparently, the potential actually exists, bringing that dangerous and thrilling adventure within human reach for the first time in recorded history.

This statement will, of course, be promptly questioned. "What," says almost any corporation executive, "do I have to do with Utopias? If we decide to make a gift to Princeton University or to the United Negro College Fund or to the American College in Beirut in the far-off Mediterranean, how do we find ourselves in competition with Plato and his *Republic*, or St. Augustine and his *City of God*, or Sir Thomas More and his *Utopia*, or Sir Francis Bacon and his *New Atlantis?* We have heard of their writings; some of us have read some of them. But we claim no familiarity with their doctrines and their philosophical premises.

"We have no sort of ambition to run the world, having plenty of headaches right in our own offices. Why not leave us out of this?" The answer is all too plain. A gift is made to Princeton — a gift to a great and free institution. "Splendid," says one board of directors. "We believe in that. In fact, one of the reasons for doing it is precisely to avoid a state-dominated system of education and thinking." Well, it seems one choice has been made. In the coming "City of God" the state is not to be the dominant factor. . . .

In the fifth century A.D. one Augustine, Bishop of Hippo in North Africa, surveyed the wreck of the Roman Empire. It had broken into vast, unstable fragments. The Roman peace and the Roman imperial order had ceased to be the framework with which life could be formed. New institutions were appearing; old ones were breaking up. In the words of the Psalmist, the foundations of the earth were out of course, and whole peoples walked in darkness.

This prelate had had full measure of experience with the phenomena of power. As bishop, he had held some himself. As ob-

server of the ebb of empire and of men who seized kingdoms or forged them, he knew quite well that power was only half the story of human organization. Aside from its ecclesiastical implications his study, *The City of God*, was a striking and simple statement of a hypothesis of political science. Underlying, entering, complementing, ultimately controlling every tangible institutional organization of affairs there was inevitably a moral and philosophical organization which continued from age to age and which ultimately directed power. This philosophical content alone gave permanence to institutions; this philosophical organization survived institutional creation. This Augustine christened "The City of God." Because it worked directly on the minds of men wherever and however placed, it could exact action from them within any framework and thus guide any institution. It is, perhaps, the first great source book for the theory of dichotomy of power which has entered this study from time to time.

We have not, up to the present, been accustomed to think of the modern corporation as an institution at all, let alone a political institution. We have thought of it merely as an enterprise (or perhaps combination of enterprises) within a community. American political thought has been frightened, and corporations themselves have been frightened, at any suggestion that they might emerge as political institutions in their own and separate right. So we have not been accustomed to place over against each other, as necessarily interrelated facts, the pragmatic concept of the corporation and the philosophical concept of the desirable community. Corporate executives rather resent being assimilated to politicians; still more they resent being called to account by philosophers. They belong to one of the few groups in history to which political power came unsought, or at any rate as a by-product rather than a main objective.

It is probable that when Mr. Harlow

Curtice and Mr. Alfred P. Sloan, Jr., wrote in General Motors Annual Report for 1953, that "with the elimination of controls and with the trend away from a centrally managed economy, industry is possessed of the opportunity to make its maximum contribution to the forward march of our country," they did not think they were talking politics at all. Still less, perhaps, would they consider they had assumed in substantial measure the philosophical burden of judging what is and what should be the "forward march" of a very great country. But they had done just that.

Herein lies, perhaps, the greatest current weakness of the corporate system. In practice, institutional corporations are guided by tiny self-perpetuating oligarchies. These in turn are drawn from and judged by the group opinion of a small fragment of America — its business and financial community. Change of management by contesting for stockholders' votes is extremely rare, and increasingly difficult and expensive to the point of impossibility. The legal presumption in favor of management, and the natural unwillingness of courts to control or reverse management action save in cases of the more elementary types of dishonesty or fraud, leaves management with substantially absolute power. Thus the only real control which guides or limits their economic and social action is the real, though undefined and tacit, philosophy of the men who compose them.

Fifteen hundred years ago, St. Augustine made the same observation concerning the men and groups who achieved power in the fragmented territories of the empire that had once been Rome. But he also knew, as the men in power in his time frequently did not, that whatever institutions they built derived permanence, continuity and significance from the philosophy more than from the power; and he endeavored, in the diffuse scholastic fashion of the time, to set the Christian philosophy over against the contemporary power institutions; and he gave impetus and direction to the whole of the Middle Ages.

The lesson, I think, is as valid for the twentieth as for the fifth century. Capitalism is not a way of life, but a method of achieving economic and social results — a method indeed evolving so rapidly that the capitalism of 1954 has but a bowing acquaintance with that of 1854 and little if any real resemblance to the capitalism of 1804. The institutional corporation collectivized capital, and like most collectivisms concentrated power into a small directing group. The aggregate of such groups — a couple of hundred or so — have proved to be the chief instruments of the twentieth-century revolution in the western world outside the Iron Curtain. As yet the community has not created any acknowledged referent of responsibility, no group from which they take their power mandate or get instructions in dealing with serious streams of events they can and do affect. There is no recognized body of doctrine by which they themselves must test their choice as they act from day to day.

View of a rapidly expanding subdivision outside Los Angeles, 1953

A CORPORATE SOCIETY

The wartime expansion of productive capacity, with its attendant prosperity and the savings made possible by restricted domestic production, merged easily into a postwar prosperity based on consumer goods, with a huge backlog of demand and continued high employment. Business boomed steadily in the 1950s with the exception of small recessions in 1953-1954 and 1957-1958, and such growth was encouraged by the Eisenhower policy of "dynamic conservatism," a phrase that, however enigmatic it might seem in theory, signified in practical terms a return to laissez faire as far as established New Deal policies would allow. New corporate forms emerged as technological and organizational advances established power in a small and relatively new managerial class. Individual corporations grew to unheard-of size; some achieved an income greater than the gross national products of most countries.

(Above) Typical scene at a large suburban shopping center; (below) all the sales representatives who visited one family during their first week in Lakewood in Los Angeles County, California

(Top) Customers in the television department of a Washington, D.C., store; **(bottom left)** jewelry display catches the eye of a wealthy woman in Miami; **(bottom right)** cartoon from the Cleveland "Plain Dealer" in 1957

Technological advances kept by wartime necessity from the consumer market opened whole new areas of production and consumption in the 1950s. Of these, television was most prominent and most far-reaching in its effects. In the new suburban sprawl the shopping center developed as a new pattern of marketing directly dependent on the automobile.

Me and My Shadow

(Above) Shoppers in a busy department store; (below) saleslady in a Woolworth store

The vast consumer market, with its new products and its proliferation of instant brand names, masked a marked change in the manner of competition for patronage. Quality considerations, already largely obviated by standardization and mass production, slowly receded as products competed more and more on the basis of attractive packaging, endorsements by popular figures, and mass advertising that generally succeeded in suggesting miraculous attributes for the most mundane products.

(Top) Residence of James Ford in Lincoln, Mass., designed by Gropius and Breuer; (center) Frank Lloyd Wright with a model of a prefabricated house he designed to be built for $50,000, 1958; (bottom) "Falling Water," a house designed by Wright located in Bear Run, Pa.

There They Are - - - Still up There!!!

Wartime full employment and high wages had not, as during World War I, depleted union membership; consequently labor was in a good position to join the postwar cost-of-living inflation battle. There were relatively few really major strikes during the 1950s; the prosperity of the period allowed producers to pass on increased labor costs to consumers, and the feared "slave-labor" provisions of the 1947 Taft-Hartley Act failed to develop teeth. Influenced by McCarthyism, labor rooted out Communists; it was less successful in dealing with labor racketeering.

(Top left) John L. Lewis inspects a coal mine in Illinois; (top right) Cleveland "Plain Dealer" cartoon reacting to the economic conditions of 1958; (bottom left) newspaper headlines relate the Supreme Court's intervention in the strike of 1959; (bottom right) workers at the Homestead, Pa., steel plant, one which Truman nationalized in 1952 to prevent a strike

(Above) George Meany and Walter Reuther raise hands in celebration of the merger of the AF of L and CIO into one union, 1955; (below) Senate Labor Rackets Commission in session; from left are Senators Goldwater, McClellan; Counsel Robert Kennedy; Senators Kennedy, Curtis, and Mundt, 1957

(Above) Engineers of the Ford Motor Company laying out plans for the production of the new Falcon in 1959; (below) designers study mock-ups of parts of the planned automobile

(Above) High-ranking officers of the Ford Motor Company meet with Robert McNamara, president of the company, to discuss plans for future, 1959; (right) restricted area at the Detroit plant where new designs are being developed

AUTHORIZED PERSONNEL ONLY

John D. Rockefeller could only with difficulty have recognized the giant business corporation as it grew in postwar America. No longer really a private enterprise, the corporation was "owned" only nominally by large numbers of stockholders whose sole function was to receive dividends, and was managed by a staff of salaried administrative and technical experts. Profit became but one of several aims as a dedication to existence and growth for their own sakes signalled the evolution of the business corporation from a money-making arrangement to an autonomous, organic institution. In these new terms, governmental regulation was accepted, even requested, as necessary for a peaceful society of corporations. The manner of competition changed as well from price wars and economic coercion to advertising persuasion and increasingly subtle appeals to consumers.

(Top right) Cameramen at work photographing the new Falcon for advertising campaigns; (center) the Falcon on display at an automobile show; (bottom) the Falcon proceeds along the assembly line as the new model goes into production for consumer consumption

Cornell Capa from Magnum

Cornell Capa from Magnum

Cornell Capa from Magnum

(Above) Supervisor examines production on the assembly line at Ford; (below) the Edsel, introduced by Ford in 1957, which failed to gain public appeal and was discontinued in 1959

Don't forget, Sam, every barrel has a bottom.

(Above) Typical scene along a U.S. highway, this one outside Newark, N.J.; (left) cartoon by C. D. Batchelor for the New York "Daily News" reflecting U.S. general disregard for natural resources

The corporate society slowly became aware of several shortcomings in the system it had developed. A number of people began to question whether it was altogether wise to deplete the land of its resources with no provision for the future; whether commercial interests must hide the land behind billboards; whether progress really depended upon water and air and land pollution; and, not the least, whether the public good could compete with corporate interest. Business was arrogating to itself unprecedented powers; major corporations, for example, maintained foreign relations with other countries and thus influenced to an indeterminable but undeniably important degree the foreign policy of the United States. The challenge presented by the Russian Sputnik in 1957 set off a public debate on the relation of an almost exclusively consumer-oriented system to scientific research and progress.

Henri Cartier-Bresson from Magnum

"They Act As If They've Been Doped"

Boom Town

(Top left) Scene in the oil country in Louisiana; (top right) cartoon by Herblock for "The Washington Post" in 1950 reflecting the government policy of granting tax benefits to oil and related industries; (left) Herblock cartoon commenting on the government's disinterest in any strong supervision of the activities of American business, 1957

USSR Magazine — Sovfoto

Let 'em eat cake
Courtesy, Edward Kuekes and the Cleveland "Plain Dealer"

(Top left) Crowds at the 1958 Brussels World's Fair view a model of Sputnik, which the Soviets launched in September 1957; (top right) cartoon in the Cleveland "Plain Dealer" commenting on Russia's space successes; (bottom) Russians view automobile at American Exhibit in Moscow, 1959

Franz Goess from Black Star

Nikita Khrushchev and Richard Nixon in a heated exchange of views while touring the United States Exhibition in Moscow, 1959. These "Kitchen Debates" contrasted the Soviets' emphasis on space achievements with America's more diversified technological advancements

Elliott Erwitt from Magnum

"Dear Boy, Where Have You Been Keeping Yourself?"

MORE MONEY FOR GOOD OLD SCIENCE

"SECURITY" METHODS

SCIENTISTS

HERBLOCK

Courtesy, Herblock, "The Washington Post"

Franz Goess from Black Star

AMERICAN "KNOW HOW"

1958 U S

'So Russia Launched a Satellite, but Has It Made Cars With Fins Yet?'
Courtesy, Ross Lewis and the "Milwaukee Journal"

(Left) Herblock cartoon from November 1957 reflecting the change of attitude following the launching of Sputnik; (above) cartoon by Lewis for the "Milwaukee Journal," October 1957; (bottom) Coca Cola exhibit in Moscow, 1959

"Hey—Don't Forget The Bottom Part, Too"

(Left) Herblock cartoon commenting on the U.S. government's subsidy of advanced scientific projects in an attempt to match the Soviets' feats; (below) Atlas rocket blows up on the launch pad in 1959. Publicity of America's inferior position in the "space race" led to many similar setbacks in the government's rush to catch up

58.

AGNES DE MILLE: Dance in America

A perennial problem for commentators on American art and civilization has been whether the predominant influence is native or foreign. Some have held that America's culture is largely an imported one, although they concede that America has made significant alterations in it; while others have argued that the really important elements in the culture are indigenous and that ideas imported from abroad have never had a real or lasting effect. Agnes de Mille addressed herself to the question in 1954 in an article dealing with the various backgrounds of the dance in America.

Source: *Profile of America*, Emily Davie, ed., New York, 1954, pp. 373-379.

FOUR INFLUENCES have shaped dancing as an art form in America — the indigenous American Indian, the African Negro, the Western European folk forms, and the European theatrical or ballet tradition.

Since the basis for all theatrical or art dancing is understandably a people's social expression, it follows that our theatrical styles rest firmly on the English and French country dances imported by early Colonists. With these immigrants came also a taste for ballet spectacle and court dancing. But lacking the means to develop, lacking all schools, theaters, and endowed institutions, creative dancing lay dormant until the end of the nineteenth century. For 200 years, our citizens had to be content with simple social dancing, minstrel shows, and a very few distinguished foreign visitors.

Our greatest indigenous source of inspiration, the American Indian, is and has been all but insensible. This is a pity but quite explicable: racially and culturally the Indians had nothing in common with their white neighbors except shared hunger and gunpowder — a tenuous relationship on which to build any art expression. But the Indians have been of mighty importance as a point of reference. The Pueblo and Plains tribes have maintained the necessity and form of their dances for several thousand years. They remind us of what we have entirely lost from our culture — dancing as a serious practice of the men of the community, dancing as magic, dancing as worship, and as a vital function in life beyond the mere requisites of courtship.

The enormous influx of the alien and powerful African aesthetic during the seventeenth and eighteenth centuries, the Negroes' persistent and persuasive contribution to music, and their reliance on rhythm in all work and play has grafted a characteristic rhythm-syncopation on our main dancing forms that has heightened and perverted them forever. It was the subtle African footwork applied to the Irish clog (jigs and reels) that produced buck and wing and tap dancing. It was the African body pulse and frank sexuality that turned the waltz into our current ballroom form. Every ten years or so from the slums, the wharves, the Negro ghettos and impalements comes a new original contribution to our folk vocabulary — the Rag, the Charleston, the Lindy-hop, the Black Bottom, the Jitterbug, the Shag, the Susie Q, the Big Apple. These are as original and as expressive as the gavotte, the minuet, or the waltz, but their most unusual aspect is the rapidity with which they develop. The English and French required 250 years to change the Elizabethan volta to the waltz. This exuberant and prolific people produce each decade a new form. No other racial group boils up constantly in such rich spontaneous gesture.

The basic forms, the mother forms on which these influences have played are, of course, the transplanted dances of Europe, most particularly those of England and Ireland. Old English longways and round country dances produced the Southern Mountain running sets and the Southwestern squares. These are almost identical with their prototypes except for two American characteristics: the tempo and the noise. Every race of people that has lived on this continent, anthropologists tell us, has been nervous, restless, and explosive in expression. American dances are raced like no dances in Europe. They are frequently stamped and clapped and shouted by the women as well as the men and the dance masters' calls, simple instructions in Europe, are here developed into a humorous lyric comment shouted or whined at unbroken speed, not only to cue the performers but to throw caustic and spicy insight into the manners of the community.

Our theater's history has been far less spontaneous. In 1842, the Viennese ballet star Fanny Elssler made a tour of the Eastern states and astonished everyone. Indeed she was probably the first great dancing artist ever seen on this continent. She found not even a legend to compete with. Audiences responded with rapture. Although she came with only two assistants and used a scratch group she picked up and rehearsed after arrival, a circumstance the professional mind quails to envisage, the members of Congress went so far as to unhorse her carriage and pull her through the streets of Washington. In 1865, a very young ballerina, Maria Bonfanti, came with her Italian troup to dance in "The Black Crook" at Niblo's Garden and thereafter there were visiting continental performers of varying rotundity and merit. When finally the Metropolitan Opera was formed, something resembling a resident company of trained ballet dancers with a ballet school attached could be organized. Now at last one was.

America, however, was a Puritan country and the forming of an opera ballet elicited no very great respect or faith. The results could have been foretold: nothing creative has come from this source, no works, no school, no great performers. The Metropolitan Ballet has always been fourth-rate and in all the years of its existence has produced from within itself neither great dancer nor choreographer. In fact the attitude toward dancing in all musical circles here has been one of unmodified and continuing condescension. Although the popular theater, which one might have hoped would have been more productive, welcomed foreign virtuosi of sorts, it remained for half a century on the minstrel-show or vaudeville level and developed no first-class creative talent.

Nevertheless, in the current century, America has led the world in a true renaissance of dancing. Four American soloists, Isadora Duncan, Ruth St. Denis, Martha Graham, and Doris Humphrey, have successively started revolutions that have influenced all forms of creative dancing and all choreographic endeavor. Although their achievements are independent and vastly different, they do have points in common — they are all women; they broke outright with tradition; they worked alone without theater, school, or patronage behind them; they approached dancing not as entertainment but as creative expression; they considered dancing as an independent art in itself and not as a supplementary or complementary adjunct to other theater forms.

They were wildcatters in a country of pioneers that valued its women and encouraged pioneers. This made their achievement possible. This perhaps explains why it has been American women and not European that have led the dance.

Duncan was the first and in many ways the most climactic figure. She did not, as is popularly supposed, discover a new type of dance nor yet revive an ancient. Her style has been called Greek simply because she chose to wear Greek tunics and referred always, when speaking, to classic sources. But her idiom was no more Greek than anything else. It was her own personal idiom of expression and for this reason it has proved ephemeral except as an influence. Her achievement was a point of view. She left no vocabulary, no works, no creative school. Her contribution was a clearing away of the accumulated debris of 600 years of artificiality. Alone she jettisoned the entire code of ballet technique, a fabrication of centuries' effort. She rediscovered the human walk, the run, the easy natural spring and jump, the emotional use of head and arms and hands. She brought the foot once more into contact with the earth. She bared the limbs so that one might see not so much naked body as revealed emotion. She refound spontaneity and individual passion. She was to her art what Luther was to Christianity — a challenging. She questioned. In an art that had been scorned and degraded for generations, she insisted on passion and purpose. She went back to beginnings.

After her and directly in response to her influence came Diaghilev, Pavlova, and Nijinsky and the overwhelming impact of the new Russian Ballet on Western Europe — a transforming experience the like of which our theater had never known before. After her came Dalcroze, the Weisenthal sisters, and the interest in expressive dancing that led to the Middle European rebirth which flowered in Mary Wigman's great school.

In less important matters, Duncan's influence has been vital — the exchange of lights and curtains for painted décor called upon the imagination of the audience and departed thereby from the European tradition of spectacle toward the classic or Oriental tradition of symbolism. The exchange of great music for the sugar-water prettiness of Delibes and Tchaikovsky made possible serious and basic themes.

Ruth St. Denis was not perhaps so great an innovator, but her influence has been strong. She brought to our attention the ritual and symbolic dances of the Far East and she reminded us what we had long forgotten — that dancing is the handmaiden of religion. Because of her greater theatricality, her influence was more readily acceptable and her imitators more numerous and flighty. Her work could be easily commercialized, and was on a wholesale scale. Duncan's could not be so successfully. When not sublime, Duncan's style proved to be silly — not to say intolerable — good only for therapy and the releasing of adolescent doubts. St. Denis was seen by more people in this country than any other dancer, possibly excepting Anna Pavlova. (Duncan was not generally popular except among the intellectuals.) And St. Denis it was who made widely acceptable the brand-new notion that dancing was not the function of expensive prostitutes but the work of artists.

Doris Humphrey, whom many critics consider our finest choreographer, was a pupil of St. Denis. Her style, however, derives very little from the early Oriental influences. Her style is lyric rather than dramatic and stresses always form rather than drama. She has experimented in pure dance; that is, nonstorytelling compositions of movement and in works of considerable scope and length. In a sense she can be considered our first symphonist.

But the great lasting contribution to our art has been made unquestionably by Martha Graham. Graham is an unsurpassed performer recalling to many Eleanore Duse at her zenith. It is, however, her creative achievements that are most noteworthy. First, her works must be reckoned among the masterpieces of our time. Beyond this, however, and possibly of more lasting importance is her expansion of dance technique. She has not merely developed traditional exercises; she has invented whole new techniques of leverage, elevation, and bodily dynamics. Graham's discoveries are already fusing with classic ballet and absorbing into the styles of the younger generation. They have got, so to speak, into the bloodstream and will undoubtedly influence all dancing for generations hence. It is the most inventive enlarging of dance idiom by any single individual in the history of the Western theater.

Her subject matter is serious and challenging, her décor and use of music experimental in the most provocative sense. In fact her influence on all aspects of our theater, though generally unrecognized, has been incalculable. It is interesting to note that she is the first dancer to make creative use of Amerindian styles and sources.

Like St. Denis and Duncan, she is a great teacher. Her pupils number the leading performers and choreographers of the new generation. Her pupils have in turn become teachers and are found in most of the women's colleges training pupils to form a demanding audience and to form intelligent criticism, both requisites to the growth of any art. It is characteristic of the pupils of both Humphrey and Graham that they tend to be creative as few ballet pupils are. Accordingly there is a composing activity now in all fields of the contemporary nonballetic dance never before evinced.

Unlike any other institution is the theater of Katharine Dunham. Dunham is an enchanting performer and a superb craftsman rather than an inventive creative choreographer. But she has brought to our attention the wealth of Negro idiom from all over the United States and the Caribbean is-

lands, and she has opened the doors of the American concert stage to the members of her race. Serious Negro dancers now have a place to perform where fifteen years ago they had none.

The growth of the ballet here has been less spontaneous. Imported ballet teachers and visiting companies recruited native talent along patterns codified in Europe. Decades passed before native creators emerged and these showed clearly the influence of strong Russian-Parisian training coupled with the styles of their great native predecessors. In the twenties Michael Fokine, of the Imperial Russian and Diaghilev ballets, opened a school in New York and girls and boys could get really first-class technical training for the first time. And they became superb technicians — their strength and virtuosity is an international byword. In the thirties the de Basil Ballet Russe de Monte Carlo began annual tours and schools and companies sprouted everywhere like mushrooms.

There are now several American ballet companies, two first-class ones, as good as anything in Europe, the City Center, developed from the earlier American Ballet Company, and Ballet Theatre. City Center ballet has provided a first-class repertoire and theater for able dancers, a school and a standard of the highest order, all badly needed in a country which has yet to establish any kind of national lyric theater.

Ballet Theatre on the other hand is heterogeneous and indigenous. A large group of choreographers are represented, classic and modern, some young ones for the first time. A new type of ballet has been there initiated and matured. In fact nearly every good performing and designing talent has during the last fifteen years passed through Ballet Theatre, which boasts, in my opinion, the most stimulating and representative repertoire of any current company.

An interesting development, although a minor one, has been the transforming, during the last ten years, of popular theater dancing into an art form. This is the only country in which major talents work in the musical comedy field. As a result, choreography, and therefore performance, as well as designing and musical arranging, are on a high level. Lacking any endowed institutions, the serious artists must rely on the popular theater for their living — and in exchange they give in all branches of the dance department polish and fervor that the popular theaters of Europe do not boast. This is becoming increasingly true of motion pictures also. With the development of the 3-D screen, it is to be hoped that the genius of our greatest choreographers will be tempted. Television is still very tentative but it could prove a rich field of discovery and achievement.

The main contribution of America, however, remains — and most gloriously — not so much individual compositions as completely new idioms and vocabularies, new styles and new, or rather old and deeply respected, approaches. That it can now be considered a serious expressive art and that its chief practitioners are women of dignity, probity, intellect, and passion, that these women attract about them as co-workers serious and impassioned men, is due largely to four pioneers. The next generation owes them much. They may serve the art with a critical standard and above all with a hope never held by dancers before.

59.

The Oppenheimer Case

Dr. J. Robert Oppenheimer, wartime head of the Los Alamos atomic laboratory, was suspended from his post as chairman of the General Advisory Committee of the Atomic Energy Commission in December 1953 as an alleged security risk. Oppenheimer was informed by AEC chairman Lewis L. Strauss that he could avoid facing charges if he resigned within twenty-four hours, but Oppenheimer refused. A special panel headed by former Secretary of the Army Gordon Gray began private hearings on April 12, 1954, and although it judged that Oppenheimer was "loyal," it decided against his reinstatement by a vote of 2 to 1. The decision was later upheld by the AEC itself by a vote of 4 to 1. The apparent contradiction involved in pronouncing Oppenheimer devotedly loyal but denying him clearance brought a storm of criticism. The selection below comprises a part of the majority decision of the AEC, upholding the Gray panel report, and a part of the dissent by Commissioner Henry D. Smyth.

Source: *In the Matter of J. Robert Oppenheimer, Texts of Principal Documents and Letters* . . . U.S. Atomic Energy Commission, Washington, 1954, pp. 51-67.

I.

Opinion of the AEC

THE ISSUE BEFORE THE COMMISSION is whether the security of the United States warrants Dr. J. Robert Oppenheimer's continued access to restricted data of the Atomic Energy Commission. The data to which Dr. Oppenheimer has had until recently full access include some of the most vital secrets in the possession of the United States.

Having carefully studied the pertinent documents — the transcript of the hearings before the Personnel Security Board (Gray Board), the findings and recommendation of the Board, the briefs of Dr. Oppenheimer's counsel, and the findings and recommendation of the general manager — we have concluded that Dr. Oppenheimer's clearance for access to restricted data should not be reinstated.

The Atomic Energy Act of 1946 lays upon the commissioners the duty to reach a determination as to "the character, associations, and loyalty" of the individuals engaged in the work of the Commission. Thus, disloyalty would be one basis for disqualification, but it is only one. Substantial defects of character and imprudent and dangerous associations, particularly with known subversives who place the interests of foreign powers above those of the United States, are also reasons for disqualification.

On the basis of the record before the Commission, comprising the transcript of the hearing before the Gray Board, as well as reports of Military Intelligence and the Federal Bureau of Investigation, we find Dr. Oppenheimer is not entitled to the continued confidence of the government and of this Commission because of the proof of fundamental defects in his "character."

In respect to the criterion of "associations," we find that his associations with persons known to him to be Communists have extended far beyond the tolerable limits of prudence and self-restraint which are to be expected of one holding the high positions that the government has continuously entrusted to him since 1942. These associations have lasted too long to be justified as merely the intermittent and accidental revival of earlier friendships.

Neither in the deliberations by the full Commission nor in the review of the Gray Board was importance attached to the opinions of Dr. Oppenheimer as they bore upon the 1949 debate within the government on the question of whether the United States should proceed with the thermonuclear weapon program. In this debate Dr. Oppenheimer was, of course, entitled to his opinion. . . .

In weighing the matter at issue, we have taken into account Dr. Oppenheimer's past contributions to the atomic energy program. At the same time, we have been mindful of the fact that the positions of high trust and responsibility which Dr. Oppenheimer has occupied carried with them a commensurately high obligation of unequivocal character and conduct on his part. A government official having access to the most sensitive areas of restricted data and to the innermost details of national war plans and weapons must measure up to exemplary standards of reliability, self-discipline, and trustworthiness. Dr. Oppenheimer has fallen far short of acceptable standards.

The record shows that Dr. Oppenheimer has consistently placed himself outside the rules which govern others. He has falsified in matters wherein he was charged with grave responsibilities in the national interest. In his associations he has repeatedly exhibited a willful disregard of the normal and proper obligations of security.

As to "character":

Dr. Oppenheimer has now admitted under oath that while in charge of the Los Alamos Laboratory and working on the most secret weapon development for the government, he told Colonel [Boris T.] Pash a fabrication of lies. Colonel Pash was an officer of Military Intelligence charged with the duty of protecting the atomic-weapons project against spies. Dr. Oppenheimer told Colonel Pash in circumstantial detail of an attempt by a Soviet agent to obtain from him information about the work on the atom bomb. This was the Haakon Chevalier incident. In the hearings recently concluded, Dr. Oppenheimer under oath swears that the story he told Colonel Pash was a "whole fabrication and tissue of lies." . . .

In 1950 Dr. Oppenheimer told an agent of the Federal Bureau of Investigation that he had not known Joseph Weinberg to be a member of the Communist Party until that fact became public knowledge. Yet on Sept. 12, 1943, Dr. Oppenheimer told Colonel Lansdale that Weinberg was a Communist Party member.

The catalog does not end with these six examples. The work of Military Intelligence, the Federal Bureau of Investigation, and the Atomic Energy Commission — all at one time or another — have felt the effect of his falsehoods, evasions, and misrepresentations.

Dr. Oppenheimer's persistent and willful disregard for the obligations of security is evidenced by his obstruction of inquiries by security officials. In the Chevalier incident, Dr. Oppenheimer was questioned in 1943 by Colonel Pash, Colonel Lansdale, and General [Lieut. Gen. Leslie R.] Groves about the attempt to obtain information from him on the atomic-bomb project in the interest of the Soviet government. He had waited eight months before mentioning the occurrence to the proper authorities. Thereafter, for almost four months, Dr. Oppenheimer refused to name the individual who had approached him. Under oath he now admits that his refusal to name the individual impeded the government's investigation of espionage. The record shows other instances where Dr. Oppenheimer has refused to answer inquiries of federal officials on security matters or has been deliberately misleading.

As to "associations":

"Associations" is a factor which, under the law, must be considered by the Commission. Dr. Oppenheimer's close association with Communists is another part of the pattern of his disregard of the obligations of security.

Dr. Oppenheimer, under oath, admitted to the Gray Board that from 1937 to at least 1942 he made regular and substantial contributions in cash to the Communist Party. He has admitted that he was a "fellow traveler" at least until 1942. He admits that he attended small evening meetings at private homes at which most, if not all, of the others present were Communist Party members. He was in contact with officials of the Communist Party, some of whom had been engaged in espionage. His activities were of such a nature that these Communists looked upon him as one of their number.

However, Dr. Oppenheimer's early Communist associations are not in themselves a controlling reason for our decision. They take on importance in the context of his persistent and continuing association with Communists, including his admitted meetings with Haakon Chevalier in Paris as recently as last December — the same individual who had been intermediary for the Soviet Consulate in 1943.

On Feb. 25, 1950, Dr. Oppenheimer wrote a letter to Chevalier attempting "to clear the record with regard to your alleged involvement in the atom business." Chevalier used this letter in connection with his application to the State Department for a U.S. passport. Later that year Chevalier came and stayed with Dr. Oppenheimer for several days at the latter's home. In December 1953, Dr. Oppenheimer visited with Chevalier privately on two occasions in Paris and lent his name to Chevalier's dealings with the U.S. Embassy in Paris on a problem which, according to Dr. Oppenheimer, involved Chevalier's clearance. Dr. Oppenheimer admitted that today he has only a "strong guess" that Chevalier is not active in Communist Party affairs.

These episodes separately and together present a serious picture. It is clear that for one who has had access for so long to the most vital defense secrets of the government and who would retain such access if his clearance were continued, Dr. Oppenheimer has defaulted not once but many times upon the obligations that should and must be willingly borne by citizens in the national service.

Concern for the defense and security of the United States requires that Dr. Oppenheimer's clearance should not be reinstated. Dr. J. Robert Oppenheimer is hereby denied access to restricted data.

II.

Opinion of Henry D. Smyth

I DISSENT FROM THE ACTION of the Atomic Energy Commission in the matter of Dr. J. Robert Oppenheimer. I agree with the "clear conclusion" of the Gray Board that he is completely loyal and I do not believe he is a security risk. It is my opinion that his clearance for access to restricted data should be restored.

In a case such as this, the Commission is required to look into the future. It must determine whether Dr. Oppenheimer's continued employment by the government of the United States is in the interests of the people of the United States. This prediction must balance his potential contribution to the positive strength of the country against the possible danger that he may weaken the country by allowing important secrets to reach our enemies.

Since Dr. Oppenheimer is one of the most knowledgeable and lucid physicists we have, his services could be of great value to the country in the future. Therefore, the only question being determined by the Atomic Energy Commission is whether there is a possibility that Dr. Oppenheimer will intentionally or unintentionally reveal secret information to persons who should not have it. To me, this is what is meant within our security system by the term "security risk." Character and associations are important only insofar as they bear on the possibility that secret information will be improperly revealed.

In my opinion, the most important evidence in this regard is the fact that there is no indication in the entire record that Dr. Oppenheimer has ever divulged any secret information. The past fifteen years of his life have been investigated and reinvestigated. For much of the last eleven years he has been under actual surveillance, his movements watched, his conversations noted, his mail and telephone calls checked. This professional review of his actions has been supplemented by enthusiastic amateur help from powerful personal enemies.

After reviewing the massive dossier and after hearing some forty witnesses, the Gray Board reported on May 27, 1954, that Dr. Oppenheimer "seems to have had a high degree of discretion, reflecting an unusual ability to keep to himself vital secrets." My own careful reading of the complete dossier and of the testimony leads me to agree with the Gray Board on this point. I am confident that Dr. Oppenheimer will continue to keep to himself all the secrets with which he is entrusted. . . . The history of Dr. Oppenheimer's contributions to the development of nuclear weapons stands untarnished.

It is clear that Dr. Oppenheimer's past associations and activities are not newly discovered in any substantial sense. They have been known for years to responsible authorities who have never been persuaded that they rendered Dr. Oppenheimer unfit for public service. Many of the country's outstanding men have expressed their faith in his integrity.

In spite of all this, the majority of the Commission now concludes that Dr. Oppenheimer is a security risk. I cannot accept this conclusion or the fear behind it. In my opinion the conclusion cannot be supported by a fair evaluation of the evidence.

Those who do not accept this view cull from the record of Dr. Oppenheimer's active life over the past fifteen years incidents which they construe as "proof of fundamental defects in his character" and as alarming associations. . . .

The most disturbing incidents of his past are those connected with Haakon Chevalier. In late 1942 or early 1943, Chevalier was asked by George Eltenton to approach Dr. Oppenheimer to see whether he would be willing to make technical information available for the Soviet Union. When Chevalier spoke to Dr. Oppenheimer, he was answered by a flat refusal. The incident came to light when Dr. Oppenheimer, of his own accord, reported it to Colonel Pash in August 1943. He did not at that time give Chevalier's name and said that there had been three approaches rather than one. Shortly thereafter, in early September, Dr. Oppenheimer told General Groves that, if ordered, he would reveal the name. Not until December 1943 did General Groves direct him to give the name. It is his testimony that he then told General Groves that the earlier story concerning three approaches had been a "cock-and-bull story." Not until 1946 were Eltenton, Chevalier, and Dr. Oppenheimer himself interviewed by security officers in this matter.

When interviewed by the FBI in 1946, Dr. Oppenheimer recounted the same story of the incident which he has consistently maintained ever since. He stated explicitly in 1946 that the story told to Colonel Pash in 1943 had been a fabrication. In the present hearings before the Gray Board he testified, before the recording of the Pash interview was produced, that the story told to Colonel Pash was a fabrication to protect his friend Chevalier. The letter which he wrote Chevalier in February 1950 concerning Chevalier's role in the 1943 incident stated only what Dr. Oppenheimer has consistently maintained to the FBI and to the Gray Board concerning Chevalier's lack of awareness of the significance of what he was doing. . . .

With the single exception of the Chevalier incident, the evidence relied upon is thin, whether individual instances are considered separately or in combination. All added together, with the Chevalier incident included, the evidence is singularly unimpressive when viewed in the perspective of the fifteen years of active life from which it is drawn. Few men could survive such a period of investigation and interrogation without having many of their actions misinterpreted or misunderstood.

To be effective a security system must be realistic. In the words of the Atomic Energy Commission security criteria:

> The facts of each case must be carefully weighed and determination made in the light of all the information presented, whether favorable or unfavorable. The judgment of responsible persons as to the integrity of the individuals should be considered. The decision as to security clearance is an overall, commonsense judgment, made after consideration of all the relevant information as to whether or not there is risk that the granting of security clearance would endanger the common defense or security.

Application of this standard of overall, commonsense judgment to the whole record destroys any pattern of suspicious conduct or catalog of falsehoods and evasions, and leaves a picture of Dr. Oppenheimer as an able, imaginative human being with normal human weaknesses and failings. In my opinion the conclusion drawn by the majority from the evidence is so extreme as to endanger the security system. . . .

The "Chevalier incident" remains reprehensible; but in fairness and on all of the evidence, this one admitted and regretted mistake made many years ago does not predominate in my overall judgment of Dr.

Oppenheimer's character and reliability. Unless one confuses a manner of expression with candor, or errors in recollection with lack of veracity, Dr. Oppenheimer's testimony before the Gray Board has the ring of honesty. I urge thoughtful citizens to examine this testimony for themselves, and not be content with summaries or with extracts quoted out of context.

With respect to the alleged disregard of the security system, I would suggest that the system itself is nothing to worship. It is a necessary means to an end. Its sole purpose, apart from the prevention of sabotage, is to protect secrets. If a man protects the secrets he has in his hands and his head, he has shown essential regard for the security system.

In addition, cooperation with security officials in their legitimate activities is to be expected of private citizens and government employees. The security system has, however, neither the responsibility nor the right to dictate every detail of a man's life. I frankly do not understand the charge made by the majority that Dr. Oppenheimer has shown a persistent and willful disregard for the obligations of security, and that therefore he should be declared a security risk. No gymnastics of rationalization allow me to accept this argument. If in any recent instances Dr. Oppenheimer has misunderstood his obligation to security, the error is occasion for reproof but not for a finding that he should be debarred from serving his country. Such a finding extends the concept of "security risk" beyond its legitimate justification and constitutes a dangerous precedent.

In these times, failure to employ a man of great talents may impair the strength and power of this country. Yet I would accept this loss if I doubted the loyalty of Dr. Oppenheimer or his ability to hold his tongue. I have no such doubts.

I conclude that Dr. Oppenheimer's employment "will not endanger the common defense and security" and will be "clearly consistent with the interests of the national security." I prefer the positive statement that Dr. Oppenheimer's further employment will continue to strengthen the United States.

I therefore have voted to reinstate Dr. Oppenheimer's clearance.

They say that when the bombs explode over Bikini, the heat will equal the interior heat of stars. This is of the utmost interest to scientists, every one of whom owes his existence to the earth's having cooled off.

E. B. WHITE, *The Wild Flag*

60.

George F. Kennan: A Cultural Curtain

George F. Kennan was named ambassador to the Soviet Union by President Truman in 1951. A career diplomat with twenty-five years of service in Eastern Europe behind him, he brought to his post not only an excellent grasp of Russian institutions and of the language but also a scholar's acute understanding of Russian history. Kennan was relieved by President Eisenhower in 1953 and returned to the United States to find himself one of the most sought-after experts on Soviet policy. In 1954 the following essay by Kennan was included in a collection of pieces on American democracy. In it Kennan warned that the anti-communism that had swept the country in the past decade involved "habits of thought and action which our Soviet adversaries, I am sure, would most like to see us adopt and which they have tried unsuccessfully over a period of some thirty-five years to graft upon us through the operations of their Communist Party."

Source: Joseph Wood Krutch *et al., Is the Common Man Too Common?*, Norman, Okla., 1954: "Seek the Finer Flavor." Copyright 1954 by the University of Oklahoma Press.

THERE ARE FORCES AT LARGE in our society today that are too diffuse to be described by their association with the name of any one man or any one political concept.

They have no distinct organizational forms. They are as yet largely matters of the mind and the emotion in large masses of individuals. But they all march, in one way or another, under the banner of an alarmed and exercised anti-communism — but an anti-communism of a quite special variety, bearing an air of excited discovery and proprietorship, as though no one had ever known before that there was a communist danger; as though no one had ever thought about it and taken its measure; as though it had begun about the year 1945 and these people were the first to learn of it.

I have no quarrel to pick with the ostensible purpose of the people in which these forces are manifest. Surely, many of them are sincere. Surely, many of them have come to these views under real provocation and out of real bewilderment. But I have the deepest misgivings about the direction and effects of their efforts.

In general, I feel that what they are doing is unwise and unfortunate, and I am against it. They distort and exaggerate the dimensions of the problems with which they profess to deal. They confuse internal and external aspects of the communist threat. They insist on portraying as contemporary realities things that had their actuality years ago. They insist on ascribing to the workings of domestic communism evils and frustrations which, in so far as they were not part of the normal and unavoidable burden of complexity in our life, were the product of our behavior generally as a nation, and should today be the subject of humble and contrite soul-searching on the part of all of us, in a spirit of brotherhood and community, rather than of frantic and bitter recrimination.

And having thus incorrectly stated the problem, it is no wonder that these people constantly find the wrong answers. They tell us to remove our eyes from the constructive and positive purposes and to pursue with fanaticism the negative and vindictive ones. They sow timidity where there should be boldness; fear where there should be serenity; suspicion where there should be confidence and generosity. In this way they impel us — in the name of our salvation from the dangers of communism — to many of the habits of thought and action which our Soviet adversaries, I am sure, would most like to see us adopt and which they have tried unsuccessfully over a period of some thirty-five years to graft upon us through the operations of their Communist Party.

These forces are narrowly exclusive in their approach to our world position, and carry this exclusiveness vigorously into the field of international cultural exchanges. They tend to stifle the interchange of cultural impulses that is vital to the progress of the intellectual and artistic life of our people. The people in question seem to feel either that cultural values are not important at all or that America has reached the apex of cultural achievement and no longer needs in any serious way the stimulus of normal contact with other peoples in the field of arts and letters.

They look with suspicion both on the sources of intellectual and artistic activity in this country and on impulses of this nature coming to us from abroad. The remote pasts of foreign artists and scholars are anxiously scanned before they are permitted to enter our land, and this is done in proceedings so inflexible in concept and offensive in execution that their very existence often constitutes a discouragement to cultural interchange. The personal movements and affairs of great scholars and artists are thus passed upon and controlled by people who have no inkling of understanding for the work these same scholars and artists perform.

In this way, we begin to draw about ourselves a cultural curtain similar in some respects to the Iron Curtain of our adver-

saries. In doing so, we tend to inflict upon ourselves a species of cultural isolation and provincialism wholly out of accord with the traditions of our nation and destined, if unchecked, to bring to our intellectual and artistic life the same sort of sterility from which the cultural world of our Communist adversaries is already suffering.

Within the framework of our society, as in its relations to external environment, the tendency of these forces is exclusive and intolerant — quick to reject, slow to receive, intent on discovering what ought not to be rather than what ought to be. They claim the right to define a certain area of our national life and cultural output as beyond the bounds of righteous approval. This definition is never effected by law or by constituted authority; it is effected by vague insinuation and suggestion. And the circle, as I say, tends to grow constantly narrower. One has the impression that, if uncountered, these people would eventually narrow the area of political and cultural respectability to a point where it included only themselves, the excited accusers, and excluded everything and everybody not embraced in the profession of denunciation. . . .

I am not condoning anyone for forgetting these obligations. But to go beyond this — to say that it is not enough to be a law-abiding citizen — to say that we all have some obligation to get up and make statements of this tenor or that with respect to other individuals, or else submit to being classified as suspect in the eyes of our fellow citizens — to assert this is to establish a new species of public ritual, to arrogate to one's individual self the powers of the spiritual and temporal lawgiver, to make the definition of social conduct a matter of fear in the face of vague and irregular forces, rather than a matter of confidence in the protecting discipline of conscience and the law.

I have lived more than ten years of my life in totalitarian countries. I know where this sort of thing leads. I know it to be the most shocking and cynical disservice one can do to the credulity and to the spiritual equilibrium of one's fellow men. And this sort of thing cannot fail to have its effect on the liberal arts, for it is associated with two things that stand in deepest conflict to the development of mind and spirit: with a crass materialism and anti-intellectualism on the one hand, and with a marked tendency toward a standardization and conformity on the other.

In these forces I have spoken about, it seems to me that I detect a conscious rejection and ridicule of intellectual effort and distinction. They come together here with a deep-seated weakness in the American character: a certain shy self-consciousness that tends to deny interests other than those of business, sport, or war.

There is a powerful strain of our American cast of mind that has little use for the artist or the writer and professes to see in the pursuits of such people a lack of virility — as though virility could not find expression in the creation of beauty, as though Michelangelo had never wielded his brush, as though Dante had never taken up his pen, as though the plays of Shakespeare were lacking in manliness. The bearers of this neomaterialism seem, indeed, to have a strange self-consciousness about the subject of virility — a strange need to emphasize and demonstrate it by exhibitions of taciturnity, callousness, and physical aggressiveness — as though there were some anxiety lest, in the absence of these exhibitions, it might be found wanting.

What weakness is it in us Americans that so often makes us embarrassed or afraid to indulge the gentle impulse to seek the finer and rarer flavor, to admit frankly and without stammering apologies to an appreciation for the wonder of the poet's word and the miracle of the artist's brush, for all the beauty, in short, that has been recorded in the images of word and line created by the hands of men in past ages? What is it that makes us fear to acknowledge the greatness

of other lands or of other times, to shun the subtle and the unfamiliar?

What is it that causes us to huddle together, herdlike, in tastes and enthusiasms that represent only the common denominator of popular acquiescence, rather than to show ourselves receptive to the tremendous flights of creative imagination of which the individual mind has shown itself capable? Is it that we are forgetful of the true sources of our moral strength, afraid of ourselves, afraid to look into the chaos of our own breasts, afraid of the bright, penetrating light of the great teachers?

This fear of the untypical, this quest for security within the walls of secular uniformity — these are traits of our national character we would do well to beware of and to examine for their origins. They receive much encouragement these days, much automatic and unintended encouragement, by virtue of the growing standardization of the cultural and, in many respects, the educational influences to which our people are being subjected.

The immense impact of commercial advertising and the mass media on our lives is — let us make no mistake about it — an impact that tends to encourage passivity, to encourage acquiescence and uniformity, to place handicaps on individual contemplativeness and creativeness. It may not seem to many of us too dangerous that we should all live, dress, eat, hear, and read substantially alike. But we forget how easily this uniformity of thought and habit can be exploited when the will to exploit it is there. We forget how easily it can slip over into the domination of our spiritual and political lives by self-appointed custodians who contrive to set themselves at the head of popular emotional currents.

There is a real and urgent danger here for anyone who values the right to differ from others in any manner whatsoever, be it in his interests or his associations or his faith. There is no greater mistake we of this generation can make than to imagine that the tendencies which in other countries have led to the nightmare of totalitarianism will, as they appear in our midst, politely pause — out of some delicate respect for American tradition — at the point where they would begin to affect our independence of mind and belief.

The forces of intolerance and political demagoguery are greedy forces, and unrestrained. There is no limit to their ambitions or their impudence. They contain within themselves no mechanism of self-control. Like the ills of Pandora's box, once released, they can be stopped only by forces external to themselves. The only permanent thing behind them all is still the naked, vulnerable human soul, the scene of the age-old battle between good and evil, assailed with weakness and imperfections, always in need of help and support, and yet sometimes capable of such breathtaking impulses of faith and creative imagination.

Finally, it lies with the devotees of the liberal arts to combat the forces of intolerance in our society; to convince people that these forces are incompatible with the flowering of the human spirit; to remember that the ultimate judgments of good and evil are not ours to make; that the wrath of man against his fellow man must always be tempered by the recollection of his weakness and fallibility and by the example of forgiveness and redemption which is the essence of his Christian heritage.

61.

Resolution of Condemnation of Senator McCarthy

The beginning of the end of Senator Joseph R. McCarthy's meteoric career came in the spring of 1954, when a series of televised hearings into his conduct of an investigation of the United States Army revealed to the people at large his methods and his general attitude toward democratic processes. The hearings themselves led to no definite conclusions, but they apparently changed the mood of the country, for in the fall of 1954 Senators Arthur V. Watkins of Utah, Ralph E. Flanders of Vermont, Wayne Morse of Oregon, and J. William Fulbright of Arkansas brought charges of misconduct against McCarthy, and a resolution of censure was introduced. In December the Senate voted not to "censure" but to "condemn" the senator from Wisconsin, who had already lost his subcommittee chairmanship as a result of the Democratic victory in the congressional elections in November. McCarthy's star descended thereafter, and he died in 1957. The Senate charges against McCarthy are reprinted here.

Source: *Record,* 83 Cong., 2 Sess., p. 16392.

Resolved, that the senator from Wisconsin, Mr. McCarthy, failed to cooperate with the Subcommittee on Privileges and Elections of the Senate Committee on Rules and Administration in clearing up matters referred to that subcommittee which concerned his conduct as a senator and affected the honor of the Senate and, instead, repeatedly abused the subcommittee and its members who were trying to carry out assigned duties, thereby obstructing the constitutional processes of the Senate; and that this conduct of the senator from Wisconsin, Mr. McCarthy, is contrary to senatorial traditions and is hereby condemned.

Section 2. The senator from Wisconsin, Mr. McCarthy, in writing to the chairman of the Select Committee to Study Censure Charges (Mr. Watkins) after the Select Committee had issued its report and before the report was presented to the Senate charging three members of the Select Committee with "deliberate deception" and "fraud" for failure to disqualify themselves; in stating to the press on Nov. 4, 1954, that the special Senate session that was to begin Nov. 8, 1954, was a "lynch party"; in repeatedly describing this special Senate session as a "lynch bee" in a nationwide television and radio show on Nov. 7, 1954; in stating to the public press on Nov. 13, 1954, that the chairman of the Select Committee (Mr. Watkins) was guilty of "the most unusual, most cowardly thing I've heard of," and stating further: "I expected he would be afraid to answer the questions, but didn't think he'd be stupid enough to make a public statement"; and in characterizing the said committee as the "unwitting handmaiden," "involuntary agent," and "attorneys in fact" of the Communist Party, and in charging that the said committee in writing its report "imitated Communist methods — that it distorted, misrepresented, and omitted in its effort to manufacture a plausible rationalization" in support of its recommendations to the Senate, which characterizations and charges were contained in a statement released to the press and inserted in the *Congressional Record* of Nov. 10, 1954, acted contrary to senatorial ethics and tended to bring the Senate into dishonor and disrepute, to obstruct the constitutional processes of the Senate, and to impair its dignity; and such conduct is hereby condemned.

———◆———

Well, I wouldn't call it a vote of confidence.
    JOSEPH R. MCCARTHY, when his condemnation was voted by the Senate, and he was asked what it meant

1955

62.

LUTHER YOUNGDAHL: *United States v. Lattimore*

Professor Owen J. Lattimore, Far Eastern expert at Johns Hopkins University and previously an adviser to the State Department, was accused by Senator Joseph R. McCarthy in 1952 of being a "Communist sympathizer" and of having traitorously worked for the victory of the Communist regime in China. At a Senate hearing, Lattimore declared he was not a "follower of the Communist line," nor a "promoter of Communist interests." He was indicted for perjury upon these statements and brought to trial — the only person accused by McCarthy actually to suffer this fate. However, federal judge Luther Youngdahl dismissed the case, on the grounds that the "sweeping . . . indictment with its many vague charges" was invalid under the Sixth Amendment's requirement of specificity of charges. Judge Youngdahl's ruling of January 18, 1955, is reprinted below.

Source: 127 F. Supp. 405.

OWEN LATTIMORE WAS INDICTED Oct. 7, 1954, on two counts of perjury allegedly committed before the Senate Internal Security Subcommittee on or about Feb. 27, 1952.

The first count charges that Lattimore perjured himself when he denied that he was a "follower of the Communist line." It avers that in his positions and policies as to political, diplomatic, military, economic, and social matters there can be found expressed in his statements and writings from 1935 to 1950 several hundred instances in which he followed the Communist line, meaning that he:

. . . followed in time, conformed to, complied with, and paralleled the posi-

tions taken, the policies expressed, and propaganda issued on the same matters by the government of the Soviet Union, the Communist Party of the Soviet Union, the Comintern and its successors, the various Communist governments, parties, and persons adhering to Communism and accepting the leadership of the Soviet Communist Party. . . .

The second count charges that Lattimore perjured himself when he testified he had never been a "promoter of Communist interests." Such a person is defined as one who:

. . . knowingly and intentionally contributed to the growth, enlargement, and prosperity of Communism by acting to further, encourage, and advance those objectives of political, diplomatic, military, economic, and social interest to the government of the Soviet Union, the Communist Party of the Soviet Union, the Comintern and its successors, the various Communist governments, parties, and persons adhering to Communism and accepting the leadership of the Soviet Communist party. . . .

Defendant moved to dismiss the indictment, alleging that each of the two counts violate both the First and Sixth amendments to the United States Constitution. The Court's holding that both counts should be dismissed on the ground of vagueness renders unnecessary a determination of their constitutionality under the First Amendment. However, when the charge in an indictment is in the area of the First Amendment, evidencing possible conflict with its guarantees of free thought, belief, and expression, and when such indictment is challenged as being vague and indefinite, the Court will uphold it only after subjecting its legal sufficiency to exacting scrutiny.

When passing upon the Motion to Dismiss, ". . . the allegations of the indictment must be accepted as they are written." This we do, and are of the opinion that it does not, as a matter of law, inform the accused of the nature and cause of the accusation against him. Neither does it charge an offense with reasonable clarity so that the accused can make his defense, nor furnish the accused with such a description of the charge that he would be able to avail himself of his conviction or acquittal for protection against a further prosecution for the same cause.

In upholding the dismissal of the first count in the prior indictment, Judge Prettyman, speaking for the Court of Appeals, aptly stated,

Not only is it a basic rule that "Criminal statutes must have an ascertainable standard of guilt or they fall for vagueness," but it is equally well established

that an indictment must charge an offense with such reasonable certainty that the accused can make his defense. The cases on the point are myriad, as reference to any authority quickly reveals.

Testing the two counts against this principle, the Court is satisfied that they fail to meet the prescribed standard of definiteness and so must fall for vagueness.

Perjury, as presently charged to defendant under 18 U.S.C. Section 1621, occurs when a person under oath ". . . willfully and contrary to such oath states or subscribes any material matter which he does not believe to be true. . . ." The substance of such crime is a defendant's lack of belief in the truth of his testimony as of the moment he made it. For a jury to conclude that perjury has been committed, in fact, it must determine what the words meant to the defendant at the time he offered them as his testimony, and then conclude that the defendant did not at that time believe in the truth of such testimony according to the meaning he ascribed to the words and phrases he used.

Under Count I, perjury is charged to the statement by Lattimore that he was not a follower of the Communist line. The government supplies a definition of this phrase in the indictment. The government is prompt to concede that no such definition was presented to the defendant at the committee hearing in 1952; that it was formulated after Lattimore testified; that it was prepared after independent research conducted by the United States Attorney's Office. The sources of such research, however, do not appear.

The government contends that it is a matter of common knowledge as to what is meant by "follower of the Communist line" and that people differ but little in their understanding of the term; that it is not a minimal requirement of following the Communist line to zig and zag with it, since it does not always zigzag; and that the Communist line means the Soviet Communist line and all other organizations that followed the Soviet line. The government claims a right to prove, by men who are familiar with the common usage of the phrase and by documents of defendants, that the definition found in the indictment was the same definition which Lattimore had in mind when he testified; that the jury should be left to determine what is the Communist line, what it means to follow such a line, what Lattimore understood as the Communist Line, what Lattimore meant by the word "follow," and lastly, having decided the above, that Lattimore, when he said he was not a follower of the Communist line, did not at that time believe in the truth of such testimony according to the meaning he ascribed to these words.

While the proper test of perjury is subjective, insofar as it is based upon the understanding of the witness himself regarding the words that he used, a criminal prosecution must have certain objective standards. Most often in perjury cases the objective standard is not hard to come by; what the accused considered his statements to mean is not in issue since the words or phrases involved have one clear, accepted, and recognized meaning. Here, the phrase "follower of the Communist line" is subject to varying interpretations. It has no universally accepted definition. The government has defined it in one way and seeks to impute its definition to the defendant. Defendant has declined to adopt it, offering a definition of his own. It would not necessitate great ingenuity to think up definitions differing from those offered either by the government or defendant. By groundless surmise only could the jury determine which definition defendant had in mind.

The Court cannot escape the conclusion that "follower of the Communist line" is not a phrase with a meaning about which men of ordinary intellect could agree, nor one which could be used with mutual un-

derstanding by a questioner and answerer unless it were defined at the time it were sought and offered as testimony. This count, even with its apparent definition, is an open invitation to the jury to substitute, by conjecture, their understanding of the phrase for that of the defendant. The meaning of such a phrase varies according to a particular individual's political philosophy. To ask twelve jurors to agree and then decide that the definition of the Communist line found in the indictment is the definition that defendant had in mind and denied believing in, is to ask the jury to aspire to levels of insight to which the ordinary person is incapable, and upon which speculation no criminal indictment should hinge. We cannot debase the principle that: "The accused is entitled under the Constitution to be advised as to every element in respect to which it is necessary for him to prepare a defense."

When elements in an indictment are so easily subject to divergent interpretation, the accused is not adequately appraised of the charges as to enable him to prepare a defense. It therefore fails to conform to the requirements of the Sixth Amendment and Federal Rules. It cannot be cured by a bill of particulars.

The second count charges that Lattimore perjured himself when he testified he had never been a "promoter of Communist interest."

Defendant contends, in essence, that this count is an identical twin of Count I, differing only in the prose in which the government has dressed it; that it really means the same thing as "follower of the Communist line," i.e., defendant allegedly followed the Communist line in that he wrote certain articles, and he promoted the Communist interests in that he followed the Communist line in these articles; that while the word "promoter" might be definite enough in an indictment when tied to certain specific acts, it has been rendered formless and indefinite by the very definition and listing of topics which the government has attached to it, *i.e.*, he encouraged and advanced the political, economic, military, diplomatic, and social policy of the Soviet Union, China, and any other Communist country, in certain situations.

The government contends that the phrase is sufficiently clear by reason of its specification of content and definition; that Count II is in no way dependent upon Count I other than in its reliance upon it for purposes of definition and topical content.

This entire perjury indictment arises out of, and is essentially founded upon, the statements, correspondence, and editorial comments of defendant. It does not rest upon alleged acts of espionage or such an act as membership in the Communist Party. The government pointed to the activities of an espionage agent as an example of how one might knowingly promote Communist interests without also being a knowing follower of the Communist line — whatever that may be. But the government was quick to state that it was not charging defendant with being an espionage agent.

It should be kept in mind that under this count only written comments and opinions are involved and are said to have produced a certain effect, namely, to have promoted Communist interests. Such writings and comments are not alleged to have produced the designated result over a short period of time, and in isolated instances, but over a fifteen-year period. By no stretch of the imagination can we comprehend how this consistent result (promoting Communist interests) could have been so attained had not the commentator been both aware of what the Communists were asserting during this extended period, and then knowingly adhered to these assertions (followed the Communist line). If defendant had contradicted the Communists' assertions, he could hardly be said to have promoted their interests.

Count II, thus dependent upon Count I, cannot stand, being anchored to, partaking

Courtesy, Hugh Hutton

"There ought to be someone more sure on his feet"; cartoon by Hutton in the "Philadelphia Inquirer"

of, and plagued by all its vagueness and indefiniteness. While some paragraphs of Count II specifically refer to Count I, either for the definition of the Communist line or for topical references wherein defendant promoted Communist interests, all of the paragraphs, realistically appraised, are rooted in, and presume a prior finding of, the meaning of the phrase "follower of the Communist line."

The charges here serve only to inform the defendant that his sworn statements are to be tested against all his writings for chance parallelism with, or indirect support of, Communism regardless of any deliberate intent on his part. They demonstrate that the government seeks to establish that at some time, in some way, in some places, in all his vast writings, over a fifteen-year period, Lattimore agreed with something it calls and personally défines as following the Communist line and promoting Communist interests.

Jury inquiries would be limitless. No charge by the Court could embody objective standards to circumscribe and guide the jury in its determination of what the witness might have meant regarding words he used. With so sweeping an indictment with its many vague charges, and with the existing atmosphere of assumed and expected loathing for Communism, it would be neither surprising nor unreasonable were the jury subconsciously impelled to substitute its own understanding for that of defendant. To require defendant to go to trial for perjury under charges so formless and obscure as those before the Court would be unprecedented and would make a sham of the Sixth Amendment and the Federal Rule requiring specificity of charges.

The indictment will therefore be dismissed.

63.

WILLIAM FAULKNER: On Privacy

The ability of the public figure to maintain a private life has decreased greatly in an age of mass communications. Some public personages who consider themselves celebrities are happy to have almost continual public attention; others would prefer to be known primarily through their work. But the conviction of the news media that the public has a right to know virtually all that can be reported has left little privacy to well-known individuals. Novelist William Faulkner dealt with the problem of personal privacy in the following article published in July 1955, originally subtitled "The American Dream: What Happened to It?"

Source: *Harper's*, July 1955.

THIS WAS THE AMERICAN DREAM: a sanctuary on the earth for individual man: a condition in which he could be free not only of the old established closed-corporation hierarchies of arbitrary power which had oppressed him as a mass, but free of that mass into which the hierarchies of church and state had compressed and held him individually thralled and individually impotent.

A dream simultaneous among the separate individuals of men so asunder and scattered as to have no contact to match dreams and hopes among the old nations of the Old World which existed as nations not on citizenship but subjectship, which endured only on the premise of size and docility of the subject mass; the individual men and women who said as with one simultaneous voice: "We will establish a new land where man can assume that every individual man — not the mass of men but individual men — has inalienable right to individual dignity and freedom within a fabric of individual courage and honorable work and mutual responsibility."

Not just an idea, but a condition: a living human condition designed to be coeval with the birth of America itself, engendered, created, and simultaneous with the very air and word America, which at that one stroke, one instant, should cover the whole earth with one simultaneous suspiration like air or light. And it was, it did: radiating outward to cover even the old weary repudiated still-thralled nations, until individual men everywhere, who had no more than heard the name, let alone knew where America was, could respond to it, lifting up not only their hearts but the hopes too which until now they did not know — or anyway dared not remember — that they possessed.

A condition in which every man would not only not be a king, he wouldn't even want to be one. He wouldn't even need to bother to need to be the equal of kings because now he was free of kings and all their similar congeries; free not only of the symbols but of the old arbitrary hierarchies themselves which the puppet-symbols represented — courts and cabinets and churches and schools — to which he had been valuable not as an individual but only as that integer, his value compounded in that immutable ratio to his sheer mindless numbers, that animal increase of his will-less and docile mass.

The dream, the hope, the condition which our forefathers did not bequeath to us, their heirs and assigns, but rather bequeathed us, their successors, to the dream and the hope. We were not even given the chance then to accept or decline the dream, for the reason that the dream already owned and possessed us at birth. It was not our heritage because we were its, we ourselves heired in our successive generations to the dream by the idea of the dream. And not only we, their sons born and bred in America, but men born and bred in the old alien repudiated lands, also felt that breath, that air, heard that promise, that proffer that there was such a thing as hope for individual man. And the old nations themselves, so old and so long-fixed in the old concepts of man as to have thought themselves beyond all hope of change; making oblation to that new dream of that new concept of man by gifts of monuments and

devices to mark the portals of that inalienable right and hope:

"There is room for you here from about the earth, for all we individually homeless, individually oppressed, individually unindividualized."

A free gift left to us by those who had mutually travailed and individually endured to create it; we, their successors, did not even have to earn, deserve it, let alone win it. We did not even need to nourish and feed it. We needed only to remember that, living, it was therefore perishable and must be defended in its crises. Some of us, most of us perhaps, could not have proved by definition that we knew exactly what it was. But then, we didn't need to: who no more needed to define it than we needed to define that air we breathed or that word, which, the two of them, simply by existing simultaneously — the breathing of the American air which made America — together had engendered and created the dream on that first day of America as air and motion created temperature and climate on the first day of time.

Because that dream was man's aspiration in the true meaning of the word aspiration. It was not merely the blind and voiceless hope of his heart: it was the actual inbreathe of his lungs, his lights, his living and unsleeping metabolism, so that we actually lived the Dream. We did not live *in* the dream: we lived the Dream itself, just as we do not merely live *in* air and climate, but we live Air and Climate; we ourselves individually representative of the Dream, the Dream itself actually audible in the strong uninhibited voices which were not afraid to speak cliché at the very top of them, giving to the cliché-avatars of "Give me liberty or give me death" or "This to be self-evident that all individual men were created equal in one mutual right to freedom" which had never lacked for truth anyway, assuming that hope and dignity and truth, a validity and immediacy absolving them even of cliché.

THAT WAS THE DREAM: not man created equal in the sense that he was created black or white or brown or yellow and hence doomed irrevocably to that for the remainder of his days — or rather, not doomed with equality but blessed with equality, himself lifting no hand but instead lying curled and drowsing in the warm and airless bath of it like the yet-wombed embryo; but liberty in which to have an equal start at equality with all other men, and freedom in which to defend and preserve that equality by means of the individual courage and the honorable work and the mutual responsibility. Then we lost it. It abandoned us, which had supported and protected and defended us while our new nation of new concepts of human existence got a firm enough foothold to stand erect among the nations of the earth, demanding nothing of us in return save to remember always that, being alive, it was therefore perishable and so must be held always in the unceasing responsibility and vigilance of courage and honor and pride and humility. It is gone now. We dozed, slept, and it abandoned us. And in that vacuum now there sound no longer the strong loud voices not merely unafraid but not even aware that fear existed, speaking in mutual unification of one mutual hope and will. Because now what we hear is a cacophony of terror and conciliation and compromise babbling only the mouth-sounds, the loud and empty words which we have emasculated of all meaning whatever — freedom, democracy, patriotism — with which, awakened at last, we try in desperation to hide from ourselves that loss.

Something happened to the Dream. Many things did. This, I think, is a symptom of one of them.

About ten years ago a well-known literary critic and essayist, a good friend of long standing, told me that a wealthy widely circulated weekly pictorial magazine had offered him a good price to write a piece about me — not about my work or works, but about me as a private citizen, an individual. I said No, and explained why: my belief that only a writer's works were in the public domain, to be discussed and investigated and written about, the writer himself having put them there by submitting them for publication and accepting money for them; and therefore he not only would but must accept whatever the public wished to say or do about them from praise to burning. But that, until the writer committed a crime or ran for public office, his private life was his own; and not only had he the right to defend his privacy, but the public had the duty to do so since one man's liberty must stop at exactly the point where the next one's begins; and that I believed that anyone of taste and responsibility would agree with me.

But the friend said No. He said:

"You are wrong. If I do the piece, I will do it with taste and responsibility. But if you refuse me, sooner or later someone will do it who will not bother about taste or responsibility either, who will care nothing about you or your status as a writer, an artist, but only as a commodity: merchandise: to be sold, to increase circulation, to make a little money."

"I don't believe it," I said. "Until I commit a crime or announce for office, they can't invade my privacy after I ask them not to."

"They not only can," he said, "but once your European reputation gets back here and makes you financially worth it, they will. Wait and see."

I DID. I did both. Two years ago, by mere chance during a talk with an editor in the house which publishes my books, I learned that the same magazine had already set on foot the same project which I had declined eight years before; I don't know whether the publishers were formally notified or if they just heard about it by chance too, as I did. I said No again, recapitulating the same reasons which I still believed were not even arguable by anyone possessing the power of the public press, since the qualities of taste and responsibility would have to be inherent in that power for it to be valid and allowed to endure. The editor interrupted.

"I agree with you," he said. "Besides, you don't need to give me reasons. The simple fact that you don't want it done is enough. Shall I attend to it for you?" So he did, or tried to. Because my critic friend was still right. Then I said:

"Try them again. Say 'I ask you: please don't.'" Then I submitted the same *I ask you: please don't* to the writer who was to do the piece. I don't know whether he was a staff writer designated to the job, or whether he volunteered for it, or perhaps himself sold his employers on the idea. Though my recollection is that his answer implied, "I've got to, if I refuse they will fire me," which is probably correct, since I got the same answer from a staff member of another magazine on the same subject.

And if that was so, if the writer, a member of the craft he served, was victim too of that same force of which I was victim — that irresponsible use which is therefore misuse and which in its turn is betrayal, of that power called Freedom of the Press which is one of the most potent and priceless of the defenders and preservers of human dignity and rights — then the only defense left me was to refuse to cooperate, have anything to do with the project at all. Though by now I knew that that would not save me, that nothing I could do would stop them.

PERHAPS THEY — the writer and his employer — didn't believe me, could not believe me. Perhaps they dared not believe me. Perhaps it is impossible now for any American to believe that anyone not hiding from the police could actually not want, as a free gift, his name and photograph in any printed organ, no matter how base or modest or circumscribed in circulation. Though perhaps the matter never reached this point: that both of them — the publisher and the writer — knew from the first, whether I did or not, that the three of us, the two of them and their victim, were all three victims of that fault (in the sense that the geologist uses the term) in our American culture which is saying to us daily: "Beware!" the three of us faced as one not with an idea, a principle of choice between good and bad taste or responsibility or lack of it, but with a fact, a condition in our American life before which all three of us were (at that moment) helpless, at that moment doomed.

So the writer came with his group, force, crew, and got his material where and how he could and departed and published his article. But that's not the point. The writer is not to be blamed since, empty-handed, he would (if my recollection is right) have been fired from the job which deprived him of the right to choose between good and bad taste. Nor the employer either, since to hold his (the employer's) precarious own in a craft can compel even him, head and chief of one of its integral components, to serve the mores of the hour in order to survive among his rival ones.

It's not what the writer said, but that he said it. That he — they — published it, in a recognized organ which, to be and remain recognized, functions on the assumption of certain inflexible standards; published it not only over the subject's protests but with complete immunity to them; an immunity not merely assumed to itself by the organ but an immunity already granted in advance by the public to which it sold its wares for a profit. The terrifying (not shocking; we cannot be shocked by it since we permitted its birth and watched it grow and condoned and validated it and even use it individually for our own private ends at need) thing is that it could have happened at all under those conditions. That it could have happened at all with its subject not even notified in advance. And even when he, the victim, was warned by accident in advance, he was still completely helpless to prevent it. And even after it was done, the victim had no recourse whatever since, unlike sacrilege and obscenity, we have no laws against bad taste, perhaps because in a democracy the majority of the people who make the laws don't recognize bad taste when they see it, or perhaps because in our democracy bad taste has been converted into a marketable and therefore taxable and therefore lobbyable commodity by the merchandising federations which at the same simultaneous time create the market (not the appetite: that did not need creating: only pandering to) and the product to serve it, and bad taste by simple solvency was purified of bad taste and absolved. And even if there had been grounds for recourse, the matter would still have remained on the black side of the ledger since the publisher could charge the judgment and costs to operating loss and the increased sales from the publicity to capital investment.

THE POINT IS that in America today any organization or group, simply by functioning under a phrase like Freedom of the Press or National Security or League Against Subversion, can postulate to itself complete immunity to violate the individualness — the individual privacy lacking which he cannot be an individual and lacking which individuality he is not anything at all worth the having or keeping — of anyone who is not himself a member of some organization or group numerous enough or rich enough to frighten them off. That organization will not be of writers, artists, of course; being individuals, not even two artists could ever confederate, let alone enough of them. Besides, artists in America don't have to have privacy because they don't need to be artists as far as America is concerned. America doesn't need artists because they don't count in America; artists have no more place in American life than the employers of the weekly pictorial magazine staff-writers have in the private life of a Mississippi novelist.

But there are the other two occupations which are valuable to American life, which require, demand privacy in order to endure, live. These are science and the humanities, the scientists and the humanitarians: the pioneers in the science of endurance and mechanical craftsmanship and self-discipline and skill like Colonel Lindbergh who was compelled at last to repudiate it by the nation and culture one of whose mores was an inalienable right to violate his privacy instead of an inviolable duty to defend it, the nation which assumed an inalienable right to arrogate to itself the glory of his renown yet which had neither the power to protect his children nor the responsibility to shield his grief; the pioneers in the simple science of saving the nation like Dr. Oppenheimer who was harassed and impugned through those same mores until all privacy was stripped from him and there remained only the qualities of individualism whose possession we boast since they alone differ us from animals — gratitude for kindness, fidelity to friendship, chivalry toward women, and the capacity to love — before which even his officially vetted harassers were impotent, turning away themselves (one hopes) in shame, as though the whole business had had nothing whatever to do with loyalty or disloyalty or security or insecurity, but was simply to batter and strip him completely naked of the privacy lacking which he could never have become one of that handful of individuals capable of serving the nation at a moment when apparently nobody else was, and so reduce him at last to one more identityless integer in that identityless anonymous unprivacied mass which seems to be our goal.

And even that is only a point of departure. Because the sickness itself goes much further back. It goes back to that moment in our history when we decided that the old simple moral verities over which taste and responsibility were the arbiters and controls, were obsolete and to be discarded. It goes back to that moment when we repudiated the meaning which our fathers had stipulated for the words "liberty" and "freedom," on and by and to which they founded us as a nation and dedicated us as a people, ourselves in our time keeping only the mouth-sounds of them. It goes back to the moment when we substituted license in the place of liberty — license for any action which kept within the proscription of laws promulgated by confederations of the practitioners of the license and the harvesters of the material benefits. It goes back to that moment when in place of freedom we substituted immunity for any action to any recourse, provided merely that the act be performed beneath the aegis of the empty mouth-sound of freedom.

At which instant truth vanished too. We didn't abolish truth; even we couldn't do that. It simply quit us, turned its back on us, not in scorn nor even contempt nor even (let us hope) despair. It just simply quit us, to return perhaps when whatever it will be — suffering, national disaster, maybe even (if nothing else will serve) military defeat — will have taught us to prize truth and pay any price, accept any sacrifice (oh yes, we are brave and tough too; we just intend to put off having to be as long as possible) to regain and hold it again as we should never have let it go: on its own compromiseless terms of taste and responsibility. Truth — that long clean clear simple undeviable unchallengeable straight and shining line, on one side of which black is black and on the other white is white, has now become an angle, a point of view having nothing to do with truth nor even with fact, but depending solely on where you are standing when you look at it. Or rather —

better — where you can contrive to have him standing whom you are trying to fool or obfuscate when he looks at it.

Across the board in fact, a parlay, a daily triple: truth and freedom and liberty. The American sky which was once the topless empyrean of freedom, the American air which was once the living breath of liberty, are now become one vast down-crowding pressure to abolish them both, by destroying man's individuality as a man by (in that turn) destroying the last vestige of privacy without which man cannot be an individual. Our very architecture itself has warned us. Time was when you could see neither from inside nor from outside through the walls of our houses. Time is when you can see from inside out though still not from outside in through the walls. Time will be when you can do both. Then privacy will indeed be gone; he who is individual enough to want it even to change his shirt or bathe in, will be cursed by one universal American voice as subversive to the American way of life and the American flag.

If (by that time) walls themselves, opaque or not, can still stand before that furious blast, that force, that power rearing like a thunder-clap into the American zenith, multiple-faced yet mutually conjunctived, bellowing the words and phrases which we have long since emasculated of any significance or meaning other than as tools, implements, for the further harassment of the private individual human spirit, by their furious and immunized high priests: "Security." "Subversion." "Anti-Communism." "Christianity." "Prosperity." "The American Way." "The Flag."

With odds at balance (plus a little fast footwork now and then of course) one individual can defend himself from another individual's liberty. But when powerful federations and organizations and amalgamations like publishing corporations and religious sects and political parties and legislative committees can absolve even one of their working units of the restrictions of moral responsibility by means of such catch-phrases as "Freedom" and "Salvation" and "Security" and "Democracy," beneath which blanket absolution the individual salaried practitioners are themselves freed of individual responsibility and restraint, then let us beware. Then even people like Dr. Oppenheimer and Colonel Lindbergh and me (the weekly magazine staff-writer too if he really was compelled to choose between good taste and starvation) will have to confederate in our turn to preserve that privacy in which alone the artist and scientist and humanitarian can function.

Or to preserve life itself, breathing; not just artists and scientists and humanitarians, but the parents by law or biology of doctors of osteopathy too. I am thinking of course of the Cleveland doctor convicted recently of the brutal slaying of his wife, three of whose parents — his wife's father and his own father and mother — with one exception did not even outlive that trial regarding which the Press itself, which kept the sorry business on most of the nation's front pages up to the very end, is now on record as declaring that it was overcovered far beyond its value and importance.

I am thinking of the three victims. Not the convicted man: he will doubtless live a long time yet; but of the three parents, two of whom died — one of them anyway — because, to quote the Press itself, "he was wearied of life," and the third one, the mother, by her own hand, as though she had said, *I can bear no more of this.*

Perhaps they died solely because of the crime, though one wonders why the coincidence of their deaths was not with the commission of the murder but with the publicity of the trial. And if it was not solely because of the tragedy itself that one of the victims was "wearied of life" and another obviously said, *I can bear no more* — if they had more than that one reason to relinquish and even repudiate life, and the man was guilty as the jury said he was, just what medieval witch-hunt did that power called Freedom of the Press, which in any civilized culture must be accepted as that dedicated paladin through whose inflexible rectitude truth shall prevail and justice and mercy be done, condone and abet that the criminal's very progenitors be eliminated from the earth in expiation of his crime? And if he was innocent as he said he was, what crime did that champion of the weak and the oppressed itself participate in? Or (to repeat) not the artist. America has not yet found any place for him who deals only in things of the human spirit except to use his notoriety to sell soap or cigarettes or fountain pens or to advertise automobiles and cruises and resort hotels, or (if he can be taught to contort fast enough to meet the standards) in radio or moving pictures where he can produce enough income tax to be worth attention. But the scientist and the humanitarian, yes: the humanitarian in science and the scientist in the humanity of man, who might yet save that civilization which the professionals at saving it — the publishers who condone their own battening on man's lust and folly, the politicians who condone their own trafficking in his stupidity and greed, and the churchmen who condone their own trading on his fear and superstition — seem to be proving that they can't.

Concerning any new thing, never consult the man whose life it is about to change.

RAYMOND LOEWY, *New Yorker*, Feb. 27, 1954

64.

James MacGregor Burns: Republicans, Democrats — Who's Who?

Traditionally, the two major U.S. political parties have been not cohesive national entities held together by fundamental agreement on the aims and methods of government, but rather collections of sectional, regional, local, economic, and social interests and factions that are able from time to time to attain enough operational unity to agree on a platform and a slate of candidates. (The exception to this rule was during the Civil War when the major parties were ideologically as well as sectionally split.) Attempts at party realignment in the modern period have never worked, the public, as well as politicians, seeming to prefer two parties of general consensus instead of ideologically committed parties such as exist in many European countries. In the following article, published during President Eisenhower's first administration, political scientist James MacGregor Burns attempted an analysis of the constituents of the Republican and Democratic parties at the time.

Source: *New York Times Magazine*, January 2, 1955.

Not long ago a London editor was trying to guide his readers through the wilderness of the American party system. There are four parties, he explained — liberal Republicans, conservative Republicans, conservative Democrats, and liberal Democrats. The first three parties, he went on, combined to elect Mr. Eisenhower President, and the last three now combine to oppose him in Congress.

The story is pertinent to the news out of Washington: McCarthy breaks with President; Knowland attacks administration foreign policy; Democrats unite in censuring McCarthy but divide over attacking President; Eisenhower solicits bipartisan support for his program of "progressive moderation."

What does this mean? Is a McCarthy third party likely? Or are we headed toward an even more fundamental party re-

alignment — toward a neater party split, with all the liberals grouped in one party and all the conservatives in another? Would this be a good thing? What *is* a Republican, anyway, and what's a Democrat?

Whether Senator McCarthy will try to split off from the Republican Party and form a third party cannot be answered by anyone — perhaps not even by McCarthy — at this early date. But whether he would succeed if he did try can be answered. The chances are strong that he would not. Third parties have never flourished in American history. If ever there were opportunity for third-party success, it was in 1948, when President Truman was beset by the Southern conservatives on the right and the Northern progressives on the left. But both Thurmond and Wallace failed ignominiously. It is significant that the anti-Fair Deal Southerners experienced far more success working for Eisenhower within the two-party system in 1952 than they had met acting independently as Dixiecrats in 1948. Seasoned politicians take such lessons to heart.

The American political system, moreover, tends to smother third-party efforts. Legal requirements, ballot arrangements, and local election officials often discriminate against such attempts. The electoral college, with its winner-take-all arrangement, gives recognition in the electoral college only if a third party has a strong concentration of votes in some state or region. McCarthy lacks such grassroots strength.

Does this mean that McCarthy would be better advised to work within the Republican Party and try to throw the 1956 presidential nomination to himself or an ally? The answer depends largely on President Eisenhower. If he wishes renomination in 1956, neither McCarthy nor Knowland can stop him; great political parties do not repudiate their standard bearers. If he fails to run, and if he refuses to exert leadership over the convention, a party fracas is likely. In such a melee, McCarthy would be at his most effective. Facing this possibility, Mr. Eisenhower is not likely to leave his party rudderless.

The chances are that McCarthy, and Knowland, too, will keep their bases of operation on Capitol Hill, where they can put pressure on the administration from positions of some strength. If so, the administration will face in acute form the problem of trying to reorganize the Republican Party so as to gain stable backing from the pro-Eisenhower elements in the party and thus disarm the President's foes.

Mr. Eisenhower would not be the first President to try this tactic. A little more than ten years ago the most successful politician in American history, plagued like Mr. Eisenhower by hostile senators in his own party, took the first tentative steps toward a party realignment. Franklin D. Roosevelt,

according to his intimate adviser Judge Samuel I. Rosenman, had decided in 1944, after thirty-five years in American politics, that the time was ripe for a party reorganization along liberal-conservative lines. Moreover, he said, he had been told by a mutual friend of his and Wendell Willkie's that Willkie, who had just lost the 1944 Republican nomination, was of like mind. "We ought to have two real parties — one liberal and the other conservative," the President said to Rosenman. "As it is now, each party is split by dissenters." He added that party realignment would take time, but that it could be accomplished. "From the liberals of both parties Willkie and I together can form a new, really liberal party in America."

Roosevelt wrote to Willkie, but nothing came of the idea. Neither of them wished to pursue the matter during the 1944 election; Willkie died before the election, and Roosevelt a few months later.

This raises the question of what we mean by "Republican" and by "Democrat." It is fashionable to say that the terms are utterly meaningless. But this is not so. Party platforms and presidential statements show that *most* Democrats stand for the increased use of government for the broader distribution of social welfare, even if it means unbalanced budgets, big government, and higher taxes, especially on the rich. They show that *most* Republicans would restrict government in order to give more scope to private initiative and investment, even if this means considerable inequality of income and even some temporary hardship for the mass of people.

This, of course, is a generalization, but a generalization that focuses on the crucial issue separating Democrats from Republicans — the extent to which government should be used to distribute social welfare.

Does this division involve foreign policy, too? More and more it does. Today the parties are substantially agreed on some of the great political and military problems such as recognition of Red China, European unity, and opposition to Communist expansion. Where they differ is in the field of foreign economic policies — tariffs, the extent of United States economic aid, the size of Point Four.

If party realignment takes place, then the only logical form would be along the lines of domestic and international economic policy. What are the chances of such a realignment? Political scientists see underlying economic, social, and political changes that may make party realignment increasingly possible as time passes. Some of these are:

Increasing urbanization. Fifty years ago most people lived in rural areas; today, twice as many Americans live in urban areas as in rural. The population of suburban areas has also increased. Politically, this means more voters who will divide over the problems involved in the government's relation to wages, prices, taxes, and social benefits.

Less sectionalism. Five or six decades ago, Americans tended to divide far more on a sectional basis than they do now. Parties were strongly rooted in certain areas and tended to embrace both the liberals and conservatives in those areas. As our politics have become increasingly "nationalized," political divisions have gradually divided voters on an economic and social, rather than on a geographical, basis.

Changes in the South. Economic and social developments are rapidly bringing the South more in step politically with the rest of the country. These are the growth of industry, the diversification and mechanization of farming, urbanization, the political organization of labor and of Negroes. While these changes vary widely from state to state, the South as a whole is moving toward the same horizontal political cleavages that cut across the rest of the population.

In the face of these developments, however, it is well to remind ourselves that somehow the American party system has survived deep-seated changes in the social and economic pattern and still has kept its essential form.

One of the elements ingrained in our system is party organization. Our parties are not centralized agencies that can be easily reformed or "purified" from the top. They are really vast holding companies for thousands of factional groups fighting for local, state, and congressional offices. The men who run the party at the base of the pyramid often have little interest in the fortunes of the party nationally; they are concerned with winning races for district attorney, mayor, sheriff, state representative, governor, county commissioner.

A second factor that will resist quick party change is the sheer weight of habit. Millions of Americans stick to their party year in and year out regardless of its changing liberalism or conservatism nationally. For example, in Republican New Hampshire there are little pockets of voters who have cast their ballots for Democrats ever since Jackson's time; "mountain Republicans" in the South have been voting for their party steadily since the Civil War.

A third factor against easy party realignment is the tendency of *both* parties to move in the same direction in the face of a strong trend in public opinion. In the 1870s and 1880s, both parties were essentially conservative parties. These days the Republicans pick national candidates — Willkie, Dewey, and Eisenhower — who take moderately liberal attitudes toward social and economic policies. The crucial changes in party development have often taken place within each of the major parties rather than between them. New England was once the spawning ground of the most conservative Republicans; now it sends to Congress some of the most liberal Republicans.

The seeming paradox of liberals and conservatives in the same party is actually the normal pattern in American parties. Early in this century the Democratic Party was split into Bryanites and Eastern conservatives, the Republican Party into Roosevelt progressives and Taft standpatters.

In the 1920s the Democrats embraced both Al Smith progressives and conservatives of the John W. Davis stripe, and the Republicans had their Hardings and Coolidges but also their "sons of the wild jackass," such as William Borah and George W. Norris. Is it strange that today there are Aiken and Javits Republicans as well as Capehart and Bridges Republicans, that there are Walter George and Richard Russell Democrats as well as Paul Douglas and Averell Harriman Democrats?

Does all this mean that party realignment is out of the question? Many political scientists think not. What we have come to, they suggest, is one of history's crucial periods when the new forces pressing for social change are in a condition of precarious balance with the forces of inertia. The outcome will depend on two elements — the nature of party leadership and the attitudes of the party rank-and-file.

The leaders of neither party show much disposition to press at the moment for the kind of change that Roosevelt sought. President Eisenhower wants backing for his policy of "progressive moderation," but he has shown little flair for the type of creative political leadership that could reorganize the Republican Party, slough off its reactionary wing, and yet keep it "slightly right of center."

Democratic leaders seem no more eager for a liberal-conservative realignment. The recent "harmony" meeting of the Democratic National Committee indicates that they would prefer to keep their Southern wing as intact as possible, even if this policy jeopardizes the allegiance of Northern Negroes and other minority groups concerned about civil rights and social welfare.

The attitudes of leaders will change, however, if the attitudes of their followers change, and it is here that important shifts may take place. The disposition of millions of workers and their union leaders to continue to work and to enlarge their influence in the Democratic Party holds tremendous implications for the strengthening of liberalism in that party. The willingness of the executive and white-collar class in the burgeoning industry of the South to turn openly and without embarrassment to the Republican Party as a vehicle for conservatism in the long run will outweigh century-old emotional attitudes toward the hated Republicans of the North. Ultimately, party realignment will turn on a rational calculation by intelligent Americans as to whether or not such a realignment on a liberal-conservative basis would benefit the general welfare.

What is the case for and against such a realignment? The essential case against ideological parties is that the present system blurs and softens the political antagonisms which divide Americans. If all people of one mind were in one party and of opposite mind in the other, the result, it is said, might be fanaticism and intransigeance. By compromising among diverse groups *within* parties rather than trying to settle differences between parties, change can be brought about easily and quietly and without tension or open hostility.

Both parties should reflect the rich diversity of our group life. It is especially important, according to this argument, that the lovers of freedom be represented in both parties so that party leaders will feel pressure from their own followers on the paramount question of civil liberties.

The opponents of a liberal-conservative party realignment grant that the present system leads to inefficiency, obstruction, and evasion. But this is the price they are willing to pay — the "price of union," Herbert Agar has called it — to maintain underlying unity in a continental nation of many diverse sections, minority groups, national backgrounds, and political attitudes. The Civil War is cited as an example of what follows when parties divide irretrievably over some crucial issue.

What is the other side of the case? How do supporters of party realignment answer these arguments?

They agree that political harmony must be preserved. They fear, however, that "me-too" parties that stand for little will disrupt American politics. If the average American comes to believe that parties will not take relatively definite and clear-cut positions on major issues, he may suspect that democratic government evades issues instead of facing and solving them. Extremist leaders and parties may arise to win the votes of such discontented people, especially in a time of economic crisis, war, or long drawn-out "cold war."

Ideological parties need not be sharply divided parties, according to this view. The British party system is cited as one that is separated essentially over ideology, but also one that compels the Conservatives to dampen down their extremists, and the Labourites to hold the doctrinaire Socialists in check.

The case for party realignment rests largely on the view that changing world and domestic conditions are confronting democratic government with new challenges that can be met only if that government is united, purposeful, and efficient. Presidents must work closely with congressmen and national officials must work closely with state and local officials. Only a united party system, it is argued, reaching into every area of the nation, can mobilize the political power that will guide and sustain and unite our leaders. And minority and individual rights can thrive best in a nation which is kept productive and strong by unified government.

It is not easy to choose between these two cases. However, many students of politics — including this one — favor party realignment because they are concerned about a central goal of democratic government — responsibility. They fear that the present party hodgepodge confuses the people and cuts them off from direct control of their leaders. An essential element of democratic government, they feel, is the presenting of relatively clear and simple alternatives to the great mass of people who are bewildered by the complexities and confusions of democratic government.

The idea of party responsibility has an even more vital implication. In a time when we desperately need a steady course abroad, we cannot afford politicians who rock the boat with shrill cries for retaliation and adventures. In a day when the crying need at home is for tolerance and harmony in the face of suspicion and witch hunts, we cannot afford politicians who earn their political living by arousing group against group.

If a party wishes to gain power on a platform of Knowlandism abroad and McCarthyism at home, it has a right to try to do so. But a party hardly has the right to beg votes for a moderate and responsible platform at the same time that it exploits the appeal of its political adventurers to malcontents. One way to curb such political adventurers is to hold their parties responsible for them. But we can hardly hold parties responsible if we allow them to serve as simple holding companies for every group across the political spectrum. To clean house a party must stand for something — otherwise it can hardly know what to keep and what to sweep out of the house.

Ultimately, in short, party realignment means party responsibility, and this in turn means the personal responsibility of political leaders to the people. As long as we must stake our hopes on the moderation and good sense of the American people, no better test of our party system can be devised.

65.

Federalism Today — A Report to the President

Among the perennial concerns of political scientists and politicians are the problems of federal-state relationships and of the balance of authority between the three branches of the federal government. The tendency since the Constitution became operative in 1789 has been for the federal government gradually to erode away the powers of the state, and attempts to reverse the trend, most dramatically in the Civil War, have never been more than temporarily successful. In 1955 the Commission on Intergovernmental Relations presented a report to the President on the status of the federal system. The first chapter of the report is reprinted in part below.

Source: *The Commission on Intergovernmental Relations,* A Report to the President for Transmittal to the Congress, June 1955: "Evolution of the American Federal System."

THE PROPER DIVISION of labor and authority between the nation and the states is the key to maintaining the federal nature of our system of government. The lines of division are not static. They have been controversial from the beginning of our life as an independent country. They remain so today. . . .

A realistic view of the prospects for a continuing federal balance compels notice of the changes that have come over our society since 1787. The changes have been physical, technological, economic, cultural, intellectual, and political. Most obvious of the main trends affecting the federal system are those, accentuated in recent decades, that have led to a great expansion in the national government and its activities, in the proportion of national income passing through the Treasury, and in the degree of attention focused on Washington. Less obvious but equally relevant is the very significant expansion of state and local governments in recent years.

The most elementary fact is the growth in total population, now over forty times what it was in 1787. This has come about through large-scale immigration, a fairly high birthrate, and a rapidly declining death rate. The remarkable rise in longevity, which in a century has perhaps doubled the average life expectancy, has helped push the population figures up. Greater population density has resulted in the multiplication of governmental functions. . . .

The growth of population has been accomplished by a continually rising standard of living, thanks mainly to the progress of science, technology, industrialization, and specialization. In the decline of the relative self-sufficiency that so conspicuously characterized the agricultural and handicraft economy of our forefathers lies a principal explanation of our demands, not only for more government services to supply what private enterprise does not provide but also to regulate many of the complex relations among the individuals and groups of an industrial society. . . .

Industrialization has made city dwellers or suburbanites out of most Americans. In 1790, nineteen people lived on farms for every one who lived in a town. Today, the farm population is less than a sixth of the total, and two people out of three live in urban areas. Cities need water supply and sewage disposal, police and fire protection, zoning and building and sanitary codes, street paving and lighting, mass transportation and off-street parking, libraries, schools, parks, and the like. City governments are commonly expected to furnish many of these services and facilities and have grown correspondingly. . . .

For the one in six who still lives on a farm, an agricultural revolution has transformed life, too. Free schools and all-weather roads, mechanization and electrification, fertilizers and hybrid and purebred strains have brought remarkable increases in productivity and changed both the farm and the farmer. With more cultivated land but fewer people working it than in 1900, farmers supply food for twice as large a total population at a far higher living standard. Subsistence farms are still numerous, but many farms are factories, and their proprietors are businessmen as well as farmers, with investments and records to keep. They provide a sharp contrast to the still surviving pattern of sharecropping agriculture. . . .

Closely allied to the revolutions in industry and agriculture is the emphasis on natural resource development and conservation which began to be felt about 1900. Land use and water use since that time have claimed much governmental attention, with programs for soil conservation, irrigation, reclamation, flood control, hydroelectric power, and stream-pollution abatement. Forests are coming to be treated as tree farms. Wildlife, parks, and recreation facilities have become increasingly important objectives of public policy.

Changes in our foreign trade likewise reflect our economic growth. Where coffee, bananas, and tin once comprised our main imports, today we look abroad for such items as iron ore, copper, bauxite, nickel, manganese, and tungsten, in addition to commodities which were never a part of our natural resources. Some of these goods are imported because the increase in consumption of all types of raw materials has sharply reduced our reserves and made it more economical to draw on foreign sources. As the population of this country grows and its standard of living rises, pressure on certain raw materials will grow even greater. A profound change in public attitudes toward foreign trade and national defense is implicit in these developments, which impose added responsibilities on the national government.

Revolutions in transportation and communications have been a fundamental factor in the changes already noted, and have had a far-reaching effect on the activities and conduct of government. . . . Modern rapid and large-scale transportation and communications facilities have helped make the population more mobile and better informed. They have helped to create national markets and have been the means of reaching them. They have transformed election campaigns. No more profound influence has been at work in changing the world the framers knew than the ability of the people to move themselves and their goods over great distances quickly and to exchange information and ideas at a distance. . . .

Overshadowing all domestic occasions for governmental action today is the new position of the United States in world affairs. George Washington warned his countrymen to avoid permanent foreign alliances: sound advice when they could not influence the outcome of events overseas and could hope to escape involvement if they gave no provocation. Jefferson and Monroe thought it still good advice, and so it remained through the nineteenth century.

Economically and politically, we played for more than a century of our national life a relatively inactive role in international relations. Before World War I our exports were chiefly agricultural commodities and our imports were manufactured goods. As a debtor nation in the balance of international payments, the United States sent abroad immigrant remittances and interest and dividends to European investors. Now, as a creditor nation, military and economic assistance to other governments, together with private investments in foreign countries, loom large in the balance of payments that sustain American exports. A substantial share of our imports is made up of raw materials, and more and more of our exports are of finished goods. Not only agricultural exports but also the level of employment in many domestic industries therefore depend importantly on the maintenance of dollar purchasing power abroad.

The familiar story of events from the Spanish-American War to the Korean invasion need not be retold here to make the point that we are at present a different country playing a different role in a different world. National defense, war, diplomacy, and foreign aid have been the province of the national government from the beginning. It is a striking change in degree, responding to a change in need, that makes expenditures for these functions now exceed all other expenditures of all governments in this country put together.

It is a testimony to the durability and flexibility of our federal system that its basic pattern has survived almost a century and three-quarters of changes of the magnitude and variety that have been sketched here. It should be no cause for surprise that in the processes of adaptation strong differences of opinion over constitutional doctrine and administrative practice have arisen. . . .

The basic constitutional question for the federal system from 1789 to 1865 was the issue of national supremacy — whether the national government was entitled to enforce, over state objections, decisions reached through its own constitutional processes. . . . Two related premises regarding the federal system underlay the judicial interpretation of national and state powers for a full half century after 1880. One was that workably clear and distinct boundaries between their respective realms of activity could be drawn in terms of constitutional powers. The other was that the Supreme Court was the final arbiter of the system.

Experience showed both assumptions to be illusory. So many judicial precedents of contrary tendency accumulated that the boundary lines became unpredictable and, indeed, a zone of governmental no-man's-land sometimes appeared to lie between them. On the major issues of national and state power the Supreme Court during the early 1900s often had a free choice in decision. Having such a choice, the Court was exposed again, as it had been on some earlier notable occasions, to a crossfire of political criticism. The clash culminated in 1937 when the Court began a series of sweeping reversals or modifications of former decisions.

Since 1937, judicial doctrine has recognized the emergence of a new concept of national-state relations, sometimes labeled "cooperative federalism" in contrast with the separatism of the previous era. The concept rests constitutionally on a broad view of national authority, on the abandonment of the due process clause as a source of substantive restraints on state regulation of economic affairs, and on the Court's refusal to entertain taxpayers' suits challenging exercises of the spending power. Coming full circle after 125 years by the route of implied powers, the Supreme Court now gives to the list of powers delegated to Congress in Article I, Section 8, of the Constitution approximately the same broad sweep of meaning conveyed by the Virginia Plan. . . . At the same time, the Court has generally refused to invoke the prerogative of review over economic policy that it exercised for 40 years prior to 1937.

State and national laws touching economic affairs are no longer held to be deprivations of due process because they conflict with natural rights of property or liberty of contract. The Court has accepted a reading of the general welfare clause that places no discernible judicial limits on the amounts or purposes of federal spending, although it does not follow that the power to spend carries with it unlimited power to regulate. The potentialities of the spending power were only dimly apprehended before the income tax and the Federal Reserve System opened up new reservoirs of federal revenues and credit. Grants-in-aid are only one characteristic use of the power, along with many other direct spending and lending programs. Finally, the Court has directed the lower federal courts to follow state law in handling litigation based on diversity of citizenship so as to minimize conflicts in the applicable rules of decision.

Under judicial doctrine since 1937 the Supreme Court has largely removed itself as a practical factor in determining the economic policies of the states and the nation. It has not, however, eliminated the historic role of judicial review in our federal system. Two remaining functions are noteworthy here, apart from its task of promoting uniformity of interpretation and filling in the gaps in federal law. One is the duty of judging when the states have overstepped and encroached on whatever area should be the exclusive domain of federal regulation, if any, or have actually legislated in conflict with federal law. The exercise of this function is as old as the Court itself and as recent as the 1955 decision that only the Interstate Commerce Commission, and not a state, can revoke the license of an interstate trucking concern to use the highways.

The other function is very recent in its present-day significance, dating only from 1925, though its roots go back to the Fourteenth Amendment. This is the guardianship of civil liberties. In the face of its withdrawal from supervision over economic policies, the Court during the past thirty years has become noticeably more stern in construing state responsibilities under the Fourteenth Amendment to protect civil and political rights. Beginning in 1925, earlier doctrine has in effect been reversed, and the guarantees of freedom of speech, press, and religion, as well as some (but not all) of the procedural safeguards in criminal cases written in the Bill of Rights against the national government, have been read also into the due process clause of the Fourteenth Amendment against the states. More recently, racial discriminations have been brought further under the ban of the equal protection clause of the same amendment.

In this whole area, in contrast to the field of economic affairs, the Congress has moved slowly, and the Supreme Court has become the principal instrument of federal surveillance. There is a surface paradox in this extension of national judicial power at the very time the Court is emphasizing its deference to state legislative policy. But the paradox disappears in a view of the purposes of our federal system which puts the strengthening and preservation of basic personal freedoms among the first objects of the Union.

What, then, is the present position of constitutional doctrine as it bears on national-state relations? Reviewing current Supreme Court interpretations in the light of their historical development, the following generalizations appear to be warranted:

First, the constitutional restrictions now applicable to any government in the United States are chiefly procedural, are quite similar in their admonitions to the nation and to the states, and consequently under the philosophy of these decisions exert no major thrust on the working division of labor and authority between them one way or the other.

These restrictions are found chiefly in the Bill of Rights and the Fourteenth Amendment. They put important limits on the permissible ways of using the coercive powers of government and on some policies related to the provision of certain services and to the conduct of elections. In the main they have been left to the judiciary to enforce. In the sense that they subject state policies and procedures to a national judicial review, they are a significant feature of our federal system. Court enforcement of them may cut across time-honored policies and deeply felt beliefs. But they do not have the effect of transferring activities from one governmental level to another. Nor do they prevent either level from pursuing substantive programs of any kind likely to be adopted in this country. The federal balance might be different if there were major disparities in the procedural restraints applied at one level in contrast with the other, or if the Congress showed any disposition to make full use of the powers conferred on it by the Fourteenth Amendment.

Second, the prohibitions on the states, express and implied, that keep them from actions deemed to encroach on powers delegated to the national government have only a minimal effect on the capacity of the states to discharge their functions.

These prohibitions set the lower limits of the zone of national responsibility for governmental action. So far as they have a nationalizing tendency, it comes chiefly from the judiciary in the form of Court review of state action. In general, these limitations keep the states out of interstate commerce, admiralty, bankruptcy, and currency matters, and prevent them from imposing burdens on federal instrumentalities. It does not follow that these prohibitions on the states automatically or necessarily compel the Congress to act in these fields; this depends on the will of Congress. They do, of course, present some borderline problems that have nevertheless proved manageable.

For one thing, the trend of recent judicial opinion outside the civil liberties field has on the whole been tolerant and accommodating to state policy: the states, for instance, can tax some interstate commerce, or set up quarantine inspections at their borders, or fix weight limits for trucks, or enforce highway traffic regulations, provided they do not discriminate against interstate commerce or burden it "unduly." Moreover, congressional waivers or administrative cessions of a national jurisdiction staked out by the Court can make flexible room for state action; this is the pattern made familiar by the Twenty-first (Repeal) Amendment. It is also illustrated in the Tidelands Act and in the refusal of the National Labor Relations Board to hear some local cases. Even where action by the states is precluded by virtue of positive congressional action, as in some aspects of labor relations, the boundary adjustments are within congressional control. Broadly speaking, the working division of duties is not determined by rigid constitutional limits on the states.

Third, the range of activities that lies primarily within the power of the states by reason of the lack of any coercive authority in Congress to deal with them is substantial. While the national government has extensive authority to regulate, especially under its tax and interstate commerce powers, there is still a broad field of regulatory activity beyond its reach. The limits of the delegated and implied national powers fix the maximum range of national action. The existence of such constitutional bounds is probably more important than their exact location for the purpose of maintaining the federal nature of our governmental system.

It is important that national powers be adequate to all truly national needs; it is also important that they do not jeopardize the proper functioning of the states. The former object is a matter of power and hence of constitutional law; the latter is primarily a matter of policy. It is improbable that judicial action would be needed to prevent the national military or taxing power, for example, from being used directly on the state governments to destroy or cripple them. The more likely danger is that the national government will dissipate its energies and prestige, or discourage the states from developing their talents, by taking on matters that lie in the field of concurrent powers and that the states can handle acceptably.

Fourth, the possibility of a significant constitutional no-man's-land in our federal system has been disposed of by judicial reinterpretations. The early child labor cases and the decisions invalidating the Municipal Bankruptcy Act and the Bituminous Coal Act during the Depression pointed for a time to subjects beyond the reach of any legislation. But apparently there are no longer any areas of economic policy barred to Congress for want of delegated power, on the one hand, and impractical or unconstitutional for the states to enter, on the other. The states are accorded more latitude now, and national powers are broadly available for all the great exigencies of government for which the Union was created: to "establish justice, insure domestic tranquillity, provide for the common defense, promote the general welfare, and secure the blessings of liberty. . . ."

Fifth, it follows that the basic problems of maintaining our federal system today lie in those areas of national and state power where both Congress and the states have real choices to make and where many alternative courses of action are open. It is in these areas that practical issues arise and tensions between interested groups and organizations are felt. Legislatures and administrative agencies within their assigned jurisdictions provide the appropriate forums for settling these issues.

Under our federal system, the division of responsibilities between the national government and the states was once thought to be settled mainly in terms of power: either one level, or both, or neither, had the authority to move; and that was enough to settle their functions. Such a decision was usually one for the judiciary. Under current judicial doctrine, there are still limits on the coercive powers at both levels, but the national powers are broad and the possibilities by means of spending are still broader.

The crucial questions now are questions of policy: Which level ought to move? Or should both? Or neither? What are the prudent and proper divisions of labor and responsibility between them? These are questions mainly for legislative judgment, and the criteria are chiefly political, economic, and administrative, rather than legal. The emphasis is on mutual and complementary undertakings in furtherance of common aims.

66.

Clifton Fadiman: King of the Tame Frontier

The problems of the city led many Americans to choose the suburbs as a place to live before and during World War II. Though the move to suburbia has never ceased, in the prosperous years after the war a new trend showed itself in some of the large metropolitan areas: the move beyond the suburbs into what was almost a rural environment. The phenomenon of the long-distance commuter was documented by A. C. Spectorsky in his book The Exurbanites *in 1955. In a review of the book, reprinted here, Clifton Fadiman discussed the exurbanites as "the frontiersmen of the 20th century."*

Source: *Holiday,* November 1955.

AFTER HAVING PASSED almost half a century trying to hypnotize myself into the belief that New York City was a proper habitat for *homo sapiens,* or even *homo stultus,* I recently threw in the sponge and removed to the pleasant town of New Canaan, Connecticut. Now, just as I am dancing cheek-to-cheek with a Locke mower, I am sandbagged by a book whose net effect is to make a Seventh Avenue subway change booth look like the Ideal American Home. After a dose of Spectorsky many a man in a gray flannel suit will become not merely discontented with his lot but homicidally inclined toward the real-estate broker who unloaded it on him.

All of which is irrelevant to the virtues of *The Exurbanites.* They are multiple. Here is a social study that can actually be read by ordinary human beings — as contrasted, for example, with David Riesman's lucubrations, which would have a tough time surviving translation into the English language. Mr. Spectorsky has marked out for himself a field of study that checkably exists; he has observed it with care, toughness and com-passion; and he writes about it with a *boulevardier* charm coating a basic seriousness. Even though he fills me with terror, I have learned much from him and urge him heartily upon all Urbanites, Suburbanites and Ruralians who contemplate removal to my own land of Exurbia.

Mr. Spectorsky's term merits inclusion in the language. What is an Exurbanite? Here is Mr. Spectorsky's answer. He is a man originally from New York City. Scorning the suburbs as neither fish, fowl nor good green country, he has settled in the Exurbs, perhaps fifty miles from Columbus Circle. The rhythm of his life is a function of the commuters' train. He lives in Fairfield County, Connecticut; or Rockland County, New York; or Bucks County, Pennsylvania; or Upper Westchester, New York; or on the North Shore of Long Island.

The typical Exurbanite is a member of a relatively new species, the Communicators. He deals in symbols — words, notes of music, pictures on paper. He sets the styles, thinks up the transient ideas, and glamorizes the objects by which we live. He makes a good deal of money — the *average* annual income in Fairfield County is $7,431. He is rarely solvent.

He suffers, says Mr. Spectorsky, "from a self-created exurban syndrome." In the first place, he is schizoid — "These short-haul expatriates really never leave town." He is a symbol-manipulator trying to live like a thing-manipulator. Continually seeking "status," he thinks to find it in liquor, foreign cars and "regional stigmata" such as salt-box houses and Rototillers. He is Republican, conformist, and increasingly, though he lives by ideas, anti-intellectual.

He drinks too much, plays too hard, and is plagued by psychosomatic illnesses. Intelligent, witty, quick-brained, often charming, he is also at bottom baffled, even miserable. His wife is in no better case. She lacks the daily stimuli which her husband presumably receives in the big city. She is overworked, overbechilded and underloved. Frustrated, she frequently seeks to sidestep her frustration in liquor, or infidelity, or frenzied absorption in the children, in housekeeping, in do-goodism.

The Exurbanites have made a partial escape from the city rat race only to find themselves confronted with a new set of problems — fiscal or emotional — which they strive courageously but with only middling success to solve. Their personal equation juggles three major factors: insecurity, obligations, and a sense that time is running out.

Mr. Spectorsky's analysis is, of course, far more detailed than this brief summary implies, and is hedged about with qualifications and subtle distinctions. As mere description of a readily observable type his book is solid. His picture is confirmed by a whole spate of recent novels, of which *The Man in the Gray Flannel Suit* is a fair sample. He observes truly and acutely. No one has ever written about a commuters' train with an eye closer to the object. He knows the country-club set, the "genius" (the ge-

nius works at home), the Saturday-night parties, the creative people of Rockland County, the ingrown moneymen of the North Shore, the conscientious school-improvers of Westchester. His book is no fantasy, no tissue of generalizations. He seems to speak from much doleful experience. He has been there.

And yet there is something incomplete about his rueful thesis. I am not sure that I know what it is, but as an Exurbanite myself, I feel driven to place Exurbia in a perspective somewhat more encouraging than Mr. Spectorsky's.

In the first place, there are a hell of a lot of pleasant, normal, nonfrenzied, nonalcoholic, sexually happy, and even financially solvent people in Exurbia. They don't rocket about in Jaguars. Their houses are not full of early American glass. They are glad to be out of the city for a reasonable part of the week. They just don't care much about Tennessee Williams' latest three-act lavatory-wall scribble. They read good books. They rear their children quietly and without tension. A few are even Democrats and not scared to say so. In other words, they're poor copy.

Now, Mr. Spectorsky knows these folks exist, and admits that they do. But, he says, the *tone* of Exurbia, particularly in my home county of Fairfield, is set by the others.

He may be correct. But, even if he *is* correct, I would suggest that his correctness is that of a limited view.

Exurbia cannot be understood or adequately defended unless we are prepared to admit now what I believe we will all be forced to admit within fifty years: that the Big City, as a place to live, is dead or dying. New York is not merely a monstrosity. It is a dying monstrosity and, except as a commercial nexus, its only appropriate form, is on the way to extinction. We have killed it ourselves, of course, by our stupidity and our greed, which is merely stupidity in a state of excitement.

The Big City is an invention. But it is not an invention like the alphabet or the number zero, whose utility is inexhaustible. It is more like gunpowder or the kerosene lamp, which are mortal. It began a long time ago, perhaps in Thebes or Babylon. It has had a fruitful, glorious career; and it has come to the end of that career in the choked, stinking, clamorous, and increasingly hideous streets of New York or Chicago. Men still love it, because they made it.

But not all men.

About thirty or forty years ago a few began to see the ugly handwriting on the dead, concrete wall. Not many; just a few. But these few were men and women with a unique ability to sense the future. There are specialized minds that can sense the future of the stock market; they understand money. There are specialized minds that can sense, often without being able to put it into words, the future of a gigantic invention like the Big City; they deal in ideas and feelings. These people do not *make* history; they merely feel it coming. They are, after the saints, the clearest-sighted people in the world, because their business requires them to deal with the nontransitory. They are artists, makers of permanent goods.

These people years ago settled in Westport, New City, New Hope, Woodstock. Without quite knowing what they were doing, they founded Exurbia. They fled the city because they could work better and (at that time) more economically in the country. But underneath this simple drive lay a vague prophetic consciousness that the Big City was accursed, accursed not only for them but, in time to come, to be accursed for all men and women.

They were numerous enough to found New York's Exurbias, but not numerous enough to settle and develop them. This was reserved (Mr. Spectorsky is perceptive on this point) for another class, a kindred class of semiartists, or quasi artists, or even pseudoartists. These are the Communica-

tors: commercial writers, TV and radio people, songwriters, advertising men, Broadway playwrights, comic-strip creators, illustrators, the manipulators of symbols, styles, slogans and popularizable ideas. To a limited extent these folk, for all their brashness, instability, commercial obsessions and questionable taste, have the same *kind* of spiritual antennae possessed by the creative artist. Just *because* they work with symbols, even if the symbols are often fake ones, they have a lucidity, a quickness of mind that is not so frequently the property of those who work with three-dimensional objects or with money. They are nervous, triggerish, energetic and — oddly enough — physically enduring, as they must be to survive Mr. McGinnis' railroad.

These people have a thousand weaknesses, but they also have one remarkable quality — the capacity, like their serener, abler cousins, the artists, to sense the future. Thus they knew, a little in advance of the rest of us, that the future included the gradual obsolescence, as living quarters, of the Big City which supported and will continue to support them economically.

The Communicators are the frontiersmen of the 20th Century. They have made the dizzy, necessary half-leap (for remember, their economic base still remains Megalopolis) into the wilderness of Exurbia. It does not matter that this is a tame wilderness of washing machines, golf clubs, croquet, bonded rye, and MG's. It is, as against New York, a genuine frontier in the sense that it requires a new kind of living if one is to survive.

The original pioneers were full of hopeful mixed-up dreams of adventure, material wealth, privacy and living near to Nature. For some these dreams were fulfilled; but all of them also encountered back-breaking toil, flood, drought, loneliness and mental starvation. Some did not have what it took; the others settled the country and forged a new way of life. Most of them did not live to enjoy the fruits of their labor, but their sons and grandsons did.

I believe firmly that the man in the gray flannel suit, the brief-case carrier, is an absurd figure only to the professional satirist, and sometimes to himself, his wife and his children. To the eye of the Muse of history he is no more absurd than Daniel Boone or Kit Carson seems to us today.

He, too, has a dream, a dream of trees and stars and green grass, of privacy, of ordered small-scale communal living. He has a vague vision of combining the philosophy of Henry Ford with that of Rousseau. He is having a hard time making that dream come true; and, because of the refractory nature of dreams, he is baffled, frustrated, often in despair. So were the other pioneers, whose experiences, including boredom, physical exhaustion, and lonesomeness, he is repeating in terms suitable to the mid-20th Century. But just as the original settlers smoothed, by their own laborious efforts, the path for their descendants, so the Exurban pioneer, himself perhaps a failure, is making it easier for the next generation. (That accounts for his almost feverish concern, so non-Megalopolitan, for the welfare of his children.)

His sons and daughters will inherit the good that will flow from the bankruptcy of the Big City. Daddy may kill himself to pay off the mortgage; but his progeny will own a mortgageless home. The motorized gimmicks that Daddy operates so clumsily they will handle with ease and efficiency. They will use the helicopters that will make the industrial wen of New York easy of access. And they will inevitably have worked out the four-day or even three-day work week that will finally make Exurbia viable.

I prefer to believe that the frictions Mr. Spectorsky so well describes are *ad interim* frictions, the sacrifice a frontiersman has to make in order to found a new culture. Boredom, excessive drinking, frenzied play, vulgar display, infidelity — these are not intrinsic to the Exurbanite, nor to the exurban situation. They are the growing pains, odd ones, I admit, that are inevitable whenever an old institution, like the City, is dying and a new one, the Exurbia of the 21st Century, is striving to be born.

So do not smile at us, at our chatter about "roots," at our fumbling gestures of do-it-yourself, at our silly status-competitions, at our shiny new small-town patriotism. We may be the most ludicrous frontiersmen in history. But we are blazing a trail and marking out new country. The 8:10 is our Conestoga, the electric hedge-clipper our ax, the portable sprayer our rifle. And make no mistake: we may complain, we may despair, we may go under — but we are not going back. We are little men confusedly engaged in something big, and we know it.

The American journey has not ended. America is never accomplished, America is always still to build; for men, as long as they are truly men, will dream of man's fulfillment. West is a country in the mind, and so eternal.

ARCHIBALD MACLEISH

67.

Unilateral Disarmament

The following selection is taken from a pamphlet, "Speak Truth to Power," published by the American Friends Service Committee in the spring of 1955. One of a series, the pamphlet argued the position that force was not the only answer to the threats posed to the nation by the Soviet Union, indeed that force was far from being the best answer. Instead, the pamphlet urged that the government and the American people consider unilateral peace moves including voluntary disarmament. The Quakers realized that the pamphlet probably would have no effect on government policy, which in fact it did not, but they hoped that its publication would inspire efforts to discover alternatives to a policy that they believed to be not only suicidal but also immoral. Portions of the pamphlet are reprinted here as reflecting an important although minority opinion of the time.

Source: *Speak Truth to Power: A Quaker Search for an Alternative to Violence,* Philadelphia, 1955.

THE CONTENT OF A NATIONAL NONVIOLENT POLICY

A GROWING PACIFIST MINORITY, and the gradual modifications of national policy that it produced, would . . . make an impact on the international scene. Our world is a dynamic world, with men and nations altering their habits, their attitudes, and their responses as the international climate shifts and changes. The pacifist wants to recognize this fact, and build policy around its existence. He suggests, therefore, that the more a minority could succeed in modifying belligerency and encouraging restraint, the more striking and unpredictable would be the resulting mutation in international relations. . . .

We . . . suggest that the more a nation focused on reconciling differences, the more creative would be the power and the life that would flow from it. A whole new dimension would be introduced into the world community just as elementary experiments have sometimes introduced whole new dimensions into the scientific community. Who could have predicted, for example, that Benjamin Franklin's early experiments with electricity would end by revolutionizing man's whole way of life?

It is a long jump from Franklin's kite to television, too long for the human imagination to have fully encompassed. Similarly, it is a long jump from our present expressions of international goodwill, such as the Fulbright program for student exchange, to its fullest possible expression in world affairs. Is this, also, too difficult for the imagination of our generation to encompass? We are certain only that its impact on the world would be fully as profound in the sphere of human relations as the impact of electricity has been in the sphere of science. Beyond that is speculation, but we can venture suggestions of the broad outlines of such a full policy of international goodwill.

1. *There would be revolutionary changes within the United States itself.* Since the nonviolent insight underlines the necessity of first attacking our own evils, it is clear that the American people would be obligated to move farther in overcoming racial discrimi-

nation and religious intolerance. We would insist on maximum freedom of thought and expression, as demanded by our democratic philosophy, and would not tolerate tendencies toward transforming the nation into a police state. We would be more sensitive to the deadening impact of our industrial life and to the inadequacy of prison systems, medical care, and housing. Instead of thinking of our democracy as something which is final and complete, and therefore belonging essentially to the past, we would think of it as a growing and developing vision, belonging essentially to the future.

We would know that it cannot be guarded behind a radar screen, but must be shared freely and dangerously with all men, whose contribution is also needed for the realization of the vision. We would discover again the wisdom of Jefferson, that error may be tolerated as long as truth remains free to combat it. Any nation which, in this fear-ridden age, had the courage to trust the democratic process instead of bartering democracy for the illusory security of an atomic stockpile would speak with undreamed power to enslaved men the world over.

2. *The United States would give its support to the great social revolutions, which are both a major problem and a major hope of our time.* Regardless of whether men strive to overthrow domination from without or outworn feudalism from within, their determination is to achieve new dignity and status as human beings and to banish the physical poverty that has so long condemned them to misery. They deserve the support of every domestic society, and they would receive the support of this country if it were freed from its preoccupation with defense and the military power struggle. If this took place, men who seek freedom would no longer conclude, as many already have, that the only source of support is from communist nations, and they would cease to be available for communist armies. American support, moreover, would make it more possi-

ble for these revolutions themselves to be nonviolent.

3. *The United States would devote its skills and resources to great programs of technical and economic assistance, carried on under United Nations auspices and with full participation in planning and administration by the receiving peoples.* The resources needed for these operations are so large that our own standard of living might be seriously affected, but the dividends would also be large. The mere fact of reducing the great economic imbalance between the United States and the poverty-stricken masses of Asia, Africa, and Latin America would itself remove one of the major sources of embitterment and strife. Our willingness to share our material blessings, without ulterior motives and to an extent well beyond our unused surpluses, would bring men to us as friends and cooperators, rather than alienate them as does present policy.

4. *The United States would get rid of its military establishment.* Various avenues might be taken to achieve this result. Many suggest that the most probable and most practical approach would be through the simple transfer of the security function to a world organization. The United Nations would assume the responsibility for defense and might well be converted in the process into a federal instrument in much the same manner as the thirteen American colonies substituted a federal government for the unsatisfactory Articles of Confederation.

Others less insistent on the importance of world federation suggest that disarmament would occur as the result of multilateral agreement: universal in character, enforceable in practice, and complete down to the level needed for internal policing. Both of these approaches are valid and both could be supported by the United States in the era about which we speculate, but in the last analysis a pacifist policy would require unilateral action if agreement could not be achieved. There is no escaping the necessity to be willing to act first ourselves if we are to have solid ground for getting others to act with us.

It will be said that for a nation to consider disarming alone in an armed world is madness; but the fact that obviously stares men in the face today is that *an armed world in this age is itself madness.* To refuse any longer to labor under the delusion that it is anything else is the beginning of common sense, as it is the counsel of divine wisdom. Moreover, it is quite possible that the Soviet Union, confronted with such a change in American behavior, might startle us with a new response. At the very least, the example of a people living without the burden of militarism and offering friendship to all, would call forth the impulses to freedom that exist in all men.

What might have happened, for example, if the remarkable East German uprising of June 1953 had had as its inspiration a United States free from involvement in the effort to rearm Western Germany and in the tragic perpetuation of an impossible division? As it was, the United States' position was a discouraging one. We welcomed the revolt, but could only stand idly by, unwilling to risk unleashing war, and yet unable to offer any other kind of encouragement. Moreover, we were so preoccupied with power concepts that one of the most striking aspects of the uprising was largely overlooked: *the fact that a group of Russian soldiers refused to fire on the unarmed and nonviolent demonstrators.* Not only were the demonstrators spared violence but a number of their grievances were recognized and corrected. How can this outcome be squared with the familiar argument that only naked power is respected by the Russians?

Nor must it be forgotten how this whole nonviolent era, about which we are speculating, would be brought about. Under our democratic philosophy . . . it would not be created by fiat, but as the result of insistence on reconciling measures by a gradually growing pacifist minority. The writers are convinced that this process in itself

would so change the climate of world opinion that no power on earth could oppose it effectively. The influence of growing programs of economic assistance, freed from the compulsions of strategy and carried forward by dedicated men and women through the operating agencies of the United Nations, would lift the heart of the world. Increasing support of the United Nations itself, as a world forum for peaceful settlement, universal in membership and inviolate of selfish national pressure, would create a new basis for an emerging world community of law. The earnest desire to negotiate differences, backed by a gradually increasing willingness to abandon our military posture, could open the way for the relaxation of tension and the achievement of disarmament. Nations which are at present hostile and threatening would be relieved of any reason for being hostile and threatening, and would face a world opinion so warmly approving of the United States that continued hostility would be difficult to maintain.

NONVIOLENT RESISTANCE

WE MUST, however, face the possibility that hatred has gone so far, and injustice penetrated so deeply, that even a revolutionary policy of peace could not prevent international aggression. A nation which had disarmed would not in that event abjectly surrender and let an invader run over and enslave it as is often alleged. On the contrary, it would have open to it possibilities of nonviolent resistance that offer more prospects of a creative and genuinely victorious outcome than is the case with violent resistance under modern conditions. It is the nation whose reliance is upon arms that now faces the bleakest prospect in the event of international aggression; for victory in any ensuing holocaust is clearly impossible for anyone. Both "victor" and "vanquished" would dwell together in a brutalized and devastated world in which the values of democratic civilization would have been largely swept away.

Nonviolent resistance, as has been demonstrated on a large scale in India and on a smaller scale in many other places, offers greater promise of confounding and overcoming an enemy without destroying our values or our world. While there are limits to the extent to which a program of nonviolent resistance can be spelled out for a nation which is quite unready to adopt it, and for a future situation whose character cannot be predicted, it is nevertheless possible to suggest the broad pattern that it would follow.

The first necessity is *noncooperation.* The population must resolutely refuse to carry out the orders of the invader. They would not run trains to transport troops. They would not operate factories to provide the invader with military supplies. They would not unload his ships. They would perform no services of any kind for him. At the same time, they would try through their words and their lives to show the meaning of a free and democratic society.

Second, the population must maintain *goodwill* toward the individual soldier of the invading forces. However difficult this is in practice, it is clear that the effective use of nonviolent resistance has always demanded that a clear distinction be drawn between hatred of an evil policy and respect for the human instrument who is caught up in its execution. Goodwill is the spiritual weapon of nonviolence just as civil disobedience is its physical weapon.

Finally, the population must be well enough disciplined to *refrain from individual acts of violence* no matter what the provocation. The whole success of the resistance depends on meeting the enemy on a level and in a manner against which he cannot retaliate effectively. He understands violence, and he is prepared to cope with it ruthlessly and drastically. He must be given no excuse to do so.

Courtesy, Lewis, "Milwaukee Journal"

"Now if they can come down as a team, too," from a "Milwaukee Journal" cartoon by Lewis

IN SUMMARY, it is certain that whatever circumstances exist in a specific instance, any campaign of nonviolent resistance will include these three elements of noncooperation, goodwill, and nonviolence. The technique is effective because it undermines the morale of the enemy and removes his will to conquer. When a soldier is received kindly, it is hard for him to continue to hate. When he faces no threat, it is hard for him to continue to kill. Moreover, he has no way to compel cooperation when faced with civil disobedience, and without cooperation the enemy will find his existence difficult indeed.

All of this is not to suggest that everything would proceed in idyllic fashion and that no suffering would occur in a nonviolent resistance campaign. We have tried to make it clear that readiness to accept suffering — rather than inflict it on others — is the essence of the nonviolent life and that we must be prepared if called upon to pay the ultimate price. Obviously, if men are willing to spend billions of treasure and countless lives in war, they cannot dismiss the case for nonviolence by saying that in a nonviolent struggle people might be killed! It is equally clear that where commitment and the readiness to sacrifice are lacking, nonviolent resistance cannot be effective.

On the contrary, it demands greater discipline, more arduous training, and more courage than its violent counterpart. Without preparation, nonviolent resistance will fail just as surely as an untrained and undisciplined army would fail in war. Not even a beginning can be made in assessing the potential of nonviolent resistance as a means of national defense until a people ready to pour billions into military preparations are prepared to put some effort into research and training of a different nature. This in turn can happen only as we make a new commitment to practice peace and recognize that the freedom worth saving is the freedom of the spirit, which can neither be protected by guns nor enslaved by tyrants.

Such is the program we would chart for the individual and for the state of which he is a part. We have not denied that it involves risk, but no policy can be formulated that does not involve risk. We have not suggested it will be easy, but only that no policy that aims at achieving peace can be easy. Finally, we have made no sweeping claims that it would work, but only that it appears to us more workable and more relevant than the barren doctrines of violence that now enslave us. We believe that it merits the consideration of thoughtful men.

68.

Dwight D. Eisenhower: Open Skies Proposal to Russia

In July 1955 President Eisenhower attended a "summit meeting" at Geneva, Switzerland, with the leaders of Britain, France, and the Soviet Union. Foremost among the issues discussed was disarmament, particularly a ban on future production of nuclear weapons. Little of value was accomplished at the meeting apart from a general easing of tensions between East and West, but at the close of the sessions Eisenhower submitted what has been called the "Open Skies" proposal as a means toward military cutback and nuclear control. Following is the text of the President's message of July 21.

Source: *Bulletin*, August 1, 1955, pp. 173-174.

DISARMAMENT IS ONE of the most important subjects on our agenda. It is also extremely difficult. In recent years the scientists have discovered methods of making weapons many, many times more destructive of opposing armed forces — but also of homes and industries and lives — than ever known or even imagined before. These same scientific discoveries have made much more complex the problems of limitation and control and reduction of armament.

After our victory as allies in World War II, my country rapidly disarmed. Within a few years our armament was at a very low level. Then events occurred beyond our borders which caused us to realize that we had disarmed too much. For our own security and to safeguard peace we needed greater strength. Therefore we proceeded to rearm and to associate with others in a partnership for peace and for mutual security.

The American people are determined to maintain and, if necessary, increase thi armed strength for as long a period as is necessary to safeguard peace and to maintain our security.

But we know that a mutually dependable system for less armament on the part of all nations would be a better way to safeguard peace and to maintain our security. It would ease the fears of war in the anxious hearts of people everywhere. It would lighten the burdens upon the backs of the people. It would make it possible for every nation, great and small, developed and less developed, to advance the standards of living of its people, to attain better food and clothing and shelter, more of education and larger enjoyment of life.

Therefore the United States government is prepared to enter into a sound and reliable agreement making possible the reduction of armament. I have directed that an intensive and thorough study of this subject be made within our own government. From these studies, which are continuing, a very important principle is emerging. . . .

No sound and reliable agreement can be made unless it is completely covered by an inspection and reporting system adequate to support every portion of the agreement. The lessons of history teach us that disarmament agreements without adequate reciprocal inspection increase the dangers of war and do not brighten the prospects of peace. Thus it is my view that the priority attention of our combined study of disarmament should be upon the subject of inspection and reporting.

Questions suggest themselves.

How effective an inspection system can be designed which would be mutually and reciprocally acceptable within our countries and the other nations of the world? How would such a system operate? What could it accomplish? Is certainty against surprise aggression attainable by inspection? Could violations be discovered promptly, and effectively counteracted?

We have not as yet been able to discover any scientific or other inspection method which would make certain of the elimination of nuclear weapons. So far as we are aware, no other nation has made such a discovery. Our study of this problem is continuing. We have not as yet been able to discover any accounting or other inspection method of being certain of the true budgetary facts of total expenditures for armament. Our study of this problem is continuing. We by no means exclude the possibility of finding useful checks in these fields.

As you can see from these statements, it is our impression that many past proposals of disarmament are more sweeping than can be insured by effective inspection.

Gentlemen, since I have been working on this memorandum to present to this conference, I have been searching my heart and mind for something that I could say here that could convince everyone of the great sincerity of the United States in approaching this problem of disarmament. I should address myself for a moment principally to the delegates from the Soviet Union, because our two great countries admittedly possess new and terrible weapons in quantities which do give rise in other parts of the world, or reciprocally, to the fears and dangers of surprise attack.

I propose, therefore, that we take a practical step, that we begin an arrangement, very quickly, as between ourselves — immediately. These steps would include:

To give to each other a complete blueprint of our military establishments, from beginning to end, from one end of our countries to the other; lay out the establishments and provide the blueprints to each other.

Next, to provide within our countries facilities for aerial photography to the other country — we to provide you the facilities within our country, ample facilities for aerial reconnaissance, where you can make all the pictures you choose and take them to your own country to study; you to provide exactly the same facilities for us and we to make these examinations — and by this step to convince the world that we are providing as between ourselves against the possibility of great surprise attack, thus lessening danger and relaxing tension. Likewise, we will make more easily attainable a comprehensive and effective system of inspection and disarmament, because what I propose, I assure you, would be but a beginning.

Now, from my statements, I believe you will anticipate my suggestion. It is that we instruct our representatives in the Subcommittee on Disarmament, in discharge of their mandate from the United Nations, to give priority effort to the study of inspection and reporting. Such a study could well include a step-by-step testing of inspection and reporting methods.

The United States is ready to proceed in the study and testing of a reliable system of inspections and reporting and, when that system is proved, then to reduce armaments with all others to the extent that the system will provide assured results. The successful working out of such a system would do much to develop the mutual confidence which will open wide the avenues of progress for all our peoples.

The quest for peace is the statesman's most exacting duty. Security of the nation entrusted to his care is his greatest responsibility. Practical progress to lasting peace is his fondest hope. Yet, in pursuit of his hope, he must not betray the trust placed in him as guardian of the people's security. A sound peace — with security, justice, well-being, and freedom for the people of the world — *can* be achieved, but only by patiently and thoughtfully following a hard and sure and tested road.

69.

Arthur Miller: The American Theater

In the following article, written primarily for non-New Yorkers, playwright Arthur Miller attempted to define "the American Theater" and to describe its spirit and makeup and the people who worked in it. For Miller, writing in 1955, the theater in America was still Broadway — and all that the word conjures up. Miller conceded that Broadway as a cultural and financial institution was not what it had been thirty years before, and he expressed the hope that the diffusion of legitimate theater throughout the country would have fruitful results in the years to come. But he emphasized the importance of one single theatrical center that would be the final test of the excellence and viability of any work of dramatic art.

Source: *Holiday*, January 1955.

THE AMERICAN THEATER occupies five side streets, Forty-Fourth to Forty-Ninth, between Eighth Avenue and Broadway, with a few additional theaters to the north and south and across Broadway. In these thirty-two buildings every new play in the United States starts its life and ends it. There will undoubtedly be many objections to this statement — you cannot say anything about our theater without fear of contradiction — and demurrers will come from professors of drama, stock-company directors, and little-theater people in New York, Texas, California and elsewhere who will claim that Broadway is not the United States and that much theatrical production is going on in other places. I agree, and repeat only that with practically no exceptions, the *new* American plays originate on Broadway. I would add that I wish they didn't, but they do. The American theater is five blocks long, by about one and a half blocks wide.

It would seem a simple matter to characterize so limited an area, but I write this with the certainty that whatever I say will appear not only new and strange to many theater people but utterly untrue. And this is because the man or woman whose tapping shoes you hear from the second-story dance studio over the delicatessen on Forty-Sixth Street is in the theater, the ballet girl hurrying to rehearsal in her polo coat with a copy of Rimbaud in her pocket is in the theater, the peasant-faced Irish stagehand sunning himself on the sidewalk with a Racing Form in his hand is in the theater, the slow-staring, bald-headed ticket broker blinking out through his agency window is in the theater, the wealthy, Park Avenue-born producer is in the theater and his cigar-smoking colleague from the West Bronx is in the theater.

In the audience itself, though the bulk of it is of the middle class, there is no uniformity either. There will be the businessman in town from Duluth sitting beside Marlene Dietrich whom he will probably not recognize and behind them two esthetes from Harvard. The word theater means different things to different groups. To some its very pinnacle is *South Pacific,* which is despised by the esthetes, who in turn cherish a wispy fantasy whose meaning escapes the Duluth man. There is a vast group of people for whom the theater means nothing but amusement, and amusement means a musical or light comedy; and there are others who reserve their greatest enthusiasm for heavy dramas that they can chew on.

The actors, directors and writers themselves are just as varied. There are playwrights who are as illiterate as high-school boys, and there are playwrights like Maxwell Anderson, who have spent a good deal of their lives studying the Elizabethan drama and attempting to re-create its mood and luxuriance on Broadway. There are fine actors who are universally admired but who have absolutely no theory of acting and there are other actors, equally good or equally bad, who have spent years studying the history of acting, taking voice lessons and learning how to dance in order to walk more gracefully.

The theater, obviously, is an entirely different animal to each of these groups. As for myself, I cannot pretend to any Olympian viewpoint about it either. I believe there is a confusion in many minds between Show Business and the Theater. I belong to the Theater, which happens at the moment to be in a bad way, but since this word, when capitalized, usually implies something uplifting and boring, I must add that the rarely seen but very real Theater is the most engrossing theater of all; and when it isn't it is nothing. I make the distinction so that the reader will be warned where my prejudice lies and discount accordingly.

The "glamour of the theater," which is and always will be its most powerful attraction, is a subject of daily reporting by almost every newspaper, gossip columnist, and radio station. Every year, around the first cool days of fall, the illustrated sections of the press and the picture magazines and newsreels run the familiar photographs of the limousines gliding up to the lighted marquees, the taxis and cars pressing into Forty-Fourth Street for the opening of some musical or drama, the inevitable montage of Sardi's restaurant at dinnertime and so on. For anyone who has made the slightest mark in this occupation there is a line of type waiting when he so much as pays his rent on time. Soon after *Death of a Salesman* opened, it was reported that I was a millionaire, which was pleasant news, if not true, and that despite my new affluence I still rode the subways. I keep wondering who was watching me going through the turnstiles. And the importance of this news still escapes me.

In fact, while everybody in the business is worried about its future — and if there is a heart of uncertainty in the country its loudest beat may be heard on these five blocks — to read the columns and the usual sources of theatrical information you would think it was all a continuous carnival of divorce, practical jokes, hilarious wit, elopements and sudden acquisition of enormous wealth.

But there is evidently no way of glamorizing the often inspiring and heart-lifting experiences of the work itself, a kind of labor that began in the Western world about three thousand years ago, and which has provided some of the most powerful insights we possess into the way men think and feel.

The net result of this image of our theater, the carnival image, is that the out-of-towner strolling these streets may quickly sense that he has been bilked. He will discover, especially if he arrives in midday, that the theater buildings themselves are tawdry-looking, and may well be disillusioned when he sees that some of the marquees do not have even the electrically lit signs of his home movie house — only temporary cardboards painted with the title of the show within. When he ventures into the outer lobby he will perhaps be shocked to discover that a seat costs six — or even eight — dollars and, if the show is a hit, that he won't get a ticket for six months or a year unless he pays a scalper twenty-five to a hundred dollars. If it is not a hit, and he buys a ticket legitimately, he may learn that he could have bought two for the price

of one; and by the time he gets inside for the performance, some of the glamour of it all may have worn a bit thin.

Once inside, however, our visitor may find certain compensations. He may recognize very important people, from statesmen to movie stars, sitting nearby, whom he would not see in the home-town movie house. He will notice a certain dressed-up air about people, a few even wearing evening clothes. There are ushers to show him to his seat, and there is a program, and possibly a little more surprising is the coat-check man waiting as he passes through the outer door. There is still a vestigial ceremony about playgoing from which one may derive a sense of self-importance if not careful, and it all may lead our visitor to feel that he is, indeed, among ladies and gentlemen.

Then, as the lights go down and the curtain rises, our visitor may feel a certain strange tension, an expectancy, and an intense curiosity that he never knew in a theater before. Instead of the enormity of the movie image before which he could sit back and relax, he is confronted by human beings in life-size, and since their voices do not roar out at him from a single point to which his ear may tune in once and then relax, he must pay more attention, his eyes must rove over a thirty-foot expanse; he must, in other words, *discover*. And if there happens to be something real up there, something human, something true, our visitor may come away with a new feeling in his heart, a sense of having been a part of something quite extraordinary and even beautiful. Unlike the movies, unlike television, he may feel he has been present at an *occasion*. For outside this theater, no one in the world heard what he heard or saw what he saw this night. I know that, for myself, there is nothing so immediate, so actual as an excellent performance of an excellent play. I have never known the smell of sweat in a movie house. I have known it in the theater — and they are also air-conditioned. Nor have I known in a movie house the kind of audience unity that occasionally is created in the theater, an air of oneness among strangers that is possible in only one other gathering place — a church.

Nevertheless, by every account our theater is a vanishing institution. We have some thirty-two houses going today in New York as against forty or more ten years ago, and between seventy and eighty in the twenties. I could weave you such a tapestry of evil omens as to make it a closed case that we will have no theater in America in two decades. What I should like to do instead, however, is to wonder aloud, as it were, why it is that each year thousands of aspiring actors, directors and playwrights continue to press into these five blocks from every corner of the country when they know, or learn very quickly, that 90 per cent of the professional actors are normally unemployed, that most of the producers are dead broke or within three cigars of being broke, and that to become a director of a Broadway show one must be prepared to gamble five to ten to fifteen years of one's life. And yet, on all the trains they keep coming, aspiring actors and eager audiences both.

As for the aspiring actors, I will not pretend to hunt for an answer, because I know it. It is simply that there are always certain persons who are born without all their marbles. Even so, the full-blown actors are merely the completed types of the secret actors who are called producers, backers, directors, yes, and playwrights. The rest of us would have been actors had we had the talent, or a left and right foot instead of two left ones, or straight teeth, or self-assurance. The actor himself is the lunacy in full profusion — the lunacy which in the others is partially concealed.

All over the country there are nine-year-old girls, for instance, who are walking around the house like my daughter is at this very moment, in high-heeled shoes with the lace tablecloth trailing from their shoulders. If mine doesn't recover before she is sixteen she will wake up one morning and something will click inside her head and she will go and hang around some producer's office, and if he talks to her, or just asks her what time it is, she may well be doomed for life.

The five blocks, therefore, are unlike any other five blocks in the United States, if only because here so many grown people are walking around trailing the old lace tablecloth from their shoulders.

If you know how to look you will find them waiting on you in Schrafft's, or behind the orange-drink counter at Nedick's. As a matter of fact, I have got so attuned to a certain look in their eyes that I can sometimes spot them on Sixth Avenue, which is not in the theater district. I was passing a truck being loaded there one day when I noticed a boy, unshaven, his hair uncombed, wearing paratroop boots; he was pitching boxes into the truck. And he looked at me, just a glance, and I thought to myself that he must be an actor. And about three days later I was sitting in my producer's office interviewing actors for *The Crucible,* when in he walked. Characteristically, he did not remember seeing me before — actors rarely do, since they are not looking at anyone but rather are being looked *at.* When asked the usual questions about his experience he just shrugged, and when asked if he wanted to read for us he shrugged again, quite as though the questions were impertinent when addressed to a great artist, and I knew then why I tabbed him for an actor. It was the time when all the young actors were being Marlon Brando. He was being Marlon Brando even when loading the truck, for a real truck driver would never show up for work looking so unkempt.

The blessed blindness of actors to everything around them, their intense preoccupation with themselves, is the basic characteristic of all Broadway, and underlies most of its troubles, which, in another industry, would have been solved long ago. But since it is glamour which brings the young to Broadway, as well as the audience, it cannot be so quickly dismissed. The fact is, it exists. But it is not the glamour you are probably thinking of.

The time is gone when the Great Producer kept four or five Great Stars in ten-room apartments on Park Avenue, and they waited in their gilded cages for days and weeks for the Impresario to call for them — for without him they were forbidden to be seen in public lest they lose their "distance," their altitude above the common things of life. The time is gone when the leading lady dared not arrive at the theater in anything but a limousine with chauffeur and lap robe, while a line of stovepipe-hatted men waited in the stage-door alley with flowers in their manicured hands. There are a few hangovers, of course, and I remember a show in Boston a few years ago whose leading lady, an hour before curtaintime, phoned the producer to say she was ill and could not play. The poor man was desperate, but there was an old-time doorman in that theater who happened to be near the phone and he said, "Get a limousine and a chauffeur." The producer, a contemporary type who was as familiar with gallantry as any other businessman, mastered his uncertainty and hired a car and chauffeur and sent a mass of roses to the lady's hotel room. Her fever vanished in roughly four minutes and she played better than she ever had, and I must confess I couldn't blame her for wanting the glamour even if she had had to make it herself.

But leading ladies, nowadays, arrive in a taxi, and a lot of them come in by bus or subway.

I have been around only ten years or so and I never knew the kind of glamour that evidently existed. But a few years ago I had occasion to visit John Golden in his office, and I saw then that there was, in fact, a kind of bravado about being in the theater, a declaration of war against all ordinariness that I can find no more.

The average theatrical producer's office today consists mainly of a telephone, a girl to answer it, an outer room for actors to wait in, and an inner room with a window for the producer to stare out of when he has nothing to produce.

John Golden's office is different. It rests on top of the St. James Theater; you rise in a private elevator, and come out in a dark, paper-cluttered reception room where an elderly and very wise lady bars you — with the help of a little gate — from entry. You know at once that behind her is not merely a man, but a Presence.

In his office the walls are painted with smoke. They are very dark and covered with hundreds of photographs, plaques, statuettes, hanging things and jutting things of gold, silver and shiny brass. There is an Oriental rug on the floor, an ornate desk at the distant end of the room, and there sits John Golden, who is now eighty years old. Behind him stands an imposing ascent of bookshelves filled with leather-bound plays he has produced. In a smaller adjoining room is a barber chair where his hair is cut, his beard shaved, and, I presume, his shoes shined. The windows are covered with drapes and obstructing statuary, because when this office was created, the man who worked in it had no time to look out into the street.

It was a time when the railroads were freighting out one after another of his productions, winter and summer, to all sections of the country. It was a time when, unlike now, important performers and even playwrights were kept on long-term contracts when a producer owned his own theater and used his own money and was therefore not an accountant, nor even a businessman, but an impresario. In short, it was the time before the masses had left the theater for the new movies, and the theater was the main source of American popular entertainment. This office is now a kind of museum. There were once many like it, and many men like John Golden.

Their counterparts, the reflected images of Ziegfeld, Frohman, Belasco and the others, appeared only later in Hollywood, for the masses are needed to create impresarios, or more precisely, a lucrative mass market. In Golden's office I saw the genesis of so much we have come to associate with Hollywood: the stars under long-term contract, the planning of one production after another instead of the present one-shot Broadway practice, the sense of permanence and even security. None of these are part of Broadway now and they appear in their afterglow above the St. James; for it is not the masses we serve any more, not the "American People," but a fraction of one class — the more or less better-educated people, or the people aspiring to culture.

Golden's eyes blazed with pleasure as he talked of plays long since gone, like *Turn to the Right* and *Lightnin'* and others I remember my father raving about when I was a boy, and finally he sat back and mused about playwriting.

"You fellows have a much harder time," he said, "much harder than in the old days; nowadays every show has to seem new and original. But in the old days, you know, we had what you might call favorite scenes. There was the scene where the mother puts a candle on the window sill while she waits for her long-lost boy to come home. They loved that scene. We put that scene in one play after another. You can't do things like that any more. The audience is too smart now. They're more educated, I suppose, and sophisticated. Of course it was all sentimental, I guess, but they were good shows."

He was right, of course, except you *can* do that now; the movies have been doing it for thirty or forty years and now television doing it all over again. I remember a friend who had worked in Hollywood writing a picture. The producer called him in with a bright new idea for a scene to be inserted in the script. My friend listened and was amazed. "But just last month you released a picture with that same scene in it," he reminded the producer.

"Sure," said the producer, "and didn't it go great?"

THE GOLDEN SPECIES OF GLAMOUR is gone with the masses; it went with the big money to Hollywood, and now it is creating itself all over again in television. The present-day actors and directors would probably seem tame and dull to their counterparts of thirty and forty years ago. David Belasco, for instance, had even convinced himself that his was a glamorous profession, and took to dressing in black like a priest — the high priest of the theater — and turned his collar around to prove it. He carried on as no contemporary director would dare to do. Toward the last days of rehearsal, when he wanted some wooden but very beautiful leading lady to break down and weep, he would take out a watch, the watch he had been displaying for weeks as the one his mother gave him on her deathbed, and smash it on the stage floor in a high dudgeon, thus frightening the actress to tears and making her putty in his hands. It need hardly be added that he kept a large supply of these watches, each worth one dollar.

The traditional idea of the actor with his haughty stance, his peaked eyebrows, elegant speech, artistic temperament and a necessary disdain for all that was common and plain, has long since disappeared. Now they are all trying to appear as ordinary as your Uncle Max. A group of actors sitting at a bar these days could easily be mistaken for delegates to a convention of white-collar people. They are more likely, upon landing in a hit show, to hurry over to the offices of a tax consultant than to rush out and buy a new Jaguar. For a few years after the war a certain amount of effort was put into aging their dungarees and wearing turtleneck sweaters and some of them stopped combing their hair, like the boy I noticed loading the truck. But you don't get Marlon Brando's talent by avoiding a bath, and gradually this fad has vanished. There are more "colorful" personalities up here in the tiny Connecticut village where I spend summers than you will find on all Broadway. The only real showman I know of is Joshua Logan, who can throw a party for a hundred people in his Park Avenue apartment and make it appear a normal evening. Logan is the only director I can name who would dare to knock a stage apart and build into it a real swimming pool, as he did for the musical *Wish You Were Here,* and can still talk about the theater with the open, full-blown excitement of one who has no reservations about it. The other directors, at least the half dozen I know — and there are not many more — are more likely to be as deadly serious as any atomic physicist, and equally worried.

There is a special aura about the theater, nevertheless, a glamour, too, but it has little connection with the publicity that seeks to create it. There is undoubtedly as much sexual fooling around as there is in the refrigerator business, but I doubt if there is much more. The notion of theatrical immorality began when actors were socially inferior by common consent; but now a Winnifred Cushing (of the Boston Cushings), the loose woman in *Death of a Salesman,* hurries home to her mother after each show.

NOT THAT IT IS AN ORDINARY LIFE. There is still nothing quite like it, if only because of the fanaticism with which so many respond to its lure. One cannot sit in a producer's office day after day interviewing actors for a play without being struck by their insistence that they belong in the theater and intend to make their lives in it. In the outer reception rooms of any producer's office at casting time is a cross section of a hundred small towns and big cities, the sons and daughters of the rich families and of the middle-class families and of families from the wrong side of the tracks. One feels, on meeting a youngster from a way-station town or a New Mexico ranch, that the spores of this poor theater must still possess vitality to have flown so far and rooted so deep. It is pathetic, it is saddening, but a thing is only dead when nobody wants it, and they do want it desperately. It is nothing unusual to tell a girl who has come to a casting office that she looks too respectable for the part, and to be greeted by her an hour later dressed in a slinky black dress, spike heels, outlandishly overdone make-up and blond dye in her hair that has hardly had time to dry. One of our best-known actresses had her bowlegs broken in order to appear as she thought she must on the stage, and there is an actor who did the same to his knees in order to play Hamlet in tights.

There is, it must be admitted, an egotism in this that can neither be measured nor sometimes even stomached, but at casting time, when one spends hour after hour in the presence of human beings with so powerful a conviction and so great a desire to be heard and seen and judged as artists, the thing begins to surpass mere egotism and assumes the proportion of a cause, a belief, a mission. And when such sacrifices are made in its name one must begin to wonder at the circumstances that have reduced it to its present chaos. It might be helpful to take a look at how the whole thing is organized — or disorganized.

EVERYTHING BEGINS WITH A SCRIPT. I must add right off that in the old mass theater that came to an end somewhere in the late Twenties, when the movies took over, the script was as often as not a botch of stolen scenes, off-the-cuff inventions of the producer or director, or simply pasted-together situations designed for some leading player. The audience today, however, demands more, and so the script has become the Holy Grail for which a producer dreams, prays, and lives every day of his life. It being so valuable, and so difficult to write, it is leased by the author on a royalty basis and never sold outright. He receives, I am happy to report, roughly ten per cent of the gross receipts, or between two and three thousand dollars a week if he has a hit. (I would add that he resolves not to change his standard of living but he has a wife, and that is that.)

Three or four times a year the playwrights have a meeting of the Dramatists Guild, their union, in a private dining room of the St. Regis Hotel. Moss Hart, the author of *Climate of Eden* and, with George Kaufman, of a string of successes like *The Man Who Came to Dinner* and *You Can't Take it With You*, is the current president of the Guild. There is probably more money represented here than at most union luncheons, the only trouble being that with a few exceptions none of the playwrights has any assets; that is, you can't write a hit every time so the three thousand a week begins to look smaller and smaller when it is averaged out over a period of unfruitful years. Oscar Hammerstein, another Guild member, put an ad in *Variety* after his *South Pacific* opened, listing a dozen or so of his failures that everyone had forgotten, and at the bottom of the page repeated the legend of show business, "I did it before and I can do it again."

Between the turtle soup and the veal scallopine, various issues are discussed, all of which are usually impossible to solve, and the luncheons roll by and we know that our profession is on the edge of an abyss because the theater is contracting; and we all go home to write our plays. Occasionally we meet with a group of producers, and Max Gordon can usually be relied on to

demand the floor; and red in the face, full of his wonderful fight, he will cut to the heart of the problem by shouting at the playwrights, "The producers are starving, you hear me? Starving!" Leland Hayward, who has scraped by on *South Pacific, Mister Roberts,* and other such titbits, will accuse me of making too much money, and Herman Shumlin, the producer of *Little Foxes, Children's Hour, Watch on the Rhine,* will solemnly avow that he is leaving the business forever unless we writers cut our royalties; and then we all go home. Once the late Lee Shubert came with the others to discuss the problems of the theater, and when he was asked if he would reduce the rentals of his many theaters, since the playwrights were willing to reduce their royalties, he looked as though the butter was, indeed, melting in his mouth, so he didn't open it. And we all went home again.

There are seemingly hundreds of producers, but actually only fifteen or twenty go on year after year. Few are wealthy, and money is usually promoted or lured out of any crack where it can be found. It is a common, although not universal, practice to hold a gathering of potential backers before whom either the playwright or the director reads the script. Established producers regard this as beneath their dignity, but some don't, or can't afford to. These readings usually take place either on Park Avenue or on swank Beekman Place, for some reason, and while I never attended one, I have known many playwrights who have, but never heard of one dollar being raised in that way.

Script in hand, then, and money either raised or on its way — usually in amounts under five hundred dollars per backer — the producer hires a director, also on a percentage with a fee in advance, and a scene designer; the set is sketched, approved, and ordered built. Casting begins. While the author sits home revising his script — for some reason no script can be produced as the author wrote it — agents are apprised of the kinds of parts to be filled, and in the producer's reception room next morning all hell breaks loose.

The basis upon which actors are hired or not hired is sometimes quite sound; for example, they may have been seen recently in a part which leads the director to believe they are right for the new role; but quite as often a horde of applicants is waiting beyond the door of the producer's private office and neither he nor the director nor the author has the slightest knowledge of any of them. It is at this point that things become painful, for the strange actor sits before them, so nervous and frightened that he either starts talking and can't stop, and sometimes *says* he can't stop, or is unable to say anything at all and says *that*. During the casting of one of my plays there entered a middle-aged woman who was so frightened she suddenly started to sing. The play being no musical, this was slightly beside the point, but the producer, the director and myself, feeling so guilty ourselves, sat there and heard her through.

To further complicate matters there is each year the actor or actress who suddenly becomes what they call "hot." A hot performer is one not yet well-known, but who, for some mysterious reason, is generally conceded to be a coming star. It is possible, naturally, that a hot performer really has talent, but it is equally possible, and much more likely, that she or he is not a whit more attractive, or more talented than a hundred others. Nevertheless, there comes a morning when every producer in these five blocks — some of them with parts the performer could never play — simply has to have him or her. Next season, of course, nobody hears about the new star and it starts all over again with somebody else.

All that is chancy in life, all that is fortuitous, is magnified to the bursting point at casting time; and that, I suspect is one of the attractions of this whole affair, for it makes the ultimate winning of a part so much more zesty. It is also, to many actors, a most degrading process and more and more of them refuse to submit to these interviews until after the most delicate advances of friendship and hospitality are made to them. And their use of agents as intermediaries is often an attempt to soften the awkwardness of their applying for work.

The theatrical agents, in keeping with the unpredictable lunacy of the business, may be great corporations like the Music Corporation of America, which has an entire building on Madison Avenue, and will sell you anything from a tap dancer to a movie star, a symphony orchestra, saxophonists, crooners, scene designers, actors and playwrights, to a movie script complete with cast; or they may be like Jane Broder, who works alone and can spread out her arms and touch both walls of her office. They may even be like Carl Cowl who lives around the corner from me in Brooklyn. Carl is an ex-seaman who still ships out when he has no likely scripts on hand to sell, and when things get too nerve-racking he stays up all night playing Mozart on his flute. MCA has antique desks, English 18th Century prints, old broken antique clocks and inoperative antique barometers hanging on its paneled walls, but Carl Cowl had a hole in his floor that the cat got into and when he finally got the landlord to repair it he was happy and sat down to play his flute again; but he heard meowing, and they had to rip the floor open again to let out the cat. Still, Carl is not incapable of landing a hit play and neither more nor less likely than MCA to get it produced, and that is another handicraft aspect of this much publicized small business, a quality of opportunity which keeps people coming into it. The fact is that theatrical agents do not sell anyone or anything in the way one sells merchandise. Their existence is mainly due to the need theater people have for a home, some semblance of order in their lives, some sense of being wanted during the long periods when they have nothing to do. To have an agent is to have a kind of reassurance that you exist. The actor is hired, however, mainly because he is wanted for the role.

By intuition, then, by rumor, on the recommendation of an agent — usually heartfelt; out of sheer exhaustion, and upsurge of sudden hope or what not, several candidates for each role are selected in the office of the producer, and are called for readings on the stage of a theater.

It is here that the still unsolved mystery begins, the mystery of what makes a stage performer. There are persons who, in an office, seem exciting candidates for a role, but as soon as they step onto a stage the observers out front — if they are experienced — know that the blessing was not given them. For myself, I know it when, regardless of how well the actor is reading, my eyes begin to wander up to the brick wall back of the stage. Conversely, there are many who make little impression in an office, but once on the stage it is impossible to take one's attention from them. It is neither a question of technique nor ability, I think, but some quality of surprise inherent in the person.

For instance, when we were searching for a woman to play Linda, the mother in *Death of a Salesman,* a lady came in whom we all knew but could never imagine in the part. We needed a woman who looked as though she had lived in a house dress all her life, even somewhat coarse and certainly less than brilliant. Mildred Dunnock insisted she was that woman, but she was frail, delicate, not long ago a teacher in a girl's college, and a cultivated citizen who probably would not be out of place in a cabinet post. We told her this, in effect, and she understood, and left.

And the next day the line of women formed again in the wings and suddenly there was Milly again. Now she had pad-

ded herself from neck to hemline to look a bit bigger, and for a moment none of us recognized her, and she read again. As soon as she spoke we started to laugh at her ruse; but we saw, too, that she *was* a little more worn now, and seemed less well-maintained, and while she was not quite ordinary she reminded you of women who were. But we all agreed, when she was finished reading, that she was not right, and she left.

Next day she was there again in another getup and the next and the next, and each day she agreed with us that she was wrong; and to make a long story short when it came time to make the final selection it had to be Milly and she turned out to be magnificent. But in this case we had known her work; there was no doubt that she was an excellent actress. The number of talented applicants who are turned down because they are unknown is very large. Such is the crap-shooting chanciness of the business, its chaos, and part of its charm. In a world where one's fate so often seems machined and standardized, and unlikely to suddenly change, these five blocks are like a stockade inside which are people who insist that the unexpected, the sudden chance, must survive. And to experience it they keep coming on all the trains.

But to understand its apparently deathless lure for so many it is necessary, finally, to have participated in the first production of a new play. When a director takes his place at the beaten-up wooden table placed at the edge of the stage, and the cast for the first time sit before him in a semicircle, and he gives the nod to the actor who has the opening lines, the world seems to be filling with a kind of hope, a kind of regeneration that, at the time, anyway, makes all the sacrifices worthwhile.

The production of a new play, I have often thought, is like another chance in life, a chance to emerge cleansed of one's imperfections. Here, as when one was very young, it seems possible again to attain even greatness, or happiness, or some otherwise unattainable joy. And when production never loses that air of hope through all its three-and-a-half-week rehearsal period, one feels alive as at no other imaginable occasion. At such a time, it seems to all concerned that the very heart of life's mystery is what must be penetrated. They watch the director and each other and they listen with the avid attention of deaf mutes who have suddenly learned to speak and hear. Above their heads there begins to form a tantalizing sort of cloud, a question, a challenge to penetrate the mystery of why men move and speak and act.

It is a kind of glamour that can never be reported in a newspaper column, and yet it is the center of all the lure theater has. It is a kind of soul-testing that ordinary people rarely experience except in the greatest emergencies. The actor who has always regarded himself as a strong spirit discovers now that his vaunted power somehow sounds querulous, and he must look within himself to find his strength. The actress who has made her way on her charm discovers that she appears not charming so much as shallow now, and must evaluate herself all over again, and create anew what she always took for granted. And the great performers are merely those who have been able to face themselves without remorse.

In the production of a good play with a good cast and a knowing director a kind of banding-together occurs; there is formed a fraternity whose members share a mutual sense of destiny. In these five blocks, where the rapping of the tap-dancer's feet and the bawling of the phonographs in the record-shop doorways mix with the roar of the Broadway traffic; where the lonely, the perverted, and the lost wander like the souls in Dante's hell and the life of the spirit seems impossible, there are still little circles of actors in the dead silence of empty theaters,

with a director in their center, and a new creation of life taking place.

There are always certain moments in such rehearsals, moments of such wonder that the memory of them serves to further entrap all who witness them into this most insecure of all professions. Remembering such moments the resolution to leave and get a "real" job vanishes and they are hooked again.

I think of Lee Cobb, the greatest dramatic actor I ever saw, when he was creating the role of Willy Loman in *Death of a Salesman*. When I hear people scoffing at actors as mere exhibitionists, when I hear them ask why there must be a theater if it cannot support itself as any business must, when I myself grow sick and weary of the endless waste and the many travesties of this most abused of all arts, I think then of Lee Cobb making that role and I know that the theater can yet be one of the chief glories of mankind.

He sat for days on the stage like a great lump, a sick seal, a mourning walrus. When it came his time to speak lines, he whispered meaninglessly. Kazan, the director, pretended certainty, but from where I sat he looked like an ant trying to prod an elephant off his haunches. Ten days went by. The other actors were by now much further advanced: Milly Dunnock, playing Linda, was already creating a role; Arthur Kennedy as Biff had long since begun to reach for his high notes; Cameron Mitchell had many scenes already perfected; but Cobb stared at them, heavy-eyed, morose, even persecuted it seemed.

And then, one afternoon, there on the stage of the New Amsterdam way up on top of a movie theater on 42nd Street (this roof theater had once been Ziegfeld's private playhouse in the gilded times, and now was barely heated and misty with dust), Lee rose from his chair and looked at Milly Dunnock and there was a silence. And the he said, "I was driving along, you understand, and then all of a sudden I'm going off the road. . . ."

And the theater vanished. The stage vanished. The chill of an age-old recognition shuddered my spine; a voice was sounding in the dimly lit air up front, a created spirit, an incarnation, a Godlike creation was taking place; a new human being was being formed before all our eyes, born for the first time on this earth, made real by an act of will, by an artist's summoning up of all his memories and his intelligence; a birth was taking place above the meaningless traffic below; a man was here transcending the limits of his body and his own history. Through the complete concentration of his mind he had even altered the stance of his body, which now was strangely not the body of Lee Cobb (he was 37 then) but of a sixty-year-old salesman, a mere glance of his eye created a window beside him, with the gentle touch of his hand on this empty stage a bed appeared, and when he glanced up at the emptiness above him a ceiling was there, and there was even a crack in it where his stare rested.

I knew then that something astounding was being made here. It would have been almost enough for me without even opening the play. The actors, like myself and Kazan and the producer, were happy, of course, that we might have a hit; but there was a good deal more. There was a new fact of life, there was an alteration of history for all of us that afternoon.

There is a certain immortality involved in theater, not created by monuments and books, but through the knowledge the actor keeps to his dying day that on a certain afternoon, in an empty and dusty theater, he cast a shadow of a being that was not himself but the distillation of all he had ever observed; all the unsingable heartsong the ordinary man may feel but never utter, he gave voice to. And by that he somehow joins the ages.

And that is the glamour that remains, but it will not be found in the gossip columns. And it is enough, once discovered, to make people stay with the theater, and others to come seeking it.

I think also that people keep coming into these five blocks because the theater is still so simple, so old-fashioned. And that is why, however often its obsequies are intoned, it somehow never really dies. Because underneath our shiny fronts of stone, our fascination with gadgets and our new toys that can blow the earth into a million stars, we are still outside the doorway through which the great answers wait. Not all the cameras in Christendom nor all the tricky lights will move us one step closer to a better understanding of ourselves, but only, as it always was, the truly written word, the profoundly felt gesture, the naked and direct contemplation of man which is the enduring glamour of the stage.

———◆———

CHARLEY: *Nobody don't blame this man. You don't understand: Willy was a salesman. And for a salesman, there is no rock bottom to the life. He don't put a bolt to the nut, he don't tell you the law or give you medicine. He's a man way out there in the blue, riding on a smile and a shoeshine. And when they start not smiling back — that's an earthquake. And then you get yourself a couple of spots on your hat, and you're finished. Nobody dast blame this man. A salesman is got to dream, boy. It comes with the territory.*

ARTHUR MILLER, *The Death of a Salesman*

70.

W. H. AUDEN: The Anglo-American Difference

The poet and critic W. H. Auden was born an Englishman and became a naturalized American citizen, thus reversing the career of his famous contemporary T. S. Eliot. As such, Auden was perhaps especially qualified to consider the perennial problem of the sources of American literature in the European past and in the culture of a new world. The essay below appeared in the first issue of a book-magazine in 1955.

Source: *The Anchor Review*, No. 1, Garden City, N.Y., 1955.

ONE OFTEN HEARS it said that only in this century have the writers of the United States learned to stand on their own feet and be truly American, that, previously, they were slavish imitators of British literature. Applied to the general reading public and academic circles this has a certain amount of truth, but so far as the writers themselves are concerned it is quite false. From Bryant on there is scarcely one American poet whose work, if unsigned, could be mistaken for that of an Englishman. What English poet, for example, in need of emotive place names for a serious poem, would have employed neither local names nor names famous in history or mythology, but names made up by himself as Poe did in *Ulalume?* Would an English poet have conceived the idea of writing a scientific cosmological prose poem and of prefacing it thus: "I offer this Book of Truths, not in its character of Truth-teller, but for the Beauty that abounds in its Truth, constituting it true. . . . *What I here propound is true:* therefore it cannot die. . . . Nevertheless it is as a Poem only that I wish this work to be judged after I am dead." (Poe: Preface to *Eureka.*)

In the same year, 1855, appeared *Maud, The Song of Hiawatha,* and the first edition of *Leaves of Grass:* no two poets could be more unlike each other than Longfellow and Whitman — such diversity is in itself an American phenomenon — yet, when compared with Tennyson, each in his own way shows characteristics of the New World. Tennyson and Longfellow were both highly skillful technicians in conventional forms and both were regarded by their countrymen as the respectable mouthpieces of their age, and yet, how different they are.

There is much in Tennyson that Longfellow would never have dared to write, for the peculiar American mixture of Puritan conscience and democratic license can foster in some cases a genteel horror of the coarse for which no Englishman has felt the need. On the other hand Longfellow had a curiosity about the whole of European literature compared with which Tennyson, concerned only with the poetry of his own land and the classical authors on whom he was educated, seems provincial. Even if there had been Red Indians roaming the North of Scotland, unsubjugated and unassimilable, one cannot imagine Tennyson sitting down to write a long poem about them and choosing for it a Finnish meter.

Leaving aside all questions of style, ther

is a difference between Tennyson's *Ode on the Death of the Duke of Wellington* and Whitman's elegy for President Lincoln *When Lilacs Last in the Door-yard Bloom'd* which is significant. Tennyson, as one would expect from the title of his poem, mourns for a great public official figure, but it would be very hard to guess from the words of Whitman's poem that the man he is talking of was the head of a State; one would naturally think that he was some close personal friend, a private individual.

To take one more example: two poets, contemporaries, both women, both religious, both introverts preoccupied with renunciation — Christina Rossetti and Emily Dickinson — could anyone imagine either of them in the country of the other? When I try to fancy such translations, the only Americans I can possibly imagine as British are minor poets with a turn for light verse like Lowell and Holmes, and the only British poets who could conceivably have been American are eccentrics like Blake and Hopkins.

Normally, in comparing the poetry of two cultures, the obvious and easiest point at which to start is with a comparison of the peculiar characteristics, grammatical, rhetorical, rhythmical, of their respective languages, for even the most formal and elevated styles of poetry are more conditioned by the spoken tongue, the language really used by the men of that country, than by anything else. In the case of British and American poetry, however, this is the most subtle difference of all and the hardest to define. Any Englishman, with a little effort, can learn to pronounce "the letter *a* in psalm and calm . . . with the sound of *a* in candle," to say *thumbtacks* instead of *drawing pins* or twenty-*of*-one instead of twenty-*to*-one, and discover that, in the Middle West, *bought* rhymes with *hot;* but he will still be as far from speaking American English as his Yankee cousin who comes to England will be from speaking the

King's. No dramatist in either country who has introduced a character from the other side, has, to my knowledge, been able to make his speech convincing. What the secret of the differences is I cannot put my finger on; William Carlos Williams, who has thought more than most about this problem, says that "Pace is one of its most important manifestations," and to this one might add another, Pitch. If indefinable, the difference is, however, immediately recognizable by the ear, even in verse where the formal conventions are the same.

> He must have had a father and a
> mother —
> In fact I've heard him say so — and
> a dog,
> As a boy should, I venture; and the dog,
> Most likely, was the only man who
> knew him.
> A dog, for all I know, is what he needs
> As much as anything right here today
> To counsel him about his disillusions,
> Old aches, and parturitions of what's
> coming —
> A dog of orders, an emeritus,
> To wag his tail at him when he comes
> home,
> And then to put his paws up on his knees
> And say, "For God's sake, what's it all
> about?"

(E. A. Robinson, "Ben Jonson Entertains a Man from Stratford")

Whatever this may owe to Browning, the fingering is quite different and un-British. Again, how American in rhythm as well as in sensibility is the stanza by Robert Frost.

> But no, I was out for stars:
> I would not come in.
> I meant not even if asked;
> And I hadn't been.

Until quite recently an English writer, like one of any European country, could presuppose two conditions, a nature which was mythologized, humanized, on the whole friendly, and a human society which had become in time, whatever succession of invasions it may have suffered in the past, in race and religion more or less homogeneous and in which most people lived and died in the locality where they were born.

Christianity might have deprived Aphrodite, Apollo, the local genius, of their divinity, but as figures for the forces of nature, as a mode of thinking about the creation, they remained valid for poets and their readers alike. Descartes might reduce the nonhuman universe to a mechanism, but the feelings of Europeans about the sun and moon, the cycle of the seasons, the local landscape remained unchanged. Wordsworth might discard the mythological terminology, but the kind of relation between nature and man which he described was the same personal one. Even when nineteenth-century biology began to trouble men's minds with the thought that the universe might be without moral values, their immediate experience was still of a friendly and lovable nature. Whatever their doubts and convictions about the purpose and significance of the universe as a whole, Tennyson's Lincolnshire or Hardy's Dorset were places where they felt completely at home, landscapes with faces of their own which a human being could recognize and trust.

But in America, neither the size, condition, nor climate of the continent encourage such intimacy. It is an unforgettable experience for anyone born on the other side of the Atlantic to take a plane journey by night across the United States. Looking down he will see the lights of some town like a last outpost in a darkness stretching for hours ahead, and realize that, even if there is no longer an actual frontier, this is still a continent only partially settled and developed, where human activity seems a tiny thing in comparison to the magnitude of the earth, and the equality of men not some dogma of politics or jurisprudence but

a self-evident fact. He will behold a wild nature compared with which the landscapes of Salvator Rosa are as cozy as Arcadia and which cannot possibly be thought of in human or personal terms. If Henry Adams could write:

> When Adams was a boy in Boston, the best chemist in the place had probably never heard of Venus except by way of scandal, or of the Virgin except as idolatry. . . . The force of the Virgin was still felt at Lourdes, and seemed to be as potent as X-rays; but in America neither Venus nor Virgin ever had value as force — at most as sentiment. No American had ever been truly afraid of either.

The reason for this was not simply because the *Mayflower* carried iconophobic dissenters but also because the nature which Americans, even in New England, had every reason to fear could not possibly be imagined as a mother. A white whale whom man can neither understand nor be understood by, whom only a madman like Gabriel can worship, the only relationship with whom is a combat to the death by which a man's courage and skill are tested and judged, or the great buck who answers the poet's prayer for "someone else additional to him" in *The Most of It* are more apt symbols. Thoreau, who certainly tried his best to become intimate with nature, had to confess

> I walk in nature still alone
>   And know no one,
> Discern no lineament nor feature
>   Of any creature.
>
> Though all the firmament
>   Is o'er me bent,
> Yet still I miss the grace
>   Of an intelligent and kindred face.
>
> I still must seek the friend
> Who does with nature blend,
> Who is the person in her mask,
> He is the man I ask . . .

Many poets in the Old World have become disgusted with human civilization, but what the earth would be like if the race became extinct they cannot imagine; an American like Robinson Jeffers can quite easily, for he has seen with his own eyes country as yet untouched by history.

In a land which is fully settled, most men must accept their local environment to try to change it by political means; only the exceptionally gifted or adventurous can leave to seek his fortune elsewhere.

In America, on the other hand, to move on and make a fresh start somewhere else is still the normal reaction to dissatisfaction or failure. Such social fluidity has important psychological effects. Since movement involves breaking social and personal ties, the habit creates an attitude toward personal relationships in which impermanence is taken for granted.

One could find no better illustration of the difference between the Old and the New World than the respective conclusions of *Oliver Twist* and *Huckleberry Finn,* the heroes of which are both orphans. When Oliver is at last adopted by Mr. Brownlow, his fondest dream, to have a home, to be surrounded by familiar friendly faces, to receive an education, is realized. Huck is offered adoption too, significantly by a woman not a man, but refuses because he knows she would try to "civilize" him, and lights out by himself for the West; Jim, who has been his "buddy" in a friendship far closer than any enjoyed by Oliver, is left behind like an old shoe, just as in *Moby Dick* Ishmael becomes a blood brother of Queequeg and then forgets all about him. Naturally the daydream of the lifelong comrade in adventure often appears in American literature:

Camerado, I give you my hand!
I give you my love more precious than
    money,
I give you myself before preaching or
    law;

Will you give me yourself? will you
    come travel with me?
Shall we stick by each other as long as
    we live?
(Whitman, "Song of the Open Road")

But no American seriously expects such a dream to come true.

To be able at any time to break with the past, to move and keep on moving, lessens the significance not only of the past but also of the future, which is reduced to the immediate future, and minimizes the importance of political action. A European may be a conservative who thinks that the right form of society has been discovered already, or a liberal who believes it is in process of being realized, or a revolutionary who thinks that after long dark ages it can now be realized for the first time, but each of them knows that, by reason or force, he must convince the others that he is right; he may be an optimist about the future or a pessimist. None of these terms apply accurately to an American, for his profoundest feeling toward the future is not that it will be better or worse but that it is unpredictable, that all things, good and bad, will change. No failure is irredeemable, no success a final satisfaction. Democracy is the best form of government, not because men will necessarily lead better or happier lives under it, but because it permits constant experiment; a given experiment may fail, but the people have a right to make their own mistakes. America has always been a country of amateurs where the professional, that is to say, the man who claims authority as a member of an elite which knows the law in some field or other, is an object of distrust and resentment. (In the field with which we are here concerned, one symptom of this is that curious American phenomenon, the class in "Creative Writing.")

Amerika, du hast es besser
Als unser Kontinent, das alte,
Hast keine verfallene Schloesser
Und keine Basalte.

(America, thou hast it better
Than our old Continent,
Hast no dilapidated castles,
No aged columns.)

Goethe, I presume, was also thinking of the absence of violent political clashes. This is a subject about which, in relation to their histories, the English and the American cherish opposite fictions. Between 1533 and 1688 the English went through a succession of revolutions in which a church was imposed on them by the engines of the State, one king was executed and another deposed, yet they prefer to forget it and pretend that the social structure of England is the product of organic peaceful growth. The Americans on the other hand like to pretend that what was only a successful war of secession was a genuine revolution (1829, though bloodless, was a more revolutionary year than 1776). There is indeed an American mentality which is new and unique in the world, but it is the product less of conscious political action than of nature, of the new and unique environment of the American continent. Even the most revolutionary feature of the Constitution, the separation of Church and State, was a recognition of a condition which had existed since the first settlements were made by various religious denominations whose control of the secular authority could only be local. From the beginning America had been a pluralist state and pluralism is incompatible with an Established Church. The *Basalte* in American history, the Civil War, might indeed be called Counter-Revolution, for it was fought primarily on the issue not of slavery but for unity, that is, not for a freedom but for a limitation on freedom, to ensure that the United States should remain pluralist and not disintegrate into an anarchic heap of fragments. Pluralist and experimental: in place of *verfallene Schloesser* America has ghost towns and the relics of New Jerusalems which failed.

Whatever one may feel about Whitman's poetry, one is bound to admit that he was the first clearly to recognize what the conditions were with which any future American poet would have to come to terms.

> Plenty of songs had been sung — beautiful, matchless songs — adjusted to other lands than these. . . . The Old World has had the poems of myths, fictions, feudalism, conquest, caste, dynastic wars, and splendid exceptional characters, which have been great; but the New World needs the poems of realities and science and of the democratic average and basic equality. . . . As for native American individuality, the distinctive and ideal type of Western character (as consistent with the operative and even money-making features of United States humanity as chosen knights, gentlemen and warriors were with the ideals of the centuries of European feudalism), it has not yet appeared. I have allowed the stress of my poems from beginning to end to bear upon American individuality and assist it — not only because that is a great lesson in Nature, amid all her generalizing laws, but as counterpoise to the leveling tendencies of Democracy.

The last sentence makes it quite clear that by the "average" here who was to replace the "knight" Whitman did not mean the mediocre, but the individual whose "exceptional character" is not derived from birth, education, or occupation, and that he is aware of how difficult it is for such an individual to appear without the encouragement which comes from membership in some elite.

What he does not say, and perhaps did not realize, is that in a democracy the status of the poet himself is changed. However fantastic in the light of present-day realities his notion may be, every European poet, I believe, still instinctively thinks of himself as a "clerk," a member of a professional brotherhood, with a certain social status irrespective of the number of his readers (in his heart of hearts the audience he desires and expects are those who govern the country), and taking his place in an unbroken historical succession. Here in the States, poets have never had or imagined they had such a status, and it is up to each individual poet to justify his existence by offering a unique product. It would be grossly unjust to assert that there are fewer lovers of poetry in the New World than in the Old — in how many places abroad could a poet demand and receive a substantial sum for reading his work aloud? — but there is a tendency, perhaps, in the former, for audiences to be drawn rather by name than a poem, and for a poet, on his side, to demand approval for his work not simply because it is good but because it is *his.* To some degree every American poet feels that the whole responsibility for contemporary poetry has fallen upon his shoulders, that he is a literary aristocracy of one. "Tradition," wrote T. S. Eliot in a famous essay, "cannot be inherited, and if you want it you must obtain it by great labor." I do not think that any European critic would have said just this. He would not, of course, deny that every poet must work hard, but the suggestion in the first half of the sentence that no sense of tradition is acquired except by conscious effort would seem strange to him.

There are advantages and disadvantages in both attitudes. A British poet can take writing more for granted and so write with a lack of strain and overearnestness. American poetry has many tones, a man talking to himself or one intimate friend, a prophet crying in the wilderness, but the easy-going tone of a man talking to a group of his peers is rare; for a "serious" poet to write light verse is frowned on in America and if, when he is asked why he writes poetry, he replies, as any European poet would, "For fun," his audience will be shocked. (In this Cambridge-on-the-Cam is perhaps a few leagues nearer Gambier, Ohio than is Oxford-on-Thames.)

On the other hand a British poet is in much greater danger of becoming lazy, or academic, or irresponsible. (One comes across passages, even in very fine English poets which make one think: "Yes, very effective but does he believe what he is saying?"; in American poetry such passages are extremely rare.) The first thing that strikes a reader about the best American poets is how utterly unlike each other they are. Where else in the world, for example, could one find seven poets of approximately the same generation so different as Ezra Pound, W. C. Williams, Vachel Lindsay, Marianne Moore, Wallace Stevens, E. E. Cummings, and Laura Riding? The danger for the American poet is not of writing like everybody else but of crankiness and a parody of his own manner.[1]

Plato said that when the modes of music change the walls of the city are shaken. It might be truer to say, perhaps, that a change in the modes gives warning of a shaking of the walls in the near future. The social strains which later break out in political action are first experienced by artists as a feeling that the current modes of expression are no longer capable of dealing with their real concerns. Thus, when one thinks of "modern" painting, music, fiction, or poetry, the names which immediately come to mind as its leaders and creators are those of persons who were born roughly between 1870 and 1890 and who began producing

1. The undeniable appearance in the States during the last fifteen years or so of a certain literary conformity, of a proper and authorized way to write poetry, is a new and disquieting symptom, which I cannot pretend to be able to explain fully. The role of the American college as a patron of poets has been discussed a good deal both here and in England. Those who criticize it, often with some reason, fail to suggest a better alternative. It would be nice if the colleges could ask no more from the poets in return for their keep than occasional pieces, a Commencement Day masque or an elegy on a deceased trustee; if that is too much to ask, then the poets themselves should at least demand that they give academic courses in the literature of the dead and refuse to have anything to do with modern literature or courses in writing. There has been a vast output of critical studies in contemporary poetry, some of them first-rate, but I do not think that, as a rule, a poet should read or write them.

their "new" work before the outbreak of World War I in 1914, and in poetry and fiction, at least, American names are prominent.

When a revolutionary break with the past is necessary, it is an advantage not to be too closely identified with any one particular literature or any particular cultural group. Americans like Eliot and Pound, for example, could be as curious about French or Italian poetry as about English and could hear poetry of the past, like the verse of Webster, freshly in a way that for an Englishman, trammeled by traditional notions of Elizabethan blank verse, would have been difficult.

Further, as Americans, they were already familiar with the dehumanized nature and the social leveling which a technological civilization was about to make universal and with which the European mentality was unprepared to deal. After his visit to America, De Tocqueville made a remarkable prophecy about the kind of poetry which a democratic society would produce.

I am persuaded that in the end democracy diverts the imagination from all that is external to man and fixes it on man alone. Democratic nations may amuse themselves for a while with considering the productions of nature, but they are excited in reality only by a survey of themselves. . . .

The poets who lived in aristocratic ages have been eminently successful in their delineations of certain incidents in the life of a people or a man; but none of them ever ventured to include within his performances the destinies of mankind, a task which poets writing in democratic ages may attempt. . . .

It may be foreseen in like manner that poets living in democratic times will prefer the delineation of passions and ideas to that of persons and achievements. The language, the dress, and the daily actions of men in democracies are repugnant to conceptions of the ideal. . . . This forces the poet constantly to search below the external surface which is palpable to the senses, in order to read the inner soul; and nothing lends itself more to the delineation of the ideal than the scrutiny of the hidden depths in the immaterial nature of man. . . . The destinies of mankind, man himself taken aloof from his country and his age and standing in the presence of Nature and of God, with his passions, his doubts, his rare prosperities and inconceivable wretchedness, will become the chief, if not the sole, theme of poetry.

If this be an accurate description of the poetry we call modern, then one might say that America has never known any other kind.

With the exception of a small group of Texans, Americans are particularly sensitive to the historical quality in the towns they visit. "If these walls had tongues," *said my taxi driver in Hollywood as we passed a big hotel, "they could tell a* *story. That building must be twenty-five years old."*
                    STEPHEN POTTER, "One-Upmanship on the Thames," *New* *York Times Magazine,* May 17, 1953

New municipal services building rises alongside Philadelphia's historic City Hall

PRESERVING THE PAST

The differential effects of progress — or, at any rate, of change — on different segments of society produced constant conflict between city and country, government and citizen, innovation and tradition. Even within the city itself, the center of civilization and hence the main source of progress, change was accompanied by controversy. Yet the forces of progress were irresistible; hopefully, then, it was the function of tradition to urge change into rational and humane channels. City planning, the rational control of man's environment, meant therefore not only the structuring of progress but also the evaluation and preservation of the worthwhile past. Away from the city, in the small-town and rural strongholds of tradition, the gradual encroachment of peripheral change — via the mass media, travel, or other such means — led often to a reaction in favor of the past, or at least against the city as the symbol of unrestrained change. The long-standing frictions between country and city were intensified by the hopeless and helpless position of the small town in an urban civilization. With no real future, the small town lucky enough to have a past found refuge there; it was, on the other hand, a rare city that did not destroy its past entirely in the pursuit of the future.

Two views of Philadelphia at the turn of the century: (Above) Market Street at 11th Avenue; (below) looking north on Broad Street from City Hall

(Above) Philadelphia's Broad Street Station in 1900; (below) railroad tracks at Broad Street Station in the downtown section of the city, 1950, before the start of urban renewal

Independence Hall in the center of a clutter of decaying commercial buildings, 1950

Philadelphia was outstanding in its response to the problems of the city at midcentury — the decay of the downtown regions following the growth of suburbia, the perpetuation of slums, choking traffic, unregulated building. The city set up a long-range plan designed to revitalize the center city and to rebuild or renovate as much as was necessary to make all of Philadelphia again pleasant to live and work in. This was by far the most extensive such city plan; "urban renewal" in other cities was typically sporadic, uncoordinated, and not uncommonly a failure.

Merchants' Exchange, Philadelphia, erected in 1832

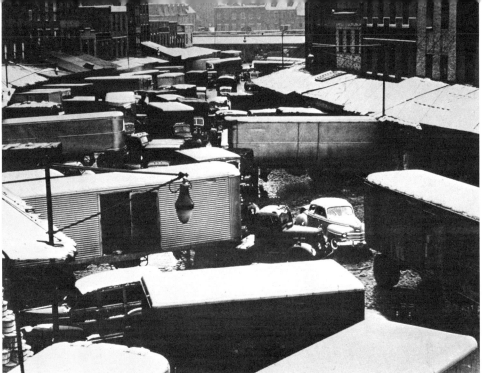

(Above) Congestion in the Food Market at Dock Street, in the Society Hill section of Philadelphia, 1954; (below) slums in Philadelphia's Mill Creek before urban renewal programs were begun

Philadelphia City Planning Commission

(Above) Plaza at Penn Center, a new commercial center for Philadelphia, replaces the railroad tracks that were previously above ground. (Below) Independence Hall stands in the middle of the new national historic park

Jordan Wilson — Pix from Publix

Franklin Williamson

(Above) Houses in the center of Philadelphia restored to their original colonial designs by private
owners; (right) boy studying a statue at Samuel
Memorial in Fairmont Park on the Schuylkill River

Franklin Williamson

(Right) New housing facilities
in the Mill Creek section of Philadelphia constructed with the
aid of federal funds

Philadelphia City Planning Commission

(Above) Walter Place, photographed in the 1880s. It was erected in 1852 by Col. Harvey Walter, a lawyer in Holly Springs who died in the yellow fever epidemic. General Grant made his home here in late 1862 while preparing his march on Vicksburg. (Left) Mother of Col. Walter. (Right) Judge Alexander Clayton, an organizer and first president of the Board of Trustees of the University of Mississippi. He secured the admission of women to the university in 1882. (Bottom) Building which housed the University of Holly Springs from 1838 to 1843, later the Chalmers Institute for Boys.

(Above) **Jousting tournament, 1869;** (center) **Dr. Chesley Daniel, who fought the epidemic**

Holly Springs is a small town in northern Mississippi. Founded in the 1830s, the town appeared destined to be a major Southern center, especially upon completion of a railroad line in the 1850s. For whatever reasons, however, it remained small. The high points of its history are its occupation by General Grant during the siege of Vicksburg, a raid by Confederate General Van Dorn, and a yellow fever epidemic in 1878. For Holly Springs the preservation of memorabilia from those times, the compilation of anecdotal histories of the town and region, and the maintenance of some of the "old South" flavor are now the major activities.

(Left) **Mrs. Lizzie Fant, designer of the "Tiger Ballot" woodcut (above) which the Democrats used to counter voting tactics of the Republicans during Reconstruction Period**

Courtesy, Mrs. L. A. Smith II

(Above) Holly Springs young people at an outing at the Gun Club, 1897; (below) medicine show in front of the courthouse, 1890. OPPOSITE PAGE: (Top) Rows of cotton bales in the town square; (center) Negro picking cotton, 1890, (bottom) Old Clapp House, built in 1858

Courtesy, Holly Springs Garden Club

(Top and center) Courtesy, Mrs. L. A. Smith II

Courtesy, Mrs. Lester G. Fant

(Both) Nicholas Sapieha, "The Delta Review"

(Above) The Mimosas, erected in 1836 as one of the first two-story homes in Holly Springs; (below) another example of the architectural styles popular in the community in the 19th century

(Above) The Montrose, a brick mansion built in 1858, now the headquarters of the Holly Springs Garden Club; (below left) antique hitching post standing outside The Montrose; (below right) K. K. Marett, a local storekeeper since the turn of the century

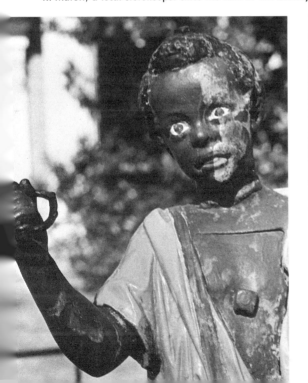

Nicholas Sapieha, "The Delta Review"

(Above) Fred Gipson, a typical Mississippi farmer, fertilizing his fields

(Left) Mrs. S. P. Gipson, mother of 15 children, all but one of whom have a college education; (below) S. P. Gipson, owner of a 60-acre farm outside Holly Springs, talks about local problems with a visiting civil rights worker from Chicago

(Both) Nicholas Sapieha, "The Delta Review"

71.

Organizing the Unorganized

On December 5, 1955, the two largest labor unions in the country, the American Federation of Labor and the Congress of Industrial Organizations, merged into one union, thus healing, temporarily at least, the breach that had occurred in the late 1930s. The following article in the Nation, *published a few days after the merger, discussed the problem of drawing the rest of unorganized labor within the union fold. But such an ambitious goal was not to be reached. The numbers of organized labor reached a high of over 18 million in 1956 and then leveled off until the 1960s when union membership began to decline, owing in part to the decreased proportion of blue-collar workers in the labor force.*

Source: *Nation,* December 10, 1955.

WHEN JOHN W. LIVINGSTON, director of organizing for the merging A.F. of L.-C.I.O., surveys his job, he will be looking beyond heavy industry, public utilities, and transportation. These, already fairly well organized, compose the bulk of the 16 million members to whom President George Meany will be pointing with pride. Livingston, the husky auto worker from the Ozarks, will be concerned rather with the 45 million wage earners outside the union fold. They include most women workers, most white-collar employees, and most of the men and women, white and Negro, employed in the South. If within the next ten years he could double the membership of the A.F. of L.-C.I.O., his name would go down in labor history alongside that of John L. Lewis.

The car you now drive, the house you live in, the meat and bread you eat — these are all pretty likely to be union-made. Likewise the electrical gadgets you live by, your means of getting hither and yon, the struc-

tures you work in, the things you read are produced, chances are, by hands that hold a union card. It's not nearly so likely that the clothes you wear (unless you insist on the union label) will be union-made. Most of the food you eat, most of the personal services you receive, the host of small and inexpensive things — these are, by and large, without benefit of union protection to their makers, processors, and handlers.

The statistics which face Livingston in his organizing drive do not give the whole picture. For instance, Chicago. This cradle of American labor is less unionized, factory-wise, than Richmond, Virginia, or Birmingham, Alabama. Enormous segments of heavy industry, particularly in oil and chemicals, remain untouched by orthodox unionism. In certain industries where both A.F. of L. and C.I.O. have competing unions, as in meat-packing, textiles, and chemicals, internecine strife has taken a heavy toll. But the key to Chicago's poor showing is the small factory. In this metropolitan area there are no fewer than 14,000 factories employing 1 million workers, and most of them have fewer than 1,000 employees.

Here unionism runs into cost factors and the law of diminishing returns. A union administrator will tell you that it costs only about twice as much to furnish union services in a plant with 1,000 members as in one with 100. The temptation here is to organize not the workers but the employers into associations to be more easily policed by association-wide contracts. Small factories are a major union problem almost everywhere; in the aggregate they may well account for 10 million unorganized workers.

Another roadblock to unionism is the white-collar employee. The factory worker tends to be output-minded and to tie this in with severely regimented wage scales, seniority, and working rules. The office workers in the big industrial plants look with no little envy on the status production workers have attained; whether unions can modify their rigid notions to fit the white collar, while the white collar abandons some of his notions of superiority, will determine union success in this most promising of all the big unconquered sectors.

Women are a problem, too. Or rather, union men are the problem in their attitude toward organizing women. The traditional male idea has been that the husband, as family breadwinner, should earn enough to support his family. Unions helped mightily to get the children out of the factories, and some of them thought woman's place, too, was in the home. However desirable this old American dream may have been, the facts of life negate it. Women constitute one-third of the labor force; one-third of women over fourteen are at work.

The new A.F. of L.-C.I.O. director of organization may know better than to try to stretch women on unionism's procrustean bed. Since he'll likely be too male-conscious to see the problem (not a single woman has

ever been elected to the Executive Board of either labor federation), perhaps there should be a woman codirector of organization. That might rectify the present situation where men are averaging $3,469 in yearly earnings against $1,252 for women, who are actually 13 percent worse off, wagewise, than they were thirteen years ago. The catch phrase, so dear to both Republican and Democratic vote-catchers, that labor never had it so good, certainly doesn't apply to women.

Whatever his other problems, Director Livingston is not going to be bothered much by the size of his organizing budget. The new federation starts with a built-in annual deficit of between $3 million and $4 million. This stems from the facts of merger. Governed by sacrosanct rules of tenure and seniority, the merged federation will enjoy no economies but rather a two-headed bureaucracy in which every officeholder is assured of his job.

The lack of money doesn't mean too much. There were hardly pennies available back in the 1930s when steel, auto, electrical, and machine workers organized themselves. Sending scads of paid organizers into virgin territory usually doesn't pay off. The paid organizers are apt to limit their efforts to getting signatures on application cards; that indeed is the criterion of success in many a union headquarters. It is assumed that there is some magic in the word "union" and that this *deus ex machina* will do the job somehow by remote control. Wherever workers have been genuinely organized into unions, they have accepted the union as a vehicle which they must pull to success by their own efforts. It is true that there are many unions organized by bureaucratic methods, but they can better be described as workingmen's business organizations which come to life once a year when the contract expires.

Unionism as a way of life, which is the biggest asset Director Livingston has in doubling the A.F. of L.-C.I.O. membership in the next decade, is a lot bigger than most union officials care to admit; in fact, there is a certain tendency to lean over backward and insist that the immediate pork chop is the sole goal of labor. A certain type of university intellectual who dabbles in labor matters fiercely loves this concept of business unionism, perhaps because it is supposed to be anti-Marxist, but few average citizens love it. It is a bit too materialistic to enlist widespread admiration among those not directly involved.

Business unionism will offer certain obstacles to Director Livingston's program. As these unions achieve a certain limited success, and their officials acquire financial and social status in rather sumptuous headquarters, bureaucratism becomes a factor. So long as the dues continue to roll in, these cumbersome machines tend to rely on their own momentum to survive. While every union covets more per capita, the imagination and drive needed for organizing become dulled and the machines become involved in contemplating their own internal problems. Unable to cope with the challenge within their own industries, they look only with vague interest toward ambitious programs for organizing women, white collars, or the South. The typical union official today is an administrator, not an organizer. The situation was highlighted when the United Auto Workers offered to toss $1,250,000 into a general organizing kitty if other unions would also chip in. The idea lies vegetating in the files and it will be interesting to see how much luck Director Livingston has in resurrecting it.

An exception must be noted. The Teamsters, an extremely self-centered and businesslike union, has garnered a rich harvest of small factories, warehouses, and processing plants. Almost any unorganized plant that a truck may enter to deliver or take away goods is subject to Teamsters' interest; so widespread has become its jurisdiction that it parallels in structure and scope the great British Transport and General Workers Union. While the Teamsters organize on a strictly self-centered basis which may afford little help to A.F. of L.-C.I.O.'s general campaigns, the success they have attained in aggressive organizing shows the possibilities lying around unrealized.

Another encouraging factor with which Director Livingston is well acquainted is the proletarianizing of the supervisory and technical staffs in heavy industry. In oil refineries, for example, there is now one supervisor for every five or six hourly workers. These, along with the technicians and professionals in the factories, are tending to become "the masses" and inclined to like the kind of protection that unionism affords.

THIS GENERATION HAS SEEN TWO UPSURGES of organization; the first growing out of the desperation of the Great Depression, the second out of World War II. In the first, workers organized themselves. In the second, the unions did the job through labor-board ballots with a powerful assist from the government which needed to have war workers mobilized for more effective direction.

The current era differs from both. It can hardly be said that the unorganized show desperation today, particularly in the North. Many of them bask in the shade of the union umbrella without having to pay dues. Perhaps as many workers enjoy the wage benefits of unionism outside the unions as inside — they are the free riders. Then there are the millions of capitalism's captives, the indentured servants of installment purchases. They feel they can't afford to risk strikes for the union because the sheriff might haul away the cherished TV, the beloved new car, or the housewife's proud badge of freedom — her machines for washing and cleaning. Not in their ranks of course are the appalling number, even in the North, who earn less than $1 an hour, but still are an influential minority among the unorganized.

Employers, too, have their umbrella, the Cadillac Cabinet in Washington, basically hostile to unionism. Lothair Teetor, former assistant secretary of commerce, whose Perfect Circle firm in Indiana believes in shooting it out with the United Auto Workers, hastily abandoned his Washington post, not, perhaps, because his hostility to the union was repudiated but because this display of pre-Rooseveltian antiunionism was embarrassing. The secretary of the interior, whose struck Oregon firm depends more on starvation than bullets to beat down the union, rides more easily in the cabinet.

Under Eisenhower, the National Labor Relations Board has become a coolly hostile force from which unions can expect no favors. Insofar as possible, they bypass the very board which was set up originally to protect their right to organize. If a minor depression should set in, the unions, under the present administration, might well find themselves entrenched in a war of self-preservation rather than in seeking more millions to organize.

Director Livingston then must face the intrinsic differences of this period, which contrasts with the 1930s and with the war years. There is an undeniable passivity among many unorganized workers and a growing intransigence among hard-boiled employers. These are high hurdles.

Any serious proposal to add millions to the labor movement must take into account the South, where industry is burgeoning, wages are low, and security generally nonexistent. The emancipation of Southern labor is the key, not only to the creation of a truly national labor movement but to the refreshment of American political life. A South brought up to national wage standards, liberated from industrial-plantation feudalists, and freed from bondage to the race issue would give a new turn to the national life.

This long overdue emancipation can be labor's greatest gift both to the South and to the country at large. It will be achieved when Southern workers find the union key. They are ready, they are good joiners, and when they have pledged their word they are loyal to it (a mighty asset on the picket line). Here especially the spiritual values that labor can express find a ready response. Southern workers are tired of being second-class industrial citizens, of being told that sunshine is a good substitute for adequate pay and the self-respect that unions bring. Nor will the chains of installment buying bind them; they have little to lose and much to win in a fight.

The textile baronies along the Atlantic Piedmont differ as sharply from the industrialized Birmingham region as does oil-rich Texas and the Southwest from either. There is no unified "South." Alongside the peonized sugar workers of Louisiana are unionized oil workers on the Gulf Coast who have wiped out the North-South wage differential. The Birmingham steel workers have just erased the wage differential; the meat-packers are narrowing the margin. Along the bayous and in the piney woods, giant new plants are mushrooming, most of them built by Northern corporations accustomed to dealing with unions up North. Any Southern organizer will tell you that a new plant is twice as easy (or half as difficult) to line up as an older one.

Nevertheless, repeated "Southern drives" have petered out. A good bit of the blame must be placed at labor's door because of its hesitant attitude toward Negroes. A firm stand has been diluted out of concern for the prejudices of the white worker; as a result neither white nor Negro is organized.

There is no disguising the stubbornness of racial prejudice; on the other hand it has been magnified out of all perspective by the racist press and agitators. It is becoming increasingly clear to Southern workers that discrimination is holding back both races.

All the way from Richmond to Corpus Christi, union leaders can give concrete examples of success in fighting discrimination. The Negro, as an ally, can decide the issue of unionism in the South; if he is left uninterested, he can defeat unionism by his mere passivity.

When the A.F. of L.-C.I.O. brings its fight for economic and political equality out of the clouds of convention oratory and pious resolutions into a genuine fighting program, the next drive in the South will need neither millions of dollars nor thousands of paid organizers. To paraphrase Marx, the emancipation of the Southern workers will be achieved by the Southern workers themselves once Negroes are assured a position in the labor movement fully equal to their white brothers.

THE MAIN REASON organized labor has made little progress in recent years can be found in "public opinion." Director Livingston will find this public opinion the all-important factor in his organizing plans. Not the public opinion so readily manufactured by the mass media controlled by the business elements, but rather that of the grapevine, of word-of-mouth that spreads among unorganized workers as they eye unionism as it is. In this, the spiritual factors far outweigh the material, odd as that may seem. The name of John L. Lewis was magic to millions in the 1930s because at last one of their own stood up, fought back, and won against the titans of his time. That exhilaration of spirit was worth more than millions in the treasury.

The image of Organized Labor as the protector of the poor, the apostle of public education, the champion of better health and welfare, the watchdog against private plunder of the national resources, the advocate of world brotherhood is the most valuable asset the A.F. of L.-C.I.O. director of organization can possibly have. That is why the business press has been so keen to show up sporadic pilfering of union welfare funds and to front-page the mansions of a few labor leaders. If the labor movement can be reduced in public estimation to a selfish, materialistic concept in which a favored class advances its own pay (and prices to the public, as the press insists) and collaborates with municipal corruptionists for special privilege, the vast majority of men and women still outside the House of Labor will remain there.

If labor's political action, in practice, seems aimed at seeking favors, in advancing the interests of political shysters, in urging expanded military expenditures so that unionized war workers in plane factories and other munitions plants may be sheltered, there will be little spark of response from the unorganized. Even if their aspirations are unverbalized, they seek security, dignity, peace.

In truth there have always been the two drives within the labor movement; the one animated by the highest concern for humanity, the other rather desperately seeking to find safety for some behind barriers. Across the country from coast to coast there are thousands dedicated to the proposition that unions are the engines of democracy in an industrial society; their voices are going to be heard increasingly as the bankruptcy in imagination and drive of the business unionists continues to breed sterility. It is to them that Director Livingston will need to be looking for the organizers, largely unpaid, of the millions who should be in the unified House of Labor.

1956

72.

Dwight D. Eisenhower: Veto of Natural Gas Bill

The Supreme Court ruled in Phillips Petroleum Co. v. Wisconsin *(June 7, 1954) that the Federal Power Commission should henceforth regulate the price of natural gas in interstate commerce. Immediate objections to this decision on the part of the natural gas producers resulted in the drafting of the Natural Gas Bill, which set a limit on the degree of government regulation of natural gas production and distribution. President Eisenhower supported the bill through Congress, but just before he was to sign it into effect, evidence came to light from Senator Francis Case of South Dakota that the passage of the bill had been owing to illegal lobbying by the natural gas producers. On February 17, 1956, Eisenhower vetoed the bill because of the questionable methods used to get it passed. The veto message is reprinted below. The bill was not repassed.*

Source: 84 Congress, 2 Session, House Document No. 342.

I AM UNABLE to approve H.R. 6645, to amend the Natural Gas Act, as amended. This I regret because I am in accord with its basic objectives.

Since the passage of this bill, a body of evidence has accumulated indicating that private persons, apparently representing only a very small segment of a great and vital industry, have been seeking to further their own interests by highly questionable activities. These include efforts that I deem to be so arrogant and so much in defiance of acceptable standards of propriety as to risk creating doubt among the American people concerning the integrity of governmental processes.

Legally constituted agencies of government are now engaged in investigating this situation. These investigations cannot be concluded before the expiration of the ten-day period within which the President must act upon the legislation under the Constitution.

I believe I would not be discharging my own duty were I to approve this legislation before the activities in question have been fully investigated by the Congress and the Department of Justice. To do so under such conditions could well create long-term apprehension in the minds of the American people. It would be a disservice both to the people and to their Congress. Accordingly, I return H.R. 6645 without my approval.

At the same time, I must make quite clear that legislation conforming to the basic objectives of H.R. 6645 is needed. It is needed because the type of regulation of producers of natural gas which is required under present law will discourage individual initiative and incentive to explore for and develop new sources of supply.

In the long run this will limit supplies of gas, which is contrary, not only to the national interest but especially to the interest of consumers.

I feel that any new legislation, in addition to furthering the long-term interest of consumers in plentiful supplies of gas, should include specific language protecting consumers in their right to fair prices.

73.

Declaration of Southern Congressmen on Integration of Schools

Southern objections to the Supreme Court's unanimous decisions calling in 1954 and 1955 for desegregation of schools were many and vehement. On March 12, 1956, a group of one hundred-one congressmen, almost all of them from Southern states, denounced the ruling in a manifesto that was presented to Congress. Considering the Court's desegregation orders to be in violation of the Constitution, the authors of the manifesto urged their states to disobey them and vowed to oppose actions to implement the orders "by all lawful means." The manifesto, called a "Declaration of Constitutional Principles," is reprinted here.

Source: *Record*, 84 Cong., 2 Sess., pp. 4515-4516.

THE UNWARRANTED DECISION of the Supreme Court in the public-school cases is now bearing the fruit always produced when men substitute naked power for established law.

The founding fathers gave us a Constitution of checks and balances because they realized the inescapable lesson of history that no man or group of men can be safely entrusted with unlimited power. They framed this Constitution with its provisions for change by amendment in order to secure the fundamentals of government against the dangers of temporary popular passion or the personal predilections of public officeholders.

We regard the decision of the Supreme Court in the school cases as a clear abuse of judicial power. It climaxes a trend in the federal judiciary undertaking to legislate, in derogation of the authority of Congress, and to encroach upon the reserved rights of the states and the people.

The original Constitution does not mention education. Neither does the Fourteenth Amendment nor any other amendment. The debates preceding the submission of the Fourteenth Amendment clearly show that there was no intent that it should affect the systems of education maintained by the states. The very Congress which proposed the amendment subsequently provided for segregated schools in the District of Columbia.

When the amendment was adopted, in 1868, there were thirty-seven states of the Union. Every one of the twenty-six states that had any substantial racial differences among its people either approved the operation of segregated schools already in existence or subsequently established such schools by action of the same lawmaking body which considered the Fourteenth Amendment.

As admitted by the Supreme Court in the public-school case (*Brown* v. *Board of Education*), the doctrine of separate but equal schools "apparently originated in *Roberts* v. *City of Boston* . . . (1849), upholding school segregation against attack as being violative of a state constitutional guarantee of equality." This constitutional doctrine began in the North — not in the South — and it was followed not only in Massachusetts but in Connecticut, New York, Illinois, Indiana, Michigan, Minnesota, New Jersey, Ohio, Pennsylvania, and other Northern states, until they, exercising their rights as states through the constitutional processes of local self-government, changed their school systems.

In the case of *Plessy* v. *Ferguson,* in 1896, the Supreme Court expressly declared that under the Fourteenth Amendment no person was denied any of his rights if the states provided separate-but-equal public facilities. This decision has been followed in many other cases. It is notable that the Supreme Court, speaking through Chief Justice Taft, a former President of the United States, unanimously declared, in 1927, in *Lum* v. *Rice,* that the "separate-but-equal" principle is "within the discretion of the state in regulating its public schools and does not conflict with the Fourteenth Amendment."

This interpretation, restated time and again, became a part of the life of the people of many of the states and confirmed their habits, customs, traditions, and way of life. It is founded on elemental humanity and common sense, for parents should not be deprived by government of the right to direct the lives and education of their own children.

Though there has been no constitutional amendment or act of Congress changing this established legal principle almost a century old, the Supreme Court of the United States, with no legal basis for such action, undertook to exercise their naked judicial power and substituted their personal political and social ideas for the established law of the land. This unwarranted exercise of power by the Court, contrary to the Constitution, is creating chaos and confusion in the states principally affected. It is destroying the amicable relations between the white and Negro races that have been created through ninety years of patient effort by the good people of both races. It has planted hatred and suspicion where there has been heretofore friendship and understanding.

Without regard to the consent of the governed, outside agitators are threatening immediate and revolutionary changes in our public-school systems. If done, this is certain to destroy the system of public education in some of the states.

With the gravest concern for the explosive and dangerous condition created by this decision and inflamed by outside meddlers:

We reaffirm our reliance on the Constitution as the fundamental law of the land.

We decry the Supreme Court's encroachments on rights reserved to the states and to the people, contrary to established law and to the Constitution.

We commend the motives of those states which have declared the intention to resist forced integration by any lawful means.

We appeal to the states and people who are not directly affected by these decisions to consider the constitutional principles involved against the time when they, too, on issues vital to them, may be the victims of judicial encroachment.

Even though we constitute a minority in the present Congress, we have full faith that a majority of the American people believe in the dual system of government which has enabled us to achieve our greatness and will in time demand that the reserved rights of the state and of the people be made secure against judicial usurpation.

We pledge ourselves to use all lawful means to bring about a reversal of this decision, which is contrary to the Constitution, and to prevent the use of force in its implementation.

In this trying period, as we all seek to right this wrong, we appeal to our people not to be provoked by the agitators and troublemakers invading our states and to scrupulously refrain from disorders and lawless acts.

74.

Herbert Ravenel Sass: Mixed Schools and Mixed Blood

Official Southern objections to the Supreme Court's demand that schools be integrated were usually based on constitutional principles, but for many Southerners the question was not political or ideological but social and, at bottom, racial. Often this was not stated explicitly, but occasionally a Southern writer would describe the feelings of his section in terms that seemed to ring true. The article published by Herbert Ravenel Sass in November 1956 and reprinted here in part is an example of this kind of Southern comment. Brutally frank, the article argued with clarity and force the Southern position on school integration and asserted that the South would never accept the intermingling of the races in its schools.

Source: *Atlantic Monthly,* November 1956.

What may well be the most important physical fact in the story of the United States is one which is seldom emphasized in our history books. It is the fact that throughout the three and a half centuries of our existence we have kept our several races biologically distinct and separate. Though we have encouraged the mixing of many different strains in what has been called the American "melting pot," we have confined this mixing to the white peoples of European ancestry, excluding from our "melting pot" all other races. The result is that the United States today is overwhelmingly a pure white nation, with a smaller but considerable Negro population in which there is some white blood, and a much smaller American Indian population.

The fact that the United States is overwhelmingly pure white is not only important; it is also the most distinctive fact about this country when considered in relation to the rest of the New World. Except Canada, Argentina, and Uruguay, none of the approximately twenty-five other countries of this hemisphere has kept its races pure. Instead (though each contains some pure-blooded individuals) all these countries are products of an amalgamation of races — American Indian and white or American Indian, Negro, and white. In general the pure-blooded white nations have outstripped the far more numerous American mixed-blood nations in most of the achievements which constitute progress as commonly defined.

These facts are well known. But now there lurks in ambush, as it were, another fact: we have suddenly begun to move toward abandonment of our 350-year-old system of keeping our races pure and are preparing to adopt instead a method of racial amalgamation similar to that which has created the mixed-blood nations of this hemisphere; except that the amalgamation being prepared for this country is not Indian and white but Negro and white. It is the deep conviction of nearly all white Southerners in the states which have large Negro populations that the mingling or integration of white and Negro children in the South's primary schools would open the gates to miscegenation and widespread racial amalgamation.

This belief is at the heart of our race problem, and until it is realized that this is the South's basic and compelling motive, there can be no understanding of the South's attitude.

It must be realized too that the Negroes of the U.S.A. are today by far the most fortunate members of their race to be found anywhere on earth. Instead of being the hapless victim of unprecedented oppression, it is nearer the truth that the Negro in the United States is by and large the product of friendliness and helpfulness unequaled in any comparable instance in all history. Nowhere else in the world, at any time of which there is record, has a helpless, backward people of another color been so swiftly uplifted and so greatly benefited by a dominant race.

What America, including the South, has done for the Negro is the truth which

should be trumpeted abroad in rebuttal of the Communist propaganda. In failing to utilize this truth we have deliberately put aside a powerful affirmative weapon of enormous potential value to the free world and have allowed ourselves to be thrown on the defensive and placed in an attitude of apologizing for our conduct in a matter where actually our record is one of which we can be very proud.

We have permitted the subject of race relations in the United States to be used not as it should be used, as a weapon for America, but as a weapon for the narrow designs of the new aggressive Negro leadership in the United States. It cannot be so used without damage to this country, and that damage is beyond computation. Instead of winning for America the plaudits and trust of the colored peoples of Asia and Africa in recognition of what we have done for our colored people, our pro-Negro propagandists have seen to it that the United States appears as an international Simon Legree — or rather a Dr. Jekyll and Mr. Hyde with the South in the villainous role.

THE SOUTH has had a bad time with words. Nearly a century ago the word "slavery," even more than the thing itself, did the South irreparable damage. In a strange but real way the misused word "democracy" has injured the South; its most distinctive — and surely its greatest — period has been called undemocratic, meaning illiberal and reactionary, because it resisted the onward sweep of a centralizing governmental trend alien to our federal republic and destructive of the very "cornerstone of liberty," local self-government. Today the word "segregation" and, perhaps even more harmful, the word "prejudice" blacken the South's character before the world and make doubly difficult our effort to preserve not merely our own way of life but certain basic principles upon which our country was founded.

Words are of such transcendent importance today that the South should long ago have protested against these two. They are now too firmly imbedded in the dialectic of our race problem to be got rid of. But that very fact renders all the more necessary a careful scrutiny of them. Let us first consider the word "segregation."

Segregation is sometimes carelessly listed as a synonym of separation, but it is not a true synonym and the difference between the two words is important.

Segregation, from the Latin *segregatus* (set apart from the flock), implies isolation; separation carries no such implication. Segregation is what we have done to the American Indian — whose grievous wrongs few reformers and still fewer politicians ever bother their heads about. By use of force and against his will we have segregated him, isolated him, on certain small reservations which had and still have somewhat the character of concentration camps.

The South has not done that to the Negro. On the contrary, it has shared its countryside and its cities with him in amity and understanding, not perfect by any means, and careful of established folk custom, but far exceeding in human friendliness anything of the kind to be found in the North. Not segregation of the Negro race as the Indian is segregated on his reservations — and as the Negro is segregated in the urban Harlems of the North — but simply *separation* of the white and Negro races in certain phases of activity is what the South has always had and feels that it must somehow preserve even though the time-honored, successful, and completely moral "separate but equal" principle no longer has legal sanction.

Until the Supreme Court decision forbidding compulsory racial separation in the public schools, the South was moving steadily toward abandonment or relaxation of the compulsory separation rule in several important fields. This is no longer true.

Progress in racial relations has been stopped short by the ill-advised insistence of the Northern-directed Negro leadership upon the one concession which above all the white South will not and cannot make — public school integration.

Another word which is doing grave damage to the South today is "prejudice" meaning race prejudice — a causeless hostility often amounting to hatred which white Southerners are alleged to feel in regard to the Negro. Here again the South, forgetful of the lessons of its past, has failed to challenge effectively an inaccurate and injurious word. Not prejudice but preference is the word that truth requires.

Between prejudice and preference there is vast difference. Prejudice is a preconceived unfavorable judgment or feeling without sound basis. Preference is a natural reaction to facts and conditions observed or experienced, and through the action of heredity generation after generation it becomes instinctive. Like separateness, it exists throughout the animal kingdom. Though the difference between two races of an animal species may be so slight that only a specialist can differentiate between them, the individuals of one race prefer as a rule to associate with other individuals of that race.

One can cite numerous examples among birds and mammals. In the human species the history of our own country provides the most striking example of race preference. The white men and women, chiefly of British, German, Dutch, and Scandinavian stocks, who colonized and occupied what is now the United States were strongly imbued with race preference. They did not follow the example of the Spanish and Portuguese (in whom for historical reasons the instinct of race preference was much weaker) who in colonizing South and Central America amalgamated with the Indians found in possession of the land and in some cases with the Negroes brought over as slaves. Instead, the founders of the future United States maintained their practice of non-amalgamation rigorously, with only slight racial blendings along the fringes of each group.

Hence it is nonsense to say that racial discrimination, the necessary consequence of race preference, is "un-American." Actually it is perhaps the most distinctively American thing there is, the reason why the American people — meaning the people of the United States — are what they are. Today when racial discrimination of any kind or degree is instantly denounced as both sinful and stupid, few stop to reflect that this nation is built solidly upon it.

The truth is, of course, that there are many different kinds and degrees of racial discrimination. Some of them are bad — outdated relics of an earlier time when conditions were unlike those of today, and these should be, and were being, abolished until the unprecedented decree of the Supreme Court in the school cases halted all progress. But not all kinds of racial discrimination are evil — unless we are prepared to affirm that our forefathers blundered in "keeping the breed pure."

Thus it is clear that discrimination too is a misused word as commonly employed in the realm of racial relations. It does not necessarily imply either stupidity or sin. It is not a synonym for injustice, and it is very far from being, as many seem to think, a synonym for hatred. The Southern white man has always exercised discrimination in regard to the Negro but — except for a tiny and untypical minority of the white population — he has never hated the Negro. I have lived a fairly long life in a part of the South — the South Carolina Lowcountry — where there are many thousands of Negroes, and since early boyhood I have known many of them well, in some cases for years, in town and country. I know how I feel about them and how the white people of this old plantation region, the high and the low, the rich and the poor, the large landowner and the white mechanic, feel about them.

I am sure that among white Carolinians there is, as yet, almost no hatred of the Negro, nor is there anything that can accurately be called race prejudice. What does exist, strongly and ineradicably, is race preference. In other words, we white Southerners prefer our own race and wish to keep it as it is.

This preference should not and in fact cannot be eliminated. It is much bigger than we are, a far greater thing than our racial dilemma. It is — and here is another basic fact of great significance — an essential element in Nature's huge and complex mechanism. It is one of the reasons why evolution, ever diversifying, ever discriminating, ever separating race from race, species from species, has been able to operate in an ascending course so that what began aeons ago as something resembling an amoeba has now become Man. In preferring its own race and in striving to prevent the destruction of that race by amalgamation with another race, the white South is not flouting Nature but is in harmony with her.

IF THE NEGRO also prefers his own race and wishes to preserve its identity, then he is misrepresented by his new aggressive leadership which, whether or not this is its deliberate aim, is moving toward a totally different result. Let us see why that is so.

The crux of the race problem in the South, as I have said, is the nearly universal belief of the Southern white people that only by maintaining a certain degree of separateness of the races can the racial integrity of the white South be safeguarded. Unfortunately the opinion has prevailed outside the South that only a few Southerners hold this conviction — a handful of demagogic politicians and their most ignorant followers — and that "enlightened" white Southerners recognize the alleged danger of racial amalgamation as a trumped-up thing having no real substance.

Nothing could be farther from the truth. Because the aggressive Northern-Negro leadership continues to drive onward, the white South (except perhaps that part which is now more Western than Southern and in which Negroes are few) is today as united in its conviction that its racial integrity must be protected as it was when the same conviction drove its people — the slaveholder and the non-slaveholder, the high and the low, the educated and the ignorant — to defend the outworn institution of Negro slavery because there seemed to be no other way to preserve the social and political control needed to prevent the Africanization of the South by a combination of fanatical Northern reformers and millions of enfranchised Negroes. The South escaped that fate because after a decade of disastrous experiment the intelligent people of the victorious North realized that the racial program of their social crusaders was unsound, or at least impracticable, and gave up trying to enforce it.

Now in a surging revival of that "Reconstruction" crusade — a revival which is part dedicated idealism, part understandable racial ambition, part political expediency national and international — the same social program is again to be imposed upon the South. There are new conditions which help powerfully to promote it: the Hitlerite excesses in the name of race which have brought all race distinctions into popular disrepute; the notion that the white man, by divesting himself of race consciousness, may appease the peoples of Asia and Africa and wean them away from Communism.

In addition, a fantastic perversion of scientific authority has been publicized in support of the new crusade. Though everywhere else in Nature (as well as in all our plant breeding and animal breeding) race and heredity are recognized as of primary importance, we are told that in the human species race is of no importance and racial differences are due not to heredity but to environment. Science has proved, so we are told, that all races are equal and, in essentials, identical.

Science has most certainly not proved that all races are equal, much less identical; and, as the courageous geneticist, Dr. W. C. George of the University of North Carolina, has recently pointed out, there is overwhelming likelihood that the biological consequences of white and Negro integration in the South would be harmful. It would not be long before these biological consequences became visible. But there is good hope that we shall never see them, because any attempt to force a program of racial integration upon the South would be met with stubborn, determined, and universal opposition, probably taking the form of passive resistance of a hundred kinds. Though secession is not conceivable, persistence in an attempt to compel the South to mingle its white and Negro children in its public schools would split the United States in two as disastrously as in the sixties and perhaps with an even more lamentable aftermath of bitterness.

For the elementary public school is the most critical of those areas of activity where the South must and will at all costs maintain separateness of the races. The South must do this because, although it is a nearly universal instinct, race preference is not active in the very young. Race preference (which the propagandists miscall race prejudice or hate) is one of those instincts which develop gradually as the mind develops and which, if taken in hand early enough, can be prevented from developing at all.

Hence if the small children of the two races in approximately equal numbers — as would be the case in a great many of the South's schools — were brought together intimately and constantly and grew up in close association in integrated schools under teachers necessarily committed to the gospel of racial integration, there would be many in whom race preference would not develop. This would not be, as superficial thinkers might suppose, a good thing, the happy solution of the race problem in America. It might be a solution of a sort, but not one that the American people would desire. It would inevitably result, beginning with the least desirable elements of both races, in a great increase of racial amalgamation, the very process which throughout our history we have most sternly rejected. For although to most persons today the idea of mixed mating is disagreeable or even repugnant, this would not be true of the new generations brought up in mixed schools with the desirability of racial integration as a basic premise. Among those new generations mixed matings would become commonplace, and a greatly enlarged mixed-blood population would result.

That is the compelling reason, though by no means the only reason, why the South will resist, with all its resources of mind and body, the mixing of the races in its public schools. It is a reason which, when its validity is generally recognized, will quickly enlist millions of non-Southerners in support of the South's position. The people of the North and West do not favor the transformation of the United States into a nation composed in considerable part of mixed bloods any more than the people of the South do. Northern support of school integration in the South is due to the failure to realize its inevitable biological effect in regions of large Negro population. If Northerners did realize this, their enthusiasm for mixed schools in the South would evaporate at once.

75.

WOODY GUTHRIE: "This Land Is Your Land"

Woody Guthrie, the famous folk singer and balladeer, wrote "This Land Is Your Land" in 1956. One of his last efforts, it is thought by many to be his best; it gained immediate popularity and soon became a perennial folk-song favorite, often being sung as the last number of folk-song programs.

Source: "This Land Is Your Land," words and music by Woody Guthrie, © Copyright 1956 and 1958, Ludlow Music, Inc., New York, N.Y., Used by Permission.

❧ THIS LAND IS YOUR LAND

As I went walking that ribbon of highway,
I saw above me that endless skyway,
I saw below me that golden valley,
This land was made for you and me.

Chorus:
This land is your land, this land is my land,
From California to the New York Island,
From the redwood forest to the Gulf Stream water,
This land was made for you and me.

I roamed and I rambled and I followed my footsteps
To the sparkling sands of her diamond deserts,
While all around me a voice was sounding, saying,
"This land was made for you and me."

The sun came shining and I was strolling,
And the wheat fields waving and the dust clouds rolling,
As the fog was lifting, a voice was chanting,
"This land was made for you and me."

76.

HARLOW H. CURTICE: Automotive Research at General Motors

*Twentieth-century technological advances in America have brought with them a train
of further problems, one of which may be called the problem of durability. Briefly, if
a machine lasts too long or is too efficient it will not soon need replacement; but the
economy is based to a large extent on increasing consumer need, and this involves
frequent replacement of necessary articles. One solution to the problem of durability
is "built-in obsolescence" — the production of consumer goods that are adequate for
their purpose and for their time but that are superseded according to a prearranged
plan by better articles somewhat later. In a speech made at the dedication of the
General Motors Technical Center on May 16, 1956, Harlow H. Curtice, president of
General Motors, discussed the problem and proposed as a solution what he called
"dynamic obsolescence." His remarks are reprinted here.*

Source: *The Greatest Frontier*, Detroit, 1956.

WE HAVE GATHERED today for a momentous occasion. The dedication of the General Motors Technical Center has great significance for us in General Motors. More importantly, it has great significance for the welfare and progress of our country and the world.

Among the traditions which are part of the rich heritage of America, perhaps none has more meaning than our belief in the importance and the inevitability of change. The urge for change — spiritual, political, or economic — was the motivating force that brought the earliest settlers to our shores. It propelled our pioneers westward, cleared our farmlands, built our great cities, created new industries and new ways of life for all of us.

Continuing emphasis on change, on a better method and a better product, in other words, on progress in technology, has been the major force responsible for the growth and development of our country. Some call this typical American process "dynamic obsolescence" because it calls for replacing the old with something new and better. From this process of accelerating obsolescence by technological progress flow the benefits we all share — more and better job opportunities, an advancing standard of living — the entire forward march of civilization on the material side.

No industry has contributed more to our nation's growth and development than the automobile industry. Its products have completely changed the face of America and the habits of all Americans. No industry has done more to raise the United States to a position of world strength and leadership. The reason is that the automobile industry, as no other industry, makes a practice of investing regularly and heavily in planned change. The importance of a continuing improvement in product and process dominates the thinking of every automobile man worthy of the name.

You are all familiar with the annual model change and its importance to our industry. Under its forced draft we have made tremendous forward strides in improving our products in every way possible — appearance, performance, comfort, durability. Of almost equal importance is the steady flow of improvements in manufacturing equipment and methods. The automobile industry is dedicated to the process of accelerating obsolescence.

General Motors has for many years been a leader in the forward march of technology. As a result, our products have been improved steadily, customers have bought them in increasing numbers. We have grown and prospered with substantial benefit to our employees, our suppliers, our dealers, and our shareholders. We also have contributed importantly to a dynamic and expanding national economy.

We expect to continue our contributions to technological progress — and at an accelerated rate. That is the purpose of this great institution — the General Motors Technical Center. The opportunity for dynamic growth rests, as never before, with the creative scientists, the researchers, and the inventive engineers who make people

dissatisfied with old products by the process of developing new and better ones.

Almost 5,000 of these scientists, engineers, designers, technicians, and other personnel are employed at the Technical Center. They comprise the central staffs of General Motors in research, advanced engineering, styling, and process development. Their work ranges all the way from pure science and basic research to the more immediately rewarding tasks of finding better things to make and better ways to make them.

The buildings at the Technical Center are furnished with every conceivable type of tool, equipment, testing device — all the very latest and the very best. Working conditions, likewise, are the very best. The campuslike atmosphere was sought deliberately, not to impress visitors but because we believe that such surroundings stimulate creative thinking and are conducive to good work.

But fine buildings, perfect tools, and pleasant surroundings alone do not make the Technical Center. Nor do just people — even well-trained, proficient people. What makes the Technical Center is a very special and dynamic kind of philosophy that we have in General Motors. We call it the "inquiring mind" approach.

The inquiring mind is never satisfied with things as they are. It assumes that anything and everything can be improved. In technology it is concerned with the creative improvement of product and process. It is always seeking to make things better and to do things better. This attitude of the inquiring mind is by no means unique to General Motors. However, we pride ourselves on having developed it to an unusual degree. We believe we can well lay claim to leadership in helping inquiry graduate from the cellar and the backyard shop, and also in pioneering the now accepted practice of setting it apart from the manufacturing process.

A small research department was established as early as 1911. In the 1920s the Corporation organized central staff styling and engineering activities. This came about largely because of the vision of Alfred P. Sloan, Jr. Many years ago, Mr. Sloan clearly foresaw the steadily increasing importance of research, engineering, and styling in this highly competitive automobile business. It was his genius also that was chiefly responsible for the concept of a centrally located Technical Center which would gather together in one place all of the forward development work of General Motors. It is a great regret to all of us that Mr. Sloan cannot be here today to witness the realization of one of his fondest dreams.

I am very happy that Mr. Charles E. Wilson is with us today, and I would like to pay tribute to him for getting the Technical Center project under way when he was president of General Motors. In a period when too many were concerned only with production to meet pent-up postwar demand, he realized the importance of continuing product development and improvement. In joining with Mr. Sloan to announce the project for the Technical Center on July 24, 1945, Mr. Wilson said: "We are hoping and preparing for an economy of plenty and not one based on the theory of scarcity. We are anxious to do our part in creating the more abundant life postwar."

Needless to say, this expression of faith and courage has been amply justified by the 60 percent growth in the country's industrial output over the past decade.

In theory the Technical Center activities are independent of the various producing divisions, just as the producing divisions operate independently of each other. In practice, however, none of them operates independently. Each derives support and gives support to the others. The result is that the whole is greater than the sum of its parts. The Technical Center is a vital and continu-

ing source of new developments for the producing divisions. In a sense, it provides the lifeblood so essential to their success.

A major General Motors research development was "Freon," the greatest forward step ever taken in the electric refrigeration field. Freon was the first nontoxic, nonflammable refrigerant and was responsible in large measure for the growth of the refrigerator industry. Even today, there is no substitute for Freon.

Another research development, of tremendous importance to the entire automobile industry, was the discovery that tetraethyl lead eliminates engine knock. This development made it possible to increase the power output of engines by raising compression ratios.

The two-cycle, lightweight diesel engine is still another outstanding research development. General Motors Research Laboratories started work on this engine as early as 1928. Our primary objective then was to develop a practical diesel truck engine that would produce substantial operating economies. Progress over the next two years indicated that diesel engines of various horsepower sizes could be designed for a great variety of applications in transportation and stationary industrial usage. That judgment of twenty-five years ago, although few would concur in it at the time, has been amply borne out by later events. General Motors two-cycle, lightweight diesel engines not only revolutionized the entire diesel industry but revitalized the railroads of the nation and saved them $600 million a year in fuel and maintenance costs alone. Railroad officials credit their present healthy financial state largely to the diesel locomotive.

In noncommercial areas General Motors research has produced the mechanical heart, used in delicate heart operations, and the Centri-Filmer for sterilizing blood plasma, polio vaccine, and other liquids.

Getting back to the automobile industry

and other Technical Center activities, the Styling Staff furnishes the creative designs which enable General Motors cars to maintain styling leadership. Practically all new styling advances in the industry — the two-door hardtop, the panoramic windshield, the four-door hardtop, to name the most recent — all of them were born in the General Motors styling section. One of the advanced engineering groups did the pioneering work which resulted in the General Motors family of automatic transmissions — one of the most important forward steps ever made in automotive technology. The V-8 higher compression engine, also pioneered by General Motors and now featured in all of its lines, was the outgrowth of the combined efforts of the Research Staff and divisional engineers.

Not all of the contributions to progress flow from the Technical Center to the divisions. The process is a reciprocal one. The divisions not only field test new developments but advance them to the point of being commercially practical and work out methods for producing them in volume. In some cases an idea originates in a division and is developed at the Technical Center. In many cases several divisions are "in" on a new project. Frequently, the work of the various groups is so interrelated that it becomes impossible to assign credit for the successive steps taken to reach the market.

We consider this interplay of ideas, this process of cross-fertilization, tremendously important. Many projects overlap, and progress in one can contribute importantly to progress in another. Often the contribution is made almost by chance and could only occur in a community where men of different interests mingle together freely. Sometimes ideas which prove to be impractical in one area are picked up by someone else and used to solve a problem in another area. A typical example is a device originally conceived as a supercharger for an automobile engine, which eventually made its appearance as a wobble plate compressor for automobile air-conditioning.

There are many projects of this type under way at the Technical Center and, of course, numerous ones representing other kinds of development work. In the interest of time, I have cited only a few scattered examples of the ceaseless activity here and the constant flow of Technical Center material to the divisions.

It is our hope and expectation that this great Technical Center will enable General Motors not only to carry on its tradition of the inquiring mind but even to speed the processes whereby many more new developments may be brought into being for the good of all. I have no doubt that from it will come many important advances in the industrial arts that will further economic progress and contribute to national defense as well. We should witness a great acceleration of the pace of technological progress as other centers of industrial engineering and research intensify their activities.

The promotion of the progress of science and the useful arts is of crucial importance and particularly right now. I have stressed the contribution of technological progress to the advancement of our material well-being. There is a *far more* vital consideration. I refer to the importance of technological progress in assuring the continuance, not only of American leadership in the free world but of the democratic processes themselves.

Today we are being put to a competitive test — a struggle for survival. We are being challenged in this one area of technological progress that we have come to regard as the source of our greatest strength.

How do we meet this challenge?

We must see to it that a larger proportion of our young people have the opportunity and the incentive for embarking on a scientific or engineering career. But quantity is not enough. We must also raise the level of quality of our technology by giving the greatest encouragement to the most talented individuals.

We must put still more emphasis on basic research. I understand that the great majority of the momentous discoveries of recent years in atomic energy, in aerodynamics, in solid state physics have had their beginnings in the abstract theorems of the higher mathematicians and the cryptic formulas of the research physicists.

General Motors has materially enlarged and broadened its research program. We are all agreed upon a well-balanced program with increasing emphasis upon fundamental research. In our research and creative engineering activities we cannot always establish specific objectives, nor do we have an exact timetable. We believe that greater emphasis on the search for fundamental scientific truths and principles will inevitably represent a good investment in tomorrow for the benefit of our country and for General Motors.

I hope you will come to regard the General Motors Technical Center in the same way I do — as one of the nation's great resources — more important even than the natural resources with which we have been endowed. The latter are exhaustible, but the "extractions" from a resource like the Technical Center are limited only by the ability and ingenuity of its scientists and engineers.

As long as this country can count on the increasing productivity of such resources, the continued expansion of our economy is assured. And likewise assured is the strength that will enable us to stand as a bulwark for the free world.

77.

Ezra Taft Benson: Price Supports and Farm Surpluses

Agricultural problems beset the Eisenhower administration as they had all previous administrations for several decades. In order to reduce surpluses and stabilize prices Congress passed the Agricultural Adjustment Act of 1954, which modified the parity system as it had existed under the Democrats. Yet the prices the farmers had to pay for their goods remained high. The farm problems naturally became a political issue in the election year of 1956, by which time the Soil Bank Act had begun to take effect. But this plan did not have the hoped-for success either. In a speech to the Pennsylvania State Poultry Federation on August 25, 1956, Secretary of Agriculture Ezra Taft Benson explained administration farm policies on price supports.

Source: VSD, October 1, 1956: "As Ye Sow So Shall Ye Reap."

Your objective as farmers is to produce an adequate living for your families — a living at least comparable to other American families. How well your family can live is a question of your annual income — not merely the price you get for one dozen eggs or one pound or bushel of any other product.

Price times volume determines your gross income. Price is just one factor. Your right to produce is just as important. Price times volume minus your costs determines your net income. And I know, as you do, that you cannot operate efficiently, and keep your costs in line, without the freedom to manage your own farms — freedom to produce as your own circumstances dictate.

Anyone — and we still have some — who would make prices the central theme of farm policy is doing a great disservice to farm families.

Today the so-called basic crops — the ones that have had the supposed benefits of rigid price supports right up to the harvest of last fall — these crops are now in more serious difficulties than are the crops and livestock that have not been price supported.

How can cotton, or tobacco, or wheat farmers, who have been sharply restricted in their acreage, produce an adequate living for their families? Actually some of them have almost been forced out of farming by the controls that have followed upon their price supports. This is a tragic circumstance. I welcome this opportunity to discuss with you some of these problems. It is imperative that they shall be more fully understood, not only by farm people but by all Americans.

This is my first public address since the national political conventions. During the next two and a half months much attention will be focused on political discussions — and that agriculture will get its share of political attention is abundantly clear. I have a feeling that a good deal of politics has been buzzing around my head for the past three and a half years. But you know by now that I am not a politician — at least many people have told you so many times. However that may be, from now until November — and I say this in all seriousness — I will be neither more political nor less political in what I say and do than I have been in the past.

Farm people — my people — have prob-

lems — serious ones. These problems have been brought on in large part by politics. They will not be solved by more political maneuvering. They will be solved only by facing facts — by sound thinking, and sound action.

The farm problem has not changed because this is a political year. I was reared on a farm. I have operated my own farm and have worked with and for farm people practically all my life. I have stated my views on what must be done to work our way out of the present difficulties of agriculture. These views have not changed because of a coming election. And I shall continue to state these views as clearly as I can, and to as many people as I can, between now and election — and after election as necessary. American agriculture is neither Republican nor Democrat. Farm people cannot, and must not, be thought of as a group who may be put on the political auction block. Their problems cannot be solved that way.

At the same time, I am glad this is a presidential election year — and I am not at all unhappy that some people are choosing to make agricultural problems an issue in the campaign. Out of all the discussion — and even controversy — will come better understanding of farm problems than we have had for a long time. I am confident of the good judgment of farm people — because they know, perhaps better than most, that "as ye sow so shall ye reap."

At the very heart of the agricultural issue is whether our farms are to continue to be operated by freemen. Or, on the other hand, to offset some very real and obvious problems that farmers now face, will government go in the opposite direction and subsidize agriculture in such a manner that it also takes control?

If price supports are to be increased, and are to be extended to more crops and to livestock, as again is being proposed in the political debate about agriculture, then farmers will be subjected to more controls. Such a result would be inescapable. Producers would have to be told how many sows they can keep and how many pigs the sows may farrow — how many hens they can keep, and how many eggs the hens may lay.

Control is the inevitable, the unavoidable, twin of the subsidy. Subsidized prices — meaning prices consistently and substantially higher than the market would pay — always lead to surpluses. This is because artificially high guaranteed prices are a green light to producers and encourage production. At the same time they are a red light to consumers and discourage consumption. If more — or even the same amount — is produced, but less can be sold, then what are called surpluses begin to accumulate. Then output has to be restricted in an effort to restore balance between supply and demand. Restricted production means that the right to produce has to be *rationed* among farmers. And this requires use of the government's police power, to restrain farmers, in our free country. This is a sequence of cause and effect that is bitter as gall to me. As a permanent condition in our agriculture it is no more necessary than it is desirable.

Our most critical farm problems — both national and for most farmers — are those rooted in our surpluses. There are other problems, as there always have been. But we could live with and surmount the others if we could get out from under the distortions and disruptions caused by the surpluses.

I would like to review five questions with you. (1) How did we get these surpluses? (2) Whose surpluses are they? (3) What are they doing to farmers? (4) Why haven't we gotten rid of them? (5) What can be done about them?

1. *How did we get the surpluses?* We have the surpluses primarily because we carried wartime incentive price supports too long into the postwar years. During World War

II price supports were raised from the prewar range of 52 to 75 percent of parity and placed at 90 percent in order to stimulate all-out production to meet war needs. Farmers responded magnificently.

War places insatiable demands on agriculture. It requires every pound, and bushel, and bale that can be produced. But after some postwar rehabilitation, the same quantities and kind of produce cannot be sold at the same prices in peacetime markets. And yet the wartime incentive levels of price supports on the six so-called basic commodities — the same rigid 90 percents — were extended year after year following the war. The final extension was in July 1952, for two years — in other words, through the marketing year for the harvests of 1954. Thus for a decade after the war — right up to the harvests of last year — the price support levels on the basic commodities were still calling on farmers to produce just as they did in wartime. And yet we did not have the wartime markets.

Surpluses began to accumulate in 1948 and 1949. Korea reversed the trend, briefly. Then the pile up became even more rapid. At first only a few items were involved — particularly wheat and cotton. But acreage diverted out of these crops threw others into surplus. Feed production was increased and stimulated overexpansion of livestock; and so the problem spread, until almost every farmer, regardless of what he produces, is adversely affected.

2. *Whose surpluses are they?* I raise this question only because some of my political opponents have been blaming this administration.

When we took office in January 1953, the inventories and loans of the Commodity Credit Corporation were about $3 billion. But our predecessors had left a time bomb. Prior to Inauguration Day, they already had announced unlimited production of wheat, corn, and cotton for 1953. Before we could do anything about it — a year later —

government-held surpluses had increased to $6.5 billion. As provided in the law, we had to subject farmers to acreage and marketing controls in 1954. This was done with great regret because I was well aware of the hardship it would work on farmers. But it was necessary and unavoidable because the rigid wartime price supports were still in effect for the basic crops. Even with the controls, the surplus stockpiles increased to well over $7 billion by the end of the 1954 marketing year.

While it was a time bomb that our predecessors left for us, it was farmers and the public — particularly farmers — who got hurt.

3. *What are the surpluses doing to farmers?* What are the costs involved in these government-held surpluses? First, the storage costs alone on the $8.5 billion stockpile we now have are more than $1 million a day. Then there are administrative costs and interest costs on the money. Deterioration costs are small, but some are unavoidable. There are losses when these products are sold for less than the government paid.

These are costs to taxpayers — to the nation as a whole. They are small compared to other costs which fall upon you as farmers.

The reason is that no one can prevent the surplus stockpiles from having a price-depressing effect upon your markets. I cannot emphasize too strongly that produce taken over by the government for price-support purposes has not actually been sold. It is merely held in a government warehouse awaiting a final use. It is still part of the domestic and the world supply. However closely it may be guarded from the market, everyone knows that sooner or later, for one purpose or another — even to meet one emergency or another — it will sometime be used. And when it is used it will add to market supplies. Consequently, the very existence of such stocks always has its depressing effect on market prices.

Department of Agriculture economists estimate that our net farm income last year was reduced at least 20 percent — at least $2 billion — by the price-depressing effect of the surplus stockpiles. This staggering sum is about *$5.5 million a day* that the surpluses are costing farmers — $5.5 million a day in reduced net income. Such tragic losses must be stopped. The cause must be corrected — because agriculture cannot be free and prosperous until it is.

4. *Why have we not disposed of the surpluses more rapidly?* Ladies and gentlemen, I can report to you that we have worked aggressively at disposal and have used every means we could devise. During the last fiscal year $2.7-billion worth of government-owned stocks were moved into use at home and abroad — in the last three years, about $6-billion worth. We have sold into the domestic market when we could. We have sold abroad for dollars — or for foreign currencies if dollars could not be had. We have bartered if we could not sell — and we have donated for relief purposes and for other worthy causes both at home and overseas.

I must call your attention to the fact that the disposal alternatives open to your government do have limits. In fact, we have only three alternatives. We can move the surpluses at home. Or, we can move them overseas. Or — well, the third is not even an alternative. It would be deliberately to destroy food and other farm products — and that would be immoral and unthinkable.

Then think a minute about the other alternatives.

When the surplus stocks are sold or given away in the domestic market, there is always the risk — an ever present risk — of lowering the prices for what you and other farmers are producing currently. Thus we have to proceed cautiously for *your* protection. And when the surplus stocks are sold or given away overseas, except in carefully controlled quantities, there is the same risk — and the risk also of upsetting markets in other countries and bringing retaliation upon us from other governments. Thus the surplus situation that has grown up as a result of unwise price supports — the wartime, rigid, incentive price supports continued too long after the wartime markets no longer existed — that surplus appears up to this point to have presented a nearly insoluble problem.

In spite of everything we have been able to do in disposal, surpluses have continued to flow into the Commodity Credit Corporation more rapidly than they could be moved out. The result has been a tragedy for farmers and a dilemma for the administration.

5. What more can be done about them? It is against this background, and to help solve the dilemma, that the Soil Bank legislation was proposed. The Soil Bank will not be a cure-all. It should be one more tool to help overcome the distortions created by the surpluses and to get agriculture back to more freedom and prosperity.

The voluntary and temporary Soil Bank provided for in the Agricultural Act of 1956 has three interrelated purposes:

First, to achieve a temporary reduction in farm output, with compensation to farmers for their participation.

Second, in consequence of smaller production, to provide an opportunity — a place in the market — to liquidate surplus stocks without depressing market prices.

Third, to shift an acreage of cropland not now needed into grass and trees and other conserving uses. The reason is to conserve and safeguard our precious heritage of soil and water resources against the future needs of the many generations yet unborn.

Unfortunately, the Soil Bank legislation was so long delayed that it could not be fully effective for 1956. Only a partial program could be established — and the partial application will have little effect this year on the surplus stocks. The real test of the Soil Bank as a means of surplus elimination will come next year.

Courtesy, F. O. Alexander, "The Bulletin"

"Still Growing"; cartoon by Alexander in "The Bulletin," Philadelphia, 1955

It *must* be made to work. It must *not* be degenerated by political pressure into a mere crop insurance or drought relief scheme — for which it was not intended — and thereby fail in its most important purpose of surplus reduction.

To restrict production is unpalatable to farmers, even for a cause as important as the elimination of surpluses. But I expect a large proportion of farmers to recognize the necessity for the Soil Bank and to accept the voluntary participation it offers. To ask farmers to restrict production is unpalatable for me. But since it must be done before the burden of surpluses hurts our farmers even more seriously, a temporary and voluntary Soil Bank seems to promise the best solution. And when the surpluses are eliminated and the distortions they have caused are behind us, there is one more essential. We must then avoid, as we would a plague, all price-support schemes or other programs of a kind that would build up surplus problems again.

I have spoken feelingly of these situations that now exist because they are so basic and fundamental to the prosperity of agriculture — and to the well-being of farm families. This administration has one broad objective in carrying out its responsibilities to our farm people. That is to do everything in our power to develop and maintain *a sound, prosperous, expanding,* and *free agriculture.* We believe that only in this way can farm life be the profitable and satisfying experience we all want it to be.

We believe there are many ways in which government can render assistance to agriculture and be a real servant of farmers. And we believe this is government's proper role. We believe that to whatever degree agriculture programs force government to control farmers, there is a corresponding risk that government will become master instead of servant. We do not believe that master is a proper role of government.

We are dedicated to reversing any such trend as rapidly and completely as possible without causing disruption to agriculture in the process. We are equally dedicated to avoiding any new programs that do not lead as rapidly as possible to restoring and maintaining farmers' own rights to operate their own farms.

We have always before us such contrasts as the inspiring example of your poultry industry *vs.* the sad plight of the so-called basic crops. You are free, expanding, and progressive. You have expanded egg production 22 percent and poultry meat 52 percent in a decade — and have increased your markets proportionately. They have had rigid price supports — and have become surplus-depressed and production-controlled. Their problems have gotten worse, not better. Your future may be interpreted anywhere in the range from encouraging to inspiring. Until their production and markets can be brought back into balance, their outlook is discouraging and bleak.

Ladies and gentlemen, the transition from war to peace is never easy for agriculture. War always brings insatiable demands and rising prices. It is easier to gear up to greater production than it is to readjust to the changing demands of peacetime. But surely no one wants war as a solution to any difficulties that readjustment may bring. Our great blessing is that we have peace — a peace achieved and maintained under the leadership of our great President. . . .

Farmers have been caught in a cost-price squeeze, the seriousness of which I would certainly not minimize. Yet never before in history has the transition from war to peace been made as smoothly or with as little distress to farmers. If it were not for surpluses, the average of farm prices would now stand above 90 percent of parity.

The percentage of farms owned by the families who operate them is at a record high level — and the number of farm foreclosures is near an all-time low. This is in sharp contrast with the years shortly after World War I. But surely it does not mean that this administration is satisfied with farm conditions as they are. In keeping with our responsibility to farmers, a whole battery of programs — some old and some new — is being operated to protect and improve the economic position of farm families. These include:

Credit — on a liberalized basis.

Conservation — for which funds have been increased.

Price supports — into which the essential principle of flexibility is being reestablished.

Assistance for perishable farm products — to relieve market gluts where such assistance will be constructive.

The Rural Development Program — for opening the doors of greater opportunity to low-income farmers.

The Soil Bank.

Drought relief.

Expanded research on production and marketing problems and technical assistance through the Extension Service.

Many of these programs are reaching to new horizons, to be of fuller service to farm families, to help achieve more efficient production and marketing — and, I pray always, to help keep farmers free as well as prosperous.

I am proud of the opportunity I have had

to serve the interests of farmers in this administration. I am proud also of my many associates in the Department of Agriculture. They, too, have worked devotedly in your interests. I am glad to have the record of our stewardship thoroughly discussed in the election campaign.

The positive, constructive programs advocated by this administration are designed to retain to farmers their full heritage of freedom and to contribute to a sound and expanding farm prosperity. They are programs founded neither on the quicksand of war nor the entanglements of bureaucracy.

78.

FREDERICK W. COPELAND: The Illusion of Owning a Business

Frederick W. Copeland, a corporation president and management consultant, analyzed in 1956 the difficulties faced by those who wanted to operate a small business in an age of giant corporations. "Much has been said about the Horatio Alger type of young man who starts his own business and progresses to fame and wealth," said Copeland, "but no one has commented on the thousands of young men who without special talents or capabilities have frittered away the years of early manhood starting their own businesses."

Source: *Atlantic Monthly*, September 1956.

AS AN ELDER BUSINESS EXECUTIVE, I am approached from time to time by young men who are emerging from educational or military training and want advice on the selection of a career.

Today's young man is no worshiper of Horatio Alger. He has watched his father carrying an increasing load of worry as he rose in prominence — always fussing about taxes, inflation, labor, and rising costs. The son's goal is simple and specific; he likes to think of himself with a wife and a couple of kids, a small house, a secondhand station wagon, a trailer, a boat, and a pair of skis. He already has definite plans for his weekends and his annual vacations. An income of $8,000 a year will suit him perfectly, and he is much more interested in reaching that point as rapidly as possible than in shooting for $100,000 a year eventually.

He does not care particularly how he earns his $8,000, and he expects to work hard. But he has one very specific reservation: "I am not going to spend my life taking orders from someone else or licking boots to get a salary raise. I am going to own my own business and work for myself."

Admittedly there is no more satisfied businessman than he who owns and operates his own established and profitable business. He has the fun of making all the decisions and of keeping all the rewards of success. He does not have to defer to the orders or moods of others, and he can exercise his own whims and moods as he sees fit. He can sleep late in the morning if he is tired and go fishing when the fish are biting. He can take out all the profits currently or leave them in the business for future growth. Within reason he can have tax-free luxuries by charging the business with club dues, home entertaining, and trips to New York, Florida, and even Europe. And, of course, the business is charged with the purchase and upkeep of his Cadillac.

When you meet this lucky man, however, and he brags about the joys of independence, you will find it interesting to draw him out on the subject of his early history. Unless he inherited the business he will be proud of the hardships and narrow escapes he suffered before he got his head above water. He will tell you how he, and usually his wife, worked twelve hours a day, seven days a week, because they could not afford to hire a stenographer, bookkeeper, or janitor; how he did not take a vacation until he was fifty; how, on various occasions, he was down to his last dollar and had to bluff his creditors or get a prepayment from a customer. And as you listen to his life story, you will recognize that his success is the result of a combination of special skill, shrewdness, willingness to gamble, hard work, personal sacrifice, and usually some luck.

Ordinarily this businessman has all his eggs in one basket: all his personal capital is invested in his business. On paper he is a wealthy man, but little of his wealth is in liquid form. What will happen to his estate if he dies? The inheritance tax people will put a high value on his company holdings, but there will not be enough cash to pay the tax. Should he sell the business while the going is good? How about straddling the issue by selling a portion of the business for cash? No, that would mean sharing ownership with a stranger and losing most of the fun. How about gradually transferring ownership to his son, so that there will be no inheritance tax? Is his son capable of carrying on the management? Suppose he conveyed ownership to his son; would his son get greedy and crowd the old man out?

If he is a manufacturer, he is always afraid that a competitor will outdesign him, steal his best man, or start a price war, and he has the constant dread of arriving at the shop some morning and finding a union picket at the gate. The personally owned company is usually too small to be diversified in products and personnel; one hard bump in the form of a lawsuit, a bad account, or the loss of a key man can do irreparable damage.

This successful man represents not more than 1 percent of the men who started their own businesses when he did. It is my best guess that out of one hundred starters, forty fall by the wayside and fifty-nine become hopelessly locked into a marginal situation, with all resources tied up in the struggle to survive, with a net profit lower than the wages they could earn outside, and with absolutely no escape because they cannot sell out. Statistics show that, in 1955, 65 percent of the total business failures were for amounts of $25,000 or less; 56 percent of the total failures were companies five years old or less. Dun & Bradstreet reports that 90 percent of all failures are attributable to inexperience and poor management.

Disregard for odds and complete confidence in one's self have produced many of our greatest successes. But every young man who wants to go into business for himself should appraise himself as a candidate for the one percent to survive. What has he to offer that is new or better? Has he special talents, special know-how, a new invention or service, or more capital than the average competitor? Has he the most important qualification of all, a willingness to work harder than anyone else? A man who is working for himself without limitation of hours or personal sacrifice can run circles around any operation that relies on paid help, particularly if it is unionized. But he must forget the eight-hour day, the forty-hour week, and the annual vacation. When he stops work, his income stops unless he hires a substitute.

Most small operations have their busiest day on Saturday, and the owner uses Sunday to catch up on his correspondence, bookkeeping, inventorying, and maintenance chores. The successful self-employed man invariably works harder and worries more than the man on a salary. His wife and children make corresponding sacrifices of family unity and continuity. . . .

IF YOU ARE BURNING WITH AN INSPIRATION to invent a new product or service, it would be a great pity not to give it a good try. But do not overlook the time-and-loss element. You must first develop the product or service to your own satisfaction; next, demonstrate it to the satisfaction of the trade; next, make the public aware of its virtues; and, finally, arrange that the willing buyer can get prompt delivery and service. In the meantime you must eat.

This brings us to the critical subject of capital. After the war several young men came to me saying, "I have saved up $10,000 and want to go into business for myself. What do you suggest as an activity?" They assumed that this amount of money had a tremendous impact. They expected to make a living wage at once, get a good return on their capital, and run a steadily growing business. Their faces fell when I suggested, in all seriousness, a filling station, a hamburger stand, a laundromat, a radio-repair service unit, or a vending machine route. They wanted something where they could hire someone else to do the legwork.

I explained that every man has two assets — his services and his capital. His services, whether he is working for himself or for an employer, have an open-market value (probably $350 per month for an inexperienced man with a college degree). The return to be expected from capital depends on the risk; 6 percent would be good if he wanted safety. Why should he expect more income unless he developed a special skill or took greater chances?

I told each man not to expect that his college degree or recent knowledge of the humanities will give any immediate edge over the high-school graduate who has already been on the job for four years; that comes later when he has caught up in ap-

plied knowledge. I explained that with few exceptions it takes money to make money in business. Someone has to put up the money for equipment, inventory, and operating expenses before there is a dollar of income. Even a free-lance commission salesman must finance his living and travel expense until he builds up an income.

The young men showed me advertisements from the Business Opportunity columns of the newspaper: "Good Business for Sale — $10,000"; also, "Want Partner in Profitable Business — $10,000 Investment." I asked, "What kind of going business do you think you can get for $10,000? Remember that your money must cover both purchase price and working capital. If it is a store or a manufacturing operation, you would be lucky to turn your capital three times a year (unless working on credit). With capital of $10,000 you might expect annual sales of $30,000 to $50,000, and a net profit of $5,000, before a salary for yourself and taxes. Now take the case of the man who is advertising for a partner with $10,000. If he had a good thing, he would not have to appeal to strangers. Selecting a partner is almost as delicate an operation as choosing a wife."

Probably the easiest and quickest way to become an independent businessman is to be a commission salesman or manufacturer's agent. You are given a sample kit, a price book, some order blanks, and a pat on the back. You are completely on your own and you sink or swim on your own. You do not have to tie up any capital in inventory or accounts receivable; neither do you get any salary or expense account. It stands to reason, however, that no one is going to give a very hot item or an established territory to an inexperienced salesman.

Some young men seem to think that if they have a new idea and good character they can borrow their starting money from a bank or from the Small Business Administration without collateral. They do not understand that any new venture is a gamble and that the lending institutions cannot see any merit in a transaction in which they stand to lose 100 percent or at best get their money back plus a small interest. Private moneylenders are not interested in advancing money to set up a business; the anti-usury laws will not allow a rate of interest commensurate with the risk. Beware of any individual who offers to lend you capital at the legal rate of interest plus outside considerations, such as a commission on sales or management fee.

I personally would rather see a young man work for someone else for ten years until he has learned the business and matured in his judgment. Then he can evaluate his own talents and the cost of getting started on his own. I hate to watch some fine young man start his career with a blind stab at a hopeless venture, and then, after sweating it out for five years, have to give up and look for a job. The personnel manager of the employing company asks him, "In what category do you classify yourself: design, production, sales, accounting, administrative?" The young man has to reply, "I have been the president of a company with three employees. I have a smattering of all functions but cannot say I am expert at any of them." How can the personnel manager place him? The general experience is valuable, but he cannot put the young man in a job above more experienced men and he cannot start him at the bottom because he is too old or cannot live on a learner's pay.

Everything I have said, so far, has been negative and discouraging to a young man contemplating starting a business of his own. I admit that in most cases my advice is: "Drop the idea of self-employment. Get yourself a job with a good-sized company and invest your money in A.T.&T. stock. If you have a yen to be an inventor, get a job as a designer; if you have already invented some gadget, turn it over to a large manufacturer on a royalty basis. If you want to be a merchandiser, get a job with Sears, Roebuck. If you think you like manufactur-

ing, try to get a job with some company in the $5 million to $10 million class, large enough to be solid, small enough to be personal. If you aim to be on your own eventually in insurance or real estate, spend some years under a first-class operator. Let someone else pay for your training and your living expenses."

If you are completely vague about a career, go to some company that is expanding in an expanding industry and say, "I want a job in this company. I will do anything, go anywhere, and accept any pay you care to give me." In an expanding company there is likely to be more rotation and upgrading. I caution against starting with a small and young company, regardless of the charm of companionship, the early assumption of responsibility, and the dream of being in on the ground floor of what may someday grow rapidly in size. When, without special ability or experience, you start a new job, you are gambling on your ability to make good. If there is a chance that your employer will fail and go out of business, regardless of your ability, you are pyramiding the odds against you. In a small company there are few openings at the top and these are closely held by the owners.

Generalizations are always dangerous because they can be refuted by exceptions. You may be the exception. If you have guts and determination and no silly scruples against long hours, dirty hands, and waiting on customers over the counter, you may be able to get into some service operation without much capital and without having to wait to get a living wage. Don't sneer at the small service operation. If you can learn that business and make good at it, you can expand indefinitely and eventually break into the big league. If you have enough capital to live on for two or three years, you should be able to set yourself up in some commission-selling operation that will snowball into a profitable business if you work hard on it. If you have substantial capital, say $50,000, you might buy a hardware store, where the assets are all in solid inventory and the momentum should carry the business until you learn how to run it.

There are always a few cases of brilliant young men who have had rapid and phenomenal success. Such men have an uncanny sense of timing and opportunity. They gamble cheerfully with their own and other people's money and start a second gamble before they know the results of the first one. After the war, one young veteran, in complete disregard of my sincere advice, used his $10,000 as a down payment and with government financing built a $100,000 apartment house. With his profit and government financing he undertook to build ten GI homes, which he sold before completion. Now he is a big operator.

Another young man secured a government development contract for a scientific product on a cost-plus basis. He did not make much profit on the transaction, but the contract financed him in building a staff and equipping a plant with which he now makes products of his own. Another man brashly contracted to buy a $100,000 business with $10,000 down (every cent he had in the world), agreeing to pay the balance out of future earnings. Another paid $5,000 for an option to buy a piece of property at $200,000; he turned around and sold it to a third party for $250,000. In all of these cases the individual gambled to the limit and would have been cleaned out if there had been any setback. We do not hear of those who gambled and lost.

79.

Interview with Billy Graham

The most famous, the most successful, and probably the most aggressive evangelist of our day is the Reverend Billy Graham. His crusades for Christianity both in the United States and in many foreign countries have brought him a devoted following, comparable only to those of men like Dwight Moody and Billy Sunday of earlier eras; at the same time, Graham's driving approach to religion has resulted in much criticism, both from those who question his own methods and from those who question the worth of evangelism itself. The editors of Look *compiled some of the recurring charges against Graham and published his answers to them early in 1956. It may be observed that the questions asked by* Look *were in many cases asked by critics of evangelism as much as two centuries ago — and that Graham's answers also have a long background in the history of American religion.*

Source: *Look,* February 7, 1956: "Billy Graham Answers His Critics," by permission of the editors of *Look* Magazine, copyright ⓒ, 1956, Cowles Communications, Inc.

CONVERTS

The criticism is often leveled at you that your "converts" don't last.

American church leaders agree that of every two persons received on confession of

faith into the church, one has been dropped as a failure. Thus the church in all the areas of its activity faces this problem. We are doing all in our power to keep those that fall away at a minimum through an extensive follow-up system. But we could fill the

Rose Bowl tomorrow with a host who have found Christ as Saviour and are on the march for Him in the cities, villages, and towns which we have visited in America. We have in our files at our office in Minneapolis thousands of letters from ministers throughout North America and Europe who have written to thank us for the newly confessed Christians in their churches.

NEED FOR A CAMPAIGN

Aren't those whom you have "converted" largely church members already? Bringing people back to God, if they really are brought back, is not the same as helping just one man find Him.

I have never converted anybody. Only Christ can change the course of a man's life. A human instrument can take the soul only so far in its relationship to God. The rest must be performed by the Holy Spirit. It is true, however, that many of the people who commit themselves in our meetings are already church members — something like fifty or sixty percent. Most of these are people who have their names on a church roll but are not faithful and loyal in the church, who probably attend church only rarely, and who have lost their interest in spiritual matters. To bring back one of these people is just as important as to get an outsider to Christ. I think most pastors would agree with this. Every church has a great list of people who break the heart of the pastor by their absence from the services or by the nature of the personal lives that they live during the week. Even if we reached none outside the membership of the church, it is my observation, gained from discussion with hundreds of ministers, that these meetings would still be worthwhile. The new vision the meetings give to the faithful church attenders, and the restoration they bring to hundreds whose names are on a church roll but who have wandered far from the teaching of Christ and loyalty to the church, certainly underscore their value.

LACK OF DIGNITY

Many have said that you rob the church of the dignity its message should have. They don't like the publicity and crowds and excitement. They claim that your meetings do not convey the idea of God to the individual, and that the better way is to worship God in a quiet chapel. In short, they prefer a more reasoned approach.

I am afraid that these people are confusing a worship service and an evangelistic mission. I, too, prefer a quiet chapel in my worship of God. But there is a vast difference between the work of evangelism and private or public worship. Evangelism seeks to win those outside to Christ and the church. To do this, the church employs various approaches. The method of mass evangelism which we use is only one of many methods. I do not believe that this is necessarily the best method, and certainly it has little value unless it actually becomes personal evangelism, but it is one method which has been employed effectively by the church through the centuries. In every other area of life, we take for granted publicity, bigness, modern techniques. Why should not the church employ some of these methods, that are used by big business or labor unions to promote their products or causes, in order to win men for Christ? I think one of the difficulties of the church in many countries that I have been to is that it has fallen far behind in the use of modern ideas. Certainly, local churches in the United States are using every type of legitimate appeal to get people to church. In one of our large crusades where all the churches are cooperating, our efforts and methods may be more concentrated and more extensive, but they are not unlike those used by the average church. I would also like to say that all the publicity in these local cities is handled entirely by local committees. We do not write the articles and only make suggestions as to the design of posters and handbills. This is all done locally. In some instances, it must be admitted that it has been overdone by local enthusiasts. Naturally, we have little or no control over what is written in the newspapers. Significantly, however, the press by and large has been friendly and sympathetic in every city that we have visited.

Billy Graham speaking to crowd in Trafalgar Square, London, during 1954 Crusade

EMOTION

The charge of too much emotion in certain types of evangelistic meetings has often been raised. It is said that people respond under the influence of emotion, and later regret their decisions.

I do not believe that this is a criticism of our meetings. Ministers and newspaper people have remarked time after time about the quietness, dignity, and absence of hysteria in our meetings. We never have any shouting or outbursts of any kind. However, there is emotion involved in everything people do. Love and hate are elements of emotion. We are trying to get men to love Christ and to hate their sins. To that extent, there is emotion involved, though we do not find in our meetings that it results in any demonstrative outbursts. I find it hard to think, however, that the preaching of John the Baptist, Christ and the Apostles set no emotion aflame. And I do not think that Christianity holds the emotions in stoic contempt, or that it leaves the emotional emptiness of modern life to be filled by secular things. But I do not think our meetings can be reduced to emotion. The content of the message is mainly distinctive Biblical doctrine. Though these doctrines may be proclaimed with a life-and-death urgency, trusting the Holy Spirit to illumine the minds of the hearers and to move their wills, most of the preaching is directed to the conscience and the will. No man can be said to be truly converted to Christ who has not bent his will to Christ. He may give intellectual assent to the claims of Christ and may have had emotional religious experiences; however, he is not truly converted until he has surrendered his will to Christ as Lord, Saviour, and Master.

USE OF FEAR

The criticism is often made that you use fear too often as a motive for conversion; that you should refer more to God's love for the individual rather than to the fear of final judgment.

I do not believe that we use the motive of fear any more than the love of God. In the New Testament, and especially in the utterances of Jesus, both love and fear were employed in His challenges to men. He not only said, "Come unto Me," but He often said, "Woe unto you." The pendulum of life swings alternately between the two extremes of love and fear. I heard Sir Winston Churchill say on the floor of the House of Commons during the debate on the hydrogen bomb that the fear of the use of this H-bomb was in itself a deterrent to war. This is a fear motive. Are we not justified in using a legitimate fear of the consequences of sin to deter men from their evil habits and sins? Jesus' teachings are full of warnings. He loved men, but He loved them enough to warn them of the wrath to come.

MONEY

The matter of your finances: scarcely a press conference is held but that this matter is discussed. Several of the more lurid "exposé" magazines have hit you on this.

I very rarely hear any criticism on this point now. We have bent over backward to keep our finances in order. When we go to a city, the finances are entirely in the hands of a local committee. Books are audited, and the entire audit is published in the press and a copy given to each minister of the city. Naturally, it costs money to do anything these days: There are auditorium rentals, advertising, accommodations, and scores of other items that involve the expenditures of funds. Again, I would like to emphasize that not one member of our team receives or spends these monies. In addition, each week we spend thousands of dollars to purchase radio and television time — we also have office expenses in Minneapolis to handle thousands of letters weekly that come from people with every type of spiritual problem. This money comes from hundreds of people who contribute to our radio program, *The Hour of Decision,* and to the other projects (such as our European crusades). This all goes to a nonprofit corporation in Minneapolis.

I personally do not receive any money,

honorarium, or stipend for any of my appearances anywhere in the world. My annual income is solely from a salary paid by our corporation in Minneapolis, and by royalties from my books.

TRAVEL

You are criticized for staying out of this country too much — particularly in recent years. Isn't there enough work to do in this country to keep you busy and effective?

John Wesley once said: "The world is my parish." Would it be right for us to limit our ministry to only the United States when there are other countries of the world that are even more spiritually in need? The United States spends billions each year in countries abroad helping them economically and militarily. It would seem the part of wisdom that, if we are going to spend so much to build up these nations economically and militarily, we should also help them spiritually and morally. Unless these countries have moral and spiritual strength, all the economic and military aid we have given will go down the drain. The American government realizes that we no longer live unto ourselves and that what happens in other countries vitally affects us. A spiritual awakening in some of the world's strategic countries will have a tremendous impact on the U.S.

LIBERAL OR REACTIONARY

The slightly more liberal school of theology, or the exponents thereof, label you as a "fundamentalist"; on the other hand, the more fundamental school of theology and its exponents make you out to be too liberal for their support. The question arises here: "Which are you?"

The terms *fundamentalist* and *liberal* need defining. There are so many shades of fundamentalism and so many shades of liberalism that it is increasingly difficult to point to a man and say he is a "liberal" or he is a "fundamentalist" without qualifying explanations. If by *fundamentalist* you mean "narrow," "bigoted," "prejudiced," "extremist," "emotional," "snake handler," "without social conscience" — then I am definitely not a fundamentalist. However, if by *fundamentalist* you mean a person who accepts the authority of the Scriptures, the virgin birth of Christ, the atoning death of Christ, His bodily resurrection, His second coming and personal salvation by faith through grace, then I am a fundamentalist. However, I much prefer being called a "Christian." The terms *liberalism* and *fundamentalism* have arisen in modern days. Neither is found in sacred Scripture.

The *liberal theology* was a partial departure from New Testament Christianity and a substitution in its place of a speculative philosophy of religion.

Fundamentalism actually has a twofold connotation. On the one side, it reasserted such crucial Christian doctrines as the deity of Christ, and it certainly championed the authority of the Scriptures. On the other hand, fundamentalism became enmeshed in a series of reactionary positions in its struggle against liberalism. It left social action largely to the "social gospelers." While concentrating on personal evangelism, it had a tendency to neglect the relevance of the Gospel to every sphere of life. At times, fundamentalism has tended to be pugnacious and to defend secondary and sometimes doubtful positions with the same zeal as primary positions and to divide over such issues. I do not identify myself with these undesirable fundamentalist features; but I stand with fundamentalism when it mirrors the great New Testament truths. Here, it is necessary to emphasize that the New Testament, not fundamentalism or liberalism or neo-orthodoxy, is the enduring Christian criterion. That is why I much prefer to be

called simply a Christian rather than to be identified by what are latter-day labels.

Since my view of the Bible is so widely discussed, particularly in Great Britain, and all sorts of positions are attributed to me, it might be well to take extra space on this question and clarify some points. The central issue ought not to be what Billy Graham thinks of the Bible nor what "Mr. Twentieth Century" thinks of it. It ought to be what the Bible thinks of us and what the attitude of Christ is toward the Holy Scriptures.

I do not share the view that Scripture has nothing to say to the scientist as a scientist or to the historian as a historian. The Bible of course is not a textbook on science or politics. It is primarily the revelation of the religion of redemption, but it speaks to us all, touching the whole of life. I must make it clear that I am not a Bible scholar. I am an evangelist, and I have been called to preach the Gospel.

I would be the last to say that we have nothing to learn from the devout and scholarly studies of the Bible in recent years, for the Christian movement can be vastly enriched in this way. Nevertheless, I have noticed that critics in one generation often give way to critics in another and that critical positions swiftly change, and I am glad that the burden of adjusting their discrepancies is not one which I bear. An evangelist is not so much concerned with the temporary conclusions at which modern scholarship has arrived as with the permanent presuppositions of life and existence which the Bible anchors in divine revelation. While I may not have the ability to prove mathematically the inspiration of the Scriptures, I settled it for myself long ago. I have accepted the Bible as fully inspired of God, *by faith!* Sometimes, faith goes beyond reason, understanding, and even logic. When this matter was settled in my own heart, a new authority came to my ministry. I find that the words of Scripture have a mysterious and wonderful power to transform human life and feed spiritually starved souls.

LINK WITH CHURCHES

It is frequently said that your work is not linked with the churches; and that the church should do its own evangelism without calling in an outsider.

This criticism came to me as quite a surprise. If it is made, it would, I feel quite sure, come from a person who is totally uninformed of our method of evangelism. We never go to a city unless we are invited by the ministers. Our work is church-integrated. We believe that the church, with all of its faults, is Christ's organization upon earth. We shall continue to do everything we can to promote and build His church on earth. All of the people who make commitments to Christ in our meetings are sent back to the church for teaching, instruction, fellowship, and worship. You mention that the church should do its own evangelism. How right you are! The fact that we are called from city to city to hold evangelistic crusades does not necessarily mean that the church is failing in its program of evangelism. It means that it is just employing another method of evangelism. Instead of the churches attempting evangelism individually on a continual basis, they decide to cooperate for a month or six weeks in a special evangelistic emphasis in the city. This is done not only through the medium of such meetings as ours but also in visitation evangelism, etc. The church should certainly be always at the task of evangelism.

SUCCESS OF "CRUSADES"

You point to the success of your crusades in terms of the sheer numbers of people who listen (2.5 million in Scotland, for instance) and in terms of those who make the "decision" for Christ. Yet is it not true that by far the greater part of these audiences are true believers, the "built-in" audience that one could find in any town; people who are predisposed to "salvation"?

You have me wrong! I am afraid that perhaps you have misinterpreted our use of the word "successful." What may seem to be successful to us may not be successful in the sight of God at all. God does not rate success by numbers, but rather He commends faithfulness. A man performing his faithful work in a small parish church may be far more successful in the sight of God than we are with our more publicized meetings. There is no doubt that the greater portion of our audiences are Christians, but the old saying is that a crowd draws a crowd; and when these great crowds of people gather, it draws in thousands of unchurched people. But these meetings also do an important thing for the Christian. When he sees 20,000 people singing the hymns of the church, praying together, listening to the word of God preached, it does something to him. It strengthens him. He goes back to his own church with a new vision. He begins to realize he is not alone in the world. While our chief objective is to win the unchurched, a secondary objective is to encourage and strengthen the Christian so that he will be a more effective witness for Christ.

CHRIST — STRONG OR GENTLE?

It is said that you portray Christ as a sort of superman rather than a meek man, a circus strong man rather than the gentlest of all men, a militant leader rather than a quiet example to the world. This portrait is hideous, is it not?

I do not know that the person who asks this question has ever heard me preach. I do not recall ever trying to make Christ a superman or a circus strong man. While He was gentle, quiet, and meek, He was also a militant leader whose influence and teaching took the shackles off the slaves, lifted woman to a new position, and shook the foundations of the Roman Empire, and whose influence has caused the fall of dictators even up to the present. I have often said that Jesus Christ was a composite man, made up of heaven's best and earth's best; and that I did not think He was like the effeminate, emaciated conceptions of some artists. But I can't remember ever picturing Him as a Rocky Marciano or a Paul Anderson.

INTELLIGENCE LEVEL

Some of your critics often claim that your sermons are intellectually empty and without any practical solution to the problems of our generation, other than the easy one of escapism into the Holy Bible.

One of the greatest problems that the church has is making contact with the masses. I seriously doubt if the average American realizes how religiously illiterate he is. The theological terminology that is often used from the pulpit today has no meaning to the average man on the street. In a recent Gallup poll in Canada, it was found that only one out of ten Canadians could give the names of six of Christ's apostles; only two out of ten could name any. More than half of the adults did not know the name of the first book of the Old Testament or the New Testament. A man may be expert in office management or brilliant in the sciences and yet be totally illiterate in religion.

Dr. Louis Evans, minister at large in the Presbyterian Church, U.S.A., has said that the average religious intelligence of an American is that of a 12-year-old. There-fore, the preaching of today must be in utter simplicity, almost as if you were talking to children. Christ ministered to an almost illiterate people, and yet He talked with such simplicity that the common people heard Him gladly. There is great need that the preaching of today get back to an utter simplicity, particularly when speaking to people outside the church.

Principal James Denny, the Scottish theologian, once said: "The man who shoots above his target does not prove he has superior ammunition — he simply proves he cannot shoot."

One of the greatest problems I face in my ministry is to maintain a simplicity of presentation so that the common people will continue to listen. However, in my preaching I touch upon almost every one of the great problems of our generation, because I firmly believe there is an answer in the Bible to every major problem we face, whether it be the problem of race, alcoholism, poverty, illiteracy, or immoral habits.

POLITICS

You have frequently been accused of seeking political position and of having political aspirations.

This is absurd! I have no political implications or aspirations. I have never taken sides politically. I have close friends in both the Democratic and Republican parties. I have made it crystal clear to them that I do not intend to get involved in politics. There was a time a few years ago when, in an immature fashion, I made political statements and entered into all sorts of controversies. I have learned better now and remain completely outside party politics, though I do not hesitate to encourage Christian men to run for political office and to incorporate Christian principles in public service.

80.

FRED ALLEN: The Life and Death of Vaudeville

One of the most successful and best-loved radio personalities of the 1930s and 1940s was Fred Allen, whose astringent criticisms of American institutions, delivered in an inimitable nasal twang, endeared him to a generation of listeners. Allen did not begin his career in radio, for he had spent many years on the vaudeville circuit, perfecting his act and developing the cast of characters that made his Sunday night show a delight to millions of Americans. In his autobiography, published in 1956, the year of his death, Allen reviewed the ups and downs of his career. The nostalgic backward look at vaudeville reprinted here is taken from the book.

Source: *Much Ado About Me*, Boston, 1956, Ch. 14.

THIS CHAPTER IS AN AUTOBIOGRAPHICAL parenthesis. It is more about vaudeville than me. . . .

Vaudeville is dead. The acrobats, the animal acts, the dancers, the singers, and the old-time comedians have taken their final bows and disappeared into the wings of obscurity. For fifty years — from 1875 to 1925 — vaudeville was the popular entertainment of the masses. Nomadic tribes of nondescript players roamed the land. The vaudeville actor was part gypsy and part suitcase. With his brash manner, flashy clothes, capes and cane, and accompanied by his gaudy womenfolk, the vaudevillian brought happiness and excitement to the communities he visited. He spent his money freely and made friends easily. In the early days, the exact degree of prosperity the smalltimer was enjoying could be determined by taking inventory of the diamonds that adorned his person. If he was doing well, the smalltimer wore a large diamond horseshoe in his tie and two or three solitaires or clusters on his fingers; his wife, dripping with necklaces, rings, earrings, and bracelets, looked as though she had been pelted with ice cubes that had somehow stuck where they landed. The smalltimer's diamonds didn't have to be good. They just had to be big. What difference if the eight-karat ring was the color of a menthol cough drop as long as the stone sparkled in the spotlight during the act? To the smalltimer, a diamond represented security. It impressed the booker, the manager, and the audience, but, more important, the diamond was collateral. Confronted with a financial crisis in a strange community, the smalltimer didn't have to embarrass himself by attempting to convince a tradesman or a hotel manager that his credentials were valid. To obtain emergency funds, he merely stepped into the nearest pawnshop, slipped the ring from his finger, and consummated a legitimate routine business transaction. When his diamonds were temporarily on location, the smalltimer avoided his friends and his usual haunts, knowing that the absence of his Kimberley gravel was an admission that the panic was on. The instant his luck changed, the diamonds were redeemed and returned to their customary places. Back in the spotlight, with the horseshoe pin and the rings sparkling, the smalltimer's necktie and his ring fingers resumed strutting their stuff.

The herd instinct was a dominant impulse in the vaudeville actor's behavior pattern. When the season closed, the smalltimers congregated at vacation resorts to revel in each other's company. The smalltimer lived in another world. He thought and talked only about his act and about show business. Nothing else interested him. If you said to him, "Do you remember the Johnstown flood?" he would probably reply, "Remember the Johnstown flood? Are you kidding? I and the wife were playing Pittsburgh that week. Eva Tanguay was the star. Walter Kelly was next to closing. After the first show the manager comes running back and says, 'You kids is the hit of the bill!' He moves us down to next to closing for the rest of the week. Kelly is blowing his top. All week long I and the wife murder them!" Everybody in Johnstown could have been swept out of town: the smalltimer wouldn't know or care. He had nothing in common with anybody who was not in his profession.

The two vaudeville centers of the country were New York and Chicago. During the summer layoff season — theaters had no air-conditioning then, and many closed during the hotter months — vaudeville colonies were formed. The Chicago acts rented or bought cottages near the lakes in Wisconsin or Michigan; the New York vaudevillians huddled together in Connecticut and down on Long Island. The most famous of the actors' colonies was founded at Freeport, Long Island. The stars first established summer homes at Freeport, and then the smalltimers precipitated a real-estate boom fighting to buy property and houses to make their home in Freeport to let the stars see how the other half lived.

The Long Island Good Hearted Thespians Society was formed. This was a social club whose members reduced the name to the Lights. The first president was Victor Moore. One of the traditional Lights Club functions was the celebration of Christmas on the Fourth of July. In December, most of the vaudeville actors were on the road, away from their homes, their families, and their friends. They spent their Christmas Days on trains, in dingy dressing rooms, or in drab hotels. Members of the Lights ignored the conventional Yule season and saved their Christmas greetings and presents until the return to Freeport. On July Fourth, though the temperature be in the nineties, the Lights' Christmas tree was decorated and lighted, Santa Claus was dressed in his heavy suit with the ermine trimmings, presents were placed under the tree, and the members and their children arrived in their furs, mittens, and earlaps, some even clattering into the club on snowshoes.

A vaudeville actor could relax and enjoy himself only in the company of another vaudeville actor. You could sit a vaudeville actor in front of a mirror and he would stay there contentedly for days on end. In cities on the road, the vaudeville performers congregated at the same boardinghouses or cheaper hotels. There was a time when the actor was *persona non grata* at the better inns, and this was especially true of vaudevillians, who were presumed to be irresponsible from the very fact that their profession was uncertain and their living precarious. It was generally understood that vaudeville performers went in for wild parties in their homes and that their domestic habits were rarely awarded the Good Housekeeping Seal of Approval. Accordingly it was deemed best for hotel clerks to smile blandly when they were asked for rooms and inform the vaudevillian that the hotel was "full up." Stage folk, except for those who had attained stellar rank, were pretty much pariahs around the decent hotels.

Duke Pohl, the manager of the Breevort Hotel in St. Louis, once told me that he was traveling in a special train to attend an annual convention of the Greeters of America, the official organization of the hotel men. Each man was asked to name his hotel and tell something about it. Duke later told me that when he announced that his Breevort catered to stage folks, "I could almost hear the gasp that went around the circle. I told them I considered stage people the most maligned persons on earth. I said that my experience with vaudevillians had been uniformly pleasant, that they paid their bills, were quiet in their rooms, were sober, sedate, and serious people trying to make a living."

Duke defended the profession at a time when many hotel and rooming-house owners were complaining that some vaudeville people were stealing towels. This practice was so common that jokes were being told about it. One joke was about the vaudeville actor who died and left an estate of eight hundred hotel and Pullman towels. Then there was the charge that actors checked into their hotels with heavy suitcases, stayed a week or two, then disappeared without paying their bills. Credit had been extended because the manager had seen the heavy suitcases; when, later, these were pried open, they were found to contain nothing but a collection of bricks and old telephone books. Indigent vaudeville actors were known to lower their suitcases out the window in the back of the hotel, then walk through the lobby empty-handed, reclaim their cases, and leave town. An actor who had a trunk in his room received an extension of credit. When the bill mounted, the actor, anticipating that the manager would tip the trunk to ascertain its contents and to try to find out if clothing had been pawned, took the precaution of nailing the trunk to the floor. Ted Healy, a comedian, once owed a sizable bill at the Lincoln Hotel in New York. Ted brought the three stooges he used in his act up to his room and ordered each stooge to don two or three sets of his underwear, two complete suits of clothes, and an overcoat. Healy followed the stooges out of the Lincoln lobby wearing three suits and one topcoat, and carrying a raincoat with every pocket bulging. Healy left the Lincoln Hotel with two mementos of his stay: an empty room and an empty trunk. Things of this kind took place occasionally, and hotel owners were suspicious, but Duke Pohl believed in befriending actors, and they showed their appreciation. As Duke used to say, "I've never lost anything by it. They all paid me eventually."

Vaudeville could not vouch for the honesty, the integrity, or the mentality of the individuals who collectively made up the horde the medium embraced. All the human race demands of its members is that they be born. That is all vaudeville demanded. You just had to be born. You could be ignorant and be a star. You could be a moron and be wealthy. The elements that went to make up vaudeville were combed from the jungles, the four corners of the world, the intelligentsia and the subnormal. An endless, incongruous swarm crawled over the countryside dragging performing lions, bears, tigers, leopards, boxing kangaroos, horses, ponies, mules, dogs, cats, rats, seals, and monkeys in their wake. Others rode bicycles, did acrobatic and contortion tricks, walked wires, exhibited sharpshooting skills, played violins, trombones, cornets, pianos, concertinas, xylophones, harmonicas, and any other known instrument. There were hypnotists, iron-jawed ladies, one-legged dancers, one-armed cornetists, mind readers, female impersonators, male impersonators, Irish comedians, Jewish comedians, blackface, German, Swedish, Italian, and rube comedians, dramatic actors, Hindu conjurors, ventriloquists, bag punchers, singers and dancers of every description, clay modelers, and educated geese: all traveling from hamlet to town to city, presenting their shows. Vaudeville asked only that you own an animal or an instrument, or have a minimum of talent or a maximum of nerve. With these dubious assets vaudeville offered fame and riches. It was up to you.

Vaudeville families endured for generations. The female of the species foaled on trains, in dressing rooms, in tank towns, and in the big cities. The show must go on. At the theater the baby slept in the top of the trunk in the dressing room. At the hotel a crib was improvised by removing a large bureau drawer and placing it on the bed or between two chairs. A large blanket filled the drawer nicely; the baby, wrapped in its quilt, rested serene in his drawer bassinet. The vaudeville baby carried its own baggage. A small valise contained milk bottles, nipples, safety pins, and emergency diapers. On a sleeper jump, vaudeville couples with a baby always had the same routine: at 1 A.M., with the train thundering through the night, a tiny cry is heard. In two berths, an upper and a lower, lights snap on instantly. The husband jumps down from his upper berth into the aisle. The curtains of the lower berth part just a crack, muted voices are heard, the clasps on the miniature valise click open, and a nippled bottle, filled with milk, appears through the curtains. The husband steadies himself as he sways down the aisle on his way to arouse the porter to warm the precious quota of milk. In the lower berth, the sounds of the mother's soothing voice and the baby's cries persist until the husband returns. The warm milk bottle is passed in, the baby gurgles and stops crying, the curtains close, the husband crawls back up into his berth. The lights go off in both berths, and it is dark and silent once again; the train hurries ahead into the night.

Arriving in the next town, and safe in their room, the family goes to work. The husband removes a small drawer from the dresser, places a rubber sheet over the drawer, and pokes it snugly down into the four corners. Then he fills the drawer half full of tepid water. The mother lowers the baby gently into the drawer to enjoy its bath after the train trip.

The smalltime vaudeville mother had the endurance of a doorknob. She did three or four shows a day as part of the act. She cared for her baby on the road and prepared its food. She did the family washing: there was always a clothesline hanging and dripping away in the dressing room and the boardinghouse, and the sinks were filled with diapers. As the family grew larger, the kids were packed like sardines into upper berths. (Midgets often traveled in clusters in upper berths; an actor in a lower berth once complained that he had been kept awake all night by a midget with insomnia who had been walking up and down in the upper berth.)

Many wives cooked the family meals in the dressing room; before electricity became promiscuous, vaudeville wives carried tin plates, cups, knives and forks, and prepared tasty meals over flaming gas jets and blazing Sterno cans in dressing and hotel rooms. Then there was a special theatrical trunk, made by the Herkert and Meisel Trunk Company of St. Louis, which was constantly adding new features to lighten the burden of the vaudeville wife. The H & M wardrobe trunk had such special innovations as a metal compartment in one drawer to hold an electric iron; a small rubber-lined compartment which enabled actors to pack wet sponges, washcloths, and soap on hurried closing nights; a hat compartment for man or woman; a flat drawer under the wardrobe section to hold shoes; a jewel box; an ironing board that could be attached securely to the trunk to enable women to iron in the theater. These, and many other features of this trunk, made life easier for the vaudeville mother.

Vaudeville families flourished. The babies teethed on greasepaint, and their sitters were other acts on the bill who watched the tots while the parents were on stage. When the babies were able to walk, they were led on stage to take their first bows. Later, they learned to imitate their parents and many other acts who played on the different bills. After completing their schooling, most of the children grew up and went into vaudeville, and had children who grew up and went into vaudeville.

The smalltimer plying his profession was exposed to many irritations. When his act laid an egg in one town, he couldn't wait to leave for the next town, where, he hoped, things would be better. When the audience was bad, the whole community was terrible; the hotel, the restaurants, the food, the newspapers, and the people all became impossible. When the smalltimer was a riot, his environment was perfect. Using the smalltimer's psychology, if his act went badly in Detroit, Detroit as a metropolis was a bust. If his act went big in Eureka, Eureka was Utopia.

Next to the audience, in its importance to the smalltimer, stood the theater orchestra. If the orchestra could not play his wife's ballad properly, if the tempo of his dance music was too fast or too slow, if the drummer didn't catch his pratfalls with a well-timed roll and crash or tear the cloth on cue as he pretended to rip his trousers, the actor fought with his wife and sulked in his dressing room until the next show. Vaudeville orchestras varied from one piece — a piano — to seven or eight pieces. The usual smalltime theater had piano, cornet, and drums. The drums were very important: they accentuated the falls and crashes of the comedians and played long rolls for the aerialists' sensational slides. For his music, the smalltimer carried eight or nine parts in cardboard or leather covers. Playing the cheaper theaters, which had only a piano and drum, only the piano and drum parts were used. After the smalltimer had played several weeks in dumps, and was then booked into a big theater, he would

occasionally brag at rehearsal in order to leave the musicians with the impression that he was accustomed to playing good theaters. He couldn't fool the musicians, however, because the minute they saw the smalltimer's music they knew where the act had been playing. The violin, clarinet, cornet, and bass parts were brand-new; the piano and drum parts were filthy. At rehearsal in a new town, the smalltimer, sensing that the orchestra wasn't too friendly, examined his music. It explained everything. The drummer in the last town had written on the drum part, "This act is lousy." The clarinet player had written, "He died here." The cornet player had summed everything up by simply writing one word: "Stinks."

The smalltimer's billing was a matter of great concern. Before the opening show at each theater he examined the front of the theater to check on the size of his name and his position in the list of acts. The vaudeville headliner often had a clause in his contract assuring him of top billing. The smalltimer's billing depended on the whim of the local manager or the man who printed or painted the theater signs. Seeing his name in runt letters could catapult the smalltimer into a three-day funk. His position on the bill was of major importance. If his act had been next to closing and he suddenly found himself second on the bill, wires were dispatched to the booking office and his agent, and the theater manager was summoned to the dressing room before the smalltimer deigned to do the first show. Headliners had clauses in their contracts that entitled them to the best dressing rooms. The smalltimer dressed where he was told. If he used the same dressing room as his wife, the smalltimer immediately examined all walls and connecting doors for holes. A few depraved actors carried gimlets and bits around with them, and drilled holes in the walls to watch the sister act or the single woman in the next room undress. If holes were discovered, the stage manager was notified and the apertures were filled with shoemaker's wax. One worry less for the smalltimer.

The censoring of his act also upset the smalltimer. When Paul Keith, after running a museum on Washington Street in Boston, opened his first theater, the Bijou Dream, he insisted on clean entertainment. Mrs. Keith instigated the chaste policy, for she would tolerate no profanity, no suggestive allusions, *double-entendres*, or off-color monkey business. As the Keith circuit grew, every theater carried a sign on the bulletin board:

NOTICE
TO PERFORMERS

Don't say "slob" or "son-of-a-gun" or "hully gee" on this stage unless you want to be cancelled peremptorily. Do not address anyone in the audience in any manner. If you have not the ability to entertain Mr. Keith's audiences without risk of offending them, do the best you can. Lack of talent will be less open to censure than would be an insult to a patron. If you are in doubt as to the character of your act, consult the local manager before you go on the stage, for if you are guilty of uttering anything sacrilegious or even suggestive, you will be immediately closed and will never again be allowed in a theatre where Mr. Keith is in authority.

Long after Mr. Keith's death the circuit was still waging its campaign against suggestive material. For many months *Variety* published a column called "You Mustn't Say That" which featured deletions in stage material ("Hell" or "Lord Epsom, Secretary of the Interior," or "An old maid taking a tramp through the woods," and so on) made by the Keith censorship bureau. As most of the gamy lines and jokes were his biggest laughs, the smalltimer would fight to the death to keep them in his act.

Many smaller acts who used one or two jokes, or a few comedy lines, and could not buy special material subscribed to *Madison's Budget*. For twenty years — from 1898 to 1918 — a man named James Madison published an annual collection of monologues, cross-fire jokes, sketches, minstrel-show afterpieces and parodies. This assortment of humorous matter sold for one dollar and was known as *Madison's Budget*. If a comedian found six or eight jokes in the *Budget* that he could adapt to his act, his dollar investment had returned a hearty dividend.

Comedy acts were always the targets of the pirates. If a comedian was original and wrote his own material, or if he frequently bought new routines and songs to keep his act up to date, he soon found that other comedians were stealing parts of his act. For many years performers had no way to protect their gags, parodies, or bits of business. Copyright laws were ignored, and good gags spread like bad news. One blackface comedian on the big time stole so much material that he couldn't use it all in his act; he hired another blackface act and paid him a salary to play the smalltime using the stolen material he had left over. There was a young comedian whose father regularly attended the opening show at the Palace. If any of the acts had new lines, jokes, or song titles, the father copied them down and wired them to his son. The act continued convulsing the Palace audience in New York, little dreaming that its best jokes were being told in Omaha, San Francisco, or wherever the son happened to be playing.

Original material was spread around in many ways. For instance, when blackface acts and other comedy teams split up, many times the men or women took new partners, and both new acts continued to do the same routines. After a series of splittings it was not unusual to find four or five teams all doing the same act. Burlesque shows lifted scenes bodily from Broadway revues. Social directors at summer camps spent the winter copying down anything they found in the Broadway theaters which they thought they could use at the camps next summer. Johnny Neff, a monologist, used to explain to his audiences how crazy comedians were to buy jokes. Johnny would relate how Frank Tinney had paid a hundred dollars for a certain joke. Johnny would then tell the joke to prove that Tinney was insane. When Johnny had finished explaining how much money Raymond Hitchcock, Ed Wynn, Jack Donahue, Leon Errol, and Richard Carle had paid for their jokes, and after he had told all these jokes himself, Johnny had a hilarious monologue that hadn't cost him a penny. And Milton Berle for years has been bragging to audiences that he has stolen jokes from other comedians. There has been no reason to doubt his word.

When Mr. Albee founded the National Vaudeville Artists, Inc., after breaking the White Rats' strike (the White Rats had been the original vaudeville performers' association), one of the inducements to attract members was the new organization's Protected Material Department. Any member could protect his act. All he had to do was to enclose a copy of his material in a sealed envelope and deliver it to the N.V.A. office. The envelope was placed in the Protected Material files. Later, if a plagiarist was brought to bay, the act preferred charges, the sealed envelope was opened, and the N.V.A. officials dispensed justice. Hundreds of acts protected their material through this service. After Mr. Albee's death, vaudeville started over the hill and took the N.V.A. club with it. Before the members vacated the clubhouse on Forty-sixth Street, some official, by whose authority nobody will ever know, sold the entire contents of the N.V.A. Protected Material Department files to Olsen and Johnson.

Superstitions and irrational beliefs influenced the vaudevillian as he made his decisions and planned his daily activities. Many credulous omens the performer treated with respect. He thought bad luck ensued if he whistled in the dressing room, found peacock feathers anywhere in the theater, saw a bird on the windowsill, threw away his old dancing shoes, and so forth. There were many other bad omens, but there were only two portents that assured the performer future happiness. Good luck was sure to follow if an actor put his undershirt on inside out, or if he touched a humpbacked person.

Vaudeville acts often assumed strange names to attract attention. An unusual name was easily remembered by bookers, managers, and audiences. A few uniquely named acts were: Fyne and Dandy (acrobats), Sharp and Flat (musicians), Willie Rolls (roller skater), Amazon and Nile (contortionists), Nip and Tuck (acrobats), North and South (musical act), Worth and While (sister act), Possum Welch (dancer), and Darn, Good, and Funny (comedy trio).

The early vaudeville performers were inventive; they had to create the unusual specialties they performed. Vaudeville grew, and new acts came along to help themselves to the ideas of the originators, and to elaborate on and embellish them. Many specialty artists, in constructing their acts, came up with some weird innovations. One of these was Orville Stamm. Not long ago I got a letter from Orville, asking if I remembered him. It was not easy to forget Orville. He billed himself as the "Strongest Boy in the World." To demonstrate his great strength, Orville played the violin; as he played, he had suspended from the crook of his bow arm an enormous English bulldog. The bulldog made graceful arcs in the air as Orville pizzicatoed and manipulated his bow. For the finish of his act, Orville lay flat on the stage and arched his back; in the better acrobat circles, this was known as "bending the crab." When Orville's chest and abdomen attained the correct altitude, a small upright piano was placed across his stomach. An assistant stood on Orville's thigh and played the piano accompaniment as Orville, in his "crab" position, sang "Ireland Must Be Heaven, 'Cause My Mother Came from There." This finish was a sensation, and I'm sure it was Orville's own idea.

Raymonde, a female impersonator, also originated an unusual finish. After doing his entire act as a girl, Raymonde took a bow and removed his wig. The audience, seeing man's hair, was amazed to find that the girl was a boy. As the applause continued, Raymonde removed the man's wig, and blond tresses tumbled down over his shoulders. The boy was now a girl again. The audience, again duped, was frantic. Raymonde took another bow or two to thunderous applause, then removed the girl's wig and was a boy again. Raymonde, emulating the manner of a female impersonator's conception of a truck driver, swaggered off the stage to absolute bedlam.

A man named Willard was billed as the "Man Who Grows." As he talked, he stretched his arms out a foot or more beyond their normal length. For his finish Willard grew four or five inches in height. I watched Willard many times backstage without being able to discover his secret. He must have been able to telescope his skin.

An inventive monologist in Chicago featured a singing goat. Following a dull fifteen minutes of talk, the monologist would introduce his partner, the Singing Goat. The orchestra would play "Mammy"; when the monologist finished the verse and started the chorus, the goat would join him in singing "Ma-a-a-my! Ma-a-a-my!" The act stopped the show. One matinee, a representative of the S.P.C.A. called at the theater and removed the goat from the premises. When the theater manager remonstrated, the S.P.C.A. man showed him the goat's lacerated buttocks; the monologist had been prodding his rump with a sharp-pointed nail.

This sort of thing often happened in animal acts. Trainers who exhibited lions and

tigers could seemingly cause them to growl and snarl on cue. The audience little suspected that the beasts worked on metal flooring, and that the lions and tigers would naturally growl or snarl after this metal flooring had been charged with electricity. Similarly, dog acts often astounded audiences when the little white terrier climbed the ladder, rung by rung, hesitated on the top rung for a second, and then jumped into space, landing in its master's arms. Little did the audience know that the top rung of the high ladder was electrified. When the little white terrier hesitated on this top rung, he wasn't kidding; he was frightened. A short shock through the rung, however, and the dog jumped.

Another great inventive act was that of Will Mahoney, who danced to his own melodies by attaching xylophone hammers to the toes of his shoes, and then danced atop the xylophone. If Will had spent the same amount of effort in thinking that he did on his xylophone, he might have discovered penicillin. I am sure that if all the hours vaudeville performers spent trying to improve their acts had been donated to science, automation would have been here fifty years sooner.

Vaudeville old-timers may not be wallowing in affluence in later life, but each smalltimer has his store of memories that will help him to escape from the unhappy present into the happy past. When the time comes that I find myself confined to the rubbish heap of humanity, I can temper my plight by conjuring up random recollections from my smalltime years. I can recall . . .

The manager of the vaudeville theater at Sandusky, Ohio. The audience there was so bad that he felt sorry for the acts. He invented an applause machine and installed it in the back of the theater. The machine manufactured applause by slapping a series of wooden paddles together. When an act finished and the audience sat there in its customary silence, the manager turned on his applause machine. To the sound of the wooden clatter, the act returned, took one or two bows, and withdrew.

The manager at Sherbrooke, Ontario, who was in the raincoat business. I remember that on the last night of my stay there he tried to talk the actors into taking their salaries in raincoats.

The manager at Torrington, Connecticut, who, on closing night, was driving me and a contortionist back to New York. Speeding through one small Connecticut town at midnight, the car was overtaken and stopped by the local policeman. The manager stepped out of the car to explain. He said, "I'm sorry, officer. I'm the manager of the theater at Torrington."

"I don't know nothin' about that," said the rube. "You was doin' sixty-five."

"I've got to get to New York," pleaded the manager. "I've got a contortionist in the car. He has to catch a train."

"You got what in the car?"

"A contortionist."

"A *contortionist?*"

"Yes."

"What's a contortionist?"

The contortionist couldn't stand it any longer. He jumped out of the car in the dark, ran around in front of the headlights, and ripped his coat off. He did a handstand, twined his legs around his neck, and ran around in circles on his hands.

The rube watched him for a few minutes and said, "That's a contortionist, eh?"

"Yes," said the manager.

"I'll be damned," the policeman said. "Go ahead!"

I can remember, too, the little theater at Lancaster, Pennsylvania, that had the bowling alley upstairs. Just as I came to the punch line of my joke, somebody in the bowling alley made a strike and the audience heard nothing but the awful crash.

And then there was the butcher in the small Ohio town who converted his shop into a theater at night and showed pictures

and Gus Sun smalltime vaudeville acts. In the window of the butcher shop he hung a sign:

Hamburger — 10ᶜ lb.
Pork chops — 20ᶜ lb.
Veal — 25ᶜ lb.
Theater tonight — 20ᶜ

There was a theater at Bayonne, New Jersey, where, during my act, a cat came down the aisle, emitted a series of blood-curdling cries, and delivered a litter on the carpet. An usher rushed down the aisle with a coal shovel, scooped up the kittens, and returned, followed by the mother, to the back of the house. The audience was in a tumult. All I could do in feeble rebuttal was to coin the line "I thought my act was a monologue, not a catalogue."

The Jefferson Theatre, on Fourteenth Street in New York, had a mongrel audience: the theater was going to the dogs. Situated between Second and Third Avenues, it attracted patrons of all nationalities. Third Avenue at Fourteenth Street was an uptown Skid Row, and should have been renamed the Bowery-Plaza. Alcoholics of all sizes and in varying conditions frequented the neighborhood and used the Jefferson as a haven from the elements and a slumber sanctuary. At some performances the Jefferson took on the appearance of a flophouse that had put in vaudeville. At one supper show, during my monologue I heard a sort of "clunk!" noise that was repeated at regular intervals. It sounded like someone dropping wet wedges into a bathtub. I'd talk for thirty seconds — then a clunk. Another thirty seconds — and another clunk. Finally I located the source of the clunks. On the aisle, in the third row, sat a simian-faced specimen. Between his feet he was holding a wooden bucket; on the seat next to him he had a bag filled with oysters. As I was struggling through my monologue, this combination bivalve addict and theater patron was shucking his oysters and dropping the shells into the bucket.

I can remember, too, *l'affaire* midget at the depot at Quincy, Illinois. The headline act, a midget troupe, was leaving to open at Galesburg. One midget on the platform was berating the manager of the act, and demanding in squeaky words that he be given a raise in salary. The train started, but the midget refused to get aboard unless he was assured of more money. As the baggage car went by, the manager calmly picked up the midget and threw him in through the open door.

When I try to clamp the lid tightly on the past, names keep popping up. There was Eddie Borden, who did an English act with a partner called Sir James Dwyer. Eddie read a magazine ad for a preparation guaranteed to cure skin blemishes. The ad claimed that you could save the expense of a trip to Hot Springs by buying a bottle of the company's elixir and taking your own curative baths at home. Eddie, who was concerned about an acne condition, mailed in the coupon. At Minneapolis, the fluid arrived with full directions. To enjoy the Hot Springs bath at home, the patient had to close the bathroom door tightly, fill the tub with steaming hot water, pour in a given amount of the magic fluid, and lie in the tub to soak for an hour or more. Eddie followed the directions implicitly, finished his soaking, and went to bed. The next morning he opened the bathroom door, and instead of the pure white bathroom he had entered the night before, he now found a room with a brown ceiling, brown walls, brown tub, brown toilet seat and bowl, brown medicine cabinet, and a brown door. The Hot Springs elixir had contained sulfur and the steam had transformed Eddie's suite into mahogany.

Jack Inglis was a funny nut comedian. One season, work was scarce. Jack lived in a rented house in Jersey with his wife and four children. A butcher friend of his knew that things were bad, and that the family wouldn't have a very happy Thanksgiving. Early in October, he gave Jack a live turkey. He told him he could keep it out in the yard in Jersey, and when the time came, he could kill the turkey for the family's Thanksgiving dinner. Jack took the turkey — a plump specimen — home, and turned it loose in the backyard. Every day for six weeks Jack's kids played with the turkey and chased it around. By the time Thanksgiving arrived, the turkey, after running away from the kids for six weeks, had lost some twenty pounds. For their Thanksgiving Day dinner that year the Inglis family had what looked like a tall sparrow.

The Billy Doss Revue was a smalltime girl act featuring Bill, a blackface comedian. I played on the bill with this act in Kansas City, Florence, Topeka, and Wichita in Kansas, and some dry oil wells in Oklahoma. The last chorus number of the revue was sung on a Southern dock with a river boat tied up in the background. On the dock there were bales of cotton, and on one of the bales sat a buxom mammy. For the act's finale the mammy jumped off the cotton bale and did an agile wooden-shoe dance to great applause. The mammy was really a boy in blackface wearing a bandana and a well-stuffed calico dress. The boy sat on his bale for three or four shows a day, looking at audiences, and with audiences looking at him. The only thing unusual about this is that the boy was wanted by the police. When they finally caught up with the blackface mammy, he was washed up for ten years, which he spent in the Ohio Penitentiary.

Nelson's Cats and Rats were a big-time act. The cats and rats, traditional enemies, performed together to the astonishment of audiences. One time, on a bill in Chicago, Fanny Brice was the headliner. As she arrived at the theater one evening and opened her dressing-room door, she shrieked. The stage manager rushed over to her and said,

"What's wrong, Miss Brice?" Fanny gasped, "A rat! There's a big rat in my dressing room!" The stage manager, no fool, called Nelson, the cat and rat authority. Nelson rushed in, cornered the rat, caught him in a heavy towel, and took the rat out of the dressing room. A few weeks later, I was on the bill with Nelson's Cats and Rats. I asked Nelson what had happened to the rat he had caught in Fanny Brice's dressing room. He said, "The next show, watch the finish of my act." I watched the finish, and saw a big black rat walk across the tiny platform carrying an American flag. "That," said Nelson, "is the rat."

The smalltimer, as he trudged through the seasons, always felt that he was getting closer to his goal. Every vaudeville actor dreamed of his personal utopia. Weekly sums were banked or mailed home against the day the smalltimer "quit the business." Then he would open his restaurant, filling station, real-estate office, chicken farm, dancing school, or other project that he had envisioned supporting him through his remaining years. Very few smalltimers saw their dreams take dimension. As the vaudeville monologist would explain it, "A funny thing happened to my savings on the way to my utopia." Sickness, relatives, going into businesses he didn't understand, meeting real-estate salesmen, joining collapsible building and loan clubs, gambling, lending money to other actors who never repaid him, playing the stock market, and a thousand other mishaps dissipated the smalltimer's savings and shattered his hopes. The few that did realize their ambitions found that after the travel and excitement of vaudeville, the dull and sedentary routine imposed on them as they tried to run some picayune enterprise in a small town was boring.

One vaudeville actor I knew couldn't wait to retire and start his own chicken farm. After he had bought a farm in California and tried to operate it for a few months, he was very unhappy. I went out to visit him one afternoon and found him sitting out in the yard under a tree, griping. Scampering around in a large wire enclosure were hundreds of White Wyandottes. The bottoms of these white hens had red circles on them; scooting by, they looked like little Japanese flags with legs on them. I asked the actor if his chickens had unusual markings. He said no, that he had seen an ad for Lay or Bust Feed that would increase the size of any hen's eggs, and that he had been giving his hens plenty of it. The hens started laying eggs that were too large for their disposal equipment. Laying the big, economy-size eggs had sprung the hens' hips and split their sphincters. "That accounts for the red circles on the bottoms of the hens?" I asked. "Yes," he answered. "I had to catch every lousy hen and dab her with mercurochrome!"

The smalltimer was never happy in retirement. Had it been within his power, the vaudeville performer would have been a timeless wanderer, spanning the generations by using the bridge of his talents.

But vaudeville is dead. Vaudeville was more a matter of style than of material. It was not so much what the two- and three-a-day favorites said and did, as how they said and did it. For fifty years vaudeville's minstrels found their way into all lands, preaching their gospel of merriment and song, and rousing the rest of the world to laughter and to tears. A few diehards who knew and enjoyed vaudeville hover over their television sets, hoping for a miracle. They believe that this electronic device is a modern oxygen tent that in some mysterious way can revive vaudeville and return its colorful performers of yesteryear to the current scene. The optimism of these day and night dreamers is wasted. Their vigils are futile. Vaudeville is dead. Period.

1957

81.

Dwight D. Eisenhower: The Crisis in the Middle East

On July 26, 1956, the Egyptian government announced that it was nationalizing the Suez Canal and would henceforth use canal revenues to finance its Aswan Dam project, from which the United States earlier had withdrawn financial support. On October 29 Israel, whose existence had been for eight years a thorn in the side of its Arab neighbors, invaded Egypt, and the next day Great Britain and France issued a joint ultimatum threatening intervention in the conflict unless an immediate cease-fire occurred and both Israel and Egypt pulled back ten miles from the canal. Israel complied with the order, but Egypt did not. British and French aircraft began bombing Egyptian targets, and Great Britain vetoed a U.S. resolution in the U.N. Security Council calling for a cessation of hostilities. The actual fighting was over quickly, and British and French troops withdrew by the end of the year. The short-lived conflict had several results. Occurring as it did at the end of a U.S. presidential campaign, it helped assure the reelection of President Eisenhower over Adlai Stevenson, the Democratic challenger; it led American policy-makers to fear the increase of Soviet influence in the Middle East; and it showed people everywhere how unstable was the peace that had followed the armistice in Korea. Eisenhower discussed both the events of the previous six months and their meaning for the world in an address to the American people on February 20, 1957, that is reprinted here in part.

Source: *Record*, 85 Cong., 1 Sess., pp. 2376-2377.

I come to you again to talk about the situation in the Middle East. The future of the United Nations and peace in the Middle East may be at stake.

In the four months since I talked to you about the crisis in that area, the United Nations has made considerable progress in re- solving some of the difficult problems. We are now, however, faced with a fateful moment as the result of the failure of Israel to withdraw its forces behind the armistice lines as contemplated by the United Nations resolutions on this subject.

I have already today met with leaders of

both parties from the Senate and the House of Representatives and we have had a very useful exchange of views. It was the general feeling of that meeting that I should lay the situation before the American people.

Before talking about the specific issues involved, I want to make clear that these issues are not something remote and abstract, but involve matters vitally touching upon the future of each one of us.

The Middle East is a land bridge between the Eurasian and African continents. Millions of tons of commerce are transmitted through it annually. Its own products, especially petroleum, are essential to Europe and the Western world.

The United States has no ambitions or desires in this region other than that each country there may maintain its independence and live peacefully within itself and with its neighbors, and, by peaceful cooperation with others, develop its own spiritual and material resources. But that much is vital to the peace and well-being of us all. This is our concern today. So tonight I report to you on the matters in controversy and on what I believe the position of the United States must be.

When I talked to you last October, I pointed out that the United States fully realized that military action against Egypt resulted from grave and repeated provocations. But also I said that the use of military force to solve international disputes could not be reconciled with the principles and purposes of the United Nations, to which we had all subscribed. I added that our country could not believe that resort to force and war would for long serve the permanent interests of the attacking nations, which were Britain, France, and Israel.

So I pledged that the United States would seek through the United Nations to end the conflict and to bring about a recall of the forces of invasion, and then make a renewed and earnest effort through that organization to secure justice, under international law, for all of the parties concerned.

Since that time much has been achieved and many of the dangers implicit in the situation have been avoided. The governments of Britain and France have withdrawn their forces from Egypt. Thereby they showed respect for the opinions of mankind as expressed almost unanimously by the eighty-nation members of the United Nations General Assembly.

I want to pay tribute to the wisdom of this action of our friends and allies. They made an immense contribution to world order. Also they put the other nations of the world under a heavy obligation to see to it that those two nations do not suffer by reason of their compliance with the United Nations resolutions. This has special application, I think, to their treaty rights to passage through the Suez Canal, which had been made an international waterway for all by the treaty of 1888.

The prime minister of Israel, in answer to a personal communication, assured me early in November that Israel would willingly withdraw its forces if and when there should be created a United Nations force to move into the Suez Canal area. This force was, in fact, created and has moved into the Canal area. Subsequently, Israeli forces were withdrawn from much of the territory of Egypt which they had occupied. However, Israeli forces still remain outside the armistice lines, notably at the mouth of the Gulf of Aqaba, which is about 100 miles from the nearest Israeli territory, and in the Gaza Strip, which, by the armistice agreement, was to be occupied by Egypt. This fact creates the present crisis.

We are approaching a fateful moment when either we must recognize that the United Nations is unable to restore peace in this area, or the United Nations must renew with increased vigor its efforts to bring about Israeli withdrawal. Repeated, but so far unsuccessful, efforts have been made to bring about a voluntary withdrawal by Israel. These efforts have been made both by the United Nations and by the United States and other member states.

Moreover, equally serious efforts have been made to bring about conditions designed to assure that, if Israel withdraws in response to the repeated requests of the United Nations, there will then be achieved a greater security and tranquillity for that nation. This means that the United Nations would assert a determination to see that in the Middle East there will be a greater degree of justice and compliance with international law than was the case prior to the events of last October-November.

A United Nations Emergency Force, with Egypt's consent, entered that nation's territory in order to help to maintain the ceasefire which the United Nations called for on November 2. The Secretary-General, who ably and devotedly serves the United Nations, has recommended a number of measures which might be taken by the United Nations and by its emergency force to assure for the future the avoidance by either side of belligerent acts.

The United Nations General Assembly on February 2, by an overwhelming vote, adopted a resolution to the effect that, after full withdrawal of Israel from the Gulf of Aqaba and Gaza areas, the United Nations Emergency Force should be placed on the Egyptian-Israeli armistice lines to assure the scrupulous maintenance of the armistice agreement. Also the United Nations General Assembly called for the implementation of other measures proposed by the Secretary-General. These other measures embraced the use of the United Nations Emergency Force at the mouth of the Gulf of Aqaba so as to assure nonbelligerency in this area.

The United States was a cosponsor of this United Nations resolution. Thus the

Courtesy, F. O. Alexander, "The Bulletin"

"The Fussy Diners"; cartoon by Alexander in "The Bulletin," Philadelphia, 1957

United States sought to assure that Israel would, for the future, enjoy its rights under the armistice and under the international law.

In view of the valued friendly relations which the United States has always had with the State of Israel, I wrote to Prime Minister Ben-Gurion on February 3. I recalled his statement to me on November 8 to the effect that the Israeli forces would be withdrawn under certain conditions, and I urged that, in view of the General Assembly resolutions of February 2, Israel should complete that withdrawal. However, the prime minister, in his reply, took the position that Israel would not evacuate its military forces from the Gaza Strip unless Israel retained the civil administration and police. This would be in contradiction to the armistice agreement. Also, the reply said that Israel would not withdraw from the Straits of Aqaba unless freedom of passage through the straits was assured.

It was a matter of keen disappointment to us that the government of Israel, despite the United Nations action, still felt unwilling to withdraw. However, in a further effort to meet the views of Israel in these respects, Secretary of State Dulles, at my direction, gave to the government of Israel, on February 11, a statement of United States policy. This has now been made public. It was pointed out that neither the United States nor the United Nations had authority to impose upon the parties a substantial modification of the armistice agreement which was freely signed by Israel and Egypt. Nevertheless, the statement said, the United States as a member of the United Nations would seek such disposition of the United Nations emergency force as would assure that the Gaza Strip could no longer be a source of armed infiltration and reprisals.

The secretary of state orally informed the Israeli ambassador that the United States would be glad to urge and support, also, some participation by the United Nations, with the approval of Egypt, in the administration of the Gaza Strip. The principal population of the Strip consists of about 200,000 Arab refugees, who exist largely as a charge upon the benevolence of the United Nations and its members.

With reference to the passage into and through the Gulf of Aqaba, we expressed the conviction that the Gulf constitutes international waters and that no nation has the right to prevent free and innocent passage in the Gulf. We announced that the United States was prepared to exercise this right itself and to join with others to secure general recognition of this right.

The government of Israel has not yet accepted, as adequate insurance of its own safety after withdrawal, the far-reaching United Nations resolution of February 2 plus the important declaration of United States policy made by our secretary of state on February 11.

But Israel seeks something more. It insists on firm guarantees as a condition to withdrawing its forces of invasion.

This raises a basic question of principle: Should a nation which attacks and occupies foreign territory in the face of United Nations disapproval be allowed to impose conditions on its withdrawal?

If we agree that armed attack can properly achieve the purposes of the assailant, then I fear we will have turned back the clock of international order. We will, in effect, have countenanced the use of force as a means of settling international differences and gaining national advantages. I do not myself see how this could be reconciled with the Charter of the United Nations. The basic pledge of all the members of the United Nations is that they will settle their international disputes by peaceful means and will not use force against the territorial integrity of another state. If the United Nations once admits that international disputes can be settled by using force, then we will have destroyed the very foundation of the organization, and our best hope of establishing a real world order. That would be a disaster for us all.

I would, I feel, be untrue to the standards of the high office to which you have chosen me if I were to lend the influence of the United States to the proposition that a nation which invades another should be permitted to exact conditions for withdrawal.

Of course, we and all the members of the United Nations ought to support justice and conformity with international law. The 1st Article of the Charter states the purpose of the United Nations to be "the suppression of acts of aggression or other breaches of the peace and to bring about by peaceful means, and in conformity with justice and international law, adjustment or settlement of international disputes." But it is to be observed that conformity with justice and international law are to be brought about "by peaceful means."

We cannot consider that the armed invasion and occupation of another country are peaceful means or proper means to achieve justice and conformity with international law. We do, however, believe that, upon the suppression of the present act of aggression and breach of the peace, there should be a greater effort by the United Nations and its members to secure justice and conformity with international law. Peace and justice are two sides of the same coin. . . .

No one deplores more than I the fact that the Soviet Union ignores the resolutions of the United Nations. Also no nation is more vigorous than is the United States in seeking to exert moral pressure against the Soviet Union, which by reason of its size and power and by reason of its veto in the United Nations Security Council, is relatively impervious to other types of sanction. The United States and other free nations are making clear by every means at their command the evil of Soviet conduct in Hungary. It would indeed be a sad day if the United States ever felt that it had to subject Israel to the same type of moral pressure as is being applied to the Soviet Union.

There can, of course, be no equating of a nation like Israel with that of the Soviet Union. The peoples of Israel, like those of the United States, are imbued with a religious faith and a sense of moral values. We are entitled to expect, and do expect, from such peoples of the free world a contribution to world order which unhappily we cannot expect from a nation controlled by atheistic despots. . . .

The present moment is a grave one, but we are hopeful that reason and right will prevail. Since the events of last October and November, solid progress has been made, in conformity with the Charter of the United Nations. There is the cease-fire, the forces of Britain and France have been withdrawn, the forces of Israel have been partially withdrawn, and the clearing of the Canal nears completion. When Israel completes its withdrawal, it will have removed a definite block to further progress. Once this block is removed, there will be serious and creative tasks for the United Nations to perform. There needs to be respect for the right of Israel to national existence and to internal development. Complicated provisions insuring the effective international use of the Suez Canal will need to be worked out in detail. The Arab refugee problem must be solved. As I said in my special message to Congress on January 5, it must be made certain that all the Middle East is kept free from aggression and infiltration.

Finally, all who cherish freedom, including ourselves, should help the nations of the Middle East achieve their just aspirations for improving the well-being of their peoples.

What I have spoken about tonight is only one step in a long process calling for patience and diligence, but at this moment it is the critical issue on which future progress depends. It is an issue which can be solved if only we will apply the principles of the United Nations. That is why, my fellow Americans, I know you want the United States to continue to use its maximum influence to sustain those principles as the world's best hope for peace.

I will not be a party to any treaty that makes anybody a slave; now that is all there is to it.

DWIGHT D. EISENHOWER, press conference, July 7, 1954

82.

Max Lerner: American Speech

Born in Russia in 1902, Max Lerner emigrated to the United States when he was five, became an American citizen in 1919, and soon began to write articles and books about his adopted country. The most massive of these, and the most noteworthy, is the two-volume work America as a Civilization, *which Lerner completed in 1957 after twelve years of writing and research. "Americans are beginning to turn a searchlight on themselves and their civilization," he wrote in the Foreword to the work, "and interpret both to the world. The present study is intended as a trial essay in this direction." The selection reprinted here deals with American speech.*

Source: *America as a Civilization*, New York, 1957, Vol. II, pp. 805-812.

THE COLLECTIVE IMAGINATION has operated with the greatest fertility in the continuous re-creation of the inherited language. American speech is surely one of the richest products of the American experience, at the base of much else that is creative in American popular culture. Abrupt, inventive, muscular, irreverent, it expresses with striking fidelity the energies and rhythm that have gone into the making of the national experience. Rarely has a new civilization taken the mature language it has inherited and adapted it so radically to its purposes. American spelling diverged sharply from British at the end of the eighteenth century, and the efforts of men like Noah Webster gave Americans the courage to break free from their cultural colonialism and assert their independence in spelling and pronunciation. While grammar and syntax in American speech have been slow in changing, the process of vocabulary-making has been a daring one: the creation of new words and expressions in the American common speech accompanied the opening of the continent. For a parallel in linguistic inventiveness, one must go to the England of the Elizabethan Age, when the speech of the common people and that of the dramatic writers burst into a new flowering, each of them affecting the other.

With all its richness, however, American speech is strikingly uniform when compared with its mother tongue. The English developed dialects so sharply divergent from one another that a traveler from one region could scarcely understand the dialect of another: it was the Midland dialect, more progressive than the archaic Southern one but less daring than the rapidly shifting Northern dialect, which came to be established as the basis of "standard" or "general" English. The Americans had no such difficulty and no need for a standard or general American speech, since a man can travel from the Atlantic to the Pacific and encounter no difficulty in being understood. The clue lies in American mobility: with so constant a turnover of people there is no chance for the hardening of local speech peculiarities. With the big media every fresh coinage or usage or pronunciation found a vast, capturable audience with which to make its way throughout the nation. Especially through TV, where the spoken word is memorably associated with a screen image, the big media have had a standardizing effect on American speech. The uniformity of speech must not, of course, be overstressed. In his "Second Supplement" to *The American Language,* H. L. Mencken gives a state-by-state roundup of homespun terms which are so local that they sound like gibberish to the rest of the nation; but the fact that this was considered a labor of affectionate erudition is in itself proof that the local diversities are marginal rather than central.

One can also overstate the separateness of the "American language" as a whole. The structure of the language spoken in America is very much like the structure of English. The basic vocabulary is the same and there is a common freightage of literary association. The differences of pronunciation are considerable, but no greater between Americans and British than (let us say) between Americans in Mississippi and in Brooklyn. Where then do the great differences lie? They do not lie in the language seen as a structure or as an instrument of literature or ideas. There is still a common literary vehicle, in which the American of John Dewey differs little from the English of Bertrand Russell, and even the American of Sinclair Lewis differs little from the English of H. G. Wells. The chief differences lie in the idiomatic vocabulary that makes up a large part of the spoken language, especially as used in the big media. They lie in rhythms and inflections, in energy intensity, in the everyday (nonliterary) associations of everyday words. What is chiefly different between the English and American languages is the common speech in its everyday usage — American speech viewed as an expressive emotional instrument.

A people's speech is the skin of its culture. It contains the indigenous vocabulary, the inflections of meaning, the tricks of rhythm, the nuances of association, that give the members of the culture the sense of belonging together and being marked off from those who use different words, rhythms, inflections, connotations. It contains — to use a military figure — the symbolic strategies that make the "we" seem superior to the "they" — a superiority that is part of the psychology of cultural nationalism. The language of American speech is, as I have said, not separate enough from the English to be called with justice an independent language. But the whole complex bundle of intangibles, which are not so much a language as a speech, forms something as distinct from the parent English as American culture is distinct from the parent culture.

Nor is it hard to see how the separateness came about. The Americans had the English language and literature to start from, yet the heritage came from a culture to which they owed no allegiance after the Revolution. Thus American speech started off with the ingredients at once of tradition and innovation, of discipline and freedom. The political release from colonialism demanded a cultural release too. Frontier farmers and backwoodsmen, land prospectors and speculators, preachers and teachers, promoters and lawyers, peddlers and country storekeepers, forge workers and innkeepers, canal bargemen, steamboat pilots, and railroad construction gangs, country editors, newspaper reporters, shrewd young men making their fortunes in the cities, storytellers — by mid-nineteenth century all of these had built a speech with an idiom, a rhythm, a pace, an inflection, a vigor and tang of its own. It was separated by more than an ocean from the speech of the England of Anne and William and Victoria. The Americans sensed that they were shaping something with a fertility and energy of its own and treated it as a plastic instrument rather than as a classical heritage.

The homespun quality of the speech

found its way into the newspapers in the late eighteenth century, into the country stores and the city streets, into Andy Jackson's talk and Abe Lincoln's anecdotes. Royal Tyler's play, *The Contrast*, depicted the gap in character and dialect between the British and the Americans. Some forty years after Tyler, Augustus Longstreet was among the first who made the spoken everyday language of Americans into a first-rate sensitive literary instrument. Lowell's *Biglow Papers* and Harriet Stowe's early short stories put New England dialect into literature. Dialect became a kind of fad in the 1880s: Mark Twain wrote the whole of *Huckleberry Finn* in dialect. But while it was amusing to the buyers and readers of books, it was not a fad for those who used it; it was their speech. Yet the writers had a function to perform. Once they had done their work, it was clear that victory had been won and that the decisive battles would never have to be fought again. There was no longer the danger that America might suffer the fate of Europe at the end of the Middle Ages, when men wrote and read in the language of the educated classes but spoke in the plebeian tongues of the new nationalities.

To be sure, some of the greatest writing by Americans was still to be done in the classical English literary tongue, and men like Henry James could make a supple literary instrument of it. Among the academic thinkers and editorial writers, political orators and literary Brahmins, the official literary language and rhythm (the "mandarin style") continued to be used without much infiltration from daily popular experience. This was more than made up by the way the popular arts embraced the new vigor of the American speech. The short story, the movie script, the vaudeville skit, the musical comedy, the newspaper column, the mystery thriller, the crime and sports reporting, the radio gagster — all came under the spell of the new idiom that had been shaped by the rhythms and mintage of American speech. Without this richness, the popular arts could not have gained their hold on Americans. Even the formal art of the novel was transformed, as witness Anderson, Lewis, Lardner, Hemingway, Farrell, Faulkner, Steinbeck, O'Hara, James Cain, Nelson Algren — to name writers widely removed in method and artistry, yet all of whom have become masters of American speech. From other genres one thinks of Hammett and Chandler, Odets and Arthur Miller and Kober, Mencken and Don Marquis, Sandburg, Broun and Damon Runyon, of Cole Porter and Hammerstein, of Ogden Nash and Perelman, and one gets a sense of a remarkably plastic language instrument that need not be cut away from the speech of the people in order to be of use to the literary craft. For American speech does not have to be split into fragments and recombined, as Joyce tried to do to the exhausted literary language of his culture in order to squeeze a desperate freshness from it. New words have cropped up out of American speech faster than they could be absorbed, so that many of them (as witness the researches of Mitford Mathews in his *Dictionary of Americanisms*) have been stuck in historical blind alleys. But every word that has survived has borne a fragment of the great hyperbolic myth of the American experience.

These accessions of richness came at first from frontier living and from the savage exaggerations and the bragging stories that grew with the opening of a continent. Then they came from the life of the growing cities, from miners, steel workers, and lumberjacks, from casual workers and stevedores, from war and the Armed Services, from the criminal rackets and from the lawless margins of business. Finally they came from big-audience sports, from the stage and the movies, and the radio, from popular music and jazz and the dance, from stock markets and the trade unions. The new words (and the new uses of old words) generally emerge from the routines of some pursuit, or from some sport or art which a few people follow with the devotion of *aficionados*. They may at the start form only a sort of jargon. But by an osmosis the jargon seeps through the general popular language to people who would never dream of mingling in the activities (crime, racketeering, gambling, vaudeville, burlesque, hot music, prizefighting) from which the new words or new uses first came.

The secret of the vigor of American speech is that the physical and social fluidity of American life have opened the sluices for a similar fluidity of American speech. In hierarchical societies the class strata operate to split the language of the culture into layers of language — clerical and secular, literary and vernacular, aristocratic and plebeian. But the openness of the American open-class system kept such divisions from rigidifying. Here was one creative activity in which even the humblest man could take a hand. The fashioning of American speech is the most popular of the popular arts since it admits of the widest participation, with no admission fee charged except a questing tongue, a feel for metaphor and color, and a bit of boldness in experimenting. Whatever other genius may be denied to the collective American spirit, the genius of the language surely belongs to it.

I do not mean to underestimate the conservative influences that have operated on American speech. The strongest is that of localism. Despite the great geographical mobility of Americans, the speech habits of the region and even the locality into which they move will in time shape the phrasing and pronunciation of the newcomers. A New England family settling in the South takes on the Southern dialect and intonation. It is surprising how clearly many of the contemporary American dialects can be traced back to England, and how little influence the large, non-English-speaking immigrant population has had on them. The American local dialects have been less tenacious than the English, partly because English history over a thousand years has covered a period when roads were bad and communication difficult, while American speech has been shaped for the greater part of its history in an age of rapid communication. As Donald Lloyd puts it, it has "leap-frogged" its way across the continent — yet, he adds, so great is the strength of localism in speech that one can draw lines, especially with respect to vocabulary, around California towns that are less than a half century old. Pronunciation is also largely local or regional.

The concept of American "speech communities," which Lloyd and Warfel have suggested in their *American English in Its Cultural Setting*, sheds a good deal of light on the differences within the larger structure of American speech. One can see America as a cluster of speech communities set apart from one another, each using subtle clues of language to detect and exclude outsiders and to make the insiders more cohesive and more comfortable with one another. Cutting across them, one should also distinguish professional (as on radio and TV) from conversational, and literary speech from the functional speech of people who must find a language for the material they deal with. One must reckon in addition with the conservative influence of the schools, which continue to resist innovations whenever the teacher can spot them. The "educated" American has a "correctionist" bent, both for his own speech and that of others: in the language democracy of America every man is a judge of language, yet if he pretends to an education he is a bit frightened about his judgment. As Americans move up the educational ladder, they move further away from the speech of ordinary people. Yet that speech has entered their lives nonetheless. They have no way of knowing what words that come to mind as they speak come from the literary tradition and what words from the speech community in which they move.

One clue to the strength of American speech is found in the relative absence of rigid principles of "correctness." There is an illustration of this in the animating spirit of the three great volumes of H. L. Mencken's *American Language*. Mencken had two basic principles in his work: that of studying American speech inductively, to find how it was actually spoken instead of how it ought to be spoken; and to scorn any notion of authoritative standards in language, other than the actual usage of the common speech. It was a curious paradox that the writer who had fought a crusade against popular democracy in politics and economics should have embraced in linguistics the principles of *vox populi, vox dei*. Since his time other students of American speech have followed the same emphasis, although one detects in them (as indeed in Mencken also) a certain snobbism in the ironic way in which they celebrate the victory of the barbarian mass. Most Americans have rejected authoritarianism here as elsewhere and have followed in the language wherever their daily experience, their image-making impulses, and the deep currents of their striving have led them. If they have thereby missed achieving an Alexandrian purity of speech, they have also largely avoided the film of gentility which after some centuries of history covers a language and presages linguistic and cultural stagnation.

There remains the question of the standard to be followed in appraising the validity of new coinages of speech even when academic standards are rejected. One can say that some change in grammar and syntax or some new word has met the inductive standards when it has come into general use. The final test is the naturalistic one of survival. Many new coinages never achieve currency and die from disuse. Among others that do, there are often shoddy or clumsy,

pretentious or synthetic words. Mencken has some delightful passages on what he calls "scented" words — such as, *realtor* for real-estate agent, *mortician* for undertaker, or *sanitary engineer* for plumber. Similarly, salesmanship has introduced the use of *contact* as a verb, while advertising has contributed *cost-wise* or *audience-wise*. These are the product of the streams of argot that flow into the language from every American activity. They are often adopted most quickly by those who hanker for gentility in speech or who pick up every linguistic fad in the hope of seeming sophisticated. What are usually called "vulgarisms," such as *it's me* or the use of the double negative, represent strong undercurrents of popular impulse which are bound to triumph despite the resistance of the educated classes. But the scented words and the pretentious argot of the genteel or the self-conscious (take, as a recent instance, the use of "fulsome" in the sense of "abundant") give American speech a quality of phoniness as the price it pays for opening its doors to all inventions. There are signs of the emergence of a new language of gentility, befitting an overwhelmingly middle-class society, in which workers have been replaced by salesmen and the insecurities of status make the newly successful people anxious to wear their words as badges of belonging.

We may speak of three classes of additions to the language: there are *functional words* — technical, occupational, or scientific, which make their way as effective short cuts to meaning, like "megabuck" from the new science of atomic production; there are *exuberant words*, notably in the coinage of the teen-agers and the jive and hepcat; finally, there are *synthetic words*, the product of cerebral inventiveness rather than of life energies in the culture. The scented words and other strainings for gentility of effect belong in the last of these categories.

This raises the question of how long American speech will maintain its vigor and its principles of growth. The fact that it still has them is shown by the way the language has spread its influence to the twelve corners of the earth and attracted the imitation of young people everywhere. There is scarcely a non-English-speaking country, whether in Asia or Africa, Europe or Latin America, in which the desire to learn English has not become an urgent one: it is as if the legend of America's wealth and influence had made it a kind of *lingua franca* over a large part of the globe — a "second language" for the educated, an aspiration for young people who have not had a chance at it.

But as the big media become the principal carriers of linguistic invention, an element of falseness far more dangerous than vulgarity of taste is coming to pervade that invention. Like the eighteenth-century court ladies in France who affected the simplicity of Rousseau's milkmaids, the grandees of American cultural commercialism are trying to make a good thing of the phony posturings. They affect a nativist mucker pose or cultivate a racy extremism of jargon which often makes them unintelligible as well as synthetic. Listen to what some of the highly paid script writers dream up for the big radio comedians. Try to follow a disk jockey on the air dishing out a "hot" record with the faded remnants of the Basin Street patois. Pick up any of the "hard-boiled" mysteries, its pages larded with the effort to duplicate the staccato mouthings of a down-at-the-heels sleuth. In all these you will get a febrile jargon contrived for money, loaded with the artificiality of a literary language but without its discipline and taste.

I do not mean to overestimate the effect of the big media on American speech. To be sure, writers, announcers, actors, and commentators working in these media are deeply affected by each other. But most of their listeners are less affected by what they hear than by the usage which is rooted in their daily life and work. Isolated words and phrases are given rapid and vast currency by TV, radio, and movies, but pronunciation and idiom grow out of conversation, and you cannot converse with a TV set. The real danger is that the synthetic may be substituted for the authentic roots of popular speech. American writers are in danger of forgetting that what gave strength to Longstreet's *Georgia Scenes* or Mark Twain's *Huckleberry Finn*, George Ade's *Fables in Slang* or Ring Lardner's *You Know Me, Al* was that the language of each had been lived by millions of people before it was re-created by the individual artist. Many of the literary artifacts of latter-day America seem to have been lived by no one. Their world is of cardboard and paste, flimsy and uninhabitable; there is no smell of earth in it and no commonalty. It is contrived without ever having been experienced, and its only life is the hothouse and penthouse life of those who, in their eagerness for the sophistication of the moment, seek pathetically to imitate the imitators.

The fault does not lie in popularization. Actually the brashness, the tongue-in-cheek satire, and the quality of wild and unashamed hyperbole are exactly what gives strength to a language. What is wrong with many of the recent affectations in American speech is not that they are too much but that they are too little the speech of the people.

———◆———

When in New York ah only dance at the Cotton Club. The only dance ah do is the Virginia reel. The only train ah ride is the Chattanooga Choo-Choo. When ah pass Grant's Tomb ah shut both eyes. Ah never go to the Yankee Stadium. Ah won't even go to the Polo Grounds unless a southpaw's pitchin'.

"Senator Claghorn," on Fred Allen's radio program

83.

Arthur J. Brodbeck and David M. White: How to Read "Li'l Abner"

The comic strip, which first saw the light in America in the 1890s, was a direct descendant of the political cartoon and employed the skills of the caricaturist, the cartoonist, the dramatist, and the storyteller. The first daily multi-panel cartoon — Bud Fisher's "Mr. Mutt" (later "Mutt and Jeff") — started appearing in the San Francisco Chronicle in November 1907. The genre soon proliferated in a variety of styles: the "gag strip" in which a constant cast of characters enacted a single joke each day ("Moon Mullins" and, later, "Peanuts"); the strip with a main protagonist, a story line, a changing scene, and reappearing minor characters ("Orphan Annie" and, later, "Terry and the Pirates"); adventure and "space" strips ("Buck Rogers"); fantasy strips ("Krazy Kat"); "serious" strips inculcating either historical ("Prince Valiant") or moral ("Mary Worth") lessons; and strips with a more or less constant cast of characters who, combined with "guest" characters, acted out one episode and then went on to the next. "Li'l Abner" falls in the last category. Its regular characters are stylized in appearance and predictable in action, and the guest characters and the story line of the episodes provide opportunities for political and social satire. The guest characters are striking examples of the use of caricature in comic strips, since most bear a resemblance to persons prominent at the moment. The selection reprinted here is a "Freudian" analysis of the characters of "Li'l Abner" and appeared in 1957.

Source: *Mass Culture: The Popular Arts in America,* Bernard Rosenberg and David M. White, eds., Glencoe, Ill., 1957, pp. 218-223.

It is a common misbelief that American comic strips consist of little more than "wish fulfillment," slick attempts to provide 100 million readers with daily dreams of adventure and happiness, power, and glory, the stuff of which dreams are made. Of course, "Li'l Abner," like other comic strips and popular art forms, *does* deal with wishes, for what are "wishes" but another name for "problems"? However, those who approach "Li'l Abner" as merely an excursion up the river toward the fulfillment of wishes will take back only a minor part of what it contains. For Al Capp's creation deals with some very painful parts of reality and, while it deals with wishes, it does not invariably fulfill them.

All art teaches us something — usually under conditions where we *think* we are being entertained. The secret of much art is that it tries to keep us off guard, subtly relaxing our shopworn critical senses, by *pretending* to be flattering our egos, while it nevertheless educates us. Art, whether in a play by Congreve or in the newer form utilized by a Harriman, a Walt Kelly or Capp, coaxes our minds to move out of their established conceptual grooves and liberates them for a fresh, creative look at reality. It tries to get us to practise a new kind of response to ourselves and the world. Yet all the while it keeps our fears down low enough by a certain amount of reassurance that things will all work out all right at the end.

"Li'l Abner" tries to do this. It may not always succeed, yet for more than two decades it has been telling millions of Americans each day something about the nature of our contemporary existence — and if we accept the "message" more easily because it is *only* a comic strip, that does not negate the artistic force of the strip.

We often go away from our daily visit to Dogpatch with renewed courage to tackle our own quarrels with urban living, deprivations to our social status, and much else of the same kind. For "Li'l Abner" stresses how far from perfect we and our real world are. But through its art it enables us simultaneously to laugh at the discrepancy, to see our human condition humbly but bravely. The ability to laugh at ourselves always has an element of bravery in it.

Although "Li'l Abner" is concerned with a multitude of the facts of American culture, from a Liberace fad to our fantastic needs to "belong" (like the rejected member of the Gourmet Club), there is nonetheless one central problem on which it hinges: *the maternally overprotected boy,* the boy with an overpowering mother.

Some years ago a British anthropologist came over to view Americans as he might view a primitive tribe, reaching conclusions which were not too different from those of Al Capp about the central American problem. Geoffrey Gorer, in *The American People,* tried to compress in a short volume the structure of American culture, the problems and pains in it, as well as the satisfactions and joys it embodied.

His conclusions have been deeply resisted by Americans, since it is seldom pleasant to have to take a good frank look at ourselves. (The Irishman, for instance, who behaves exactly like Barry Fitzgerald is most likely to look upon him as "caricaturing" the Irish personality.) Yet, there are many who believe that Gorer was not too far from the truth about us, although still more remains to be said.

Gorer tried to show first that every "red-blooded" American boy is expected to be "better" than his parents; in fact, he's supposed to "outgrow" them. It is interesting that "Li'l Abner," when it first began in 1934, started off with Mammy and Pappy Yokum as tall as their son. But within a few months a curious thing happened. Mammy and Pappy began to shrink. It was a period of great conflict, perhaps second only to Li'l Abner's marriage. For the parents never remained "shrunken." They rose — first one, then the other — back to full initial stature again, or very near it, continuing to shrink and grow unpredictably. Finally, they were permanently "dwarfed" as they are now.

It was almost as if, as Al Capp made his way toward success (as every red-blooded American boy is supposed to do) he could "afford" to shrink the parent figures, to feel it was artistically right. In order to feel one's own sense of self-esteem, we Americans more frequently than not set, as a condition of that, some signs of tangible success — a better home, more money, wider acclaim, etc. — that "prove" we have risen "above" our parents. Change between generations is built into the structure of our society. And it is sometimes hard on us indeed. "Li'l Abner" symbolizes all of this wish for social mobility by a mere picture.

But this is to oversimplify what the strip tells us. For Mammy Yokum — small, wizened, and masculinized as she is — is endowed with magical powers. She is par excellence the overprotecting mother. Or, at least, she is her son's childlike conception of such a type of mother, the *way* in which he believes in her and imagines her to be. She can handle the "monsters" four times her size by "wrasslin' Dogpatch style" — which knowledge *she*, not Pappy, imparts to her son. She is the leader of her community, ready to impress by force if necessary her and her offspring's importance upon all others. When not using her "fisks," she divines truth by supernatural incantations and brings about justice in mysterious ways. Her famous duel with "Evil Eye" Fleegle (who symbolizes the "sinfulness" of city life), in which rays of "goodness" emerge from her eyes, casts Mammy Yokum in the heroic mold. Anything you can do she can do better.

What woman could compare with her? The feminine Daisy Mae is weak and helpless. The city women are designing, shallow, and seething with lust. (Basically, says the strip, all American women, unlike Mammy, are constantly trying to put a man's potency to test, when they are not engaged in destroying his independence and innocence through such devices as "Sadie Hawkins Days.")

Beside Mammy, Li'l Abner's father is the merest caricature of a man — and to accentuate this feature, by a twist of Capp's special use of irony, Pappy is called "Lucifer," while Mammy is named "Pansy," which connotes inappropriately a shrinking, timid woman of delicate design and presents a denial of the masculinity and power of American mothers by the magic of words juxtaposed against what is so graphically otherwise.

As a matter of fact, what we are looking at is nothing but the American version of the Oedipus complex set in a mother-dominated family. To identify with Mother is to become a "Pansy"; yet, the source of strength lies nowhere else, since the protection and guidance of the son is all generated from the mother figure. Indeed, "Lucifer" is almost a cry of protest, comically contrived,

against a father who is not there in any important sense.

In the early days of the strip, when Li'l Abner put on the wedding suit of his father, as he starts out to the big city and symbolically up the social ladder, the usual Oedipal feeling would demand that the suit be oversized. Instead, it is comically small and shrunken and leads the "sassiety" people into gales of laughter when they see it. Li'l Abner succeeds through his family connections on Mammy's side (her sister) and despite the inadequacy of Pappy's bequest to him.

But the Oedipus complex comes out fully and strongly in the traditional way — feelings of active possessiveness toward the mother and competitive feelings toward the father for her favors — as Abner moves among "high sassiety" people or aristocratic foreigners from the "old country." As Malinowski discovered, just as the uncle occupies the father's position in the Oedipus triangle among the Trobrianders, so the people above oneself in the social scale, as one moves out of the family, bring out one's true, not inverted, Oedipus feelings. One's masculinity is suddenly aroused as one moves up the social ladder. The "high sassiety" women are constantly acting out their sexual feelings toward Li'l Abner, and the "bosses" and the other male aristocrats of mass society vent their spleen on Li'l Abner, and sometimes compete with him for the favors of the women.

A count who courts Li'l Abner's "high sassiety" aunt, and is continually frustrated in the courtship by Li'l Abner, finally delivers a blow (below the belt) to him, explaining that it's an "old custom" in his own land (the European land of patriarchy where the real Oedipus complex exists, instead of the American land of matriarchy where boys find their fathers nonentities). Dumpington Van Lump, a cruel, selfish, and slobbish "high sassiety" creature, tries to wrench Daisy Mae away from Abner and to destroy all of Dogpatch — the primary ego — in the process.

Gorer has tried to show that it is the overprotective, all-powerful American mother who is the source of the strengths *and* weaknesses of American men. This contributes in subtle ways to their fears of being effeminate — since they identify with and get their source of strength and self-esteem from their mothers more than their fathers. It leads them to feel "guilty" about sex which is not "idealistic" and which doesn't partake of the noble and passive relationship the American male has had with his own Mother. But it makes him strong enough to be sympathetic and kind toward the weak, as Mother was. And it makes him able to endure stress, although sometimes complaining as one would to Mother, and to blind himself to the harm that others can (and sometimes do) cause him, because of the optimistic *weltanschauung* that mother bequeathed him.

Food, Gorer has pointed out, is the way in which American mothers and sons express their love for each other: the mother by filling the child with it and the child by passively allowing himself to be filled. Food themes abound everywhere in "Li'l Abner." At crucial moments in his life, moments of crisis and danger, Abner calls for his "Po'k chops." He is calling for Mother-Love, and attempting to assuage his anxiety by recalling the strength he has gotten from Mother. He is engaged in a magical act — and we laugh at the magic of it, the palpable absurdity — and yet, it is the type of magic that operates in both high and low places in the lives of American men. The "monsters" and "high sassiety" people often deprive Abner of his food indulgences. The world is not like the nursery, even though Abner frequently expects it to be bountiful in the food of Mother-Love.

There is a Henry James complexity to the strip. Each episode, depending on which character's eyes you see it from, takes on a slightly different meaning. In this way, Li'l Abner's personality is seen from a multitude of viewpoints that exist in American society, viewpoints that condemn the results of maternal overprotection and viewpoints which beam on it. In general, however, it is the problems which the overprotected boy causes for other people with whom he must constantly interact that is stressed. The complexity of the strip thus makes us see its most exaggerated consequences. And to repeat, it does this and makes us like it — whereas, when Geoffrey Gorer did it, we were repelled.

At no time does the strip allow us to examine the themes with complete pessimism or complete optimism. Li'l Abner's courage often seems incomprehensible and his pessimistic fears seem ridiculous. True, we always tend to feel that things will really work out for the best in the end, but never without a certain amount of "comic" pain and misery first. (Watch the way Li'l Abner "sweats" unremittingly on his way through life!) Nothing comes easy, except Mammy Yokum's strength and her willingness to use it for her son.

We can never be sure about endings in "Li'l Abner." All the shmoos were killed — and the shmoo was a sort of truncated symbol for the very concept of wish fulfillment. And Truth, masquerading as the Bald Iggle, must be silenced in the end, even if it has to be by a female impersonator of Mother. And Abner does marry and so loses his boyish innocence.

No, "Li'l Abner" does not run away from reality, even when it is most fantastic; it doesn't hesitate to frustrate wishes, even when it ironically denies reality in ways in which many Americans deny it in their everyday lives. In fact, by *exaggerating* our own defenses against the painful parts of our American reality, especially those concerned with the pain in social mobility, it shows how absurd those defenses really are. It speaks in reverse English directly to our unconscious knowledge about ourselves and the world by overdoing the kind of flattery we treat ourselves to as we march through life. In his ironic "Did I say that?" type of artlessness, which is practised as a high art, Capp gets us to see what hypocrites we are, and yet doesn't force us to hate ourselves for it. It is done so tactfully, so gently, as though we were all good friends. Indeed, there is a warmness for people in "Li'l Abner," an affectionate streak and a kind one, even though the sentiment is always firmly but fantastically married to realism. The eyes of the strip do not wear rose-colored glasses.

Even the style of the strip is completely American in its fierce "individualism," which it is constantly redefining. It never quite allows us to hate or love any one character or movement wholeheartedly. It sees imperfection everywhere. No one, not even Li'l Abner, is exempt from a savage honesty of appraisal, except again Mammy Yokum — and there have even been times when the strip, perhaps without knowing what it was doing, and getting carried away by its own style, took a fast-running, critical side glance at her. The style permits of no wholehearted sentimentalization of any person, idea, or organization. Yet, though there is no *unqualified* love and adoration expressed toward anyone, there remains *warmth* and *compassion*. And is this not, truly, an American style of feeling, part of what we have come to mean by "individualism"? The very best we have in American Life? The very heart of the complexity of our spiritual quality existing among our technological and materialistic way of living?

Without plunging into the pros and cons of popular culture and mass society, let us not forget that Shakespeare was once an element in Elizabethan popular culture and that it took dozens of decades before the guardians of high literary standards allowed him to rise in respectability and permitted us to see his permanent worth. Any art, no matter how popular, which has the kind of complexity that is the substance of "Li'l Abner," and has learned to communicate the complexity to us so simply, so matter-of-factly, is bound to have a certain amount of lastingness, even though it is embodied in a particular time and place, even though it makes concessions to the "mass mind."

Does Capp altogether know what he is saying through his comic strip? Is it perhaps a case, more than with Shakespeare, of one person's unconscious speaking through a large circulation to millions of others? The answer is bound to be moot. Writers often learn an astonishing amount from their critics about what they have written. Since "Li'l Abner" depicts so much of the unconscious and unrecognized forces at work in American life, some of it is bound to well from Capp's own unconscious itself.

But reading "Li'l Abner" is much different than listening to the free associations of a single gifted exponent of American culture. These associations have become, through Capp's artistic talents, transformed and universalized. He is not talking to an analyst, but he is communicating with twenty to thirty million fellow American citizens. The artistic transformation means that whatever is unique in one's associations must be communicated by more universal symbols or else it cannot be shared. The artist need not be ashamed of the sources of his inspirations and we do not need to know what they are in order to judge the quality of his finished product.

It is often said that our "mass society" has produced a greater leisure than ever before for the general run of mankind; but the people have turned away from "the higher art" and "the better culture" to indulge themselves in the tawdry *kitsch* of the mass-media industry. Surely, the gulf between the higher and the popular arts is not quite so wide, and some of the elements of "good" art are present in Capp's comic-strip fantasies.

But may the public have turned away

from the "higher art" because it is so full of pessimism and unhappy ending and no resolutions to the problems of life? It may be not so much that people want to be flattered, as they may want some *help* and *guidance* in finding solutions to the problems that confront them. The "higher art," many times, only reiterates the conflicts which they already feel and leaves them at the same, or even worse, impasse than that at which they were already. Hollywood takes over precisely because the most gifted and complex of artists share a grotesque form of pessimism about life's problems and present only masochistic reveries for people.

It is indeed fortunate that there is someone like Capp to fill the gap, until the "higher art" begins to offer solutions again to the woe-begotten state of life it depicts. If anything, Capp should not be criticized too much for the pleasantness of his comic reveries. Instead, like the "higher art," he frequently in his more recent work destroys hope and courage and becomes more devoid of solutions to the American dilemmas. One might wish him to be more optimistic, without losing his complexity. There never was a time when Americans, Mass or Elite, needed it more, if there are some realistic grounds on which it can be maintained.

84.

Harvey Swados: The Myth of the Happy Worker

Every era of American history has entertained its special myth about the workingman. In the 1930s he was a noble — or despised — proletarian; in the '40s he was a patriot; but in the '50s he became, in the eyes of many, a full-fledged member of the middle class. The statistics seemed to bear out the myth, but according to Harvey Swados, a free-lance writer, but also a factory worker at various times during his life, the myth was just that — a myth. "There is one thing that the worker doesn't do like the middle class," asserted Swados: "he works like a worker." And as long as the worker is not able to escape the "degradation" of "repetitive work," and attain the freedom of the real middle class, he will continue to be unhappy, whatever social or economic class he is supposed to belong to. The article reprinted here, in which Swados makes this and other points about the workers of the present day, was first published in 1957.

Source: *Nation*, August 17, 1957.

"From where we sit in the company," says one of the best personnel men in the country, "we have to look at only the aspects of work that cut across all sorts of jobs — administration and human relations. Now these are aspects of work, abstractions, but it's easy for personnel people to get so hipped on their importance that they look on the specific tasks of making things and selling them as secondary. . . ."

— *The Organization Man*, by William H. Whyte Jr.

THE PERSONNEL MAN who made this remark to Mr. Whyte differed from his brothers only in that he had a moment of insight.

Actually, "the specific tasks of making things" are now not only regarded by his white-collar fellows as "secondary," but as irrelevant to the vaguer but more "challenging" tasks of the man at the desk. This is true not just of the personnel man, who places workers, replaces them, displaces them — in brief, manipulates them. The union leader also, who represents workers and sometimes manipulates them, seems increasingly to regard what his workers do as merely subsidiary to the job he himself is doing in the larger community. This job may be building the Red Cross or the Community Chest, or it may sometimes be — as the Senate hearings suggest — participating in such communal endeavors as gambling, prostitution and improving the breed. In any case, the impression is left that the problems of the workers in the background (or underground) have been stabilized, if not permanently solved.

With the personnel man and the union leader, both of whom presumably see the worker from day to day, growing so far away from him, it is hardly to be wondered at that the middle class in general, and articulate middle-class intellectuals in particular, see the worker vaguely, as through a cloud. One gets the impression that when they do consider him, they operate from one of two unspoken assumptions: (1) The worker has died out like the passenger pigeon, or is dying out, or becoming acculturated, like the Navajo; (2) If he *is* still around, he is just like the rest of us — fat, satisfied, smug, a little restless, but hardly distinguishable from his fellow TV viewers of the middle class.

Lest it be thought that (1) is somewhat exaggerated, I hasten to quote from a recently-published article apparently dedicated to the laudable task of urging slothful middle-class intellectuals to wake up and live: "The old-style sweatshop crippled mainly the working people. Now there are no workers left in America; we are almost all

middle class as to income and expectations." I do not believe the writer meant to state — although he comes perilously close to it — that nobody works any more. If I understand him correctly, he is referring to the fact that the worker's rise in real income over the last decade, plus the diffusion of middle-class tastes and values throughout a large part of the underlying population, have made it increasingly difficult to tell blue-collar from white-collar worker without a program. In short, if the worker earns like the middle class, votes like the middle class, dresses like the middle class, dreams like the middle class, then he ceases to exist as a worker.

But there is one thing that the worker doesn't do like the middle class: he works like a worker. The steel-mill puddler does not yet sort memos, the coal miner does not yet sit in conferences, the cotton-mill hand does not yet sip martinis from his lunchbox. The worker's attitude toward his work is generally compounded of hatred, shame, and resignation.

Before I spell out what I think this means, I should like first to examine some of the implications of the widely-held belief that "we are almost all middle class as to income and expectations." I am neither economist, sociologist, nor politician, and I hold in my hand no doctored statistics to be haggled over. I am by profession a writer who has had occasion to work in factories at various times during the Thirties, Forties and Fifties. The following observations are simply impressions based on my last period of factory servitude, in 1956.

The average automobile worker gets a little better than two dollars an hour. As such he is one of the best-paid factory workers in the country. After twenty years of militant struggle led by the union that I believe to be still the finest and most democratic labor organization in the United States, he is earning less than the starting salaries offered to inexperienced and often semi-literate college graduates without dependents. After compulsory deductions for taxes, social security, old-age insurance and union dues, and optional deductions for hospitalization and assorted charities, his pay check for forty hours of work is going to be closer to seventy than to eighty dollars a week. Does this make him middle class as to income? Does it rate with the weekly take of a dentist, an accountant, a salesman, a draftsman, a journalist? Surely it would be more to the point to ask how a family man can get by in the Fifties on that kind of income. I know how he does it, and I should think the answers would be a little disconcerting to those who wax glib on the satisfactory status of the "formerly" underprivileged.

For one thing, he works a lot longer than forty hours a week — when he can. Since no automobile company is as yet in a position to guarantee its workers anything like fifty weeks of steady forty-hour paychecks, the auto worker knows he has to make it while he can. During peak production periods he therefore puts in nine, ten, eleven, and often twelve hours a day on the assembly line for weeks on end. And that's not all. If he has dependents, as like as not he also holds down a "spare-time" job. I have worked on the line with men who doubled as mechanics, repairmen, salesmen, contractors, builders, farmers, cab drivers, lumberyard workers, countermen. I would guess that there are many more of these than show up in the official statistics; often a man will work for less if he can be paid under the counter with tax-free dollars.

Nor is that all. The factory worker with dependents cannot carry the debt load he now shoulders — the middle-class debt load, if you like, of nagging payments on car, washer, dryer, TV, clothing, house itself — without family help. Even if he puts in fifty, sixty, or seventy hours a week at one or two jobs, he has to count on his wife's paycheck, or his son's, his daughter's, his brother-in-law's; or on his mother's social security, or his father's veteran's pension. The working-class family today is not typically held together by the male wage earner, but by multiple wage earners, often of several generations, who club together to get the things they want and need — or are pressured into believing they must have. It is at best a precarious arrangement; as for its toll on the physical organism and the psyche, that is a question perhaps worthy of further investigation by those who currently pronounce themselves bored with Utopia Unlimited in the Fat Fifties.

But what of the worker's middle-class expectations? I had been under the impression that this was the rock on which Socialist agitation had foundered for generations: it proved useless to tell the proletarian that he had a world to win when he was reasonably certain that with a few breaks he could have his own gas station. If these expectations have changed at all in recent years, they would seem to have narrowed rather than expanded, leaving a psychological increment of resignation rather than of unbounded optimism (except among the very young — and even among them the optimism focuses more often on better-paying opportunities elsewhere in the labor market than on illusory hopes of swift status advancement). The worker's expectations are for better pay, more humane working conditions, more job security. As long as he feels that he is going to achieve them through an extension of existing conditions, for that long he is going to continue to be a middle-class conservative in temper. But only for that long.

I suspect that what middle-class writers mean by the worker's middle-class expectations are his cravings for commodities — his determination to have not only fin-tailed cars and single-unit washer-dryers, but butterfly chairs in the rumpus room, African masks on the wall, and powerboats in the garage. Before the middle-class intellectuals condemn these expectations too harshly, let them consider, first, who has been utilizing every known technique of suasion and propaganda to convert luxuries into necessities, and second, at what cost these new necessities are acquired by the American working-class family.

Now I should like to return to the second image of the American worker: satisfied, doped by TV, essentially middle class in outlook. This is an image bred not of communication with workers (except as mediated by hired interviewers sent "into the field" like anthropologists or entomologists) but of contempt for people, based perhaps on self-contempt and on a feeling among intellectuals that the worker has let them down. In order to see this clearly, we have to place it against the intellectual's changing attitudes toward the worker since the Thirties.

At the time of the organization of the CIO, the middle-class intellectual saw the proletarian as society's figure of virtue — heroic, magnanimous, bearing in his loins the seeds of a better future; he would have found ludicrous the suggestion that a sit-down striker might harbor anti-Semitic feelings. After Pearl Harbor, the glamorization of the worker was taken over as a function of government. Then, however, he was no longer the builder of the future good society; instead he was second only to the fighting man as the vital winner of the war. Many intellectuals, as government employees, found themselves helping to create this new portrait of the worker as patriot.

But in the decade following the war, intellectuals have discovered that workers are no longer either building socialism or forging the tools of victory. All they are doing is making the things that other people buy. That, and participating in the great commodity scramble. The disillusionment, it would seem, is almost too terrible to bear. Word has gotten around among the highbrows that the worker is not heroic or idealistic; public-opinion polls prove that he

wants barbecue pits more than foreign aid and air-conditioning more than desegregation, that he doesn't particularly want to go on strike, that he is reluctant to form a Labor Party, that he votes for Stevenson and often even for Eisenhower and Nixon — that he is, in short, animated by the same aspirations as drive the middle class onward and upward in suburbia.

There is of course a certain admixture of self-delusion in the middle-class attitude that workers are now the same as everybody else. For me it was expressed most precisely last year in the dismay and sympathy with which middle-class friends greeted the news that I had gone back to work in a factory. If workers are now full-fledged members of the middle class, why the dismay? What difference whether one sits in an office or stands in a shop? The answer is so obvious that one feels shame at laboring the point. But I have news for my friends among the intellectuals. The answer is obvious to workers, too.

They know that there is a difference between working with your back and working with your behind (I do not make the distinction between handwork and brainwork, since we are all learning that white-collar work is becoming less and less brain-work). They know that they work harder than the middle class for less money. Nor is it simply a question of status, that magic word so dear to the hearts of the sociologues, the new anatomizers of the American corpus. It is not simply status-hunger that makes a man hate work which pays *less* than other work he knows about, if *more* than any other work he has been trained for (the only reason my fellow workers stayed on the assembly line, they told me again and again). It is not simply status-hunger that makes a man hate work that is mindless, endless, stupefying, sweaty, filthy, noisy, exhausting, insecure in its prospects and practically without hope of advancement.

The plain truth is that factory work is degrading. It is degrading to any man who ever dreams of doing something worthwhile with his life; and it is about time we faced the fact. The more a man is exposed to middle-class values, the more sophisticated he becomes and the more production-line work is degrading to him. The immigrant who slaved in the poorly-lighted, foul, vermin-ridden sweatshop found his work less degrading than the native-born high-school graduate who reads Judge Parker, Rex Morgan, M.D., and Judd Saxon, Business Executive, in the funnies, and works in a fluorescent factory with ticker-tape, production-control machines. For the immigrant laborer, even the one who did not dream of socialism, his long hours were going to buy him freedom. For the factory worker of the Fifties, his long hours are going to buy him commodities . . . and maybe reduce a few of his debts.

Almost without exception, the men with whom I worked on the assembly line last year felt like trapped animals. Depending on their age and personal circumstances, they were either resigned to their fate, furiously angry at *themselves* for what they were doing, or desperately hunting other work that would pay as well and in addition offer some variety, some prospect of change and betterment. They were sick of being pushed around by harried foremen (themselves more pitied than hated), sick of working like blinkered donkeys, sick of being dependent for their livelihood on a maniacal production-merchandising setup, sick of working in a place where there was no spot to relax during the twelve-minute rest period. (Some day — let us hope — we will marvel that production was still so worshiped in the Fifties that new factories could be built with every splendid facility for the storage and movement of essential parts, but with no place for a resting worker to sit down for a moment but on a fire plug, the edge of a packing case, or the sputum- and oil-stained stairway of a toilet.)

The older men stay put and wait for their vacations. But since the assembly line demands young blood (you will have a hard time getting hired if you are over thirty-five), the factory in which I worked was aswarm with new faces every day, labor turnover was so fantastic and absenteeism so rampant, with the young men knocking off a day or two every week to hunt up other jobs, that the company was forced to over-hire in order to have sufficient workers on hand at the starting siren.

To those who will object — fortified by their readings in C. Wright Mills and A. C. Spectorsky — that the white-collar commuter, too, dislikes his work, accepts it only because it buys his family commodities, and is constantly on the prowl for other work, I can only reply that for me, at any rate, this is proof, not of the disappearance of the working class but of the proletarianization of the middle class. Perhaps it is not taking place quite in the way that Marx envisaged it, but the alienation of the white-collar man (like that of the laborer) from both his tools and whatever he produces, the slavery that chains the exurbanite to the commuting timetable (as the worker is still chained to the time clock), the anxiety that sends the white-collar man home with his briefcase for an evening's work (as it degrades the workingman into pleading for long hours of overtime), the displacement of the white-collar slum from the wrong side of the tracks to the suburbs (just as the working-class slum is moved from old-law tenements to skyscraper barracks) — all these mean to me that the white-collar man is entering (though his arms may be loaded with commodities) the gray world of the workingman.

Three quotations from men with whom I worked may help to bring my view into focus:

Before starting work: "Come on, suckers, they say the Foundation wants to give away *more* than half a billion this year. Let's do and die for the old Foundation."

During rest period: "Ever stop to think how we crawl here bumper to bumper, and crawl home bumper to bumper, and we've got to turn out more every minute to keep our jobs, when there isn't even any room for them on the highways?"

At quitting time (this from older foremen, whose job is not only to keep things moving but by extension to serve as company spokesmen): "You're smart to get out of here. . . . I curse the day I ever started, now I'm stuck; any man with brains that stays here ought to have his head examined. This is no place for an intelligent human being."

Such is the attitude toward the work. And toward the product? On the one hand it is admired and desired as a symbol of freedom, almost a substitute for freedom, not because the worker participated in making it but because our whole culture is dedicated to the proposition that the automobile is both necessary and beautiful. On the other hand it is hated and despised — so much that if your new car smells bad it may be due to a banana peel crammed down its gullet and sealed up thereafter, so much so that if your dealer can't locate the rattle in your new car you might ask him to open the welds on one of those tail fins and vacuum out the nuts and bolts thrown in by workers sabotaging their own product.

Sooner or later, if we want a decent society — by which I do not mean a society glutted with commodities or one maintained in precarious equilibrium by overbuying and forced premature obsolescence — we are going to have to come face to face with the problem of work. Apparently the Russians have committed themselves to the replenishment of their labor force through automatic recruitment of those intellectually incapable of keeping up with severe scholastic requirements in the public educational system. Apparently we, too, are heading in the same direction; although our economy is not directed, and although college education is as yet far from free, we seem to be operating in this capitalist economy on the totalitarian assumption that we can funnel the underprivileged, undereducated, or just plain underequipped into the factory, where we can proceed to forget about them once we have posted the minimum fair-labor standards on the factory wall.

If this is what we want, let's be honest enough to say so. If we conclude that there is nothing noble about repetitive work, but that it is nevertheless good enough for the lower orders, let's say that, too, so we will at least know where we stand. But if we cling to the belief that other men are our brothers, not just Egyptians, or Israelis, or Hungarians, but *all* men, including millions of Americans who grind their lives away on an insane treadmill, then we will have to start thinking about how their work and their lives can be made meaningful. That is what I assume the Hungarians, both workers and intellectuals, have been thinking about. Since no one has been ordering us what to think, since no one has been forbidding our intellectuals to fraternize with our workers, shouldn't it be a little easier for us to admit, first, that our problems exist, then to state them, and then to see if we can resolve them?

When I was a boy I used to do what my father wanted. Now I have to do what my boy wants. My problem is: When am I going to do what I want?

SAM LEVENSON

Street scene on New York's lower east side, 1957

THE STRAIN OF AFFLUENCE

The life of the nation in the 1950s has yet to be fully described, explained, or assessed. Elements of the national culture of the postwar Cold War period persist as a sort of cliche folklore; cultural change is so swift and strong that there exists already a generation capable of feeling nostalgia toward the late 1950s. It is safe to say, however, that the central fact of the period was the incredible success of the American economy, a patchwork of capitalism, government regulation, fiscal management, and social welfare, all based on the consumer market. This success — the creation of the "affluent society" — and the problems and reactions that attended it, form the framework of American culture. Disregarding for the moment, as was quite generally done during the decade, the objection that America's affluence was not complete, that poverty persisted in many areas and levels of society, the main question that was raised, consciously and otherwise, coherently or not, was: After affluence, what? The automation upon which much of the nation's wealth rested created technological unemployment; it accelerated the migration of the largely unskilled rural population to the crowded cities; and it increased leisure time without educating anyone to its use.

(Above) Shoppers at an open-air produce display outside a Hoboken, N.J., grocery; (below) the scene in a Hoboken bar

Bruce Davidson from Magnum

Eve Arnold from Magnum

(Above) Kite-flying in Central Park, New York; (right) chess game in a Greenwich Village square

Naturally enough, different groups and classes of people had varying reactions to leisure. Groups and communities with well-established patterns of social activities were less disturbed than those more fragmented. Television was so successful in absorbing free time, particularly among children, that it became a point of controversy for educators and parents. Many observers drew a connection between increased leisure and the weakening of the family as a social unit; this was seen as a primary middle-class phenomenon. The young, as a group, seemed most affected; they had, of course, the least established set of habits and reactions. Such a lack of direction and identification seemed to lie behind much of highly-publicized juvenile delinquency of city gangs and suburban vandals.

(Above) A sandlot baseball game in the Italian-American section of Hoboken; (below) couple on park bench in Central Park, New York

A study of New York City's young people: (Top left) Teenage boy; (top right) young couple; (bottom) two members of a teenage gang

(Top) Marlon Brando (center) with members of his motorcycle gang in the film, "The Wild One"; (bottom left) teenage singing idol of the mid-1950s Elvis Presley performing in Hollywood; (bottom right) movie actor James Dean in a scene from "Giant"

A period of affluence and leisure naturally gives rise to fads, cults, and generally spectacular productions. As the Twenties had had hot jazz and Flaming Youth, the 1950s had rock and roll and Teenagers. While manufacturers were discovering that the young constituted a new, potentially highly profitable, and virtually unexploited market, sociologists and psychologists were examining them in search of the bases of their generally bizarre behavior. Among older youth, those of college age, a startlingly different observation was made: the political awareness and activism, the tendency to experiment with radical doctrines that had characterized students of the 1930s and 1940s seemed to be gone. This group was dubbed the "Silent Generation" in their apparent dedication to personal comfort and security. Yet another fringe group appeared to challenge this image; rejecting the bland and "phony" middle-class life, the Beatniks continued the long line of American bohemianism into the 1950s.

David Seymour from Magnum

(Right) **Film star Audrey Hepburn; (below) Monsignor Barthe, bishop of Monaco, celebrates Nuptial Mass at the marriage of former American actress Grace Kelly and Prince Rainier, 1956**

UPI — Compix

Eyerman, "Life," © Time Inc.

(Above) Looking down from the mountains on the sprawling metropolis of Los Angeles; (below) ladies attending an outdoor fashion show at a suburban shopping center in California

Eyerman, "Life," © Time Inc.

Henri Cartier-Bresson from Magnum

Exercising on Muscle Beach, California

Henri Cartier-Bresson from Magnum

Henri Cartier-Bresson from Magnum

(Above and right) Two groups of members of a private social club in Miami, Fla. OPPOSITE PAGE: (Top) Relaxing in a short-order restaurant; (bottom left) Northwestern fans at a football game; (bottom right) outfielder Ted Williams at bat for the Boston Red Sox in 1959

Myriad ways were discovered to turn leisure into profit as soon as it became apparent that large numbers of people were willing to have their pastimes provided for them. A new boom in retirement towns boosted the economy in Florida, California, and Arizona; here the "senior citizen" was provided with constantly varied activities and spared the boredom of retirement. Spectator sports of all kinds made huge gains in attendance and gate receipts, raising speculation that the nation was becoming generally sedentary and uninterested in active participation. It should be remembered, however, that the new leisure was primarily a phenomenon of the new middle class, and largely urban — or suburban — in appeal and extent. Among the poor and in rural areas, life was only marginally affected.

(Above) A scene in the hills of eastern Tennessee; (below) William Faulkner, American writer who treated many aspects of Southern society, photographed at his home in Oxford, Mississippi

85.

James H. Gray: A Canadian Looks at America

Americans have often pointed with pride to their country's relations with Canada, which, they sometimes boast, are an example to the world of what international amity could be. And it is true enough that mutual peace and prosperity for both Canada and the United States have been the norm for more than a century, and that such neighborly friendliness is rare on this strife-torn earth. These self-congratulatory feelings are not shared, however, by Canadians — at least to anywhere near the same extent. At best, many citizens of America's northern neighbor charge the U.S. with ignorance of Canadian problems, and, at worst, with a fundamental lack of concern with Canada's needs. Such charges were leveled by James H. Gray, editor and publisher of the Calgary Western Oil Examiner, *in 1957. In so doing he revealed some of the disadvantages to a smaller country of being "owned" by the U.S. — disadvantages that were also pointed to in the next decade by Europeans like President Charles de Gaulle of France.*

Source: *Atlantic Monthly,* March 1957: "A Canadian Looks Us Over."

Living next door to a boy learning to play a fiddle can frazzle the nerves of even the most friendly neighbors. Living next door to a nation which is trying to learn how to be a great power can have the same effect on another nation. The transformation of the United States from an isolationist nation into the leader of the free world has been a fascinating thing to watch from Canada. But the leftovers from the isolationist days, the unchanged thought patterns of American politics and business, periodically give Canadians conniption fits.

The latest example erupted just before Christmas over tolls for the use of the St. Lawrence Seaway. As all the Seaway advocates have been saying for thirty years, the purpose of the St. Lawrence Canal is to give the whole Great Lakes industrial area and the consumers of the mid-continent the benefit of lower costs that come with ocean transportation. From this premise several conclusions follow. The first is that the cost of the project must be kept down so that tolls may be set at the lowest possible point; high tolls mean high shipping rates. The second is that there must be the maximum freedom of movement of all ships into and out of the area. The third is that the whole purpose of the waterway will be defeated if shipping is restricted.

The Canadian view has always been that the ships of the world will ply the waterway with freedom of call. This will encourage ships to come in for long-haul exports and will speed the movement of short-haul domestic freight. But when Canadians sat down to discuss canal tolls, they discovered that the United States has no great burning ambition to permit that to happen.

American taxpayers subsidize their shipping to the extent of about $100 million a year. Whenever it is decided that a sea route is "essential to the trade and economy of the nation," ships using the route are entitled to a subsidy which will amount to about $750 per day. This is in addition to the usual grant of 40 percent of the building costs and 50 percent cargo preference. When the United States, early in 1956, promulgated the Great Lakes-Northern Europe and Western Europe route as "essential to the trade and economy of the nation," Canada regarded it as an unfair act, one that violated the spirit of the St. Lawrence agreement.

American coastal laws will not permit goods to be moved between U.S. ports in foreign bottoms. Through the Canal American ships will monopolize American trade. And because they are subsidized, U.S. ships will grab off much of the Canadian trade. Canada's exchange problem would thus be substantially worsened. Its trade deficit with the United States is currently out of balance by $1 billion a year. It makes up for this in part by selling more than it buys from the United Kingdom and Western Europe. It is in Canada's interest to let non-U.S. foreign ships pick up Canadian cargo and earn Canadian dollars with which to buy Canadian goods.

The joker in all this for U.S. taxpayers is that 95 percent of American ships will be unable to use the Seaway if they are fully laden. In the last generation the trend in marine architecture has been to large vessels which draw a maximum draft of thirty feet or more. Most ships of the American merchant fleet fall into the modern category. European shipping, however, has not followed this trend so closely. The European tramps are generally smaller and may draw only twenty-two to twenty-six feet fully laden. To compete with them, the American ships must sail partly loaded. That will boost their costs, make their operations along the route uneconomic. This, Canada fears, is bound to cause the U.S. to seek higher tolls to discourage foreign shipping.

In applying the subsidy regulation to the St. Lawrence Seaway, the United States sowed seeds of doubt as to its good faith in future operation of the Seaway. There is reason to believe that this doubt led to the Canadian decision to reject American protests and proceed with the construction of the Cornwall link at a cost of $17 million.

That link will become part of an all-Canadian system of locks. The United States regarded such construction as unnecessarily adding to the cost of the Seaway. The Canadians have always held that two sets of locks are essential, one on the American side and one on the Canadian side. With the United States insisting on retaining one end of the Canal in its control, despite Canadian protests, Canada decided it could not afford to remain vulnerable to ill-conceived or politically inspired action in Washington which might harm Canadian interest. It notified Washington it would build the Canadian link immediately.

Canada expects that ships will use the waterway right up to Fort William. This will save large sums now expended in rail freight from Montreal to central Canada. Moreover, it expects some foreign ships to participate in the local coastal trade — to pick up material at Toronto and deliver it to Fort William, or at Buffalo for shipment to Fort William. In the other direction, these ships will be able to load grain at Fort William for shipment to Europe. But if they are discouraged from entering the waterway by high tolls or competition from subsidized American bottoms, they will not be able to move out Canadian grain, which was one of Canada's main reasons for building the Canal.

THE SHIPPING SUBSIDY is an almost perfect example of how domestically motivated legislation can fog up international relations. Other sections of Canada have lately been affected by other examples. American agricultural price-support programs have created surpluses which have been dumped on world markets to unsettle international trade. Quotas have been imposed against Canadian imports. Efforts to export Canadian gas to the United States have been endlessly delayed by clashing local interests.

Of particular importance in rousing widespread Canadian reaction against Washington has been the recent attempt, by the U.S. Bureau of Internal Revenue, to force an American-owned Ontario company to pay back taxes to the United States on income that the Canadian government ruled was tax exempt sixteen years ago. If the U.S. courts sustain the U.S. government, the reciprocal tax agreements between the two countries, which are the foundation of Canadian-United States industrial relations, will be abrogated. The confusion such abrogation could create would involve thousands of companies and billions of dollars. So important did Canada consider this matter that Prime Minister St. Laurent himself protested to Washington. Yet at last reports the case was bound for American court decision.

In themselves irritations of this kind may be inconsequential when compared with the bonds of friendship that exist. The collective result of this continual wrangling, however, is to tarnish the vital prestige of American leadership in world affairs. That was seen in Canada when the English and French invaded Egypt.

Canadians generally reacted to American denunciation of the invasion with: "What would the Americans have done if some tin-pot dictator in Panama had announced he was nationalizing the Panama Canal? Waited for the United Nations to devise a formula to appease him sufficiently so that he would permit some nations to use the canal? In a pig's eye they would!"

So long as the United States was an isolated nation living largely to itself, the laws it made were its own business. But a world power must reconcile the laws it passes with the role it has to play in the world. That role, moreover, must be recognized by American business, which also is expanding rapidly abroad.

Because they have become accustomed to trading in interstate commerce, American businessmen tend to regard the rest of the world as just another state. What works in Texas must work in Canada. The reason it is not working must be that Canadians don't know about it. So it becomes the first chore of all newly appointed managers of American branches in Canada to enlighten Canadians. After they have discovered the endless differences between Canada and the United States, they spend the next couple of years trying to explain Canadian idiosyncrasies to their bosses back home.

The manager of a Canadian subsidiary which had been in business in western Canada for forty years got a letter last fall from his sales manager. The latter had seen a three-line item in a Chicago paper reporting that Canada was harvesting a bumper wheat crop. This was enough to impel the sales manager to urge his Canadian outlet to increase its orders and launch a special drive to get the company's share of the flush farm income.

"What's the use?" the branch manager asked. "Here we've got our elevators jammed with wheat from last year. All over western Canada grain is piled in the fields because there is no place else to store it. I've told them that. I've explained how Canadian farm spending is now spread over a full year because farmers can't market their grain in the fall of the year they grow it. I've explained our quota system. What's the use!"

Of greater importance than the ignorance of some sales managers is the application of company rules to Canadian operations. In most U.S. multi-plant operations, one branch is usually designated as the export branch. All inquiries from abroad are channeled through this branch. Canada has a small army of trade commissioners scattered around the world drumming up Canadian trade. They bombard Ottawa with reports of markets for exports and supplies of goods available for importation. Ottawa gives these bulletins to Canadian business.

Last fall, follow-up surveys disclosed that many of the needs were being filled by American instead of Canadian factories. The Canadian branches had sent the information home to the U.S. and ultimately the designated export branch had got onto the sale. Why? Because Canadian branches were not permitted to sell Canadian-made goods for export. When this became bruited about Ottawa, roofs were dented all over the Trade and Commerce Department. As the Rt. Hon. C. D. Howe, Minister of Trade and Commerce, said later, "Too often, I regret to say, our trade representatives abroad turn up export opportunities for a subsidiary company operating in Canada only to find that the United States parent does not permit the export business to be done from the Canadian plant. Mind you, we do not object to doing occasional export promotion for United States corporations, but you will agree that it is rather difficult to justify the expense to the Canadian taxpayer!"

Mr. Howe, who is one of the greatest Canadians of this century, recently went to Chicago and Milwaukee to make two speeches to American businessmen — obviously in the hope of dampening down some of the anti-American feeling that has been aroused in Canada. His speeches were appeals to Americans to try to understand Canada and Canadians. That he should have felt the need to make such speeches is an indication of the work that is required on Canadian-American relations. Mr. Howe, himself American-born, gave up a lucrative engineering business to enter politics in 1935. He built the Trans-Canada Airlines, was in charge of the entire Canadian wartime industrial expansion and muni-

tions production, has singlehandedly carried through the Trans-Canada gas pipeline, has actively supported American investment in Canada, and has pushed the industrialization of Canada with ceaseless vigor. Here is Mr. Howe's appeal to American business:—

Anyone who does business in Canada should reckon with the pride, and the legitimate pride, of Canadians in their country. In other words, they should reckon with the normal feeling of nationalism which is present in Canada, just as it is in the United States. Canadians do not like to be excluded from an opportunity of participating in the fortunes, good or bad, of large-scale enterprise incorporated in Canada but owned abroad. They may not buy many shares, but they resent the exclusion. They do not like to see large-scale Canadian enterprises entirely dependent upon foreign parents for their research and top management. They do not like to see the financial results of large-scale Canadian enterprises treated as if they were the exclusive concern of the foreign owners.

I make bold therefore to offer three suggestions for the consideration of United States corporations establishing branch plants in Canada or searching for and developing Canadian natural resources:

1. Provide opportunities for financial participation by Canadians as minority shareholders in the equities of such corporations operating in Canada.

2. Provide greater opportunities for advancement in U.S.-controlled corporations for Canadians technically competent to hold executive and professional positions.

3. Provide more and regular information about the operations of such corporations in Canada.

Shortly after these speeches were made by Mr. Howe, I happened to attend a convention of one of the biggest American industries, which has a multi-billion-dollar investment in Canada. I asked the delegates for their reaction to the Howe speeches. In three days none was found who had heard of Mr. Howe, let alone the speeches.

BEHIND MR. HOWE'S APPEAL to American business lies an economic problem which only American business can solve. That problem is the threat posed to the economic life of Canada, and friendly political relations between Canada and the United States, by the snowballing American investment, which has now reached $13 billion, and the Canadian trade deficit of $1 billion a year with the United States. Before the war, American investment in Canada was barely $3 billion. It only reached $4.9 billion by 1945 but has doubled in the last ten years and is now increasing, almost by geometric progression, at a rate of $700 million a year. Capital inflow accounts for only half that figure. The rest is made up of growth of continuously reinvested profits.

The trade deficit is accounted for by Canada's unprecedented boom. Because much of its industry is based upon processing parts imported from the United States into finished products sold in Canada, the greater the prosperity, the larger the deficit. Only the steady inflow of investments, and export surpluses elsewhere, have enabled Canada to keep her trade in reasonable balance.

But what happens to Canada's foreign exchange position when the inflow of capital stops and Americans start taking their earnings home instead of reinvesting them? When that happens, as someday it must, Canada will face its worst exchange problem in history, with political implications impossible to predict. Canadians seeking a solution habitually point to obvious but relatively unimportant impediments to trade — high U.S. duties on wheat, quotas on beef cattle and dairy products, restriction on fish, the duty of 10 cents a barrel imposed on Canadian crude oil for the oil-short U.S. Pacific Coast. Yet if all these things and more were permitted duty-free entry into the United States tomorrow, it would not begin to solve the problem.

What dams up Canadian exports to the United States is not only tariffs and quotas but the policy decisions of the American owners of so large a segment of Canadian industry. American capital owns the Canadian automobile industry; the electrical, aluminum, asbestos, chemical, nickel, rubber, paint, machinery and machine tools industries; most of Canadian petroleum production, refining capacity, and gasoline marketing; plastics, glass, and an endless variety of other manufacturing.

What keeps Canadian Fords, Chevrolets, and Plymouths from being sold throughout the United States is not tariffs or duties but policy decisions of Ford, General Motors, and Chrysler. It is neither the tariff nor patent rights that stop Canadian chemicals from being marketed extensively in Chicago, Detroit, Akron, and Cleveland. It is the decisions of du Pont, Dow, Monsanto, and Goodyear. It is not the duty on crude oil that keeps it out of the Chicago and California refineries. It is the decisions of Standard of Indiana and Standard of California not to use any of their Canadian crude in their U.S. refineries.

No Canadian branch can operate as efficiently as the American factories because none enjoys a market of similar size. If Canadian operations were integrated with American operations, the companies would benefit from greater profits from their Canadian plants. Some years ago, thoughtful Canadian economists who saw this problem arising suggested that the automobile industry was one which would lend itself most effectively to across-the-border integration.

All Canadian plants duplicate machinery and methods used in the United States. If General Motors, for example, decided to integrate, it could follow many possible routes. Today it makes all its Buicks in the United States and serves the Canadian market with exports. Suppose, instead of making Chevrolets and Pontiacs and some trucks in both countries, it moved all its truck-making to Canada and all its car-making to the vacated truck plants in the U.S. Sales of Canadian-made trucks to the United States might balance, exchangewise, the cost of importing American cars. What happens now is that the American parts content of every Canadian car is an exchange liability and there is no offsetting credit for anything sold to the United States.

The chemical industry, which is in its infancy, is admirably suited to this sort of international production rationalization. Instead of erecting Canadian plants to duplicate American plants, surely the logical approach would be to have Canadian plants specialize in one process while American plants specialized in others.

Some such solution as this is imperative if Canada is to obtain a vast increase in the *kind* of exports to the United States it must have. Canadians who agitate for greater American purchases of agricultural products — particularly wheat, meat, and dairy products — ignore the fact that the need is for high-value exports, which alone can bulk large enough to overcome the trade deficit. Ultimately Canada must convert its billion-a-year deficit into a billion-a-year surplus if American investors are to be paid interest and sinking funds on their Canadian investments. These investments are substantially represented by goods exported to Canada. They can only be repaid in goods — and high-value goods.

This problem was not created by American big business, American small business, one industry, or a group of industries, so it cannot be solved completely by automobiles, rubber, steel, or chemicals. Perhaps the problem has now grown so large that it is beyond solution. Certainly as long as thousands of Canadian branch plants are barred from selling their production in the United States by head office ukase, political discussions about tariff concessions are but exercises in applied futility.

Once that is understood, it becomes easier to appreciate the value to American industry of Mr. Howe's second suggestion — that places be opened at the policy level for Canadian employees of proved ability. The process of converting domestic industry into a world-trading industry must begin at the policy level. The impact of even one foreigner on the boards of directors of a thousand American companies could be important. And while the process of educating the directors proceeds, it would do no harm to follow Mr. Howe's first piece of advice. If American industry is opened to Canadian equity investors, the external debt may be reduced painlessly right now. And it will do American industry no harm to have a small army of investors on the loose in Canada while solution to the debt problem is worked out by men of goodwill on both sides.

———————◆———————

That long [Canadian] frontier from the Atlantic to the Pacific Oceans, guarded only by neighborly respect and honorable obligations, is an example to every country and a pattern for the future of the world.

WINSTON CHURCHILL, speech in honor of R. B. Bennett, Canada Club, London, April 20, 1939

86.

Ernest Gruening: Alaska's Fight for Statehood

The United States bought Alaska from Russia in 1867, for the then considerable sum of $7,200,000 — and promptly, as Ernest Gruening points out in the article reprinted below, forgot it. Writing nearly ninety years later, Gruening had a woeful tale to tell of unkept promises, unjust treatment, and unexploited riches. Alaska did not have to wait much longer: the long-sought prize was won on January 3, 1959, when the vast territory became the forty-ninth, and largest, state of the union. Gruening himself is one of the most distinguished Alaskans of the century; he served as Alaska's appointed governor from 1939 to 1953, and was elected the state's first U.S. senator.

Source: *Atlantic Monthly,* January 1957: "Alaska Fights for Statehood."

Ninety years ago, in the Treaty of Cession by which we bought Alaska from Russia, the United States pledged that "the inhabitants of the ceded territory . . . shall be admitted to the enjoyment of all the rights, advantages, and immunities of citizens of the United States." The United States has not carried out that pledge. Alaskans, having unceasingly sought its fulfillment, or a substantial portion thereof, during the nine decades under the American flag, are now resorting to a procedure which was last invoked nearly a century ago. They are sending to Washington two senators and one representative, elected by Alaskans last October, to seek admission to the Congress.

The event will not be unprecedented in American history. In the past, five areas destined to become states of the Union have, in advance of action by the Congress admitting them to statehood, elected their senators and representatives and sent them to the national capital to request admission. Tennessee began it in 1796, followed by Michigan in 1835, by California — which had not even been granted territorial status — in 1849, by Oregon in 1858, and by Kansas in the years preceding its admission in 1861. In all five instances this tactic was,

after varying intervals of time, successful. In every case it hastened the coming of statehood.

Alaska's history has been one of neglect by a distant and uninterested federal government. Worse, it has been a history of continuing discrimination, which makes Alaska today a flagrant example of colonialism. In the first seventeen years after the purchase, Congress passed only two laws relating to Alaska. One extended the commerce and navigation laws and made Alaska a customs district. The other turned over the fur-seal fisheries of Alaska's Pribilof Islands to the secretary of the treasury, who leased them as a monopoly to a private concern in San Francisco.

While four presidential administrations and eight Congresses came and went, it was not possible in Alaska for a hopeful settler to acquire title to a square foot of land. No pioneer could clear a bit of the forested wilderness and count on the fruits of his labor, or build a log cabin with the assurance that it was his. No prospector could stake a mining claim with security for his enterprise. Property could not be deeded or transferred; the lovelorn could not marry; no injured party could secure redress except by his own acts; crime could not be punished. This period — unique for any area under the American flag — has become known in Alaska as the "era of no government."

Such authority as existed was exercised, without legal warrant, by the commanding officer of the troops stationed at Sitka. And when, in 1877, he and his troops were removed from Alaska to put down an uprising of the Nez Percé Indians in Idaho, there remained not even a semblance of government. Fearful of a similar uprising in Alaska, the white settlers appealed to their government in Washington for the dispatch of a gunboat to maintain order. When the federal authorities ignored repeated requests, the frontiersmen appealed to their neighbors, the Canadians, who complied. For months one of Her Majesty's men-o'-war performed the function that it was the duty and obligation of a United States warship to perform. The incident was prophetic of eighty years of subsequent federal indifference to the Alaskans' welfare. When an American cruiser ultimately arrived, the commander of that vessel, and his successors for four years, acted as Alaska's chief executive, with no legal warrant whatever.

Finally, in 1884, Congress decided to give Alaska a form of government, and adopted an Organic Act. It proved almost worthless. Application of land laws was specifically forbidden, thus preventing settlement. Grand and petit juries were not legally possible under it. The position of governor, a presidential appointee, was created, but he was given little authority and no means with which to function. Establishment of a legislature was denied. For the next fourteen years the reports and messages of five successive governors were urgent pleas to enact some body of workable law for Alaska. All in vain.

But in the late '90s Congress was roused from its thirty-year lethargy in regard to Alaska by the discovery of gold in the Klondike. When 60,000 Americans rushed northward and found no law to satisfy their needs, they began writing to their senators and representatives, and because they were still constituents — and therefore voters — their caustic letters brought action.

However, the new legislation, enacted at a distance of 5,000 miles by men who had no firsthand knowledge of Alaska, proved largely . . . unworkable. So there arose a demand for someone who could speak officially for Alaska, a voteless delegate, such as every other territory had had from its beginnings. But four Congresses debated this modest proposal without action. Not until 1906 was that office established.

Invariably, in Alaska's annals, such minor concessions as it has received from its federal overlords have been "too little and too late." Before long, Alaska's 60,000 inhabitants, a population doubled by the gold rush, felt that some form of self-government was long overdue. Their demand for a legislature, such as every other territory had had from its birth, was finally granted in 1912. It had taken forty-five years to accord Alaska the minimum of home rule to which every American community is entitled.

The Organic Act of 1912, although a substantial improvement over its unworkable predecessor — the Act of 1884 — was still notable for the things it *forbade* Alaskans to do. The Alaska legislature was forbidden to enact any basic land laws — a lamentable omission in an area one-fifth as large as the United States, consisting of large areas of public domain and crying for settlement. At the behest of the powerful canned-salmon lobby, which has always fought and continues to fight every increase in Alaskan autonomy, the management of Alaska's natural resources, the fisheries and wildlife, was kept under federal control — a withholding not visited on any other American territory. Congress likewise retained control of the judiciary. Alaska's lower-court judges, however, were not to be paid a salary, but were compelled to subsist on the fees they could collect from the Alaskan

"I thought men didn't go for that sack style"; cartoon by Lewis in the "Milwaukee Journal," 1958

people — a source of revenue insufficient for all but five or six of these fifty-odd federal judicial officials. Alaskans were forbidden to create counties. There were numerous other prohibitions. In fact it was a far more restrictive act than had been granted any other territory, including the act given twelve years earlier to the newly annexed territory of Hawaii.

When the first legislature assembled in 1913 and found vast fields into which it was forbidden to tread, it memorialized Congress to enact obviously required legislation. It asked for revision of the land laws — laws adopted for the states half a century earlier and not suited to Alaska, and therefore impeding settlement. It asked for federal highway construction — an appropriate request in a region over 99.9 percent public domain. It asked for an end to reservations and withdrawals which further impeded entry and settlement. It asked for action looking toward reasonable transportation rates. It requested that the lower-court judges — the United States Commissioners — be paid a salary. It requested transfer of the management of the fisheries to Alaska.

Over forty years later, not one of these

requests, all reasonable, proper, essential to Alaska's development, repeated by successive legislatures, and obtainable only through congressional action, had been granted.

But there was worse to come. New discriminations, which intensified Alaska's colonial status, were to be imposed by the federal authorities. The federal income tax, passed in 1913, included Alaska though it excluded Puerto Rico, which in addition received in its treasury all the excise taxes and customs receipts collected by the federal government. Alaskans neither sought nor wanted such favor, but they were shocked when they found that Alaska was excluded from the federal aid highway legislation enacted in 1916.

This highly important and beneficent legislation coincided with the development of the automobile and the consequent necessity to create a new, nationwide transportation network. The Congress correctly foresaw that there would have to be a national system of highways of a uniform and reasonably high standard, and that this could be accomplished only by joint federal and state enterprise. So, by authority of the new act, the federal government began appropriating vast sums to match funds provided by the states — no state receiving less than 50 percent matching. But the Western states, in which a varying proportion of land remains public domain and therefore unavailable for tax revenue, receive a larger proportion of federal funds, based on a complex formula in which area extent of public domain, population, and existing highway mileage play a part. Alaska — alone among the states and territories — was excluded.

As a result, Alaska, compelled to rely on its own revenues and parsimonious annual federal appropriations, has only a negligible road mileage. Virtually the only highway construction it has secured through the federal government has been that required for military purposes.

The discrimination in federal highway legislation has been further increased, currently, by Alaska's exclusion from the mammoth superhighway bill sponsored by President Eisenhower during the 83rd Congress and revised and brought out in a different form in the 84th. There was a conflict of opinion between the President and Congress as to the method of financing: the President urged long-term bonding; the Congress preferred "pay as you go," through higher taxes on gasoline, tires, trucks, and trailers. But, in one respect, executive and legislative branches agreed; while Alaska was to be excluded from participation in this measure's benefits, it was to be included in the taxation. Thus every Alaskan will pay his share of the multibillion-dollar program for the benefit of all the states from Alabama to Wyoming every time he stops for gas or buys a truck or a new tire.

Toward the close of the 84th Congress, Alaska was finally included, *but on a reduced and discriminatory basis, and only in a part* of the federal aid highway legislation. An amendment by Senator Richard Neuberger of Oregon proposed that Alaska be included henceforth, but that in calculating Alaska's quota of federal funds only half of Alaska's area be counted. In return for this reduction — not applicable to any state or to Hawaii or Puerto Rico — Alaska would be allowed to use federal and its own matching funds for road maintenance as well as construction, a reasonable arrangement. But on motion of Senator Francis Case of South Dakota, Alaska suffered a further reduction, its share to be based on only one-third of its area. That was the best deal obtainable for Alaska.

Small wonder that the comment forty years ago of Judge James Wickersham, one of Alaska's earlier delegates, is still pertinent: "Alaska is only a redheaded stepchild in the national family, and the other children covet its estate and take it."

The Congress imposed a similar exclusion on Alaska in maritime transportation four years after the initial exclusion of the territory from the Federal Aid Highway Act.

The Maritime Act of 1920, known in Alaska as the Jones Act, after its sponsor, the late Senator Wesley L. Jones of Seattle, Washington, provided a unique discrimination by the insertion of the words "excluding Alaska." Under that law, all areas, foreign and domestic, were permitted to use interchangeably American or foreign rail or marine carriers to transport freight across the country and beyond. Alaska, however, was forced to use the rail and shipping services in and out of Seattle only, and denied the more convenient and far less costly use of nearer Canadian ports. In consequence a number of budding industries in Alaska were put out of business, and their reestablishment or the creation of others has been foreclosed ever since.

The Alaska legislators deemed this discrimination violative of the commerce clause of the Constitution, which specifically forbids giving preference to one port over another. Therefore, when they assembled in 1921 for their fifth biennial session, they ordered the territorial attorney general to take the issue to court. The Supreme Court, before which it finally came, declared that the action of Congress regarding Alaska in the Maritime Act of 1920 was clearly discriminatory, but that the Court could discover no prohibition in the Constitution of discrimination against a territory, and that the fathers, in drawing up the Constitution, did not visualize extension of its provisions "to the ports of entry of colonial dependencies."

So the highest court of the land, the ultimate dispenser of "equal justice under law," ruled that it is proper and legal to discriminate against a territory! And the Court's language affirmed Alaska's colonial status.

In that respect the Court was at least realistic. The Jones Act and its accompaniments of federal bureaucratic action have burdened all Alaskans with the highest freight rates in the world. Putting the entire population of a dependent area at an economic disadvantage for the profit of privileged groups in the "mother country," which are able through their superior political power to have special benefits enacted into law — this is the quintessence of colonialism. The United States is guilty of it on many counts in Alaska.

FOR THE LAST THIRD OF A CENTURY every Alaskan delegate has sought to rectify these discriminatory injustices. In virtually every Congress the delegate has introduced bills (1) to include Alaska in federal aid highway legislation; (2) to abolish the discriminatory language in the Jones Act; (3) to reform the land laws for Alaska to suit them to its needs; (4) to pay the lower-court judges a salary; (5) to transfer the management of the fisheries to the territory. Every one of these efforts, unremittingly sought for nearly two generations, has failed, except as above noted.

The federal land laws still make settlement of Alaska extremely difficult. Despite the protests of Alaskans, federal reservations and withdrawals total nearly a hundred million acres, an area larger than the state of Montana. Yet members of Congress oppos-

ing statehood have in debate reproached Alaskans for their "failure" to transfer more public land to private ownership.

Administration of justice, the cornerstone of a free society, continues to suffer gravely in Alaska. The lower-court judges are still unsalaried; the discredited fee system provides only one-tenth of the judges a living wage. In the States, the number of federal judges has been increased steadily to keep pace with population growth. But in Alaska the number of judges — and federal judges being the only judges that colony is permitted to have, their duties are more extensive than those of federal judges in the States — remains the same as it was fifty-eight years ago when the population was less than a third its present size. Every attempt to get Congress to give Alaska even one additional judge has failed.

Under the joint control of a politically potent absentee industry and a federal bureau which the industry dominates, instead of being regulated by it, Alaska's greatest natural resource, and once the nation's greatest fishery resource, the Pacific salmon, is being destroyed. The Alaska salmon runs reached in 1955 the lowest point in nearly half a century, although there was a slight upturn in 1956. President Eisenhower for three successive years has had to proclaim Alaska's fishing communities disaster areas.

In neighboring British Columbia and in the states of Washington and Oregon the salmon industry is thriving and growing, despite the handicaps of power dams, pulp and paper mills, the sewage of large communities, and other accompaniments of modern industrial development which Alaska lacks, thereby illustrating the superiority of home management which Congress persists in not according Alaska.

Thus "a long train of abuses and usurpations" of their promised rights as Americans has led Alaskans to conclude that only statehood — and the equality it would bring — will satisfy their needs, end the injustices which they suffer, and validate the unfulfilled pledge of the Treaty of Cession to admit them to "all the rights, advantages, and immunities of citizens of the United States."

Those rights, advantages, and immunities would entitle them to vote for President and Vice-President, which they cannot now do; to representation in the Congress by two senators and a representative, whom they do not now have; and to immunity from the legalized disadvantages outlined above.

The major party platforms have pledged statehood to Alaska — the Democratic in 1948 and both the Democratic and the Republican in 1952 and 1956. Gen. Dwight D. Eisenhower, in a ringing public address in Denver in 1950, declared: "Quick admission of Alaska and Hawaii to statehood will show the world that America practises what it preaches." But after taking the presidential office, he dropped espousal of Alaskan statehood and urged statehood for Hawaii only. This reversal Alaskans attribute to President Eisenhower's close friend and trusted adviser, Gen. Lucius D. Clay, chairman of the board of the Continental Can Company, one of whose principal customers is the Alaska canned-salmon industry.

In contrast to governmental opposition, public opinion in the United States overwhelmingly supports statehood for Alaska.

The failure of Congress and the President to act, not merely on statehood but on a variety of lesser measures, has led the people of Alaska to the point where, after ninety years of neglect, discrimination, and violation of platform pledges and of treaty commitments, they believe that patience has ceased to be a virtue. They know that they have long since demonstrated their readiness for statehood — that every congressional committee which has studied the question through extensive hearings has returned a favorable report. They point out that Alaska's population of 209,000 is greater than was that of two-thirds of the thirty-five

states of the Union admitted after the original thirteen, at the time of their admission. Of this Alaskan population, six-sevenths originated in the forty-eight states — men and women of pioneer instincts who, following the oldest American tradition, moved westward in search of greater freedom and opportunity. The remaining one-seventh, descendants of the aboriginal population, are no less worthy, no less capable of assuming the responsibilities of full citizenship.

Alaskans feel in their hearts that what progress they have made in Alaska — and it has been substantial — has been made in spite of the federal impositions and largely because of the fiber and character of their fellow Alaskans, who brought to "the last frontier" the very qualities that have made America. They have now determined to do everything in their power to secure the validation of the most basic of American principles, that of government by consent of the governed.

Alaska's Americans deeply feel that the great destiny of Alaska is to be not merely a bulwark of defense for the Western Hemisphere but also — and perhaps even more important — a citadel of the American idea, a firm outpost of democracy most befittingly located in those distant Northern latitudes once under Russian rule and now within naked-eye view of the totalitarian tyranny of the Soviet police state. But they are no less deeply convinced that this challenging objective, to make Alaska a shining example of all that is best and attainable in our free society, can never be achieved while Alaska remains a colony. Moreover, they firmly believe that America's leadership in the interest of peace is gravely jeopardized by the contrast between preachment and practice, and that the national interest will be served by validation through deeds of American principles and professions — specifically by the prompt admission of Alaska as a state of the Union.

87.

DWIGHT D. EISENHOWER: The Little Rock School Crisis

Following the Supreme Court's decisions of 1954 and 1955 calling for integration of schools, Southern opposition solidified into massive resistance. During a few months in 1956, five states adopted forty-two segregation measures: for example, Georgia made it a felony for school officials to spend tax monies on integrated schools, Mississippi declared it illegal for any organization to begin desegregation proceedings in state courts, and Virginia closed down the public schools in some counties rather than integrate. In Arkansas, in late summer of 1957, Governor Orval Faubus ordered the state guard to prevent Negro children from attending white schools. A federal judge ordered the troops withdrawn, but mobs of whites refused to allow Negro students to enter a high school in Little Rock. On September 24 President Eisenhower took over command of the Arkansas Guard and ordered it and federal marshals into Little Rock to restore order. His address of the same day to the American people is reprinted here.

Source: *Public Papers of the Presidents of the United States: Dwight D. Eisenhower, Containing the Public Messages, Speeches, and Statements of the President, January 1 to December 31, 1957*, Washington, 1958, pp. 689–694.

FOR A FEW MINUTES THIS EVENING I want to speak to you about the serious situation that has arisen in Little Rock. To make this talk I have come to the President's office in the White House. I could have spoken from Rhode Island, where I have been staying recently; but I felt that, in speaking from the house of Lincoln, of Jackson, and of Wilson, my words would better convey both the sadness I feel in the action I was compelled today to take and the firmness with which I intend to pursue this course until the orders of the federal court at Little Rock can be executed without unlawful interference.

In that city, under the leadership of demagogic extremists, disorderly mobs have deliberately prevented the carrying out of proper orders from a federal court. Local authorities have not eliminated that violent opposition, and, under the law, I yesterday issued a proclamation calling upon the mob to disperse. This morning the mob again gathered in front of the Central High School of Little Rock, obviously for the purpose of again preventing the carrying out of the court's order relating to the admission of Negro children to that school.

Whenever normal agencies prove inadequate to the task and it becomes necessary for the executive branch of the federal government to use its powers and authority to uphold federal courts, the President's responsibility is inescapable. In accordance with that responsibility, I have today issued an executive order directing the use of troops under federal authority to aid in the execution of federal law at Little Rock, Arkansas. This became necessary when my proclamation of yesterday was not observed, and the obstruction of justice still continues.

It is important that the reasons for my action be understood by all our citizens.

As you know, the Supreme Court of the United States has decided that separate public educational facilities for the races are inherently unequal, and, therefore, compulsory school segregation laws are unconstitutional. Our personal opinions about the decision have no bearing on the matter of enforcement; the responsibility and authority of the Supreme Court to interpret the Constitution are very clear. Local federal courts were instructed by the Supreme Court to issue such orders and decrees as might be necessary to achieve admission to public schools without regard to race — and with all deliberate speed.

During the past several years, many communities in our Southern states have instituted public-school plans for gradual progress in the enrollment and attendance of school children of all races in order to bring themselves into compliance with the law of the land. They thus demonstrated to the world that we are a nation in which laws, not men, are supreme. I regret to say that this truth — the cornerstone of our liberties — was not observed in this instance.

It was my hope that this localized situation would be brought under control by city and state authorities. If the use of local police powers had been sufficient, our traditional method of leaving the problems in those hands would have been pursued. But when large gatherings of obstructionists made it impossible for the decrees of the court to be carried out, both the law and the national interest demanded that the President take action.

Here is the sequence of events in the development of the Little Rock school case.

In May of 1955, the Little Rock School Board approved a moderate plan for the gradual desegregation of the public schools in that city. It provided that a start toward integration would be made at the present term in high school, and that the plan would be in full operation by 1963. Here I might say that, in a number of communities in Arkansas, integration in the schools has already started and without violence of any kind. Now, this Little Rock plan was challenged in the courts by some who believed that the period of time as proposed in the plan was too long.

The United States court at Little Rock, which has supervisory responsibility under the law for the plan of desegregation in the public schools, dismissed the challenge, thus approving a gradual rather than an abrupt change from the existing system. The court found that the School Board had acted in good faith in planning for a public-school system free from racial discrimination. Since that time, the court has, on three separate occasions, issued orders directing that the plan be carried out. All persons were instructed to refrain from interfering with the efforts of the School Board to comply with the law.

Proper and sensible observance of the law then demanded the respectful obedience which the nation has a right to expect from all its people. This, unfortunately, has not been the case at Little Rock. Certain misguided persons, many of them imported into Little Rock by agitators, have insisted upon defying the law and have sought to bring it into disrepute. The orders of the court have thus been frustrated.

The very basis of our individual rights and freedoms rests upon the certainty that the President and the executive branch of government will support and insure the carrying out of the decisions of the federal courts, even, when necessary, with all the means at the President's command. Unless the President did so, anarchy would result. There would be no security for any except that which each one of us could provide for himself. The interest of the nation in the proper fulfillment of the law's requirements cannot yield to opposition and demonstrations by some few persons. Mob rule cannot be allowed to override the decisions of our courts.

Now, let me make it very clear that federal troops are not being used to relieve local and state authorities of their primary duty to preserve the peace and order of the community. Nor are the troops there for the purpose of taking over the responsibility of the School Board and the other responsible local officials in running Central High School. The running of our school system and the maintenance of peace and order in each of our states are strictly local affairs, and the federal government does not interfere except in a very few special cases and when requested by one of the several states. In the present case, the troops are there, pursuant to law, solely for the purpose of preventing interference with the orders of the court.

Courtesy, Lewis, "Milwaukee Journal"

"Order in the Courtroom"; cartoon by Lewis for the "Milwaukee Journal," 1958

The proper use of the powers of the executive branch to enforce the orders of a federal court is limited to extraordinary and compelling circumstances. Manifestly, such an extreme situation has been created in Little Rock. This challenge must be met and with such measures as will preserve to the people as a whole their lawfully protected rights in a climate permitting their free and fair exercise.

The overwhelming majority of our people in every section of the country are united in their respect for observance of the law — even in those cases where they may disagree with that law. They deplore the call of extremists to violence.

The decision of the Supreme Court concerning school integration, of course, affects the South more seriously than it does other sections of the country. In that region I have many warm friends, some of them in the city of Little Rock. I have deemed it a great personal privilege to spend in our Southland tours of duty while in the military service and enjoyable recreational periods since that time. So, from intimate personal knowledge, I know that the overwhelming majority of the people in the South — including those of Arkansas and

of Little Rock — are of goodwill, united in their efforts to preserve and respect the law even when they disagree with it. They do not sympathize with mob rule. They, like the rest of our nation, have proved in two great wars their readiness to sacrifice for America.

A foundation of our American way of life is our national respect for law. In the South, as elsewhere, citizens are keenly aware of the tremendous disservice that has been done to the people of Arkansas in the eyes of the nation, and that has been done to the nation in the eyes of the world.

At a time when we face grave situations abroad because of the hatred that Communism bears toward a system of government based on human rights, it would be difficult to exaggerate the harm that is being done to the prestige and influence, and indeed to the safety, of our nation and the world. Our enemies are gloating over this incident and using it everywhere to misrepresent our whole nation. We are portrayed as a violator of those standards of conduct which the peoples of the world united to proclaim in the Charter of the United Nations. There they affirmed "faith in fundamental human rights" and "in the dignity and worth of the human person" and they did so "without distinction as to race, sex, language or religion."

And so, with deep confidence, I call upon the citizens of the state of Arkansas to assist in bringing to an immediate end all interference with the law and its processes. If resistance to the federal court orders ceases at once, the further presence of federal troops will be unnecessary, and the city of Little Rock will return to its normal habits of peace and order, and a blot upon the fair name and high honor of our nation in the world will be removed.

Thus will be restored the image of America and of all its parts as one nation, indivisible, with liberty and justice for all.

88.

WALTER LIPPMANN: The Portent of the Moon

In both the United States and the Soviet Union the development of missile technology after World War II was essential to the larger satellite and space probe programs. As preparations progressed for the International Geophysical Year (IGY, 1957-1958), both countries announced that they would launch satellites during the year. The race was feverish, although most Americans, when they thought about satellites at all, were certain that the United States would be first to launch a "rocket" (as they were then called) into space. But the first satellite, the famous "Sputnik," was Russian; it flashed across the sky on October 4, 1957, after a series of heartbreaking failures with the American Vanguard. The Russian "victory" was a profound shock to Americans in all walks of life and resulted in a radical change in American thinking on such subjects as scientific education, government support of basic research, and military preparedness. The dismay felt by many of his countrymen is well expressed in the following essay by Walter Lippmann, published only six days after Sputnik I went up.

Source: *The Essential Lippmann,* Clinton Rossiter and James Lare, eds., New York, 1963, pp. 66-74.

THE FEW WHO ARE ALLOWED to know about such things, and are able to understand them, are saying that the launching of so big a satellite signifies that the Soviets are much ahead of this country in the development of rocket missiles. Their being so much ahead cannot be the result of some kind of lucky guess in inventing a gadget. It must be that there is a large body of Soviet scientists, engineers, and production men, plus many highly developed subsidiary industries, all successfully directed and coordinated, and bountifully financed.

In short, the fact that we have lost the race to launch the satellite means that we are losing the race to produce ballistic missiles. This in turn means that the United States and the Western world may be falling behind in the progress of science and technology.

This is a grim business. It is grim, in my mind at least, not because I think the Soviets have such a lead in the race of armaments that we may soon be at their mercy. Not at all. It is a grim business because a society cannot stand still. If it loses the momentum of its own progress, it will deteriorate and decline, lacking purpose and losing confidence in itself.

The critical question is how we as a people, from the President down, will respond to what is a profound challenge to our cultural values — not to the ideal of the American way of life but to the way in fact we have been living our life. One response could be to think of it all in terms of propaganda, and to look around for some device for doing something spectacular to outmatch what the Russians have done. The other response would be to look inward upon ourselves, and to concern ourselves primarily with our own failings, and to be determined not so much to beat the Russians as to cure ourselves.

The question then might be defined in this way: Why is it that in the twelve years that have passed since the end of World War II, the United States which was so far in the lead has been losing its lead to the Russians who at the end of the war were so nearly prostrate? Mr. Khrushchev would say, no doubt, that this is because communism is superior to capitalism. But that answer really begs the question, which is not why the Soviets have moved ahead so fast but why we, who had moved very fast, have not been moving fast enough. For while our society is undoubtedly progressive, it has not in the postwar years been progressive enough.

I do not pretend to know the whole answer to what is for us and for our future so fateful a question. But I venture to think that even now we can discern certain trends that since the World War have appeared in American life and must be taken into account.

We must put first, I think, the enormous prosperity in which, as the politicians have put it to the voters, the private standard of life is paramount as against the public standard of life. By the public standard of life I mean such necessities as defense, education, science, technology, the arts. Our people have been led to believe in the enormous fallacy that the highest purpose of the American social order is to multiply the enjoyment of consumer goods. As a result, our public institutions, particularly those having to do with education and research, have been, as compared with the growth of our population, scandalously starved.

We must put second, I think, a general popular disrespect for, and even suspicion of, brains and originality of thought. In other countries, in Germany and in most of Europe and in Russia, it is an honor, universally recognized, to be a professor. Here it is something to put a man on the defensive, requiring him to show that he is not a highbrow and that he is not subversive.

What McCarthyism did to the inner confidence of American scientists and thinkers has constituted one of the great national tragedies of the postwar era. It is impossible to measure the damage. But the damage that was done was very great. It was done in the kind of thinking where the difference between creation and routine lies in the special courage to follow the truth wherever it leads.

With prosperity acting as a narcotic, with Philistinism and McCarthyism rampant, our public life has been increasingly doped and without purpose. With the President in a kind of partial retirement, there is no standard raised to which the people can repair. Thus we drift, with no one to state our purposes and to make policy, into a chronic disaster like Little Rock. We find ourselves then without a chart in very troubled waters.

89.

"Oh Russia, Let That Moon Alone!"

The first Russian Sputnik, launched October 4, 1957, was hailed by most of the world as a major technological breakthrough, and the United States immediately initiated a feverish attempt to "catch up" in the space race to the moon. However, a minority opposed the vast appropriations for space exploration, asserting instead that the money should be used to improve the lot of man on earth. Still others objected on the grounds that man was never intended to live in space, and that the effort to reach the moon was morally and spiritually wrong, as well as expensive. The following Negro folk song, which expressed the latter attitude, was first recorded in New Orleans toward the end of 1957.

Source: *Negro Folk Music U.S.A.*, Harold Courlander, ed., New York, 1963.

OH RUSSIA, LET THAT MOON ALONE

Oh Russia, let that moon alone!
Oh Russia, let that moon alone!
Moon aint worryin' you!
Oh Russia, let that moon alone!
God told you go till the earth,
God didn't tell you to till the moon!
You got to let that moon alone!
Oh Russia, let that moon alone!
You can make your sputnickles
And your satellites,
You can't get God's moon!
Let God's moon alone!
The moon aint worryin' you!
The moon aint worryin' you!
God told man to till the earth,
God didn't tell you to till the moon!
You better let God's moon alone!
The moon aint worryin' you!
Oh people in Russia, get out on your knees and pray!
And let God's moon alone!
The moon aint worryin' you!
The moon aint worryin' you!
God put the moon up there to give you light by night!
Oh let God's moon alone!

90.

Eugene Kinkead: "Brainwashing" in Korea

"Brainwashing" is a process of intensive psychological indoctrination that has probably been used for centuries, but that aroused American indignation when it was discovered that a large proportion of U.S. prisoners in Korea had been compelled by its use to collaborate more or less fully with their Communist captors. A thorough study of the technique and effectiveness of brainwashing was undertaken by the U.S. government during the Korean War and was completed in July 1955. It resulted in a new emphasis on psychological training of soldiers in the hope that, if they were captured, they would be able to withstand any and all efforts to make them defect. The following selection is taken from an article on brainwashing that appeared in the New Yorker *on October 26, 1957.*

Source: *A Reporter at Large: The Study of Something New in History,* New York, 1957.

IN EVERY WAR but one that the United States has fought, the conduct of those of its servicemen who were held in enemy prison camps presented no unforeseen problems to the armed forces and gave rise to no particular concern in the country as a whole. In some of those camps — among them British camps during the Revolution, both Union and Confederate camps during the Civil War, and Japanese camps during the Second World War — our men were grievously treated and fell victim to starvation and disease, yet there was no wholesale breakdown of morale or wholesale collaboration with the captors. Moreover, whatever the rigors of the camps, in every war but that one a respectable number of prisoners managed, through ingenuity, daring, and plain good luck, to escape.

The exception was the Korean War. As everybody knows, twenty-one of the Americans captured as members of the United Nations forces decided to remain with the enemy — the only time in history that American captives have chosen not to return home because they preferred the enemy's form of government to our own. What was even more shocking — for, after all, the twenty-one men could be regarded as ideological cranks — was the fact that roughly one out of every three American prisoners in Korea was guilty of some sort of collaboration with the enemy, ranging from such serious offenses as writing anti-American propaganda and informing on comrades to the relatively innocuous ones of broadcasting Christmas greetings home, and thereby putting the Communists in a favorable light, because such broadcasts had to include a report of good treatment at their hands.

Then, when the war ended and the prisoners began to return, it became clear that some of them had behaved brutally to their fellow prisoners, and for a time the newspapers carried reports of grisly incidents in the prison camps, including the murder of Americans by other Americans. (The most notorious offender, perhaps, was Sergeant James C. Gallagher, who was convicted by a court-martial of killing two seriously ill fellow prisoners by throwing them out into the snow.) Furthermore, during the entire Korean conflict not one of our men escaped from a prison camp.

And, finally, to mention another calamity that might not, on the face of it, seem to point to any moral or disciplinary weakness among the prisoners, 38 percent of them — 2,730 out of a total of 7,190 — died in captivity. This was a higher prisoner death rate than that in any of our previous wars, including the Revolution, in which it is estimated to have been about 33 percent.

All in all, regrettable things happened in the prison camps of North Korea, and the public has been inclined to attribute them solely to the cruelty of the Communists and, in particular, to the mysterious technique known as brainwashing. The officials involved, however — in the Defense Department and especially in the Army, which, because of the nature of the operations in Korea, supplied more than 90 percent of the American servicemen who fought there — could not accept an explanation as simple as that. For one thing, there was evidence that the high death rate was due primarily not to Communist maltreatment but to the ignorance or the callousness of the prisoners themselves. For another, the prisoners, as far as Army psychiatrists have been able to discover, were not subjected to anything that could properly be called brainwashing. Indeed, the Communist treatment of prisoners, while it came nowhere near fulfilling the requirements of the Geneva Convention, rarely involved outright cruelty, being instead a highly novel blend of leniency and pressure. If our prisoners had behaved strangely, then, the explanation was bound to be a complex one.

That some of them were behaving strangely had become evident surprisingly early in the hostilities — at 11:55 A.M., Greenwich time, on July 9, 1950, to be precise, or only four days after our ground forces first engaged the enemy in Korea — when an American Army officer, taken prisoner some forty-eight hours before, made a 900-word broadcast in the enemy's behalf over the Seoul radio. Purportedly speaking for all American soldiers, this man said, among other things, "We did not know at all the cause of the war and the real state of affairs, and were compelled to fight against the people of Korea. It was really most generous of the Democratic People's Republic of Korea to forgive us and give kind consideration for our health, for food, clothing, and habitation." Service authorities were dumfounded — parts of the statement, of course, were actually treasonable — but a tape recording had been made of the broadcast and there was no mistaking the officer's voice.

Within a few weeks, many statements of this sort were picked up by American listening posts in the Far East, and the Army immediately began collecting data for a formal study of the behavior of our Korean prisoners of war in all its aspects — medical, psychological, propagandistic, and legal. The study turned out to be a massive one — it was not completed until July 29, 1955, two years and two days after the signing of the armistice at Panmunjom — and as it went along, its findings produced a serious dispute within the armed services concerning the degree to which a captive might collaborate without being ultimately answerable to his government. In May, 1955, to resolve the dispute, the Defense Department set up an Advisory Committee on Prisoners of War, composed of five civilians and five retired generals and admirals, which thereupon conducted an intensive three-month survey of all the prisoner-of-war problems that had arisen in Korea. On August 17, 1955, shortly after the committee had turned in its report, President Eisenhower issued the following six-point Code of Conduct for members of the armed forces in combat and captivity:

I am an American fighting man. I serve in the forces which guard my country and our way of life. I am prepared to give my life in their defense.

I will never surrender of my own free will. If in command I will never surrender my men while they have the means to resist.

If I am captured I will continue to resist by all means available. I will make every effort to escape and aid others to escape. I will accept neither parole nor special favors from the enemy.

If I become a prisoner of war, I will keep faith with my fellow prisoners. I will give no information or take part in any action which might be harmful to my comrades. If I am senior, I will take command. If not, I will obey the lawful orders of those appointed over me and will back them up in every way.

When questioned, should I become a prisoner of war, I am bound to give only name, rank, service number, and date of birth. I will evade answering further questions to the utmost of my ability. I will make no oral or written statements disloyal to my country and its allies or harmful to their cause.

I will never forget that I am an American fighting man, responsible for my actions, and dedicated to the principles which made my country free. I will trust in my God and in the United States of America.

Like the events in Korea that inspired it, the Code of Conduct was unprecedented — the principles of conduct prescribed for our soldiers had always been covered in regular training manuals, and no other President had found it necessary to restate or clarify them — and it has led, in each of the services, to unprecedented courses of training designed to teach our servicemen how to survive captivity, and not buckle under it.

Behind all this lay the Army study, and not long ago, feeling that the study itself constituted a neglected bit of American history, I went down to Washington to find out what I could about it. When I got there, the Army Information Office suggested that I see Hugh M. Milton II, as-

sistant secretary of the Army for Manpower and Reserve Forces, who had been directly in charge of the study, and had later become a member of the Advisory Committee. Mr. Milton, I was told, would give me a general idea of what the Army had discovered. . . . When I called at his office in the Pentagon, Milton, a tall, dark fifty-nine-year-old Kentuckian, offered me a chair, sat down at his desk, and plunged into his subject.

The Korean War, he told me, marked the first time in history (this phrase, it seems, is bound to keep occurring in any discussion of the prisoner-of-war situation in Korea) that the American Army had been confronted by an enemy who attempted to manipulate the minds of prisoners, thus extending what might well be called combat tactics into the prison camps. Soon after the propaganda broadcasts from our men began, the Communists revealed that they had other tricks up their sleeves. In February of 1951, small groups of American captives began returning to our lines, and in the course of investigation by counterintelligence officers it was discovered that they had been heavily indoctrinated and had come back prepared, with the aid of propaganda leaflets, to put pressure on our troops to desert. (These men were closely questioned, and provided the Army with its first direct information about the Communists' way with prisoners.)

Meanwhile, back in the States, people were receiving letters from prisoners that harped on a single theme — the hope for an early restoration of international peace — and that sounded wholly unlike the men who had unmistakably written them. Then articles by captive GIs praising life under Communism started appearing in newspapers in India, North Africa, Indonesia, and elsewhere. It was clear, Milton said, that all these acts were part of a highly coordinated Communist scheme to demoralize both our fighting men and our civilian population, and, at the same time, to win over the diplomats and nationals of non-Communist countries. "The articles and statements by our soldiers got around," Milton said. "One of them — something to the effect that the Communists were nice fellows and we were warmongers — was even reprinted as a United Nations Security Council document in 1950, when Jacob Malik, of the Soviet Union, headed the Council. But what was probably worse was the effect those statements had in neutral countries. You can imagine what a problem it was for our government to refute such lies — backed, as they were, by the names, and even photographs, of American soldiers — in the hinterlands of Asia, say, where the free way of life has such a tough ideological struggle anyway. It is hard to tell how much damage those soldiers did."

This sort of thing — American troops turning renegade in such large numbers, and apparently so casually — was unthinkable, Milton went on, and yet it was happening. The Army, in puzzlement, resolved that if we ever got those men back, every one of them would be put through a series of searching questions about his experiences after capture and about the Communist techniques of handling prisoners. "The resulting Army study was the first in history to go into the background and prison experiences of every American soldier captured during a war," Milton said.

. . . I will say this much: After it was completed, we knew a great deal more than we had known about Communist methods and about the way our men reacted to them. No limit was set on the length of the men's answers to our questions, and all told they must run to several million pages. The data is extremely valuable, and it may be unique in the world. From it we learned, among other things, how the Communists managed to persuade most of the captives to attend classes where Communist theory was drummed into them. The Army calls this "indoctrination." The alternative term, "brainwashing," has become a catch phrase, used for so many things that it no longer has any precise meaning — and, as you'll find out, a precise meaning is necessary in this case.

We also learned about the special Communist uses of interrogation. Interrogation is a legitimate method of trying to elicit military information, of course, but the Communists used it not so much for this as to produce a state of mind that would be vulnerable to indoctrination — in other words, to change a man's political views and obtain his collaboration. The Communists rarely used physical torture — you'll hear more about that as you go along — and the Army has not found a single verifiable case in which they used it for the specific purpose of forcing a man to collaborate or to accept their convictions. The enemy did, however, apply many forms of mental pressure and physical hardship — withholding food, medicine, and hospital care, for example — and, of course, using such techniques to change political views is not only illegal by all the recognized codes for prisoner handling but completely contrary to the basic tenets of humanity. But say what we will, condemn it as we like, it is a cold, hard fact of Communist practice. It may sound trite, but if America is going to survive, Americans must learn to cope with this practice.

I asked Milton if he could estimate the percentage of prisoners who had collaborated, and he replied,

If we use as a standard the committing of some perhaps understandable act of "technical" collaboration, such as broadcasting Christmas greetings to relatives at home, the percentage might run as high as 30 percent. One man in every seven, or more than 13 percent, was guilty of serious collaboration — writing disloyal tracts, say, or agreeing to spy or organize for the Communists after the war. . . .

As you can see, the picture isn't a pretty one. But it has its compensations. For one thing, the Army has met a Communist enemy for the first time, and that has given us a good insight into Communist methods of handling prisoners. We have learned that they play no favorites. What they did to us they do to their own people. Now that we know what they do, we've found that the Army's training and previous standards of conduct, while essentially right and proper, did not go far enough. We have therefore taken additional steps to prepare the men for the kind of thing they encountered in Korea, and we are confident these will be helpful. I also ought to say at this point that after we had learned more about the Communists' handling of prisoners and had begun to understand it, we were very pleased that so many of our men had stood up so well, when they had nothing to fall back on but their own staunch characters and our insufficient training.

Milton told me that while the Army is still concentrating, first and foremost, on producing a healthy, hardy, well-disciplined, and properly motivated soldier who will avoid capture — a captured soldier has naturally failed in his primary purpose, which is to destroy the enemy — it has changed its policy on telling men what to do in case of capture. In the past, there was strong resistance among the authorities to giving them such information; the argument against it was that if a man knew what to do he was more likely to surrender. The Korean experience and the changing nature of warfare in general have, the Army feels, made this argument an outmoded one. With greater mobility of troops in combat and with the increased use of paratroopers, the risk of capture has mounted. Reasoning in the old way, it is felt, is like arguing that a sailor should be forbidden to learn to swim because his superiors want him to stay with his ship until the last possible moment. Suppose an enemy torpedo dumps him into the water and he finds himself six feet from a life preserver? Figuratively speaking, this occurred too many times in the Korean prison camps.

"Experience has shown that the Commu-nists will humiliate and debase anyone in their hands," Milton said.

The soldier's best defense against this treatment, of course, is his own raw courage. But the Army now realizes that a man's nerve can be greatly stiffened if he is taught exactly how his captors will go about trying to break that nerve. Their step-by-step undermining of loyalty will be made much more difficult if our troops are forewarned. Returned prisoners have agreed that one of the best possible defenses against Communist tactics would be mental preparation. That sounds elementary, yet it is a new concept, resulting from a new set of international conditions and from the new experiences we had in Korea.

Our servicemen in prison camps must work together as disciplined units to resist the enemy's demands — mentally and morally. They may be deprived of sleep, food, and medical attention in a prison camp, and they should expect this and have the will to live while these things are lacking. If there's nothing else to support life, they must not balk at whatever food and drink — however unpleasant — the enemy offers them. They should have some familiarity with nutrition, first aid, and preventive medicine. On the spiritual side, *esprit de corps* and a feeling of comradeship are great aids to morale. So are faith in democracy and adherence to religious beliefs. Many of the men said that in prison camps these intangibles were of greater help to them than anything else. Now, much more than in the past, such things bulk large in Army training.

A number of measures have been taken as a result of the prisoner of war study. Perhaps the most important are based on the President's six-point code, and deal with the education of the whole Army in the proper conduct of troops after capture. "Many of the men who collaborated in Korean camps pleaded innocent of misconduct on the ground that they had acted on orders from their superiors," said Milton. "One of the hardest things to make clear, both legally and logically, is that a man has a loyalty to discipline but also an independent loyalty to his country. The two should be reconciled, and they must be reconciled if our men are to cope with a devious enemy like the Communists, who, naturally, try to see to it that orders favorable to their own ends will be issued by weak officers and that weak men will obey them. With our new program, the Army feels that this reconciliation between the two kinds of loyalty can be accomplished."

In connection with this program, the Army has issued a basic pamphlet explaining Communist indoctrination and interrogation methods in detail and suggesting simple ways to render them ineffective, and has also prepared several training circulars and films presenting techniques that will help men trapped behind enemy lines to evade capture or, if they are captured, to escape. Tackling the problem from another direction, the Army has instituted a group replacement policy, known as Operation Gyroscope, whereby units, instead of individuals, are rotated in assignments at home and abroad. This, it is believed, enables a soldier to identify himself more strongly with his unit, and thus greatly increases his loyalty to it; the unit should consequently be more effective in combat, and also, if any of its members are captured, they should be more able to resist pressure in a prison camp.

The Army has decided to adhere to its policy of authorizing prisoners to give the enemy nothing more than their name, rank, serial number, and date of birth. This decision was reached after months of investigation and soul-searching as to the best course to follow, both practically and ethically. "You can argue about such things till doomsday, but the Communist challenge has got to be met," said Milton. "And it's got to be met in an American way — no compromise with evil. If this means that our troops must withstand emotional pressure and psychological pain, then, for the good of the country, these must be borne. If the Communists alter their methods to include physical torture, that, too, must be endured."

The Army, Milton went on, wants as many people as possible to think about these matters. "Overcoming Communism is not simply an Army problem," he said. "It's a truly national problem. And don't forget — the battle against Communism is waged largely at the level of the individual, and the earlier the preparation the better. The Army would like to see every American parent, teacher, and clergyman work to instill in every one of our children a specific understanding of the differences between our way of life and the Communist way of life, and, even more important, give every child, in the blunt, old-fashioned spirit, a firm regard for right and an abiding distaste for wrong. The Army's period of training is too brief to make changes in the habits of a lifetime. By the time a young man enters the Army, he should possess a set of sound moral values and the strength of character to live by them. Then, with Army training, he may become something very close to military perfection — the ideal citizen soldier."

The time not to become a father is eighteen years before a world war.
E. B. WHITE, *The Second Tree from the Corner,* 1953

1958

91

Lyndon B. Johnson: Political Credo

When Lyndon B. Johnson wrote the following political credo in 1958 he had served in Congress for twenty-one years: from 1937 to 1949 as a Democratic representative from the 10th district of Texas, and from 1949 on as one of his state's U.S. senators. He was the Senate minority leader in 1953-1954, and majority leader from 1955 to 1960, when he was elected Vice-President. His political experience was thus very wide, and he was known as the man who perhaps above all in the Congress understood the workings of our democratic legislative system. That system is based, of course, on party politics, and it is therefore all the more interesting to find Johnson, in the eloquent paragraphs reprinted here, disavowing the spirit of party, at least in the way, as he suggests, that many of his contemporaries comprehended it. The impulse to affix labels — political and otherwise — to men during the 1950s is said to have been a hangover of the McCarthy Era, when guilt by association became a weapon in the hands of those who seemed to desire to destroy, as well as of those who wished to save, the country.

Source: *Texas Quarterly*, Winter 1958: "My Political Philosophy."

I AM A FREE MAN, an American, a United States senator, and a Democrat, in that order.

I am also a liberal, a conservative, a Texan, a taxpayer, a rancher, a businessman, a consumer, a parent, a voter, and not as young as I used to be nor as old as I expect to be — and I am all these things in no fixed order.

I am unaware of any descriptive word in the second paragraph which qualifies, modifies, amends, or is related by hyphenation to the terms listed in the first paragraph. In consequence, I am not able — nor even the least interested in trying — to define my political philosophy by the choice of a one-word or two-word label. This may be against the tide, but, if so, the choice is deliberate.

At the heart of my own beliefs is a rebellion against this very process of classifying, labeling, and filing Americans under headings: regional, economic, occupational, religious, racial, or otherwise. I bridle at the very casualness with which we have come to ask each other, "What is your political philosophy?"

I resent the question most often, not because I suspect it of guile and cunning but for its innocence, the innocence that confuses dogma with philosophy and presumes that the answer can be given in a word or two. Our political philosophies, I have found, are the sum of our life's experience. God made no man so simple or his life so sterile that such experience can be summarized in an adjective. Yet we seem bent today on reducing every man's philosophy to a mere vital statistic, to the next question asked — of professors, students, public officials, job applicants, business executives, labor leaders, and many more — after age, weight, height, and color of eyes and hair.

Inquiries of men's philosophies do not fit this context.

It is a part of my own philosophy to regard individuality of political philosophy as a cornerstone of American freedom and, more specifically, as a right expressly implied in our nation's basic law and indispensable to the proper functioning of our system.

Our basic law — the Constitution — is distinctive among the basic law of all nations, even the free nations of the West, in that it prescribes no national dogma: economic, social, or religious. Free enterprise, for example, is not mentioned. Nor are our parties or the party system. Nor is there any provision to require allegiance to any dogma or doctrine. Yet government is an expression of philosophy, and active governments are inevitably guided by philosophers. As I see it, the mandate of our system — and, perhaps, the ultimate genius of it — is that the American people should be the true philosophers of the American government within the limits upon governmental powers set by our Constitution.

This is an ennobling concept, yet like many things noble and beautiful, it has certain frailties and we seem quick now to crush it. We crush out the individuality of our political beliefs and, by this process of high-speed sorting and classifying of Americans, automate our choice of courses and sterilize our explorations of the reasons why.

Some might suggest that my rebellion against this process is a show of the provincial Texan in me. I would disagree. Texans are independent and individual, but not the monopolists of these virtues that we sometimes suppose ourselves to be. The traits are American in origin and, fortunately for the republic, are deposited quite widely, not part of certain regional hoards. Thus, I believe it is the American in me — even more than the Texan — that now reacts so strongly against the merging of the individual American into the mass in the name of dogma.

I realize, as I say this, that others might point to the Senate where I serve — and where I am, in fact, a designated leader of the majority party — and suggest that the example there of a two-party, two-philosophy system contradicts or is in conflict with this thesis. The opposite is so. Had I not been privileged to serve in Congress, I might never have come to hold the respect for individuality of philosophy that I do.

The very purpose of Congress, in our governmental form, is to arrive at national decisions by bringing together some 531 individuals, representing 170 million individuals, to achieve a consent on the way the nation should go. Were we bound by rigid dogmas, whatever their name, there would be no more cause for assembling Congress than for bringing the Soviet Presidium together. We are not so bound, and it is part — a great part — of my own philosophy that the Congress reaches a very dubious decision when its choices are made solely by head counts of the partisan division.

This leads to a listing of the tenets of my own beliefs, the specific tenets of my own philosophy. I would set them down this way:

First, I believe every American has something to say and, under our system, a right to an audience.

Second, I believe there is always a national answer to each national problem, and, believing this, I do not believe that there are necessarily two sides to every question.

Third, I regard achievement of the full potential of our resources — physical, human, and otherwise — to be the highest purpose of governmental policies next to the protection of those rights we regard as inalienable.

Fourth, I regard waste as the continuing enemy of our society and the prevention of waste — waste of resources, waste of lives, or waste of opportunity — to be the most dynamic of the responsibilities of our government.

These tenets, I concede, are simple. They are certainly personal. For these are not tenets I have embraced or adopted, but, rather, beliefs I have — over fifty years — developed and come to follow from my own experience.

In the instance of the first listed, I realize that — in these times — the notion that each American has something to say and the right to an audience may seem excessively idealistic. I do not believe that is so, either in principle or in practice.

I am reminded always in my work at Washington of my own origins. I was born to the Hill Country of Texas, a remote region then, still remote today, although less so. My neighbors, friends, and relatives there live independently, self-contained if not self-sufficient. They are distant from many national issues, yet neither their distance nor their limited information on any given subject makes them any less a party to the national decisions we reach in the halls of Congress. Knowing the folks at Johnson City and Blanco and Stonewall and Hye as I do, I know that it would be much more difficult for me to secure a unanimous agreement among them than among the senators in Washington.

Yet, in this individuality, my neighbors — or the constituency of all of Texas — are not different from Americans everywhere. There is likely to be merit in the views of the minority, quite as much as there is wisdom in the views of the majority. We have, as I see it, an obligation to seek out that merit, if it is there, and not merely to content ourselves with obliging the majority, for the majority's wisdom — however wise — is never the sum of all wisdom.

What we do, too often now, is oblige our patience with expedients. To grant audiences to 170 million Americans would be exhausting. So we make our divisions, our classifications, and our cross-classifications which permit us to forgo the listening and the searching we ought to do. Trouble compounds when, having made our divisions on one basis, we extend the application to other issues and other decisions. Here we adopt in our American political philosophy the pattern not of philosophy but of cults devoted to dogma, and we construct false equations which produce false answers.

This equation process is much a part of our party systems and contributes to the myth of the concept that "there are two sides to every question." True, there are two parties. That is not the same as two sides. But, by maintaining the two-side concept, we satisfy our consciences — again as a matter of convenience — that when a partisan majority has prevailed there is no need to examine either the majority's side or the minority's side again. Our reasoning is that since there are two sides, either side would have been acceptable, and hence the answer decided by political strength does not require closer scrutiny.

I think otherwise. This popular view is, I

feel, very much counter to our American philosophy based on the thinking of men like Jefferson and Madison. I do not believe we have arrived at an answer until we have found the national answer, the answer all reasonable men can agree upon, and our work is not done until that answer is found — even if the process requires years of our lives.

Here fits the third tenet of my philosophy — and the fourth. Had America been bound by the Constitutional Convention to the philosophies of the eighteenth century — and by the limits of the wisdom and vision of those times — we would not have the nation that is ours today. Our rising greatness through more than 180 years has come from our freedom to apply our accumulating knowledge to the processes of our self-government. Or, to state it another way, this has come because America's course has been left to the living. Thus, the eighteenth-century philosophy of our Constitution has allowed for growth so that it is still strong, still good for our twentieth century.

Our nation, like all nations, is possessed of certain resources — resources of nature, resources of position, and resources of the human mind. Without conquest or aggrandizement, we cannot add to these basics. Thus whatever we are to be we must build from those things at our disposal, and to content ourselves with less than the ultimate potential is to deny our heritage and our duty.

Obviously, having come from a land like Texas, I feel this strongly. Of all endeavors on which I have worked in public life, I am proudest of the accomplishments in developing the Lower Colorado River during the 1930s and 1940s. It is not the damming of the stream or the harnessing of the floods in which I take pride but, rather, in the ending of the waste of the region.

The region — so unproductive and insig-

nificant in capacity in my youth — is now a vital part of the national economy and potential. More important, the wastage of human resources in the whole region has been reduced. New horizons have been opened for the fulfillment of young minds, if by nothing more than the advent of electricity into rural homes. Men and women have been released from the waste of drudgery and toil against the unyielding rock of the Texas hills. This is fulfillment of the true responsibility of government.

Conversely, the elimination of waste of this sort carries with it a continuing obligation for government — at all levels — not to create waste itself by extracting from the people the fruits of their new opportunities through improvident excesses in spending and taxing. This is an increasingly critical area for American government, but one to which we sometimes apply false standards.

Government can waste the people's resources by inertia quite as much as by vigor. Government can, for example, fall into a state of complacency over the relative positions of strength between nations in the world. An international stalemate with Communism would, I believe, be the greatest of waste of American resources and the resources of freedom, even though stalemate produced no war. A vital government cannot accept stalemate in any area — foreign or domestic. It must seek the national interest solution, vigorously and courageously and confidently.

These tenets are the tenets of my political philosophy.

Some who equate personal philosophies with popular dogmas might inquire, endlessly, as to my "position" on this issue or that issue or some other. Philosophies, as I conceive them at least, are not made of answers to issues but of approaches more enduring and encompassing than that. By these approaches I have set down, I can seek and, I believe, find answers to the issues of 1958 or 1978, as they arise.

By personal choice, I am a Democrat, for I can in that party best apply and express my beliefs. As for being anything else, the definitions of what I am will have to be applied by others as they see fit, for I make no such distinctions myself.

I am, as I said in the beginning, a free man, an American, a United States senator, and a Democrat, in that order, and there, for me, the classifying stops.

92.

Norman Cousins: Wanted — Two Billion Angry Men

That world peace is not possible without a world government has been maintained by a few writers and thinkers in the West for centuries, but the main effort to create such a government, based on the United Nations, came after World War II. For a few years after the war, world federalist groups were active in many countries, but by the 1950s the movement had largely petered out, mainly owing to the apparent impossibility of doing anything about the profound opposition between the United States and the Soviet Union. However, men like Norman Cousins, editor (since 1942) of the Saturday Review *and a vigorous opponent of nuclear warfare and of everything that pointed in its direction, had not given up hope even by 1958, when the Russian success with its hydrogen bomb and with its Sputniks seemed to make the necessity for some resolution of the arms race even more dire. The following editorial by Cousins appeared in the* Saturday Review *early in 1958.*

Source: Saturday Review, February 1, 1958.

THERE IS NO POINT in talking about the possibility of a war breaking out. The war is already being fought. It is being waged by national sovereignties against human life.

It is true that national sovereignties are arrayed against each other under conflicting ideological banners. But the consequence of this conflict will not be victory by one over the other. The consequence can only be a mass cheapening of life or its elimination from this planet.

Everything being done by the national sovereignties to advance their supposed security succeeds only in intensifying the peril to life on earth. The weapons they are making are an advanced form of the competition between the sovereignties. Should these weapons be used, the nations behind the sovereignties will be pulverized and the humans along with them. The hope of the statesmen, of course, is to create a balance of terror so that neither side will dare to attack. But the same hideous momentum that produced the weapons can lead to their use. Neither side will be made secure by the fact that the other side possesses the means of instantaneous, devastating attack. Neither side will feel under the obligation to wait until it is hit first. It is upon such a frail reed that the cause of life on earth is now made to rest.

It is wrong to say that nuclear explosives are being tested; they are being used. Every time one of the explosives is fired human beings are hurt. Just in the act of exploding a test nuclear bomb, life-destroying materials are put into the air. These explosions form no ordinary clouds; they are not dispersed by the winds; they retain their ability to poison and kill for more than two dozen years. With each bomb the canopy of poison above the earth grows heavier. Not long ago only one nation was involved in this kind of experimentation. Today, three nations are contributing to the general poisoning. Tomorrow, perhaps a half-dozen or more national sovereignties will insist on their right to add their own portions of poison to the sky.

There is no disagreement about one aspect of such general testing. All experts agree that at some point the burden of poison will become heavier than human life can sustain. The only disagreement has to do with when that point will be reached. Also, whether the amount of poison already in the air has caused widespread harm or only limited harm. In short, whether 10,000 persons will die this year of leukemia produced by the bomb poisons in the atmosphere or whether only one-fourth or one-fifth that number will die.

The men at the head of sovereign nations are helpless to deal with the onrushing peril. They are part of something unworkable as it concerns the making of world peace, for unfettered sovereignty today is an unworkable concept. It makes no difference how benign or well-intentioned are the men who represent the sovereignties. So long as their ultimate aim is to maintain the present station of a nation above law, the statesmen will work at opposite ends from what human life requires in order to be sustained on this planet.

In a very real sense, the statesmen are trying to deal with the problems of yesterday rather than the problems of today and tomorrow. It is true that the Second World War was brought on in large part because the free nations of the world were weak and disarmed. But if disarmament a generation ago was no answer, neither is an armaments race today the answer. If an arms race leads to war and if war leads to the liquidation of both freedom and life, then the arms race offers not military security but the prospect of mutual suicide.

Here the advocates of unfettered national sovereignty argue that they would rather take their chances with an arms race ending in mutual suicide than with the danger of being disarmed in the face of almost certain Communist world conquest. If these were the only alternatives then something might be said for the arms race. But these are not the only alternatives. Neither disarmament nor armament can create a peace. Real peace depends on the amount of support that can be mobilized in the world for transforming the United Nations into a body with the effective powers of world law.

So long as peace is pursued under present methods; so long as each nation is allowed to retain the right and the capacity to destroy millions of human beings; so long as nations are allowed to engage in the kind of acts which are forbidden inside their countries to individual citizens; so long as lawlessness is the normal way of life among nations — so long as these conditions prevail there can be no peace.

It is not true that only the totalitarian states are opposed to a world under law. The free nations have yet to make the specific proposals that go as far beyond sovereignty as is necessary to make world law work.

Meanwhile, what the world needs today

are two billion angry men who will make it clear to their national leaders that the earth does not exist for the purpose of being a stage for the total destruction of man. Two billion angry men can insist that the world's resources be utilized for human good. They can demand that the nations stop using the sky as an open sewer for radioactive poi- sons, and that an end be put to the uncon- trolled devices that pursue future genera- tions by way of damaged genes. They can compel the nations to end the long age of the cave and begin a real civilization. A war is now being waged against the world's peoples and they have the need and duty to defend themselves.

93.

Hubert H. Humphrey: First Step Toward Disarmament

In March 1957 the Soviet Union proposed a general "reduction of armaments and armed forces and the prohibition of atomic and hydrogen weapons." In August of that year the United States, Great Britain, and France replied with their own "package plan" for partial disarmament. Both the Western and the Soviet plans called for reduction of military manpower and conventional armament under the supervision of an international body; but where the Soviet plan would have banned nuclear weapons entirely, the Western plan merely banned the development of new weapons and concentrated on the creation of an effective inspection system. The Soviets rejected the Western proposals and pressed their own more comprehensive ones in a United Nations General Assembly debate in the autumn of 1957. In July 1958 a conference of scientists from eight countries, including the U.S. and the U.S.S.R., met at Geneva to work out a detection system. By that time the U.S., the U.S.S.R., and Great Britain had all stopped nuclear tests in the hope of reaching a formal agreement. It was against this background that Hubert Humphrey of Minnesota, then serving his second term in the Senate, made the following plea for a disarmament agreement in an article published in May 1958. At the time Humphrey was chairman of the Subcommittee on Disarmament of the Senate Foreign Relations Committee.

Source: *Nation*, May 24, 1958.

SEVEN MONTHS AGO the Soviet Union launched the earth's first artificial satellite. This Sputnik inspired dreams throughout the world of future explorations in space; but it also cast an ominous shadow on earth, for it demonstrated the Soviet deter- mination and ability to perfect the ICBM, a missile which could carry a nuclear warhead from one continent to another.

The shock of the Soviet launching had repercussions which were in large part ben- eficial, and which I hope will not die out now that we too have successfully launched earth satellites. The Soviet Sputniks pro- pelled us into a reexamination of our educa- tional systems and scientific endeavors which may result in a renaissance of intel- lectual efforts. On the defense front, we were given ample proof that defense needs should be determined primarily by the threat rather than by the requirements of a balanced budget. To those hoping for progress toward disarmament, however, the reaction to the Sputnik launching, at first glance, appeared unfortunate, for it gave a fresh impetus to the arms race.

Our security system at the present time is built on the ability to retaliate effectively against, and thus deter, any attack. As long as the Soviet Union chooses to increase its capacity for attack, we have no choice but to continue to strengthen ourselves militarily and plug important loopholes in our defense system.

Many have asked me whether we could seriously demand greater progress toward disarmament at the very time when we were also demanding greater progress in missiles. My answer to this is not only that we can but that we must.

A security system based on massive strength, a "balance of terror," is not satisfactory as a permanent security system. It is extremely wasteful of money, talent, and energy. We cannot help but deplore the vast expenditure of funds and effort for weapons that become outdated almost as soon as they are in production and that we hope will never be used. How much better if we could use the resources for urgently needed schools, houses, hospitals, roads, libraries, laboratories, and aid to underdeveloped countries.

An even stronger objection to our deterrent policy is that it simply does not provide real security. No matter how far our rockets can travel or how many nuclear warheads we have, a terrible risk remains. If the deterrent fails, it means a nuclear war in which most of the people of this country and the Soviet Union would probably perish, and residual radiation would threaten the safety of survivors and their posterity throughout the world.

During the seven months immediately following the Sputnik's launching, disarmament negotiations were in great jeopardy. Talks within the United Nations broke down when the Soviet Union vowed it would not continue with them until the United Nations agreed to the Kremlin's version of a reconstituted Disarmament Commission. The United States and the Soviet Union each proposed negotiations at levels which were unacceptable to the other. The anxiously waiting world did not see how the cause of peace could be advanced in such an atmosphere.

The outlook for negotiations is only slightly more hopeful now, and many questions are yet to be resolved. But whatever the form, whoever the participants, there are certain qualities which the United States can demonstrate if it wishes to help create an atmosphere in which negotiations can be conducted.

One of these qualities is flexibility. When one policy has been given a reasonable trial without success, then we should search for an alternative. To maintain that a policy which was valid five or six years ago must necessarily still be valid today, is pure nonsense. Our mentalities have got to be flexible enough to adjust to evolving reality.

The adoption of a much more positive attitude by us could also improve the atmosphere. No government, least of all the government of the United States, should be negative about the possibility of limiting the arms race. Proposals of the Soviet Union should not be lightly or impatiently brushed aside, even when they are exasperatingly rigid or unreasonable. The densest armor has chinks and it is the task of statesmanship to find them.

One of the few diplomatic victories which the United States has scored in recent months came as a result of demonstrating some flexibility and positive thinking. I refer to our timely proposal for mutual aerial inspection of the Arctic in response to Soviet complaints of the flights of the Strategic Air Command in the area. The Soviet veto of this proposal indicated to the people of the world that the Soviet Union is just as capable of responding negatively to disarmament proposals as is the United States.

The lack of respect for its bonded word which Moscow has shown time and again necessitates another quality on our part, prudent caution. I do not think we should become so skeptical of the Soviet record that we refuse to deal with her. Even Russia keeps some of its agreements — for instance, the Peace Treaty of 1947 with Finland and the Austrian Peace Treaty. The key to making effective agreements with the Kremlin is to confine them to those situations where it is to the interest of the Soviet Union, as well as to the United States and other countries, to keep the agreement. If we exercise prudent caution we will not endanger ourselves.

In regard to disarmament, prudent caution requires that we should not jeopardize our security by putting our signatures to any agreement that depends on good faith alone for its fulfillment. Adequate inspection must be provided for wherever appropriate to make discovery of violations so certain that they would not be attempted.

This does not mean that an inspection system must be absolutely perfect. I do not believe we can hope to establish a 100-percent foolproof inspection system. Among human beings, very little can be that certain. However, I believe that with respect to many arms-control measures we can establish an inspection system which would make the probability of detecting violation so great that the Soviet Union would abide by the agreement rather than risk the ignominy of being caught cheating. Moreover, we should always remember that any inspection system established in the Soviet Union would be a tremendous step toward raising the Iron Curtain. It could pave the way, not only to additional inspected disarmament measures but also to a general

"opening up" of the Soviet Union and to greater mutual understanding. Despite Russian assertions that inspection is really intelligence and thus proposed for purposes of spying, could there be any better political breakthrough than to conclude a first-step disarmament agreement with inspection safeguards?

Right now we should concentrate our efforts on making that first step. If we really want to base our security system on armaments control rather than on armaments alone, we must recognize that a task of such complexity cannot be achieved overnight or all at once. The most we can hope for at this time is to make a beginning. In fact, unless we concentrate on reaching agreement on a small first step, we shall make no progress at all.

For some time this country has talked of offering so-called first-step proposals. In practice, however, we have not been able to abandon our "get rich quick" dream. Instead of proposing first steps which would be feasible, we have put forward measures which, when coupled with the elaborate inspection systems necessary to assure their observance, were so far-reaching as to be virtually unattainable.

For example, the Western proposal for a first-step disarmament agreement offered at the London disarmament negotiations included various nuclear-control measures, an inspection system to provide against surprise attack, a reduction of armed forces and the transfer of some armaments to international depots, and the establishment of a committee to study ways to insure that objects sent into outer space would be used exclusively for peaceful purposes. All the measures were tied together in such a way that each proposal was contingent on acceptance of all the other proposals.

To expect the Soviet Union to accept a package such as that as a "first step" would be like expecting a baby to take its "first step" two days after birth. Since it would be excessively optimistic to press for agreement on our total disarmament hopes all at once, I have suggested that the package be broken up into small parcels and presented bit by bit. The support I have received for this approach from the American people is overwhelming.

One of the most meaningful measures, and one which would prove our earnest desire for disarmament, is the suspension of nuclear-weapons tests, with inspection on both sides. Public opinion throughout the world favors stopping the tests in order to check the rising level of radioactive fallout in the atmosphere. Suspension of tests would also be an effective measure of arms control. It would freeze or retard nuclear-weapons development in those countries which have produced live weapons — the United States, the Soviet Union, and the United Kingdom. Since we have been assured that we are not behind in nuclear-weapons technology, a test ban should not be to our disadvantage. It would retard, and I hope prevent, the spread of nuclear-weapons production to other countries. Otherwise, the day is certain to come when these lethal devices will fall into many hands which by accident, irresponsibility, or malevolent intent might trigger off an Armageddon.

Adequate assurance that the Soviet Union was observing a test-suspension agreement would require monitoring stations within the Soviet Union equipped with seismographs, microbarographs, and radiation-measuring and other equipment, but it would not require much intermingling of inspectors with the Soviet people, a prospect which the Soviet government greatly fears. The closer together such stations were placed, the more certainly we could detect violations. But even with relatively few stations, I believe we could make the chances of detecting clandestine tests good enough to discourage Soviet cheating.

In view of the energy with which the So-

viet Union has been calling for a separate ban on nuclear tests, we should at least call their bluff to see if they are willing to do what is necessary or if they are just spreading a propaganda hoax. The move is just as necessary now that the Soviets have announced that they are temporarily stopping weapons tests unilaterally. If the Soviets really want to bring an end to testing, they will agree to an inspection system. An opportunity to move forward may have been provided by Mr. Khrushchev's note of May 9, in which he expressed an apparent willingness to set up the joint study of inspection for a test suspension which had been proposed earlier by us.

Control of outer space is another avenue along which we can pursue disarmament. Now is the time to make sure that our new technical ability to send vehicles to outer space is dedicated to peaceful purposes alone. If we fail to bring under control weapons designed to travel through outer space, the new discoveries, instead of opening up new horizons to us on earth, may bring an end to our existence.

To keep man's differences on earth from contaminating outer space, the United States, as a separate and independent project, should take the lead in marshaling the talents and resources of the world for space research and exploration under the auspices of the United Nations. The cooperative endeavor of the International Geophysical Year has laid a foundation of experience. This "Year" should be extended until a more advanced structure can be erected, an agency similar to the International Atomic Energy Agency, which promotes world cooperation on developing peaceful uses of the atom.

All nations should be invited to participate in what may be man's greatest enterprise. Our experience in setting up the International Atomic Energy Agency has demonstrated that such joint undertakings for world peace and welfare exert a magnetic force that compels even the reluctant to join. An international space research and exploration agency would absorb energies and divert resources that might otherwise be expended in military rivalry.

My second proposal in the field of outer space is that the nations of the world should unite in a priority program for an earth reconnaissance satellite. Under the supervision, guidance, and control of an international organization, such a satellite could cross national borders and climb over Iron Curtains and expose to the wholesome gaze of the world military preparations of all nations. This watcher in space would make preparations for surprise attack, especially by conventional forces requiring mobilization, much more difficult. In this way, developments in space could help control armaments on earth.

My third proposal is that all flights of long-range missiles and outer-space vehicles should be placed under international surveillance to insure that no clandestine tests of rockets or outer-space devices are conducted for military ends. The United Nations would be the proper body to assume responsibility for this task. Until long-range missiles have reached a state of perfection, test firings are necessary. Since the missiles rise to great heights and travel great distances, long-range radar now under development could in all probability fulfill much or all of the surveillance necessary to insure only authorized flights.

Difficulties would be compounded, however, if inauguration of an inspection system were delayed until the long-range missiles were perfected, for then multiplication of their numbers could proceed without field tests. Location and inspection of factories would then be necessary to discover illegal production, and it is uncertain whether any inspection system could detect hidden stockpiles of completed missiles.

Time is already growing short, and I consider it necessary to get a program under way as soon as possible to work out the details of a control and inspection apparatus to prevent stockpiles of long-range ballistic missiles from adding to the threat that nuclear stockpiles already hold for the world. The United States should continue to pursue its proposal, thus far ignored by the Soviet Union, to create a joint study commission with the U.S.S.R. to devise machinery that can insure that no further tests of long-range missiles are conducted for weapons purposes.

It should be pointed out that any of these proposals entails risks. I feel strongly, however, that in these days the greatest risk, an immeasurable risk, lies in doing nothing — in letting the armaments race continue with no control whatever. The first step, perhaps, is the hardest, but until we take it we shall never progress toward a security system based on the control of armaments rather than the fear of armaments.

———◆———

The only war I ever approved of was the Trojan war; it was fought over a woman and the men knew what they were fighting for.

WILLIAM LYON PHELPS, Sermon

94.

Edward Teller and Albert L. Latter: For Continued Experimentation with Nuclear Weapons

United States-Soviet discussion of disarmament proposals during 1957 and 1958 provoked sharp disagreement both among American government officials and in the scientific community. Among the scientists, the leaders of the two main opposing positions were J. Robert Oppenheimer and Edward Teller. Oppenheimer, who had directed the production of the first atomic bomb, tried to resist the production of the hydrogen bomb, but without success. The principal promoter of the hydrogen bomb was Teller, who had not only developed its theory but also agitated for its production. A staff member at Los Alamos (under Oppenheimer) during World War II, Teller was an adviser to the Atomic Energy Commission and wrote widely on nuclear weapons and their use. The following selection is taken from Our Nuclear Future, *published in 1958 by Teller and Albert L. Latter, a theoretical physicist with the Air Force's Rand Corporation. The book, which strongly advocated the continuation of nuclear tests, was criticized by many reviewers, but it probably reflected the view then prevailing in influential government circles.*

Source: *Our Nuclear Future*, New York, 1958, pp. 137-145, 168-173.

MANY PEOPLE feel that [nuclear] tests should be discontinued. This feeling is widespread and strong. The question of tests is obviously important. It may influence our security as individuals. It certainly will influence our security as a nation. If in a free, democratic country the majority believes that something should be done — it will be done. The sovereign power in a democracy is "the people." It is of the greatest importance that the people should be honestly and completely informed about all relevant facts. In no other way can a sound decision be reached. The basic and relevant facts are simple. The story can be presented without unnecessary frills or undue emotion. When this has been done, the right decision will be reached by common sense rather than by exceptional cleverness.

Unfortunately much of the discussion about continued experimentation with nuclear explosives has been carried out in a most emotional and confused manner. One argument concerning tests is so fantastic that it deserves to be mentioned for that very reason: It has been claimed that nuclear explosions may change the axis of the earth.

Of course, nuclear explosions do produce such changes. Only the changes are so small that they are impossible to observe and even difficult to estimate. Searching for effects connected with past tests that may displace the axis of the earth, or the position of the North Pole, we could find no effect that would have caused a change of position even as great as the size of an atom. One could design tests with the specific purpose to produce such a change, but these man-made effects could not be compared even remotely with the forces of nature. The motion of the Gulf Stream has a small effect on the North Pole; but this effect is incomparably greater than what any nuclear explosion could accomplish. It is good to know that the old top on which we live does have some stability.

The argument about worldwide radioactive fallout is more serious. It is asserted that fallout is dangerous and that we are ignorant of the extent of the danger.

In a narrow, literal sense both these statements are correct. But in the preceding chapters we have seen that the danger is limited. We do not know precisely how great it is. We do know, however, that the danger is considerably smaller than the danger from other radiations to which we continue to expose ourselves without worry. The danger from the tests is quite small compared with the effects of X rays used in medical practice. The fallout produces only a fraction of the increase in cosmic ray effect to which a person subjects himself when he moves from the seashore to a place of higher altitude like Colorado. People may or may not be damaged by the fallout. But it is quite certain that the damage is far below a level of which we usually take notice.

Fallout in the vicinity of the test sites did cause damage. In the past this damage was not great although in one Pacific test it was serious. Precautions have been increased and we may hope that future accidents will be avoided altogether. The safety record of the Atomic Energy Commission compares favorably with other enterprises of similar scale.

It seems probable that the root of the opposition to further tests is not connected with fallout. The root is deeper. The real reason against further tests is connected with our desire for disarmament and for peace.

There can be no doubt that the desire for peace is most deep, and this desire is felt by all thinking and honest people on our earth. All of us certainly hope that the catastrophe of war can be avoided. This great and universal wish for peace is the driving force behind the desire for disarmament. In the minds of most people it would be an important step toward disarmament if the testing of nuclear weapons were stopped by all nations. This belief is widely held, but it is not necessarily well-founded. In fact, there are arguments on the other side which should be considered carefully. . . .

If an agreement were made to discontinue the tests, the United States would surely keep such an agreement. The very social and political structure of our country excludes the possibility that many people would collaborate in breaking an international undertaking. Whether Russia would or would not keep such an agreement would depend on the ingenuity of the Russians, on their willingness to make economic sacrifices, and on their honesty. Of these three factors we can have a firm opinion about the first. The Russians are certainly ingenious enough to devise secret methods of testing. As to the other questions, whether the Russians will want to invest the effort and whether they will be bound by their word, we feel that each man is entitled to his own opinion. According to past experience, an agreement to stop tests may well be followed by secret and successful tests behind the iron curtain.

In a more general way we may ask the question: Is it wise to make agreements which honesty will respect, but dishonesty can circumvent? Shall we put a free, democratic government at a disadvantage compared to the absolute power of a dictatorship? Shall we introduce prohibition in a new form, just to give rise to bootlegging on a much greater scale? It is almost certain that in the competition between prohibition and bootlegging, the bootlegger will win.

All of these arguments, however, would become irrelevant if it were true that further testing would not accomplish any further desirable result. It has been said and often repeated that we now possess adequate nuclear explosives to wipe out the cities of any enemy. What more do we need?

Our main purpose in further experimentation with nuclear bombs is not, of course, to make city-busters more horrible. We would prefer not to have to use our nuclear weapons at all. We keep them as a counterthreat against the danger that we ourselves should be subjected to a devastating attack. To understand what we are actually trying to do in the tests, we have to take a closer look at some military problems.

In the Second World War strategic bombing was used for the first time on a really massive scale. It may well be and, in fact, it is probable that such strategic bombing will not be repeated in the future. There are two military reasons for the bombing of cities. One is that factories are located in cities, and these factories support the war effort. The other reason is that cities are centers of transportation through which the supplies of war materials pass. By destroying these centers the flow of the war supplies can be interrupted.

Nuclear warfare is likely to be quite different from past conflicts. The great concentration of firepower which a nuclear weapon represents makes it possible to attack an enemy anywhere, at very short notice. This is true no matter what the particular target is, whether one is trying to attack the planes, ships, tanks, or troop concentrations of an enemy. The great mobility of nuclear firepower makes it highly probable that the nuclear conflict will be short. What the factory produces during this conflict will not affect the outcome of the fighting. The only weapons on which anyone can rely are the weapons which are already stockpiled.

Therefore, it will be militarily useless to bomb factories.

The same fact of mobility also implies that no great flow of war material will need to be maintained. Practically all movement can be executed by light and fast methods, by planes, submarines, and small battle groups. Under these conditions the cities will lose their importance as centers of transportation. The only purpose in bombing cities will be to spread terror among the enemy. This was rarely done in past wars. In fact, terror is self-defeating because it provokes retaliation from the other side.

We believe that the role of nuclear weapons in a future war is by no means the killing of millions of civilians. It is rather to stop the armed forces of an aggressor. This is not easy to do because it requires not only nuclear weapons, but very special kinds of nuclear weapons which are hard to develop and harder to perfect. But with proper experimentation and proper planning the defensive use of nuclear weapons is possible.

The idea of tactical nuclear weapons is not new. The possibility of using nuclear explosives in small wars has been frequently discussed. What kind of weapons do we need in order to fight these small wars and to defend the freedom of people wherever such defense becomes necessary? It has often been suggested that in small wars, small weapons will be used, while big weapons are appropriate for big wars. Such a statement is much too simple and has no relation to reality. In every case the right kind of weapon is the one which performs the job of stopping the enemy's armed forces without inflicting unnecessary loss on the innocent bystander. For this purpose we need a great number of weapons which are adaptable to specific purposes, which are easy to transport and easy to deliver, and give rise to the kind of effect which the situation requires.

For instance, a nuclear weapon may be carried by a fighter plane and used to shoot down an attacking bomber. Since the carrying capacity of the fighter plane is severely limited, the weapon for this purpose must be small and light. A major objective of the test program is to develop such purely defensive weapons.

The encounter between the fighter plane and the bomber may well take place in our own country over populated areas. This possibility would fill most people with alarm lest the population underneath the explosion should be hurt. Fortunately, in a recent nuclear test in Nevada, five well-informed and courageous Air Force officers demonstrated that there is complete safety to people on the ground. They did this by standing directly beneath the explosion at ground zero. . . .

In order that nuclear weapons should be effective against armed invaders, it is clear that great numbers of these weapons are needed. Such great numbers of weapons, some of which must be ground-burst, will produce a considerable amount of radioactive contamination, and this contamination will endanger friend and foe alike. In particular, the radioactivity is likely to kill people in the very country whose liberty we are trying to defend. For this reason it is most important that we should be able to use nuclear weapons which cause the least possible contamination. In recent nuclear tests more and more attention has been paid to the development of such clean weapons, and most fortunately these efforts are well on the way toward success.

The radioactive fallout from nuclear testing gives rise to a possible danger which is quite limited in size. The danger from the fallout in a nuclear war, however, would be real and great. If we stop testing now, and if we should fail to develop to the fullest possible extent these clean weapons, we should unnecessarily kill a great number of noncombatants. Not to develop the explosives with the smallest radioactive fallout would, indeed, be completely inexcusable.

The only alternative is that nuclear weapons should not be used at all. Since these weapons have been presented as purely evil instruments, most people hope that they will never be used, and indeed one should hope that wars, and therefore the use of these weapons, can be avoided.

But in our conflict with the powerful communistic countries which strive for world domination, it may be too much to hope for uninterrupted peace. If we abandon our light and mobile weapons, we shall enable the Red bloc to take over one country after another, close to their borders, as opportunities arise. The free nations cannot maintain the massive armies throughout the world which would be required to resist such piecemeal aggression. On the other hand, the flexible power of clean nuclear explosives would put us in a position where we could resist aggression in any part of the world, practically at a moment's notice.

The announced policy of our country is to maintain peace and stability in the world. By being patient and prepared we are trying to arrive at a world order based on law and justice for all peoples. There is no doubt that this policy is supported by the overwhelming majority of Americans. Our armed forces need the greatest possible flexibility in order to give strength to this policy. Such flexibility we can possess only if we have in our possession the strongest, best-developed weapons which are also the cleanest, so that they may be used for defense rather than for random destruction.

If we renounce nuclear weapons, we open the door to aggression. If we fail to develop clean explosives, we expose people to disaster from radioactive fallout in any serious military conflict. To our way of thinking these are weighty arguments in favor of continued experimentation and development of nuclear weapons. But still another, more general, point of view should be considered.

The spectacular developments of the last centuries, in science, in technology, and in our everyday life, have been based on one important premise: to explore fearlessly any consequences to which greater knowledge and improved skills can lead us. When we talk about nuclear tests, we have in mind not only military preparedness but also the execution of experiments which will give us more insight and more ability to control the forces of nature. There are many specific political and military reasons why such experiments should not be abandoned. There also exists this very general reason — the tradition of exploring the unknown. We can follow this tradition, and we can at the same time be increasingly careful that radioactivity, carelessly dispersed, should not interfere with human life.

THE FUTURE DEPENDS ON PEOPLE. People are unpredictable. Therefore, the future is unpredictable. However, some general conditions of mankind depend on things like the development of technology, the control won by man over nature and the limitations of natural resources. These can be predicted with a little greater confidence. The future is unknown but in some respects its general outline can be guessed. Such guesses are important. They influence our present outlook and our present actions.

The nuclear age has not yet started. Our sources of energy are not yet nuclear sources. Even in the military field, where development has been most rapid, the structure of the armed forces has not yet adjusted itself to the facts of the nuclear age in a realistic manner. In politics the atomic nucleus has entered as a promise and as a menace — not as a fact on which we can build and with which we can reckon.

Some technical predictions seem safe:

Nuclear energy will not render our older power plants obsolete in the near future. But nuclear energy will make it possible to maintain the pace — even the acceleration — of the industrial revolution. It will be possible to produce all the energy we need at a moderate cost. Furthermore — and this is the important point — this energy will be available at any place on the globe at a cost which is fairly uniform. The greater the need for power, the sooner will it be feasible to satisfy the need with the help of nuclear reactors.

Nuclear energy can be made available at the most outlandish places. It can be used on the Antarctic continent. It can be made to work on the bottom of the ocean.

The expanding front of industrialization has been called the "revolution of rising expectations." That nuclear energy should be involved in the current and in the turbulence of this expanding front, is inevitable.

One can say a little more about the effects of scientific and technological discoveries on the relations among the people of the globe. With added discoveries raw materials will no longer be needed with the old urgency. For most substances substitutes are being found. This may make for greater economic independence. On the other hand, new possibilities will present themselves. We shall learn how to control the air and how to cultivate the oceans. This will call for cooperation and more interdependence.

The dangers from radioactive by-products will act in a similar direction. The radioactive cloud released from a reactor accident may be more dangerous than a nuclear explosion. Such a cloud will not stop at national boundaries. Some proper form of international responsibility will have to be developed.

What effect the existence of nuclear weapons will have upon the coexistence of nations is a question less understood and less explored than any other affecting our future. Most people turn away from it with a feeling of terror. It is not easy to look at the question with calm reason and with little emotion.

A few predictions seem disturbing but are highly probable:

Nuclear secrets will not keep. Knowledge of nuclear weapons will spread among nations — at least as long as independent nations exist.

Prohibition will not work. Laws or agreements which start with the word "don't" can be broken and will always be broken. If there is hope, it must lie in the direction of agreements which start with the word "do." The idea of "Atoms for Peace" succeeded because it resulted in concrete action.

An all-out nuclear war between the major powers could occur but we may have good hope that it will not occur if we remain prepared to strike back. No one will want to provoke the devastation of his own country.

Atomic bombs may be used against cities. But there will be no military advantage in destroying cities. In a short and highly mobile war neither centers of supply and communication nor massive means of production will count. If cities are bombed, this will be done primarily for reasons of psychological warfare. We must be and we are prepared for this kind of war but only as a measure of retaliation. There is good reason to believe that as long as we are prepared for all-out war, our civilian population will not suffer from a nuclear attack.

The certainty of a counterblow gives real protection against all-out war. No such protection exists against wars limited in territory and in aims. In the history of mankind such wars have been most frequent. There is no indication that these limited wars have ended. We must be prepared for these conflicts with effective and mobile units, and this requires the use of nuclear firepower. Nuclear weapons will certainly have a pro-found effect upon such limited warfare. Not all of this effect need be and indeed it must not be in the direction of greater devastation.

In a nuclear war it will not make sense to use massed man-power. Any such concentration will provide too good a target for atomic weapons. To use big, costly, and conspicuous machines of war will be unwise. Such machines will be defeated by nuclear explosions in the same way as the mailed knight went down before firearms.

Any fighting unit in a nuclear war will have to be small, mobile, inconspicuous, and capable of independent action. Such units whether on sea, land, or in the air cannot rely and will not rely on fixed lines of supply. There will be no possibility and no need to occupy territory and to fight at fixed and definite fronts. If a war should be fought for military reasons and for military advantage, it will consist of short and sharp local engagements involving skill and advanced techniques and not involving masses that slaughter and are being slaughtered.

If an invader adopts extreme dispersion, it will become impossible to defeat him with atomic weapons. But a very highly dispersed army can be defeated by a determined local population. Therefore the main role of nuclear weapons might well be to disperse any striking force so that the resistance of people defending their homes can become decisive. Nuclear weapons may well become the answer to massed armies and may put back the power into the hands where we believe it belongs: the hands of the people.

AT THIS POINT we are brought back to the main topic of this book: radioactivity. In a limited nuclear war the radioactive fallout will probably kill many of the innocent bystanders. We have seen that the testing program gives rise to a danger which is much smaller than many risks which we take in our stride without any worry. In a nuclear war, even in a limited one, the situation will probably be quite different. That noncombatants suffer in wars is not new. In a nuclear war, this suffering may well be increased further due to the radioactive poisons which kill friend and foe, soldier and civilian alike.

Fortunately there exists a way out. Our early nuclear explosives have used fission. In the fission process a great array of radioactive products are formed, some of them intensely poisonous. More recently we have learned how to produce energy by fusion. Fusion produces fewer and very much less dangerous radioactivities. Actually the neutrons which are a by-product of the fusion reaction may be absorbed in almost any material and may again produce an assortment of radioactive nuclei. However, by placing only certain materials near the thermonuclear explosion, one may obtain a weapon in which the radioactivity is harmless. Thus the possibility of clean nuclear explosions lies before us.

Clean, flexible, and easily delivered weapons of all sizes would make it possible to use these bombs as we want to use them: as tools of defense. When stopping an aggressor we would not let loose great quantities of radioactive atoms which would spread death where we wanted to defend freedom. Clean nuclear weapons would be the same as conveniently packaged high explosives. They would be nothing more.

The possibility of clean explosions opens up another development: the use of nuclear explosives for the purposes of peace. Conventional high explosives have been used in peace fully as much as in war. From mining to the building of dams there is a great variety of important jobs that dynamite has performed. Nuclear explosives have not been used in a similar way. The reason is the danger from radioactivity. Once we fully master the art of clean explosions peaceful applications will follow and another step will be made in controlling the forces of nature.

All this is of course only a small part in the process of the increasing power of man and the increasing responsibility of man. As the impossible of yesterday becomes the accomplished fact of today we have to be more and more aware of our neighbors on this shrinking planet. The arts of peace may lead to conflicting interest as easily as they may lead to fruitful cooperation. If we ever learn to control the climate of the world, a nation may find itself in the same relation to another nation as two farmers who have to use the waters of the same river.

Rivals are men who fight over the control of a river. When the same word "rivals" comes to mean cooperation for the best common use of the river or any other resource — that will be the time of law and of peace. Surely this sounds like Utopia and no one sees the way. But the general direction in which we should go is not to consider atomic explosives and radioactivity as the inventions of the devil. On the contrary, we must more fully explore all the consequences and possibilities that lie in nature, even when these possibilities seem frightening at first. In the end this is the way toward a better life. It may sound unusually optimistic in the atomic age, but we believe that the human race is tough and in the long run the human race is reasonable.

———◆———

Thinking About the Unthinkable.
HERMAN KAHN, title of book, 1964

95.

EARL WARREN: Federal Court Congestion

Included among the federal courts' jurisdiction are two main kinds of cases: in criminal actions where the offense charged is against a federal law and in civil cases where the parties are citizens of different states. Congress has tried to reduce the number of cases in the latter category by establishing that unless the amount in contest is greater than $10,000, the action must be tried in a state court. Nevertheless, the case load of the federal courts has steadily increased as economic, social, racial, and religious questions have resulted in legal actions. There is also, as Alexis de Tocqueville observed long ago, an American propensity for turning all political questions into legal ones. The enormous case load pressing on the federal courts was the subject of the following address by Chief Justice Earl Warren of the Supreme Court, delivered before the American Law Institute on May 21, 1958.

Source: *Record, App.,* 85 Cong., 2 Sess., pp. A4797-A4799.

THE DELAY and the choking congestion in the federal courts today have created a crucial problem for constitutional government in the United States. It is so chronically prevalent that it is compromising the quantity and quality of justice available to the individual citizen and, in so doing, it is leaving vulnerable throughout the world the reputation of the United States for protecting and securing these rights and remedies.

We have made some progress, but the truth is that for every inch we gain, the normal healthy economic and population growth of our country extends a yard, leaving in its wake a whole new volume of litigation for the courts. . . . The federal judiciary is simply unable — as long as it lacks a sufficient number of judges, improved administrative and procedural techniques, and ample supporting staff — to keep pace with the dynamic growth of our country.

The business of the district courts is the best evidence of this. If we go back to the prewar year 1941 — the first year that complete statistics were compiled in the administrative office — we can trace a veritable upward surge in the volume of litigation in our federal trial courts.

You know, of course, that I am not referring to the criminal business of the courts because, despite its importance, it takes only a minor portion of the court time. Criminal business has priority and is promptly disposed of. It is, rather, the civil business of the courts which has skyrocketed since 1941. In that year, 38,000 civil cases were filed, and an equal number of cases were disposed of. The pending caseload at the end of the year was 29,000. The time interval — the vital issue-to-trial period — during which time the case is entirely in the control of the court, was only five months for the average or median case. In that year, 1941, we had approximately 200 trial judges.

Today — sixteen years later — the number of cases filed annually has increased to 62,000, and the pending backlog of business totals some 66,000 cases. We have, in our federal trial courts, 250 judges. In other words, the numbers of cases filed annually in federal district courts has increased more than 60 percent since 1941. The backlog of cases has risen more than 125 percent. But, in contrast, there has been but a 25 percent increase in the number of judges to handle the increased volume of business. This also applies generally to supporting personnel.

The inevitable result has been a most discouraging increase in the length of time for getting a case heard. From five months in 1941, the interval from issue-to-trial for the median case has risen to nine months. At the present time, over 38 percent of all the civil cases in the Federal courts are subject to undue delay — that is, delay from one to four years between the date of filing and the time of trial. This delay is chiefly in our large metropolitan areas. For example, in Brooklyn the delay is forty-two months; in Pittsburgh, thirty-three months; in Cleveland, thirty months; in New York City, twenty-six months; Philadelphia, twenty-six months; Milwaukee, twenty-six months; Denver, twenty months; Chicago, eighteen months; and in San Francisco, thirteen months.

The Judicial Conference, as you know, has established an objective standard of six months for a normal case from the time it is filed until it is tried. Unfortunately, there were but seven out of ninety-four districts which met the six months' standard in 1957. They include the Middle District of Alabama and the Southern District of West Virginia, and such populated areas as Memphis, Tulsa, Albuquerque, Dallas, and Fort Worth. The actual median case throughout the United States takes twelve months. The median time interval in the courts of appeal from filing of the complete record to final disposition ranges from 3.8 months in the fastest circuit to 10.4 months in the slowest.

This time must be added before final disposition of the case is reached.

The upward trend in the number of appeals seems to be leveling off, at least temporarily, but in the Second, Fourth, and Fifth Circuits the additional judges recommended by the Judicial Conference must be supplied or the growing pressure of business will surely force these courts behind.

Now, after the interested parties have exhausted the appellate procedure, they have a right to seek a review in the Supreme Court. That also takes a considerable period of time. Fortunately, because of our discretionary power on certiorari, the Court has been able to keep abreast of its work every year since 1928. While the work has increased very greatly since that time, in recent years the flow of cases has been somewhat uniform.

The number of cases docketed in the Court during the past year has continued at the same high level of the preceding two years. As of May 19, there were 1,013 cases on the appellate docket and 781 cases on the miscellaneous docket, an increase of 25 as of the same time last year. There have been 154 cases argued before the Court compared to 145 in the preceding year, an increase of 9. On May 19, we had disposed of 1,391 cases from both dockets, compared to 1,380 at that time last year. On the appellate docket, 567 petitions for certiorari have been denied and 90 petitions have been granted. On the miscellaneous docket, 571 petitions for certiorari and applications for leave to file extraordinary writs have been denied and 19 petitions have been granted. We have every reason to believe that at the last session of this term we will be able to say, as the Court has said every year since 1928, when it acquired the certiorari jurisdiction, that all cases ready for argument have been heard and decided.

However, until the discretionary writ of certiorari was authorized by the Congress, the Supreme Court found itself falling further and further behind, as are the other courts in the federal system. We can all derive satisfaction from that innovation in court administration because I have no doubt that if it were not for that change, the Supreme Court would be suffering from the same congestion that confronts the other courts in our judicial system. As a remedy was found for the congestion in the Supreme Court, so we must search day by day and year by year for remedies to put the district courts and the courts of appeals on a current basis. There is no single answer, but I have the confidence to believe that if the bench and bar come to a realization of the dangers involved, that we can and will find the remedy. If we really believe in our system, we must have that faith. . . .

The backlog in civil business has already increased by more than 5,000 cases in the district courts this year, and it is continuing to spiral upward. But, I should emphasize, the total number of cases is not an entirely satisfactory criterion for measuring the problem of congestion. The type of case is important, too. For example, during the war and shortly thereafter we had on our dockets a large number of government price and rent control cases, which took a minimum amount of time. Studies that we have made show that, on the average, cases between private individuals, the majority of them under the diversity of citizenship jurisdiction, take three times as much time to handle as government cases. These private cases, therefore, are the most important factor in the caseload. And it is this group which has increased most rapidly. Between 1941 and 1957, private civil cases based upon diversity of citizenship jurisdiction increased from some 7,000 per year to over 23,000. The backlog has increased 150 percent.

Bankruptcy matters, while usually handled by the referees, are also an important part of federal court business. The number of bankruptcy cases has not increased significantly excepting cases involving wage earners. Although it is true that during the fiscal year 1957 the total backlog of bankruptcy cases of all types rose from 59,000 to 68,000 cases, the fact is that about 80 percent of the total are employee-type cases and almost 20 percent of these were filed under Chapter 13 as wage-earner plans for the payment of indebtedness. If it seems somewhat misleading to lump the Chapter 13 proceedings with ordinary bankruptcy, it should be borne in mind that each of them constitutes another case for the courts to handle no matter what section of the act may be relied upon.

These statistics are a record of delay piled upon delay in the federal courts. But, serious as they may be, they are no accurate measure of the extent to which our administrative weaknesses have caused injustice. They do not reflect the hardship and suffering caused to unfortunate victims of such delays, nor the inadequate settlements which individuals are frequently forced to accept on that account. Neither do these figures include what are probably the worst and most numerous cases of all: those instances in which citizens with causes that cry for justice under law have turned from our court system in despair and have sought ways of working out their problems without resort to the courts at all.

It is evident that if this condition is not remedied it will seriously undermine what we have described as "the keystone of America's strength," and will dilute what we have proclaimed as "our main claim to moral leadership in the world community." Certainly we must be gravely concerned when our judicial machinery is facing an outlook of this kind. . . .

This brings me to the steps we have taken since I met with you last May to improve our own administrative machinery.

First, I should like to mention that we have strengthened the Judicial Conference of the United States by the addition of district judges — a district judge selected to represent each circuit, thus doubling the membership of the Conference. The importance of this, of course, is that we now have as members trial judges who are experiencing daily the complex problems which plague the courts. Already, we have availed ourselves of this increased membership to establish a budget committee to study, appraise, and make recommendations as to the overall needs of the judicial branch. Second, we have moved to strengthen the Administrative Office of the United States Courts. . . .

I have mentioned a more flexible use of federal judgepower by transfer from one district to another. This is not a satisfactory permanent solution to the lack of a sufficient number of judges to carry on our business, but it can be of great help in taking care of the situation until Congress has acted. We have, in the federal courts in those districts having purely federal jurisdiction, 13 districts where in 1957 the number of private cases filed per judge exceeded 200. We also have 31 districts where it was less than 100, the average for the country per judge being 151. To bring about an adjustment of this situation is one of the challenges to the Judicial Conference and to the Circuit Councils.

A greater and more effective use of pretrial procedure is another measure to expedite court business. . . . The Conference has been urging that pretrial should be used in every civil case before trial, except where the district judge expressly enters an order to the contrary. . . . The exception when it is not used should be unusual and should result from the particular nature of the case rather than on account of the predilections of the judge.

I should also like to mention in the category of long-range improvements in judicial administration the proposal endorsed by the Judicial Conference of legislative authorization for it to participate in the rulemaking function of the Supreme Court. The bill does not alter the rulemaking power of the Court. It merely authorizes the Judicial Conference to maintain continuing studies of the rules, through committees, and to recommend needed changes in the rules for consideration of the Supreme Court. That Court can adopt, modify, or reject the Conference recommendations.

If the bill is adopted, the restudy of the court rules will call for close cooperation of the bench and bar to make the judicial rulemaking process more nearly a science. I am hopeful that the bill will pass this session of Congress. If it does, your individual assistance in the rulemaking process will be called for and will be greatly appreciated.

The Judicial Conference has also recommended an amendment of the statutes conferring federal question and diversity jurisdiction on the district courts. It may eliminate a number of cases that are not of sufficient importance to challenge the jurisdiction of the federal courts on such grounds. It must be remembered that when the jurisdictional amount of $3,000 was fixed in 1911, the purchasing power of the dollar was about three times what it is now. It is, therefore, appropriate that there should be a corresponding increase in this amount, and the Judicial Conference is recommending it be raised to $10,000. The bill, which was approved by the Conference and is now pending in Congress, would have a considerable effect on the cases where a corporation is involved by providing that "a corporation shall be deemed a citizen of any state by which it has been incorporated or the state where it has its principal place of business."

It is hard to say just what this will accomplish, but at all events it should be helpful because there are many corporations doing a strictly local business with a foreign charter, and the necessity for diversity jurisdiction in litigation affecting them in the state where they do business would no longer seem to exist. The phrase "principal place of business" was used following the words of the Bankruptcy Act which employs this same language as a basis for jurisdiction in a bankruptcy case. There are a number of cases in the books which construe this language. These provisions would give at least some measure of temporary relief to the federal courts because they would decrease the number of federal question and diversity cases filed and these are on the average the most time-consuming type of cases for the courts.

In making this overall report to you, I am not criticizing individual judges, because I firmly believe that by and large judges are as devoted public servants as can be found anywhere. However, in a sprawling, detached judicial system such as ours is, with 250 judges dispersed from Maine to California and from Washington to Florida, judicial administration and modern procedures, as well as sufficient personnel, of necessity play a large part in the efficiency of the system, and it is to promote your continued interest in this field that I feel justified in taking the time of the members of this important Institute to give you these dry but important statistics.

96.

Proposal to Limit the Power of the Supreme Court

The power of the Supreme Court may be checked, according to Article III, Section 2, of the Constitution, by congressional limitation of the cases that the Court may hear on appeal. The Judiciary Act of 1925 restricted the kinds of cases the Court is obliged to review, thereby broadening its discretionary reviewing power. In 1957 Senator William E. Jenner of Indiana introduced a bill to limit the Court's appellate jurisdiction. The bill was largely prompted by dissatisfaction with Court decisions on the investigatory power of Congress, on regulation of the Communist Party, and on states' rights. The following selection is in two parts. The first comprises remarks by Jenner in a speech in defense of the bill, delivered July 26, 1957, and in testimony before the Subcommittee on Internal Security of the Senate Committee on the Judiciary on February 19 and March 5, 1958. The second part comprises portions of the testimony of Senator Thomas C. Hennings, Jr., of Missouri, before the same subcommittee on March 4. Senator Hennings opposed the bill, which was not passed.

Source: *Congressional Digest*, May 1958.

I.

WILLIAM E. JENNER: For Limiting Appellate Power

THE SUPREME COURT has dealt a succession of blows at key points of the legislative structure erected by the Congress for the protection of the internal security of the United States against the world Communist conspiracy. Time after time, Congress has acted to shore up these legislative bulwarks; and time after time, the Supreme Court has knocked the props out from under the structure which Congress has built.

There was a time when the Supreme Court conceived its function to be the interpretation of the law. For some time now, the Supreme Court has been making law — substituting its judgment for the judgment of the legislative branch. Laymen and lawyers, the legislative branch and the executive branch of government, have come to recognize the predilection of the Supreme Court for making new law. Even the lower courts have come to expect it, with the result that it has become commonplace for decisions to be held up in lower courts waiting for the Supreme Court to make some new law that will apply to the case.

By some of these decisions, antisubversive laws and regulations have been rendered ineffective. States have been denied the right to fight subversion and have been denied the right to bar Communists from practising law. Violators of federal antisubversive laws have been turned loose on flimsy technicalities. Confidential files of the FBI and of other investigative and law-enforcement agencies have been opened up to fishing expeditions by defendants and their counsel. The Court has challenged the authority of Congress to decide upon the scope of its own investigations and the right of a congressional committee to make up its own mind about what questions to ask its witnesses.

Many pending cases may be affected, and an undetermined number of cases already settled may be reopened, as a result of recent decisions of the Supreme Court, regardless of what Congress may find it possible to do toward curing the situation, because while Congress cannot make a new law that will affect a case already tried, the Supreme Court can, and does. The Supreme Court can change overnight a rule of law 100 years old, and can make the new rule apply to all cases underway, and provide a basis for reopening cases already tried which involved the point covered by the new rule.

There is no way for Congress to invalidate or repeal a decision of the Supreme Court of the United States, even when that decision is legislative and policy making in nature. Congress can in some cases strike down judge-made law by enacting new law or by correcting the Court's error, respecting the intent of Congress, by a new declaration of intent. This power of the Congress should be exercised to the maximum, of course, but it will not fully meet the situation. The Court has become for all practical purposes a legislative arm of the government, and many of its feats are subject to no review.

In the Watkins case, the Court struck a devastating blow at the power of Congress to inform itself.

In 1933 the federal government employed about half a million persons. The annual budget totaled about $4 billion. And there were ninety-six senators who were members of this body. In 1957, the federal government employs about 2.5 million persons. The annual budget totals about $70 billion. But there are still only ninety-six senators.

The federal establishment has engulfed the Congress, to the mortal danger of our government's constitutional balance. Congress, today, appropriates only about 1 percent of total appropriations for its own purposes. The other 99 percent goes elsewhere.

It is physically impossible today for members of Congress to keep currently informed about the other branches of government. To preserve the constitutional balance, to turn back the tide of engulfment, Congress has resorted more and more to the use of investigating committees, staffed by professional personnel. Investigating committees also are used more and more to study facts as a basis for legislative activity. But in the Watkins case, the Supreme Court has dealt this committee function a body blow by making it possible for reluctant witnesses to stop an investigation in its tracks.

The chief justice's opinion in the Watkins case makes it clear that Mr. Warren does not even know the history of the House Committee on Un-American Activities. This committee did not come into existence after

World War II. It was founded in 1938 to dig out the Reds who were crawling into the wood all over Washington. And it was preceded by other Senate and House committees, which began investigating Red subversion only a year or two after the 1917 Bolshevik Revolution.

Worse than its misstatement of facts is the holding in the Watkins decision that a committee must explain the pertinency of a question to the understanding of a witness before he may be required to answer it. The effect of this was immediate. At the very next hearing of our Subcommittee on Internal Security, witnesses used the Watkins decision as a blueprint of how to avoid answering legitimate questions. They made it clear that hereafter, unless Congress can find a way to reassert its independence, any witness, anytime, can switch any investigation onto a siding by telling his interrogator, as Watkins did, that the question is not "relevant," or by the simple device of playing dumb and claiming not to understand why a question is pertinent.

This severely cripples, if it does not wholly smash, the congressional power to investigate. By doing so, it multiplies the danger of constitutional imbalance.

Anyone who can read should know by this time that communism is a continuing worldwide conspiracy, that American communism is subordinate to Soviet communism, and that American Communists are under discipline to their Soviet masters. All three branches of the United States government have affirmed this to be the fact in a host of findings and decisions. Consequently, questions about party membership are not questions about beliefs. These are questions about deeds. When a man joins an international organization which seeks to destroy his own country, he is voluntarily performing a conspiratorial act. This is and always has been the basic issue, since the first rudimentary investigations of bolshevism, which began here thirty-seven years ago.

Reasonable men may err. If the Court had erred only once or twice in these decisions involving the greatest threat to human freedom which history ever had to look upon, reasonable men could find excuses for it. But what shall we say of this parade of decisions that came down from our highest bench on Red Monday after Red Monday?

The Senate was wrong. The House of Representatives was wrong. The secretary of state was wrong. The Department of Justice was wrong. The state legislatures were wrong. The state courts were wrong. The prosecutors, both federal and state, were wrong. The juries were wrong. The Federal Bureau of Investigation was wrong. The Loyalty Review Board was wrong. The New York Board of Education was wrong. The California bar examiners were wrong. The California Committee on Un-American Activities was wrong. The Ohio Committee on Un-American Activities was wrong. Everybody was wrong except the attorneys for the Communist conspiracy and the majority of the United States Supreme Court.

The objective of my bill S. 2646 is to check judicial legislation in certain fields where it has been damaging the internal security of the United States. Utilization by the Congress, as this bill proposes, of the power conferred by paragraph 2 of Section 2 of Article III of the Constitution to regulate the appellate jurisdiction of the Supreme Court is the only effective way to reply to the Supreme Court's usurpation of legislative power in these fields.

This authority did not get into the Constitution by chance. It was specifically inserted as a part of the system of checks and balances which distinguishes the Constitution of the United States. The purpose of this provision could only have been to put the Congress in a position to divest the Supreme Court of its appellate jurisdiction when, in the discretion of the Congress, circumstances required such action. In fact, under the interpretation of this clause which has been uniform since 1796, the Congress can withhold appellate jurisdiction from the Supreme Court simply by not in terms granting it. Thus, all the appellate jurisdiction the Supreme Court has it holds by virtue of congressional act; and, of course, what the Congress has granted, the Congress may take away.

It has been said, by way of argument against my bill, that the factor of primary importance in connection with appellate jurisdiction is uniformity of decision and preservation of *stare decisis*. But it is the recent decisions of the Supreme Court which have upset the principle of *stare decisis* and given us confusion, rather than uniformity, in decisions. This has been the result of the Supreme Court's attempts to legislate its opinions into the law of the land. By taking from the Supreme Court the right to enforce these novel items of judicial legislation, my bill would restore *stare decisis* and help to preserve the uniformity of decisions.

In connection with this point, we must consider the nature of the cases in which my bill would take from the Court its appellate jurisdiction. With respect to the investigatory power of the Congress, the Court never should have such appellate powers. As Mr. Justice Clark said in his dissenting opinion in the Watkins case:

> So long as the object of a legislative inquiry is legitimate and the questions propounded are pertinent thereto, it is not for the courts to interfere with the committee system of inquiry. To hold otherwise would be an infringement on the power given the Congress to inform itself, and thus a trespass upon the fundamental American principle of separation of powers.

Mr. Justice Clark declared that the majority "has substituted the judiciary as the grand inquisitor and supervisor of congressional investigations," and asserted "it has never been so."

Substantial portions of my bill have to do with areas involving states' rights and the performance by states of functions which are primarily of concern to the states. So it is with the matter of home rule in the administration of schools and so it is with respect to actions by state legislatures to combat subversion within the boundaries of their respective states; and so it is with respect to the powers of states to control the practice of law within their boundaries. There is no need for any national uniformity with respect to these matters. They are things for each state to decide for itself. Leaving the decisions in each state to the highest court of that state and taking from the Supreme Court of the United States any power to step in and impose an arbitrary rule can only be a salutary thing, a step away from regimentation and back toward freedom of the individual.

The purpose of this bill is not to punish the Court; the purpose of this bill is to utilize one of the basic check-and-balance provisions of the Constitution for the purpose of restoring a balance which has been seriously upset by the actions of the Supreme Court. The Court has repeatedly sought to legislate. The people of the United States are unhappy about this. They do not have to be lawyers to understand that it is the job of their elected representatives to legislate, and not the job of the Supreme Court; and they do understand this.

It is not any particular decision or the provisions of any particular decision which I am attacking, I am attacking the problem of how to overcome a trend toward judicial legislation by the Supreme Court of the United States. I concluded that the only way to check this trend was to utilize the provision of the Constitution which I believe was placed there for the purpose of permitting the Congress to act in just such a situation as we now find ourselves in.

Enactment of the bill S. 2646 will not repeal or reverse any of the decisions of the Supreme Court about which many have complained. This kind of an act cannot reach and affect a decision of the Supreme Court. I have never thought that my bill would change any of these decisions or any of the Court's interpretations. What my bill will do, I hope, is to push the Supreme Court out of the field of legislation and back into the area where it was constitutionally intended to operate. My bill is not punitive; it is wholly remedial in purpose.

It has been argued against my bill that it would have the effect of "freezing" the various Supreme Court decisions in the fields which the bill would affect. This argument depends upon the assertion or the assumption that all lower courts would be absolutely bound by these decisions, even in cases where the lower courts might consider the decisions to be bad law. This argument is just another way of saying that the Supreme Court can make law which neither the Congress nor any other court can change; but that the Congress can do nothing to change a law which the Supreme Court has made, and that the judge of a lower court must adhere to a decision of the Supreme Court rather than to the Constitution as he understands it.

I say that is not the case. The Congress can act, in any one of several ways, and my bill is one of the ways. And a lower court can act in a way contrary to a Supreme Court decision, because what the judges of our courts are sworn to uphold is the Constitution of the United States, not the Supreme Court of the United States.

The founding fathers understood that if any one branch of the government got complete ascendancy, we would not have a government of checks and balances but an oligarchy which would lead unquestionably and irresistibly to tyranny.

The genius of the Constitution is that it does not provide for a final arbiter; it does provide for checks and balances which may be used by the different branches of the government, one against the other, to guard against or to repel encroachments. It is this very system of uneasy balances which gives the citizen his best guarantee that his rights will continue to be observed. For once all power is put in a single place, so, surely as

"power corrupts and absolute power corrupts absolutely," the individual rights of citizens are doomed from that day on.

II.

THOMAS C. HENNINGS, JR.: Against Limiting Appellate Power

I HAVE COMPLETE CONFIDENCE in the ability and common sense of the nine men who occupy the highest bench in the land, the Supreme Court of the United States. All of the nine justices have been confirmed by the United States Senate. If one man sits on that bench who does not understand the nature of the Communist conspiracy, then the appointing President and the Senate have been utterly remiss in the performance of their duty. I do not believe that either had acted with such irresponsibility.

The Communist conspiracy, as we all know, is an ever present danger to our government. It seeks to destroy our traditional democratic processes. It is absolutely necessary that we have laws which will protect our nation against such destruction. But I believe in establishing barriers against the destruction of our system; let us not ourselves destroy one of the great bulwarks of our country.

For over 170 years the Supreme Court has been the court of last resort respecting the meaning of the Constitution. This, of course, is our traditional legal system, which is part of our democratic processes. And even though Congress has had the power to limit the Supreme Court's appellate jurisdiction, it has always given to the Court broad appellate jurisdiction over cases where the Constitution is involved. Only once has the Congress limited the Court's appellate jurisdiction. Only once has this power of jurisdiction been limited and this limitation went only to the Court's power to review denials of writs of habeas corpus. It did not cut out the Court's review power over a complete area of law.

S. 2646, if enacted, would result in the Constitution meaning one thing in one place and something else in another. The ultimate effect of the bill would be to destroy a significant part of our legal system, a part of our democratic processes. Therefore, to meet the threat against our system of government posed by the Communist conspiracy, this bill proposes that the Congress destroy an integral part of the traditional system itself.

I most emphatically do not believe it is necessary to take from the Supreme Court a part of its jurisdiction to meet the threats of the Communist conspiracy. Furthermore, and to the contrary, such a step would belittle our system of government in the eyes of the rest of the world. The Court does not dwell upon any high plateau of infallibility. Under our system, the Court is open to criticism and the Court should, like all of us, be subject to criticism by men of goodwill and learned in the law and who are informed on these matters.

Now, let us go back for a moment to another era, in the main, almost 100 years ago, when Congress enacted the only statute limiting the Court's jurisdiction. That was during the early Reconstruction period. The Supreme Court in *ex parte McCardle* upheld the power of Congress to limit the appellate jurisdiction of the Court. Congress had withdrawn from the Court its jurisdiction to review on appeal a denial of a writ of habeas corpus. I think it must be remembered that in such cases the defendant had the opportunity to raise all constitutional questions in the original trial and to appeal the same to the Supreme Court. The limitation enacted in 1867, during the days of Reconstruction, merely took from the Court its power to hear appeals in one collateral action.

S. 2646, on the other hand, would completely destroy the privilege to appeal to the Supreme Court in the five areas of the law. If a person claimed that his constitutional rights had been violated in any of these areas, he could not go to the Supreme Court with his grievance. The final determination of his claim would be made by a state Supreme Court or a federal Circuit Court of Appeals. So, then, the decision would depend upon which court had the last say. There would no longer be conformity as to the meaning of the Constitution. The constitutional issue involved in almost every case in these areas is the due process clause of the Fifth or Fourteenth Amendment.

Now, Congress was given the power to limit the Supreme Court's appellate jurisdiction by Article III, Section 2 of the Constitution. This power of the Congress became effective upon the ratification of the Constitution. The people of our nation in 1789 had certain misgivings as to the power which they had bestowed upon the government, as we all know from reading the debates of the Constitutional Convention. They quickly engrossed upon the Constitution what we now know as the Bill of Rights. The Bill of Rights limits the powers given to the government by the original Constitution. Therefore, the power of Congress to limit the appellate jurisdiction of the Supreme Court is subject to the restrictions, several restrictions, of the Bill of Rights.

In *United States* v. *Bitty* (203 U.S. 393), decided in 1907, the Court in constructing Article III, Section 2, said:

> What such exceptions and regulations should be, it is for Congress in its wisdom to establish, having, of course, due regard to all the provisions of the Constitution.

The Supreme Court has held that the due process clause is satisfied by one judicial determination. So, in this respect, an appeal is not guaranteed by the Constitution and its amendments. However, I have very serious misgivings as to the constitutionality of S. 2646. Due process of law, I believe, requires that the Constitution mean the same to everyone within the four corners of our nation. A proposal such as we have here will destroy the philosophy of equal justice under law which is basic to our system of jurisprudence, Anglo-Saxon jurisprudence.

A bill which will result in the Constitution requiring certain safeguards in one part of the nation and not requiring the same safeguards in another would be repugnant to the due process clause. Therefore, it might well be declared void on that ground. Congress must always keep in mind that the amendments to the Constitution restrict the powers originally given to it by the Constitution.

This bill would establish a very dangerous precedent and would be a first step toward the destruction of our present judicial system. By S. 2646, we would take from the Supreme Court its appellate jurisdiction in certain areas because of disagreement with its decisions in these respective areas. The next step might be to take from the Supreme Court its jurisdiction in other areas where there is disagreement with its decisions. Furthermore, if the Supreme Court's jurisdiction is limited, I can also visualize an attempt to limit the jurisdiction of the United States Circuit Courts, if they should reach decisions which are contrary to the views of the proponents of this bill. And this sequence logically could easily lead to the piecemeal destruction of our independent judiciary. Our courts would possess only limited power, and the guaranties of the Constitution, from a practical point of view, I think would become meaningless.

The Butler amendment to S. 2646 cannot really be looked upon as an amendment because four of its five provisions do not limit the Supreme Court's jurisdiction but amend present federal statutes. The proposed amendment would not change the original proposal to take from the Supreme Court the power to review cases involving bar admissions. Everyone will agree that a state has the power to determine who can practise law and be officers of its courts. However, the use of this power is limited to the extent that it must conform with the Constitution of the United States. The limitation is inherent in a constitutional form of government and has been judicially recognized for almost 100 years. The only procedure which will insure to prospective lawyers the protection of their constitutional rights in this area is to leave intact the present jurisdiction of the Supreme Court.

No one contends that a person has a constitutional right to practise law. The practice of law is a privilege, not a right. However, a person does have the right not to have the privilege to practise withheld from him in violation of the Constitution. The legal profession traditionally has held the role of protector of the people against arbitrary governmental action. It is unwise to establish more limited procedural safeguards respecting the legal profession than other fields of endeavor and other legal relationships between the citizen and his government.

Mere disagreement with a decision of the Supreme Court is not grounds for withdrawing jurisdiction. The powers of the state are limited by the Constitution, and the Supreme Court has traditionally been the final authority on the construction of the Constitution. Violence will be done to the spirit of the U.S. Constitution even by this limited withdrawal of jurisdiction and a dangerous precedent will be established.

Section 2 would be most undesirable. One of the essential elements of the crime as provided by the present statute is the pertinency of the question under inquiry. As held in *Sinclair* v. *U.S.* (279 U.S. 263), the question of pertinency is a question of law to be determined by the Court. It is a judicial question which must be determined by the judiciary. A committee cannot be given the power to make a binding determination of the legal significance of one of its questions for purposes of a criminal trial for contempt. The present proposal would do just this. I have no doubt as to the constitutionality of such a provision under the due process clause of the Fifth Amendment.

If Section 3 were adopted, we would create a legal monstrosity. We would be approving a provision which would authorize the head of any department or agency of the government in his absolute discretion, and when deemed necessary in the interest of national security, to suspend, without pay, any civilian officer or employee of eleven enumerated agencies. Our civil service laws were adopted to provide a competent work force for the federal government. To allow summary discharges without procedural safeguards directly contravenes the purposes of our civil service laws. We lay open to destruction our whole civil service system. Our nation has always stood for justice and fair play. The procedures established under these acts, as interpreted by the courts, not only insure these but also, if only indirectly, protect our nation.

Section 4(a) is intended to restrict the rules of statutory construction which the courts have developed in applying the doctrine of the supremacy of federal law to situations where a federal statute is alleged to have restricted concurrent state activity.

The essential weakness of this is that it comes about 100 years too late. Over the past decades Congress has created complex and elaborate systems for the regulation of labor relations, interstate carriers, communications, and a multitude of other areas of national interest and scope. Interwoven within these regulatory statutes are a large number of judicial decisions which have passed on the question of when particular fields are subject to exclusive regulation by federal law, and when they are subject to concurrent regulation by federal and state law.

These adjudications are now an integral part of our federal regulatory law. Section 4(a) would provide the basis for disrupting this existing framework of law affecting some of the most vital areas of our national life. For example, in the labor field, the states do not now have concurrent power to determine representative disputes or to prevent unfair labor practices which come within the jurisdiction of the NLRB. Section 4(a) would open up these two areas to state activity. It is hard to conceive of anything but chaos and confusion resulting from this multiplicity of tribunals and diversity of procedures and substantive law.

There are several cogent reasons for not disturbing the Nelson decision. Communist subversion is, admittedly, a national problem, and for this very reason should be handled on a national basis by the federal government. The federal government is fully equipped to do the job of prosecuting individuals for subversive activity, and it alone is in a position to coordinate effectively this task. The states are still free to cooperate with the federal authorities in exposing subversion, but the responsibility of prosecuting individuals for subversive activities directed against the government of the United States should be left solely to the federal government.

Section 5(a) states that the Congress finds the distinction between advocacy of the forcible overthrow of the government as an incitement to action and advocacy of such overthrow as mere abstract doctrine is "subtle and difficult to grasp." Other than the fact that the courts have dealt with this distinction for fifty years, there is another reason for the perpetuation of this distinction. This distinction is necessary for compliance with the First Amendment.

The First Amendment contains the most basic individual liberties. It guarantees freedom of speech, freedom of press, and freedom of assembly. If a free society is to exist these three freedoms must be closely guarded. It is true that these freedoms can be restrained, but this can be done only under the rarest conditions. The "clear and present danger" doctrine, in this connection, first arose in *Schenck* v. *U.S.* (249 U.S. 47). The question to be determined, where there is an attempt to restrict the freedom of speech, is whether the words used are used in such circumstances and are of such a nature as to create a clear and present danger that will bring about substantive evils that Congress has a right to prevent. In my opinion, the advocacy or teaching of the overthrow of the government as a mere abstract doctrine is not a clear and present danger.

97.

EARL WARREN: *Perez* v. *Brownell*

Among its several provisions, the Nationality Act of 1940 declared that an American could forfeit his citizenship by voting in a political election in a foreign state. In Perez v. Brownell (1958) the Supreme Court upheld the constitutionality of the 1940 act in a 5 to 4 decision. The petitioner, although born in Texas, had resided outside the country from 1920 until 1943, and had voted in a Mexican election in 1946. Chief Justice Warren, in a dissent reprinted here in part, said that since citizenship is a man's basic right because it is the right to have rights, a government based on the sovereignty of the people cannot take away citizenship. On May 29, 1967, Warren's dissent became the law of the land when the Court in Afroyim v. Rusk declared the Nationality Act of 1940 unconstitutional. In this more recent case Justice Hugo Black's majority opinion (in another 5 to 4 decision) went beyond the case at issue and stated that the Fourteenth Amendment makes a citizen's nationality inviolate unless he voluntarily gives it up. Black noted that "Citizenship is no light trifle to be jeopardized at any moment Congress decides to do so under the name of one of its general or implied grants of power. The very nature of our free government makes it completely incongruous to have a rule of law under which a group of citizens temporarily in office can deprive another group of citizens of their citizenship."

Source: 356 U.S. 44.

THE CONGRESS of the United States has decreed that a citizen of the United States shall lose his citizenship by performing certain designated acts. The petitioner in this case, a native-born American, is declared to have lost his citizenship by voting in a foreign election. Whether this forfeiture of citizenship exceeds the bounds of the Constitution is the issue before us. The problem is fundamental and must be resolved upon fundamental considerations.

Generally, when congressional action is challenged, constitutional authority is found in the express and implied powers with which the national government has been invested or in those inherent powers that are necessary attributes of a sovereign state. The sweep of those powers is surely broad. In appropriate circumstances, they are adequate to take away life itself. The initial question here is whether citizenship is subject to the exercise of these general powers of government.

What is this government whose power is here being asserted? And what is the source of that power? The answers are the foundation of our republic. To secure the inalienable rights of the individual, "Governments are instituted among men, deriving their just powers from the consent of the governed." I do not believe the passage of time has lessened the truth of this proposition. It is basic to our form of government. This government was born of its citizens, it maintains itself in a continuing relationship with them, and, in my judgment, it is without power to sever the relationship that gives rise to its existence. I cannot believe that a government conceived in the spirit of ours was established with power to take from the people their most basic right.

Citizenship *is* man's basic right, for it is nothing less than the right to have rights. Remove this priceless possession and there remains a stateless person, disgraced and degraded in the eyes of his countrymen. He has no lawful claim to protection from any nation, and no nation may assert rights on his behalf. His very existence is at the sufferance of the state within whose borders he happens to be. In this country the expatriate would presumably enjoy, at most, only the limited rights and privileges of aliens, and like the alien he might even be subject to deportation and thereby deprived of the right to assert any rights. This government was not established with power to decree this fate.

The people who created this government endowed it with broad powers. They created a sovereign state with power to function as a sovereignty. But the citizens themselves are sovereign, and their citizenship is not subject to the general powers of their government. Whatever may be the scope of its powers to regulate the conduct and affairs of all persons within its jurisdiction, a government *of* the people cannot take away their citizenship simply because one branch of that government can be said to have a conceivably rational basis for wanting to do so. . . .

My conclusions are as follows. The government is without power to take citizenship away from a native-born or lawfully naturalized American. The Fourteenth Amendment recognizes that this priceless right is immune from the exercise of governmental powers. If the government determines that certain conduct by United States citizens should be prohibited because of anticipated injurious consequences to the conduct of foreign affairs or to some other legitimate governmental interest, it may within the limits of the Constitution proscribe such activity and assess appropriate punishment. But every exercise of governmental power must find its source in the Constitution.

The power to denationalize is not within the letter or the spirit of the powers with which our government was endowed. The citizen may elect to renounce his citizenship, and under some circumstances he may be found to have abandoned his status by voluntarily performing acts that compromise his undivided allegiance to his country. The mere act of voting in a foreign election, however, without regard to the circumstances attending the participation, is not sufficient to show a voluntary abandonment of citizenship.

The record in this case does not disclose any of the circumstances under which this petitioner voted. We know only the bare fact that he cast a ballot. The basic right of American citizenship has been too dearly won to be so lightly lost.

I fully recognize that only the most compelling considerations should lead to the invalidation of congressional action, and where legislative judgments are involved, this Court should not intervene. But the Court also has its duties, none of which demands more diligent performance than that of protecting the fundamental rights of individuals. That duty is imperative when the citizenship of an American is at stake — that status that alone assures him the full enjoyment of the precious rights conferred by our Constitution. As I see my duty in this case, I must dissent.

Three men in a rundown section of a Southern town

THE RIGHTS REVOLUTION

The average citizen in the mid-1950s, concerned as he was with the horrors and injustices of communism in Russia and Eastern Europe and with the specter of Communist infiltration in his own government, was doubtless taken by surprise when questions of justice and democracy were raised within the United States itself. Led chiefly by the NAACP, a campaign was begun to bring equal rights and opportunities to Negro citizens, beginning with an attack on public school segregation. The sudden violent reaction of Southern white citizens proved what Negroes had known for four hundred years — they were considered, at best, as second-class citizens. The civil rights movement rapidly gained momentum in the second half of the decade as the nonviolent direct-action tactic preached by the Rev. Martin Luther King, Jr., was used to desegregate schools and public accommodations throughout the South. King and his followers — Southern Negroes, Northern liberals, college students both black and white — were met with violence at every turn; when police did not attack directly, they stood idly by as white mobs did. While the nonviolent movement gained legal reforms, few practical results could be seen in the lives of Negroes in the South or in Northern cities. Basic change was clearly necessary. By 1960 a note of militancy was creeping into the movement as the efficacy of nonviolence began to be doubted.

(Above) Negro woman picking cotton in an Arkansas field in 1953; (below) Negro workers in New Orleans in the 1920s; photograph by Arnold Genthe

(Above) Crowd of whites watching the lynching of two Negroes somewhere in the South in the 1920s; (below) scene in Whitley General Store, Wendell, N.C., 1939

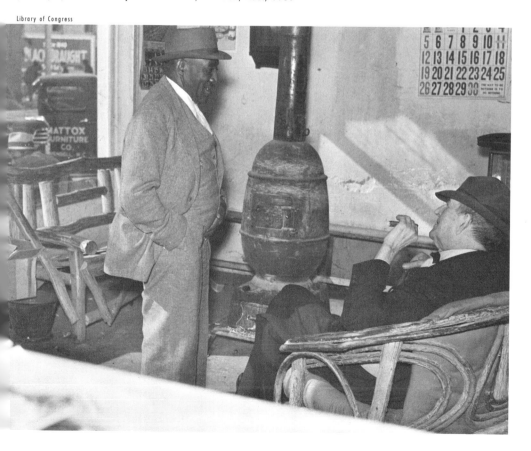

(Above) Scene in Harlem, N.Y., in the 1940s; (below) apartment houses and a funeral parlor in a Negro section of Chicago, 1941

(Above) A group of young girls playing on a Harlem street; (below) lonely man on a bench in New York's Central Park

(Left) Marcus Garvey, leader of a "Back to Africa" movement in the 1920s. He was deported in 1927; (above) Father Divine, who sought to relieve the Depression by planning outings and picnics for residents of Harlem; (below) sign in a Harlem bookstore

(Above) Negro mother leads her child past segregationist pickets outside a public school in Nashville, Tenn., as integration begins in fall 1957; (left) first day of integration in Oklahoma

In 1954 the Supreme Court handed down a unanimous decision reversing the "separate but equal" doctrine that the court had sanctioned in 1896. The immediate reaction in the states affected was outrage. Nullification was revived as "interposition" and several states completely ignored orders to desegregate public schools. The climax in Little Rock, Arkansas, in 1957, aroused public opinion around the world; the successful desegregation of Central High School by federal troops did not, however, end segregation in the South. Legal delaying tactics and the loss of public attention allowed Southern authorities to avoid compliance with Supreme Court rulings apparently indefinitely.

(Above) Restless youths of Little Rock, Ark., at the beginning of school integration, 1957; (left) National Guard forces the school to remain open and orderly in the face of local protest; (below) Herblock cartoon, 1956

"Tsk Tsk—Somebody Should Do Something About That"

National Guard keeps order in Cicero, Ill., after an outbreak of racial disturbances

(Above and below) Two incidents during the attempt to integrate Levittown, N.J., 1957

(Above) Mrs. Rosa Parks, whose actions began the bus boycott; (right) Martin Luther King arrested in Montgomery; (below) boycott leaders ride an integrated bus, December 1956

In December 1955 Rosa Parks, a seamstress in Montgomery, Alabama, refused to give up her bus seat to a white man; she was arrested and fined for violating local segregation ordinances. Rev. Martin Luther King, Jr., organized a boycott of the municipal bus company that culminated a year later in a federal district court's decision that segregated intrastate transportation was unconstitutional.

98.

John D. Williams: The Nonsense About Safe Driving

The automobile killed upwards of 35,000 Americans each year during the 1950s, a fact that deeply distressed many of the survivors. The issue of traffic safety did not explode into the headlines until the publication of Ralph Nader's slashing indictment of the American automotive industry, Unsafe at Any Speed, *in 1965, by which time the yearly toll was approaching its present level of 50,000 men, women, and children. However, there was another side to the argument, as revealed in the article reprinted below. Written by the head of the mathematics division of the Rand Corporation and first published in 1958, the article discussed some of the "myths" of the automobile's critics and suggested that many of the proposed solutions of the problem were nothing more than emotionally based panaceas. Williams' remarks, of course, should be read in the light of subsequent research, much of which is reported on in Nader's book. Nevertheless, the view here represented by Williams is more than merely iconoclastic.*

Source: *Fortune*, September 1958.

EVERY OUNCE OF ENERGY I have seen devoted to the subject of automobile accidents has been aimed at reducing the present level. I should like to make the point that this may or may not be a useful aim. Most campaigns now are based on nonsense premises, such as cut-down-the-horsepower-and-save-lives. These are groping attempts to place an absolute limit on speed, and this is a strictly antisocial concept. I am sure that you cannot eliminate automobile accidents without eliminating the automobile. I am sure that there is, in effect, a desirable level of automobile accidents — desirable, that is, from a broad point of view; in the sense that it is a necessary concomitant of things of greater value to society.

We accept it as a creed that human life is priceless and react involuntarily against anything that kills. In so doing we confuse the values of the individual and of society. For instance, my life is priceless to me: there are probably things for which I'd give it up, but it isn't something I regard as part of my normal stock in trade. It is worth a lot to my family, but clearly it is less fundamental to them than to me. It is worth less to my associates than to my family, less to my community than to my associates, and so on. The loss of my life would not produce an observable effect on society, and this is literally true for most of us.

The automobile kills about 100 people a day, which seems terrible to the individual. But society is more used to death and recognizes the obvious need for it. Over 4,000 of our citizens die every day — and over 10,000 are born every day. (In the end we may be standing on each other's heads, an exercise poorly suited to the old people who will dominate society.) In any case, I doubt that the present total number of deaths, of which the automobile accounts for 2 or 3 percent, is undesirably large for the well-being of society, and it may in fact be undesirably small. From these facts we at least gain the perspective that the automobile is not exterminating us, so we can afford to approach the problem calmly.

A few years ago someone conceived the idea of a national No Death Day for automobile traffic. To be against this would seem like being against Mother's Day, so men of goodwill everywhere supported it. But if the program were serious, we would just have to take the vehicles off the road for twenty-four hours. It would be a day long remembered. On a normal day tens of thousands go to hospitals, but on this day tens of thousands would not. Doctors normally see hundreds of thousands of patients at home or office, but not this day. Firemen normally control thousands of fires, but not this day. Police normally control thousands of criminals and malefactors of all kinds, but not this day. And so on. In fact, we should be pretty lucky if the deaths in the population rose by only a thousand on No Death Day.

This gives us some clues to the importance of the automobile to our society. The automobile has a large credit balance at the end of each day in precisely the coin we tend to worry about: lives. (Incidentally, the conspicuous lifesaving operations — which would be absent in the No Death Day drama — tend to be carried out at relatively high speeds and more frequently than not under dangerous traffic conditions.)

Does the 100 deaths per day figure suggest that we are conducting the technical operation of mass transportation in a grossly careless manner? The general tone of public statements would certainly imply that this is so. Almost every person who has had access to and used mass media of communication to discuss traffic safety has contributed to the impression that the American motorist is grossly careless and thought-less, and even bent on homicide. I don't read the record that way. Practically all of the people in the country from teen-age children to old men and women drive automobiles. The quantity of kinetic energy loose on our roads — taking into account the increased numbers, weights, and speeds — is perhaps ten times what it was a quarter of a century ago. It is a significant fact that the daily traffic death rate has remained fairly constant at about 25 deaths a year per 100,000 of population over this same long period. Whatever else this proves, it should scotch the canard that today's driver is maniacal.

Our overt efforts at control of this symptom of a large operation — psychological attacks, legal and police action, and such — have had little to do with this record. The dominant factor has been the improvement in the physical equipment. There have been improvements in the vehicles, but the most important improvement has been in the roads, which have tended to get wider, straighter, and smoother.

The important fact about the automobile is not that it kills 100 people a day but rather that it has been a crucial factor in the development of a fantastically complex and rich society. It has given us a new degree of personal mobility that we have exploited to develop the industrial complex, to provide ourselves with agreeable homes, a social life rich in choices, and a new degree of personal safety from the hazards of life. The important point about the new federal highway system is not that it will cut down accidents but that it will greatly stimulate our economy — and enlarge the choices we, as individuals, will have to make. . . .

The physical factor of greatest significance is unquestionably speed — precisely the item we have the strongest instinct to tamper with in the interest of reducing accidents. For consider that, while we move great loads of goods and people by road, the vehicle most characteristic is one that contains one person bent on a personal mission. If speed were not the critical factor, this vehicle could be replaced completely and literally by a horse. The physical and social structure of the country would be almost frozen in its present attitude were we to freeze the speed of the automobile.

Speed is one of the really crucial factors in our society. As with any crucial factor, it is promising to look for more — in this case, more speed. I cannot help but believe that we would manage better if we were conscious of the need for more speed rather than believing the exact contrary.

There is an almost involuntary impulse immediately to add, "But not too much speed." Now no one could advocate "too much" speed — that's bad by definition — but the question of when speed does become "too much" is a very thorny question. I encounter situations where, in my opinion, 10 mph is too much, and others where 80 mph is not too much, and the variations in the situations are too great to be controlled very intelligently by fiat and in advance. The speed at which vehicles have in fact operated from time to time has been determined principally by the drivers, who want very much to live, who have substantial personal investments in their hands, and who also know that any injury they do to other persons or property will entail very unpleasant consequences. Their intelligence, judgment, and skill are not always a match for the situations, but in general they have managed to exploit the equipment available without undue damage. They generally drive faster than those who seek to control speed think they should, but as the interested parties on the spot, their views are probably more nearly right than those of their critics. They are burdened by some feelings of guilt about the letter of the law, and they are subject to assault in the form of a fine or imprisonment if they are caught out

of bounds. This business of making us into a lot of lawbreakers has been an unfortunate aspect of the development of the use of vehicles.

The situation may become intolerable as the technical devices of detection and control, such as radar, improve; intolerable in the sense that the utility of the vehicle may be lessened by strong enforcement of inappropriate, however well-intentioned, laws. Our laws tend to be aimed at the limitation of speed rather than at the promotion of traffic flow.

Psychological factors also seem to play large roles in the use of automobiles. Consider the phenomenon of new communities. As our mobility has increased, we have built more cities. It would not be astonishing to discover, after the fact, that we average a new city when we average an increase of one mile per hour in speed. Consider this example: Suppose it is ten miles from a prospective homesite to work. It will require fifteen minutes of travel time if the traveler can average 40 mph, or twenty minutes if he can average but 30 mph. This is the kind of example that anti-speed advocates love. It is obvious that the five minutes saved at 40 mph isn't worth much, directly. If the man earns $5 an hour, it is apparently worth 42 cents, and he may expend rubber worth this much in one high-speed stop. The kinetic energy of the automobile increases as the square of the speed, so it is up by a factor of 16.9, an increase of almost 80 percent, which may be a fair measure of the increased hazard. So why travel at 40 mph?

Such an analysis would miss an essential point: the driver is not motivated by those five minutes as minutes. In fact, he may not know within five minutes how long it takes. But the experience strongly affects important decisions. It may be that he has a feeling of well-being when moving rapidly and that he has one of intense irritation while sitting and staring at a red light. He may as a consequence decide not to live in that particular spot after all. If many others feel as he does, a community may not develop. So the five minutes, which means nothing to the individual driver and which is not very significant even when thousands of drivers are aggregated, may have a major effect on society. Thus there is an apparently irrational factor that tends to increase the importance of speed. Or one may look on speed as a catalyst that triggers other forces. It has undoubtedly been strongly instrumental in developing our urban civilization. Unfortunately it is so sensitive that the lawmaker who frames an unnecessarily inhibiting regulation, the local authority that installs in the hamlet two unnecessary, ill-timed traffic signals, or even the man who paints a white line on the highway in the wrong place, can inadvertently impose a loss on society.

I have belabored the subject in this fashion because the viewpoint is not the conventional one among persons concerned with traffic safety. Yet it seems to me that a simple, direct approach to traffic safety is likely to lead to a misformulation of the problem, which in turn leads to solutions that do more harm than good.

If, on the contrary, one recognizes that the central problem is to promote the smooth and rapid flow of lots of traffic, one is likely to devise measures that will in fact operate in this direction — and it will probably have reasonable safety. I cannot resist mentioning a few measures that have occurred to me, though they are mostly obvious ones, and of uneven importance.

Separation of traffic lanes is very important. The overwhelming bulk of our roads still mix opposing streams of traffic. It is a wonder that the death toll from head-on collisions alone is not much greater than 100 a day. It is not greater because the drivers want to live, so they tend to match their speeds to those of the slower vehicles.

Thus the cost to society of two-way roads is vastly greater than one would infer from the death toll on them, even when that toll is relatively high.

There are important unsolved management problems regarding our roads. We have, for example, very rudimentary means for coping with trouble. Anything from a vapor lock to a major accident can lead to a snarl tying up thousands of vehicles for hours. We need powerful means for unsnarling these knots quickly, even at the expense of deferring (and possibly compromising) the questions as to what happened and why. Simple tow equipment and helicopter ambulances seem like natural tools. The ubiquitous policeman could do more with a nylon towrope than he could with his gun and notebook.

The traffic light is a useful device to promote the flow of cross traffic when the density on two roads is at a certain level, but it isn't the best device for all levels of density and for all purposes. It is used indiscriminately by the million for purposes deliberately inimicable to traffic flow — like a left turn. And since traffic lights never seem to disappear, we need a man with the authority and responsibility to collect and junk unnecessary ones.

The useless ritual around school zones has some of the elements of No Death Day — notably, high emotional content and little reflection. Most of the time that children are at school they are required to be inside the school in fixed groups and outside the building they are kept in supervised play areas (fenced, or they should be fenced). They are safer from vehicles than at any other time in their waking lives. The time they need extra protection is during the periods they are in transit between home and school. The problem is soluble in ways more useful to society than posting school zones with extraordinary speed restrictions. Perhaps if the energy and money now spent on superfluous traffic lights were spent on school-crossing-in-use lights, the restrictions on the speed of vehicles could be confined to times when they could do some good.

I have argued that safety is a secondary matter from the viewpoint of society. However, it is a legitimate personal concern for the individual and he may help himself to things that will ameliorate the dangers, *e.g.,* seat belts (or better, shoulder harnesses), crash helmets, and roll bars. They are probably more useful to the average driver than to the racing driver because they are more likely to be effective in a low-speed crash than in a high-speed one.

The National Safety Council may do all sorts of unpublicized good works, but the only thing it is generally known for is its activity as a spoilsport. On the formal holidays of our society the council stands about deploring the number who will be killed by automobiles, the implication being that if we would only be sensible this wouldn't happen. I question the value of these warnings. They don't even have the professional merit of being difficult to make! What organizations like the National Safety Council should be doing is putting on campaigns for shoulder harnesses, crash helmets, or any other equipment they feel is useful — campaigns aimed at both the individual and the automobile manufacturer.

We should urge the manufacturers to invent more advanced signaling equipment. The brake-operated rear light has been standard equipment for a third of a century, the turn indicator for a tenth of a century. Is that all they can think of? Automobiles traveling at high speed slow up abruptly when the driver lifts his foot from the accelerator. How about a slowing-up light?

Let us be done with attempts to restrict horsepower. They are pretty silly attempts: it is surprising how little horsepower it takes to go 100 mph if you design for it. The principal function of lots of horsepower is to increase maneuverability, which may either increase or decrease safety in a specific instance, but which in general we should presume increases it; there must be some net advantage in having vehicles that will more often do what you want them to do when you want them to do it.

Safety is a nice thing to have in specific cases, but one can easily overdo its use — just as, in using our wonder drugs, one must not try to kill all the bugs. The motto of everyone concerned with traffic should be "Keep It Moving." The odds are that no matter what one does to that end, something good will come of it. The odds are that whatever one does that is contrary to the motto will have a detrimental effect.

Drive carefully; the life you save may be your own.
Common highway sign, U.S.

Have all the traffic lights on the streets turn red — and keep them that way.
GEORGE S. KAUFMAN, solution for the New York traffic problem

99.

Health and Medical Care

Concern about the status of America's health and medical services was particularly marked during the 1950s. President Truman had proposed a government-sponsored medical care program in 1945, but American conservatives, and particularly the doctors themselves (under the leadership of the American Medical Association), opposed such proposals vigorously. The question at issue was not only whether American medicine was good enough in itself but also whether it was as good as that of other Western countries. An evaluation of the quality of American medical services was undertaken by the Rockefeller Brothers Fund in the mid-1950s, the results of which, along with a program for the next fifteen years, were published in 1958. A portion of the report is reprinted here.

Source: *The Challenge to America: Its Economic and Social Aspects,* Special Studies Project Report IV, New York, 1958, pp. 312-315.

HEALTH IN ITS BROADEST ASPECTS has an importance to our nation second only to our national security. The advances in this field during the past few decades have been remarkable. The gradual extension of the average lifetime offers ample evidence of the results of medical research, preventive medicine, and health education. The infectious diseases have ceased to be major causes of death; the hazards of childbirth have been largely overcome.

But the more rapid our progress is, the greater the necessity that we think ahead in the field of health. The broad national policies that such a "look ahead" suggests are outlined below.

Medical Research

The toll of today's leading killing and crippling diseases, such as cancer, cardiovascular diseases, and mental illness, is staggering in both human and economic terms. In addition, many new types of health problems and opportunities are emerging today that demand intensive investigation.

The acquisition of new knowledge is basic to advancing national health. We recommend, therefore, continued expansion of our medical research programs as rapidly as the supply of scientific talent will permit.

As we step up medical research efforts, equal strides must be taken toward putting their results to use more rapidly. We recommend that public health authorities and private medical groups join in a study analyzing the extent of the time lag between the acquisition of new medical knowledge and its practical availability to the general public, identifying the causes of delay and delineating measures to reduce it.

Medical Manpower

We are short of doctors in many parts of the country and also of many categories of medical specialists. The number of doctors should increase in relation to total population, whereas it appears now to be constant or declining in relation to population. We urge immediate steps to overcome this trend, including maximum possible utilization of the facilities of existing medical schools and immediate planning for the inauguration of new medical schools.

The existing medical schools are having serious financial difficulties. If private fund-raising efforts and indirect government aids prove inadequate, we would recommend consideration of a federal-state program of assistance to the operational budgets of the medical schools.

Federal and state loan and scholarship programs, in addition to increased scholarship funds from private sources, commend themselves as a means of helping the student to overcome the high cost of medical education, which is not recouped by the student for many years. Similar measures to encourage the training of more professional and practical nurses should be continued and expanded.

Medical Facilities

Subject to the limitations imposed by personnel shortages (particularly nursing and technical personnel), we need in most areas of the country more hospitals and other health facilities of many kinds. The increase in chronic disease and the needs of an aging population highlight the necessity for substantial expansion of facilities for long-term care, particularly of high quality nursing homes for the care of the aged with moderate impairments.

We recommend the use of a portion of available hospital construction funds for developing radically new types of medical facilities, such as hospitals permitting maximum self-help and community care centers offering diagnostic services and extensive outpatient treatment and homemaker services.

At the same time, modernization and re-

habilitation of existing hospitals — particularly older ones in large cities — must be a major target of the next decade. We suggest consideration of low-interest state loans for this purpose.

Paying the Costs of Medical Care

As medical practice has become more complex and specialized, it has become apparent that cooperative efforts among practising physicians can enhance the quality of care given. The first question is how best to achieve this. The second is how to pay for high quality medical care so as to spread costs among a large group of individuals and families, and over years of high and low health costs for each individual or family. The increasing costs of hospital and medical care lend urgency to this question.

One approach, adopted effectively in some communities, is group medical practice, affiliated with a common hospital, and with essentially all costs prepaid by the subscribers through family health insurance premiums. The range of physician services covered by the fees should be comprehensive in scope. The resulting incentives tend to emphasize preventive care and early diagnostic services and to minimize unnecessary hospitalization. We believe that this group-practice prepayment approach, although by no means suited to all communities, could be advantageously adopted by more communities.

Health centers established by industry and labor in connection with a place of employment also offer great possibilities for improved health care.

Irrespective of the form through which physician's services are provided, we urge as a major objective of prepayment plans over the next decade the coverage of doctor's and nursing care *outside* the hospital. Such coverage can serve as a real encouragement to early discovery and treatment of physical defects and illness, thereby resulting in better health and lower costs, and to shorter periods of hospitalization.

More people should be covered by the newer "catastrophic illness" plans, designed to help meet extraordinary costs of accident or illness over and above the costs met by a comprehensive basic plan. The cost of this protection, when spread over a large group, is relatively small — provided that the underlying basic plan is broad in the scope of services covered and encourages rather than discourages early use of diagnostic services and facilities.

For the present needy aged and for the "medically indigent" who cannot afford to pay for protection even under basic health prepayment plans, financing from general tax revenues — federal, state, or local, or a combination of the three — seems essential.

100.

LAWRENCE GOWING: The White of American Painters

Abstract Expressionism, the first major American contribution to painting in the Western world, was in part a result of America's artistic isolation in the years between the world wars. The international impact of the new style made New York the painting capital of the West. Although the school was trying to break away from a "typically American" style, there is much in their work that suggests that it could only have been produced in America. This was particularly true of certain characteristics of Abstract Expressionism (for example, the giant canvases, the boldness of design, and above all the use of white paint), in the opinion of such European critics as Lawrence Gowing, a British painter and art historian. He published some observations on American art in an article published in 1958 and reprinted here in part.

Source: *New Statesman*, May 24, 1958.

NOTHING ATTRACTS LIKE AN IDEA. When artistic Europe saw itself falling for American abstract painting and, enraptured, plunged deliberately head over heels, what captivated it was not any visible picture or painter but the American idea. The tributes that European painters paid and are paying to paint itself, to the automatic splash and trickle of it, and the glamor of its crude nature as it comes from the tin, are tributes in fact to the logical necessity of a certain line of thought.

The infatuation has proceeded almost independent of its real object. The idea of American painting has worked an extraordinary liberation, a liberation from ideas about painting, which has a particular force for the self-conscious painter in Europe. But it is doubtful if there is a painter in Europe who loves many real American pictures. It is not easy here even to know many, and books . . . with good reproductions of large numbers of good examples of both fashionable and other kinds are needed. At present, when a representative collection of American pictures is imported, it is not much enjoyed. There seem to be too many pictures, or too few by too many artists, or the wrong ones (even when they are the best). The size of the gestures they make looks out of scale. *Something* is always wrong. In Europe one might suppose that the American achievement consisted in nothing so much as its idea, in the cynical realism with which it has boiled down the aesthetic of the age. Here in Europe the paint to which painting is reduced embodies a principle — a faith pursued to its fatalistic extremity (and the fatalism is chic) — but not much else.

Seen in America, American painting embodies something very different. Quite another meaning fills it. The program and the line of talk are seen to serve something else, which no one has been able to imitate or export.

In any art anywhere there is something more radical than the idea. There is a visual substance older than the intention, older than the skills and devices: it is there before style can be there. The essential base of art is in the place before there is an artist; understanding art, we comprehend both together — the common substance and the specific expression. Just as it was possible once for Europe to borrow the Corinthian order whole, from curling head to foot, without understanding the Renaissance in the least, for lack of its Italian substance, so now the flourishes of the American style travel everywhere, but without the meaning which they derive from the imaginative landscape of a specific community at a certain time.

To know anything about this art (about any art, perhaps) one must know almost everything. One may start anywhere. Look, for example, at the paint itself in its most famous manifestations — at the indispensable strand of white paint in Jackson Pollock's net, or the white strips in the paint-

ing of Bradley Tomlin. Grasping the substance that this one color possesses in its own world, we have to reconstruct elements which are there effortlessly assumed and retrieve something immemorial (of which perhaps no American will tell us). First, as always, we have to share senses of structure and material which are native to the place; we have to recognize the abstracted physique of forms and qualities which are everywhere supplied by building.

When De Tocqueville, a century and a half ago, found that the little marble palaces along the shore of the Hudson River were made of wood, it seemed to him the final give-away, the clearest sign of what democracy, the rule of quantity over quality, does to the arts. One of the few disappointments in the welcome new collection of Sir Herbert Read's essays is that when he read De Tocqueville on American art he felt there was no more to say. It is the quality of wood which has lasted in America and remains as strong as ever, a quality as definite and pervasive as marble ever gave to a country, and one that similarly supplies the base of life and imagination. The classical material of American building is wood and the characteristic structure is clapboard, framed surfaces of overlapping strips. It is painted white. Here at the outset we have elementary preconceptions (our bungalows, *potting-sheds*) and an elephantine condescension to discard. We have also, even though we recognize that American architecture is the great architecture of the last two hundred years, a deeper adjustment to make, an adjustment of fantasy as well as sense to a new direction, as positive as the direction that we associate with De Tocqueville's marble and opposite to it, a direction which only to us seems uninhabited by marble's lovely associations. The adjustment may be hardly possible without the place to give the clue.

If we can make the adjustment, the conception of building takes on a new and spe cific meaning. In America the idea of structure envisages a broad assembly of slender parts, standing squarely, but with a quality of light attentiveness, independent but aware. The construction balances vertical against horizontal, major upright members against the delicate level ruling of boarded surfaces. In the balance there is the most lively serenity: it is recognizably embodied in the color, the white paint.

All this formal meaning — the counterpart of a certain human stance and frame of mind — is contained in American white paint. It was there almost from the start, in the broad American canvases of Copley, in their sharp white planes with thin overlapping edges and the level grooves of human features, the signs of an incomparably sharp and level vision. Copley raises to great art the qualities of whiteness and striplike straightness and thinness — the qualities of linen and straight looks from lined faces — which make beautiful the symbolic presentations (very near to the common base of art) of the journeymen-portraitists who were also house painters.

The other implication of architectural whiteness, the balance of vertical against horizontal, and the togate stoicism of mood, was similarly fixed in painting at the outset, in the early style of Benjamin West who carried an essential quality of Pennsylvania, naïvely preserved within him, to Rome and London. It remains the strongest of all the country's patterns, and unimaginably stronger in America than in any other place or style. The frame of horizontal and vertical which building makes, now more than ever, is communicated to every structure, every visible system of intervals, every surface. Its meaning, its regular reference is communicated to forms which are not rectangular at all but freely curving and capricious, the freer for the presence of the frame. The clapboard frame house (any house, old or new, of those around almost any town) sets up a rhythm which extends beyond it, sideways and also upward, among the trees (typically, the house is built among trees, wood among wood). The rhythms catch hold among the branches; trunks and limbs are claimed in order by the same system. (The trees take on a special, different look; no doubt they are different; no doubt they originally gave some of their special character to building.)

The white-painted building imparts its order high into the threading arabesque, and the clear gray of sun-brightened bark which is the natural accompaniment of white in America and American painting (the random symmetry produced involuntarily and invariably by Pollock never looks arbitrary again after this), and out into the sky. The sky is the far, continental sky, which the European never sees, with its distant, extreme blue. Wherever there is white paint, this color too is in mind. When the colors come together, with their peculiar, fluorescent-seeming sharpness, in the canvases of Bradley Tomlin, the combination is immediately recognized.

The whiteness of building and paint is enriched with still further associations. Their whiteness is also the white of paper. The black and white of print, and its characteristic forms, contribute to the white and black of painting. The bold, bad letter forms (as they look in Europe, where graphic style is fixed in a shape as clearly cut as De Tocqueville's marble) have a serious force which here we can hardly read, the force of a communal ideal in which independence and ungoverned enterprise are inseparable. (There is more of American art on the reverse of a one-dollar bill than in any European commentary.) The broad letter, with its fat vertical stroke balanced, naturally, against thin horizontals, forms the concentrated basis of a new style, resting, as style does anywhere, on the style of the society.

The natural graphic consistency of America, the unity of free, disparate shapes — the consistency of the clustering proliferation of signs over any sidewalk — belongs to a country in which the natural consistency and unity is simply the new, unknown consistency of human behavior let loose in an immense and empty space. This style is cut, not as marble is but in the manner that sheet metal is cut, in the same sharp manner as the cluster of signs — the metal arrows pointing with internal fluorescent light to this or that, metal seafood, dry goods, and the curling metal signatures of soft drinks — are cut out against the continental sky. Seen in place, the cut shapes of Stuart Davis call to mind, never the *papiers collés* of Matisse but their own grand, fluorescent source. Seen there, it is precisely the serif-like terminations to Bradley Tomlin's strips of paint that give them the quality of characters spelling out the consistency of natural disorder and representing with material realism a real place.

In some such way the resources of painting snowball, accumulating meaning and depositing it in the raw material of art. All this, and more, is contained in the white of American painters. It is already in the tin when they buy it. It is on the canvas before they touch it. To reconstruct in Europe the artistic substance of America may be hardly possible; its connection with our own is often slight. Its antecedents are no more than half European; its birth and rebirth are wholly American. No other art is likely to be born again in just this way, in the American shape. The paint in its pot is different.

Why did the American idea not occur to anyone before? It did; it was in the air in Europe for a quarter of a century. It required to be filled with the unique American substance, the material poetry of the country, to gain its present force.

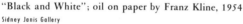

"Black and White"; oil on paper by Franz Kline, 1954
Sidney Janis Gallery

1958 - 1959

101.

Statehood for Hawaii

Statehood for Hawaii and Alaska had been often proposed but never very seriously considered by the Congress until the Republicans urged it in their platform in 1952. After his election, President Eisenhower retreated somewhat and suggested that Hawaii alone become a state, and the issue was argued throughout most of his administration. Alaska was finally admitted as the forty-ninth state on January 3, 1959, and Hawaii, as the fiftieth, on August 21 of the same year. The following selection, in two parts, comprises some remarks by an opponent of Hawaiian statehood, Senator George W. Malone of Nevada, inserted into the Congressional Record *on March 21, 1958, and a statement in favor by Secretary of the Interior Fred A. Seaton, given before a Senate subcommittee in February 1959.*

Source: *Record,* 85 Cong., 2 Sess., pp. 5041-5042.
       Record, 86 Cong., 1 Sess., pp. 3394-3395.

I.

GEORGE W. MALONE:
Against Statehood

THE COMMITTEE on Interior and Insular Affairs has reported S. 50 favorably to the Senate, and is expected to report S. 49 the same. I voted in committee against these bills to provide statehood for Hawaii and Alaska, and submit herewith for consideration by the Senate the reasons for my opposition.

Since first elected to the United States Senate, I have consistently voted against Hawaiian and Alaskan statehood mainly because this nation has never granted statehood to any noncontiguous territory; and it is not conceivable to me that at this time we could ever have a homogeneous people through the acceptance of offshore areas widely separated from the mainland, where perhaps not over 1 percent of the inhabitants would ever visit the mainland. In these noncontiguous areas, a great bulk of the people have no direct knowledge of life and conditions in the United States, and because of this their ways of life are different from ours. Consequently, they are much more vulnerable to infiltration by the exponents of ideologies and theories which are contrary and dangerous to the American philosophy of life and government.

In Hawaii, the Communist-infiltrated International Longshoremen's and Warehousemen's Union is all-powerful. The political life of the islands is controlled and dominated by this union, and through Hawaiian statehood, Moscow, in effect, could achieve representation in the United States Senate.

The acceptance of a noncontiguous territory like Hawaii or Alaska — and they would all be clamoring for admission if we granted the privilege to one — would result in a disruption of the balance of power in our legislative form of government. It is entirely within the realm of possibility that a group of senators, representing a way of life not in accord with ours, could easily control a balance of power in the United States Senate. Hawaii has one three-thousandth of the population of the United States, and if admitted to the Union would be given one forty-ninth of the total vote and power in the Senate. If Alaskan statehood, which is also before the Senate, is approved, both the territories would be given one twenty-fifth of the total vote and power in the Senate.

In denying statehood to these noncontiguous territories, I do not propose that we keep them as subject colonies. In 1953 I introduced a self-government bill for Hawaii and a similar bill for Alaska was introduced by the late Senator Hugh Butler of Nebraska. I have introduced in this Congress S. 35 and S. 36 to provide for the election of a governor and for the adoption of a constitution, approved by the Congress of the United States and by the people of the territory involved, for both Hawaii and Alaska. The bills also provide for the appointment of the justices of the Supreme Court of the territories by the governor and with the consent and advice of the Senate of the territories in each case.

Senate Bill 36 provides that the people of the Territory of Hawaii may organize a government pursuant to a constitution of their own adoption and specifically states that such a constitution shall provide a republican representative form of government and shall include a bill of rights subject to the approval of the Congress of the United States.

I believe that is the proper step in government for all territories of the United States which are of sufficient size and importance to merit such self-government.

The commonwealth status that my bill provides does not impose second-class citizenship upon the residents of Hawaii. Quite the contrary; they would be almost completely independent. They would govern themselves and they would have from $135 million to $140 million a year that now goes into federal taxes to improve an economic system which has been operating in the red for some time. As a self-governing state freely associated with the United States, using the same postal system and with the courts of law associated with our federal courts, as our state courts are at the present, Hawaii could develop to the full extent of its capabilities through the foundation of new industries to utilize its reservoir of skilled labor, and the same situation may be made applicable to Alaska.

I was one of five Senators who visited Puerto Rico in 1947. The question of statehood for that area was just as hot then as the Hawaiian and Alaskan question is now. At that time we recommended against statehood and suggested complete autonomy, subject, of course, to the provisions of the United States Constitution. This was done and in 1952 Congress approved the Puerto Rican constitution.

Today, after seven years of self-government, Puerto Rico has raised itself from a situation once described by our committee as unsolvable because it was ridden with disease, slums, and poverty, to a standard of living reported to be the highest in the Caribbean. Puerto Rico has not forgotten statehood by any means, though its government is working very well and the people are not complaining.

If we admit Hawaii and Alaska to the Union, we will be establishing a precedent that will be used by other noncontiguous and island areas as support for their statehood arguments. I should like to emphasize strongly that our own independence of thought and action is involved. Our own independence to determine the course which the United States wishes to pursue in national and international policy is indelibly linked to what we do with the Hawaiian and Alaskan statehood bills.

It has been argued that the way to stop wars is for the United States to take in many outside areas, foreign nations or states, and that by taking them into a "United States of the World" and giving them representation on the Senate floor we would stop the incentive for wars. Many international organizations, believing as they do that the sovereignty of this nation should be sacrificed to a world organization, are sincere in their advocacy of even European nations being admitted as states.

Once we had relinquished the rule that we shall not take into the Union any territories outside the North American continent, what reason could we give, once a precedent was established in Hawaii and Alaska, for not granting similar statehood to the Philippines, Okinawa, Samoa, Guam, and many others? The French people started the practice of admitting their colonial areas' representatives to their assembly many years ago. The resulting instability of that body should make other countries wary of the practice.

We are dealing with a much wider question with broader implications than those who support these bills would have the Senate believe. I am firmly convinced that once we break the precedent on noncontig-

uous areas, there is no stopping place. We must remember that granting statehood to Hawaii is an irrevocable act, and once it is done it cannot be undone.

Congress must proceed with the utmost caution and with the fullest deliberation of these issues which effect such a radical change in the structure of our government and our external relations.

II.

FRED A. SEATON:
For Statehood

THERE CAN BE no possible question concerning the position of the administration on Hawaii statehood. Since this Congress convened, the President has on several occasions urged the Congress to admit Hawaii into the Union as a state. You are dealing this year not with an enabling act but with an admission act. We of the executive branch wholeheartedly concur in this approach and recommend that the bill before you be dealt with as expeditiously as possible. . . . To me, there can be no question properly raised as to whether Hawaii should become a state. The question is simply when shall Hawaii become a state?

As a personal observation, I believe that the language we all use in referring to the admission of Hawaii into the Union is not technically correct. Hawaii is as much a part of this Union today as any state. As an incorporated territory, and the only one we have left, Hawaiians are subject to all of the obligations imposed upon any citizen in any state by the federal government. The problem arises because they are denied some of the most precious prerogatives of freemen, among them equal representation and the right to vote in national elections.

The record is also clear on another aspect of the subject before you. Since the incorporation of Hawaii into the Union, Hawaiians have developed their islands at a rapid pace. Any part of the Hawaiian economy, culture, philosophy, or political institutions that is examined today will be found to be a duplicate of or modeled after the way of life in vogue in the continental United States. Hawaii is the picture window of the Pacific through which the peoples of the East look into our American front room.

This will be particularly important in our future dealings with the peoples of Asia, because a large percentage of the population of Hawaii is of Oriental or Polynesian racial extraction. The participation of the people of Hawaii in the full measure of the benefits of American citizenship will bring a fresh, new, informed outlook to our councils. More significantly, the peoples of those eastern lands washed by the waters of the Pacific will look through that front window of ours and take renewed notice that we do, indeed, practise what we preach. There can be no finer way to demonstrate the dynamic nature of our Union and the everlasting validity of the principles upon which our republic was founded than by the admission of Hawaii as a state in this session of Congress.

While I have mentioned the racial background of some Hawaiians, let me hasten to point out that it would be both unfair and inaccurate to conclude that the objectives of Hawaiian people are in any way foreign to those of any other American group. No conclusion could be further from the truth. The overwhelming majority of Hawaiians are native-born Americans — they know no other loyalty and acclaim their American citizenship as proudly as you and I.

Their economy is self-sustaining — Hawaii is adequately prepared, financially, for the burdens of statehood. More than a million tons of sugar, worth nearly $150 million, are produced annually from over 200,000 acres of cane. Capital investment in this industry amounts to nearly $200 mil-

"Aloha!"; cartoon by Hutton in the "Philadelphia Inquirer," 1959

lion, of which about $50 million is in irrigation facilities alone. In sugar-production techniques and per-acre production, Hawaii leads the world, and its hourly rated employees receive the world's highest year-round agricultural wages.

Hawaii also produces 85 percent of the total U.S. supply of canned pineapple products; which is to say 65 percent of the world's production. Pineapple production utilizes about 75,000 acres of intensely cultivated land and provides employment for over 22,000 people annually. The annual value of the output, estimated at about $115 million, gives pineapples second rank to sugar.

Although other specialty crops for export may be considered as minor in comparison to those already named, they add annually about $10 million to Hawaii's gross income.

Aside from agriculture and the processing of farm products, a second major source of income for the people of Hawaii is the tourist trade. In 1922, the total number of visitors was less than 10,000. As late as 1941, the peak prewar year, it was only 32,000. . . . One hundred and thirty-three thousand tourists visited Hawaii in 1956 . . . in 1957 it had reached a total of 169,000, more than five times the number of sixteen years before. That 169,000, incidentally, represents the number of persons staying two days or more. They spent nearly $80 million in Hawaii in that year, and thus put tourism next to sugar and pineapples as a source of income from private industry.

Most of Hawaii's economic possibilities are already well-developed, and the territory is already a tax-paying partner, carrying a full share of the burden of supporting the federal government. Federal internal revenue collections in Hawaii last year amounted to $166,306,000, a figure higher than in ten of the present states: New Hampshire, Vermont, North Dakota, South Dakota, Montana, Idaho, Wyoming, New Mexico, Nevada, and Alaska.

The geographical area of Hawaii is comparatively small (6,423 square miles), although not so small as three of our present states — Rhode Island, Delaware, and Connecticut. The territory is thickly settled, comparatively, with a population estimated in June 1958 at about 635,000 — larger than that of six of the present states: New Hampshire, with 584,000; Delaware, 454,000; Vermont, 372,000; Wyoming, 320,000; Nevada, 267,000; and Alaska, approximately 214,000. In fact, Hawaii today has a greater population than that enjoyed at the time of admittance by any of the states — other than the original thirteen — with the single exception of Oklahoma.

It is with some difficulty that I proceed with the balance of my statement. When testimony is limited to new material, it is extremely difficult to approach the subject of what can, today, be stated as an argument against statehood for Hawaii. So far as I am aware, there are no new arguments

against Hawaii. There are none which were not thoroughly discussed in this committee in 1957, and thoroughly considered by the full Senate when the Hawaii bill was passed in 1954. With the exception of one subject, I would venture to state that every argument that is currently raised against Hawaii was in fact raised during the debates which led to the incorporation of Hawaii into our Union as an organized territory in 1900. Many of these same arguments were made in opposition to the admission of Louisiana in 1812, which, as the members of this committee well recall, was the first state to be admitted from territory outside of that embraced by the original thirteen states.

One argument against Hawaiian statehood, that of Communist infiltration, seems to demand explanation here today. Historically, even this is not a completely new subject in debate and consideration of statehood, because the question of loyalty to the United States has, indeed, been raised in regard to other states prior to their admission. Debate in the Congress as to the extent of French influence in Louisiana and that of the Spanish-speaking people of New Mexico are significant examples. The Communist question, of course, presents a new ramification of the subject of loyalty not presented in the past, and that is whether any substantial segment of Hawaii actually is committed to a doctrine which advocates the violent overthrow of the very government in which the overwhelming majority of Hawaiians seek to permanently become a full partner.

For myself, I believe that this committee and all advocates of Hawaiian statehood will squarely face the Communist issue.

The people of Hawaii have time and time again rejected completely the Communist philosophy and have thwarted every attempt of the Communists to influence their government. The proposed constitution of the state of Hawaii contains a far-reaching prohibition against any Communist holding public office or public employment of any kind.

A perennial target of alleged Communists in Hawaii has been the law enacted by the 1949 territorial legislature, following a prolonged dock strike, which empowered territorial government to seize Hawaiian docks in the event of a strike. Notwithstanding four general territorialwide elections for the legislature, those laws are still on the books in Hawaii today. In each election the laws were an issue, and in each legislative session attempts have been made to repeal them. This is a prime example of the dogged determination of Hawaiians to stand firm on what they consider to be a matter of principle.

This committee needs no exposition of the rebuttals to the argument based on noncontiguity, upon the loyalty of Hawaiians, or upon the subject of whether approximately 635,000 people deserve equal representation. Normally, this last argument is directed at whether 635,000 people deserve to have two senators when New York's almost 16 million, California's 13 million, and Pennsylvania's 11 million people have but two senators. A succinct answer to the last argument can be presented by any student aware of the wise compromises agreed to in the Constitutional Convention by our founding fathers.

It helps, I believe, to keep the Hawaiian statehood movement in the proper perspective. In my opinion, statehood for Hawaii will bring as much good to the other forty-nine states as it will to Hawaii itself. The admission of any fully qualified partner does strengthen the whole Union. As every one of the thirty-six states, which have been admitted since the original thirteen, entered, the Union has become more vibrant and has enjoyed at the very least a great moral uplifting.

We teach our children in our homes, churches, and schools to think in terms of fair dealing, and in terms of devotion to the principles of our Declaration of Independence and our Constitution. Hawaiians are teaching their children the same thing, but what will all this come to mean to these Hawaiian children if they witness again and again the denial of their petition for equal rights and privileges?

Gentlemen, in my opinion the major question before you is a question of when to take action. It is a moral question and one which raises serious implications throughout the world. It is my firm hope that the Hawaiian cause, which really involves a plea for simple justice, will be answered forthwith with the only remedy available — that which is granted by the Constitution to the Congress exclusively: the power to admit new states into the Union.

We have no other territory which is incorporated and ready for statehood, and Congress itself must first grant to any other territory the basic status of incorporation into the Union before any new apprenticeship can begin.

As you continue your deliberations, please feel free to call upon me or the personnel of the Department of the Interior for any information or assistance you may desire. We stand ready to assist in any way to bring about the immediate admission of Hawaii as a state.

———————◆———————

The old, men and women, and little children could sleep safely in the highways.
ANON., description of reign of King Kamehameha I, early 19th century

1959

102.

John Foster Dulles: Peace Through Law

John Foster Dulles was President Eisenhower's secretary of state from 1953 until a few weeks before his death in 1959. As such, Dulles was the leading architect of American foreign policy during the 1950s, and his ideas continued to mold that policy into the following decade. Basing his conception of America's role in the world on the proposition that there is a fundamental opposition between the moral force of democracy and the immoral ambitions of the Communists, Dulles fought the Soviets and their allies at every turn. He also had deep confidence in the ultimate triumph of the right, a belief that is reflected in the selection reprinted here. In the speech from which it is taken, delivered before the New York State Bar Association on January 31, 1959, Dulles discussed America's relations to the United Nations and upheld the thesis that lasting peace in the world could never be attained by force, but only under law.

Source: Memorial Brochure published by New York State Bar Association, January 31, 1959.

WHILE WE HAVE, through collective security arrangements, largely deterred the Communist bloc from using force, we have found no effective means of persuading or inducing the countries of that bloc to accept the principles of justice and law and peaceful change.

This is not true as respects the nations of the Free World. There, the twin concepts of the renunciation of force and the affirmative role of justice and international law have, generally speaking, prevailed. The reasons for this are not difficult to understand. The peoples of the Free World have respect for religion; they recognize moral law; and they have a decent regard for the opinions of mankind. As a result, the nations of the Free World have not only evidenced a healthy respect for the principles of international law but they have also promoted a remarkable amount of "peaceful change" to conform to concepts of justice and morality.

Since January 1, 1943, for example, twenty-one new nations have come into existence in countries formerly ruled by other Free World countries and have been accepted into the community of nations. Others are scheduled to gain their independence and sovereignty in the near future. During the spring of the past year, eighty-six nations met in Geneva to review the principles governing the law of the sea. While a number of the established rules of law in this field were reconfirmed by the conference, it is equally important to note that significant changes — responsive to the requirements of new conditions — were agreed upon.

Peaceful change and development are, therefore, significant among the nations of the Free World. Perhaps, indeed, the pendulum is swinging too far in the direction of change. Law serves, not merely to settle specific disputes but to provide a sense of security in daily living. A measure of stability is an essential ingredient of peace and order.

Change — even political and social change — should not be so impetuous as to paralyze forward planning or to wreak unnecessary injury upon established rights. While law is and should be subject to an orderly process of change, as required by justice, it should be a shield and a protector of those who rely in good faith on international engagements.

Let us now look ahead and consider what can be done to promote a fuller recognition of the role of justice and law in international affairs.

First, I would say that there is a pressing need among the membership of the United Nations for more condemnation and less tolerance of the double standard in the United Nations which has been created by the actions and activities of the nations of the Soviet bloc. Those nations should be made to feel the weight of public disapproval of their attitude. The position they have taken strikes at the foundation of man's promising and essential effort to abolish resort to force and to replace it by the processes of justice and law. I say in all seriousness that the United Nations and the

world can, perhaps, survive a limited phase of double standard. But they cannot survive a permanent double standard. Unless the United Nations becomes, for all, an instrumentality of peace through justice and law, as it was designed to be, then, as the founder declared, some alternative must be found.

Second, there is a real need to intensify, within the Free World, the development of the processes of justice, giving due regard to the need for stability and to the coequal need for an orderly process of change, in accordance with the requirements of justice. This, in my view, is sometimes overlooked in the deliberations and the actions of the General Assembly of the United Nations. The General Assembly can be and is powerful when it represents a genuine moral judgment. On the other hand, that same Assembly could become feudal or even tyrannical if it were to develop into a system of bloc "voting" in terms of geographical areas or in terms of the "haves" as against the "have-nots."

Third, there is a serious need for all of us to develop a respect for law as a basis for stability and confidence. Those nations which do have common standards should, by their conduct and example, advance the rule of law by submitting their disputes to the International Court of Justice, or to some other international tribunal upon which they can agree. . . . We are closely examining the question of our own relationship to the International Court of Justice with the view of seeing whether ways and means can be found to assure a greater use of that Court by ourselves, and, through our example, by others.

The United States was born as a nation because the colonists believed men possessed, under law, certain basic freedoms and certain inalienable rights. As a nation we have, more than any others, striven for the supremacy of law as an expression of justice. Now, we are seeking to establish world order based on the assumption that the collective life of nations ought to be governed by law — law as formulated in the Charter of the United Nations and other international treaties, and law as enunciated by international courts.

Your fellow bar association, the American Bar Association, has set up a committee under the chairmanship of Mr. Charles Rhyne, its past president, charged with the duty of looking into the question of what can be done to advance the rule of law among nations. The government welcomes this action and will give full and serious consideration to any recommendations made by that committee.

To accomplish peace through law will take patience and perseverance. It will require us at times to provide an example by accepting for ourselves standards of conduct more advanced than those generally accepted. We shall be misunderstood and our motives misinterpreted by others who have had no such training as we in doctrine of law. In this task the members of the legal profession will have a special responsibility and unique opportunity.

There is no nobler mission that our nation could perform. Upon its success may depend the very survival of the human race. We can, therefore, dedicate ourselves to this mission with supreme confidence that we shall thus fulfill our national destiny.

103.

Henry B. du Pont: The Greatest Invention of Them All

The main theme of the following address, delivered by industrialist Henry B. du Pont at the Franklin Institute of Philadelphia on April 15, 1959, is that the invention of the business corporation must be reckoned a vital factor in America's technological progress. According to du Pont, the corporate form of business organization is the principal force behind the tremendous increase in production that has characterized American manufacturing since the onset of the Industrial Revolution; the business corporation aids technological progress in that it supplies the necessary financial resources and the legal and administrative framework required for efficient industrial organization.

Source: VSD, July 15, 1959.

There is, I suppose, no more appropriate place than the Franklin Institute for a discussion of technology. The Philadelphia Story is rich in technological history, for much of it was enacted — at least in its early stages — within a relatively short distance of this room.

I am thinking not only of Dr. Franklin's work. His contributions would be remarkable anywhere, anytime. I am thinking, as well, of the astonishing number of other scientists and inventors who worked in or near Philadelphia in the early days of the country.

There was the naturalist John Bartram and, a little later, John Audubon, whose interest in ornithology began while he was living in Mill Grove, near Mount Carmel. There was Benjamin Rush, the physician. There was David Rittenhouse with his planetarium, and Owen Biddle with his telescope at Cape Henlopen. There was John Fitch, a transplanted Connecticut Yankee, puffing along the Schuylkill and the Delaware in a fire-breathing contraption called a steamboat. A few miles downstream, on Brandywine Creek, there was Oliver Evans, who built a flour mill which operated almost without human attention. Among his neighbors was E. I. du Pont, recently arrived from France, who went into the powder business at the urging of Jefferson and made important contributions to the manufacture of explosives then badly needed to clear the forest lands, build the roads, and defend the nation.

There was Thomas Paine, remembered as the pamphleteer of the Revolution, but due equal honors for his engineering contributions. One of Paine's more imaginative schemes was an engine driven by a continuous series of tiny gunpowder explosions, actually a sort of internal-combustion engine. Unfortunately, the "Internal-Explosion Engine" did not work out. I say "unfortunately" because the du Pont Company was mighty close to bankruptcy for many of its early years, and a large-scale development in this field would have created a welcome new market. However, let us not criticize Citizen Paine for his mistakes. He also developed the iron bridge and had some worthy thoughts about planing machines, cranes, and carriage-wheel construction.

The list of Philadelphia contributors could be extended indefinitely, for, in the eighteenth and nineteenth centuries, this small sector of the American geography was the home of dozens who were instrumental to the progress of technology.

It could be argued that "technology" is not the word to use for the scientific contributions of a Franklin or a Bartram, so let me define my terms. Technology is much more than engineering. It is much more than invention, much more than the nuts and bolts, as is sometimes said. Technology,

as I see it, is the sum total of man's work in developing the tools and techniques which lend leverage to human effort. Whether a man be a research scientist, or engineer, or an "inspired tinkerer" as some were called, he contributes to and is an integral part of the technology which has shaped this nation.

America in 1800, despite its vast potential wealth, was one of the poorest of the have-not nations, although few nations of that day were well-off. The natural resources which we know today were underdeveloped and many of them were unsuspected. In 1800, standards of living even for the well-to-do were crude; and for the mass of the population, they approached the hand-to-mouth level. Farming occupied the attention of more than 90 percent of the population, and the primitive equipment used would have been recognized by any farmer from the time of Julius Caesar. Manufacture had hardly reached a level where it deserved the title "industry." In 1814, in a report prepared for the United States Senate, a Philadelphian named Tench Coxe estimated that the output of manufacturing in the United States came to a value of something less than $175 million a year. That meant an average of $35 worth of manufactured goods for each man, woman, and child in the population, hardly an impressive amount.

The real poverty of the nation, however, lay in the inadequacy of its human resources to meet growing needs. Tench Coxe was among those who saw that technology held bold possibilities of enriching the nation, and he pleaded for the development of laborsaving machines to lift human burdens and increase output. Men simply could not be spared from the fields. Manpower was so scarce that in a textile mill, for example, Mr. Coxe said that not more than one employee in eight could be an adult male; the rest of the work had to be done by women and children. Before we send Mr. Coxe to the pillory for suggestions which would shock us today, let me add that no less noble a man than Jefferson shared these views. Coxe was simply stating facts. Men were needed to raise food and could not be spared for manufacture.

In such a restricted economy, there was obviously little money and little time to expend in research and development. The men whose enthusiasm carried them into science or engineering did so, for the most part, on their own initiative, just as we today might take music lessons or write poetry. But, for the necessities of life, they had to turn to other fields. Some of the most significant work done in America came about as a result of the two-job practice we would now describe as "moonlighting."

Samuel Morse, for example, was a portrait painter by day and a scientist by night. John Fitch sold maps as he traveled the Eastern seaboard looking for someone, anyone, to invest in his fire-breathing boat. Eli Whitney earned his living as a schoolmaster before he earned a nickel from his inventions. Joseph Henry, another part-time scientist, deplored the fact that his experiments had to be confined to the summer months when the school in which he taught was closed. Oliver Evans got along by operating a store and an iron foundry; and Paine, who first had plied his trade as a staymaker, later eked out a living by his writing and political work.

Few scientists were as well-situated as Franklin, whose early successes in publishing enabled him to live amid comforts while indulging his interest in such diverse subjects as the Gulf Stream, electricity, and bifocal spectacles. Most were obliged to expend so much of their energies to earning a livelihood that their most memorable achievements were made on borrowed time. The strain told. Fitch died poor, by his own hand, broken by years of frustration and want. Elias Howe, while enduring hunger and privation, was worn out by toil and died at the age of forty-eight.

To add to the difficulties of these early technologists, poor communication led to frequent duplication of effort, with the result that many things were invented several times by different people who were ignorant of each other's work. When Eli Whitney set up his factory to make guns with interchangeable parts, he spent a large amount of time working out machine tools which already had been developed, or at least anticipated, in other countries. He had no way of knowing that they even existed. Fitch worked for years on a double-acting steam engine, apparently ignorant of the fact that James Watt and Matthew Boulton had already solved many of the problems he faced. Oliver Evans started from scratch and had no access to technical books, although many had been written in the fields in which he worked. Henry worked for six years on magnetism and electric currents before discovering that Faraday, an ocean away, was doing the same research.

Inevitably, when two or more men brought forth the same discovery at approximately the same time, there were conflicting patent claims. This produced some of the stormiest and most extended legal battles in history. No doubt, it provided amusement for many interested spectators. But it was costly national fun because it dissipated the creative energies of men who could not easily be replaced or duplicated. Genius is too rare a commodity to be squandered lavishly or used inefficiently.

Looking back to the conditions of the eighteenth and nineteenth centuries, it should cause little wonder that technical progress came slowly. The marvel is that anything was accomplished at all, and our respect and admiration for the talents and persistence of the men involved grows as we come to appreciate their handicaps. They earned every tribute we pay them. I cannot help but wonder how different our history might have been if these extraordinary minds had been unleashed for full-time experiment and invention.

If we were asked to construct a list of the technological developments most fundamental to America's progress, it would be difficult indeed to single out any group upon which we could present a clear case. The nominations most meaningful would be those representative of broad application, spanning all categories of human need. For, the most notable thing about the technical development of America is that its industrial revolution was not confined mainly to manufacturing, as was the case in Europe. Instead, American technical development was spread broadly across the entire economic and scientific field.

The growth of our industrial technology was accompanied by parallel gains in agriculture, in communications, and in transportation. There was no single stream of technological advance. Instead, America's progress resulted from the converging of many streams, uniting to produce a flood tide of inventive achievement. In this great creative outpouring, it is difficult to identify any small group of inventions which would be judged outstanding in importance.

Everyone has his own list of "greatest inventions," and every invention has, I suppose, its partisans. My own list has three virtues to commend it. First, it is brief; second, most of my selections are simple; and, third, it is based, not on scientific preeminence but on the universal importance to our economic revolution.

I would include, for example, the steel plow. A humble device, perhaps — John Deere simply hammered it out of an old circular saw blade. But it speeded the work of the farmer and was the predecessor of a host of other laborsaving farm equipment — the reaper, the binder, the tractor, the combine. Some might argue that these were more significant and, in a way, they would be right. But the important thing about the steel plow is that it was the first in a long line of major advances which lifted man from the subsistence level of agriculture, thus freeing increasing numbers of people

for other occupations. Improved farm tools, supplemented by insecticides, weed killers, fertilizers, and better planting and irrigation techniques, have multiplied the efficiency of the farmer by a factor of twenty-five.

Second, I include Oliver Evans' wonderful flour mill, the precursor of automatic control. In terms of scientific merits, it was a modest accomplishment. But it showed the world how a whole series of production operations could be linked together, driven by machinery, and tended by one or two men. All of the technologists who followed Evans, and the millions of consumers who use mass-produced goods, are eternally indebted to this extraordinary man.

The steam locomotive, of course, put power on wheels and gave man a wholly new mobility of special significance in a nation spanning such great distances. The locomotive was not unique to America, and it was more a compendium than an invention, but it should not be ruled out on that score. After all, no nation can claim many major inventions which are all its own, created without outside help. Technology is a cumulative force. To credit all of the people who made the locomotive possible, we would have to track down the inventors of the lever, the wheel, and the inclined plane, not to mention the steam engine and similarly modern developments. Incidentally, some of the most important contributions to railroad development came from this area. George Westinghouse, the inventor of the air brake, was a Pennsylvanian by adoption if not by birth. Matthias Baldwin, the locomotive builder and one of the men who helped found the Franklin Institute, was a Philadelphian. John Edgar Thompson, who did as much as any man to build the Pennsylvania Railroad, was born and raised in Delaware County. In the hands of men like these, the railroad reached a high level of development in the United States and, with the vast distances of the continent falling beneath its iron wheels, the locomotive counts more heavily in our history than many inventions we like to think of as 100 percent homegrown.

Fourth on the list is the telegraph, which presaged the telephone and did more to speed communication than any device since the printing press and movable type.

I have mentioned here four basic inventions covering each of the major fields. There is a fifth which pertains to all. I think in any list of inventions we should include this one which, strictly speaking, is not an invention at all but a legal fiction. Yet, it seems to me to equal in importance any specific invention in history. This is the development of the modern corporation.

The industrial corporation, as we know it today, is a creature of technology just as certainly as the flying machine or the cotton gin, and it has proved the most effective device for extending technology which man has ever known. Its contributions have been unique. For the modern industrial establishment is the agency which made the pursuit of technology a full-time job, and not for a few men but for hundreds of thousands. Industry employs today more than 550,000 scientists and engineers, a majority of the nation's technical work force. Such figures amaze few today. But, in contrast to the struggling little band of amateurs of the early days, it is a vast army.

Development of the industrial organization as we now recognize it came too late to aid the earlier inventors. In some ways, the "corporate" form of organization dates from medieval times, but it was not until the twentieth century that the corporation came into wide usage as the structural form of large-scale organization. In this century, it has changed the world. It has provided a focal point for the development of technology, taking it out of the sideline class and making it a full-time profession. The corporation has brought to the support of technology an extraordinary number and variety of services and resources. In our own company, as an example, we have about 2,400 technically trained employees in research and development, assisted by more than 3,500 specialists and technicians. We spent $90 million last year to underwrite their work.

All the facilities which can be mustered are employed to assist the research worker and make his effort more productive. No longer does he work in ignorance of what others are doing. Today, few developments throughout the world escape notice, for there is a constant interchange of information, and scientists have major reference publications at their fingertips. Our own technical libraries stock over 800 different periodicals, and we have one divisional group whose sole function is to keep track of research discoveries elsewhere and pass on pertinent information. Whether new ideas originate in our own laboratories or elsewhere, they are eagerly studied and their applicability is appraised quickly. If one man's experience is insufficient to evaluate the work, another's frequently will prove to be, offering, as it does, a different background and perspective.

What is true in du Pont is true in many other companies today. Large corporations consolidate information from many disciplines of science and engineering and bring to scientific development a breadth of vision extending far beyond any one man's capacities. The individual scientist is stimulated and encouraged. His discoveries no longer are left to languish on the laboratory shelf while their creator goes out to search for a sponsor.

In addition, the development of the modern corporation has created the national resources which support technology in many other types of institutions. The research efforts of universities, private foundations, and government laboratories contribute importantly to the advancement of American science and engineering, but these institutions could not exist were it not for the wealth generated by American industry.

The size of the institutions furthering technology has become an important element in our progress. With its engineering and production resources, the modern industrial organization can direct large groups of technologists — people skilled in many areas of science — to projects no one individual technologist could undertake. For example, it is possible to produce penicillin in a one-man laboratory in quantities sufficient to save a few lives. Produced in major pharmaceutical plants, penicillin has saved the lives of millions. I remember from my early interest in flying that a number of enterprising individuals built airplanes in backyard garages. Perhaps some still do. They would be the first to admit, however, that their efforts, in scale or in volume, are not quite comparable to the accomplishments of North American or Boeing.

Some of my colleagues at du Pont, given a few days' notice and a small set of laboratory apparatus, could formulate a kind of nylon and spin a bobbin or two of yarn. But, to supply a national market, this would be like trying to feed an army with the grain you could raise in a flowerpot. Moreover, the factor of size also has an important value to national defense. During World War II, for example, the government asked du Pont to build the atomic materials plant at Hanford, Washington. More recently, we were asked to undertake the construction of the Savannah River hydrogen-materials plant. These were perhaps the most ambitious engineering projects in history; they could not have been completed without the services of a large institution employing thousands of specialists in dozens of fields.

Quite obviously, all of the technological efforts of companies like du Pont are not of this magnitude. And, obviously, not all of the technological jobs required for the nation's advancement require large institutions. Some of the most significant accomplishments have come, and will continue to come, from smaller organizations. In technology, as in other facets of American life, there is a need for business units of every size. Small firms supply companies like du Pont with tools, materials, and special services, which are basic to large-scale research and production efforts. At the same time, the small are important customers of the large, buying products which only the large firms can produce in a volume sufficient to meet national needs. Very often, the small firm makes its contribution to technology and finds its route to commercial success by developing and marketing a product created in the research laboratories of a large company. Thus, small and large business units work as a team to expand America's technology, with each contributing its special talents.

Four years ago, the Swiss economist William Rappard set down his views on the causes of America's prosperity. Most important of all, he wrote, were the application of science to production, the "passion" for efficiency in industry, mass production to bring large quantities of goods to people at low cost, and the spirit of competition. It is worth noting that the development of large industrial units is a factor in each of Professor Rappard's considerations. These organizations, consolidating many talents, have provided to technology and the technologist a whole new dimension of performance and potential. They have elevated the horizons of science and engineering, and they have literally extended man's reach into the boundless areas of outer space.

When the history of our era is written, the birth and development of the modern corporation must be recorded as a vital factor in our technological progress. Indeed, the corporation may well prove to be the greatest invention of them all.

104.

Hyman G. Rickover: Education, Our First Line of Defense

The quality of American education became a matter of deep concern to professional educators in the years after World War II. Selective service boards had to reject many draftees for illiteracy, and the armed forces had to institute training programs designed to raise many others to the level of functional literacy. Educational deficiencies were particularly evident when it became impossible to fill government and military positions demanding competence in mathematics, science, and foreign languages. The public at large did not become disturbed until the Russians launched their first Sputnik, in 1957, after which a near panic occurred in the United States because of the apparent superiority of the Soviets in science and technology. Admiral Hyman G. Rickover was one of those who was most deeply concerned to improve the quality of American education, a subject discussed by him in the following selection, first published in January 1959.

Source: *Education and Freedom*, New York, 1960, pp. 15-38.

WHENEVER MAN MAKES a major advance in his age-old effort to utilize the forces of nature, he must simultaneously raise his education, his techniques, and his institutions to a higher plateau. Let me illustrate this by giving an example of a past upgrading necessitated by a shift from one energy source to another.

If you obtain your power from human muscle, wind, or water, you need almost no technical knowledge. To drive a gang of galley slaves, to manage a windmill or water mill do not even require literacy, but putting Faraday's invention of the dynamo to practical use in a central-station power plant needed fifty years of engineering effort by highly trained people. The men who run such plants use their minds a great deal more and they need much better minds than the quondam miller or slave driver. Similarly, from the splitting of the atom in the 1930s to the bomb in the 1940s, to the

practical nuclear power plant in 1953, a vast amount of intellectual effort of a high order had to be expended. Highly trained nuclear engineers are needed to design, build, and run nuclear power plants. Still greater demands on the human mind will be made if and when we obtain energy from hydrogen fusion.

It is obvious that the kind of American who thoroughly mastered his environment on the frontier in the muscle, wind, and water state of technology would be totally ineffective in the atomic age which is just around the corner, and the fusion age which is still a way off. Social workers in big cities into which people from our last-frontier regions have been pouring are fully aware of the inadequacy of these human beings in an urban environment for which their simpler life had not prepared them.

The consequence of technological progress is that man must use his mind more and his body less. We still think in terms of a more primitive era; we overvalue physical prowess and undervalue intellectual competence. This has a profound effect on our attitudes toward education. The kind of school which prepares young people adequately for life in a less complicated environment is of little use today. Nor do we need schools that concentrate primarily on adjusting the children of immigrants to this new country; on helping them become Americans quickly and painlessly. Today we must have schools which develop in all children — talented, average, and below average — the highest level of intellectual competence of which they are capable; schools that help young people to understand the complex world of today and how it came to be what it is. This means that our schools must return to the traditional task of formal education in Western civilization — transmission of the nation's cultural heritage, and preparation for life through rigorous training of young minds to think clearly, logically, and independently.

For as long as I have worked in the atomic-energy field I have been absorbed in educational problems. Indeed, I found the two so intertwined that I would have had to be most unobservant not to have gotten myself involved with American education. When I started on the work of harnessing the energy of the atom for propulsion of naval ships and generation of electricity in civilian power plants, I had in my group a handful of men with training in nuclear engineering. We knew that our project would present difficult technical problems, particularly since I deemed it necessary to speed the work by telescoping the usual pattern of development which proceeds from theoretical to applied research, to laboratory experimentation, and finally to practical application. We designed and built reactors directly for practical use in ships and power plants, skipping the stage when theory is tried out on laboratory models. To the lay-

man — and alas even more so to the public-relations man — such models always seem to be equivalent to the working, finished product. This is not so. This country has many laboratory reactors — reactors producing some electricity under ideal laboratory conditions, and much is to be learned from them. There is a vast difference, however, between a research or experimental reactor and a reactor which must actually produce useful power for a ship or an electric grid. Whereas laboratory conditions favor the new project, reality is troublesome.

When I set up my reactor group twelve years ago, I put all my energy into finding the right people and wasted no time creating an "ideal" organization. In fact we still have no formal organization. We have excellent people, carefully chosen, thoroughly trained for their job, and strongly motivated because of their intense interest in the work. Such people cannot be fitted into the usual hierarchic organization which exists in most industrial and government complexes. They must be given freedom to work out their own problems and to assume responsibility for what they do. They need an environment that allows them to be venturesome and does not stifle their initiative with routines; in a novel development project there can be no routine.

Our country will not be able to make rapid technological progress unless we reorganize our institutions. These must be pried from their exaggerated veneration for routine and protocol and made to see that provision must be made for both routine work and for new and creative work; for routine workers and for people with specialized knowledge who must be allowed to operate outside routine procedures. We have not yet solved this problem; chiefly, I believe, because it is relatively new, a consequence of two new phenomena — the scientific revolution and organizational growth necessitated by population expansion.

The scientific revolution now engulfs us

though not all of us are fully aware of this. We must expect that science will influence our mores in ever increasing degree. There will be some unemployment in the ranks of people whose principal qualification is their ability to get along, to fit into organizational structures, and to adjust. The man of the future on whom we shall depend more and more is the technical expert. Today he is still subservient to nontechnical leaders in government and industry, and his work is hampered and sometimes destroyed by men in whom is vested great power but who cannot understand the realities of the new, artificial, technological age. But the "verbal" men are on the way out; the men who can handle the intricate mysteries of complex scientific and engineering projects are on the way in. That applies all along the line down to the skilled workman on whose judgment, concentrated attention, and responsibility may depend the functioning of some new and gigantic piece of engineering. To put this in military terms: we shall need more technical sergeants and fewer martinets. In our naval nuclear program we have taken cognizance of this demand for a different kind of man and we have set up schools to train the officers and men who will run the new atomic navy.

Another relatively new phenomenon in American life which compels us to find room for creative people in our institutions is the sheer mass of our people. Government and industry must in some manner organize and manage our huge population to prevent chaos and insure safety and efficiency. No other industrial democracy has to cope with a problem of quite such staggering dimensions for none is so populous or grows at such dizzying speed as we do.

Our Founding Fathers knew that size endangers democratic institutions and they had some misgivings as to whether democracy would function in as populous a country as ours. In the mid-eighteenth century, when plans for an independent America be-

gan to ripen, we *had 1.2 million people* — exactly twice the population of the only then existing democracy, Switzerland. All other democracies had been small city-states — Plato's republic was to have had 5,040 citizens! Where Switzerland had quadrupled its population in 200 years, we *increased more than a hundred fold.* We can be proud of our record of maintaining democratic processes, even expanding them, despite this enormous increase in population. While we have been highly successful politically, economically there has of necessity been a gradual loss of personal freedom. Each year fewer people are self-employed; more become submerged in huge organizations. In fact, nothing grows faster than organization. Increasing specialization aggravates this trend. Even professional people have been losing independence and increasingly work as members of a team. Without organizations run by competent administrators we simply could not get along. This presents few problems if the work is routine. A capable administrator can learn enough about the techniques of routine production or service to organize it efficiently; he knows how to oil the machinery and dovetail individual work into the whole. The people under him do not know more than he about the essentials of the routine procedures in which they are engaged.

It is entirely different with experts having specialized knowledge. Few administrators know enough about the work of subordinate experts to be competent to administer or manage them efficiently. Most administrators reach their positions in the organizational hierarchy because they understand routine personnel problems, know how to keep people working contentedly, and are always subservient to the wishes of their superiors. The typical administrator is used to "group-think" in committees — whether brainstorming or ordinary — and has limited his own originality so severely that he has no understanding of the freedom essential to the creative worker. His mental processes are the very opposite of those of the expert, especially the scientist or engineer. Men whose minds have been trained to respect intellectual honesty and scientific fact simply cannot submit to the orders of administrative superiors whose intellectual honesty they may not respect and whose "scientific facts" they may regard as fable. *There is no hierarchy in matters of the mind.*

This causes a great deal of friction. What appears to the organization man as an almost criminal insubordination is to the trained professional a vital necessity; unless he is allowed to follow his own judgment in matters pertaining to his specialty, he becomes a hack. His intellectual freedom is so intimate a part of his nature that to yield to a superior lacking technical knowledge is to degrade himself and become unfree. Actually, administrators can contribute very little that is useful to the work of creative people. In fact, nobody can waste as much time as a super-efficient administrator trying to run a group of "eggheads."

I fear that we have gone far toward lowering the output of our brainworkers by overorganizing them. We are drowning in paper work. We are talking ourselves into a standstill in endless committees — those pets of the administrator. We are losing the genius we once had for improvisation. Nowadays nothing can be done without elaborate preparation, organization, and careful rehearsal. We have been diluting responsibility for making decisions by piling layers of supervisory administrative levels, pyramid fashion, upon the people who do the real work. All this delays new developments. To the technical difficulties of creating something new are added the constant frustrations of interference by men who do not understand technical matters. If we are to regain ground lost to the Russians in important developments, we must learn how to run organizations with sufficient flexibility so that routine work may proceed efficiently without interfering with creative work. Somehow every organization must make room for inner-directed, obstreperous, creative people; sworn enemies of routine and the *status quo,* always ready to upset the applecart by thinking up new and better ways of doing things. They are troublesome mavericks, unloved by the administrator who cannot forgive their contempt for conventions. However, unless these people are permitted to lead the way, there will be stagnation.

It was men of independent mind and venturesome spirit that I set out to find for my nuclear propulsion group. From the start it was evident that no experienced men of this type were available. Before we could tackle our work, we therefore had to find young people showing *potentialities* of growth whom we could then ourselves train intensively for work on reactor design. This took time, but in the end it has proved far more satisfactory than the usual custom of raiding the small hoards of already qualified people accumulated by other government agencies or industries. We set up special schools and turned ourselves into teachers, discovering in the process that the fundamentals of a good liberal arts education had been skimped in the education given these bright young men. The search for and training of promising young people still take up much of my time and that of my leading engineers for we are constantly expanding and there are of course losses through attrition. These, fortunately, are few so that we reap pretty much of a full harvest from our educational efforts.

Among the young engineers we interview we find few who have received thorough training in engineering fundamentals or principles; but most have absorbed quantities of facts — much easier to learn than principles but of little use without application of principles. Once a principle has been acquired it becomes a part of one and is never lost. It can be applied to novel problems and does not become obsolete as do all facts in a changing society. American education in general emphasizes learning factual know-how at the cost of absorbing fundamental principles, just as it stresses conditioning of behavior at the cost of developing the ability to think independently. Most of our schools have lost sight of the fact that a well-trained mind can cope with many unforeseen problems. Instead, they try to foresee every possible future difficulty a young person may encounter and then give a special course in how to deal with it. This is a hopeless endeavor, for in a rapidly changing world no one can foresee what future problems will have to be met.

I have interviewed more than two thousand young men in the last twelve years. My naval-reactor engineering group presently numbers about 150. Since the men I interviewed had already passed through a number of previous interviews which weeded out all but the best, it can be seen that those who could not meet the requirements of the nuclear-power project — and hence inferentially of *any* new development project — vastly outnumbered those who qualified.

This experience made a deep impression on me. It led me directly to a study of why our educational system produces so few men who are qualified to do the work which we must do if we are to progress. Our schools are the greatest "cultural lag" we have today. When I read official publications put out by the men who run our educational system — booklets such as *Life-Adjustment Education for Every Youth* or *Education for All Youth* — I have the strange feeling of reading about another world, a world long since departed if it ever existed at all. I sense the kindly spirit, the desire to make every child happy, the earnest determination to give advice on every problem any young person might ever meet in life — and withal so complete a misunderstanding of the needs of young people in today's world that it frightens me. If I speak out against this mistaken concept of what 20th-century American education must be, I do so out of no desire to find fault with those who misread the demands of the times but from anxiety for the future of our children. I am worried about the chances which young people, so poorly equipped to deal with modern life, will have when things become more complex and difficult, as they surely will before very long.

Today's big problems for young people are not how to choose the proper tie, or how to be socially popular — these are minor problems which any mother can teach her children with little difficulty. They are piddling problems. The important problems our young people will have to meet in life cannot be foreseen; the only way to prepare for them is to make sure that all our children will be truly "educated." By that I do not mean the same thing as some of our educationalists. Witness the statement of a teachers' college dean, quoted in John Keats' revealing book *Schools Without Scholars:* "An educated man is one who is well adjusted and helpful in his community." When the dean was asked "whether a man who was well adjusted and helpful could be considered educated *without also being able to count his fingers or write his name,*" the dean said, "Yes."

Apart from the life-adjustment fallacy so prevalent among American educationists, our schools seem unable to concentrate on training young minds because of partiality for so-called useful knowledge. This utilitarian concept of education is to be found among parents no less than among educationists. It may be in the nature of a revolt against liberal-arts education which many consider suited only for gentlemen of leisure and hence out of place in a democracy. An extraordinary lot of nonsense is said and believed about European education which stresses the liberal arts. European education is dismissed as aristocratic and exclusive, perhaps in order to avoid having to stand the test of comparison which might necessitate eventual upgrading of American education. Unfortunately, constant repetition that ours is the only democratic and universal education has been lulling and persuasive. It has been so effective that we have the oddest delusions about academic life abroad. In American folklore the European student becomes a golden youth in blazers and white flannels, living in ivy-clad seclusion amid shady campuses while the vast majority of young people are sternly excluded from this higher education. This is an unreal concept of European university life as it is today and as it has been in the past. Far from being islands of aristocratic privilege, European universities have always been intellectual workshops of austere aspect. In the long and honorable history of learning which sets Western civilization apart from all others and to which the Western world owes its dynamic quality, the scholar and the student have more often been poor than rich. The medieval and renaissance universities which shaped the crude intellect of Europe through association with the polished mind of Greece and Rome offered no more nor less than a chance to seek truth — to achieve liberation of the mind from ignorance and superstition. . . .

No plaything for the idle gentleman is this liberal-arts education based on the humanities and the sciences. It makes little sense for us to go on refusing to profit from Europe's educational experiences. By even the most pragmatic of tests her education has proved itself. Consider that in but one single branch of learning — theoretical physics — Europe has produced some fifteen to twenty men of high originality in the last one hundred years. The United States, writes Lancelot Law Whyte, produced "only one: J. Willard Gibbs (1839-1903), the great physical chemist, a lonely figure who did not found a school." Much

of our superior standard of living has been owing more to the fact that we applied European techniques to a vast, fabulously rich land than to any superiority of Americans in competence, determination, industry, or education. It is only now, when Russia has begun to apply European techniques to her own vast land, that we are meeting competition on equal terms.

We have of course done exceedingly well with our natural riches; we can be proud of what we have accomplished. But, unless we understand the important part played by America, the land, in our enviable life, we shall not be able to keep moving forward as fast as we did in the past, for our land now has far fewer natural resources and far more people. In just half a century we have changed from an exporter to an importer of many vitally needed raw materials. Daily we become more dependent on other countries for the sinews of our economic and military power. We are deficient in eighteen of the thirty most important industrial minerals and we lack five completely; our oil production will pass its peak about 1965, twenty years before this happens in the world at large. Then we shall have to import oil or undertake the costly process of utilizing shale-oil deposits. It is possible that we may then have to operate with energy which is more expensive than that used elsewhere. This will adversely affect our standard of living and our political power. Imperceptibly some of the foundations supporting our present prosperity and world position have been getting weaker. As always happens when things are turned upside down, it takes a while for people to readjust their beliefs to changed conditions.

Most Americans still think of ours as an empty, fabulously rich country and of our people as superior to all others, if not in everything at least in everything technical. Yet, a healthy baby born today may well live to see a population density in this country as high as that of Europe, excluding

Russia. We have much semiarid and eroded land; Europe has no semiarid regions and she has preserved her soil, her forests, and her water supply. We lost almost 3 percent of our most fertile farm lands in fifteen short years (17 million acres), but small Holland has been wresting a whole new province from the North Atlantic. Charles Morrow Wilson estimates that the acreage in roadsides of the United States, not including other rights of way, is equal to the size of the state of Georgia, the largest state east of the Mississippi. Our rapid urbanization alone destroys annually 1 million acres of land which will never again produce a crop. Much of it was good farm land. In the past we could afford to be wasteful but in the future we may have to follow Europe's example and condemn only the poorest land for housing or factory development. The day may come when future Americans will even deplore our fine new interstate highway system which will cost us 2 million acres of land.

The use a people makes of its natural resources is basically a matter of education and wisdom. We have not done so well as Europe in this matter. We still think there are no limits to expansion in this country, even though the warning signals are here for all to see. Our wastage of water alone will soon bring us up against a really serious problem. Last year distilled water was sold in Dallas, Texas, at 50 cents a gallon!

There is but one way out of our worsening raw materials position and that is to develop to their utmost our human resources — the minds of our young people. They will need far more highly trained minds than the ones we get by with in order to cope with the poorer and more crowded world we are bequeathing to them. One of the ways in which we can ease their problems is to provide ahead of time for eventual replacement of natural resources by artificial, man-made substitutes such as atomic energy, which may to some extent replace fossil fuels when these are finally exhausted. Every day we waste in fighting those who interfere with development of substitutes for the irreplaceable resources we ourselves are using up will hurt future Americans. For the sake of our descendants, we must get on with this work and not let ourselves be stopped or slowed by outdated attitudes, institutions, or hallowed procedures.

Our present educational system does not produce enough trained people to carry forward new projects of this kind. We would be wise to investigate how Europe educates her children, for she prepares them better than we do for the more difficult life we must expect in the future. Yet she maintains a decent and comfortable standard of living on her very limited resources and her crowded land. It is not too early to prepare for a time when our children must be as well equipped as Europe's because our future is her present.

We often personalize countries when we want to make a point. Countries do act through human beings and analogies therefore have some validity. To paraphrase Donne, no country is an island, entire of itself. We are not so great and wise that we cannot profit from the experience of others, especially from countries that have lived longer than we and that have had some measure of success. We are nearly all of us children of Europe. Like young people the world over, younger countries go through a phase when they reject everything the parent country stands for, believes in, and does. But we are growing older. Has not the time come when we can associate with Europe as grown-up children do with their parents? I am reminded of what Mark Twain said:

"When I was a boy of fourteen, my father was so ignorant I could hardly stand to have the old man around. But when I got to be twenty-one, I was astonished at how much the old man had learned in seven years."

Never rich in land or raw materials, Europe achieved enormous power, prosperity, and world influence through cultivation of brain power. It seems advisable to me that we observe how she did this.

We can learn from her respect for the superior human mind — the kind of mind we need to move our techniques to higher levels and thus to offset loss of tangible national wealth. For the first time in history the mind is really coming into its own. Only countries which understand and respect the creative processes of the intellect will be able to maintain themselves in decency in this overfull world. Only those who give free scope to men who work creatively will progress. It is strange that the importance of intellectual freedom and creativity should have been better understood in authoritarian Prussia and totalitarian Russia — bent on exploiting human intelligence for the benefit of power-hungry rulers — than in our own humane democracy. Prussia and imperial Germany were pioneers in establishing an excellent public educational system, adequate for the masses and highly conducive to development of superior scientific achievement by the talented few. It was so good that many European democracies adapted it to their own needs. Russia has now adopted our ideal of universal education and combined it with the excellence of the European educational system, and in but twenty-five years she has worked wonders. We do not want her school system. We must devise one suited to our own needs. In it we, too, must combine the ideals of universal education and of scholastic excellence.

At different levels of civilization, different degrees of popular education are needed. A future dependent on creative brains obviously must have an educational system quite different from the one needed when men of brawn and physical courage exploited this continent. With hindsight we now see the mistakes of the past; we realize that we would now have better soil, cleaner rivers, and more extensive forests had there

been some infusion of informed thinking, some consideration of future needs when our natural wealth was expropriated during the great westward movement. Past Americans have mined our incredibly rich soil, ravaged our forests, and squandered our mineral and fuel resources with reckless, with truly heroic abandon. Future Americans will have to make shift with less natural wealth. They will manage this if we prepare them for greater intellectual exertion by providing a vastly better educational system.

Our schools have done a fine job making Americans out of motley groups of foreigners from all corners of the globe and doing it in record time. This job is finished. The schools must now tackle a different job. They must concentrate on bringing the intellectual powers of each child to the highest possible level. Even the average child now needs almost as good an education as the average middle- and upper-class child used to get in the college preparatory schools. The talented child needs special schooling to move him rapidly through the period of absorbing knowledge into the period when his fine mind can turn this knowledge into new ideas, new discoveries, new ways of life. We need creative thinkers in the humanities no less than in the sciences. Living in crowded areas demands more of us in tolerance, in consideration, and in acceptance of necessary rules than life on a frontier. Perhaps our children — certainly our grandchildren — will have to live with fewer material possessions. It is not too early to turn to inner resources which are limitless: to art, music, literature, good conversation; to cultivation of a more contemplative way of life.

Democracy is a growing force. It never reaches perfection. It ever finds new objectives. To achieve it in a small, homogeneous farming community is one thing. To maintain it in a metropolitan, highly industrialized country is another. We must not make shibboleths of words such as "democracy" and "equality." I think that Erich Fromm gave us a wonderful definition for both. In an interview with Mike Wallace he said that democracy is consent by the governed, active participation and responsibility of each citizen in the whole social life; not being a little cog who is satisfied that he is manipulated the right way, by persuasion and not by force. But I like his definition of equality best. It means, he said, that we are all created in the image of God, and "that no man must be the means for the ends of another, that every man is an end in himself." That, he said, "is the only equality there is."

This democracy and this equality do not require that we deny to the minority of people with creative minds the right to use them in their own way and to their fullest potential. They do not mean that we cannot accept the rare contributions which creative people are able to make merely because not everybody can do the same thing. Nor should the great ideas of democracy and equality be vulgarized into exaction of conformity to the opinions and tastes of the majority on pain of being considered odd, undemocratic, stuck up, or maladjusted. People who use their minds successfully ought not to be expected to pretend they are just like everybody else — except, of course, for the one matter in which they excel. We have gone quite far in forcing unusual people to buy acceptance from us by making a show of their simple tastes, their conformity to popular views of what constitutes a "normal" person. It is often by this form of crude flattery alone that they win permission to do their work. The people rule and they rule as absolutely as the Bourbon kings of France. France was not run very well when everyone had to win the king's permission for necessary actions by flattering him. Then, too, the most effective flattery was imitation. Nothing the king did was too silly or trivial not to be immediately copied by every ambitious courtier.

Here celebrities of one kind or another must all win the people's permission to be themselves by similar imitation. It is seldom enough that a woman is both beautiful and a gifted actress. To keep her public happy she must also make a great show of domestic virtues — perhaps feign to like scrubbing her kitchen floor. It isn't enough for a brilliant scientist to have made a discovery which will bring great benefit to millions of average people; he must also pretend that he shares all the endearing little foibles and simple pleasures of the average man. Everyone who is in any way unusual suffers from the arrogance of mediocre people. I have before me a resumé of a "research" project undertaken by certain educationists in which they set themselves up as judges of the character and personality of scientists of note. What strikes these judges is the alleged poor social adjustment of these unusual people, and one is made to feel that this defect far outweighs any possible contributions the scientists may have made to the common good.

Recently an eminent scholar made some pertinent observations about American life. At least one commentator chose to report on this solely in terms of the color and shape of the scholar's socks. A small amount of respect and tolerance would lessen the estrangement now existing between the "eggheads" and the public at large. Last year Viscount Hailsham proposed a toast to the Royal Society in which he talked back at some of these detractors of intelligence. Many an American "egghead" must have felt like cheering. "Eggheads of the world, unite!" urged the viscount. "We have nothing to lose but our brains. A country neglects its eggheads at its peril. For it is the egghead who is the greatest realist. It is the egghead who invents the Sputnik, not the captain of the football team." That very egghead is considered "unfit for the society of successful politicians, hardheaded men of business, simple soldiers, silent sailors or working journalists, and all the other kind of folk who make such a botch of this practical world by refusing to think about the theoretical problems involved in the art of living."

We might get some very practical results if we tried to understand our brainworkers better; if we stopped thinking of science as a mere "comfort-grinding machine," a term coined by Huxley in a moment of anger; if we respected the true scientist's thirst for knowledge for the sake of knowledge and his irritation when we keep asking "will it be useful for us?" . . .

Our timidity in the face of organized pressure tactics by groups whose interest it is to silence all comment on matters they wish to order to their own satisfaction, without regard to the possibility that this may do damage to the nation as a whole — this timidity continues to this very day. Robert M. Hutchins warns us that we must realize that "an uncriticized culture cannot long endure." It would indeed be tragic if democracy deteriorated into mass tyranny over the unconventional individual. We should then lose the diversity from which spring all great ideas; we should rob ourselves of the precious quality that distinguishes man from all other orders — his determination to think for himself; *to be different.*

105.

ROBERT H. THAYER: America's Cultural Relations Abroad

America's foreign trade expanded greatly during and after World War II, and its interest in its "image" abroad increased proportionately. One of the main items of export was American "culture" — for example, the margin of profit of most American moviemakers in the postwar period was foreign sales — but others besides businessmen were concerned that the nations of the world not only buy American products but also understand the country's deep and age-old commitment to peace and freedom. Above all, the government was convinced that the Cold War must be waged with ideas as well as with weapons and money. Robert H. Thayer, special assistant to the secretary of state for the Coordination of International Educational and Cultural Relations, discussed these and related matters in an address before the Virginia Women's Forum of Richmond on November 5, 1959. Portions of his speech are reprinted here.

Source: *Bulletin*, November 23, 1959.

FROM AN OFFICIAL POINT OF VIEW I have looked forward with great anticipation to the opportunity of talking to you about the new position that I hold, its objectives, and most of all the part that every one of you ladies here can play in this very vital work. I believe very sincerely that there is something akin to a crusade to be waged in the field that I am engaged in, and I know enough of American history to appreciate that there is no group of individuals more enthusiastic in espousing a crusade, or more effective in carrying it out, than the ladies of the state of Virginia.

Let me tell you about this crusade. It is a new way of waging peace. It is the way in which mutual understanding between the peoples of the world can be so firmly established that not even the totalitarian monster of international communism can drive them apart into misunderstanding and war. It is the way in which people under the Communist yoke are going to find freedom of thought and spiritual release from the bondage of dialectical materialism. It is the way in which the people of the new countries that are springing into being in Africa and Asia are going to be helped to take their rightful place beside us in the free world as equal partners in a modern, up-to-date civilization. It is the way in which the concept of a free world with no underdeveloped countries, no East and West or North and South as separate areas, can be brought to realization.

What is this way? I call it "cultural diplomacy" — a new type of international relationship, a relationship of people to people as distinguished from government to government, a relationship in which every American citizen can and should play just as important a part as did the great diplomats of the early days of our American history — Benjamin Franklin, Thomas Jefferson, Washington Irving, and James Russell Lowell. Cultural diplomacy is the normal, logical development of the relationship between nations in the modern world of today. . . .

Can anyone say that economic aid alone is winning us the cold war? Can we say that these relationships really have succeeded in building a world where peoples of all races and backgrounds can live in understanding and peace? The answer is obviously no. The old types of diplomacy, the old methods of dealing between nation and nation, have not succeeded. The existence of an embassy within a country — the appointment of ambassadors assisted by a staff of Foreign Service officers, the contacts between these ambassadors and their staffs and foreign government officials — does not insure mutual understanding between peoples of the countries concerned. It does not even assure mutual understanding between governments.

Now let us examine this cultural diplomacy of which I speak. What is it exactly? It is not complicated. It is simple — and therein lies its strength and potential for success. It is the act of arranging the broadest and closest possible contact between the people of America and the peoples of the rest of the world — and the mutual communication through this contact of every facet of the life of these peoples, the one to the other.

This concept is not complicated or obtuse; it is simple. To implement it is, alas, not simple, but every single person here today can make a personal contribution toward this implementation.

I have a very great personal friend who holds a high position in one of the leading activities of American life today. He has told me repeatedly that he will never travel to a foreign country other than the British Commonwealth because he cannot submit, even temporarily, to the confusion and personal embarrassment of living in a country whose language he cannot understand. And yet I know that the warmth and magnetism of this individual's personality, his sincere love of his fellowman, his dedication to the elements that are common to all human relationships, would make him able, by his own example, to explain America clearly and effectively to any people with whom he might come in contact.

What is it that makes it so difficult for an American to understand and to communicate with someone from a country outside of the United States? We have been physically isolated from the rest of the world for a long time, it is true, but the United States is a big country and there are hundreds and thousands of Americans in New England who have never been to California. Furthermore, I would venture to say that one might, on analysis, find as many differences between a citizen of the state of Virginia and a citizen of the state of Montana as one might find between a Bostonian and an Australian. The psychological aura of Americanism that makes a Virginian and Montanan, upon meeting, relaxed and receptive to each other's efforts to communicate — which insures that communication, in fact — that same Americanism seems automatically to raise an artificial barrier between Americans and the people of other nations. And let me emphasize that it is artificial, a kind of psychological block, which is unnatural, unnecessary, and more easily removable than anyone realizes.

I was talking on this subject the other day with a high-ranking official of the United States government. He told me the story of his first trip to Europe, which so echoed my own experience that it startled me. He described the shock of familiarity that greeted his first trip to England — the ride from Southampton in the boat train, the familiar countryside with its hedges and checkerboard fields, the little villages and church steeples, and London with its chimney pots and even its smells that made him certain he had been there and seen it all before — and then the sudden dawning that indeed he had been there before as a boy, in Charles Dickens and Meredith and Trollope and Thackeray. And in this dawning there dropped from him all the psychological inhibitions of an American outside his own environment and there came on him a relaxed receptivity, an ability to give and receive communication. . . .

Cultural diplomacy seeks to build up a social environment of mutual trust in which peoples can attempt to understand each other and thrash out their problems without resorting to force. Cultural diplomacy is de-

signed to develop in all peoples a world outlook, a basic awareness of community matters as they affect the larger area of world affairs.

To coordinate the government's efforts in this field, the Department of State has created the office which I now hold as head of the Bureau of International Cultural Relations. Under my jurisdiction in the bureau is the well-known International Educational Exchange Program, which provides for the exchange of approximately 6,500 students, teachers, professors, and specialists between the United States and about 100 countries each year. It includes the famous Fulbright and Smith-Mundt programs. Some of you may have personal knowledge of these programs because of family members or neighbors who have won Fulbright and Smith-Mundt grants to travel abroad. I wonder how many of you here today have children in the classrooms of the six foreign teachers from England, France, Germany, and Canada who are teaching in Virginia this year. Our teacher from France is right here in Richmond, and the others are in Winchester, Charlottesville, South Norfolk, Princess Anne, and Waynesboro. . . .

The International Educational Exchange Program also provides support to American-sponsored schools in other countries. Many of these schools are staffed by American teachers and provide an introduction to the American way of life to thousands of foreign students who might never have a chance to visit the United States.

The program has been building slowly but surely since the war. More than 65,000 of its alumni, in every state of the Union and in every corner of the globe, are constant sources of truth about the countries they visited. This group is a steadily growing bulwark against the harsh effects of Communist false propaganda and the psychological block of which I spoke. The exchange program is one of our most valuable tools in our long-range effort to build a lasting peace.

There is also the President's Special International Program for Cultural Presentations. This program assists American performing artists and athletes to appear in other countries. Most of you have read, I'm sure, of the outstanding success of the New York Philharmonic Symphony Orchestra in its recent tour of Europe and the Soviet Union and of the National Symphony Orchestra in South America. Many other attractions have gone abroad under this program, including the San Francisco Ballet, the Roger Wagner Chorale, the Woody Herman Jazz Band, and Blanche Thebom, the Metropolitan Opera singer. . . .

Outside the Bureau of International Cultural Relations — in organizations like the United States Information Agency, the International Cooperation Administration, the Defense Department, the National Institutes of Health, the Library of Congress, and a host of others — there are many activities that involve the movement of people and cultural materials between the United States and other countries.

The International Cooperation Administration brought 8,000 foreign citizens to the United States for training last year and sent more than 3,500 American technicians abroad to teach skills to the peoples of other countries. Under its various information programs the United States Information Agency arranges for the translation and sale of American books in other countries, the teaching of English to about 200,000 foreign students each year in 55 countries, the purchase of American textbooks for foreign educational institutions, and the maintenance of libraries and reading rooms in hundreds of foreign cities.

The first Americans to visit the Soviet Union as members of cultural delegations in 1958 were caught flatfooted by the question, "What do you think of Willis Conover?" None of the visitors had ever heard of Willis Conover, much less thought anything about him. They later found out that Willis Conover is heard regularly by millions of people outside the United States who listen to his broadcasts of jazz music over the Voice of America. Although his broadcasts are in English and he used to be hampered by radio jamming, Willis Conover is one of the best known and most popular representatives of American culture abroad.

Outside of the government — in the private sector — the exchange programs of universities, foundations, service clubs, sororities, and fraternities are greater in scope than those of all government agencies combined.

Last year, more than 47,000 foreign students were enrolled at American institutions of higher learning. Less than 5 percent had United States government support. We know also that approximately 78,000 foreign nationals came to the United States in 1958 for cultural purposes. In addition to the students and teachers engaged in academic pursuits, there were business executives who came for training, journalists and authors on temporary assignments, professional people attending international conferences, performing artists and athletes, and doctors holding internships and residencies at American hospitals.

Traveling in the other direction were approximately 28,000 Americans engaged in cultural projects. Add to this figure the military, government, and business employees stationed abroad and you have a picture of 2 percent of the American population living among other peoples, providing a daily image of the United States to millions of foreign citizens in all walks of life. . . .

May I enlist the active help of everyone here in this great work? There are two things to be done: We must educate ourselves and our children for world responsibility, and we must bring the peoples of the world right into our own communities. We must teach our children to think of foreign lands with the same naturalness and anticipation and delight as they think of their own. We must turn every town and hamlet of the United States into a Burns, Kansas, which has become known all over the world as a town where foreigners are welcomed in every house and at every table.

What can you do in this work? As community leaders and mothers, one of your primary concerns is education. Many of you sit on school boards. Most of you belong to parent-teacher associations. All of you are interested in education. Reexamine the educational systems in your area from the international point of view. Are they adequate to maintain United States leadership in a rapidly changing world? Is there sufficient foreign language instruction? Are the cultures of the Middle East, Latin America, Africa, and Asia being presented properly, if at all? Do you have foreign students and teachers in your schools to inject different ideas and stimulate interest in other peoples? We need more cultural ambassadors. Are your schools doing the job?

How many of you have come into contact with foreign students in your own communities? There were 331 enrolled at 32 universities and colleges in Virginia last year. They must be made to feel at home and be given a chance to gather firsthand knowledge of our institutions — our homes, theaters, sporting events, churches, shopping centers, factories, elections, and every other aspect of our way of life. There is only one way to do this, and that is to invite them. Organized hospitality for foreign visitors is one of the most important contributions any community can make to the successful conduct of our foreign policy. I am sure you are doing this, but do a great deal more. A foreigner who has tasted the hospitality of a Virginia home will not easily forget America.

I urge you all, therefore, to think about the relationships of your communities to the rest of the world. Remember that in this most important task of developing an atmosphere of confidence and trust among peoples the government's basic role is to provide guidance and coordination. The heavy burden of cultural diplomacy is on the individual and the community.

This is, indeed, a crusade. It is not one to which governments can draft their peoples; it is a crusade of all the peoples on earth joining in a common effort to establish mutual understanding.

Our children and grandchildren and great-grandchildren must find it just as easy and natural to sit down and share a meal with a man from Istanbul or Athens or Rome or Moscow as to dine with a man from San Francisco or Dallas or Chicago or, yes, even Boston!

We must bring up our youth to drop the word "foreign" from their vocabulary. We must teach them to speak many languages. But languages are no barriers to the very young. Rockets will take future generations in a few minutes or seconds over distances over which ships carried our ancestors in weeks or months.

But, while we watch with awe and admiration the progress of physical communication, let us not neglect a far more important element — in fact, the very basis of human relationships — that is, the mental and spiritual communication which leads to understanding.

An American's country does not end with the Statue of Liberty or the Twelve Mile Limit.

SAMUEL PUTNAM

1960

106.

Dwight D. Eisenhower: The U-2 Incident

*Nikita Khrushchev's trip to America in 1959, during which he visited an Iowa farm,
Hollywood (but not Disneyland), as well as the United Nations in New York, combined
with the announcement of plans for a summit meeting in May 1960, led to widespread
hopes that relations between the U.S. and the U.S.S.R. were finally improving.
However, on May 5, just eleven days before the meeting in Paris was to occur, the
Soviet premier announced that an American plane had been shot down over Russian
territory. U.S. officials immediately replied that the plane was on a meteorological
mission and had strayed off course. Khrushchev then announced that he had material
proof, as well as a confession from the pilot, Francis Powers, that the flight was
a military reconnaissance mission collecting data for "aggressive purposes." The
U.S. State Department then issued a surprise statement conceding that Powers had
been on an intelligence mission. On May 25 President Eisenhower broadcast an
address to the American people, in which he not only accepted full responsibility
for the flights but also presented a moral justification for them. The summit meeting
did take place as planned. Eisenhower's address is reprinted here in part.*

Source: *Bulletin,* June 6, 1960, pp. 899-903.

My Fellow Americans:

Tonight I want to talk with you about
the remarkable events last week in Paris,
and their meaning to our future.

First, I am deeply grateful to the many
thousands of you, and to representatives in
Congress, who sent me messages of encouragement and support while I was in Paris,
and later upon my return to Washington.
Your messages clearly revealed your abiding
loyalty to America's great purpose — that

of pursuing, from a position of spiritual,
moral, and material strength — a lasting
peace with justice.

You recall, of course, why I went to Paris ten days ago.

Last summer and fall I had many conversations with world leaders; some of these
were with Chairman Khrushchev, here in
America. Over those months a small improvement in relations between the Soviet
Union and the West seemed discernible. A

possibility developed that the Soviet leaders might at last be ready for serious talks about our most persistent problems — those of disarmament, mutual inspection, atomic control, and Germany, including Berlin.

To explore that possibility, our own and the British and French leaders met together, and later we agreed, with the Soviet leaders, to gather in Paris, on May 16.

Of course we had no indication or thought that basic Soviet policies had turned about. But when there is even the slightest chance of strengthening peace, there can be no higher obligation than to pursue it.

Nor had our own policies changed. We did hope to make some progress in a summit meeting, unpromising though previous experiences had been. But as we made preparations for this meeting, we did not drop our guard nor relax our vigilance.

Our safety, and that of the free world, demand, of course, effective systems for gathering information about the military capabilities of other powerful nations, especially those that make a fetish of secrecy. This involves many techniques and methods. In these times of vast military machines and nuclear-tipped missiles, the ferreting out of this information is indispensable to free-world security.

This has long been one of my most serious preoccupations. It is part of my grave responsibility, within the overall problem of protecting the American people, to guard ourselves and our allies against surprise attack.

During the period leading up to World War II, we learned from bitter experience the imperative necessity of a continuous gathering of intelligence information, the maintenance of military communications and contact, and alertness of command.

An additional word seems appropriate about this matter of communications and command. While the secretary of defense and I were in Paris, we were, of course, away from our normal command posts. He recommended that under the circumstances we test the continuing readiness of our military communications. I personally approved. Such tests are valuable and will be frequently repeated in the future.

Moreover, as President, charged by the Constitution with the conduct of America's foreign relations, and as commander in chief, charged with the direction of the operations and activities of our armed forces and their supporting services, I take full responsibility for approving all the various programs undertaken by our government to secure and evaluate military intelligence.

It was in the prosecution of one of these intelligence programs that the widely publicized U-2 incident occurred.

Aerial photography has been one of many methods we have used to keep ourselves and the free world abreast of major Soviet military developments. The usefulness of this work has been well established through four years of effort. The Soviets were well aware of it. Chairman Khrushchev has stated that he became aware of these flights several years ago. Only last week, in this Paris press conference, Chairman Khrushchev confirmed that he knew of these flights when he visited the United States last September.

Incidentally, this raises the natural question — why all the furor concerning one particular flight? He did not, when in America last September, charge that these flights were any threat to Soviet safety. He did not then see any reason to refuse to confer with American representatives. This he did only about the flight that unfortunately failed, on May 1, far inside Russia.

Now, two questions have been raised about this particular flight: first, as to its timing, considering the imminence of the summit meeting; second, our initial statements when we learned the flight had failed.

As to the timing, the question was really whether to halt the program and thus forgo the gathering of important information that was essential and that was likely to be unavailable at a later date. The decision was that the program should not be halted. The plain truth is this: When a nation needs intelligence activity, there is no time when vigilance can be relaxed. Incidentally, from Pearl Harbor we learned that even negotiation itself can be used to conceal preparations for a surprise attack.

Next, as to our government's initial statement about the flight, this was issued to protect the pilot, his mission, and our intelligence processes, at a time when the true facts were still undetermined.

Our first information about the failure of this mission did not disclose whether the pilot was still alive, was trying to escape, was avoiding interrogation, or whether both plane and pilot had been destroyed. Protection of our intelligence system and the pilot, and concealment of the plane's mission, seemed imperative. It must be remembered that over a long period these flights had given us information of the greatest importance to the nation's security. In fact, their success has been nothing short of remarkable.

For these reasons, what is known in intelligence circles as a "covering statement" was issued. It was issued on assumptions that were later proved incorrect. Consequently, when later the status of the pilot was definitely established and there was no further possibility of avoiding exposure of the project, the factual details were set forth.

I then made two facts clear to the public: First, our program of aerial reconnaissance had been undertaken with my approval; second, this government is compelled to keep abreast, by one means or another, of military activities of the Soviets, just as their government has for years engaged in espionage activities in our country and throughout the world. Our necessity to proceed with such activities was also asserted by our secretary of state, who, however, had been careful — as was I — not to say that these particular flights would be continued.

In fact, before leaving Washington I had directed that these U-2 flights be stopped. Clearly their usefulness was impaired. Moreover, continuing this particular activity in these new circumstances could not but complicate the relations of certain of our allies with the Soviets. And of course, new techniques, other than aircraft, are constantly being developed.

Now, I wanted no public announcement of this decision until I could personally disclose it at the summit meeting in conjunction with certain proposals I had prepared for the conference.

At my first Paris meeting with Mr. Khrushchev, and before his tirade was made public, I informed him of this discontinuance and the character of the constructive proposals I planned to make. These contemplated the establishment of a system of aerial surveillance operated by the United Nations. The day before the first scheduled meeting, Mr. Khrushchev had advised President de Gaulle and Prime Minister Macmillan that he would make certain demands upon the United States as a precondition for beginning a summit conference. Although the United States was the only power against which he expressed his displeasure, he did not communicate this information to me. I was, of course, informed by our allies.

At the four-power meeting on Monday morning, he demanded of the United States four things: first, condemnation of U-2 flights as a method of espionage; second, assurance that they would not be continued; third, a public apology on behalf of the United States; and, fourth, punishment of all those who had any responsibility respecting this particular mission.

I replied by advising the Soviet leader that I had, during the previous week, stopped these flights and that they would not be resumed. I offered also to discuss the matter with him in personal meetings, while the regular business of the summit might proceed. Obviously, I would not respond to his extreme demands. He knew, of course, by holding to those demands the Soviet Union was scuttling the summit conference.

In torpedoing the conference, Mr. Khrushchev claimed that he acted as the result of his own high moral indignation over alleged American acts of aggression. As I said earlier, he had known of these flights for a long time. It is apparent that the Soviets had decided even before the Soviet delegation left Moscow that my trip to the Soviet Union should be canceled and that nothing constructive from their viewpoint would come out of the summit conference.

In evaluating the results, however, I think we must not write the record all in red ink. There are several things to be written in the black. Perhaps the Soviet action has turned the clock back in some measure, but it should be noted that Mr. Khrushchev did not go beyond invective — a timeworn Soviet device to achieve an immediate objective, in this case, the wrecking of the conference.

On our side, at Paris, we demonstrated once again America's willingness, and that of her allies, always to go the extra mile in behalf of peace. Once again Soviet intransigence reminded us all of the unpredictability of despotic rule and the need for those who work for freedom to stand together in determination and in strength.

The conduct of our allies was magnificent. My colleagues and friends — President de Gaulle and Prime Minister Macmillan — stood sturdily with the American delegation in spite of persistent Soviet attempts to split the Western group. The NATO meeting after the Paris conference showed unprecedented unity and support for the alliance and for the position taken at the summit meeting. I salute our allies for us all.

And now, most importantly, what about the future?

All of us know that, whether started deliberately or accidentally, global war would leave civilization in a shambles. This is as true of the Soviet system as of all others. In a nuclear war there can be no victors — only losers. Even despots understand this. Mr. Khrushchev stated last week that he well realizes that general nuclear war would bring catastrophe for both sides. Recognition of this mutual destructive capability is the basic reality of our present relations. Most assuredly, however, this does not mean that we shall ever give up trying to build a more sane and hopeful reality — a better foundation for our common relations.

To do this, here are the policies we must follow, and to these I am confident the great majority of our people, regardless of party, give their support:

First, we must keep up our strength, and hold it steady for the long pull — a strength not neglected in complacency nor overbuilt in hysteria. So doing, we can make it clear to everyone that there can be no gain in the use of pressure tactics or aggression against us and our allies.

Second, we must continue businesslike dealings with the Soviet leaders on outstanding issues, and improve the contacts between our own and the Soviet peoples, making clear that the path of reason and common sense is still open if the Soviets will but use it.

Third, to improve world conditions in which human freedom can flourish, we must continue to move ahead with positive programs at home and abroad, in collaboration with free nations everywhere. In doing so, we shall continue to give our strong support to the United Nations and the great principles for which it stands.

Now as to the first of these purposes — our defenses are sound. They are tailored to the situation confronting us. Their adequacy has been my primary concern for these past seven years — indeed, throughout my adult life. In no respect have the composition and size of our forces been based on or affected by any Soviet blandishment. Nor will they be. We will continue to carry forward the great improvements already planned in these forces. They will be kept ready — and under constant review. Any changes made necessary by technological advances or world events will be recommended at once.

This strength — by far the most potent on earth — is, I emphasize, for deterrent, defensive, and retaliatory purposes only, without threat or aggressive intent toward anyone.

107.

The Super-City

America's population has shown a steady movement from the country to the city for at least the last century. But during the second quarter of the twentieth century a new trend began to show itself, in the relegation of business and administrative activities to the "central city," and the flight of the populace to the suburbs — "dormitory cities," as they came to be called. The new phenomenon was no longer "urban" in the old sense, and a new term — "the metropolitan area" — was applied to it. The metropolitan areas of America ignored geographical and especially political bounds — for example, the New York metropolitan area includes previously independent communities in three states, New York, New Jersey, and Connecticut — and thereby created new and unprecedented political as well as economic problems. The following report on recent developments in the American city was prepared by the Committee for Economic Development, an organization financed by members of the business community for the purpose of studying current social and economic issues. Part of the report, which was published in 1960, is reprinted here.

Source: *The American City*, Charles N. Glaab, ed., Homewood, Ill., 1963, pp. 461-473.

BACKGROUND AND BASIC TRENDS

1. *Background.* Within the span of a century America has gone through two great changes in its living patterns. In the last quarter of the nineteenth century and the first quarter of the twentieth century we shifted from a predominantly rural to urban society.

The second change in American life during the twentieth century is from a basically urban to metropolitan condition. Prior to the metropolitan era, cities were centers of industrial and commercial activity. The workers lived in closely built houses and tenements within walking distance of factories or of trolley-car and subway lines that went out only relatively short distances from the hub. Sanitation problems of this pattern of urban concentration were met by a central public sewer system. There was little question where the city ended and the country began. Outside of city boundaries there were no large population concentrations, and government structure outside these boundaries was designed for a basically rural condition.

The metropolitan area is in effect a new community. Its boundaries often are hard to define. In some instances they change and expand frequently. The area ignores old geographic boundaries, jumping over and around rivers and land masses. It ignores the political lines of districts, villages, towns, cities, counties, and states.

The metropolitan area reflects a new kind of society resulting from higher average incomes, the development of new tastes in living standards, and technological means for releasing people from the old patterns. The private automobile has freed many from dependence on local public transportation. The greatly increased use of septic tanks has, temporarily at least, freed dwellers from dependence on a central public sewer system. The location of industrial plants outside the core city has diffused job opportunities throughout a wide area. Suburban shopping centers have changed the marketing pattern.

These tendencies have increased rather than decreased the problems of government. As our population grows and our technology advances, the decisions about the use of land and of public revenue become increasingly complex. The governmental machinery to make these decisions and the governmental influences on private market decisions have not kept pace with this complexity. As a result, we are faced with increasing traffic congestion, blight in our central cities, unequal public burdens of suburban expansion, duplication of public facilities, and an inefficient use of public and private resources.

2. *Population Growth.* Two trends have dominated the long-term growth of population in the United States; an ever larger proportion of our people live in urban areas; and within urban areas, the suburbs and fringe are growing relatively faster than

the central districts. Urbanization of our population has been in process for more than a century. In 1850 only 15 percent of our people lived in urban places. By 1900 the proportion had risen to 40 percent and twenty years later passed the halfway mark.

Today two out of three Americans live in urban areas. The growth of urban population — both relatively and in absolute terms — shows no sign of abating. It is a reflection not only of the shift of population from rural to urban areas but of the tendency of urban populations to expand by natural increase.

Metropolitanism is a twentieth-century phenomenon. Technological advances, primarily in the field of transportation, have made possible a diffusion of plants, homes, and shops in a wide expanse around the older central city. As of June 1959, the Bureau of the Census recognized 192 standard metropolitan areas — central cities of 50,000 or more together with their contiguous suburban areas. Within these areas, slightly more than half of the population still reside in the central cities, but 80 percent of the population growth in metropolitan areas since 1950 has been registered in the suburbs, and the day is fast approaching when a majority of our metropolitan population will reside outside the central cities.

Where are these trends taking us? An intermediate projection by the Bureau of the Census is for a population of 220 million in 1975, an increase of roughly 40 million over 1960. If metropolitan areas continue to get three-fourths of this national growth, our metropolitan population in 1975 will approximate 140 million persons. Central cities will still hold great concentrations of people — in the aggregate, perhaps 60 million. But the balance will have shifted to areas outside present central-city boundaries: 80 million people will live in the suburbs and fringes of metropolitan districts.

By the year 2000, only forty years from now, the population will exceed 300 million according to intermediate estimates of demographers, an increase of 120 million. As many as 100 million of these will be added to the present population of our metropolitan areas.

3. *Urbanization.* Two large questions must be examined: First, will the forces making for urbanization be sustained? Second, how will various activities — manufacturing, wholesaling, retailing, business services, home building — be spatially distributed within metropolitan areas?

The forces which have transformed the United States into an urban nation within the lifetime of many of us are still ascendant. Barring several events — nuclear war, a national program for dispersal, or a pronounced shift in values — existing urbanmetropolitan regions will continue to grow. For such concentrations are evidently necessary to take maximum advantage of technological opportunities that give us a high and rising standard of living. The economies of mass production and distribution which are made possible by large urban markets are widely recognized.

We are perhaps less aware of the importance of external economies of aggregation in urban areas. These are savings available to the individual concern in the form of services or facilities outside the plant and shared with other producers. Among these are middlemen and distributors, bankers, legal experts, accountants, advertising services, and market analysts. Also, our transportation facilities, waterworks, sewerage plants and other massive overhead investments, and the availability of research facilities and technicians concentrated in university, library, and laboratory yield economies of this type.

Urban growth in the United States has become a cumulative process. The precondition for this growth, of course, was a marked rise in productivity on the farm with the introduction of new types of agricultural machinery in the second and third quarters of the nineteenth century. This not only yielded a surplus to feed large urban populations but released labor to the mills and shops of the city.

Meanwhile, as markets grew, mass production methods in manufacturing became more feasible. The resulting increases in output per worker were reflected in rising income for the community. This in turn made effective new consumer wants. To fill these demands a host of service industries emerged in the fields of recreation, education, personal and medical care. Commerce and industry also required more and different skills and services. Partially offsetting the economies of urban living are certain "diseconomies" which have required additional services — building inspectors, settlement-house workers, laundries, traffic police, and window washers.

The growth in urban-type activities is revealed in the changing composition of the nation's labor force over an eighty-year period. In 1870 slightly more than half of all gainfully employed workers were engaged in farming; by 1950 the proportion had dropped to one in eight workers. Meanwhile, workers employed in trade, finance, and related industries increased from 6.4 to 21.2 percent, professional service workers rose from 1.6 to 6.3 percent, and government employees increased from 2.0 to 7.9 percent. Since 1950 the largest relative gains have continued to be registered in service-type, urban-linked industries, particularly medical care, engineering and business services, public education, and other government services. These economic trends underlie the growth of urban areas at a rate considerably faster than the nation as a whole during the past half century.

The growth of urban areas continues to be fed by large-scale movements from the farms and small towns. The net migration from farms to urban areas in the United States between 1920 and 1955 amounted to about 24 million people. Most of the migrants are young adults. Many come from the rural South and Puerto Rico to the urban centers of the Northeast, the North Central region, and the West. These migrants are a major source of unskilled and semiskilled labor and have contributed significantly to the economic expansion of the urban areas. But the movements have also entailed social costs resulting from lack of experience with urban living and frequently from insufficient income to afford decent housing.

4. *The Pattern Of Development.* Within metropolitan regions, we are witnessing a significant redistribution of economic activities from the older central districts to the fringe areas. Home building and industrial plant construction are leading this outward movement; retail trades and household services, warehousing and other industrial services are rapidly adapting to the new patterns of development.

The statistics on home building and retailing since the end of World War II simply confirm our everyday observations. Of 13 million dwelling units erected in nonfarm areas from 1946 through 1958, approximately 11 million, or 85 percent, have been located outside of central cities. In retailing, data for the New York region are illustrative of the national trend. Both sales and jobs in retail lines have dropped steadily in the core as a proportion of the New York region over a twenty-five-year period with the outer rings registering the corresponding gains. In 1929 the core area accounted for about 69 percent of retail employment as well as sales; in 1954 these were down to about 60 and 55 percent respectively.

A gradual but unremitting relative decline in manufacturing jobs located in central cities is also discernible. Of total production workers in forty-eight standard metropolitan areas, 66.5 percent worked in the central cities of the areas in 1929; in 1954 the ratio was down to 53.6 percent. In the postwar years between 1947 and 1954, cen-tral cities like Cleveland, Chicago, St. Louis, and San Francisco have experienced *absolute* drops in manufacturing employment of 3 to 8 percent.

Certain types of activities, however, show little inclination to deconcentrate. Business and governmental services requiring face-to-face relationships or dependent upon a large pool of female labor continue to exercise a strong preference for office space in the core of large metropolitan areas. In eight leading standard metropolitan areas, about 80 percent of all employment in finance, insurance, and real estate in 1956 was in the central cities.

Further evidence of this tendency for office-type activities to concentrate in or near the central business district is found in figures on office-building construction. From 1946 through 1958 a total of 65 million square feet of new rentable office space was put on the market in twenty-four of the larger cities of the nation. Of this new space, some 27 million, or 42 percent of the total, went up in the nation's leading central business district, the island of Manhattan in New York City.

Central locations have also retained their hold on manufacturers of unstandardized products and those dependent upon a diversified mix of skills and materials. In six major central cities — Baltimore, Chicago, New York, Philadelphia, St. Louis, and San Francisco — total manufacturing employment in the central cities was 62.3 percent of manufacturing employment in the corresponding metropolitan areas in 1947, but for nineteen industrial central-cities employment averaged 85 percent of total area employment. Among those with the highest percentages in the central city were: fur goods — 99.2 percent; footwear cut stock — 98.9 percent; printing trade services — 96.1 percent; millinery — 95.9 percent; periodicals — 95.4 percent; miscellaneous publishing — 90.1 percent.

Between the business core and the rapidly growing suburbs lies a large expanse of older districts — the "gray areas." In the more compact city of 1920 these areas housed most of our families. Increasingly, since 1945, middle-income families with children have been departing for the suburbs; lower-income groups, including substantial numbers of racial minorities, have taken up the slack. But while there are few vacancies, physical deterioration of housing and supporting facilities is much in evidence. The gray areas are experiencing capital consumption and their economic future is in doubt.

What is the shape of things to come in metropolitan areas? In our mixed economy, investment decisions reflect a combination of factors — changes in industrial techniques, consumer preferences, and public policy. With regard to the location of new investment in metropolitan areas, the net effect of these factors in the postwar period has been to encourage a more dispersed pattern of development. For industries dealing in standardized products, the shift to horizontal-line processing in single-story plants has compelled a search for larger sites available only in the outer reaches of the metropolis. At the same time, the clustering of plants in new industrial districts has yielded some of the external economies formerly available mainly in the central city.

The strong desire for lower-density living on the part of families with children has led many to choose a suburban home. Federal policies in the field of mortgage insurance, which have generally favored single-family construction as against apartment developments, have strengthened this outward movement. So, too, have public policies in the fields of highway construction and education. On balance, these and related factors portend a more and more widely dispersed pattern of metropolitan development in the years ahead.

METROPOLITAN PROBLEMS

THE LARGE-SCALE BREAKOUT of residences, commercial activities, and manufacturing from the bounds of the central city has produced a number of major problems. Each part of the metropolitan area is faced with problems peculiar to itself. This diversity may strengthen the feeling of mutual antagonism between city and suburb. The area as a whole, however, faces problems which cannot be dealt with adequately on a piecemeal basis. Yet, so far, few areas have developed institutions which can adequately deal with these problems, and the prevailing antagonism between city and suburb inhibits the development of such institutions.

1. *Central City Problems.* The public service requirements of central cities are shaped by a unique set of pressures. One is the burden of handling a daytime population 30 to 50 percent greater than the residential population. The continuous decline in use of mass-transit facilities is making this task enormously more difficult. Between 1950 and 1958 transit riding in American cities fell from 17.2 billion to 9.7 billion rides per year, a drop of 43 percent. More and more people are getting to work or shopping by car.

The principal response of the cities has been to facilitate this shift by building or planning to build expressways to the core district and by adding to the supply of parking space. But discouraged by the growth of congestion, some cities like Washington, D.C. and San Francisco are considering a new emphasis on rapid-transit systems. For central cities, the provision of good access to the central business district can be expected to have a high priority in capital improvement programs in the years ahead.

An historic function which the central city continues to perform is that of reception center for low-income migrants from outside the region. A steady stream of people from the rural South and Puerto Rico has replaced earlier migrations from abroad as the chief source of unskilled and semiskilled labor in urban centers. The majority of these migrants characteristically settle in the central cities. Thus the cities carry a major share of the responsibility for helping newcomers adapt to an urban environment. It follows that city expenditures for social services, health clinics, welfare agencies, and public housing are considerably higher per capita than in suburban areas.

Another major concern of the central cities is the relentless spread of blight and obsolescence both of public and private facilities. In New York City, for example, almost half of the current capital budget is allocated to the replacement of outworn and outmoded public facilities. The prevention of excessive depreciation of private investments such as housing is a responsibility the municipality now shares with private owners.

Blight may afflict residential, commercial, or industrial areas. It involves neglect of property by owners and it may result in the development of unsafe and unsanitary conditions. Generally, large areas are afflicted. The law of contiguity, a Gresham's Law of land-use whereby poor uses drive out good, prevents private redevelopment in small parcels. Under favorable circumstances one activity would replace another when it could make better use of the site. But thousands of acres of built-up land in the central cities of our metropolitan areas are under-utilized and not filling needed functions. To restore land to sound use, redevelopment of a large acreage is generally required to overcome the impact of bad neighborhood influences.

Private ownership commonly finds it very difficult to redevelop on the scale necessary to establish new dominant uses. Owners of plots in such areas frequently have a price expectation far above market realities; many small plots must be accumulated; a few holdouts can make the cost inordinately high; and there are large demolition costs. Any major shift in land use requires a combination of capital, foresight, willingness to risk, and the full cooperation of the local government.

The public interest in restoring land to sound use and generally to a higher tax-paying basis is considerable. Not only does this increase vital functions in parts of the central city but it also reduces the heavy burden of providing fire protection, police protection, public facilities, and other services which a seriously blighted area requires.

The development of effective programs to check blight and obsolescence would entail substantial increases in municipal efforts to enforce building and housing codes, relocate displaced tenants, prepare community-wide and neighborhood plans and zoning ordinances, and related activities. Few, if any, cities are yet geared to handle this immense job. Thus, continuous pressure on city budgets may be expected from this field of municipal activity.

While the needs of central cities are growing, their revenue sources are not keeping pace. Property tax income is checked by the exodus of upper- and middle-income families and the establishment of retail shopping centers, new factories, and "clean" industries, such as research laboratories, outside the city limits. The resulting squeeze on taxpayers in some cases has sent property taxes so high as to make new private construction almost uneconomic. Without new construction to support and encourage new economic activity, the city finds it increasingly difficult to meet its revenue needs.

2. *Suburban Needs.* With more than eight out of ten new homes being erected in suburban communities, it is these places which

are feeling the brunt of demand for new schools, water systems, sewage-disposal plants, fire stations, streets, and utility lines. Each new house in a suburban development requires a package of public services which entail capital outlays ranging in cost from $2,500 to $3,500 or more, depending upon the density of development and degree of utilization. Thus, capital expenditures run substantially higher in suburban communities than in the central city or nonmetropolitan areas.

In the New York region, for example, suburbs made capital outlays in 1955 of $68 per capita compared with $44 in the central city and $38 in the nonmetropolitan sections. Considering these expenditures, it is no surprise that many communities try to effect their own salvation by screening out moderate-priced housing and forestalling a need for public sewerage systems and other facilities through such devices as two-acre zoning. For rapidly growing suburbs the good design of neighborhoods will provide long-lived improvement at minimum cost. Failure to take these steps now will prove very costly in ten to twenty years.

3. *Areawide Problems.* Some services essential to metropolitan living cannot be provided separately by each municipality. The size and geographic extent of the capital investment, the economic forces at work, the nature of the physical environment, or the claims for use by the residents of the area make it almost impossible for communities to provide services or meet these needs separately. Among these are the provision of areawide transportation systems, the control of air and water pollution, the reservation of open land for outdoor recreation, broad land-use planning, a fair distribution of tax resources, and the stimulation of growth in the economy of the area.

(a). Transportation. The transportation of goods and people is basic to the life of a metropolitan area. The most important transportation problem is the movement of people within the area to places of employ-

ment and for shopping. Recreational and other personal travel needs are generally adequately met by the facilities provided for the first two purposes.

Historically, public transportation and rail-commuter travel developed in our older metropolitan areas before the general use of the automobile. In these areas increased use of private automobiles has put financial strain on mass-transit and rail-commuter facilities. Some of our newer metropolitan areas have come to rely predominantly or almost exclusively on the private automobile supplemented by bus systems. In all areas increased use of the automobile has posed a serious congestion problem.

In the allocation of land and public revenues to various means of transportation three questions arise: (1) How shall facilities and travel be divided among highway, transit, and rail commuter? (2) Where shall facilities be located? and (3) How shall the cost be covered?

In planning for population growth and higher incomes, public agencies need to determine how to strike a balance among programs which expand highways, provide mass transportation, or shore up commuter facilities. At some point the additional space required for private automobile travel will so encroach on other land uses that mass transportation will have to be provided or improved to handle the additional travel. In some major metropolitan areas, rail-commuter services transport a significant number of people into the central city daily. Yet the abandonment of commuter lines under the provisions of the Transportation Act of 1958 is forcing more people to turn to the private automobile. A wholesale abandonment of commuter runs by railroads would greatly increase the expenditure and the land required for the highway system.

Commuter lines are suffering financial difficulties, with no easy solution. The property tax on roadbed and terminal facilities used by commuter lines is a competitive burden, for the highways used by alternative forms of travel are tax-free public facilities. But rail-commuter facilities share roadbed with rail freight and with long-distance passenger traffic.

Public responsibility for the problems of the commuter railroads is divided among the federal government, the state governments, and the many communities through which the rights-of-way run. As with mass-transit systems, the benefits are enjoyed by users, businesses dependent on commuter travel for employees and customers, and the general public.

Transportation networks within metropolitan areas are basic, the capital costs of new construction are high, and the operating costs of rail and mass transportation are heavy. Yet in most metropolitan areas there is no single public agency able to study the relative needs for highway, mass transit, or rail. There is no single body able to allocate costs among users, business, and the general tax funds. No authoritative body is able to balance transportation capacity and the traffic-generating uses of land. Under these circumstances many ills are apparent: undue congestion, duplicated facilities, poor service, financial difficulties, inequitable sharing of burdens, and inadequate anticipation of future needs and costs.

(b). Control of air and water pollution. The winds that blow across the Hudson River are no observers of municipal or state boundary lines. Any program to control smoke or other pollution of the air in and around New York obviously must be areawide. Each metropolitan area has a similar problem. The same holds true for control of the degree of contamination in fresh- or saltwater bodies in or on the boundaries of metropolitan areas. No individual municipality can influence the water flowing into it or washing its shores, except by cooperative effort with other municipalities, or through an areawide or state governmental body.

(c). Land-use planning and open land. Vacant land on the fringe of metropolitan areas is being absorbed at a rate of approximately 1 million acres a year. Current investments in housing, shopping centers, plants, streets, and public facilities are fixing the environment for two generations or more. But in few, if any, metropolitan areas is the magnitude of this responsibility matched by adequate preparation, planning, and land-development controls on a metropolitan scale. In consequence, transport facilities, sewerage and water systems, and schools have been overtaxed in many areas; commercial ribbon-developments have sprung up alongside metropolitan highways, choking traffic and blighting the countryside.

Equally important, few areas have reserved sufficient space for parks and recreational needs, and rights-of-way have not been set aside for future expressways and utility lines. All too frequently, land only recently developed in the outskirts of a metropolis has had to be purchased for a right-of-way at a price 5 to 10 times as much as the cost of the raw parcels. These costs as well as the uprooting of families and businesses are avoidable through advance planning and acquisition by the government of rights in land.

(d). Industrial development. The expansion of income-generating activities is desired by practically all metropolitan areas — both to provide more jobs and to provide an expansion in the tax base. The most important economic activities generally sought are expanded or new manufacturing plants.

The success of local communities in attracting new industry is partly dependent upon the expansion of the national economy and the region's economy, and some factors in industrial location are beyond the control of individual localities. But other influential factors can be controlled within the metropolitan area. Among these are space for industry, traffic, public services, the attractiveness of the community as a place to live, and local taxes.

Allocation of space for industrial use takes

place partly through the free workings of the real estate market. It can be strongly influenced by industrial zoning provisions which limit or exclude other uses. Thus the small percentage of land in a metropolitan area which is most suitable for industrial use can be reserved for such use. Where a clear conflict exists between two good uses not easily satisfied by most land, such as watersheds, industrial and waterside recreation uses, some mechanism for careful decision should exist so that allocation is not made by default.

Taxes in any community in a metropolitan area may become an influence on industrial location when they are excessively high or abnormally low. Abnormally high taxes may be the result of inequitable assessments or of an inefficient local government; but they may also be the result of the community having to carry an undue share of the metropolitan area costs for welfare, for highway maintenance, for mass transit, for schools, or for other public purposes.

Abnormally low taxes in some areas may result from an avoidance of responsibilities which are passed on to others to carry; or they may reflect a reluctance to provide positive services in the nature of good schools, recreational facilities, and the like. The absence of good public services of this type may reduce a community's attractiveness for new industry.

108.

Kenneth Allsop: Black, White, and the Blues

Negroes streamed northward from the economically blighted towns and rural areas of the South in ever increasing numbers after World War II, seeking not only economic opportunity but also political freedom. They came to Washington, and New York, and Cleveland, and Detroit, and other Northern cities (and also to Los Angeles in the West), but perhaps especially to Chicago, the metropolis at the top of the Mississippi Valley that had been a magnet for immigrants for over a century. With them came Southern "poor whites" from the exhausted lands of Kentucky and Tennessee and the no longer efficient factories of West Virginia, and together they began to create what could almost be called a sub-culture in Chicago, one that the city had never known, or not known for a long time. The morals of this sub-culture may have been "bad" and its habits "un-American," but its music was superb — a fact pointed to with admiration by the Englishman Kenneth Allsop, who wrote the following "Letter from Chicago" for publication in an English magazine in 1960. The piece is reprinted here in part.

Source: *Encounter*, April 1960.

On Michigan Avenue, on Chicago's South Side, a young Kentuckian wearing long Presley sideburns and a black leather jacket, and carrying a half-empty bottle of muscatel, boarded a late-night bus. He lurched down the aisle, fell into a seat and peered opaquely around. His wine-muzzy eyes lit on a Negro opposite, and a mild sort of illumination spread across his face. "Hey, you there!" he called, and an uneasy twitch of apprehensive attention galvanized all the passengers, white and colored. But no race incident was about to erupt. The Kentucki-an took a pull from the bottle and leaning forward, said to the Negro emotionally: "You and me, boy, we're together. We're surrounded."

It would be heartwarming to be able to report that the Negro stepped across the aisle and that black and white hands gripped in brotherliness, whereas in fact the Negro stared straight ahead in glassy embarrassment in the hope of discouraging the drunk's confidences. He did, for the youth slumped into a muttering doze, and everyone's gaze drifted back to the bleak, neon-glaring drabness beyond the window, where lay the city fiefs of racial and economic segregation.

Yet this random pulse of melodrama unexpectedly made real for me one small, strange aspect of the social turmoil that is still today as desperate a problem as it has ever been in Chicago's brief and violent history.

Immigration, the process of blood transfusion from all the world's nations that has given America both its vitality and its overheated, accelerated metabolism, has in this decade entered a new phase in Chicago. Between 1910 and 1920 the Negro population of Chicago doubled as a result of the demand for Southern labor to replace the influx of European immigrants stemmed by World War I. In the Depression years of the Thirties, the population growth of the city, including that of the Negro, ground to a halt, but in the postwar years Northern industries again tapped the South for their supplies.

What consequently happened is described by a local demographer (Professor Philip M. Hauser, of the University of Chicago) as a "population explosion," a "rapidity of growth, a change in population composition, and a mushrooming of physical problems practically unique in human history." And one bizarre element in this present sociological ferment is the creation — probably extremely tenuous and temporary, but

still an actuality for the moment — of a bond of sympathy between poor white and poor black from the rural South, lost and lonely in the metropolitan asphalt jungle, thrust into unfamiliarly frightening and ferocious conditions, a feeling of unity that so far all the federal integration legislation has failed to achieve in Little Rock and the Dixie hinterland.

Any day and every day the scene is the same at Chicago's railroad termini — the uncertain surge forward through the gates of entry of the newest batch of arrivals, family groups with string-lashed suitcases and bulging bundles. The Negroes are field-hands and levee laborers from the Mississippi Valley here to try their urban luck, whose wage rates have been $3 a day (not subsistence level in the United States) and who in recent years have heard reiteratively two alluring and challenging things in letters from friends and relatives who had earlier gone North: that $2.50 an hour can be earned in Illinois factories and that "If you can't make it in Chicago, you can't make it anywhere." It is a matter of fine degree, but the white invaders tend to be less literate and less skilled than the Negroes. Lumped together by Chicagoans — and there's a good deal of contempt in the term — as "hillbillies," but also variously known as backwoodsmen, Appalachians, poor white trash, mountain hicks, and red-necks, they are pouring in, in pursuit of jobs and the much-advertised American Good Life, from the declining coal-pit and scratch-farm regions of Missouri, Mississippi, Kentucky, Arkansas, Alabama, and Tennessee.

The Southern migrants are arriving in Chicago at the rate of 2,000 a week. There are estimated to be 65,000 hillbillies resident, but the number is hard to check for they crowd houses as subtenants, are disinclined to send their children to school, and do not register as voters. The Negroes are swelling a black population which already numbers 800,000 — 21 percent of the city's total — and which is thickening and expanding Chicago's black core. At a quickening rate the established white white-collar class is shifting outward to the suburbs, evacuating what a generation ago were prosperous residential districts and which are now fast becoming decaying ghettos. Nor are all the newcomers finding the jobs they expected: 75 percent of those on county welfare aid are Negroes.

Chicago is an illusory city. To drive into it by car through the great complex of eight-lane freeways that swing airily across cloverleaf junctions and coiling flyovers, and then down on to the surpassingly beautiful Lake Shore Drive, is to infer that little can ail a metropolis of such radiant magnificence. For mile upon mile the rainbow cars ooze with their big-engine casualness along those lakefront tree-arcaded boulevards, on one side the white sails of that now obligatory household accessory, the small boat, flecking Michigan's blue waters; on the other the glinting, soaring sierras of skyscraper apartment houses and office buildings, a lovely and splendid cliff range of towering white stone, glass, and metal. They made me think of white teeth that shine in a skull. At almost any point in those resplendent frontage miles you have to divert only a few blocks to be in the city's squalid interior, a complex of interminable, ugly, shabby streets which for long sections slide into some of the worst festering slums to be found anywhere, including Glasgow and the Middle East.

A truer sense of what you are entering is gained if you reach Chicago by train, as on this occasion I did from New York. As you approach the industrial fringes the rails fray out wider and wider into a vast skein, the convergence of 19 trunk lines, a 1,750-square-mile sorting center for 221,000 miles of national rail arteries that end and start here, and where 45,000 goods cars are loaded and unloaded every day. Presumably you already know that you are 1,745 miles from the West Coast and 713 miles from the East Coast, but what suddenly drives home

that this is the very belly of the Middle West, the central transit point of this enormous land, and so the arrival point for job seekers from everywhere, is the sight of the banked processions of freight trucks that pass you and which are passed.

For me, the insignia on their sides were a distillation of all the romance and wonder of American history, the symbols of distance and lunging frontiers and restless adventurousness. CHESAPEAKE & OHIO, PENNSYLVANIA, B & O, SANTA FE, OVERLAND ROUTE, MID-AMERICA, ROCK ISLAND, THE CHIEF, FLORIDA EAST COAST, ARMOUR STOCK EXPRESS, SOUTHERN PACIFIC, MOBILE AND OHIO, THE ROUTE OF THE HIAWATHA, TEXAS AND PACIFIC, WABASH, LOUISVILLE AND NASHVILLE, EVERYWHERE WEST — BURLINGTON ROUTE . . . the rumbling litany gave me a private satisfaction, for it seemed to ring with the authentic clangor of folk history, to be the essential stuff of that aspect of the American legend that is made up of such ingredients as Big Bill Haywood's itinerant union organizers — the "Wobblies" of the IWW — New Deal construction camps, the big exoduses of *The Grapes of Wrath* period, the bums produced by the big strikes and lockouts of the 1890s and the Depression hoboes riding the rods and the boxcars across the continent, the mythological John Henry, Casey Jones, and Paul Bunyan, the "fast Western" piano style of the Carolina turpentine camps, blues-minstrels like Blind Lemon Jefferson and Leadbelly, the breakout of jazz from the Mississippi Valley in the Twenties, radical guitarists like Woody Guthrie, the period of the Dust Bowl and the migratory harvest workers and loggers . . . all the movement and mixture under economic pressures, all the fluid patterns which are only just beginning to congeal into a recognizable American image.

Chicago, geographically a corradial center for so much of this flux, is still far from congealed. To talk of minorities, meaning the racial and foreign-stock inhabitants, is misleading. It is native-born Chicagoans who are the minority. In the city's 3.7 million population — 6.5 million within the standard "metropolitan area" — only 40 percent are what might be called for want of a better ethnic label Anglo-Saxon American. Of the rest 15 percent are foreign-born (Polish, German, Italian, Russian, Scandinavian, and Irish in order of numbers), 24 percent second-generation foreign, and 21 percent Negro. Conditions of living are not so neatly packaged as those figures. The colored "quarter" is no longer clearly demarcated. The poverty-tide of the colored and foreign immigrants has broken through at many points into the "respectable" areas of the city and washes hungrily around eroding middle-class islands. The University of Chicago, down on the South Side at Hyde Park, is encircled now by Negro tenements. Adjacent to the Newberry Library on the Near North Side is a public school which has among its pupils Japanese, Negroes, Puerto Ricans, Greeks, Gypsies, Spaniards, Germans, Poles, Mexicans, and Chinese. Many of the Southern new arrivals are colonizing freshly invaded districts on the West Side.

The reason for this "population explosion" is what might be called with equal justification an "industrial explosion." It is certainly true, but impossible for the mind to grasp, that just 126 years ago this present metropolis was a village of 350 people and a few onion fields reclaimed from swamp at the junction of a river and a lake, and whose Indian name meant "the smell of skunks." In 1837, when the population had climbed to 4,179, it was incorporated as a city. Eleven years later Chicago was connected with canals and railroads, and its development as a grain and meat center began. Its population shot up. By 1860 — only twenty-three years later — it had reached 100,000; by 1910, 2 million; by 1930, 3 million. The latest spurt upward has been brought about by the opening of 5,000 new factories since 1939, by the increase of retail trade from $2 billion to $8 billion in sixteen years, by a still expanding steel industry that employs half a million men, and by an annual handling of 72 million tons of waterborne cargo — a figure which will be vastly expanded by the completion of the St. Lawrence Seaway, connecting the city direct with the Atlantic, and which, it has cautiously been predicted, will result in a fresh "economic breakthrough" and push the population up to 7 million in the next five years.

The peculiar paradox is that Chicago's mood is not in harmony with this bounding momentum of prosperity and material progress. Today this does not seem the swaggering frontier town, brassy with arrogant self-confidence and bursting vitality, that has been its reputation. A banker, one of the richest and most influential political figures in Illinois, said to me: "We're not so cocky as we once were." This is also the town whose mayor, Big Bill Thompson, threatened in 1927 to "bust the snoot" of the King of England if he showed up there, which last year turned out in millions to cheer the Queen of England. There is less pride today in the city's lurid past, the long "open town" history of unhindered prostitution, gambling, and drinking, and there is a general sensitive resentment toward inquiries about the fourteen years of Prohibition, when the corrupt alliance between crime and politics was expressed in law flouting of a blatancy and violence unparalleled in any other American community.

This new sobriety may be due to a number of factors. Perhaps to the knowledge that the racketeer, behind his contemporary facade of legitimate business, still has a powerful grip upon the administration and upon civic life — a prominent lawyer whose activities are mostly in the catering field alleged to me that "there isn't a night club or restaurant in Chicago that isn't paying protection to the hoods," and a writer, who has lived in Chicago all his life, said: "This city is as full of complicity as it ever was. The whole city's under the table. Nobody makes it legitimately." Perhaps the change is also due to the nagging knowledge that, despite that lakefront skyline of glittering pinnacles, despite piecemeal slum clearance and rehousing projects, internally the second city of the United States is a sleazy mess — decaying, declared a recent report, "not structure by structure, but by whole neighborhoods and communities at a time." Perhaps, furthermore, it is due to the racial tensions that appear to paralyze effective improvements in so many spheres.

It is no doubt logical in the light of the present situation that the anxieties of so many white Chicagoans are morbidly fixed upon the swelling voting strength of the Negroes. A Civil Rights Commission survey admits that "the Negro population in Chicago is probably as segregated as in any large city of the United States and, perhaps, more so than in most," but the point is how much longer will the Negro stay — and, those who are honest, say can he be kept — in what the survey calls "discernible enclaves"? It is estimated that if the intake continues at its present rate, by 1975 Negroes will form one-third of the population — "I figure," one businessman said to me gloomily, "that we have about twenty years left before we get our first black mayor, and then things will get really tough for the rest of us." . . .

Although "black supremacy" is an idea that is juggled about with widely different emotions by many white and colored Chicagoans, its practical application appeared to me to be far distant from realization. For what are immediately striking are the schisms that run jaggedly through the black community of Chicago. To the established Negro resident, who has possibly had a college education and pulled himself up by his bootstraps to at least a replica of the *Saturday Evening Post* cover way-of-life — good income, good house, good cars, good deep freeze, good stereo system — the rough, unsophisticated arrivals from the South are an embarrassment and a drag. As much as

he can he dissociates himself from the new settlers, who, he feels, have more affinity with the equally poor and illiterate hillbillies, Puerto Ricans, Gypsies, and Navajo, Hopi, Sioux, and Mandan Indians who in some numbers are trying to turn themselves into urban workers and are cramming together in the La Salle Street and Clark Street areas.

A young Negro recording company executive said to me: "There are internal race problems here. Because the hillbillies are dirty and lawless and dangerous when drunk, every white Chicagoan isn't identified with them. But when the Southern Negroes misbehave, we get blamed for what they do. You see, I've got the same badge of my face."

There is another, less serious but to me equally regrettable, consequence of these divisions of sympathy and understanding, which can be seen to be economically horizontal as well as racially vertical. That is the obliviousness that exists among the educated Chicagoans of both colors of a subculture renaissance that is burgeoning in the side-street bars and cafes deep in the slum belts. There is a new, late flowering of folk music. By this I don't mean the kind of smooth folksy cabaret dispensed at the smart Gate of Horn night club by such professionals as Josh White and the Kingston Trio, but authentic, rough, rural stuff well below the line of potential commercialization. This has two distinct forms. In the hillbilly clubs and saloons west of Broadway near Belmont Street, where Confederate flags are hung over the bar, the entertainment is a local brand of country-and-western imported from the Kentucky highlands. . . . In the Negro bars in the area of Cottage Grove Avenue and Halsted Street the blues are being sung and played with a volume and variety to be found nowhere else in the United States, not even in the Mississippi Valley where the blues were born. . . .

There are scores of places — sawdust

dives into which a white man won't get admission unless escorted by a Negro known there — where blues in the old manner, crude, funky and sad, are to be heard any time after midnight. The stars in this underground and strictly zoned entertainments industry are people like Muddy Waters, Memphis Slim, Little Walter, Jimmy Reed, and Howling Wolf; but there are a hundred others, mostly immigrant Southerners, middle-aged and more, who work for the Post Office or drive delivery vans during the day, who after midnight play the blues on a guitar or mouth organ, and shout variations on such perennial themes as:

You been sweet to me and you ain't
    never run aroun'
Said you been sweet to your daddy and
    never run aroun'
But will you still be my baby when this
    lousy deal goes down? . . . .

The blues are a plaint, a protest music that grew out of suffering, indignity, and rotten living conditions. There is still good cause for the blues to be sung in modern Chicago. When the blues die and are heard no more, it will probably be a melancholy day for such folk-song hunters as I; but then Chicago will be a healthier city.

109.

William D. Workman, Jr.: The Case Against Forced Integration

The Supreme Court's school integration decisions in 1954 and 1955 were met by well-organized opposition, not only in the South but also in some Northern cities. By 1962, less than one-half of one percent of Southern Negroes attended previously all-white schools, and almost nothing really effective had been done about the de facto segregation in the North. Negroes were understandably impatient, and they began to charge the judicial process with being slow, cumbersome, and expensive; but at the same time segregationists intensified their attacks on the programs, such as big-city bussing, for enforced integration. William D. Workman, Jr., argued the South's position in a book from which an excerpt is reprinted here.

Source: *The Case of the South*, New York, 1960, pp. 285-302.

It is a fair and practical question to ask now whether anything constructive can be salvaged out of all the unpleasantness which has stemmed from the fight over racial integration. The answer might well be "Yes," a qualified "Yes."

The prospect of improving race relations in the face of intense resistance to integration is admittedly difficult under present pressures and hostilities, yet there are changes which can and should be made, not only for the improved welfare of Negro Southerners, but also for the justification of many arguments used by white Southerners against forced integration.

In any attempt to approach this delicately balanced situation, the advocate of change or relaxation immediately runs head on into a major division of opinion. There are those who contend that any concession whatever will tend to weaken the South's position, to crack the dike of resistance, and to make for an ultimate flooding as the dam breaks. On the other hand, there are those of equal sincerity who argue that SOME abridgments of the adamant segregation pattern MUST be made if the South is to successfully defend its main line of resistance, i.e., the schools. Despite these contrary positions, there IS some hope of improved race relations by virtue of the fact that these two groups BOTH oppose racial integration in the schools. It may be that in joint resistance against a common foe they might find a basis for agreement on certain changes which might ease the situation, improving the lot of the Negro without damaging the lot of the white man.

For one thing, there should be some relaxation of both the legal and the social barriers which obstruct voluntary association of whites and Negroes. Much of the Southern argument against the Supreme Court decision has been based on the interpretation (whether correct or incorrect is beside the point) that enforcement of the decision would deny to the Southern man a freedom of choice as to where his child should attend school. Along with that has gone an extension of the same line of reasoning and its application into other fields — housing, churches, and so on. The essence of the white man's argument has been this: The individual should be protected in his right of freedom of association, and correspondingly, of freedom to AVOID unwanted association.

But by the same token, if the Southern segregationist wants to be free in his determination of associates, so should the Southern integrationist be free in HIS determination of associates provided, of course, that such associations are mutually acceptable, and provided further that the circumstances and conditions of integrated associations are not such as to endanger the public peace.

Much of the legislation enacted in the Southern states in both the immediate and

the distant past has been aimed basically at preserving domestic tranquillity as well as racial integrity. This is especially true in the fields of education and recreation, where indiscriminate mingling of the races is bound to bring discord and strife. Whatever the future may bring, and whatever may be the judgment of non-Southerners, the governmental agencies of the South are acting wisely when they seek to prevent mass mingling of the races in schools, pools, and parks. And distressing though it may be, the closing of such institutions in many cases would be the sensible alternative to the emotional, social, and physical upheaval which would follow on the heels of forced race mixing.

But where there is willingness to mix, and where such mixing would not jeopardize the public peace nor infringe upon the rights of others NOT to mix, some concessions are in order. Neither the written law of the political agency nor the unwritten law of the social community should stand in the way of whites and Negroes foregathering to confer, to discuss, or even to dine together with each other's consent and cooperation. The fact that such biracial activities might be distasteful to a large percentage of Southern whites should not be allowed to stand in the way of the integrationists' exercise of the right of peaceable assembly.

If an area of biracial activity can be carved out of the no-man's-land which now separates the two races by law in most Southern communities, there seems no cause for undue alarm. If the South is to protect the right of some (most) white people to move within segregated circles, then in all fairness it should permit other white people to move within integrated circles if that be their wish. For many years to come, the impetus of such movement will have to be from the whites to the Negroes, but the Southern argument against compulsory integration should apply with equal validity against compulsory segregation of those inclined, however mistakenly, toward racial commingling, so long as the rights of all are protected with respect to preference of association.

The white Southerner can contribute importantly to the easing of the segregation tenseness, and to the ultimate adjustment of the racial problem itself, by the simple expedient — the word is used deliberately — of extending to the Negro Southerner a larger and more adequate share of personal dignity and decency. This can be done with loss to neither, and with gain to both. Courtesy requires only intent and effort, and the application of those two in even small doses would repay the expenditure a thousandfold.

Many a Negro reduces his racial complaint to this basic emotion: "I just want to be treated like a man." There are those, of course, who want much more than that, who want special privilege, who wish to inject themselves into a white society which is not willing to accept them, who wish to break down every racial barrier that can be found, preferably by force — but these do not reflect the broader and more basic desire of the Southern Negro, which is simply to be accorded a better opportunity to make for himself whatever place he can in his community.

This will necessarily mean a revision of attitude on the part of those whites who say, with altogether too much condescension, "I've got nothing against the Negro, so long as he stays in his place." The fact of the matter is that the Negro is entitled to make his own place, and it ill behooves the white man to do other than help his black neighbor along.

This, too, is important: That a mere change of attitude on the part of white Southerners will aid materially in easing racial tensions. A change of attitude does not entail any change of conviction, or lessening belief in the desirability of racial segregation in the schools, and wherever else it may be needed in the particular community. A change in attitude means only that a white man can help himself, his neighborhood, and his Negro associates by simply substituting an attitude of cooperation for the old pattern of condescension.

Along with this must go a measure of insistence that the Negro play his part in what could be a new and improved level of communication. If the Negro genuinely desires to be treated with greater dignity, then his own conduct must be such as to warrant it. He cannot expect to receive dignity along with indulgence. The burden of performance rests finally upon him. He cannot continue in his improvident ways, squandering his relatively small earnings on drink, trinkets, and carousing, forsaking his family when the mood strikes him, "forgetting" legal and moral obligations — and still look for the sort of treatment reserved for more worthy persons.

Many a white man is convinced that the Negro does not have it in him to break off his old habits, to buckle down to the demanding task of becoming a more laudable citizen, to raise his standard of personal conduct to an acceptable level. But the fair-minded white will show himself willing to meet the Negro fully halfway toward the higher level of communication.

In doing so, the white Southerner himself may gain a fairer and clearer picture of Negro capabilities. There is a Southwide tendency among white people to attribute to ALL Negroes those characteristics of the Negroes with whom they habitually come into contact. Since those contacts are for the most part with Negroes in menial or very subordinate positions, there is little awareness among whites that there are Negroes whose capacities and conduct are such as to warrant better treatment from their white neighbors.

As a corollary of improved communication between the two races, with accompanying better appreciation of each other's merits, there should be the offering of greater opportunity to the Negro to participate in both the planning and the execution of programs aimed at community development. It does not require any great amount of imagination on the part of a fair-minded white man to appreciate the resentment which naturally arises among manifestly capable and decent Negroes when they are denied all opportunity to take part in the formulation of policies and decisions which will bear directly upon them. The solidly American slogan of "no taxation without representation" has a bearing here, and Negroes would be something less than Americans if they did not feel the basic unfairness of complete exclusion from the area of community betterment on the grounds of color alone. . . .

In the field of race relations, the white Southerner's major shortcoming in recent years has been by way of omission rather than commission. When the Negro complains of having been denied even the outward trappings of dignity and decent treatment, he is justified in very large measure. It is to the discredit of the white man that he has provided no place in the Southern order of things for the colored man who, by his own efforts, has brought himself up to the level of decency and achievement demanded by white society.

Old habits and old associations die hard, and few Southerners outside the ministry and, to a lesser degree, the world of education have seen fit to bring the Negro into their counsels in ANY capacity. Understandably, the capable Negro who KNOWS his own capacity has become resentful of whites who will accord him no recognition of achievement nor any degree of participation in community development, be it segregated or nonsegregated.

In all justice, however, it must be recorded that here and there about the South, degrees of recognition and participation were being accorded Negroes in slow but growing measure. A documentation of the biracial enterprises being conducted throughout the South in the years immedi-

ately preceding the Supreme Court decision presents a surprisingly long list of joint efforts. Yet the list fell far short of what could have been, and what should have been, an effective coordination between the races in every community of the region. Now, unhappily, the list has been cut to shreds by the revival of distrust and animosity engendered by the Supreme Court decision and the subsequent attempts to force integration on areas not prepared to accept it. . . .

One of the blind spots in the make-up of the average white Southerner is his ignorance of the attitudes and workings, and in large measure of the very existence, of a middle class Negro group. Yet these Negroes presumably have much the same outlook on life as that held by the white middle class: a preoccupation with education, for themselves and their children; an adherence to strict (or professedly strict) codes of morality; and a consuming desire to be accepted as desirable elements of the community. Because of these feelings, which are judged desirable by members of the white middle class, it comes as a shameful thing to these Negroes who, upon actually attaining such middle-class status, nevertheless are treated as being inferior to the lower-class whites who make no pretense of subscribing to the same standards of values.

Unfortunately, at this stage of the game, these able and cultured Negroes are not strong enough in either numbers or influence to set the tone of the Negro community, whether it be located North or South. Consequently, any such community of appreciable size is much more likely to reflect the habits, attitudes, and values of the lower class. And since the lower Negro classes lean noticeably toward licentiousness, there is no strong pressure of community opinion to guide individual Negroes into an acceptable mode of conduct.

It may well be that, figuratively speaking, the Negro in the South now is passing from a prolonged period of civic adolescence into his maturity. The extended length of that growing period has been due both to the paternalistic attitude of the Southern white and to the childish attitude of many a Southern Negro. Just as parents frequently are somewhat bewildered and irritated by the behavior of their own children as they move from childhood into the trying days of adolescence, so have white Southerners been puzzled by the growing restiveness and resentment of Negro Southerners. So also have many white Southerners been unwilling to recognize the fact that the Negro may be "growing up."

ONE OF THE CHIEF RALLYING CRIES of the NAACP and its fellow travelers is that of "first-class citizenship" for the Negroes of America. The catch phrase is appealing and has been used effectively to enlist the support of well meaning persons whose heartstrings are pulled by the caterwauling which constantly arises from the professional champions of the Negro. Without in any way condoning the undeniable instances in which Negroes have been denied some of their rights, not only in the South but in the North and elsewhere about the nation, let's take a look at the reverse side of the coin and see whether the Negroes have themselves earned a categorical reputation as "first-class citizens." In the process, we might learn whether there is not a tendency among Negroes to confuse citizenship with social privilege. Citizenship is a conditional, not an absolute, right. It comes unasked as a blessing to those fortunate enough to be born in the United States, and to certain others under varying conditions, so there is no real credit attached to BECOMING or BEING an American citizen. It generally stems from the accident of birth. But even so, the right of citizenship can be forfeited, or abridged, by misconduct in any of a number of ways, and therein may lie some basis for distinction between "first-class" and "second-class" citizens.

First-class citizenship demands more than the simple payment of taxes and the rendering of obligatory military or civil service as the need arises. It demands a fulfillment of society's unwritten as well as its written responsibilities. It involves a civic consciousness which contributes to community welfare, a code of personal and family conduct which meets the standards of decency and self-respect, and a willingness to participate in as well as partake of the benefits of the social organization.

On the other hand, the citizen may lose his status, or at least his right to vote or hold office, if he is convicted of any of a number of disqualifying crimes. The list varies from state to state, but to list some which appear in many jurisdictions, there are such offenses as "burglary, arson, obtaining money or goods under false pretenses, perjury, forgery, robbery, bribery, adultery, bigamy, wife-beating, housebreaking, receiving stolen goods, breach of trust with fraudulent intent, fornication, sodomy, incest, assault with intent to ravish, miscegenation, larceny, or crimes against the election law." (S[outh] C[arolina] Constitution)

Conviction of any of those crimes automatically places an individual in the role of a "second-class citizen" regardless of race, but there are other offenses which rightfully establish offenders as something less than "first-class" citizens. And here again, as in a great number of the crimes cited above, the Negro offends out of all proportion to his numbers and far beyond the limits of provocation. Unfortunately, he has been *permitted* to do so not only through the laxity of his own standards, but by the indulgence of white persons in positions of authority. In far too many instances, white officials have tolerated intraracial crime and immorality among the Negroes out of a sense of humoring those whose pattern of life differs in such a large measure from that of white persons.

The time is at hand when such indulgence should stop short, for the good of both races. Prolonged tolerance of immorality and criminality among Negroes tends to perpetuate their inadequate social patterns and to threaten the patterns of white neighbors.

Consequently, if Negroes by and of themselves launch an all-out campaign against their own shortcomings, they can contribute to several desirable goals at one and the same time: They can materially improve the community standing of their racial group by reducing the incidence of venereal disease, illegitimacy, sexual promiscuity, indolence, and so on; they can demonstrate to themselves, and to the world at large, that they have both the capacity and the will to raise their own standards; they can enlist the support of other groups in campaigns manifestly designed for community betterment; and — this is important — they can virtually disarm their critics who employ the stereotype device against them. A stereotype label is bound to lose effectiveness in the face of statistical proof that it is factually wrong, and many of the charges brought categorically against Negro conduct are subject to statistical appraisal.

All of this presupposes that the Negro can meet the challenge, and to that extent, the suggestion accepts at face value the assertions of the NAACP and of the modern-day sociologists and anthropologists who insist that the Negro race, as a race, is not inferior to the white. Here, then, is an opportunity for them to prove the truth of that contention, and to prove it in a manner which can be understood and appreciated by the layman. They can do so by an unflagging insistence that their race measure up to community standards. This means that there is a burden of performance and respectability imposed upon the Negro if he is to qualify as a first-class citizen in fact as well as in legal standing.

But if the challenge of self-improvement confronts the Negroes themselves, there is much which can be done by the white Southerners who hold the political and economic reins of the region.

For one thing, there is a dire need for improved housing facilities for Negroes. Even the most cursory study of the Negro shift in population bears out the obvious but virtually ignored fact that Negroes are moving in great numbers from the country to the city. This is no new development, and it shows no signs of either moderating or ceasing in the near future. Furthermore, it is a massive sort of flow which cannot be readily stemmed or controlled by appeals to reason or by the raising of obstacles. The impact of these incoming Negroes is being felt in city after city throughout the South as well as in the North, and there is need for both planning and action to adjust to their influx.

Since few Negro communities in metropolitan areas now have decent or adequate sections for residence, the continuing immigration of newcomers has the effect of piling-up more and more residents into areas of already high population density. With this comes added problems of public health, morality, crime, and general conduct, to say nothing of the added demands for educational, social, welfare, and medical services.

Adequate planning and preparation by both white and Negro businessmen, real estate agents, community organizations, and city officials would make possible an orderly expansion of Negro residents into new areas, and might even make for gradual rather than sudden and hostile displacement of white families. One of the main complaints of white occupants and property owners in a given area threatened by Negro invasion is the abrupt and seemingly inevitable falling of property values once the neighborhood becomes "mixed." That in itself is due in no small part to the fact that the internal pressure in the "containers" of Negro population builds up to such a point that any breakout becomes anything from a spurt to a torrent, rather than a regulated flow. The need for housing is so great that, once access is obtained to other accommodations, there is a veritable deluge of Negroes into such newly available quarters. A further complication is the fact that these new or once-white quarters frequently demand a higher rental or purchase price than the average Negro family can meet. Consequently, additional families or wage earners are crowded into the housing units in order to provide a greater rent-paying potential per square foot of occupancy. All of this combines to hasten the conversion of the recently acquired housing into veritable slums, which depress property values throughout the entire neighborhood.

It seems that cooperation of the type suggested above might meet this situation through the establishment of rigid zoning ordinances which would limit the occupancy of individual housing units, require the maintenance of adequate standards, and in general insure the maintenance of the area on a respectable basis for residential use.

White landlords all too frequently show interest only in draining a heavier financial return from their investment and accordingly fail to maintain their holdings in decent repair. But if these white property owners can be accused of being niggardly, their tenants in too many instances can be accused of being "niggerly," to use a word at once offensive and descriptive. The proper maintenance of housing requires joint effort by both owner and occupant, and that state of affairs very seldom prevails in the field of Negro housing. The landlords complain of Negro irresponsibility in matters of both finance and household care, while Negroes complain of indifference and callousness on the part of the white owners. Here is an area in which much work is to be done by way of persuasion and regulation on the parts of municipal leaders, whether political or not. Intelligent use can be made here of existing Negro civic groups, and others can be brought into the field to heighten the feelings of self-respect and pride of appearance which make for pleasant and healthful residential areas.

City planning, although anathema by its very title to many a rugged individualist, nevertheless can play an important role in helping communities anticipate and solve such housing problems before they reach the acute stage. One major need in this field is to plan for spatial expansion of Negro housing areas so as to serve the dual purpose of providing living space for Negroes without forcing them into white residential areas.

Today, thousands upon thousands of Negroes in the "piled-up" slums and ghettos of the North are finding that their freedom is indeed a serious thing. They find few of the helping hands, white or black, to which they could turn in their former rural settings. They are exposed to all the meanness, the grubbing, the grasping, and the greed of congested urban life, and they frequently wallow in their own helplessness and ineptitude. For them, competent guidance, advice, and instruction could mean the difference between existing and living. Whether the helping hands should be black or white, or both, and whether they should be provided by the local, the state, or the federal governments, or jointly by them all, these are questions to be answered only after more study — but tax monies expended wisely in this sort of urban demonstration work could well be bread cast upon the waters. . . .

Short of utter amalgamation of the races, a thing utterly unacceptable to white Southerners, there is no *solution* to the problem of race relations; there can only be a continual adjustment and readjustment of relationships. The sense of race, no less than those of religion or of nationality, is so deeply embedded in man's nature — both conscious and unconscious — that it cannot be eradicated in the foreseeable future, if indeed it *should* be eradicated. Some persons, whose impulses can be regulated or whose incentives can be manipulated, may rise above, or descend below, race consciousness, but the masses are not likely ever to shed their recognition of race.

Whatever may be the future of race relations in America, this much seems evident: That neither satisfaction nor peace can come from any coercive mingling of the white and black races against the will of either, and that little hope can be entertained for any assimilation of one in the other. There remains, then, only the prospect of accommodating their differences in a pattern of peaceful coexistence based upon a friendly tolerance and helpful understanding. It is the recognition of racial distinctions, not their denial, which will lessen the tensions and enhance their adjustment.

There is serious need now for a thorough reassessment of the entire picture of race relations — North and South — and for what the phrase makers might call another "agonizing reappraisal" of the costs and the consequences of the nation's forced march toward integration. The time is ripe for both sides — for all sides — of the several controversies to inventory their successes and their failures. Fresh decisions need to be made in the light of matters as they stand now, and as they seem likely to develop in the near future.

These are some of the questions to be answered before the making of new decisions, or the reaffirmation of old ones, if that be the course taken:

1. Are the people of the East, the West, and the North willing to persist in driving a divisive wedge between themselves and those of the South through endorsement of anti-Southern legislation which inevitably will perpetuate sectionalism?

2. Is the Supreme Court of the United States so convinced of the wisdom of its school integration decision that it will continue to insist upon the sociological upheaval of communities which are being transformed from peaceful neighborhoods into writhing centers of racial conflict?

3. Is the National Association for the Advancement of Colored People so determined to compel race-mixing that it cares not for the regeneration of bitter race hatred, which had been diminishing steadily for years, but which now is being planted in the hearts and minds of white youngsters and which will be a scourge to the NAACP and to the Negro for years to come, not only in the South but everywhere?

4. Are the two national political parties so base in their competition for partisan advantage that they are willing to offer up the white South as a sacrifice to the unreasoning demands of minority blocs in the North, and thereby to drive white Southerners into a third political party?

5. Is the national government prepared to display to the world at large an inability to treat fairly with the inhabitants of one-quarter of the nation, and a willingness to coerce with military might those citizens whose only fault is their insistence on preserving their racial integrity and the remaining vestiges of the local self-government presumably guaranteed to them by the Constitution of the United States?

6. Is organized labor willing to write off the South as a target for future unionization by continued agitation for "civil rights" and other class legislation?

7. Are the churches of America so confident that integration is the only Christian answer to the eternal question of race relations that they will risk driving into other denominations and other associations those equally sincere Christians who have received no divine admonition to mix the races?

8. Are the Negroes of the land so devoid of self-respect and pride that they stand ready to admit that their children cannot develop and improve except in the presence of the white race?

9. Are the teachers of America prepared to abandon the precept that learning is enhanced where students share similar values and backgrounds, and to embark upon the instructional ordeal of teaching discordant groups of dissimilar children?

10. Are the parents throughout the South, or throughout the nation for that

matter, ready to surrender all hope of transmitting their own cultural heritage to their children, and to accept an agglutinated cultural compound distinctive only in its lack of all distinction?

11. Are the people of America so obsessed with determination to force integration upon an unwilling South that they will support their federal government in the use of bayonet-studded force to overcome resistance? . . .

"If the two races are to meet upon terms of social equality, it must be the result of natural affinities, a mutual appreciation of each other's merits, and a voluntary consent of individuals."

110.

KARL SHAPIRO: What Is American Poetry?

American writers and critics continued in the 1960s, as they had done for close to 200 years, to ponder the question whether there was, or is, an "American" literature. Karl Shapiro, a noted poet in his own right, addressed himself to the subject in the Introduction to an anthology of American poetry that he edited in 1960. So compelling has the question been to all American writers, Shapiro concluded, that "any discussion of American poetry resolves itself into a search for the meaning of 'American.'" And he added that "this quest for self-definition might be said to be the main theme of all American literature." The conclusion might be disputed by many modern writers, but it is represented here as typical of an important body of current opinion.

Source: *American Poetry*, New York, 1960, pp. 1-8.

WHEN I THINK of American poetry, the first thing that comes to my mind is the witticism of a modern British poet: "American poetry is a very easy subject to discuss for the simple reason that it does not exist." Nowadays, when American poets feel so sure of themselves, the malice of this epigram has a kind of charm. American poets repeat it and even use it in their writings. Not very long ago — a generation or two — such a quip would have been met with indignation.

To say that American poetry does not exist is simply a roundabout way of saying that our poetry still belongs to English literature. On the face of it this seems a likely argument. We still use the English language to the exclusion of any other, and despite the radically new idiom of American speech, ours is obviously a not too distant version of the mother tongue. When we consider the amazing linguistic and racial mixtures of the American people it is surprising that our language has remained as "English" as it has; for there is scarcely a corner in the United States where people speak anything else. The English writer naturally feels a proprietary interest in American literature, though it cannot be said that our poetry has been well understood in England.

The use of the same language for English and for American poetry is misleading to the student of our literature unless he bears in mind that the contents of the two poetries are quite unlike. Or rather, it is the struggle to free itself from English convention which has given our poetry its character. It is no exaggeration to say that any discussion of American poetry resolves itself into a search for the meaning of "American." This quest for self-definition may be said to be the main theme of all American literature. It is a unique theme: we do not find the Roman or the French or the British writer debating the question What is a Roman, What is a Frenchman, or What is an Englishman. But few American novelists and poets have been able to resist the theme What is an American.

At the risk of emphasizing the obvious let us look at the language situation for the American writer and poet. At the time of the founding of the United States our white population was of 90 percent British stock (the blacks were not counted in the population). A generation after independence the Germans and the Irish began to arrive in large numbers on our shores. From the midcentury on, hordes of Irish, Dutch, Danes, Swedes, Norwegians, Swiss, and Jews entered America as homesteaders and factory laborers. Toward the end of the century still larger waves of Italians, Russians, Poles, Austrians, Bohemians, and Hungarians entered the new land. All of these people, almost without exception, were foreign-speaking or dialect-speaking peoples. And though the Englishman proper was the least represented in these grand influxes of refugees, English remained the language of education, government, and literature in the United States. The vast majority of these stocks were white Europeans, the Asiatic races having been excluded by law and by prejudice. By 1900 we were no longer what had once been known as New England; we were New Europe.

Generally speaking, the New World immigrants did not belong to the lettered classes to begin with, and during the century of heavy immigration literature was left to the "Anglo-Saxon" minority, as in the early years it was left to the governing classes and the clergy. The nineteenth-century refugees from famine, political op-

pression, and military conscription did not come to the United States to write novels or poems nor, for that matter, to read them. A fair part of our political or semipolitical writing was done by the newcomers but almost none of the pure literature. It is not until the twentieth century that "foreign" names begin to decorate the literary anthology.

One of the most extraordinary facts about the new America was and is the rapid disappearance of Old World traits and the evolution of a common American personality. Writers have from time to time appeared shocked at this cultural amnesia and have frequently interpreted it as "materialism," "isolationism," or just an ordinary lapse into frontier barbarism. American folklore, with its love for the shooting cowboy, the gangster, and the boy who goes from rags to riches, tends to corroborate the image of the American without a past. The image is repeated in serious American literature as well with the heroic Huck Finn lighting out for the frontier to escape civilization, and the martyred Billy Budd who cannot comprehend the mores of organized society. Only among antiquarians do we find any considerable nostalgia for the home country or for the cultural past.

American poetry is a poetry of departure from the past. It is a poetry still struggling for freedom from the past and from its own enemies, the American "expatriates." It has thus far only partly succeeded in creating the appropriate poetry of the New World. The high point of our literature was reached a century ago with *Leaves of Grass.* Whitman's book was a part of a renaissance that included Emerson's *Representative Men* and Thoreau's *Walden.* Emerson, Whitman, and Thoreau have a great deal in common. Hawthorne and Melville were a part of that renaissance also and they too, in their preoccupation with innocence and newness, have a kinship with these other three writers. But there is a darker side to Hawthorne and Melville which casts shadows over the sunny landscape and on occasion caused them to be satiric at the expense of their contemporaries who were insufficiently aware of the inevitable limitations in any human situation, American or otherwise. By and large, the modernist poets, those in the Pound-Eliot line, have overstressed this darker side, and caused the waste land image to dominate not only twentieth-century poetry but all of twentieth-century literature.

Our cultural amnesia is held in contempt by most Europeans and by our noisy handful of expatriate writers, but on the whole our insistent forgetfulness of the past is the first characteristic of the American. To break loose from the grip of the old religions, the old forms of government, the old manners and morality, is still the American aim. It is no accident that America has been used from the beginning as an experimental station for every conceivable kind of utopia, religious, political, scientific, and even literary. What dream or crackpot plan has not been tried, or is not still being put into action in the U.S.? And compare the American sense of social pioneering with that of our neighbors — the Canadians to the north and the Spanish-Americans to the south. How are we to account for the mysterious dynamism of the Middle Americans, almost all of them refugees from Europe?

Our poetry is very new, raw, full of the clumsiest trials and errors and yet it has become one of the most vital in the world. Is ours a vital and influential poetry because it is great poetry in itself, or because it is the poetry of a people upon whom the eyes of the world are constantly focused for other reasons? Have we produced a "poetry for the ages" or a mere challenge to the past? American poetry is no more than a century old (a century and a half at a liberal estimate) yet it has attracted more attention in that time than literatures ten times older. Beyond a doubt it is the label "American" that accounts for the bulk of this interest.

The reader will find this anthology top-heavy on the modern side. We have included only a few poets from the seventeenth century and only one from the eighteenth! The bulk of the poetry that is more American than English comes toward the middle of the nineteenth century and thereafter. As this is not an historical survey it appeared useless to reprint the usual poets whom we remember for some historical reason rather than for literary merit. The tendency to repeat is the vice of the anthologist, and in this collection we are attempting to recast the list of American poets, emphasizing the American element. Many, if not most, of our poets have followed the literary fashions of England unthinkingly. In the seventeenth century we had our Metaphysical poets; in the eighteenth our Neo-Classical wits; in the nineteenth century our Romantics. Imitation was the rule up to the time of Poe, Emerson, and Whitman. A fair amount of competent American verse, for example Bryant and Longfellow, is mostly poetry *à la mode*, poetry that has nothing fundamentally American about it, even when it talks about honeysuckle or Hiawatha. Longfellow has always been more respected by English writers than by Americans.

Our seventeenth-century literature, by and large, is a theology-centered literature. Our eighteenth-century literature is a politics-centered literature. But in the nineteenth century there is a flowering of literary consciousness which takes two forms, one led by the intellectualizing Poe, the other by the humanizing Whitman. And twentieth-century poetry is either a "Poe" poetry or a "Whitman" poetry, with the Whitman being very much out of favor in the first half of our century.

SEVENTEENTH CENTURY

THE DARK DETERMINISM of the Puritan, with his bitter vengeful God and his fanatical devotion to hardship and hard work, set the tone of our early poetry, which we can still detect in some of our moderns. The New

England child was taught his letters and his theology in the same breath with the baleful words:

> In Adam's fall
> We sinned all.

This was the opening of the famous *New England Primer,* also called "The Little Bible of New England." And it is typical of New England poetry that the first book published on this side of the ocean was a versified translation of the Psalms. Poetry, in other words, was tolerated if it could be made useful. The preacher Michael Wigglesworth celebrated the Calvinist hell fire in an endless series of couplets which New Englanders committed to memory by the page. It is doggerel poetry and we do not include it here, except for this sample:

> The mountains smoke, the hills are shook,
>   the earth is rent and torn
> As if she should be clear dissolved or from
>   her center borne.
> The sea doth roar, forsakes the shore, and
>   shrinks away for fear;
> The wild beasts flee into the sea, so soon
>   as He draws near . . .

> It's vain moreover for men to cover the least
>   iniquity;
> The Judge hath seen, and privy been to all
>   their villainy.
> He unto light and open sight the work of
>   darkness brings;
> He doth unfold both new and old, both
>   known and hidden things.

> Thus he doth find of all mankind that stand
>   at His left hand,
> No mother's son but hath misdone, and
>   broken God's command.
> All have transgressed, even the best, and
>   merited God's wrath,
> Unto their own perdition and everlasting
>   scath.

This kind of naïve verse is somewhat redeemed by other New England writers. Nearly every American anthology of poetry begins with Anne Bradstreet, a very competent and frequently charming poetess, a Puritan of a more sophisticated type. She is still read today, if only by poets and scholars, and a twentieth-century American poet (John Berryman) has rediscovered Mistress Bradstreet for himself and has written what in effect is a love poem to his three-hundred-year-old sweetheart. Both Anne Bradstreet and Edward Taylor, who is the best of our seventeenth-century poets, are very conscious of our religious dogma. Taylor even left a request at his death that his poems be left unpublished, and it is only recently that they have come to light. In their richness of imagery and attention to worldly beauty there may be something that points to the death of the God-ridden Puritan world.

EIGHTEENTH CENTURY

As ENGLISH-SPEAKING and English-reading people (Americans are notorious for their lack of interest in languages), we tend to overlook our deep relationship to France. Our great political visions and ideals have more to do with French social visionary thinking than with English. Our law is basically derived from English law but not our sense of liberty. Herman Melville wrote an attack on the Articles of War of the U.S. Navy which we had swallowed whole from English maritime law. His account of our naval discipline in *White Jacket* was a deciding factor in *humanizing* our military regulations and turning them away from the authoritarian practices of the past. English law remains the foundation of our legal thinking, but our idealism comes from elsewhere. Rousseau, Chateaubriand, Crèvecoeur are as Americanized as Lafayette, and whether their ideals were good or bad, true or false, they are part and parcel of American social thought. It is no accident that the literary genius of America in its early years went not into poetry but into political writing. Pamphleteers like Tom Paine (if we can claim him) were men of journalistic genius, to say the least; Franklin, John Adams, and Jefferson bent their literary gifts toward shaping the documents upon which the democratic world would stand. The *Declaration of Independence* was Jefferson's proudest accomplishment and one of the most sweeping revolutionary writings in human history. In effect, the *Declaration,* with its premise that the "laws of nature and nature's God" entitled us to separation from the past, called for a new human order throughout the world, the rule of man rather than the rule of God and the God-anointed kings.

The American poets of the eighteenth century are weak. There is something frivolous and irrelevant about our eighteenth-century poets, especially the so-called Hartford Wits. They imitate the fashions of eighteenth-century English wit and satire; they do not appear to understand the magnitude of the drama taking place before them, and on the whole they are more sympathetic with England than with America. The general mediocrity of their verse detracts from whatever position they may occupy even in a purely historical scheme of things.

The only poet we represent from this period is Philip Freneau, the critic and opponent of the Hartford Wits, revolutionary, sea captain, and the first American poet who tried in poetry to write without benefit of the British example.

NINETEENTH CENTURY

IT IS THE HABIT of modern anthologists, editors, and poets to tell their readers that American poetry reaches its high point in the twentieth century. This is a mistaken view of our poetry, in my opinion. In the nineteenth century we produced the one American poet who is a world poet, Walt Whitman. In the nineteenth century we produced also the school of Moderns who derive from Poe, and who are the antithesis

of Whitman. The immense poetic activity of our time is probably a reflection of statistical literacy more than it is a spontaneous growth of poetic consciousness. We must not be misled by the size and the cleverness of the contemporary anthology.

One of the best critics of American literature is D. H. Lawrence. Speaking of the rhythm of American art-activity Lawrence says that there are two forces at work:

1. A disintegrating and sloughing of the old consciousness.
2. The forming of a new consciousness underneath.

And Edgar Allan Poe, says Lawrence, had only the first disintegrative force in his work. This makes Poe almost more a scientist than a poet. Poe is a man who must reduce everything to knowledge; he must *know* even at the expense of killing in order to know. Poe is credited with inventing the "whodunit," the modern detective story; he is also the father of *ratiocinative* criticism, the "scientific" criticism which is the fashion in the twentieth century.

Walt Whitman, on the other hand, celebrates the new consciousness of man, the American consciousness. To Poe, God is a great and terrifying Will. To Whitman, man and the universe are divine. All of Poe is dressed in mourning for the terrible funeral of the old consciousness; while Whitman clothes the world and everything in the world with light.

Walt Whitman is one of the most misinterpreted writers in all literary history, and he has been less understood in America than in any other country. The most common error about Whitman which we find in textbooks is that *Leaves of Grass* is primarily a political document celebrating the size and the glorious might of these States. He is thus mistakenly considered a kind of historical poet, or a self-styled Poet Laureate of America. Among modern critics, T. S. Eliot and Ezra Pound have done much to encourage this distorted view of Whitman. But even our scholars have misled us about Whitman to a large degree. The tradition of rationalism which pervades our scholarship has led scholars to overlook the central meaning of Whitman, which is *mystical and irreligious*. It is in this significant respect that Whitman is related to Emerson, Thoreau, the primitivist Melville, and the whole tradition of mystical literature from the *Bhagavad-Gita* up through Blake. This literature is taboo to the Modernist critic and scholar, who see in it the destruction of institutions and a threat to civilization itself. Whitman and the "Transcendentalists" are in fact enemies of society and of organized religion and of all that is left over from the historical lumber-room of Europe, as Hegel called it. They are the carriers of the American dream of the new free race of men.

Beyond question the poem "Song of Myself" records an actual mystical experience of the author. The modern critic, who is embarrassed at any mention of a "mystical experience," turns away from the poem and its meaning. In so doing he departs from that element in our thinking and writing which is perhaps the most authentic American element. The underlying idealism of equality, freedom from the past, and the sense of "nature's law" are extended in Whitman's poetry to a vision of the universal America and to the cosmic harmony of all things. The Modernist, who sees everything in terms of historical struggle and inherent evil, naturally disdains Whitman's Americanism. The Modernist turns rather to Poe.

Poe's reputation as poet and critic has always been higher in Europe than in this country. Because of Charles Baudelaire's fascination with Poe, Poe may be considered the godfather of Symbolist poetry and thus one of the godfathers of twentieth-century poetry. The morbidity of Poe's poems and tales was very attractive to the author of *Flowers of Evil*, who found in them a reflection of his own despair. The somewhat phony aristocratic pose of Poe also at-

tracted the democracy-hating Baudelaire. And the cold rationalism of the American lent a kind of Faustian "scientific" glamor to the analysis of society which the Symbolists were to make one of their fields of interest. But above all, it was Poe's discovery of the "effect" in poetry which was to influence Symbolist and Modern poetry and to turn it into the most obscure poetry in history. The modern idea that the thing is not as important in a work of art as the effect of the thing is a doctrine of Poe's which has led to many grotesque forms of poetry in our age. Add to this the psychological nostalgia of Poe for the splendors and vulgarities of the past, and his worship of the perverse in human nature, and we have all the trappings for the founding of a new school of poetry. It was easy for the French poet Baudelaire to turn Poe's images into a replica of man's fall from grace and from civilization. Modern civilization especially was to be the enemy of the new poetry; the villain was Progress.

TWENTIETH CENTURY

TWENTIETH-CENTURY poetry (the first half of it certainly) belongs to the modernists or, as they shrewdly call themselves, the Modern Classicists. These Classicists are led by Ezra Pound and his disciple T. S. Eliot, both of whom follow a kind of esthetic-political-religious platform laid down by an English essayist named T. E. Hulme. The planks of this platform are these: a belief in Original Sin or in the natural brutality of man; a belief in aristocratic institutions and in the leadership principle; a belief in the poet or artist as a priest of civilized culture and the interpreter of history.

The anti-Americanism of Eliot and Pound manifests itself in various ways in contemporary American verse. In E. E. Cummings, for example, the salesman, the politician, the soldier, the businessman, and the scientist are all mercilessly lampooned. Nobody in modern America, in fact, is left unscathed by this satirical poet except the poet himself, members of his family, and a few isolated individuals who have never been drawn into the "system." Following the lead of Eliot and Pound, many other modern poets write out of their contempt for modern life. Most of these poets, also following the lead of Eliot and Pound, consider Whitman a provincial flag-waving rustic who never learned how to write a respectable line of verse.

But this snobbish and expatriate brand of anti-Americanism is not the only kind in the modern anthology. There is a more native variety which we see in poets like Edwin Arlington Robinson and Edgar Lee Masters. Masters describes in his *Spoon River* portraits the degeneration of the pioneer spirit in the Middle West into the petty self-centered and vicious lives of villagers. Robinson takes a somewhat similar view of New England men, though with a good deal more subtlety. And Robinson Jeffers, following the intellectual fads of the early twentieth century (Freud and Spengler with their sexual and historical pessimism) condemns not only America but all the works of man. Jeffers dreams of a world in which man himself is no more — the not uncommon nihilistic image in so much popular writing of our day.

There are virtually no poets of the twentieth century who carry on the Whitman-Emerson-Thoreau view of American man. A poet like Robert Frost, for all his genius and control, is really more of an English than an American poet, more of a Victorian than a contemporary. The New England mask which he wears and which becomes him perfectly is, after all, only a literary device for talking about man in general philosophical terms. There is nothing of the visionary or the seer in Frost, nor of the revolutionary, nor even of the idealist. Frost has discovered the balance of man in the New England landscape, yet it is a specialized man — the white, Protestant, small farmer of Anglo-Saxon stock. Frost is with-

out words when it comes to, say, the Bostonian or New Yorker, the New England Irish Catholic, or the Negro, or the Middle Western farmer. In symbolizing the American through his New England countryman he does not so much oversimplify our situation as to ignore the twentieth-century world. Frost really sees America through the eyes of the nineteenth-century rural New Englander.

Whitman has a minor following in poets like Sandburg, Fletcher, and Lindsay, though these men seem to miss the real import of *Leaves of Grass*. They are fascinated by imagery and the rhythms of American speech. Sandburg celebrates the free immigrant but in rather heavy-handed journalistic poetry; Lindsay is virtually the only American poet to date who has seriously adopted the rhythms of the Negro and the Midwest hymnal.

The most respected though probably least read of the modern followers of Eliot and Pound are Marianne Moore, Wallace Stevens, and Archibald MacLeish. Stevens is the nearest thing to the French Symbolists we have and thereby shares a relationship with Eliot. Marianne Moore has stuck to the dry prose statement and the image which Eliot early recommended to her. MacLeish has followed Eliot, Pound, and the contemporary French poet St. John Perse in the use of "mystic method"; his beliefs, however, are hard to ascertain, though it is clear that he takes the aristocratic view of Poe, Baudelaire, and Eliot, without somehow completely violating his interest in democracy.

Every attempt to revive the Whitman influence in our time has thus far been defeated by the "new criticism," an immense collection of writings embodying the Pound-Eliot-Hulme esthetic and politick. An example in passing is Hart Crane's *The Bridge*, an epic work which has been consistently denigrated by the new critics and Classicists. The Hart Crane influence is therefore considered by the Eliot faction to be a weakening, undisciplined, "Romantic" influence. At the same time Hart Crane, more than other twentieth-century poets, except perhaps D. H. Lawrence, is a symbolic figure for the modern visionary and the poet who sees beyond civilizations and history into the great significance of man.

But perhaps it is an exaggeration to say that the Whitman vision has been defeated by the New Criticism. The fact is that we have had no poets, other than Crane and William Carlos Williams, who have been successful in reestablishing the Whitman influence.

It appears possible that the remaining years of the twentieth century will manifest an increasing reaction against the European anism of twentieth-century American poetry, and a return to the mystique of the American vision as it is expressed in "Song of Myself." The definition of *American* is given us in varied works from our own brief past and not merely in poems. We find its nature and essence in Whitman above all, but also in the political documents of the founding fathers, in *Huckleberry Finn*, in Melville's islanders, in Thoreau, in Hawthorne's *The House of the Seven Gables*, in the poetry of Crane and William Carlos Williams. These writers, and their works, are only beginning to assume their proper importance for us. Each of these writers has attempted a partial definition of what it is to be American.

111.

DAVID RIESMAN: The Uncommitted Generation

The problems of American youth have been a subject of almost obsessive concern to their elders for nearly a century, at no time more so than at the present day. Youth have been called everything and have been said to believe everything, almost as if they were a different species, insects, as it were, exposed for examination upon a laboratory table. This obsession with its youth, indeed, is one of the most marked characteristics of the United States in the twentieth century. However, all writing and talking about youth has not been as good, as honest, and as authoritative as the following article by the distinguished sociologist David Riesman, which was published in Encounter *in 1960. It is interesting to observe that things can change very fast; in the years since 1960 American college students have made just the sort of attempts that Riesman said they were not making — to change their school environment, their relations to their elders, and the politics of their country.*

Source: *Encounter*, November 1960.

IN A RECENT LECTURE, addressing myself primarily to students, already a highly self-conscious group, I was reluctant simply to list once more the labels the older generation has already pinned on them: apathy, conformity, security-mindedness, "coolness," "beatness," and so on. Such labels do have a certain truth, and I shall try to delineate what it is; but they also conceal about as much as they reveal. They conceal the fact that the college generations of the 1920s and 1930s, now nostalgically admired, were on the whole far less responsive, serious, and decent than students in comparable institutions today. They conceal the fact that the apparently negative qualities of apathy and conformity must be seen as an aspect of the high intelligence and sensitivity of this generation of students, who know more than their elders did and who have, justly, more to be afraid of. . . .

My principal theme, however, was not to defend students against the common ethnocentrism of their elders but to help explain them to themselves, and to show how some of the students' attitudes toward the world, as shaped in school and college, are not so much a reaction to that world as it is, but a "reaction-formation" in the psychoanalytic sense: that is, a defense which has become unrealistically overgeneralized. College students today often act as if they believed that work in large organizations and, beyond that, work in general, could not be basically or humanly satisfying (or at times even honest), but was primarily a way to earn a living, to find a place in the social order, and to meet nice or not-so-nice people. This is a conclusion which, I shall suggest, is partly projected upon the occupational scene as the result of their experience with the curriculum in college and university — and as the result of experience also with college and university as organizations which are viewed as bureaucratic, monolithic, and unchangeable, at least by many students.

I do not think it is the primary task of education to prepare students for their later occupational roles, or indeed any narrowly specialized roles, nor to teach them to enjoy work regardless of its quality and meaning. Rather, the relation of education to later life should be a dialectical and critical one. If, however, one result of going to college is to become alienated from work per se and defeatist about the possibility of altering one's relation to it, then it seems to me one ought to reexamine academic institutions

themselves and see whether anything in them or in one's own attitudes or both might be changed.

Some time ago several hundred interviews were done (at the behest of *Time* magazine) with seniors at twenty colleges throughout the country, most of them colleges of some or of great distinction. The seniors were supposed to be reasonably representative, but what this was taken to mean and how it was applied at various colleges and universities varied greatly. A good many student leaders were chosen, a good many bright people, but hardly any women got in (a questionnaire circulated by *Mademoiselle* gave me somewhat comparable data concerning college women).

When I first examined the interviews, and now again when I have once more gone over them, I have been struck by what appears to be a not quite conscious ambivalence toward work in large organizations. On the other hand, the majority are planning to enter large organizations in pursuit of their careers: big corporations, big governments, big law offices, and so on. Only a few seek independence in their work, either in terms of old-fashioned ideals of entrepreneurship or in terms of the desire to become a foreign correspondent, to enter politics, or to follow some other individualistic or exotic calling. (Moreover, hardly anyone expresses resentment against his prospective Army service on the ground that the Army is a large organization: there is no eagerness for service, but rather resignation to it as one of the givens of life.)

And yet, when these young people are asked about their lives outside of work, a very different picture emerges. There, bigness and scale are definitely *not* valued. Only a tiny fraction want to head for the metropolis, even if their careers might make such a location convenient. They want the suburbs — not later, after some bachelor start has been made in the big city, but now, on graduation. The great majority either are already married or plan to get married soon (even if there is no special one in mind at the moment); they plan to start having children at once, and to begin building a community-centered life in the suburbs. They envisage a two-car but usually not a two-career family, in which the prospective wife will be active in the Parent-Teachers' Association, with subsidiary assistance from the husband, and in which both spouses will concern themselves with a manageable bit of real estate — a suburban neighborhood in which they can at once be active and hope to make a difference. It does not occur to them that they might be gifted and energetic enough to make a difference even in a big city. Rather, they want to be able to work through a face-to-face group — the post-collegiate fraternity of the small suburbs.

Correspondingly, the very emphasis on family life which is one of the striking and in so many ways attractive qualities of young people today is an implicit rejection of large organization. The suburban family with its garden, its barbecue, its lack of privacy in the open-plan house, is itself a manifesto of decentralization — even though it makes use of centralized services such as TV, clinics, chain stores, and *House Beautiful*. The wish to build a nest, even if a somewhat transient one, is a striking feature of the interviews, in contrast with the wish to build a fortune or a career which might have dominated some comparable interviews a generation earlier.

This pattern — the acceptance of large organizations combined with tacit and uncrystallized resistance to them — appears not only in the respondents' emphasis on the family but also in what they say about their plans and attitudes toward their future work. I get a sense from the material, and from other comparable data, of a certain withdrawal of emotional adherence from work. To be sure, it has become fashionable to speak of one's work or other activities in

deprecatory terms and to adopt a pose of relative indifference to the larger goals of an organization. In an era of political, economic, and cultural salesmanship, such deprecation is a way of guarding against being exploited for ends outside oneself. It is as if one had constantly to conduct psychological warfare against an outside enemy. But, as in any such process, students become to some extent the victims of their own defenses. They come to believe that work cannot really be worth doing for its own sake, whether or not it is done on behalf of a large impersonal organization — a fear of overcommitment to one's work even while one is at the workplace. In the course of getting rid of earlier collegiate or rah-rah enthusiasm, these young people have come to feel that work is not worth even their part-time devotion, and perhaps that nothing, except the family, deserves their whole-hearted allegiance.

We see the same attitudes, of course, among the junior echelons now engaged in work. One hears them talk of their benevolent company as "a mink-lined rattrap," or speak of "the rat race," or refer to fights over principles as "ruckuses" or "blow-ups" — if somebody cares, he is said to "blow his top." In a number of business novels, of which *The Man in the Gray Flannel Suit* is representative, it is taken for granted that a sensible fellow, and indeed an honest one, will prefer suburban domesticity and a quiet niche to ulcerous competition for large business stakes, despite the view from the top and the interesting climb.

Attitudes such as these are, of course, an aspect of a general cultural shift, not confined to students and not confined to those who seek employment in large organizations; similar attitudes turn up in some measure even among those who, studiously avoiding such organizations, look for a professional career in which they hope to be their own masters. Scholars, for example, are not immune to distaste for their work, nor are architects or physicians. But while I don't intend to imply that a life without any boredom is conceivable, except for a very stupid person, still I think we are witnessing a silent revolution against work on the part even of those relatively privileged groups who have been free to choose their work and to exercise some freedom in the doing of it. This reflects, in part, the fact that much work is meaningless per se, save as a source of income, prestige, and sociability; but it also indicates, as I have already implied, that people too readily accept their work as it comes, without hope of making it more meaningful.

What I want to stress is the fact that not all large organizations are alike, despite the sorts of institutional similarities investigated by sociologists; and of course that not all positions in them are alike. Many, although their top executives clamor for creativity and independence of mind, largely manage to process these qualities out of "their" people in the lower ranks. Others stockpile talent and expect it to keep as gold keeps at Fort Knox. Still others make products or provide services which are either antisocial or useless. But here and there one finds companies which face real and not contrived problems and apply to them an intelligence which is often remarkably disinterested and, in the best sense of the term, "academic."

Young people in search of challenge and development would do well to seek out such relatively productive climates rather than to assume offhand (as is true of so many brand-name products) that they are all alike except for the advertising and the label. And this search is necessary precisely because many of the motives which impelled work in the older generation have fortunately become attenuated — motives such as money for its own sake, power, and fame — goals, that is, whose emptiness became evident with their attainment. Our industrial and commercial plant no longer

"needs" such compulsive attachments to work which are based not on any genuine creative impulse but on the drying up of other alternatives.

There is a further issue concerning work in large organizations where again differentiation is required. I refer to the conception that work in organizations requires surrender of independence of judgment, if not of integrity. When I was in college, there was a prevalent feeling among the more sensitive that this was true only of business and commercial organizations, not of governmental or philanthropic ones, and young men debated whether they would enter Wall Street and make money or enter government or teaching and be saved. This dichotomy has in large measure vanished, although traces of it do survive among the less cynical. For instance, I have known many graduate students in social psychology who believe that if they teach they can be honest, but that if they work in market research they will serve manipulation and corruption, and will have no power over their own work.

Such judgments oversimplify the ethical dilemmas of any calling, and are in addition snobbish: one can find "hucksterism" (often hypocritically veiled) among academic people in search of reputations, grants, and promotions, as well as among market researchers and other businessmen. Indeed, I am inclined to think that at present many observant young people don't need to be persuaded of this; many are actually over-persuaded to the point of believing that *every* occupation is a racket, and that at best some of the racketeers are less pious about it than others. And this, I suspect, is one of the reasons they tend to withdraw emotional allegiance from their work: with the impression that they have no control over it anyway, that all is in the hands of mysterious men upstairs who run the show. If there is greater wisdom in the belief that all occupations, like all forms of power, are corrupting in some degree, there is also greater resignation, greater passivity and fatalism.

Where are such attitudes learned and confirmed? Even at some of the leading colleges, the more intellectual colleges — the colleges which produce literary magazines — the relation of students to the curriculum has a certain alienated quality, in the sense that the students do not believe they have any control over their own education.

Let me give a few examples. In the last few years I have visited a number of colleges of high quality — colleges which turn out eminent professional men, scholars, and scientists; and I have made it my business to talk with students informally, to read their student newspapers and, where possible, student council reports. At a number of these institutions, the livelier students complain of the educational fare they are getting, of the very little contact the curriculum makes with the problems that are meaningful to them. Sometimes they feel that opportunities for a civilized and intellectual life on campus are wanting — for example, that there are few inviting places to study or to talk, that social pressures in dormitories force any intellectual life out of the group setting, that student publications are either dominated by the school administration or devoted to "campus news" and trivia, that the bookstore is inadequate, or that the library is geared to research needs, rather than to attract undergraduate browsers. They often feel they have no access to the faculty for other than merely routine matters. Sometimes students complain about the prerequisites of a department, which serve its monopolistic aims or protect its mediocre teachers from boycott, rather than serve any defensible pedagogic aims.

Yet when I ask such students what they have done about these things, they are surprised at the very thought that they could do anything. They think I am joking when I suggest that, if things came to the worst, they could picket! They think I am wholly unrealistic when I say that many on the faculty might welcome student initiative in revising the curriculum, or that it might be possible to raise modest sums of money among alumni or others to bring visiting lecturers, poets *et al.*, to the campus, or to furnish commodious rooms for interest-group meetings. When I tell them that the Harvard House plan came about in considerable measure because of the report of a Student Council committee in 1926 which caught the attention of the philanthropist Edward Harkness, they shrug — that must have been a golden era, they say; nothing like that could happen now. Of course, as long as they think that, they will conduct themselves accordingly.

What is perplexing in this outlook is that the students appear to be so very realistic about the organization they are living in. They harbor no illusions about the faculty, the administration, the trustees. Yet they act as if the structure these men have created or inherited were part of the universe. It seems hardly ever to occur to students that a faculty is not a unit but a set of factions, often in precarious balance, and that student activity might conceivably help tip the balance. And in spite of all that they know intellectually (and as children of vulnerable parents) about their power over their teachers, they don't put this power to use to improve the quality of their education.

At a low-level college it may be that the students have too much power. My colleague Everett C. Hughes has investigated institutions supposedly devoted to higher education where students make it impossible for the professor to demand anything of them beyond routine and comfortable performance; for instance, if they are asked to read a book they consider too difficult, they will turn in blank pages on an examination concerning it. Professors even at good and serious colleges have to preserve their own autonomy like any other professional group, and I am not recommending that they conduct "customer research" and guide themselves by a popularity poll. But I don't think it follows from this that they must remain innocent of educational sociology and psychology, unaware of the harm they do, or indifferent to the indifference they help breed.

In fact, it is the very quality of some of these professors and of the institutions at which they teach that helps to create in a paradoxical way feelings of passivity and helplessness among their students. Not only have students become better in the better colleges in recent decades but professors have become ever so much more erudite and competent. One seldom finds any longer at a first-rate university the platform ham actors or dreary pedants who were all too common even when I was an undergraduate. The most difficult and avant-garde books — often those considered not long ago subversive or ribald — are on the freshman reading list at many institutions, and while the market for textbooks is better than ever because education is everywhere such a boom industry, there are also many textbooks which take account of new knowledge and are reasonably sophisticated. "Sophisticated" is in fact the word for much current higher education: the professor is one-up on the student and the student knows it. This is one of the cases where general social advance brings unanticipated negative consequences in its wake. Vis-à-vis such professors, students feel even less able than heretofore to influence their fate as students; and so they tend to leave matters in the hands of the constituted authorities, preserving (like GIs in the Army) only their privilege of griping. . . .

At work here is a characteristic social pattern in which individuals, hesitant to reveal feelings they have scarcely voiced to themselves, are misled about what in effect could be done if they expressed themselves, there-

by discovering others who might share their views. (Sociologists refer to this process as "pluralistic ignorance.") Leadership, of course, whether in politics or in other affairs, often serves to help a group change its apparent mood to conform to its actual or potential but repressed views — but leadership also may, and frequently does, serve to continue enforcing the repression. Even in a large organization, radical and what were previously regarded as "impossible" changes come about almost instantaneously once people discover that views they had previously regarded as unacceptable or idiosyncratic are in fact widely shared.

The students know that there are many decisions out of their conceivable control, decisions upon which their lives and fortunes truly depend. But what I am contending is that this truth, this insight, is overgeneralized, and that, being believed, it becomes more and more "true." Not only do we fail to spot those instances in which intervention might change things quite substantially, but we fail to develop the competence and the confidence in ourselves that are necessary to any large endeavor. In that sense, despite our precociousness, we fail to grow up; we remain the children of organization, not the masters of it.

For Americans, there is something paradoxical about this development. Americans in the past have not been overimpressed by mechanical achievements. Workers in a steel mill are not awed by the giant rollers, and we take for granted that we are not awed by any large physical construction of our hands and brains. Contrary to the prevalent impression abroad that we are slaves to our machines, we are actually relatively uninvolved with them, and we surely do not feel dominated by them. But it seems to be different with the organizational machines. These are as much the product of our thinking and our imagination as any technological feat; yet, as Erich Fromm has said, we worship like idolators the product we have created — an image not of stone but of other images.

It is a commonplace observation that in organizational life we use arguments to convince others which we think will appeal to them, even though they don't convince us. We try to persuade people to behave justly to Negroes because "discrimination makes the United States look bad in the Cold War" — as if that were why we ourselves behaved decently. Or we persuade businessmen to give money to colleges for all sorts of public-relations reasons, playing on their fear of radicalism or federal control or whatnot, whereas we ourselves devote our lives to education for quite different reasons. All arguments of this nature have two qualities: they patronize the other person and they perpetuate "pluralistic ignorance." It can be contended that there may be occasions when we must appeal to others as they are, not as we would like them to be — when there isn't time for idealism. But, in our realism, we often make mistakes about what others will actually respond to, and we sacrifice the integrity and clarity of our argument to our false image of what will go over. The result: we conclude that one can't be honest while working for an organization, that one can be honest only when one is at home with one's family in the suburbs.

There is another result as well, namely, that we often end up in doubt as to what we ourselves think. We come to believe what we say to others and thus become "more sincere" in the subjective sense, but at the price of becoming still more confused as to what is actually so: we are the first victims of our own propaganda. No wonder we end up without emotional ties to what we do, for it is no longer we who do it, but some limited part of ourselves, playing a role. Not recognizing that we have done this to ourselves, we attribute to organizations the power and the primacy we have lost. And then . . . we strike back, not directly, but by a kind of emotional attrition, in which we lend to our work willingness without enthusiasm, conscientiousness without creativity. . . .

Let me again make it quite clear that I understand the positive functions of what sometimes appears as mere apathy or passivity among students; for passivity toward revivalist manias and crusades is a sensible reaction, a sign of maturity. Moreover, as I noted at the outset, students are not at all apathetic about many fundamental things, among them personal relations, family life, and in many cases the arts. But even these attachments may be in danger. If one is apathetic about one's work, with all that such an attitude implies for one's relation to social and personal creation, it is hard to prevent this apathy from spreading to other areas. . . .

My concern is that young people today, by "playing it cool" and fearing to be thought "squares," may create a style of life, not only in work but in every dimension of existence, which is less full, less committed, less complex, and less meaningful than mid-century opportunities allow.

I have lived some thirty years on this planet, and I have yet to hear the first syllable of valuable or even earnest advice from my seniors.

HENRY DAVID THOREAU, *Walden*, 1854

112.

John F. Kennedy: Address to the Ministers of Houston

Although John F. Kennedy's candidacy for the Democratic nomination for President in 1960 was not announced until January of that year, it was widely recognized much earlier. Early interest in Kennedy's political aims centered on the "issue" of his religion. He was only the second Catholic to gain the nomination of a major party; the first, Alfred E. Smith of New York, had been badly defeated in 1928, and there was speculation that Kennedy's religion would prove an insurmountable obstacle. During the campaign there were rumors to the effect that, as President, Kennedy would be subject to control by leaders of his church and would be a tool for the implementation of its policies. The issue was brought into the open on September 7, 1960, when a group of 150 Protestant ministers and laymen of Houston, Texas, issued a statement asserting that Kennedy would be influenced by the Catholic Church in making political decisions. Kennedy replied to the charges in the following address, delivered on September 12, before the Greater Houston Ministerial Association. The frankness with which he discussed the matter probably turned the "religion issue" in his favor.

Source: *New York Times*, September 13, 1960.

WHILE THE SO-CALLED religious issue is necessarily and properly the chief topic here tonight, I want to emphasize from the outset that we have far more critical issues to face in the 1960 election: the spread of Communist influence, until it now festers ninety miles off the coast of Florida; the humiliating treatment of our President and Vice-President by those who no longer respect our power; the hungry children I saw in West Virginia; the old people who cannot pay their doctor bills; the families forced to give up their farms; an America with too many slums, with too few schools, and too late to the moon and outer space.

These are the real issues which should decide this campaign. And they are not religious issues, for war and hunger and ignorance and despair know no religious barriers.

But, because I am a Catholic, and no

Catholic has ever been elected President, the real issues in this campaign have been obscured, perhaps deliberately, in some quarters less responsible than this. So it is apparently necessary for me to state once again, not what kind of church I believe in, for that should be important only to me, but what kind of America I believe in.

I believe in an America where the separation of church and state is absolute — where no Catholic prelate would tell the President, should he be a Catholic, how to act, and no Protestant minister would tell his parishioners for whom to vote; where no church or church school is granted any public funds or political preference; and where no man is denied public office merely because his religion differs from the President who might appoint him or the people who might elect him.

I believe in an America that is officially

neither Catholic, Protestant, nor Jewish; where no public official either requests or accepts instructions on public policy from the pope, the National Council of Churches, or any other ecclesiastical source; where no religious body seeks to impose its will directly or indirectly upon the general populace or the public acts of its officials; and where religious liberty is so indivisible that an act against one church is treated as an act against all.

For, while this year it may be a Catholic against whom the finger of suspicion is pointed, in other years it has been, and may someday be again, a Jew — or a Quaker — or a Unitarian — or a Baptist. It was Virginia's harassment of Baptist preachers, for example, that helped lead to Jefferson's Statute of Religious Freedom. Today I may be the victim, but tomorrow it may be you, until the whole fabric of our harmonious society is ripped at a time of great national peril.

Finally, I believe in an America where religious intolerance will someday end; where all men and all churches are treated as equal; where every man has the same right to attend or not attend the church of his choice; where there is no Catholic vote, no anti-Catholic vote, no bloc voting of any kind; and where Catholics, Protestants, and Jews, at both the lay and pastoral level, will refrain from those attitudes of disdain and division which have so often marred their works in the past, and promote instead the American ideal of brotherhood.

That is the kind of America in which I believe, and it represents the kind of presidency in which I believe — a great office that must be neither humbled by making it the instrument of any religious group nor tarnished by arbitrarily withholding it — its occupancy — from the members of any one religious group. I believe in a President whose views on religion are his own private affair, neither imposed upon him by the nation nor imposed by the nation upon him as a condition to holding that office.

I would not look with favor upon a President working to subvert the First Amendment's guarantees of religious liberty; nor would our system of checks and balances permit him to do so. And neither do I look with favor upon those who would work to subvert Article VI of the Constitution by requiring a religious test — even by indirection — for if they disagree with that safeguard, they should be openly working to repeal it.

I want a chief executive whose public acts are responsible to all and obligated to none — who can attend any ceremony, service, or dinner his office may appropriately require of him to fulfill, and whose fulfillment of his presidential office is not limited or conditioned by any religious oath, ritual, or obligation.

This is the kind of America I believe in — and this is the kind of America I fought for in the South Pacific and the kind my brother died for in Europe. No one suggested then that we might have a "divided loyalty," that we did "not believe in liberty" or that we belonged to a disloyal group that threatened "the freedoms for which our forefathers died."

And in fact this is the kind of America for which our forefathers died when they fled here to escape religious test oaths that denied office to members of less favored churches; when they fought for the Constitution, the Bill of Rights, the Virginia Statute of Religious Freedom; and when they fought at the shrine I visited today, the Alamo. For side by side with Bowie and Crockett died Fuetes and McCafferty and Bailey and Bedilio and Carey — but no one knows whether they were Catholics or not. For there was no religious test there.

I ask you tonight to follow in that tradition — to judge me on the basis of fourteen years in the Congress — on my declared stands against an ambassador to the Vatican, against unconstitutional aid to parochial schools, and against any boycott of the public schools — which I attended myself. And instead of doing this, do not judge me on the basis of these pamphlets and publications we have all seen that carefully select quotations out of context from the statements of Catholic Church leaders, usually in other countries, frequently in other centuries, and rarely relevant to any situation here, and always omitting, of course, the statement of the American bishops in 1948 which strongly endorsed church-state separation, and which more nearly reflects the views of almost every American Catholic.

I do not consider these other quotations binding upon my public acts — why should you? But let me say, with respect to other countries, that I am wholly opposed to the state being used by any religious group, Catholic or Protestant, to compel, prohibit, or persecute the free exercise of any other religion. And that goes for any persecution at any time by anyone in any country. And I hope that you and I condemn with equal fervor those nations which deny their presidency to Protestants and those which deny it to Catholics. And rather than cite the misdeeds of those who differ, I would also cite the record of the Catholic Church in such nations as France and Ireland — and the independence of such statesmen as De Gaulle and Adenauer.

But let me stress again that these are my views; for, contrary to common newspaper usage, I am not the Catholic candidate for President. I am the Democratic Party's candidate for President who happens also to be a Catholic. I do not speak for my church on public matters — and the church does not speak for me.

Whatever issue may come before me as President if I should be elected — on birth control, divorce, censorship, gambling, or any other subject — I will make my deci-

sion in accordance with these views, in accordance with what my conscience tells me to be in the national interest, and without regard to outside religious pressure or dictates.

And no power or threat of punishment could cause me to decide otherwise.

But if the time should ever come — and I do not concede any conflict to be remotely possible — when my office would require me to either violate my conscience or violate the national interest, then I would resign the office. And I hope any other conscientious public servant would do likewise.

But I do not intend to apologize for these views to my critics of either Catholic or Protestant faith, nor do I intend to disavow either my views or my church in order to win this election.

If I should lose on the real issues, I shall return to my seat in the Senate, satisfied that I had tried my best and was fairly judged.

But if this election is decided on the basis that 40 million Americans lost their chance of being President on the day they were baptized, then it is the whole nation that will be the loser in the eyes of Catholics and non-Catholics around the world, in the eyes of history, and in the eyes of our own people.

But if, on the other hand, I should win this election, then I shall devote every effort of mind and spirit to fulfilling the oath of the Presidency — practically identical, I might add, to the oath I have taken for fourteen years in the Congress. For, without reservation, I can "solemnly swear that I will faithfully execute the office of President of the United States, and will to the best of my ability preserve, protect, and defend the Constitution . . . so help me God."

Index of Authors

*The numbers in brackets
indicate selection numbers
in this volume*

ACHESON, DEAN (April 11, 1893-   ), lawyer and public official. Undersecretary of the treasury (1933) under F. D. Roosevelt; assistant secretary of state (1941-45) under Roosevelt; undersecretary of state (1945-47) and secretary of state (1949-53) under Truman; wrote *Power and Diplomacy* (1958). [13] See also Author Index, Vol. 16.

ALLEN, FRED (May 31, 1894-March 17, 1956), humorist. Began in vaudeville as juggler and humorist, touring U.S. and Australia; became radio entertainer (1932); starred in motion pictures and musical comedies; wrote *Treadmill to Oblivion* (1954), *Much Ado About Me* (1956). [80]

ALLSOP, KENNETH (?-   ), English author. Literary editor (1940s and 1950s) of the (London) *Daily Mail*; contributor to *Encounter*; wrote *Adventure Lit Their Star* (1950); *The Angry Decade* (1958), *The Bootleggers* (1961), and *Scan* (1965). [108]

AUDEN, W. H. (Feb. 21, 1907-   ), poet. Born England; to U.S. (1940); professor of poetry (1956-   ) at Oxford University; wrote *Look Stranger* (1936), *Another Time* (1940), *The Age of Anxiety* (1947), *Nones* (1951), *The Shield of Achilles* (1955), *The Dyer's Hand and Other Essays* (1962). [70]

BELL, DANIEL (May 10, 1919-   ), sociologist. Staff writer (1940) and managing editor (1941-44) of the *New Leader;* managing editor (1945) of *Common Sense;* taught social sciences (1945-48) at the University of Chicago; labor editor (1948-58) of *Fortune;* lecturer (1952-58) and professor of sociology (1959-   ) at Columbia; wrote *The New American Right* (1955), *The End of Ideology* (1960), *The Radical Right* (1963). [47]

BENSON, EZRA TAFT (Aug. 4, 1899-   ), public official. Economist and marketing specialist (1930-37) of the state of Idaho; organizer and secretary (1933-38) of the Idaho Cooperative Council; executive secretary (1939-44) of the National Council on Farmer Cooperatives; secretary of agriculture under Eisenhower. [77]

BENTON, THOMAS HART (April 15, 1889-   ), painter. Teacher (1935-41) at Kansas City (Mo.) Art Institute; painted murals, including Whitney Museum, New York City (1932), Missouri state capitol, Jefferson City (1935), Truman Library, Independence, Mo. (1959); wrote autobiography, *An Artist in America* (1937; rev. ed., 1951), and articles for magazines. [24]

BENTON, WILLIAM (April 1, 1900-   ), businessman, educator, and statesman. Founder (1929) with Chester Bowles of Benton and Bowles advertising agency;

vice-president (1937-45) of the University of Chicago; publisher (1943-   ) of *Encyclopaedia Britannica;* assistant secretary of state (1945-47) under Truman; U.S. senator from Connecticut (1949-53); ambassador to UNESCO (1963-   ). [26] See also Author Index, Vol. 16.

BERLE, ADOLF A. (Jan. 29, 1895-   ), lawyer and diplomat. Consultant (1918-19) to the Paris Peace Commission; assistant secretary of state (1938-44) under F. D. Roosevelt; ambassador to Brazil (1945-46); professor (1927-   ) at Columbia University Law School. [57] See also Author Index, Vols. 15, 16.

BRODBECK, ARTHUR J. (fl. 1957), journalist. [83]

BURNS, JAMES MACGREGOR (Aug. 3, 1918-   ), political scientist. Professor (1947-   ) and chairman of the department of political science and professor of history and public affairs at Williams College; wrote *Congress on Trial* (1949), *John Kennedy: A Political Profile* (1960), *Four-Party Politics in America* (1963). [64]

CAMPBELL, PAUL (fl. 1951), folk singer and songwriter. [23]

COMMAGER, HENRY STEELE (Oct. 25, 1902-   ), historian. Professor of history (1939-56) at Columbia and (1956-   ) at Amherst; wrote *The Growth of the American Republic* (with S. E. Morison, 1931-42), *Freedom, Loyalty, Dissent* (1954), *The Nature and the Study of History* (1965); edited *Documents of American History* (1934, 1940, 1949). [3] See also Author Index, Vol. 16.

COPELAND, FREDERICK W. (fl. 1956), businessman and management consultant. [78]

COPLAND, AARON (Nov. 14, 1900-   ), composer. Lecturer on music (1927-37) at the New School for Social Research and (1935-44) at Harvard; director of the American Music Center; composed ballets (*Appalachian Spring,* 1944), operas, chamber music, orchestral works, and music for the theater and motion pictures. [38]

COUSINS, NORMAN (June 24, 1912-   ), editor. Literary editor and managing editor (1935-40) of *Current History* magazine; executive editor (1940-42) and president

and editor (1942-   ) of *Saturday Review;* vice-president (1961-   ) of McCall Corp.; wrote *Who Speaks for Man?* (1953), *In Place of Folly* (1961). [92]

CURTICE, HARLOW H. (Aug. 15, 1893-Nov. 3, 1962), auto executive. Controller (1915-29) and president (1929-33) of AC Spark Plug Div. and president (1933-48) of Buick Motors Div. of General Motors; vice-president (1948-53) and president (1953-58) of General Motors. [76]

DAVENPORT, RUSSELL W. (July 12, 1899-April 19, 1954), editor and author. Editorial staff member (1923-24) of *Time* magazine; reporter (1924-25) for *Spokane* (Wash.) *Spokesman Review;* editorial staff member (1930-37), managing editor (1937-40), and chairman of board of editors (1941) of *Fortune;* chief editorial writer (1942-44) of *Life;* publishing consultant (1944-47) for CBS; editor (1948-51) of Life Round Tables; director (from 1951) of Institute for Creative Research, Inc.; wrote *Through-Traffic* (1930), *The Dignity of Man* (1955). [21]

DE MILLE, AGNES (1908-   ), dancer and choreographer. Choreographed ballets, stage productions, and motion pictures; head of the Agnes De Mille Dance Theater; wrote *Dance to the Piper* (1952), *The Book of the Dance* (1963). [58]

DEWEY, JOHN (Oct. 20, 1859-June 1, 1952), philosopher, psychologist, and educator. Professor of philosophy (1894-1904) at the University of Chicago and (1904-30) at Columbia University; founder and director (1896-1904) of the University of Chicago Laboratory School; wrote many works, including *Democracy and Education* (1916), *Problems of Men* (1946). [37] See also Author Index, Vol. 12.

DOUGLAS, WILLIAM O. (Oct. 16, 1898-   ), jurist. Engaged in bankruptcy studies for U.S. Department of Commerce (1929-32); professor of law (1931-39) at Yale; member (1934-36) and chairman (1936-39) of the Securities and Exchange Commission; associate justice (1939-   ) of the U.S. Supreme Court. [27] See also Author Index, Vols. 16, 18.

DRUCKER, PETER F. (Nov. 19, 1909-   ), management consultant. Professor of philosophy and politics (1942-49) at Ben-

search in Contemporary Cultures; author of *Movies: A Psychological Study* (with M. Wolfenstein, 1950). **[8]**

LERNER, MAX (Dec. 20, 1902-   ), author and lecturer. Taught social sciences (1932-35) at Sarah Lawrence College and (1933-35) at the Wellesley Summer Institute; editor (1936-38) of the *Nation;* professor of political science (1938-43) at Williams College; radio commentator (1943-48) and newspaper columnist (1948-49); professor of American civilization (1949-   ) at Brandeis; syndicated columnist (1949-   ). **[82]**

LIPPMANN, WALTER (Sept. 23, 1889-   ), editor and author. Assisted in preparation of the Fourteen Points and the League of Nations plan for the Paris Peace Conference (1918-19); a co-founder (1914) and editor of the *New Republic;* syndicated political columnist (1931-67) for the *New York Herald Tribune;* wrote *Public Opinion* (1927); *A Preface to Morals* (1929), *The Good Society* (1937), *U.S. Foreign Policy: Shield of the Republic* (1943), *Essays in the Public Philosophy* (1955). **[88]** See also Author Index, Vols. 13, 14, 15, 16, 18.

LODGE, HENRY CABOT (July 5, 1902-   ), diplomat. Member (1933-36) of the Massachusetts General Court; U.S. senator (1937-44, 1947-53); U.S. representative to the United Nations and to the Security Council (1953-60); Republican Party candidate (1960) for Vice-President of the United States; ambassador to South Vietnam (1963-64, 1965-67). **[2]**

MACARTHUR, DOUGLAS (Jan. 26, 1880-April 5, 1964), army officer. Commanded 42nd Division in France during World War I; superintendent (1919-22) of U.S. Military Academy; commanded Philippines Department (1928-30); chief of staff of U.S. Army (1930-35); supreme Allied commander in the Pacific (1942-45) and of occupation forces in Japan (1945-50); commander of UN forces in Korea (1950-51). **[15, 19]** See also Author Index, Vol. 16.

McCARTHY, JOSEPH R. (Nov. 14, 1908-May 2, 1957), public official and politician. U.S. senator from Wisconsin (from 1947); instigated congressional hearings on his charges that Communists had infil-

trated the U.S. State Department, the military, and other government offices; condemned by the Senate (Dec. 2, 1954) for conduct "contrary to senatorial traditions." **[5]**

MACDONALD, DWIGHT (1906-   ), author. Founded and published (1944-49) *Politics;* contributor to the *New Yorker* and *Esquire;* wrote *Memoirs of a Revolutionist* (1957), *Against the American Grain* (1962). **[49]**

MALONE, GEORGE W. (Aug. 7, 1890-May 19, 1961), engineer and public official. Nevada state engineer (1927-35); consultant to the secretary of war during World War II; U.S. senator (1947-59). **[101]**

MANSFIELD, MICHAEL J. (March 16, 1903-   ), public official. Miner and mining engineer (1922-30); professor of history and political science (1933-42) at Montana State University; U.S. representative from Montana (1943-53); U.S. senator (1953-   ) and Democratic majority leader (1961-   ). **[46]** See also Author Index, Vol. 18.

MARSHALL, CHARLES BURTON (fl. 1952), government official. Staff member of U.S. State Department. **[28]**

MILLER, ARTHUR (Oct. 17, 1915-   ), playwright. Wrote *All My Sons* (1947), *Death of a Salesman* (1949), *The Crucible* (1953), *A View From the Bridge* (1955), *After the Fall* (1963), *Incident at Vichy* (1964). **[69]**

MORSE, WAYNE L. (Oct. 20, 1900-   ), lawyer and public official. Taught at Wisconsin, Minnesota, and Columbia universities; professor (1929-44) and dean of the law school (1931-44) at the University of Oregon; U.S. senator from Oregon (1945-69). **[4]**

MURRAY, JOHN COURTNEY (Sept. 12, 1904-Aug. 16, 1967), Roman Catholic clergyman. Professor of theology (from 1936) at Woodstock College; editor (from 1941) of *Theological Studies;* wrote *The Problem of God: Yesterday and Today* (1964), *The Problem of Religious Freedom* (1965). **[22]**

OPPENHEIMER, J. ROBERT (April 22, 1904-Feb. 18, 1967), physicist. Professor of physics (1929-43) at the University of California and California Institute of

Technology; director (1943-45) of Los Alamos Scientific Laboratory, where he directed scientific efforts to develop the atom bomb; professor of physics (1947-66) and director of the Institute for Advanced Study, Princeton University. **[43]**

POTTER, DAVID M. (Dec. 6, 1910-   ), historian. Professor of history (1942-61) at Yale and (1961-   ) at Stanford; wrote *Nationalism and Sectionalism in America* (with T. G. Manning, 1949), *People of Plenty: Economic Abundance and the American Character* (1954). **[56]**

RANDALL, CLARENCE B. (March 5, 1891-August 4, 1967), lawyer and businessman. With Inland Steel Company (from 1925), president (1949-53) and chairman of the board (1953-56); chairman (1956-61) of the Council on Foreign Economic Policy; special minister to Turkey (1956); special emissary to Ghana (1961). **[33]**

RICKOVER, HYMAN G. (Jan. 27, 1900-   ), naval officer and author. Served with atomic submarine project of the Atomic Energy Commission (1946-47); head (1947-   ) of the Nuclear Propulsion Division of the U.S. Bureau of Ships; chief of the naval reactors board of the Atomic Energy Commission; wrote *Education and Freedom* (1959), *Swiss Schools and Ours* (1962), *American Education — A National Failure* (1963). **[104]**

RIESMAN, DAVID (Sept. 22, 1909-   ), lawyer, sociologist, and author. Professor of law (1937-41) at the University of Buffalo; deputy assistant district attorney (1942-43) of New York County; associated (1943-46) with Sperry Gyroscope Co.; professor of social sciences (1946-47, 1954-58) at the University of Chicago and (1958-   ) at Harvard; wrote *The Lonely Crowd* (1950), *Faces in the Crowd* (1952), *Thorstein Veblen* (1953), *Individualism Reconsidered* (1954), *Abundance for What?* (1964). **[111]**

ROOSEVELT, ELEANOR (Oct. 11, 1884-Nov. 7, 1962), diplomat and humanitarian. Wife of Franklin D. Roosevelt; delegate (1945-52) to the United Nations and chairman of the commission to draft the Universal Declaration of Human Rights; wrote "My Day," a syndicated newspaper column, *This Is My Story* (1937), and

The Moral Basis of Democracy (1940). **[30]** See also Author Index, Vol. 16.

ROSENBERG, HAROLD (1906-   ), painter and art critic. Interpreter and critic of the Abstract Expressionist movement. **[39]**

SASS, HERBERT RAVENEL (Nov. 2, 1884-Feb. 18, 1958), naturalist and author. Contributor to the *Charleston* (S.C.) *News and Courier* and to the *Atlantic Monthly;* wrote several books on South Carolina history. **[74]**

SEATON, FRED A. (Dec. 11, 1909-   ), public official. Nebraska legislator (1945-49); U.S. senator (1951-53); assistant secretary of defense (1953-55), presidential administrative assistant (1955-56), and secretary of the interior (1956-61) under Eisenhower. **[101]**

SELDES, GILBERT (Jan. 3, 1893-   ), author and editor. Associate editor (1919) of *Collier's* magazine; editor (1920-23) of the *Dial;* columnist (1931-37) for the *New York Journal;* director of television programs (1937-45) for CBS; dean (1959-63) of the school of communications at the University of Pennsylvania. **[9]**

SHAPIRO, KARL (Nov. 10, 1913-   ), poet. Professor of writing (1947-50) at Johns Hopkins University; editor (1950-56) of *Poetry* magazine; professor of English (1956-   ) at the University of Nebraska; wrote *Poems* (1935), *V-Letter, and Other Poems* (1944), *Trial of a Poet* (1947), *The Bourgeois Poet* (1964). **[110]** See also Author Index, Vol. 16.

SMYTH, HENRY D. (May 1, 1898-   ), physicist. Professor (1924-   ) and chairman of the department of physics at Princeton University; associate editor (1927-30) of *Physical Review;* consultant (1940-45) to U.S. Office of Scientific Research and Development and (1943-45) to the Manhattan Project; member (1949-54) Atomic Energy Commission; U.S. representative (1961-   ) to the International Atomic Energy Commission; wrote *Atomic Energy for Military Purposes* (War Department report, 1945). **[59]**

STEVENSON, ADLAI E. (Feb. 5, 1900-July 14, 1965), lawyer, public official, and diplomat. Special assistant (1941-44) to the secretary of the Navy; assistant (1945-46) to the secretary of state; U.S. delegate to the United Nations (1945-47); governor of Illinois (1949-53); Democratic Party candidate (1952, 1956) for President of the United States; ambassador to the United Nations (from 1961). [40] See also Author Index, Vol. 18.

SWADOS, HARVEY (Oct. 22, 1920-   ), author. Faculty member (1958-   ) of the literature division of Sarah Lawrence College; wrote *On the Line* (1957), *Nights in the Gardens of Brooklyn* (1961), *A Radical's America* (1962), *A Story for Teddy, and Others* (1965). [84]

TANSILL, WILLIAM R. (fl. 1950), author. [16]

TELLER, EDWARD (Jan. 15, 1908-   ), physicist. Professor of physics (1936-41) at George Washington University, (1946-49, 1951-52) at the University of Chicago, and (1953-60) at the University of California; assistant director (1949-51) of Los Alamos Scientific Laboratory; staff member (1952-   ) at the Radiation Laboratory of the University of California. [94]

THAYER, ROBERT H. (Sept. 22, 1901-   ), lawyer and diplomat. Assistant ambassador to France (1951-54); minister to Rumania (1955-58); special assistant (1958-61) in U.S. State Department; associate director (1961-   ) of American Field Service International Scholarships; consultant to the secretary of state (1961-   ). [105]

THOMAS, DYLAN (Oct. 27, 1914-Nov. 9, 1953), Welsh poet. Wrote *Eighteen Poems* (1934), *Twenty-Five Poems* (1936), *The Map of Love* (1939), *Deaths and Entrances* (1946), *In Country Sleep* (1952); sketches and short stories, radio play *Under Milk Wood* (1954). [50]

TRUMAN, HARRY S. (May 8, 1884-   ), political leader and statesman. Thirty-third President of the United States (1945-53); presiding judge (1926-34) of Jackson County (Mo.) Court; U.S. senator from Missouri (1935-45); Vice-President of the United States (1945) under F. D. Roosevelt; succeeded to the presidency upon Roosevelt's death (April 12, 1945). [1, 11, 12, 17, 18, 31, 53] See also Author Index, Vol. 16.

VAN DOREN, MARK (June 13, 1894-   ), writer and editor. Instructor (1920-24) and professor (1942-59) of English at Columbia University; literary editor (1924-28) and motion picture critic (1935-38) for the *Nation;* wrote poems (*Collected Shorter Poems,* 1939; *Collected Longer Poems,* 1948), novels and stories (*Collected Stories,* 2 vols., 1962, 1965), plays (*The Last Days of Lincoln,* 1959), and criticism (*Shakespeare,* 1939; *Liberal Education,* 1943; *The Noble Voice,* 1946). [25] See also Author Index, Vol. 18.

WARREN, EARL (March 19, 1891-   ), public official and jurist. Deputy district attorney (1920-25) and district attorney (1925-39) of Alameda County, Calif.; attorney general of California (1939-43); governor (1943-53); chief justice (1953-   ) of the U.S. Supreme Court; chairman (1963-64) of the Presidential Commission to Investigate the Assassination of John F. Kennedy. [55, 95, 97] See also Author Index, Vol. 18.

WHITE, DAVID M. (June 28, 1917-   ), journalist and educator. Professor of journalism and chairman of the department (1946-49) at Bradley University; professor (1949-   ) and chairman (1964-   ) of the division of journalism at Boston University; special elections editor (1954-   ) for Associated Press; consultant (1954-   ) to the department of mass communications, UNESCO. [83]

WILLIAMS, JOHN D. (fl. 1958), head of mathematics division of the Rand Corporation. [98]

WOLFENSTEIN, MARTHA (fl. 1950), sociologist. Participant in the Columbia University Research in Contemporary Cultures; author of *Movies: A Psychological Study* (with N. Leites, 1950). [8]

WORKMAN, WILLIAM D., JR. (fl. 1959), author. [109]

YOUNGDAHL, LUTHER W. (May 29, 1896-   ), jurist and public official. Judge (1930-36) of Minneapolis Municipal Court; judge (1936-42) of Hennepin County District Court; associate justice (1942-47) of the Minnesota Supreme Court; governor (1947-51); judge (1951-   ) of U.S. District Court for the District of Columbia. [62]